6-90

Enjoy, Dad
& have a good
Day

Love Lema Dn

MW01169297

GREAT LAKES BOOKS

ORVIE

*Orville L. Hubbard looks west down Michigan Avenue
outside the Dearborn City Hall, 1967.
(Courtesy of the* Detroit News. *Photo by Charles T. Martin.)*

ORVIE

The Dictator of Dearborn

The Rise and Reign of
ORVILLE L. HUBBARD

David L. Good

WAYNE STATE UNIVERSITY PRESS   DETROIT   1989

93   92   91   90   89   5   4   3   2   1

Library of Congress Cataloging-in-Publication Data

Good, David L., 1942–
    Orvie : the dictator of Dearborn : the rise and reign of
Orville L. Hubbard / David L. Good.
       p.   cm. — (Great Lakes books)
    Bibliography: p.
    Includes index.
    ISBN 0–8143–2289–1.   ISBN 0–8143–2290–5 (pbk.)
    1. Hubbard, Orville Liscum, 1903–1982.
    2. Mayors—Michigan—Dearborn—Biography.
    3. Dearborn (Mich.)—Politics and government.
I. Title. II. Series.
F574.D2H834   1989
977.4'33—dc20
[B]
                            89–30495
                                CIP

For Marcie, Leslie, Chris and Janet,

with whom I look forward to spending a lot more time.

Biography appeals to the child in all of us—that craving for "and then, and then, and then."

—Edmund Morris

Contents

Illustrations

Maps

Tables

Acknowledgments

There are a great many ways to write a book; one I wouldn't recommend is to spend 18 years at it. As a spare-time project that devoured weekends and vacations, this one took exactly half as long to finish as it took Orville L. Hubbard to live it during his 36-year tenure as mayor of the Detroit suburb of Dearborn, Michigan. I'd have much preferred to do it faster.

Although I'd grown up in Dearborn hearing about Hubbard—he took office the same year I was born—I first met him in 1967, when my editors at the *Detroit News* assigned me to Orvie's territory as a suburban beat reporter. I'd already voted against him once, and I was prepared not to like him much in the flesh.

I was wrong. I was absolutely taken by Hubbard's personal magnetism, his outspokenness and his knack for telling a story. He soon became one of my favorite people, no matter how much I found myself disagreeing with some of the things he said.

Three years later, just before I left the Dearborn beat, I decided to do this book—with or without Hubbard's input. To my surprise, he agreed— with no conditions whatsoever—to a series of occasional taped interviews that eventually spanned a couple of years. They ended when a massive stroke robbed Hubbard of his remarkable gift of gab in 1974.

Hubbard's words from those interviews appear with conventional attribution in the first part of the book, an overview of various aspects of his life; in the second part, a chronological account, his quotes are set off by italics without attribution. I should note that although the words are all his, I have frequently condensed and reorganized them; otherwise we'd be here all year.

11

Inevitably, I have a long list of people to thank for their help. Hubbard's public relations director, Doyne E. Jackson, provided many shortcuts in gathering both information and city photographs. Gary Woronchak, editorial director of the *Dearborn Press & Guide*, gave me access to decades of bound copies of Dearborn's weekly papers. Frank Hubbard, the mayor's son, cooperated in every way I asked, as did other members of the family. Their names are included in the interview section of the bibliography, along with those of other principals, Hubbard friends and foes, who were kind enough to talk to me for the oral history portions of this book. Among others who went out of their way for me are Angelo Arella, Jeanette Bartz, Donald Baut, Joseph J. Burtell, William J. Coughlin, Herschel P. Fink, Draper Hill, John Klemanski, Carl Levin, Helen Mamalakis, Charles Press, Ed Roose, Philip W. Spitzer and Ronald R. Stockton.

Finally, I'd like to note particularly the years-long encouragement and many insights provided by political scientist John W. Smith. A good kick in the pants never hurt anybody.

Prologue:
America's Defense Arsenal

Exclusive: Scoop rips lid off America's biggest vice scandal!

—Cover headline, *Dan Gillmor's Scoop*[1]

The way police figured it, the car had been sitting there in the woods, 300 yards off the highway, for about three days. Someone had set the brakes and left the motor running, then pitched a soft drink bottle and a green prescription medicine bottle out the driver's side window.

Now, on this sweltering July day in 1941, flies swarmed around the massive Lincoln Zephyr. The gas tank was empty. In the trunk was a bottle of wine, partially drunk. On the ground nearby were the other two bottles, both of them empty. On the front seat was unmistakable evidence that someone had been convulsed in a wave of nausea. And behind the wheel was the stiff, unnaturally bloated carcass of Charles W. Slamer, chief inspector of police of the city of Dearborn, Michigan.

Slamer, 60 at the time of his death, was born on George Washington's birthday, and he once claimed he had never told a lie in his life. Indeed, a few years earlier, the newspapers could find nothing more remarkable to report about him than that he liked bowling and Jimmy Cagney movies and didn't like potatoes or white bread.

But today the death of Charles W. Slamer was national news, and it was fast becoming clear that telling the truth had not been one of his hallmark virtues. A New York–based police magazine, *Dan Gillmor's Scoop*, summed up the case with a cover illustration of a female—conspicuous in her depravity, cigarette in mouth and drink in hand. The magazine trumpeted news of Slamer's suspicious death and the trail of corruption leading up to it over five pages of its November 1941 issue. The article's title: "Vice gangs rule America's defense arsenal."[2]

No one could know it then, but the finger-pointing exposé in *Scoop* helped set up a chain of events that for the next four decades would shape one of America's most happily endowed suburbs, eventually transforming it into a town reviled nationally as a fortress of northern racism, studied as a test-tube case of homeowner-pampering boss rule, and laughed at as a sort of sanctuary for political buffoonery.

As reported in *Scoop* and the local papers, Dearborn—the town where Henry Ford lived, created his auto empire and soon would centralize the war production effort—was a wide-open den of gambling, prostitution and corruption—and had been for some years. That was quite a revelation for many of the home folks. Dearborn always had considered itself a staid, upright community, tax-supported by the huge Ford Rouge industrial complex in the southeast corner of town but untainted by it, just as it was untainted by the big-city corruption of Detroit, its neighbor on its eastern boundary. Except for auto and labor news, the city seldom had made headlines since the merger of old Dearborn and adjacent Fordson in 1929.[3]

Things changed fast after a wild auto chase through the streets of Dearborn in late May 1941, two months before Slamer's body was found near semirural Flat Rock, south of Detroit.

Two policemen spotted a suspicious-looking car on Miller Road near the Rouge plant. The two men inside were exchanging what looked like money and envelopes with men in other cars. As the officers drew alongside, the car suddenly lurched off, slamming into the open door of the police vehicle and ripping it off its hinges. The lawmen, Louis Cruzen and Thomas Davey, finally overtook the speeding auto after blasting out the left rear tire with a shotgun. Police later found three envelopes containing $642.91 in the car and another envelope containing policy betting slips in the grass along the route of the chase.

Back at headquarters, the two suspects were booked on minor disorderly charges under city ordinance and released immediately—by Slamer himself.

It didn't take long for news of Slamer's magnanimity to spread. The Detroit metropolitan area already was caught up in a wide-sweeping vice investigation under three separate grand juries overseen by Wayne Circuit Judge Homer Ferguson, later to be elected a U.S. senator. The next day Slamer was ordered before one of the grand juries. Why, he was asked, had he released the two men, and why had they not been charged under state law with a more serious offense? Ferguson already had cited Slamer for contempt the year before, accusing him of "evasive and contradictory" answers in another matter, and the judge obviously didn't like what he heard this time much better.

A few days later he indicted Dearborn Police Chief Carl A. Brooks, along with two vice squad detectives, a former member of the vice squad and nine alleged underworld characters. Slamer was named an unindicted coconspirator. The charge: the Dearborn Police Department was taking graft for protecting the National Daily Bankers, the biggest mutuels numbers racket in Michigan, with a reported yearly take of $500,000 in Dearborn alone.

Mayor John L. Carey suspended Brooks and Slamer immediately, along with the other two officers. But Brooks, arrested on his farm outside of town, collapsed on the way back to Dearborn and never even made his arraignment. He died of a heart attack within three weeks.

Slamer got his chance to talk, however, as did the others. Though Brooks had told reporters he had "never taken a quarter" from anyone, testimony suggested that he was raking in up to $10,000 a year from the racketeers. In contrast, Slamer admitted taking only $50 or so a month from gamblers and brothel keepers. He didn't get more, he said, because the "old man" (Brooks) "was awful greedy and wanted it all."

Other testimony depicted Dearborn as a haven for dice games, baseball pools, slot machines and some 30 bordellos controlled by the racketeers.

Scoop magazine went so far as to implicate Harry Bennett, chief of Ford Motor's head-busting security force, in the affair. Bennett, *Scoop* asserted, had used "his position . . . to bring into Dearborn a horde of criminals and gangsters, thereby helping to create the conditions that bred the wholesale vice and corruption of the city government."[4]

The only others charged with wrongdoing in Dearborn, however, were the secretary of the city's Public Safety Commission and a city councilman. Neither was convicted. In truth, except for Brooks's heart attack and Slamer's mysterious death, Dearborn was hardly even noticed amid all the other investigations. Speculation about how Slamer died kept his name in the papers for weeks. The body, it was noted, bore no marks of violence, and there were no signs of poisoning.

Was it suicide? His widow and son didn't believe it. Though he had been suspended from the force, they said, he was to start a brewery job on the day he was last seen alive. Besides, his fingerprints didn't show up on the bottles near his car.

Was it an accident? He had been drinking heavily, the autopsy showed, and he had ingested large quantities of chloral hydrate, or "knockout drops." The medical examiner concluded it was "highly unlikely it could have been accidental."

Was it murder? A hospital pathologist who conducted tests on the body said, "My conclusion would be that a second person was in the car to administer the poison." But there was no sign of a struggle, and the quantity of drugs Slamer had consumed could hardly have been sneaked into his drinks.

Finally, the clues started to make sense. Twice the preceding month Slamer had collapsed, diagnosed as a victim of chloral hydrate poisoning. A nurse who was a friend of his said he had complained of being jittery three days before his death, and she'd bought him a bottle of 100 chloral hydrate tablets at his request. Detectives found he had been drinking morosely at four places the day before he died, and a witness turned up who said he had seen Slamer looking around the woods near Flat Rock and then driving away, also on the day before he died. Several acquaintances said Slamer was brooding about "killing Carl Brooks by becoming a witness for the grand jury."

Charles W. Slamer, the authorities concluded, apparently had taken his own life.[5]

The Ferguson grand juries issued more than 500 indictments and heard more than 7,000 witnesses utter more than 30 million words of testimony from 1939 to 1941. Dozens of racketeers went to jail, and so did a number of prominent officials, including former Detroit Mayor Richard W. "Double Dip" Reading and a police superintendent, county sheriff and county prosecutor.[6]

And if the grand juries didn't uncover much in Dearborn, still they shocked the good citizens there into realizing it was time to turn the rascals out, if only someone could find a challenger willing to take on Bennett and city hall.

Part
I

An Overview

1

The Old Pro

He went about doing good. Acts 10:38
—Sign above the door to the office of the mayor
of Dearborn

The polls in Dearborn had been closed for nearly an hour now, and Mayor Orville L. Hubbard looked about as mad as a winner could look. He looked much madder than the time the *New York Times Magazine* said he looked like a Berkshire hog.[1] Or the time Roy Wilkins of the NAACP vilified him as the nation's "meanest man in race relations."

Never mind that at his peak weight of perhaps 350 pounds he did look a little like a Berkshire—albeit a well-groomed one—or that he had built a national reputation for keeping the "niggers" out of town. Orville Hubbard was not the sort of man you engaged in a name-calling contest if you hoped to emerge unscathed.

On this particular night, a night he was making history of sorts, there was no name-calling, but Orville Hubbard was scowling blackly anyhow. The target of his wrath: a TV set. Or, more precisely, a TV newscaster droning on about the latest demands being made of Richard Nixon by Watergate investigators.

As Hubbard sat simmering in his office at city hall, his immense, bulbous form looked for all the world like some occidental Buddha in bow tie and starched shirt. The pale skin of the fleshy cheeks and jowls was smooth and soft, filled out with layers of fat accumulated over seven decades and masking the once-regular features. The reddish-brown hair, though dyed, was full and thick, slicked back like that of a young man from an earlier era. The fingernails were immaculate. Despite the age and bulk, here was obviously a man of great personal vanity, a man with the assurance and command presence of a drill sergeant, a man used to speaking his mind without the slightest fear of contradiction or retribution.

Finally, Hubbard, unable to sit silently any longer, banged his big fist against the long hardwood conference table in his office. It was a maneuver that always seemed to have the desired effect on his flinching subordinates, but the newscaster kept right on talking.

"If I were Nixon, I'd tell 'em to go to hell," Hubbard barked out over the sound of the TV, obviously talking as much to himself as to the two dozen or so aides and well-wishers assembled in his suite. "Do any god-damn thing. If they want to have an indictment, have it. Get it over with. Whether you like Nixon or don't like him—I was a Wallace man—who in the hell can you think of who could do a better job?"

He wasn't really expecting an answer, but up piped one of his aides with the right one. "You," rejoined Maureen Keane, a well-endowed blonde nearly 40 years Hubbard's junior, with no detectable trace of sarcasm in her voice.

"No, honestly," Hubbard continued. "Who's going to do a better job? Jerry Ford? I don't think so. If you impeach Nixon, what are you going to do? This government is ready to collapse. The system was good in 1789, but is it good today? It's better than everyone running around with guns— I admit that—but they're pretty close to that, too."[2]

The irony of Hubbard's apocalyptic discourse undoubtedly was lost on all but a few members of the assembled throng. He himself had thrived by taking his own advice to Nixon: telling 'em all to go to hell—councilmen, judges, federal attorneys, county sheriffs and prosecutors. Anybody he couldn't outshout, he'd figure out other ways to deal with. Anything he did always seemed to be just fine with the voters. And now, while the president of the United States struggled with events that had dropped his popularity to an all-time low and soon would cost him his job, the mayor of Dearborn, Michigan, population 104,000, could hardly have felt more secure.

At age 71, Hubbard already had been administrative head of one of the state's most affluent cities since 1942, after winning his first election in the power vacuum created by the old Ferguson grand jury investigations. He already held a share of the record for most consecutive years in office by any full-time mayor in U.S. history.[3] And on this night, November 6, 1973, he had just been assured of another four years—his fifteenth term, enabling him to run his total to 36 years.

He'd had some hard-fought campaigns over the years, but this election hardly qualified as one of them. The only question was whether he'd come closer to 80 or 90 percent of the vote. Given all that, Hubbard could be excused if he'd rather get mad at a TV set than soak up adulation for his own rather tame victory. After all, this was a man who, over the years, was willing to do almost anything for excitement, especially if it meant getting his name or his picture in the papers.

The pundits and headline writers had gleefully dubbed him "Orvie" and "Little Orvie" years before. To his subordinates, supporters and even his friends, however, he was seldom anything but "Mayor," only rarely "Orville." And yet, to thousands of people who knew him only through the newspapers, "Orvie" he remained.

You wanted a publicity photo with white bunnies? Orvie would cover himself with white bunnies. You wanted Orvie to jump up and down on a subpoena he'd been served with? He'd already kicked it away once, but get the photographers set and he'd do it even more convincingly a second time. You wanted Orvie and a couple of other fat guys to put on identical clown masks so pursuing sheriff's deputies wouldn't know who was who? Sure, and if the photo made all the papers, it would make the hassle worthwhile.

It was more than just public relations. It was politics as theater—and not always good theater, either. Life in Dearborn city hall was one long Punch and Judy show under Hubbard.

There was a more serious side to Orville Hubbard, to be sure. Indeed, he had established an image as the consummately successful suburban politician in an era of burgeoning financial problems and white flight from the big cities. While neighboring Detroit struggled to survive, Hubbard was overseeing middle-class, lily-white Dearborn, home of the Ford Motor Company, as the city became the self-proclaimed provider of the "world's best public service," as well as the seat of the nation's last vestiges of old-style boss rule and the most notorious segregationist rhetoric north of the Mason-Dixon line.

Orville Hubbard survived—and flourished—by being tougher than anybody else—tougher than a group of city councilmen who passed a "gag" ordinance designed to keep him from talking to constituents; tougher than Ford's, which he claimed once tried to help recall him from office and wound up enmeshed with him in a "dirty tricks"-style campaign that made Nixon's better-publicized efforts seem like sophomoric pranks; even tougher, in a sense, than the federal government, which once brought him to trial on a charge of conspiring to violate a civil rights law dating back to Reconstruction times.

Through it all, Orville Hubbard practiced his own peculiar style of what might be called the politics of confrontation. If there was a path of least resistance, he seldom took it. If there was an excuse for a fight, he almost always tried to pick one. When he got mad at Ford Motor, Orvie ordered his fire chief to take an ax to the office door of Henry Ford II. When an antagonistic judge attended a convention in Dearborn, Orvie sent him a letter inviting him to "get out and stay out" of town. When another judge fined him more than his annual salary for libeling a prominent local attorney, Orvie refused to pay, then set up a "government in exile" in Canada while evading arrest.

There is a real question whether these were the acts of a rational person—or at least one who had arrived fully matured into adulthood. But

21

there is no question about the power or the resourcefulness of the man who committed them.

If Richard Daley had been boss in Chicago, or Frank Hague in Jersey City, or Thomas J. Pendergast in Kansas City, Orville Hubbard was the dictator of Dearborn. "There used to be a saying in Dearborn—'Hitler, Hague and Hubbard,'" Hubbard once said with obvious relish. "But Hitler and Hague are gone. I'm the only one left."[4]

It was no accident that Orville Hubbard headed what could be considered America's longest-running elected dictatorship, marking one of the only times in U.S. history that a majority of voters effectively chose one-man rule—and kept on doing so for more than three decades. After all, Hubbard knew exactly what the voters wanted, and he gave it to them. If Mussolini made the trains run on time in Fascist-ruled Italy, Orville Hubbard got the snow plowed and the garbage picked up promptly in Dearborn. And in doing so, he took Henry Ford's hometown and turned it into almost his own personal fiefdom.

Whether his dictatorship was a benevolent one or not, most of Dearborn's voters wanted things just the way they were. They loved his commitment to keeping them happy—or, as he occasionally had said, to "keep the trees trimmed and take care of barking dogs." They loved his continual nose-thumbing at the establishment, even though in his town he *was* the establishment. And, though not all of them would admit it, many loved his status as a symbol of Jim Crowism in suburbia.

All these elements contributed to the Hubbard mystique through the years, although on this day—the last time he would sit and wait for results of his own election—his success seemed more a matter of voter habit than anything else.

November 6 started out cool and windy, with the temperature in the mid-30s and about 32,000 of Dearborn's 65,000 registered voters expected to go to the polls. The mayor had voted himself that morning a bit after seven o'clock, then attended to some routine chores at the office.

A woman phoned to complain that Hubbard campaign workers had stuffed her mailbox with literature, and the mayor dispatched somone to pick up the offending materials. An 83-year-old man felt sick but still wanted to vote, and the mayor was able to "fix him up" with an absentee ballot.[5] Then one of the councilmen "came in and sat around and took up about three hours of my time doing nothing." Finally, after meeting with several judges who were reconnoitering the city as a possible circuit court site, he completed his daily chauffeured drive around town. Then lunch back in his office. Yes, he was still on his rice-and-fruit diet. No, it wasn't helping much. He had been telling everybody he had gotten down to 270—probably a good 80 pounds less than his all-time high (even he wasn't sure how much that was)—but some city hall insiders were positive he was still over 300.

"Between now and a year from now, I'm going to peel off about 75 pounds for sure," he said, sounding just like a beginner at a health club. "Without fail. I owe it to myself and my constituents."

Late that afternoon, with an aide again driving him, he visited all but one of the city's 38 polling places, shaved a second time and finished his final bit of primping for the evening: he left to get his hair done. (His barber said his new left-side part made him look years younger than his usual no-part style.)

Then, about 7:45 P.M., the mayor returned to city hall with Keane and several others. Smiling broadly, he navigated his ponderous form past the green chalkboard that would inform visitors of the vote tally for "Hubbard" and "Opponent," past the lobby bulletin board filled with newspaper stories of interest ("Convictions of Miranda ruled valid," "46 beaten, several die in African war on thefts," "New Year's wedding whirl—Dearborn's Hubbard marries 12 couples") and finally past the tidbit of scriptural inspiration emblazoned over the door of his own office: "He went about doing good. Acts 10:38."

Then he removed his dark blue suit jacket in his back office and finally passed into the conference room, where a small crowd had gathered to watch for results on TV. He was dressed as he always dressed: immaculately pressed powder-blue shirt, starched in front; white-on-blue polka-dot bow tie; dark blue trousers hiked up over his ample midsection. First order of business: replace the TV set, which was on the fritz.

"Son of a bitch," Hubbard muttered. "The damn thing works for two years, and then the one night you want to use it, it goes out like this." Then, to the multitude: "Sit down. There's not much to do, but no smoking, please."

It was 8:20 P.M. when the first partial results came in, brought by Fire Chief Chester Swanger, handed to public relations aide Doyne Jackson and then to the mayor. Jackson read the results: with 15 of 104 precincts reporting, Hubbard was leading his opponent, a high school government teacher named John A. Pazzanese, 5,014 to 845. And on Proposition A, a ballot proposal to raise the mayor's pay from $25,000 to $35,000, the vote was 2,610 yes, 2,611 no.

"Yep, one vote, yeah, yeah," intoned Hubbard. "We'll be lucky if it ever passes, I'm telling you, the way people feel about it."

With that, Hubbard went to work editing the "modest victory statement" Jackson had started preparing the day before. "A little fuzzy there," Hubbard said, marking over several sentences.

More vote results kept coming in—Hubbard for years called his hand-delivery system the "pony express"—and it became clear that the mayor would come close to beating his own personal record (87 percent against a real estate salesman who hardly campaigned) and that the pay increase would be a matter of just a few votes either way.

It was sure enough, at any rate, that the mayor's victory party could begin. No bands, no refreshments, no speeches. But old friends—as well as old antagonists—moved in to greet him. Among them was 78-year-old Homer Beadle, one of his old foes on the City Council, who had been run out of politics by Dearborn's dictator years before.

"Let me be the first to congratulate you," Beadle said in a self-consciously dramatic-sounding note of genuflection. "You ran a hell of a race today, but you made it."

"Thank you, Homer, thank you," responded the mayor, grinning ear to ear and adding a non-sequitur riposte that only he and Beadle could appreciate. "I always liked you ever since I first saw you. You got your ass shot off in World War I."

From another well-wisher, attorney Michael J. Berry, longtime kingpin of the powerful Wayne County Road Commission and once an officer in the citizens' committee allied with Ford's in trying to remove Orvie from office more than two decades before: "Aren't you getting tired of pounding your opponents into the ground, Mayor? You're running out of enemies."

Hubbard smiled graciously, accepting the compliments in a style polished by 30 years of repetition. Then, taking a slip of paper from an aide, he adjusted his reading glasses and tried to make himself heard over the din in the room.

"Here's the final, plus absentees: mayor 24,760, opponent 5,334; pay raise 14,211 yes, 14,312 no. One hundred votes." Then, to Jackson: "What does the percentage show? Have you figured out the percentage?" Jackson replied, "It's about 82."[6]

Hubbard, his shirt sleeves rolled up now, crossed his arms in front of his chest, smiling faintly. He was disappointed. Not about the pay raise. The vote. He had been hoping to do better against Pazzanese, whom no one had taken seriously.

"Some people said 90 percent," the mayor acknowledged. "You like to feel your work's approved. Everyone likes to have 100-percent approval if they can get it. We try like hell to please every way we can. You have to be sort of a Boy Scout. You have to do a good turn daily for every person."

He insisted that the pay raise defeat didn't bother him.

"That's the way human nature works. I don't think it would have made any difference if it had been one dollar. Maybe people will feel sorry for me now. If I'd got it, they'd say, 'You rich son of a bitch.'" As for tomorrow, the mayor told friends before leaving the room, "We just carry on. We've got nothing to celebrate. We've got leaves to pick up. In the west end, Christ, I've never seen so many leaves in my life."

His next immediate chore: deal with a TV interviewer, Robert Vito of Channel 4. The cameras were set up in front of a yellow-and-red banner proclaiming, "A King of All Mayors," and Hubbard began to describe his feelings. "Well, I've been in the business too long to be excited about it. Of course, we kind of thought we might win."

Vito: "There must be, I would guess, a disappointment to this election in the sense that Proposition A, which proposed a $10,000-a-year pay raise . . ."

Hubbard: "No, it's not a disappointment to me. . . . Of course, I never made much anyway. If I'd made it in the past, it's probably the worst thing that could have happened to me. But I don't feel bad about it at all. Matter of fact, I wouldn't know what to do with the money."

Finally, with only a few close aides and supporters left, Hubbard sat at the end of the table and started going over the precinct returns. In the ethnic south end, traditionally a Hubbard stronghold when it was dominated by East European immigrants and still so now that a large Arab community had sprung up, he got a subpar 73 percent of the total vote, compared to 70 percent in the Country Club Estates.

"The Country Club Estates?" Hubbard said in mock anger. "Those rich bastards. Let 'em pick up their own leaves." Then, laughing at an observation that he got 88 percent in the new Fairlane development area: "Eighty-eight? What the hell's wrong with the other 12? Son of a bitches just moved in. Tell 'em we're going to annex 'em to Melvindale right away."

Finally, Hubbard had to stifle a yawn. If he could maintain only a modicum of academic interest in his own election, so be it. He really was as much interested now in the other three dozen or so elections being carried on across the state. Detroit, for instance, was in the midst of electing its first black mayor, Coleman A. Young, a former state senator who was pitted against ex–Police Commissioner John F. Nichols, a white.

To Hubbard, the prospect had an aura of inevitability about it. Told by a staffer that Nichols was still leading two-to-one with 44 percent of the vote in, he replied, in something of a mixed metaphor, "Wait till those black votes come in. Then you'll see the clouds come up out of the west."

Actually, Hubbard had been predicting for months that Young would beat Nichols.

"It was just bound to be. I don't think Nichols came across on TV too good. I would've voted for him, I think, if I'd been there, but maybe just because he's white. But this guy Young has been in the game a long time, and he's been kicked around. Well, he's gonna find out he's got one of the toughest jobs he ever had in his life. The Detroit blacks are gonna expect so much of him. It's a lot easier to advocate than it is to administer. The problems are crime among his own people. He's got to take a strong stand or he can't do anything at all. But he can be tough, too. He's sort of a knock-'em-down, drag-'em-out type."[7]

A bit later, hearing that Mayor John Canfield had won reelection in neighboring Dearborn Heights over attorney G. Daniel Ferrera, Hubbard mused, "Well, I'll be goddamned. I'll be goddamned. Ferrera did better than I thought he'd do, but he didn't punch hard. He had to punch under the belt line. . . . But he'll learn. You have to learn. It's a long, hard game."

Next, after taking phone calls from the Detroit papers, the mayor heard from a number of constituents. "Joanna! I'm looking to see more of you. Thank you very much. I'll let you buy my dinner some night when Keane goes away . . ."

Then Hubbard looked over the results of some of his running mates on the City Council, including John Baja. Interjected Keane, "Know what Baja said? He said last time he ran fifth and this year he ran on your ticket and ran sixth."

"Well," Hubbard said, his voice rising, "why doesn't he run alone, then? Goddamn bunch of ingrates. Then he could've been eighth or ninth. You just love people that . . ."

"Look at Coleman Young," Keane broke in, gesturing toward the TV. "They're neck and neck, 93 percent in, 203,000 to 219,000."

"The niggers have it," Hubbard declared, raising his beefy hands in mock triumph.

"The niggers have it," echoed Keane. "That'll be headlines tomorrow."

Everybody chuckled. Times were changing, all right, but Dearborn and its mayor remained secure. And somehow Hubbard didn't look at all mad anymore.

2

Keeping Dearborn White

I have sometimes wondered why, if God was able with
a simple command to bring light to the universe, he
does not do the same thing to the minds of Orval Fau-
bus and Orville Hubbard.
— John C. Dancy, former executive director, Urban
League of Detroit[1]

Through the half-drawn blinds in his mayoral suite at city hall, Orville
Hubbard could see mainstream America.

He could see the storefronts along historic Michigan Avenue, once the
main Detroit-to-Chicago auto route, known during the stagecoach era as
the Chicago Road and before that, during Indian days, as the Sauk Trail.

He could see the housewives at the neighborhood shops, the businessmen at the lunch spots, the auto workers at the bank, the retirees on the
benches and the youngsters on the municipal playground equipment. He
could see it all. And he could see that it was white.

In a sense, Orville Hubbard's view was no different from that in any of
a dozen or more other segregated suburbs that ringed the city of Detroit—
or in hundreds of other such communities scattered across the country.

But Orville Hubbard saw the cityscape and knew it was more than just
a view. He knew it was a lever for self-perpetuation. And while the racism
of Orville Hubbard was not the racism of the Ku Klux Klan, of the cross
burners and the lynch mobs, it was just as insidious in its way, representing
as it did the stranglehold of the white power structure on the political
machinery of the suburbs of northern America.

In Dearborn the political machinery was housed in a three-story, brick,
colonial-style city hall built in 1922 and distinguished chiefly by a cupola
inspired by the one at Philadelphia's Independence Hall.

Inside, lettered above the front entryway, was an immediate reminder
of the influence of Henry Ford: his inspirational saying, "People get ahead
during the time that others waste." To the right, down the hall from a spiral

stairway, lay the mayor's office. Past a paneled wooden door stenciled with an invitation to "Walk In," a pair of industrious-looking secretaries awaited to intercept visitors.

The dingy green walls of the office were decorated with a mix of clippings and slogans, including the Preamble to the U.S. Constitution and a quotation on human kindness. There was also a map of Southeast Asia for quick reference on the Vietnam War, a Marine insignia arrangement and a large color photo of three young women waterskiing in 1950s-style tank suits. For good measure, there was a time clock with a card exhorting, "You asked for work. You have a job. Dig in or dig out. —Mayor Hubbard." And, as insurance against confusion on busy days, there was a "Please Take a Number" standard and a "Now Serving" numerical display. Beyond a swinging gateway, past the long table in the conference room, was the mayor's inner sanctum.

There, behind a neatly ordered desk near the windows that looked out on the erstwhile Indian trail, next to a pair of large wall mirrors and a couple of old maps of the United States and Florida, sat Orville L. Hubbard, onetime high school athlete, ex-Marine, nonpracticing attorney, self-acknowledged expert on matters from the milking of cows to the history of the American Revolution, and personal symbol of suburban America's resistance to racial integration.

This sunny fall morning in 1972 was no different from most. The mayor had a visitor, and, as always, he was ready to impart his peculiar wisdom to whoever was within earshot.

Most of Hubbard's conversations soon turned into rambling, disjointed discourses, often profane or scatalogical, but nearly always compelling. Although his voice was flat and adenoidal, he was a master storyteller, even when he mumbled or skipped words, as he sometimes did in his declining years. He was witty, apt of phrase, insightful in his analysis of human nature, unequivocal in his opinions. His musings were invariably an intriguing melange of folksy epigrams, barnyard humor, historical references and character assassination.

When Hubbard talked, he didn't just talk. He regularly worked himself into a desk-pounding fury, spewing out a machine-gun barrage of cuss words as he recalled past transgressions, real or imagined, by opponents or subordinates. Then he would regain his composure and meander off into childhood reminiscences, anecdotes about historical figures or general philosophizing, often pausing along the way to check a date or a spelling with an aide.

An interview with Orville Hubbard wasn't so much a question-and-answer session as it was an occasional effort to nudge a monologue back toward a topic that may have seemed all but abandoned hours before.

In one-on-one conversations, Hubbard often appeared obsessed with the race issue. At least that was how he struck me during a two-year series

28

of interviews we set up to talk about his life, and this morning was typical. As usual, he was flipping through the morning paper as we began. And as usual, he had found something that set him off.

This time it was a story about Detroit Mayor Roman S. Gribbs declaring the birthday of Dr. Martin Luther King Jr. a city holiday. With a touch of incredulity in his voice, Hubbard began reading aloud Gribbs's description of the slain civil rights leader: "'A man of our times. . . . A man for all times. He advocated and lived nonviolence.'"

Hubbard's squinty, gray-blue eyes peered out from behind his reading glasses, his swivel chair squeaking loudly as he shifted around to face me directly. "That son of a bitch," he said in measured tones. "Truman said that Martin Luther King was just a troublemaker. He certainly stirred up violence everywhere."

Then he read more of Gribbs's commentary: "'He struggled for and he gained equality. He resisted and he overcame hatred.'" Again, Hubbard looked up. "He did like hell," he snapped.

Finally, adding his own practical reflection on the folly of Gribbs's gesture: "That's a lot of holidays. And they're broke? I wouldn't vote to give 'em the time of day. That goddamn mess in Detroit can never be straightened out. Never, never, never, never."

Orville Hubbard was rolling now. Spotting a story about 65 Haitian refugees being blown ashore on the coast of Florida, he immediately clicked back to his own days as a Marine in the Caribbean. He had served a year and a half in the Virgin Islands, "where it's 99 and 44/100ths percent black," and where he recalled with some chagrin having to step deferentially off the street to make way for the locals to pass. He also drew some lasting impressions from a couple of days stationed on duty in Haiti, which he still mispronounced as "HAY-tie."

"Boy, that's some country," he said enthusiastically as he launched into an impromptu history lesson about "HAY-tie." "It was settled by the French, you know, and then the niggers all overthrew 'em one night—massacred 'em. For years they just lived down there by themselves. They started eating each other. Cannibalism. The Marines went down there in 1914, and they ate a few Marines. There was a General Russell that was in charge of 'em at that time. Gave orders to go through those hills and shoot every goddamn thing that moved. That brought 'em under complete control then, settled 'em down."[2]

A few minutes later, the mayor came to a story about a 26-year-old Detroit woman who was awarded $740,000 after a bungled operation turned her into a mental patient. "Jesus Christ Almighty," he thundered. "Society can't stay in business. Because the niggers are revolting, we just give it away."

This was vintage Orville Hubbard, all right. If he was trying to cement his reputation as the nation's most outspoken segregationist outside the Deep South, he certainly was succeeding. It was exactly the kind of performance you might expect of a man who supposedly once had examined the bullet-riddled body of a black man and called it an open-and-shut case of suicide.[3]

Or a man who, during the Detroit race rioting of 1967, had ordered Dearborn police to "shoot looters on sight."

Or a man who, the stories go, sometimes used to discourage blacks who had just moved into Dearborn by providing police and fire protection that was a little too good—wake-up visits every hour or so through the night in response to trouble calls.

Despite his record, Hubbard, intriguingly, saw himself as almost a moderate on the race issue, even while giving in to racist invective of the worst sort. "I'm not a racist," he once protested to his assembled department heads, "but I just hate those black bastards."

In fact, in discussing blacks privately, Hubbard often slipped into a pattern of familiar racial slurs—"niggers," "snowballs," "jigaboos"—and occasionally he fell into the habit in the presence of reporters. Once, when this was pointed out to him by an aide, he replied, "Well, what the hell. A nigger's a nigger. If he's black, he's black. That's all right with me. I'm not against him."

Indeed, Hubbard was known as a generous tipper where blacks were involved. He often slipped a few dollars to the black shoeshine boy at his barber shop, for instance. And once, in an apparent effort to show a group of appointees and a reporter how broadminded he was, he approached a black parking attendant at one of his favorite luncheon spots and, with a flourish, kissed the man on both cheeks. "See," the mayor told his entourage, "I don't hate niggers."

In his later years, Hubbard seemed to take genuine umbrage at the label with which he was inevitably tagged. When Roy Wilkins pinned the "meanest man in race relations" tag on him in 1969, Hubbard declined public comment. But when I asked him about it later, he was palpably irked. "He's full of shit," he said, adding somewhat extravagantly, "I'm probably the kindest human being that ever dealt with people anywhere in the world." A year after the Wilkins incident, when a Dearborn attorney named George Lewis upbraided Hubbard at a City Council meeting as "a bigot who is too gutless to admit it," Hubbard responded with a threat to "roll one off your goddamn nose."

And while Hubbard never did become completely reconciled to the civil rights movement, he was willing to make accommodations to it in his later years. If he looked at Dr. King as an agitator, he also once extended a cordial greeting to the Reverend Ralph D. Abernathy, Dr. King's successor as head of the Southern Christian Leadership Conference.

When Abernathy arrived one afternoon in 1969 to speak at the Dearborn Inn, Hubbard told him, "We'd like to have you living here."[4] Hypocritical, perhaps, but it also was another indication that the ogre of Dearborn could—and often did—relate well with individual blacks.

Hubbard had few contacts with blacks when he was growing up. One of his most vivid childhood recollections in the rural Michigan community of Union City, he told me, was a huge sign depicting "a nigger kid eating a watermelon."

But by the time he got into politics, his feelings on the subject had been hardened by a streak of shameless opportunism. Although he took no public position on the racial issue until he'd been in office for a few years, he soon became willing to seize on it as one more political advantage in a homogeneous community where many voters undoubtedly felt threatened by the presence of thousands of black auto workers at the Ford Rouge plant.

While the anti-Semitic sentiments of old Henry Ford all but evaporated from the public mind after Dearborn's most famous citizen made a brief and unsuccessful foray as a U.S. Senate candidate, the whites-only rhetoric of Orville Hubbard tinged the mayor's entire career. Even his first successful run for the mayor's job in 1941 was marred by rumors—unfounded, he always said—that he was a member of the Klan and the even more notorious vigilante group the Black Legion. Shortly after that, he began using a campaign slogan originally intended to refer to illegal activities in town before the Ferguson grand juries came in. "Our first slogan said, 'Keep Dearborn Clean from Vice, Graft and Corruption,'" Hubbard explained to me. "That's exactly what it means." But a few years later, the slogan had evolved—in its familiar short form, "Keep Dearborn Clean"—into something that most observers took to mean "Keep Dearborn White." Probably the most charitable interpretation of that evolution is that the mayor never worked very hard at dispelling the impression.

Hubbard's years in office were marred by a long list of racist pronouncements. In what was arguably the low point, he opposed construction of a low-income housing development in 1948 on the grounds that it was a "racial gamble" that could turn into a black slum. He went so far as to have his aides pass out leaflets urging citizens to "keep the Negroes out of Dearborn" by voting against a referendum on the project.[5] One of his favorite stories, in fact, concerned a former council member who, he said, worked at a polling place while wearing a hat with the same exhortation on it. But there were no other politicos in town who could even think of outbigoting Orville Hubbard.[6]

Orvie became a national figure of sorts on the race issue in 1956, when he told an Alabama newspaperman that he was "for complete segregation, one million percent." In 1965, the federal government tried him—unsuccessfully—on charges of conspiring to violate the civil rights of a Dearborn man whose house was vandalized during a mob scene stirred up by rumors that he had sold to blacks. A bit later, Hubbard became the first target of the fledgling Michigan Civil Rights Commission after he refused to remove race-related news clippings he had posted on city bulletin boards.

Despite all that, however, Dearborn's history of outright discrimination or harassment against blacks—by either Hubbard, his underlings or his constituents—fell well short of the city's national image as a bastion of northern racism. A much-repeated story throughout Hubbard's tenure in office dealt with routine mistreatment of blacks traveling in Dearborn or trying to live or shop in the city. In fact, however, the public record contained little to back up the story.[7]

The mayor had a way of explaining his position on the basis of justice and equity without realizing his words were loaded with irony. "Goddammit," he once was quoted in the *New York Times Magazine*. "I don't hate niggers. Christ, I don't even dislike them. But if whites don't want to live with niggers, they sure as hell don't have to. Dammit, this is a free country. This is America."[8]

Usually, though, when quoted for print, Hubbard spoke temperately, if patronizingly, on the subject. "I just don't believe in integration," he told the *Detroit News* in 1967. "When that happens, along comes socializing with the whites, intermarriage and then mongrelization."[9] But, he added, "the Negroes who work here are well treated. They're welcome in our restaurants and motels. One Negro told me that he never received more polite treatment than when he was stopped by one of our policemen. And go talk to the Negro family who was slipped into the city by some civil rights group. We treat them well."[10]

The race issue came up repeatedly during our series of interviews, sometimes at length but more typically interspersed with other subjects. During one three-and-a-half-hour session, for example, the conversation started off focusing on his segregationist leanings, became enmeshed in such other topics as a visit to a brothel (he was just visiting with friends who went there, and nothing happened, he said), no-fault divorce (he favored it), lawyers (he hated them as a class, even while continuing to identify himself as one on city stationery) and doctors (he thought they were all phonies). Eventually, he had covered dozens of subjects, but the race issue continued to pop up. Among his comments were the following:

On a federal official who pushed for the low-income housing project in 1948: "He looked like a scurvy goddamn poor white trash. He had a warped mind."

On his response to Dearborn clergymen after they criticized his statements on race in 1956: "I said, 'I'll tell you this. If you want [black] people here, get 'em. You start bringing 'em here, you aren't going to have a church very long. Your people aren't going to put up with it.'"

On the exit of a black minister and his family—the one he said was slipped in by a "ruse"—after renting a house on Dearborn's east side: "He wasn't accepted because his kids raised hell. He didn't take care of his property, either."

In spite of his frequent segregationist declarations, Hubbard was not, strictly speaking, a white supremacist. He never said blacks were inferior—just that they should be kept apart from whites. As for assessing his role in keeping Dearborn white, he occasionally claimed "credit" for the feat in his earlier years as mayor. But he became more modest about the "accomplishment" later in life.

"I don't keep the niggers out of Dearborn," he told me. "I don't keep anybody out of Dearborn. I haven't done anything to encourage 'em. I don't do anything to discourage 'em.

"I would think eventually they'll overrun the place—in another 20 years, I wouldn't be surprised. We're surrounded now. Christ, we're just a little postage-stamp community here. I would say the attitude of Dearborn is no different than of any other community. This town has probably got the greatest diversity of nationalities in the country—45, according to the 1970 census report. That's almost as many as the United Nations.

"I believe in freedom of choice. Most people want to be accepted, and the only way to be accepted is to fit the pattern. I'm not against any human being in the world. I've never taken a stand against a person because he was red, white or yellow, whatever his color is. I've taken this stand; I've never changed it: I don't believe in one group of people forcing themselves upon another. The average fellow with good sense doesn't go where he's not welcome and not wanted. I don't care who he is, where he lives, you or me. People upon this world have lived among their own people. That's the pattern. That's the whole history of the world.

"What the hell's a racist? You're a racist because you don't believe in forced segregation? If you are, I guess I'd be a racist. Do I think the black man is inferior? No, I don't. I think any normal-born human being that has an equal opportunity would develop as much as anybody else regardless of who they are. I think environment's the whole story in life. Human beings—I don't care what color they are, but they must be accepted on their own merits. If you're going to be a bum, be a bum. If you're going to try to do something, you're recognized for doing something. Be proud of who you are and how you live, and people will be proud of you."

That's the kind of stuff many of the folks in Dearborn loved to hear—the blue-collar conservative groups in the heavily ethnic east-side precincts as well as at least a share of the WASP-ish white-collar and professional types on the west side. It was a formula for racial separation without all the guilt feelings engendered by outright vituperation. And it well may have helped pull Hubbard through an election or two in the early years of his career.

To those who knew Orville Hubbard well, the irony of this strong ethnic support was inescapable. Of several long-standing secrets he kept from his constituents, the best kept was that he harbored a wide-ranging personal contempt that extended far beyond the black race. He looked down on a variety of ethnic and religious groups, including many that turned out heavily for him at the polls. If he had not remained on guard to mask his considerable prejudices about all kinds of white groups, he would never have seemed so easy to pigeonhole as a white bigot.

Indeed, during our interviews, Hubbard frequently let slip asides or anecdotes that revealed his deep-seated dislike of many non-WASP groups. Sometimes he caught himself, and sometimes he did not.

"They say the Jews own this country, the Irish run it and the niggers have all the fun," he once observed. Then he added, "There's more truth to that. And if there's ever any corruption—it's not a good thing to say, make a lot of people mad, but it's true—the Irish are all involved. I've noticed that over the years. In the police department, they seem to be more corrupt even than the Dagos."

Once as we talked, he referred to a former city official as a "goddamn Polack liar," then recovered quickly with: "Don't write the word *Polack*. It'll come out, make people mad, and I get a big Polish support." Other such references dotted his conversations: "those fucking Irishmen," "damn Jews," "goddamn narrow-minded Methodists," "goddamn raw-necked Catholics," not to mention "goddamn Polacks." He also had built up an active dislike for the city's burgeoning Arab enclave in the east end, allowing once that "some people think the Syrians are even worse than the niggers."

Observed Judy Cord, an office secretary for Hubbard from 1959 to 1970: "I don't think he liked anybody. I mean you were either a Polack or a Dago or a Jew or a nigger or a potato digger, or you were cheap or you were a son of a bitch. Whatever you were, that was the excuse. So I don't think you could say specifically he disliked blacks, because it expanded to everybody."[11]

As an aside, however, let it not be said that Orville Hubbard remained totally blind to the evils of prejudice. At one point, he remarked with totally unintentional irony, "Those Irish Catholics are the worst of them all. They're so goddamn prejudiced. They talk about the Irish Mafia, about what's going on in Ireland. They can never settle that stuff because of the goddamn narrow-mindedness."

But a question remains. Was Hubbard's own racial stand really just calculated for political effect? There can be no doubt that he believed what he was saying publicly, and yet, in light of his privately expressed revulsion toward other ethnic groups, there's equally little question but that he would have been saying it differently had circumstances been different.

One clue comes from the mayor's own musings about his dealings with blacks on a personal and political level. "Christ," he sputtered, "when I ran for office back in the early days [as a township justice of the peace in 1936], the Negroes all voted for me. I knew 'em all. I get along with everybody. I say if Negroes lived here, they'd be all voting for Hubbard."

Blacks voting for Hubbard?

Perhaps. In another town, under different circumstances, why not? But left unanswered is the question of what sort of community would elect such a man on such a racist platform as Orville Hubbard implicitly ran on—and keep on electing him.

3

The Company Town

History is bunk.
—Henry Ford I, testifying in his libel trial against
the *Chicago Tribune*[1]

From the white-spired tower of old Independence Hall to the little cycle shop where the Wright brothers built their first flying machine, the scene looks as though it has been snatched from some impossible time warp. The hall, as it happens, is an architectural knockoff of the original in Philadelphia. But, like nearly all the other buildings in the 252-acre complex, the cycle shop is the real thing, transplanted in this case from Dayton, Ohio, and spliced into what the brochures used to call "an inspiring village which vividly portrays three centuries of American life," but which now concentrates on history and technology from 1800 to 1950.

It all provides an intriguing panorama for the million or so visitors who come from around the world to Dearborn every year to visit the Henry Ford Museum and Greenfield Village, the paired historical shrines of Americana established in 1929 by Henry Ford in spite of his much-quoted notion equating history and bunk.

But Dearborn's real historical centerpiece lies down the road a few miles to the east, where tourists once trekked by the thousands but where, since the beginning of the 1980s, they have no longer been welcome.[2] Visitors who never catch a glimpse of the belching smokestacks of the Ford Rouge plant miss a landmark that, more than Henry Ford's romanticized village and museum complex, marks the Detroit suburb as perhaps the most emphatically American of any of the nation's twentieth-century industrial cities. It is the Rouge plant, after all, that is depicted in one of the most widely celebrated series of paintings of American industry, Diego Rivera's assembly-line murals at the Detroit Institute of Arts.

As the city's most famous historical attraction, Greenfield Village may be partly ersatz, but Dearborn's links with Henry Ford, the man who put America on wheels, are real enough. This is the place where Ford was born, resided and eventually produced the cars that transformed America from a rural nation to an urban one. At the turn of the century, six of ten Americans lived on farms. Fifty years later, six of ten lived in cities. To a large extent, that was the work of Ford and the auto manufacturing processes he developed in Dearborn.

While that was happening—and while the automobile also was helping to create the ultimate expression of mid-twentieth-century life, the suburb— Henry Ford's hometown was undergoing exactly the same metamorphosis as it had stimulated in the rest of the country. Dearborn began as a little farming village that expanded with the advent of local industry. And then, as the automobile became commonplace, the town bloomed into the most visible suburb of Detroit.

For sheer visual impact, Dearborn's 24.5-square-mile expanse is little different from hundreds upon hundreds of other suburban communities around the country. The museum-village complex is a walled enclave, and the Ford plant is tucked away in the southeast corner of the city. The rest of Dearborn—with its neatly kept homes, close-clipped lawns and neighborhood parks and playgrounds—extends out from its east-west axis, Michigan Avenue.

The town is segregated into two distinct sectors, generally characterized as a white-collar west end and a working-class, ethnic east end. In between twin downtowns lies a two-mile-wide greenbelt that once was owned exclusively by Ford and now accommodates the village and museum, along with Ford's old Fair Lane estate and the headquarters of the Ford Motor Company. In more recent times, parcels were given over as campuses for the University of Michigan–Dearborn and Henry Ford Community College, as well as the sprawling, 2,360-acre Fairlane shopping center with its upscale stores, hotels and offices.

Most of the changes visited on Dearborn over the years were witnessed by the man who, second only to Henry Ford, had the most influence on the burgeoning city.

Orville Hubbard liked to call himself a country kid who came to the city and left his mark, but the city itself was growing in the years that he was establishing himself there as an energetic young man with a gift of gab and a streak of combativeness. When Hubbard arrived in Detroit in 1920 to work in an auto factory, Dearborn was still a village of slightly more than 3,500 souls. By the time he became mayor in 1942, the city had passed the 63,000 mark.

Dearborn's earliest days were typical of the development of much of the Midwest. Though there is no reason to suspect that he ever visited, the community is named for Major General Henry Dearborn, who served with distinction in the Revolutionary War and the War of 1812 and was secretary of war for Thomas Jefferson from 1801 to 1809. The earliest names for the place came from the woodland Indians—Ottawa, Potawatomi, Wyandotte, Chippewa, Saux-Fox—who camped along the two river branches that wound through the meadows and forests there. *Minosa Goink*, some of them called it: "Singeing Skin River," the place where game was dressed. The first white settlers were mostly French farmers who came in 1795 to claim narrow ribbons of land that fronted on the river—they knew it as the Rouge—and protruded back toward the woods. Later came the English, Irish and Scottish. Many traveled by water, particularly after the Erie Canal was completed in the 1820s, providing access to the Great Lakes from the East. Others came by wagon down the rugged, muddy Chicago Road, the onetime Indian path that ranked as the oldest toll road in the Midwest. The local Ten Eyck Tavern became one of its best-known stagecoach stops.

Dearborn originally consisted of parts of two townships, Springwells to the east and Bucklin to the west, laid out and named by Lewis Cass, governor of the Michigan Territory, in 1818 and 1824, respectively. During a succession of political subdivisions and name changes, the village of Dearbornville was incorporated in 1838 from a part of Bucklin Township that had been renamed Dearborn Township in 1833. Dearbornville reverted to unincorporated status in 1846 and was incorporated again in 1893 as the village of Dearborn. For years before that, however, residents often referred to the area simply as Dearborn.

Life changed in Dearbornville in the 1830s, when the U.S. government took steps to consolidate its hold by erecting the Detroit Military Arsenal, a high-walled complex of 11 buildings on a plot of 230 acres right on the Chicago Road. There followed a construction boom that attracted dozens of skilled tradesmen. Many of the area's 200 or 300 settlers decided to stay and farm, continue their trades or start businesses. The thick clay along the riverbanks encouraged the startup of the area's first industry, brickmaking.

Though the arsenal was manned by fewer than 75 men at its peak, the little hamlet was becoming a veritable military-industrial complex. And in 1837, the year the arsenal was finished, the town knew it had arrived: the Michigan Central Railroad came through, prompting a new wave of activity. By the Civil War, the arsenal was used as a training center for Union Army recruits. By 1875, the military abandoned the facility, but the commandant's quarters were put to a succession of other uses, including a municipal office, police headquarters, jail and kindergarten.

From the 1880s through the turn of the century, a variety of businesses flourished along the old Indian trail, now known as Michigan Avenue. These included meat markets, shoe stores, grocery and dry goods stores, hardware stores, blacksmith and harness shops, lumber companies and a barber shop. By 1897, Dearborn had an electric rail line.

But the biggest changes were still ahead. A young man born in 1863 on a Springwells Township farm eventually joined the legion of hopeful mechanics who had begun tinkering with internal combustion engines. In 1893, he constructed a one-cylinder gasoline model in the kitchen of his Bagley Avenue home in Detroit. By 1896, he had built his first car, a frame that held together an engine and four bicycle wheels. Although young Henry Ford was about 10 years behind Karl Benz's work with gasoline autos in Mannheim, Germany, he soon caught up, and his success became Dearborn's success. He held 25 percent of the stock when the Ford Motor Company incorporated in 1903, operating out of a factory at Bellevue and Mack in Detroit. By 1906, he held 51 percent of the stock, and he recapitalized the firm in 1919, arranging it so that his family held all the shares. That fall the first car—the latest of Ford's already famous Model T's—came off the assembly line at the 1,200-acre plant he had built in the south end of Springwells Township.

The Ford Rouge plant worked on the revolutionary principle of vertical integration. The idea was to unload iron ore, coal, sand, limestone and other raw materials at the plant's docks on the Rouge and days later to turn out finished autos at the end of a moving assembly line. This method of modern mass production enabled the Rouge in four years to outstrip the Krupp Steel Works in Germany as the world's largest manufacturing complex operated by a single company. The Rouge was a magnet for job seekers after World War I, but the village of Dearborn and neighboring Springwells Township were scarcely ready for the masses who poured in from the South, from Europe and later from the Middle East.

In 1920, the little communities had volunteer fire brigades, skeleton police forces, unpaved streets and no public sewers. But Springwells incorporated as a village in 1921, became a city in 1923 and was renamed Fordson in 1925 in honor of Henry and his son Edsel. Dearborn, meanwhile, had annexed a chunk of Dearborn Township in 1925 and then incorporated as a city in 1927. By the end of the decade, the combined population had mushroomed 15 times to slightly more than 50,000, and Dearborn was recognized as the fastest-growing community in the nation.

In March 1929, the Rouge plant was employing a staggering total of 102,811 workers, its all-time high. It was during these times that Ford pushed for one of the city's most important decisions. With Detroit annexing land willy-nilly on its western borders, Ford concluded that the metropolis soon would ingest the tax plum represented by the millions of dollars of assessed valuation in the Rouge Plant. At his behest, voters approved a merger of Dearborn and Fordson in 1928, thus providing Dearborn with an industrial base and protecting Fordson against Detroit's appetite for land.

The city hall slate that took office in January 1929 was led by Clyde M. Ford, a pudgy-faced, resolute-looking man who had served as mayor of the old city of Dearborn since 1927. One of the problems facing Clyde Ford was bootlegging. Until Prohibition ended in 1933, Dearborn, like most communities, was beset with rumrunners and illegal drinking emporiums. Indeed, one national magazine charged that the mayor had knowledge of some 30 "blind pigs" operating in town. Despite his troubles, Ford was reelected twice more, serving until John L. Carey became mayor in 1936.

Dearborn also was a target for labor unrest during the 1930s. The Depression had all but erased the memory of the sensation Ford caused when he announced the five-dollar workday in 1914. In 1930, an army of some 20,000 unemployed men rioted at the Rouge after camping out all night to wait for job offers that never materialized. In 1932, a group of as many as 5,000 hunger marchers descended on the Rouge, which had shut down in the Depression's worst year. Dearborn police waded in with billy clubs and tear gas, and in the ensuing melee they shot five men to death and wounded up to 100 more. In 1937 came the infamous Battle of the Overpass, in which Ford toughs under Harry Bennett brutalized Walter Reuther and other United Auto Workers organizers at the Rouge plant. As a company town in all but the most extreme sense, Dearborn maintained a close working relationship with Ford Motor throughout the 1930s and '40s. The City Council passed an ordinance under Carey prohibiting union organizers from passing out leaflets at plant gates. City police also were accused of helping Ford goons beat up union sympathizers. Finally, the UAW organized Ford in 1941, eventually boasting the world's largest union, Ford Local 600, with 87,000 members.

During World War II, the Rouge plant was transformed into the hub of the war production effort, and the Detroit area became known as the Arsenal of Democracy. In World War I, Ford had built submarine-chasing "eagle boats" at its Detroit plant. Now, along with the other auto firms, it stopped building cars and started making tank and aircraft engines, jeeps, military trucks and armored cars. When peace came, the first postwar U.S. car was built there.

From Dearborn's earliest days, Henry Ford remained a generous benefactor to the town he had helped create. In one Depression year, he instructed the city fathers to raise the Rouge assessment by a million dollars so they could pay city employees. And through the decades, he and his company, which once owned nearly one-quarter of all the land in the city, donated more than 1,000 acres for public purposes.

Ford's relationship with city hall changed not long after the upstart new mayor was elected in 1941, the same year the company was unionized. Ford took a wait-and-see stance toward Hubbard at first and in 1945 allied with him against a plan to condemn Ford land for a federal housing project. But another housing project, this one proposed by Ford in 1948, pitted the firm's money against Hubbard's racially tinged scare campaign, creating hard feelings that lingered for nearly a decade.

In 1950, Hubbard's fire chief said the mayor had ordered him to break into Henry Ford II's office with an ax and find code violations to embarrass the company. The next year came the low point in the firm's relations with Hubbard, when Ford backed a broad-based but unsuccessful recall campaign against him. A few months later, Hubbard threatened to punch out a Ford vice-president in a controversy over a parcel of company land.

Gradually, though, as Henry Ford II realized that Hubbard was in city hall to stay and as Hubbard came to see the increasing advantages to the city if he were on good terms with its largest taxpayer, the two sides developed a rapprochement.[3]

The firm continued to donate land to the city, including 50 acres for a civic center and 15 acres for a Henry Ford Centennial Library. And the mayor, who at first had opposed the Ford Fairlane project ("Here we are, the only city in the world with its inner core vacant and beautiful, and they want to make it congested"), gave his grudging blessing to the development in the early '70s, thus launching the city's biggest building boom.

Meanwhile, Dearborn had continued to grow in population—to more than 94,000 by 1950, more than 112,000 by 1960 and an unofficial peak of about 115,000 by 1968. Within a decade after that, it fell back to less than 100,000. The city fluctuated between fourth and seventh place among Michigan's largest cities during its highest-population years.

What kind of people lived in Henry Ford's hometown? The census reports showed that, like most of Detroit's other suburbs, Dearborn was overwhelmingly white, more than 99 percent. Through the last years of Hubbard's tenure, the number of black families in town was less than 20.

In addition, about one of every seven Dearborn residents was foreign-born, coming primarily from Canada, Britain, Poland, Italy or Germany. Over recent decades, an already established Arab enclave grew to dominate much of the east end, including many refugees from the long-running Lebanese civil war.

In general, Dearbornites have been older, more prosperous and better educated than average. Their ranks swelled with residents who moved in decades before, Dearbornites have had a median age some six years higher than the state as a whole. Their median family income has been about a third higher than in Detroit, though somewhat lower than in some nearby communities.

Family life has been stable: more than three-fourths of the residents traditionally have lived in their own homes, divorce rates have been unusually low, and most families have tended to stay in town. There have been no slums, and, except for cyclical downturns in the auto industry, only a small percentage of families have lived below the poverty level.

Historically, Dearbornites have tended to vote Democratic, belying a long-standing reputation for intolerance that dates back to Henry Ford's anti-Semitic tirades in his old *Dearborn Independent* magazine.

Many of Orville Hubbard's enemies have attributed his success at the polls to his stand on the race issue. Attorney John J. Fish, who helped lead the opposition in several of Orvie's early campaigns, once told me, "We took a poll one time among the engineers of the Ford Motor Company, and, lo and behold, the majority were for Hubbard, and the principal reason as we could determine it was because of his attitude towards the colored. Now here are educated people. I was amazed. But I think his underlying strength in the community has been his attitude, this racial attitude. And the average voter—the Pole and the Italian in the community—thinks he keeps the Negro out of Dearborn."[4]

Despite Hubbard's image as a sort of living dead-bolt lock against racial integration, a 1964 telephone poll indicated that West Dearbornites had views on civil rights similar to those of other northern suburbanites, as reflected by a recent Gallup poll. A 1969 mail survey of one of West Dearborn's Roman Catholic parishes produced comparable results.

Those findings were corroborated by attitudinal surveys conducted among Dearbornites between 1974 and 1976 under the supervision of two political scientists, Ronald R. Stockton and Frank Whelon Wayman of the University of Michigan—Dearborn.

The surveys, as described in the Stockton-Wayman book *A Time of Turmoil: Values and Voting in the 1970's*, suggested that Dearbornites are a lot like suburbanites everywhere; the authors concluded that "opinions in the community are fairly typical of northern urban whites."[5] The book also indicated that residents of Dearborn espouse a new value system typical of many Americans:

> They report high levels of personal happiness. They are distrustful, however, of the large institutions around them—especially the government, politicians, and the news media, but also big business and labor. They are "conservative" in thinking that government programs are wasteful and inefficient. But they are "liberal" on their support of "New Deal" government programs that put money in their pockets: government aid to education, social security, unemployment compensation, medical insurance, and even guaranteed jobs to those who want to work. The people we studied support various aspects of sexual liberation, such as abortion and sex education. In this respect they are liberal. They oppose a variety of other radical or anti-traditional movements: the women's liberation movement, homosexuals, and black militants. In the same vein of conservatism, they support the police, the military, and law and order. The majority are free of classical racial prejudice; they do not think that blacks are genetically inferior. But they have stereotypes of black neighborhoods as dens of crime and vice, and they strongly oppose busing and housing integration.[6]

Significantly and surprisingly, on the race issue, the authors also found that although Dearbornites may have negative feelings about black militants, they "view blacks warmly to lukewarmly."[7]

If those findings truly reflect Dearborn's collective conscience over the years, then Orville Hubbard's success with his electorate cannot be explained away simply as a demagogue's pandering to a racist cadre of single-issue supporters. The findings suggest instead that Hubbard, as he himself had declared in his half-joking aside that blacks would vote for him if there were any in Dearborn, might have found a touchstone with voters almost anywhere.

4

The Hubbard Machine

This country needs a dictator. I'm sorry I'm too old to
be it.
        —Orville L. Hubbard, on a drive to his hometown
                        of Union City, Michigan[1]

Seven forty-nine A.M.—sharp—and Orville Hubbard had glided into the chair
at the head of his conference table to face his trusted cadre of key appointees. Years before, as he described it to *Life* magazine, Hubbard had insisted
that his department heads closet themselves into solitary "think sessions"
for a half-hour every morning at that time, but now they were simply
assembled for their regular daily meeting with the boss. Accordingly, Dearborn's top bureaucrats rose en masse to sing one of Orville Hubbard's favorite inspirational songs, "Do What You Do, Do Well." Then, with all the
decorum of some obscure lodge ritual, they solemnly repeated their own
peculiar Oath of Allegiance to Orville, which the mayor had borrowed—
perhaps from turn-of-the-century essayist Elbert Hubbard—and incorporated into the daily routine of municipal government: "No matter how
much you have to offer, if you don't deliver it when and where needed, it
isn't worth much."[2]

That done, they could get down to the business at hand—selecting the
tile color for the interior lobby walls of the proposed new Henry Ford
Centennial Library. The land had been donated by Ford; the plans for the
immense, white marble edifice had been completed; and now, on this morning in 1966, Hubbard and his staff were down to the detail work.

Normally, it might be brushed off as a matter of small consequence, to
be decided perhaps by a functionary of the library or public works department. But in Dearborn, such decisions were not taken so lightly. This would
be the product of the collective wisdom of Dearborn's policymakers—with,
naturally, appropriate input from the city's elective head.

As it happened, Hubbard knew exactly what he wanted: a particularly dark marbleized green that looked almost black. The only problem was that few of the department heads liked it much, if at all. In fact, one of them, longtime loyalist Harold DeWyk, went so far as to observe that he "had been in whorehouses that had better-looking tile than that."

Hubbard didn't always encourage his appointees to speak their minds thus, but this time he had, and now he was regretting it. Of the 22 or so present and voting, only 9 or 10 were going along with the mayor's choice.

Eventually, as one of the aides recalled it, "it got to be right around lunchtime, and he started getting hungry and he wanted to get that damn thing in. The vote kept coming up something like 12–10, 13–9. And so finally, Hubbard got tired of it, and he cast 8 votes for the green tile. That was the end of discussion, and we all went to lunch."

So this was the dictator mayor of Dearborn at work—the man who, for almost as long as he had served his community, had been compared by his enemies with nearly all the tyrants of the twentieth century and some before that: Hitler, Stalin, Mussolini, Napoleon, Caesar.

Well, admittedly, this was not so momentous a decision as Hitler's orders to eradicate the Jews or Stalin's directive to starve the Ukraine. But Orville Hubbard was elected by the people, and if he sometimes had to struggle to remember that he ruled in a democracy, he liked at least to give the superficial impression that decisions in city hall—even the little ones—occasionally were reached by means other than imperial decree.

There had been a time when Hubbard did not deal well with the dictator comparisons. His foes in the 1949 campaign had provoked him into a libelous rage by promulgating their "Hitler, Hague and Hubbard" slogan. Later on, he was able to look at the situation with a touch of humor when his 1957 opponent, newspaperman Bill Mills, used his *Dearborn Independent* to circulate a lengthy article entitled "How Dearborn Got a Dictator Mayor." Typical of the article:

> Hubbard, the candidate, was building himself up politically when Adolf Hitler, Benito Mussolini, Joseph Stalin, Juan Peron and others were . . . gaining power. . . . The world stood aghast a few years later at the cruelty of these men. . . . Hubbard during those years was campaigning for office. He too was out to win. It was only natural that the pattern set by the world leaders of that time should be studied and where possible their methods applied.[3]

Hubbard this time contented himself with calling press conferences and making a great show of ripping up copies of the offending publication. Even better, during a subsequent political rally, he put Mills on the defensive for a change by seizing on his opponent's squat, bullet-domed appearance and shouting out, "Look at that bald head. Did you ever see anybody that looked more like Mussolini than that guy?"

In an unguarded moment, Orvie occasionally would let slip his real feelings about his place in the cosmos. Once, as I tagged along during a 1973 visit he made to his hometown of Union City, Michigan, he proffered this: "This country needs a dictator. I'm sorry I'm too old to be it."

During formal interviews, Hubbard was always quick with disingenuous denials that he was anything more than a servant of the people. But even his most ardent supporters had to concede that he exercised almost complete administrative control of Dearborn. Everybody in town knew Orville Hubbard ran things by manipulating the City Council and bullying his department heads.

And it was no secret that the Hubbardian tentacles reached out well beyond the city limits. Twice, in fact, he had stretched his grasp to limits believed unprecedented in U.S. municipal experience, acquiring for his city a large wooded tract in another county and, later, a building in another state. These two extraterritorial acquisitions had been all too well publicized. Camp Dearborn, a 626-acre "citizens' country club" in neighboring Oakland County, was acquired in several purchases beginning in 1948. And Dearborn Towers, an apartment building in Clearwater, Florida, was bought from the federal government in 1968, then survived a lawsuit challenging the city's right to acquire and own property out of state. Another time, Hubbard toyed with the idea of buying two privately owned links across the Detroit River between the United States and Canada—the Ambassador Bridge and the Detroit-Windsor auto tunnel.

Of more direct influence on the day-to-day lives of Dearbornites, however, was a much less well publicized aspect of Hubbard's operations. Even many longtime residents never realized that Orville Hubbard was the architect of a network of pools, parks and playground facilities built to his personal specifications; that like the green library tile, many of the details— right down to the placement of swings and slides—resulted from the quirky preferences he developed over three decades in office.

By the same token, the whims of Orville Hubbard also found their way into the city's building code, considered the most rigid in Michigan. For decades, Dearborn builders and homeowners discovered that their blueprints had to fit into the "harmonious neighborhood" concept. If they wanted to build, the home had to be brick, not frame (and, for a few years, red brick at that); if they wanted walls, they had to be plaster, not drywall; if they wanted awnings, they had to be canvas, not aluminum; and such items as garbage disposals, 100-amp electrical service, kitchen and bathroom vent fans and bathtub "grab bars" were not only de rigueur, they were legal requirements. Motels had comparably stringent mandates. [4]

Hubbard's likes and dislikes were even translated into consumer choices available at Camp Dearborn. One of his son Frank's favorite examples concerned the "canteen" at the camp: "One day he went to the canteen and he got an ice cream cone. He saw a kid that got a double-dip, and one dip fell on the cement there. So from that point on he ordered that nobody could have a double-dip ice cream cone anymore because the kid dropped it, he lost his money and it made a mess."[5]

Acknowledged Doyne Jackson, "In his own way, if you're talking about strictly power, power per capita, if you will, Hubbard was a hell of a lot more powerful than the president of the United States or the mayor of Detroit or Chicago or any other city, or probably kings of different countries. He didn't have to answer to anybody. He didn't worry about what the media did. He really had absolute control over which street was paved, and garbage routes, and how many cops you had, and all that other. He was a tremendously powerful man. He was king."[6]

Dictator? King? Perhaps. Though there's a certain amount of hyperbole in many of the pejorative terms flung at Orville Hubbard through the years, it is nonetheless true that he was as pervasively influential as just about any of the old-style political bosses who dominated American politics from the late nineteenth century through the middle of the twentieth.

William Marcy "Boss" Tweed in New York. Big Bill Thompson and Richard Daley in Chicago. George B. Cox in Cincinnati. Ed Crump in Memphis. James M. Curley in Boston. Frank Hague in Jersey City. Tom Pendergast in Kansas City. At various times, the bosses ruled almost all the big cities.

Many had similar formulas. They all had a machine—a hierarchy of political stooges, generally linked with a political party and tied in with smaller ward or precinct organizations that reached from city hall into the neighborhoods. And they often dispensed hundreds, sometimes thousands, of patronage appointments. They handed out jobs on the city payroll as well as on municipal construction projects for sewer lines, streets, trolley tracks, hospitals, libraries, schools and municipal buildings. They sometimes depended on intimidating voters, buying votes and stuffing ballot boxes.

And yet, as author William V. Shannon points out, the bosses and their machines also accomplished considerable good, sometimes in spite of themselves: "The boss ran a kind of ramshackle welfare state. He helped the unemployed find jobs, interceded in court for boys in trouble, wrote letters home to the old country for the illiterate; he provided free coal and baskets of food to tide a widow over an emergency, and organized parades, excursions to the beach, and other forms of free entertainment."[7]

Orville Hubbard took the mold for the turn-of-the-century big-city political boss and totally retooled it for a mid-twentieth-century suburb. He demonstrated that one man could take over a town, even a company town run by an American legend like Henry Ford and his minions, without a traditional party organization and the external trappings of a machine. "I can't lick him," former Ford Board Chairman Henry Ford II once was quoted as saying about Hubbard's influence in maintaining Dearborn's lily-white character, "and I'll be damned if I join him."[8]

Though a longtime Republican precinct delegate, Hubbard was a pariah with the state GOP because of his history of publicity stunts and political feuds; and besides, the city ballot was nonpartisan. His patronage appointments consisted only of some 20-odd department head jobs. His "machine" was essentially a one-man operation consisting of Orville Hubbard himself.[9] "Everybody talks about the Hubbard machine," said Jackson. "Well, there was no Hubbard machine. There was Hubbard—and about 20 guys who would react to his orders, and not always effectively. The way he ran government was like a boot camp. He was a general; everybody else was a lieutenant. No majors or captains, all lieutenants. The Hubbard machine was one person—with a lot of mechanics."[10]

Almost by the sheer force of his personality, Hubbard orchestrated his small, hand-picked group of hatchetmen and political operatives, along with a few professional administrators, and he found a way to extend his influence across the entire spectrum of municipal government, including the City Council and, to a lesser extent, the courts. He seized on the strategy of the personal favors performed by the bosses by broadening the range of legitimate municipal services far beyond that of most cities. He overlayered his approach with a theme that drew many voters together under his mantle: the threat of black encroachment into an all-white city.

Ask him how he succeeded in maintaining his taut hand over Dearborn, and he remained circumspect. Ask him point-blank if he considered himself a political boss, and he'd say, "I don't know why they call me the boss. I don't think I'm that type of person. I'm the administrative leader of the city. We consider ourselves the people's mayor, if you want to use that expression."

As for the so-called Hubbard machine, he said, "If there is, it's the registered voters of the city. Everyone who votes for Hubbard is part of the organization. You can call it a machine if you want to. I don't like to call it that. We call it a team."

One of the epigrams attributed to him—"No stone moves unless I kick it"—is undoubtedly apocryphal, though he might as well have said it, since he was free to operate unilaterally whenever the mood struck him.

But did he really model himself after the much-reviled characters he was always being compared to? Did he actually admire Hitler? Hubbard typically reacted with disdain ("That's a lot of bullshit") when asked such questions. "I hated Hitler," he snapped—and then elaborated in a way that left a listener wondering whether the mayor were insulted more by what he perceived as Der Fuehrer's military ineptitude than by his crimes against humanity. "Hitler was a corporal. Dumb bastard should have known better than to invade Russia. If I'd had his army, I'd have won that war. I'd have crossed the English Channel at all costs and had England down to their knees."

While professing a certain respect for Napoleon ("A real go-getter, wasn't he? Sort of a ruthless bastard, though"), Hubbard was more an admirer of Washington: "Washington is one of the great people I've admired all my life. He could've been king. If we'd listened to his advice, we wouldn't be in the mess we are today: 'Beware of foreign entanglements; be strong enough to knock anyone on his ass.'"

As for contemporary Americans, Hubbard admired General Douglas MacArthur, but he said he had never met Hague or Crump or most of the other bosses, never was a "student" of Louisiana Governor and U.S. Senator Huey Long, liked Daley and Curley but most looked up to Fiorello LaGuardia: "LaGuardia had courage. He had vision. He was a dedicated public servant, and he was as honest a man as ever breathed in public office. I really loved the man."

Hubbard's own political philosophy was an almost incoherent mixture of socialist ideals, Democratic sympathy and Republican party loyalty. "I've always been an independent," he declared. "I was just born that way. Whether you're a Democrat or a Republican, what the hell difference does it make? It's all hocus-pocus anyway. No one does anything different that I know of.

"I worked like hell as a Republican delegate, but I voted for Roosevelt every time, if that makes me a good Republican. Hoover before that. Dewey in '48, Stevenson '52, Eisenhower '56, Nixon '60, Goldwater '64, Nixon '68 and '72.

"But I'm even more of a Democrat than the Democrats are. I'm just plain socialist is all. Look at everything I've done. Camp Dearborn: if it isn't, what is it?

"People are looking for a stronger government. I wouldn't be surprised if the thing winds up in a dictatorship. I don't know if the military or who's going to run it.

"But something's going to happen. Hoover said, 'You think this depression's bad? You wait till the next one comes.' And I think he's right. All of a sudden you're out of everything. If everybody missed a credit payment one month, that alone might break it. I think the whole goddamn thing's going to go down the drain. The whole life that we live."

Regardless of ideology, Hubbard's control of Dearborn depended largely on the strong-mayor/weak-council charter adopted by the city in 1942, his first year in office. It permitted him to appoint department heads—a power not granted under the city's previous weak-mayor charter. However, the charter allowed no further patronage.

The new mayor wasn't shy about usurping some additional administrative powers, though. Although the charter provided no mayoral control over employment—and in fact set up one of the strongest local Civil Service systems in the nation—Hubbard sometimes was accused of trying to subvert hiring procedures.

One of his best-known eccentricities was to require each new city employee to write a 200-word essay on Elbert Hubbard's moralistic tract, *A Message to Garcia*. He read all the essays himself, and he could be a tough grader when writers failed to find appropriate inspiration on loyalty and initiative in their reading. One oft-repeated story told of an applicant who copied his essay from an article by a Yale professor with six degrees. Asked how the mayor liked it, the applicant replied, "Oh, he said it was OK. He gave me 82 percent."

Less well publicized were Hubbard's attempts to manipulate Civil Service. Through the mid-1950s, Hubbard actually interviewed prospective city employees himself before hiring decisions were made. Civil Service tests would pare candidates down to the top three, and the mayor typically would indicate which of those he wanted appointed. When Hubbard disagreed with a decision, a new hire often would find that paperwork on his appointment was being held up in the mayor's office.

In his later years, a firmly entrenched Hubbard no longer took such pains, although department heads knew they needed the mayor's OK on key hires, Civil Service or no Civil Service.

Hubbard's department heads, all serving at his pleasure, regularly were pressed into duties that seemed emphatically more political than administrative. At election time, for example, their jobs suddenly became geared to electioneering. They all helped cover the city with Hubbard's floridly written campaign literature. And each had three or four voting precincts to oversee, making sure that volunteers were available to hand out literature and that cars decked out with Hubbard signs were parked within sight of voters.

The public relations man—Alex Pilch and then his successor, Doyne Jackson—made sure the main billboards were all committed to Hubbard and paid for a year in advance. It was a luxury most of the opposition couldn't afford.

Another of Hubbard's favorite gimmicks was an election eve rally held at Fordson High School, usually featuring political speeches and entertainment highlighted by "starlets of stage and TV" and emceed by a local comedian.

Toward the end of his reign, Orvie contented himself with billboards and door-to-door flyers, along with newspaper ads.

Although he was accused of leaning on local businessmen for donations and even accepting contributions from local gamblers in his early campaigns, the way he raised money from the mid-1950s or so on was all but painless. Not only was there no need to beg money from merchants or individual contributors, but the mayor never even bothered to hold fundraisers.

"If people want to help our campaign," Hubbard explained, "we let 'em pay a bill. We don't take in cash. Oh, there are a few people that give you donations. Very few. They'll get a bill, made out to them, as their receipt."

That modus operandi sometimes worked to Hubbard's advantage, according to one observer: "I remember one Armenian guy came in a couple years after an election, said, 'Goddammit, I contributed to your campaign. Your building inspectors are giving me shit. What the hell's going on here?' Hubbard didn't like Armenians anyway. He said, 'You contributed to my campaign, my ass.' The guy said, 'I gave you X hundred dollars.' Hubbard said, 'You did, like shit. You obey the law.' And he would do things like that."

Another source of campaign funds was the department heads themselves. Based on the mayor's whims and his evaluation of their performance, most were given election bills to pay, just as voluntary contributors were.

Hubbard's tactics antedated the 1976 Michigan Campaign Finance Act, designed to require disclosure of the sources of campaign contributions and to discourage large contributions. "Candidates did have to file a report with Wayne County on the expenditures," Jackson said. "I can remember Hubbard filing a report one year where he had zero expenditures and we'd run a $25,000 campaign. Now he could honestly say we had zero expenditures, and that's what he filed on. Most years it would be a couple hundred bucks."[11]

The primary reason for Hubbard's lack of money worries, of course, was the fact that he was a lead-pipe cinch at the polls. Every one of his elections after his first one fit today's definition of a landslide—55 percent of the vote. And in many of those, he was elected by a ratio of more than three to one. "Elections were really a farce as far as the mayor goes," Jackson observed. "He didn't even have to work. He just put his name on the ballot, and he was going to get elected. We didn't even bother with the election till two months in advance. But by today's standards, they were amateur affairs."[12]

What was not the least bit amateurish, by yesterday's standards or today's, was Hubbard's willingness to use all his force of personality—and his guile—to win. The mayor himself always insisted he was no dirty campaigner. The closest he ever came to admitting it was an afterthought tacked onto one of his standard denials: "We don't attack the opposition. I used to do a little bit of it."

But Orvie's immense personal popularity and his willingness to get personal with his enemies discouraged many of the city's most capable residents from running against him. Many of those who did, or who aided those who did, paid a heavy price for it.

The long list of the targets of Hubbard's political wrath included Municipal Judge George Martin, who stood up to years of petty vindictiveness and name-calling; attorney John J. Fish, who sued Hubbard for libel and won; and a Ford public relations man whom the mayor labeled a sexual deviate in public.

After overcoming his major bloc of council foes in the 1940s, Orvie controlled at least four and as many as all seven councilmen from 1953 on, largely by running them on his slate and using the coattail effect to get them elected: "Vote for 7 from these 18 to help Hubbard Keep Dearborn Clean."[13]

Hubbard blamed himself for not refining his slate system until the late 1940s. Instead, he recounted, he would include opposition candidates in on political rallies, then distribute literature that credited them, just as though they were allies. "I helped elect some of the opposition by doing it," he recalled. "It was several years before I got smart enough to drop the bastards off my slate."

Hubbard exercised absolute control over which candidates made his slate. Sometimes, however, he changed his mind at the last minute about whether he really wanted to support them. In the 1970 election, for example, one of Hubbard's "opposition" councilmen, John Baja, got a boost from Orvie's department heads at the expense of a certain Hubbard slater. When it began to look as though the slater would beat Baja, Orvie told his aides, "Wait a minute. I want a son of a bitch I know on that council, not that asshole, even though he's on our team." So the Hubbard machine did a last-minute distribution that helped Baja edge the slater for a spot on the council.

Hubbard also picked some of his mayoral opposition. Before his final election, as he was discussing his prospective 1973 campaign with department heads, the mayor was so concerned about the dearth of opponents that he was talking about finding candidates to run against him. "I'm sitting there and I can't believe it," one department head recounted. "He's recruiting opposition. He didn't ever want to run unopposed, because he felt very strongly you build that momentum for the council slate. And Hubbard says, 'We'll use the approach we used for [name deleted].' I said, 'What approach was that, Mayor?' 'Hell,' he says, 'I was going unopposed. I sent [two aides] to talk to him to run for mayor so we'd have some opposition.' Jesus Christ, was I taken. I voted for [name deleted]."

That single insider's vote, meted out in a fit of pique against Orvie in the 1960s, wasn't enough help for the loyal opposition candidate, who hardly bothered to campaign and finished well back. Another unsuccessful opponent, John Pazzanese, an old schoolmate of the mayor's son Henry, was encouraged by the mayor to run in 1973 to enhance his name recognition.

Hubbard also believed strongly in trying to co-opt the opposition, often offering jobs to foes after an election. "When the game's over, you got to join hands," he said. "I may spout off a little bit, but I don't carry grudges against anybody. Otherwise you have a war. You drop your ballots and pick up your bullets. Did we make terms with Japan and Germany? We bought 'em off. Politics and war make strange bedfellows."

To keep his allies in line, Hubbard used techniques of psychological blackmail, offering and withholding such favors as publicity in the local papers, donations from department heads and the use of free city cars.

As Jackson told it, "One of the rewards that Hubbard had for council people was pictures. In those days, neither one of the local papers had a photographer on staff. Anything we gave 'em they used.

"We got mad at Tom Dolan one year. He had too much to drink, and he made a crack. And Hubbard decides to punish Dolan. His punishment is a chill. Tom Dolan's name didn't appear in news releases, no pictures, and it was getting closer to election, and Tom Dolan is panicking.

"So he goes in to make peace with Hubbard, and Hubbard would make peace, but you got to 'prove yourself' before you get the benefits again. And he's sitting there talking to Tom, and my hot line goes off, and I pick it up, and he says, 'Goddamn you, Jackson, aren't you taking Dolan's pictures?' And I'm under orders not to. So I know right away that Tom's sitting there. 'You son of a bitch. All these goddamn literary eggheads. They don't know what it is to deal with politicians and get elected.' Gives me the big speech. And he says, 'Dolan's coming up there. I want you to schedule some pictures for him.'

"After he left Hubbard's office, hot line rings, says, 'You take that fucker's picture and it's your resignation.'

"I no more than hung up the phone when Dolan comes running up, panting. Dolan used to tell that story. Says, 'I ran up the stairs. Jackson shrugged his shoulders. I knew I was dead.'

"We used to cut 'em off, too, when they voted wrong. [One councilman] would react every time you'd cut his pictures off. He'd get back in line."[14]

Hubbard also expected department heads to volunteer contributions to councilmen at Christmastime, perhaps totaling $200 for each aide to distribute among the seven lawmakers.

Somewhat more subtly, he also required his department heads to butter up council allies; for instance, attendance was enforced at the annual kielbasa-and-sauerkraut dinner parties that longtime supporter Edward Dombrowski held every Christmas.

Orvie also had his department heads operating year-round in an administrative equivalent to an ad hoc ward system, with each one assigned to his own district, which he periodically traded off with a colleague so that each would get to know the entire city as intimately as possible.

"The city's divided into about 20 to 24 districts," Hubbard explained. "Every fellow has a district. He's the mayor of his district. No calls go unanswered. One of the many important things the fellows have to do is count every Coca-Cola sign they see in their district. Develops the power of observation.

"They report hole in street, sidewalk need repair, curb need repair, rusty sign in the street. They observe construction; they check and see if permits have been issued on it. Here's another important thing we do: we make a record of all houses for sale by the month. They drive around at least once a week. I don't know anyplace in the world they do that.

"We require all of our fellows to belong to some civic or luncheon group in town. Those are good listening posts. Any grumbling, you'll get 'em there. We know what goes on. I think we have a member in every civic club in town. We say don't take over the jobs. Don't try to be the president. Work with the fellow who's the leader."

Hubbard augmented his department head system by encouraging residents to participate in a wide variety of permanent and ad hoc governmental boards and commissions. With a total membership of more than 250 citizens, the 28 bodies were primarily creatures of the mayor's office, though some were specified in the charter as regulatory. Many of the commissioners earned $15 per meeting under the charter in effect under Hubbard.

"I think on a per-capita basis, no city in the world has as many people working on a volunteer basis as we do," Hubbard bubbled. "When people are involved in things, I think they take a greater, deeper interest. That's the secret. When you've got government like that, you've got better government.

"We wouldn't have Camp Dearborn if it wasn't for a volunteer citizens' group. I wrote a letter to every club in town to ask 'em to name someone who was interested in camping, and we wound up with 45 members on our camp commission. As a result of that, they found this site, and, you see, that is one of the most popular things we run in Dearborn today."

For all Hubbard's good-government protestations, the setup still had its rub-off effects politically. Commission members often became campaign workers, for one thing. Additionally, the commissions, in a very real sense, were a sort of minor-league system for council hopefuls.

Of Hubbard's slate of 14 candidates in 1967, for instance, 6 won and he appointed 6 of the others to commissions. Of 16 candidates in 1970, 5 won and he appointed 7 of the others to commissions. Of 14 candidates in 1973, 6 won and he appointed 7 of the others to commissions. As Jackson pointed out, "Most people were put on for one of two reasons: they approached him or were referred to him because they wanted to serve the community, or they were out raising hell and he put 'em on there to get 'em quiet. Some of the biggest bitchers, when they found out what was going on and why, became his biggest supporters."[15]

Hubbard's administrative formula as head of the city was simple: keep voters happy through unparalleled city services and low taxes. He carried it out not by being an efficient administrator but by being the indirect beneficiary of the largesse of the Ford Motor Company and other industries in town.

For decades, Dearborn had an industrial base equaled almost nowhere else, with Ford paying more than half the city taxes, down from about three-quarters in the early Hubbard years. To ensure that homeowners—that is, voters—would bear an even more disproportionately small tax burden, Hubbard worked unflaggingly at keeping a two-tiered property system in force, grossly overassessing business and industrial properties and underassessing residential properties. Ford did not actively oppose this system until after Hubbard was out of office.[16]

53

Orvie cultivated the image of being a cost cutter through an ongoing series of attacks on city unions, especially the fire fighters, and the employees' pension system. "We've never catered to city employees," he said. "We take 'em on, nose to nose, if necessary."

Hubbard's management style was to take a direct personal hand in as many matters, both important and small, as was humanly possible for one man to do. Part of it was his ready willingness to tackle detail work, and part was his reluctance to delegate responsibility to his aides.

Frequently, he refused even to trust some of his professional people. Besides being mayor, he was, in effect, his own public works director, his own city engineer, his own recreation director. In recreation, for instance, his aides typically had to clear every detail with him on new parks or "tot lots," new equipment or new policies.

Take, once again, the Henry Ford Centennial Library, for example. With its multihued spray of water playing off the fountain, just east of a statue of the elder Ford, the structure is a fitting memorial to the man who put the world on wheels and Dearborn on the map. But in a more subtle sense, the way the building was planned and completed is something of a testament to Orville Hubbard's compulsive need to control the very fabric of the city, right down to the smallest detail.

Hubbard had harbored fears that the library, a Ford gift, would turn out to be a white elephant imposing a perpetual drain on the city just to pay utilities. Consequently, he took an interest in it from the beginning, even to the point of overseeing the positioning of the cement footings. The city engineer "must have staked that thing out and surveyed it 200 times," one department head recalled. "He'd stake it and Hubbard would go by there and say, 'No, you got to move that pole over there 20 feet to the left,' which affected all the other poles. He'd move it and then Hubbard would come by the next day at lunch and he wouldn't like that, either. He was like that in almost everything."

There are similar stories about the time Hubbard made a Camp Dearborn work crew redig a hole for the swimming pool because he wanted it perpendicular so that the sun would be less of an annoyance to swimmers; and the time he argued with subordinates, for similar reasons, about the direction in which a lighted softball diamond at Ford Field should face.

The mayor often involved himself in those kinds of municipal minutiae in the course of taking his chauffeured ride around town nearly every afternoon with the city engineer, city plan director and other key appointees. That way, he could keep abreast of whatever city problems might come up.

To proceed as he did, Hubbard had to be more than just a confirmed workaholic. He was also a bear of a man whose enthusiasm and physical stamina, despite his great bulk, seemed almost boundless. He punched a time clock for most of his career and, according to his own count, averaged 12-hour workdays.

Running a city as a one-man shop, of course, hardly produces municipal efficiency, as many of his overworked and exasperated subordinates observed. "The general perception is he was a great administrator," Jackson said. "The truth is he was a lousy administrator. If you could have one person do it, Hubbard would find a way to have three people do it. I think at one time he had 11 or 12 clerical types in his office. You see, Hubbard would do things like he'd get a girl to type a letter, and that girl might type that same letter 20 times during the day till it got where it looked just right to him. And the letter was notifying somebody that he would attend a fiftieth-anniversary party or something, which he could've done with a phone call. But that attention to detail was also why a hell of a lot of people loved him."[17]

Whether they loved him or hated him, Hubbard's associates, as well as interested observers who knew him only casually, generally agreed that he was a phenomenon. "World-class," enthused Joseph J. Burtell, who left his job as Dearborn's acting city attorney (Hubbard refused to promote him to fill a vacancy) and won election as a district judge. "I call him a Stradivarius. He was brilliant, and I think there probably won't be anybody like him for another 50 or 100 years. I put him in the same category as Daley, Boss Tweed. He makes a guy like [Michigan Governors] George Romney or William Milliken or G. Mennen Williams look like minor leaguers. The man was a genius in his own way."[18]

Even Doug Thomas, a mayoral opponent and longtime foe of city hall who denigrated Hubbard as "a man who had no class," noted, "He had to have a very, very brilliant mind. It's more than street smarts. It went beyond that. As a politician—the greatest, small town or big town."[19]

In an assessment that might be discounted totally had it come from a more typically doting son, Jim Hubbard went so far as to say he thought his father could have been president. "He could've run the country," he told me. "These so-called eastern people couldn't touch Orville Hubbard in his youth. I'm talking about Jack Kennedy. And I'm talking about Eisenhower. These guys couldn't touch him."[20]

Even a detached observer with an academic background and strong liberal sensitivities had to give Orvie his due. Mel Ravitz, longtime Detroit city councilman and sociology professor at Detroit's Wayne State University, had the chance to observe Hubbard during meetings of the county Board of Supervisors, on which both held ex-officio seats. "I found him to be much more reasonable a person in person than his image indicated," Ravitz said in an interview during Hubbard's next-to-last term. "I have a sneaking hunch he doesn't believe all he says. He's a good mayor. He works at being mayor."

As for Orvie's intellectual gifts, Ravitz assessed him as "shrewd" rather than "smart." "I don't see any great intellectual depth to the man," he said.

"He strikes me as an Elbert Hubbard type—mottos, sayings—who likes to pontificate on occasion. And he's more of a practical man, concerned about staying in office. He could have moved out into the state and been a force in politics, but he's been content to stay in his own bailiwick."[21]

Part of Orville Hubbard's charm, of course, was that he felt more comfortable in a smaller setting, a setting where he could not only control events around him but also do things for people.

5

The Personal Touch

Good public service is the best politics.
—A favorite Hubbard slogan

The rains of April had been buffeting Dearborn for days, swelling the Rouge River and sending its stinking waters spilling out across streets and lawns and into homes. At the spacious Fair Lane estate where Henry and Clara Ford had lived for three decades, the floodwaters had cut off the power. On this sodden evening in 1947, the 83-year-old auto magnate lay dying of a cerebral hemorrhage in a room lit by candles and kerosene lamps.

A few miles away, on Brandford Lane in the plush Springwells Park neighborhood, another Dearborn couple were having their own troubles. Their basement was flooding rapidly, and they had been unable to find relief during a series of agitated calls to plumbers, contractors, manufacturing plants, friends and the fire departments of both Dearborn and Detroit. Finally, out of options, the anxious couple looked up Orville Hubbard's phone number and called him at home. Was there any possibility, the woman wanted to know, that he could find a way to have their basement pumped out?

The mayor of Dearborn had had more than his share of special requests that week, but he told her he'd see what he could do. Five minutes later, the city's public works director appeared at her door. Within a half-hour, the pumps themselves arrived, and another happy Dearborn taxpayer was left, slightly bedazzled at the beneficence of city hall, to sing hosannas to his miracle-working honor, Orville Hubbard.

"You can readily see how impressed and grateful we were," gushed the woman in a letter she wrote on behalf of her husband and some neighbors. "Efficient service like this is not soon forgotten."

Hubbard tried without much success to stifle a sarcastic guffaw as he finished rereading the letter, a relic of gratitude from 25 years before. "Three years later," he recounted, "the recall came along and every goddamn one of 'em signed. . . . 'You haven't done anything for me lately.'"

Hubbard could afford to see the humor in that little vignette, of course. It was a distinct anomaly among the more enduring expressions of gratitude made by Dearborn voters for the mayor's good turns over the decades. Political favors turned into Hubbard votes year after election year. Orville Hubbard's personal brand of city service had put thousands of old-line Dearbornites in his debt, and many of them truly lionized the mayor for his good works.

Hubbard, in turn, always insisted that he was a champion of the under-dog, and, indeed, he seemed to get a genuine kick out of being able to help the ones he considered the little people. There was, for example, the time Hubbard had a visit from George Romney on behalf of John Dempsey's congressional campaign against incumbent John Dingell in 1966. A public relations man had set everything up weeks before, right down to making sure the TV cameras were there to record the event. The only problem was that Hubbard had something else he needed to do first.

A constituent—"this little Italian lady right out of Hollywood casting," one aide had called her—had come in with a problem. When city crews salted her alley in wintertime, it seemed, the sloppy residue would splash onto her tomato patch. For almost a half-hour, Hubbard listened to the woman complain about her stunted tomatoes, while out in the anteroom the governor—along with the cameramen—waited to see him.

City annals do not record that Orville Hubbard was able to help the woman grow bigger and juicier tomatoes, but when she left, she was happy— simply because he listened to her. As for Hubbard, he had no qualms about letting the politicos know they meant less to him than a lone voter's problem.

Service, in any case, was the professed keystone of Orville Hubbard's strategy for staying in office. "I'm just an A-1 garbage and rubbish collector," he was fond of saying.

To be sure, there were those who cried foul at Hubbard's actions, whether they were complaining about favoritism or accusing him of retaliating against recalcitrant voting precincts by, say, ordering rubbish collectors to skip whole neighborhoods. But these gripers were mostly the sore losers or, as Hubbard liked to call them, political disappointees.

In 1957, for example, one of Orvie's challengers, Eugene Keyes, berated him for playing favorites. In an election flyer, Keyes, a dentist-physician-attorney who had served two terms as Michigan's lieutenant governor in the 1940s, pontificated:

He has subsidized more than half the electorate by favors, gifts, appoint-ments to commissions of dubious usefulness, thousands of free passes to

Camp Dearborn, the summer stock playhouse starring the "fat boy." . . .
Do you think it is being completely honest to vote for this man because
he has done you a favor at the expense of the rest of the taxpayers? Do
you ever stop to think of the big favors he has done others at your
expense? Are you aware that this is the system of the dictators and that
its perpetuation will completely destroy democratic philosophy upon
which our free elections are based?[1]

Based on the handful of votes they gave him during that campaign,
Dearbornites apparently saw little merit in Keyes's argument. They loved
the idea of being able to phone or write the mayor to complain or ask a
favor, and have a reasonable expectation of getting results.

Whether it was an elderly couple with a flooded basement, an expectant
mother out of coal in the middle of a strike or, most likely, an angry taxpayer
with a missed garbage pickup, the Hubbard mythology is replete with story
after story of the mayor's delighting and mystifying homeowners by answering their requests with alacrity, sometimes in person.

He was not above making public relations events out of the occasion,
either, such as the time during a 1940s dairy strike when he personally
delivered a bottle of milk to an opposition councilman who was sick at
home.

One story, perhaps apocryphal, had the mayor taking a phone call from
a man complaining that his garbage had not been picked up. Promising,
"I'll take care of it right away," he appeared at the man's home, whisked
away the rubbish, drove it over to the office of the city public works director
and dumped it on his desk, snapping, "You missed Mr. DiSilva's garbage.
Make sure it doesn't happen again."[2] Another much-circulated story told of
a homeowner calling to complain that the city had failed to follow through
on a request to spread some gravel in his rear alley. The next morning,
Hubbard showed up to have a cup of coffee with him (he hated coffee),
and when the two went out together to inspect the alley, the gravel, obviously on the mayor's personal order, already had been dumped and spread.

Hubbard himself took many of the calls that came in, sometimes after
his secretaries fielded them. And he often worked Saturdays in his office.
He liked to tell of taking a call in 1972 from a woman who refused to
believe it was he answering his own phone. "Orville wouldn't like it if he
knew you were fooling people like that," she told him. He replied, "Ma'am,
please write a letter to the mayor and tell him you talked to an SOB in his
office Saturday and ask him to chew me out."

"No calls go unanswered," he explained in one of our talks. "I may not
be able to take 'em all, but no calls go unanswered. I get a conversation
and I get the department and say, 'You see how fast you can get over to this
address and see that woman about so and so.' I say, 'Madam, I think if you
take a look out the door, maybe you'll find him there.'" Then, in his best

falsetto, he said, pounding the table, "'Just pulled up, just there, can't believe it.'"

Longtime mayoral secretary Judy Cord confirmed the impact of the strategy on potential voters: "The department head, whosever district that was, would have to go out and maybe pick up somebody's garbage and put it in the trunk of their car. He [Hubbard] then would call the person back. He was a great talker. Oh, they loved it. You know, he was their idol. He was their god. Probably you couldn't tell them anything wrong about the man; there was just nothing that this town didn't have or that he didn't do. 'Oh, Mr. Mayor, I love you. I would do anything for you.' He was always gracious. He'd charm the socks right off you."[3]

As Hubbard explained it, "We're elected to do a job, and we don't have any other interest in the world except this job. I put my mind to be the best mayor the world ever had, anywhere, in any circumstances at any time. That has been my ambition. It's still my ambition. And every day we try to do whatever we do better all the time.

"After all, people want service. Good public service is the best politics. Our job is here, right here. That's what we're elected for. What's life about? Just to be a son of a bitch? Make people happy. We'll do anyone a favor that we can if in the process we don't harm somebody else. Any legal favor.

"It's one thing if you have a smaller community like this. A big mayor, all he can do is run to New York and sign bonds and make speeches. What the hell else can he do? We try to give 'em as much personal attention as humanly possible."

Often the service began as soon as a new Dearborn resident arrived in town. A 1952 mayoral opponent named James Christie distributed literature describing how one newcomer was greeted on his first day in Dearborn by a Hubbard department head delivering a package—containing thimbles, rulers, a box of soap and some slightly used comic books—all labeled, "Compliments of Orville Hubbard." The next day, the man was taken down to shake hands with the mayor.

Visitors to his office typically received keepsakes such as beer, matchbooks, sewing kits, plastic thimbles, newspaper reprints, famous quotes, dirty jokes and inspirational tracts.

He also used to make a production out of handing out courtesy passes to Camp Dearborn. In 1949, the *Dearborn Independent* asserted during a political campaign that he was using the camp "for all it is worth." Applicants were to pick up a green permit card from the mayor, after registering to vote at the city clerk's office. Then, according to the paper, "the green card is graciously presented by His Highness and Lordship with an obeisance that would put to shame Mr. Columbus when he appealed to Queen Isabella of Spain for ships and funds."[4]

Orvie also found a way to make himself one of the family with thousands of Dearborn voters. He sent them birthday cards, all bearing a smaller version of the familiar, flowing signature he typically wrote with green ink in letters an inch high. Hubbard's system for sending out the cards (he said he did it instead of exchanging Christmas cards) was elaborate and expensive in terms of city personnel use. The birthday card file was for years the province of a full-time secretary. A large rotating file held perhaps 5,000 or more names on three-by-five cards containing information, much of it gleaned from forms sent in by residents who had requested city services. Much of it also came from information Hubbard had wheedled during personal meetings or telephone calls with constituents.

"Sometimes I used to think that everybody in Dearborn got a birthday card," said Judy Cord. "There had to be 10 or 20 a day go out, signed with an autopen. Later on they were printed. They sent cards and they sent letters. Different color paper every year and some simple little message."[5]

Hubbard insisted that the files be kept rigorously updated against obituaries and his own current feelings, often influenced by whether the person in question had signed a recall petition against him in 1950. "One of my jobs as the receptionist was to go through the obituary column every week and send an obituary card to the deceased," Cord explained, "and then check it against the birthday file and the sticker file—that was for Camp Dearborn stickers—and then cross it off on the birthday file. If the card came back 'deceased,' then we'd remove it, but most of the time we caught that through the obituary column. When people would call on the phone, he'd write you to go and check that recall list. If they were on that list, before he'd terminate the conversation, he would get them to apologize, and then he would take and write on that card that they had apologized, and then go ahead and send 'em a birthday card."[6]

Toward the end of his career, Hubbard put more energy into marrying couples than he did providing traditional services. By his own count, he performed 1,745 weddings from 1972 to 1974. "Son of a bitch, that's the most interesting thing I've ever done in my life," he bubbled. "Oh, Christ, that's a big business around here. We had 19 Saturday, from 9:30 to 4. My ass was really dragging around here."

Hubbard wrote his own version of wedding vows from a rough outline provided by an Oakland County judge. Afterward, he continued to try to refine and rework it. It was hardly a traditional service, although he had "The Wedding March" and songs such as "Get Me to the Church on Time" and "By the Light of the Silvery Moon" piped into his conference room, which he had transformed into a wedding chamber. Though he insisted, "I don't make a joke out of it," he included his own corny lines ("Now that you're joined as one, in a short time you'll know who won"), and he gave each couple a lottery ticket afterward.

"It's the novelty of it," he said, explaining why he enjoyed the activity so much. "It's fun. It's nice to make a real first-class ceremony out of it."

Hubbard's standard fee for a wedding was two dollars, which he turned over to the city clerk, as provided by law. "One guy gave me \$40 once," he recalled. "Most people probably give you 20. Don't write about that, though. People think you're getting rich out of the marriage business."[7] Orvie sometimes teased about his rights at the weddings. In planning a mass ceremony in 1974, he quipped, "The mayor gets the first night with the bride. That's the old feudal system."

Hubbard's preoccupation with public service covered a much wider range than just weddings or quick responses to individual requests, of course. The city was famous for its efficient trash collection and snow removal, including sidewalk snow plowing and leaf pickup in the streets. And his insistence on keeping Dearborn "clean"—in a strictly nonracial sense—resulted in the formation of a City Beautiful Commission that helped earn the city runner-up honors three straight years in the National Cleanest Town contest in the late 1950s.

What he billed as the "world's most courteous police force" drove in cars carrying the slogan "Be Nice to People." On New Year's Eve, police provided free transportation for celebrants too drunk to drive themselves. And during the last decade of his tenure, he had all city cars equipped with gasoline cans to help stranded motorists. For shoppers, there was free baby-sitting as well as free parking. City health services included fluoride treatments for youngsters' teeth. And in a curious mixing of state-church relations, he had city workers periodically pave the parking lots of virtually all the town's churches.

Hubbard came to office as a young father not yet 40 and oversaw, in addition to the creation of Camp Dearborn, the development of parks (six), pools (seven), ice rinks (seven, plus one arena), a multipurpose building he dubbed the Youth Center, and a network of "tot lots" scattered around the city. As he matured, he shifted his emphasis to low-rent senior citizen apartments (three in the city plus the one in Florida). He railroaded through city budgets that were heavily skewed toward recreation. For instance, from 1941, the year he first was elected, to 1974, the last year he effectively governed, the police budget rose about tenfold, from \$394,689 to \$3,924,954, slightly less than the rate of increase for the total budget in 33 years of inflation and rising employee costs; meanwhile, the recreation budget was up nearly 35 times, from \$38,010 to \$1,325,147. As Hubbard was fond of saying, every dollar spent for recreation was a dollar you didn't need to spend on police.[8]

Orvie's willingness to spend money on recreational programs and other "frills" was perhaps the hallmark of his administration, according to Jackson. "I really believe when people look back, he'll be remembered as an innovator," Jackson said. "We were eons ahead of anybody else. Just constant innovation. We would be challenged to come up with ideas for new programs. You know what that means? We were being challenged to find ways to spend money. He had the guts to try different programs. Camp

Dearborn was probably the classic example. There's no other city in the country that's got a Camp Dearborn."[9]

In the view of political scientists Wayman and Stockton, Hubbard's administration amounted to a "massive program of municipal socialism":[10]

> Leaving aside the flamboyance of his remarks, the Mayor's views typify in many ways the new suburban populism. The Mayor is liberal—even "socialistic"—on the role of government in the economy. To him the New Deal is taken for granted, for it is assumed that the government has an important role to play in providing social services to the citizens. This posture makes the Mayor a liberal. On the other hand, the Mayor emerges as a conservative on many of the new issues of the sixties and seventies: crime, law and order, race and busing. These new issues are ones that cut across party lines and create the potential for realignment or disintegration of the party system. The typical [Dearborn residents'] views are similar to the Mayor's on these issues. . . .[11]

> There is a danger of course in mistaking the views of. . . a mayor for the views of a whole community. . . . A mayor is frequently elected because he picks up the garbage on time, sends out birthday cards, or runs the city efficiently. In many cases his position on political issues is a relatively minor thing.[12]

Several observers have contended that the mayor linked his services to elections. Political scientists Charles R. Adrian and Charles Press wrote in *Governing Urban America*, "It is a policy of Hubbard to start at least one new service before each election."[13] But the record bears this out only spottily.

Trying to corroborate Adrian and Press, a *Dearborn Guide* columnist cited instances he said contributed to what could become known in textbooks as "the Hubbard style." Among them were the sidewalk snow removal and the Dearborn Navy of World War II. But the sidewalk snow removal started up in December 1952, almost exactly midway between the mayoral elections of 1951 and 1953. And Hubbard had no connection whatsoever with the so-called bathtub navy except to scuttle it.[14]

But regardless of his timing, Orvie remained so closely identified with good services that, as longtime Hubbard slate Councilman Ed Dombrowski observed after the mayor suffered a debilitating stroke, people were convinced that the quality of services had declined proportionally. "Two weeks after the mayor got sick, we had the biggest snowfall in Dearborn's history," he told reporters in 1977. "It took two days to clear it. But the people complained that if the mayor was not sick, it would have been cleared faster."

Given his record, perhaps it would, at that.

6

The Perks of Office

By political standards, the man is a saint.
—Doyne E. Jackson, Dearborn director of research and
information, on Orville L. Hubbard's honesty[1]

They said he accepted bribes from gamblers. They said he demanded kick-backs from his appointed stooges. They said he extorted campaign contributions from shopkeepers and finagled money from businesses in return for lower tax assessments.

They said he fixed traffic tickets. They said he conned old people into making him the beneficiary of their wills. They said he siphoned gate receipts out of Camp Dearborn.

They said he turned city hall into a tacky municipal marriage bureau so he could get rich from raking in wedding fees. And they said he found city jobs for relatives and tried to set up a family dynasty in city government.

Orville Hubbard spent a good deal of his energy over his 36 years in office fending off accusations about venality and nepotism and various breaches of ethics and violations of the law. Occasionally, he had to tell his side of the story in court. Most of the time, however, he contented himself with telling it to the newspapers, radio and TV.

If he sometimes sounded less than persuasive, it was not through any lack of conviction on his part. When, for instance, he began spewing a torrent of expletive-filled vitriol at *Dearborn Press* Editor Joyce Hagelthorn about abuses of the press in 1972, he hardly missed a beat in interjecting the most emphatically wide-sweeping self-endorsement imaginable. "This administration does no wrong to anybody," he declared with a tone that defied anyone to contradict him. "All we do here is work day and night trying to serve people. . . . We run the cleanest, most honest, decent government in the whole wide world right here."[2]

Sadly, however, and despite all his protestations, Hubbard probably will be remembered as a small-stakes wheeler-dealer and conniver even though his record hardly supports that view.

If not quite the paragon of public virtue that he himself insisted he was, Orvie nonetheless broke from the stereotype of the municipal boss by proving that one-man government could be operated essentially without regard for personal monetary gain. Considering his longevity in office, with as many sub rosa opportunities as he must have had to enrich himself, Hubbard's career was essentially free of evidence that he did so.

Even such an unswervable foe as John J. Fish, an attorney whom Hubbard once libeled in a campaign circular, conceded to me, "I think he's got a clean city. I don't think he allows vice or gambling or anything like that."[3]

And Bill Mills, Orvie's caustic-witted opponent in a hot mayoral race in 1957, told me, "He's not a thief. . . . I don't think money was ever a big factor with him. A lot of people felt that, oh, he must be mopping up—and he could've mopped up, but I don't think he ever did on any big scale. It could've run into millions, but it didn't."[4]

In point of fact, nobody was ever able to pin any wrongdoing of real substance on Hubbard. And it wasn't for lack of trying—witness the recall attempt, the grand jury investigation, the governor's removal hearings, the civil rights trial and, finally, the state audit of his administration.

But all they ever got on him was that he accepted a TV set from a clothing store whose assessment he ordered reviewed in 1950, resulting in a reduction of more than $220,000; and, in apparent violation of state law, he kept more than $30,000 in fees for weddings he performed from 1972 to 1974, the last two years in which he actively governed the city. In neither instance was he prosecuted.

When he died, Orvie left such a modest estate—only about $200,000, including the family home—that even his children were surprised. Several of his heirs insisted he must have left deposits in secret bank accounts around the country, in a manner reminiscent of misanthropic comedian W. C. Fields. Nothing of the kind ever was discovered, though.

When it came to helping out family members and friends from his office at city hall, Orvie was somewhat less circumspect. All four of his sons were on the city payroll for various periods, and even though he was never accused of helping them get jobs, there seems little question but that he provided encouragement that would not have been afforded to strangers.

When his son John ran successfully for a city councilman's seat, Orvie declined to help him. But later, when a vacancy for city clerk came up, Hubbard's puppet council appointed his son. John's daughter Susan later was elected to the council. Of Orvie's other sons, Jim retired as a city police corporal whose last assignment was essentially to be available to run errands for the mayor; Frank had been appointed by his father to the City Plan Commission (which netted a nominal fee for each meeting attended), a springboard to his subsequent election as a school board trustee and then as city treasurer; and Henry worked as head of motor transport, a Civil Service job. Hubbard's only daughter, Nancy, worked briefly for the city as a teenager; a daughter of hers was a secretary in Hubbard's office for a few years, and she and the mayor's wife Fay were assigned city cars in violation of the city charter.[5]

Beyond that were accusations that Henry Hubbard and Maureen Keane profited in technically illegal city land deals, although Orvie himself was not implicated.

But if the traditional perquisites of a big-city boss never accrued to Orville Hubbard, he certainly reaped ample rewards of a less tangible nature. He could, after all, do or say almost anything—and see it in the papers a day or so later.

7

Lies of the Press

Editors are the most corrupt sons of bitches in the United
States today.
—Orville L. Hubbard, reacting to an unfavorable news-
paper story[1]

Time magazine reporter Ben Cate was doing his darnedest to get some
response, any response, out of Orville Hubbard. What, he wanted to know,
was the mayor's role in a racially motivated mob scene a couple of months
earlier on Labor Day 1963? It was this incident that eventually led the
federal government to file its civil rights case against Orvie.

Backed up by a pair of free-lance photographers he'd brought along,
Cate cornered the mayor at the back door of city hall and introduced himself. "I've got nothing to say," Hubbard snapped, underscoring the point by
ducking into an unmarked men's room.

Cate stood his ground, and for the next half-hour he observed a parade
of men going through the lavatory door. Most, it seemed to him, were going
in and only a few—the mayor not among them—coming out. Then, as if on
signal, about eight of them barreled out and confronted him.

No, he conceded to mayoral secretary Bert Schlaff, he didn't have an
appointment. He was just after a quote and a new photo of Hizzoner. The
last one *Time* had used, during an altogether unfriendly piece the magazine
had run at the time of the 1951 recall, was out of date. At that, the unlucky
Cate learned in what esteem national magazines were held around Dearborn city hall. Two Hubbard lieutenants hustled him out the door and sent
him sprawling down the steps.

Later, the mayor and his aides seemed not the least bit contrite. One
official, told that Cate had gone to Henry Ford Hospital for examination of
a skinned knee and other injuries, inquired whether doctors had "looked
inside his head." And Alex Pilch, the city's publicity director, blamed it all

on *Time's* track record. *"Time* lies," he said. "It has gone out of its way to be nasty, and its stories about the recall stunk."[2]

Years afterward, the mayor himself would acknowledge only that his men "pushed him a little, I believe." But just the same, that incident marked the low point in Orville Hubbard's decades-long love-hate relationship with the news media.

Things had begun on a much more buoyant note. Even before he was elected to anything, Orvie was always trying to get his name or his picture in the paper, and he succeeded more often than he had any right to expect.

As mayor of Dearborn, Hubbard quickly stamped himself as perhaps the most reckless, I'll-try-anything-once self-promoter in the history of municipal politics. The stories were not always favorable by the time they found their way into the Detroit papers and then, through wire service reports, into other papers across the country, but there was no denying that they drew attention to Dearborn and its mayor, and that was all Orville Hubbard really wanted.

One national magazine article, for example, prompted a local community college dean to write Orvie: "Everywhere I go in different parts of the country, you are known and people always ask me about 'our mayor.' It is amazing how many people in the country seem to know Dearborn's mayor by name."

Some of the headlines stemmed legitimately from his accomplishments: establishing the Florida apartment complex, innovating sidewalk snow plowing and shopper babysitting, stirring up support for the concept of federal revenue sharing. But many others resulted from his adolescent pranks or unabashed showing off: buying dinner for the jury that acquitted him on civil rights charges stemming from the Kendal Street incident, for example.

Even his less spectacular capers sometimes caught on with publications around the world. When, in 1974, Hubbard had gotten his weight down to a comparatively svelte 283 pounds—and then required all his department heads to lose weight themselves—the story became front-page news in Los Angeles ("Dearborn Mayor Orders an End to Waist in Government," *Los Angeles Times*) and Miami, and the story eventually hit papers in France, Germany, Hong Kong, Mexico, Argentina, Canada and across the United States. He also did live interviews on the "event" with ABC-TV, NBC-Monitor radio, CBS radio and the British Broadcasting Co., and he turned down interview requests from CBS-TV and NBC-TV.

Sometimes his mayoral doings produced publicity bonanzas totally unrelated to the subject at hand. During the early 1950s, when he ordered department heads to lock themselves in their offices for half-hour "think" sessions, *Life* magazine published a two-page photo spread that also happened to catch his platinum-haired daughter, Nancy. The publicity generated an offer—though one that never panned out—for her to come to Hollywood for a screen test.

In contrast to the rough handling he usually got from magazines such as *Time* and *Newsweek*, Hubbard was given kid-glove treatment in "Dearborn's Madcap Mayor," a profile run in 1958 by the now-defunct *Coronet* magazine.[3] Writer Edward E. Malkin noted that Orvie had been called the "most colorful, provocative and irrepressible mayor in the U.S." and assessed him as an able administrator, invulnerable because of his city services, and handsome and youthful despite his bulk. Hubbard gloried in the article, circulating reprints wherever he went.

Flattering or not, publicity was what Hubbard's administration was all about. Political scientists Charles R. Adrian and Charles Press assessed politics under Hubbard as "one long publicity stunt."[4] That wasn't far off the mark.

His knack for getting reporters to like him and work with him at publicizing his snappy one-liners and his escapades helped get him entrenched and continued to bring him attention of one sort or another throughout his tenure in office. When, for example, exasperated Dearborn city councilmen passed a "gag ordinance" to try to rein in their loudmouthed new rival in the mayor's office, Hubbard got himself arrested for talking to constituents. The resulting trial attracted national attention that made him look like a civil rights crusader.

Hubbard at first typed out his own press releases and for years maintained an open-door policy for reporters. But, although he never forgot the value of good press, he soon became embittered at what he perceived as an ongoing campaign by the local weekly newspapers and the Detroit dailies to make him appear ridiculous. As if he needed the help.

Orvie began losing the cooperation of the two Dearborn papers, the *Press* and the *Independent*, a few years after he took office.[5] Both papers took to running front-page editorials attacking him, and the *Press*, particularly, often slanted stories against him, not deigning even to mention his name but instead referring to him simply as "the chubby mayor."

When a third paper, the *Guide*, expanded from a shopping guide and entered the Dearborn media competition in the late 1940s, its impartial editorial policy was such a contrast that it was tabbed almost instantly as a "stooge rag" for Hubbard. As Hubbard solidified his hold on city hall in the early 1950s, he began to fare better with the other papers, too. The *Press* and the *Independent* changed owners and became more even-handed in their coverage.[6]

Hubbard's major coup in his early battles with the locals was to get the City Council to set up a publicity department under Pilch in 1948. The job was abolished for a year, but when an again-friendly council let Hubbard rehire Pilch, the mayor quickly turned the department into his personal arm. Indeed, recall leaders later compared his administration to Hitler's, saying he was "as adept at propagandizing as Goebbels." At any rate, hundreds upon hundreds of stories cranked out by Pilch and his successor,

Doyne Jackson, found their way into the papers virtually word for word.

Many of the words, it should be noted, emanated from Hubbard himself. Even routine news releases sometimes bore the Hubbard touch, perhaps adding an obscure historical reference or inserting a date; and anything that mentioned his name had to pass his inspection before it was sent out.[7]

When it came to politics, Hubbard was his own pamphleteer. Orvie's ear for effective language—the same gift that often made his verbal statements so memorable—translated directly into overblown, yet undeniably effective, campaign literature. "He'd have made a great advertising PR man," noted Jackson. "His spelling and English weren't the greatest, but the words were tremendous."[8]

After several years on the job, Hubbard did his best to intimidate local editors by trying to make them dependent on city press releases, which he dispensed according to his whim. When the *Guide* began publishing, for example, Hubbard tried to help out the new paper by routing his most timely releases to its editors, while cutting out the *Press* and the *Independent*. But in 1951, just after Hubbard's recall victory, Police Chief Ralph B. Guy denounced all three local weeklies (along with the *Detroit News*) as "unworthy of being called newspapers" and denied them access to police reports for a few days.

One of Orvie's most time-honored responses to unfavorable stories was highly theatrical. He would throw a tantrum, which he usually orchestrated for the benefit of his subordinates or for photographers, highlighted by his tearing up the offending publication and jumping up and down on its remains. He also took to giving reporters excerpts he had drawn from an obscure attack on the press by Thomas Jefferson. The mayor titled it "Lies of the Press."[9]

There were accusations through the years that Hubbard had key city officials try to intimidate the local weeklies by pressuring businessmen to pull their ads and by demanding that publishers fire certain reporters or editors. Once Hubbard supposedly doubled the tax assessment on a local editor's home in retaliation for unwelcome commentary. But those charges remained largely undocumented. Orvie much preferred trying to manipulate what appeared in the papers.

In 1968, the *Guide* complained that Hubbard had temporarily cut off recreation releases because he was unhappy with what was printed about the city's Florida apartment building. The next year, he invoked a form of censorship in reacting to an unflattering story in the *New York Times Magazine*.[10] Complaining that the story contained "43 major errors and as many minor miscues," he announced that before being granted any more interviews with him, reporters must agree to turn over finished copies of their stories before publication. He had a "reporter courtesy agreement" run off for distribution to ensure "a check of the facts" with city hall. A Hubbard press release said of the errors in the *Times* story, "All that and more will

---

go down as history, and someone researching the files will accept it as fact. . . . The more I see of history being written and recorded by newspapers, the more I am convinced that Mr. Ford was absolutely right when he claimed that 'history is bunk.'"[11]

Orvie soon began ignoring his own decree, and things were back to normal. Although he had for years derided newspaper editors and the "scandal sheets" they published, his most flamboyant denunciation of the press came in 1972, when the *Detroit News*, acting on a tip, published a story about conflict-of-interest implications entailed in the sale of houses to the city by the mayor's son, Henry Ford Hubbard, and by Maureen Keane.[12]

Hubbard went into a blue funk, snarling into a tape recorder operated by *Dearborn Press* Editor Joyce Hagelthorn: "I'd like to blow up the goddamn *Detroit News*, and I'd like to find the son of a bitch that started that story and shoot him right between the goddamn eyes. If I had my way, I'd close the whole goddamn press up. Look what they do in politics: just sensationalism, to get people to buy their papers. They don't care who they smear or where they smear, and that's wrong.

"I think the newspapers have done more to ruin the country than any other single force in the nation today. Even the advertising is false. Jefferson said it a long time ago: 'It is better to be uninformed than misinformed.'

"Editors are the most corrupt sons of bitches in the United States today, and I think the average citizen would agree. If you put a question in the *Free Press*, 'Do you think that the newspapers are honest?' you'd see the vote you'd get on it. They'd get all their employees to call and they'd say no, too."[13]

It was hardly the kind of performance that might be expected of an elder statesman of Orville Hubbard's standing, but then, if he hadn't said it, he wouldn't have been Orville Hubbard.

8

The Rough Log

I *am* the king.
—Orville L. Hubbard, in an unguarded moment with
friends[1]

There was no getting around it: Orville Hubbard was a charmer. If he wanted you to like him, or if he wanted something from you, whether it was your vote or your goodwill, he would wither your resistence and you would be his.

For example, there was the time he telephoned a woman from one of Detroit's northern suburbs, Sterling Heights, to set the record straight on the subject of George Washington. Hubbard earlier had tossed off one of his typical double entendres, a slightly disrespectful speculation that Washington is known as the father of his country because of the number of progeny he produced while he slept here or there.

But now he needed to deal with a woman who had decided that his witticism, as reported in the Detroit papers, was not one bit funny. So here he was, on a brisk November afternoon in 1972, phoning her, turning on the charm to a critic who, by reason of geography, wouldn't even be able to vote for him.

"I apologize to you," he said meekly. "That was supposed to have been sort of a wisecrack. I didn't know they'd print it that way." And with that, he began to blather on about Washington, who, as he had made clear many times before, actually was one of his heroes. He urged her to read one of his favorite biographies of Washington—available, he pointed out, in paperback.

"Bless your heart," he gushed. "You read that and call me on it. I want to be your friend, and I'd like to have you be my friend, 'cause certainly nothing in the world was ever meant by it. If you can't get the book, I'll let you borrow mine."

If the woman was perturbed before the phone call, her anger had no chance against the folksy, sincerity-laced, almost naive charm of Orville Hubbard. "Your apology is accepted, and thank you for calling," she replied.

How could anyone think ill of such a man? Certainly the Sterling Heights woman never would after this, and the same was true of thousands upon thousands of constituents who watched him in action as he exchanged small talk with them or graciously doled out favors godfather-style. These were people who refused to believe the frequent reports about Orville Hubbard's eruptive temper and his capacity for carrying a grudge for years. They totally discounted headlines about the name-calling bouts and petty feuds in the first two decades of his career. They laughed off whining complaints that he was a sadistic martinet who liked to make his staff grovel before him. And they quickly forgot about stories that his wife had accused him of physical and mental abuse.

Bill Mills, a mayoral opponent he had steamrollered in 1957, once declared that the only people who voted for Hubbard were the ones who didn't really know him. If so, based on his record, Orvie was a stranger to most of the people in Dearborn. But what did it all mean? Could it be that the private Orville Hubbard was really so well hidden?

One former department head, who remained an admirer even though he was a frequent target of the mayor's barbs, acknowledged to me, "Of course, the public image—the nice, benevolent, kindly old person—is just so different from the person that he was. At times he was a tyrant."

John Fish, an attorney who once won a libel judgment against the mayor, had this explanation: "Hubbard is a Jekyll and Hyde. He has a charming personality. He's a great actor. He can present two faces to people. His lip will curl and he'll snarl like a dog when he's mad or makes out he's mad. He can be ruthless at the same time he can be charming."[2]

Secretary Judy Cord noted about the facets of her boss's personality, "He had lots, like a Rubik's Cube. He was a real charmer on the surface. He was whatever you wanted him to be, really. And he could be a monster at the same time."[3]

Even his grown children felt the same way. "He had two personalities— he was two people," declared Hubbard's oldest son, Jim, a retired Dearborn police corporal. "I think most of us have a dark side and a bright side. And we show the bright side. I didn't like the side of him that was cruel. He was cruel to people who were close to him."[4]

But both sides had served a purpose for the mayor of Dearborn through most of his adult life. Hubbard the charmer seldom failed to make his mark with those whose favor he was currying or with others who posed no threat to him. Hubbard the tyrant buffaloed his way through everybody else.

To a large extent, I concluded, Hubbard's charming persona was simply a facade, a mode he turned on and off as it suited him. Several of his associates pointed out, for instance, that he often complimented people to

73

their face, only to mock them unmercifully behind their backs. For instance, on one occasion during our interviews, he chummily received a call from a local physician serving in a volunteer capacity with the city, then told me in a whispered aside, "I have to be nice to him." After hanging up, he declared acidly, "I wouldn't let him operate on my pet guinea pig."

Certainly, Hubbard's dark side was one I had seen flashes of as he talked about his life and people who had crossed him. But as he talked, it wasn't always easy to reconcile the Hubbard who had been a chip-on-the-shoulder young hothead with the agreeably irascible Hubbard of 70 who sat in front of me. And even though I realized that in part he was "performing" for me, it was all but impossible for me not to like and admire him.

Of course, I didn't work for him or live with him. I was not, for instance, one of the appointees he constantly tried to emasculate. At one department head meeting I was allowed to attend, I could only think how lucky I was to be an observer instead of an appointee. "Jesus Christ, how'd I get such a bunch of goddamn dumbbells working for me?" he grumbled in exasperation when his office staff couldn't find a box of insulated pots. "I must be dumb myself, or I wouldn't have hired 'em. Come here, Ken, before you lose your nuts."

As one observer told me, "I'd see him absolutely belittle his department heads. It was terrible treatment, but he was consistent. He was not charming one hour and then a miserable SOB the next. He was always a miserable SOB. He made life miserable for them, though I really think he liked his people."

Saying that Hubbard humiliated his underlings is like saying that Attila the Hun raided a few villages. Sometimes he did it as a sort of joke. He once made a department head get down on all fours and bark like a dog. Another time, he made one pick up some marbles he himself had spilled from a game, and then, when the unfortunate man came up a few short, Orvie proceeded to berate him for his incompetence—while hiding the missing marbles in one of his hands. Yet another time, he took a new department head out to Camp Dearborn, stood him atop a hill with his arms extended out to help the mayor check from various angles how a new totem pole would look on the site, and was left standing there as Hubbard and his driver abruptly returned to Dearborn. The man quit a couple of days later.

Not quite so much fun were the frequent demonstrations of fealty the mayor required of his appointees: rousting department heads out of bed to go change a spare tire for a constituent, making them pick him up at the airport or play chauffeur for somebody else, scheduling them for "gate duty" at Camp Dearborn in three-hour shifts every other Sunday in the summer.

Sometimes he orchestrated a group emasculation. One summer, he had arranged an early-morning assembly at Camp Dearborn for his department heads. As the auto caravan approached the front gate, Hubbard's car screeched to a halt. He bounced out and excitedly gathered the flock around him.

"Who did it?" he demanded in a manner reminiscent of Jimmy Cagney's paranoid captain in *Mr. Roberts*.

"We don't know, Mayor. Who did what?" came a chorus of responses.

"You don't know?" he replied in disgust. "You're supposed to keep your eyes open on everything that happens here."

And he went down the line, asking, "Did you do it?" as each denied culpability for whatever offense the mayor had in mind.

"You bunch of dummies," he snapped. "I have nothing but a bunch of incompetent dummies around me."

Then, with the camp director hastily summoned to Hizzoner's presence, he finally let the other shoe drop. Someone had moved a boulder from the left side of the entrance road to the right side, and Orvie wanted things rectified. "Who moved that boulder from over there?" he barked at the director. "I told you that I want that boulder *there*."

"Well, Mayor, the cars were hitting that boulder and . . ."

"I don't care if they were hitting the boulder. I want it over *there*."

And so it went.

With subordinates as well as acquaintances, Hubbard had a real gift for sizing up their inadequacies, for targeting the best way to pull their chains. And he liked to know all the gossip about everybody. He encouraged his department heads to spy on each other, for instance, and let him know who had been seen in which bar or who was having marital problems. He also worked at keeping his secretaries at odds with each other. A current management expert might call it "creative tension." With Hubbard, however, it was hardly intended as a route to office efficiency.

For the most part, Orvie did not socialize with his appointees, and his inner circle of confidants was a minuscule one. When I asked him who his closest friends were, he had difficulty coming up with any names at all. My conclusion, sadly, was that he was a man whose absolute control of his city insulated him from intimate social contacts. He trusted almost no one; after all, a king can hardly afford to have friends.

As Jim Hubbard observed, "Orville's first and only love and confidant in his whole life was himself. He loved Orville Hubbard better than anything else on earth. Everybody else, well, he used."[5]

But a more sympathetic picture of him emerged from others whom he had social contacts with—a Hubbard who was an earthy, direct, yet often immensely likable companion. The consensus among the mayor's few regular social acquaintances was that he was a man of simple tastes, crude mannerisms, an innate if unschooled intelligence and intellectual curiosity, a touch of gentleness and kindliness that generally went unnoticed, and a remarkable—if often raunchy or totally bent—sense of humor.

"You only know him as a rough, tough mayor," declared Maureen Keane, who was seen with him often enough that the Detroit dailies began referring to her as the mayor's "constant companion." "But he's really very gentle. He really is. And he's very simple."[6]

In many respects, Orvie never outgrew his farm background. One friend, Annette Ross, often called him a "rough log."

He was a man who, while not at all religious, performed small kindnesses for people in ways that were totally divorced from the political process.[7] Who took up many charitable causes totally unconnected with his city and its residents, often raising money for Catholic parishes and soup kitchens in Detroit.

He was a man who loved to catnap and yet seemed to be able to find almost unlimited stamina when he needed to focus his energy. Who economized around the office by using scrap paper and insisting he and his staff use old manual typewriters. Who was notorious among his associates for his male chauvinist attitude. Who never stopped being a Marine, even 50 years after his discharge from the corps.

He was a man who followed rigid routines for assembling parties for lunch, for taking early-morning drives to Camp Dearborn, for attending a travelogue series on Sundays. Who was particularly fond of hamburgers and black bean soup and who cheated on his rice diet by gobbling up drawers full of candies he stored in his office suite.

He was also a man who liked to sneeze explosively and pass gas loudly in his office, then run out, gasping for air. Who would tell the same dirty stories over and over again, to females as well as males. Who sometimes would remain behind his desk while greeting visitors, knowing they were unaware he had taken his trousers off and was sitting in his undershorts.

Hubbard's sense of humor manifested itself in his everyday routine. He loved a good laugh, and he didn't care at whose expense he got one.

For nearly a year in the 1950s, he raised parakeets in his office, much to the consternation of some visitors. One day, a couple of Detroit Edison representatives paid a call to discuss new street lights, spreading blueprints out across his desk. "Excuse me. Just keep talking—I can hear you," he reassured his guests as he disappeared into the next room to start chirping back at his birds and calling them by name. At that, the mayor of Dearborn began opening cages, shooing out perhaps six dozen parakeets, which promptly began flying around the ducking Edison men and even, outrageously enough, targeting the pate of one of them with a load of doo-doo. A less than fully contrite Hubbard scolded the offending bird, "Henry, don't do that. Don't shit on that guy."

Orville Hubbard's social acquaintances had a way of overlooking his personality quirks and the more egregious flaws in his character. That was true even when he had trouble distinguishing between work situations and social outings.

When he arranged his daily lunches with his department heads and others (almost always totaling 4, 8 or 12 to make the seating in the cars and at the tables come out even), he typically ordered for everybody—and then made the department heads split the cost of his lunch and any guests'.

When he was out on purely social occasions, he still tried to run everything, from the itinerary (an auction house in the Clearwater area was the required nightly destination when he traveled to Florida once with three others) to the menu (he decreed that everybody should eat lobster three nights in a row while on a private Great Lakes cruise with several couples).

Though Maureen Keane spent more time with him than anyone else did, in fact Orvie usually had other people tagging along. Often it was Michigan Bell public relations executive James Helmrich and his wife, Mary. Sometimes it was *Dearborn Guide* Publisher Bill Ross and his wife, Annette. Others he associated with regularly included Floyd Haight, a retired Dearborn teacher and fellow history buff; J. L. Bowles, a retired builder who often picked up the dinner tab for the mayor; and a young Dearborn newspaperman and later a department head, Fred Hoffman.

Helmrich saw more of the private Hubbard than did most of the mayor's entourage at city hall. He estimated he and his wife traveled out of town with Hubbard and Keane perhaps 60 times in the late 1960s and early '70s. "He was fun to be with," he said. "He was enjoyable; he was a fountain of information. He was an interesting person because he was opinionated as hell."[8]

Hoffman, who took over as editor of the weekly *Dearborn Times-Herald* at age 16, had to maintain balance between his association with Hubbard as news source and as mentor. "He was kind to many people, and particularly the people at the bottom end of the totem pole," Hoffman said. "We spent an awful lot of time together, and we were genuinely friends."[9]

Annette Ross, who stayed on at the *Guide* for several years in the 1970s after her husband died, said that despite differences with Hubbard, she "always was fond of him." Although he had a ferocious temper, she said, "he was very good to children, and he was very good to old people; he really loved people."[10] Ross retained her affection for Hubbard despite his prejudices. Once, she said, he unconsciously told an anti-Semitic story when she and her husband were present, then, in an uncharacteristic instance of mortification, he apologized profusely, recalling they were Jewish.

Only rarely did his cavalier treatment of his friends bring much of a protest, and then the apologies were considerably harder earned than with either the Rosses or the woman from Sterling Heights. Once in the late 1960s, for example, Hubbard was on a car trip in southern Indiana with Keane, recently appointed as his service bureau head, and the Helmriches. At one point, Hubbard chewed out Helmrich for failing to top off the gas tank when it was half full. At that, Mary Helmrich accused the mayor of crossing the bounds of friendship and told him he had no right to "order us around."

"Nobody talks to me the way you do," snapped back Hubbard, who was sharing the back seat with the woman. "I *am* the king." After a half-hour of dead silence, Hubbard finally said, "Mary, I apologize. You are absolutely right. I have no right talking to Jim this way."

For Keane, the turn-about was an eye-opener of sorts. "I have never heard him apologize," she later told Helmrich. "Never."[11]

Indeed, as difficult as Orville Hubbard obviously found it to apologize for his occasional gaffes involving his friends and acquaintances, he found it next to impossible to make up to the members of his immediate family for his long-standing transgressions against them.

9

The Family Man

I didn't know him intimately. Nobody did.
—Jim Hubbard, discussing his father[1]

It was 1949, Orville Hubbard was running for reelection, and if there was ever one big happy family, the Hubbard clan, as shown in the city hall photo, seemed to be it.

On the mayor's right were his wife, Fay, and his teenaged son, John, his arm around his mother. Close by on the mayor's left were his youngest son, Henry, and his platinum-blonde daughter, Nancy. On the mayoral desk were glossy photos of his two oldest sons, Jim and Frank, both serving on active duty in the Marine Corps. And in the center was the mayor himself, enjoying a long-distance call with the absent heroes as the rest of the family brightly crowded around to hear.

Hubbard had worked assiduously throughout his career to shield his family from publicity, ordering them not to talk about family affairs outside the home and hoping instead to manufacture in his campaign brochures precisely the kind of Ozzie-and-Harriet image conjured up by the photo.

Yes, it was true that Fay Hubbard had filed for divorce that year, complaining that her husband beat her and the children and had brought his young secretary to live with the family for a time, but the happy couple were reconciled now, with the children to keep them together.

Or so the mayor hoped it would seem.

In fact, however, the most generous description of Orville Hubbard's domestic life is that when it came to loving his family, he had his own way of showing it. He seldom had time for them after he became mayor of Dearborn, and what time he did have he spent making their lives miserable. He was even harder on them than he was on his appointees.

He had regularly manhandled his three oldest sons, and one big reason why Jim and Frank were in the Marines was that they couldn't wait to get away from the tyranny of their father.

But the public got only a glimpse of any of this. Fay filed again for divorce in 1953, for instance, complaining that Orville "is a devil to live with," but she withdrew the suit a day later. Later the newspapers gleefully jibed Hubbard ("All the world loves a lover, with the possible exception of Dearborn Mayor Orville L. Hubbard") when they latched onto a rift between him and his daughter over her elopement in 1955.

Orville and Fay Hubbard had married in 1927 and begun their family in 1928 when Jim was born. Two years later came Frank, then John, Nancy, and finally, in 1942, the year Orville took office, Henry. Although the Hubbards never divorced or legally separated, they stopped living together in the early 1960s.

Fay Hubbard broke silence about her family life only once or twice in the press. In 1975, she reflected bitterly with the *Dearborn Times-Herald* about her life with Orville Hubbard.[2] "Living with Orville Hubbard changes your whole personality," she said. "When I lived with him, I was a nervous wreck. I guess it's much better now that he is gone. I just couldn't stand all that turmoil. He loves turmoil. Orville likes to pit one person against another. He thrives on turmoil. Orville is very poor husband material. He was never any fun to be with at home. He could never sit down and relax. He has bought me a piano, but I could never play it when he was around. He doesn't care for music. He has no appreciation for anything. I used to cry a lot when we were first married because he would be gone all hours to night school and then work all day. I'm happy now that he has left. Orville's only love in life is to be mayor of Dearborn, but I think that job went to his head. He thinks he outgrew me, and he thinks he outgrew his family. If anyone has ever envied me for the type of life I lead, they shouldn't."

Hubbard's oldest children have similar misgivings about life with Orville, although they emphasized that their early years were happy. As they described things to me after their father left office, the Hubbard sons have fond memories of growing up in the Depression, taking Sunday rides and extended vacation trips.

"I can remember as a little toddler around the house, how much time and effort he spent with the family," recalled John.[3]

Frank explained, "We have a lot of good memories from the '30s. Before he was elected and became a very busy man, he took us out on picnics to Rouge Park; he took us to visit his aunts in Colon [Michigan]."[4]

Added Jim, "He loved history, and he exposed us to history. He took us to Civil War and Revolutionary War battlefields as young people. He was an exciting person to be around. You never knew what the hell he was going to do."[5]

But with the mayor of Dearborn making only $6,500 a year, the family was not well off. The kids slept in the unheated, unventilated attic of their modest East Dearborn home, and a downstairs remodeling project left the walls stripped of plaster right down to the studs for years.

Unsurprisingly, as a father Orville Hubbard was a strict disciplinarian. He had iron-clad house rules, he wanted his kids to be readers, and he wanted to instill a bit of the military in the boys.

"When I went out," related Nancy, "he said, 'You be in this house at 12 o'clock or the door will be locked.' And it was locked. When you left the house, you had to leave a name who you were going with, where you were going to be and a phone number where you could be reached. That worked for everyone. That's just the way he was.

"We used to have to read 20 minutes every day in front of the mirror and then put the book down and tell what we read—which was a good thing to do.

"But the thing with my dad—and he realized this later—is that he said you have to do this, you have to do that. So as a result, no one wanted to do anything. For years he'd call my mother on the phone, he'd say, 'You know, Fay, I raised all the kids wrong. I wish I could do it again.' But you do the best you can."[6]

Said Jim, "He demanded a lot from us that we weren't at that time ready to give. He was short on his patience. He wasn't flexible. We avoided him a lot."[7]

"We'd hear his car door slam in front of the house," remembered Frank, "and we'd all yell out, 'The old man's home,' so everybody grabbed a book. One day he walked in, and poor Jim was standing there and the book was upside down. The old man says, 'You're not fooling me. You're not reading.'"[8]

Jim: "There was an alley in the rear of our house, and sometimes when the door slammed, we all made a beeline for the back door and left our poor mother stuck with explanations why we vacated, and there'd be a cloud of dust in the alley. We just didn't really feel comfortable in his presence."[9]

When they were still shy of their teens, Hubbard taught his older boys close-order drill the way he had learned it in the Marines. The boys would take turns doing right-shoulder-arms and left-shoulder-arms with the family BB gun, while their father sat next to them. If they didn't get it right, he'd whack them in the leg with a ruler. "We were terrified," conceded Jim.[10]

In the mornings, the mayor would roust the family out of bed with a recording of reveille. He even had inspections, insisting the boys put out their underwear and other clothes and make their beds so tautly he could bounce a coin off the blankets.

Recalls Nancy, who thrived on the routine: "He was a stickler about shoes. I never went to school unless my shoes were polished. My shoelaces I took out every night and washed them. He showed us the right way."[11]

Even Fay Hubbard couldn't escape. The towels had to be stacked properly and the medicine bottles lined up just so. "It drove my mother nuts," said Jim. "She was a neat person, but she wasn't quite the way he wanted it. She was a stabilizing force in this whole thing. Her presence made the whole thing bearable. She was always in the background doing her duty as a woman. With her, the kids came first."[12]

That wasn't the way it was with their father. "Once he got into the political life," observed Frank, "he had a new family that was the city of Dearborn. That came first. He was married to his job. That was his baby; that was his life. He just immersed himself so much into it, he lost contact with everything but what he had to do in the city of Dearborn."[13]

"He had his hands full with his public life," Jim said. "I think he said himself, a man in public life probably shouldn't have a family."[14]

And his methods of discipline were hardly calculated to instill self-confidence in his offspring. "You didn't know one day whether you were gonna be yelled at or patted on the back," said Frank.[15]

"And he'd pit us against each other," Jim recalled. "Frank emerged as his favorite in terms of correct report cards and proper education. The rest of us sort of slackened off. And my dad could never stand the fact that Frank could beat him in chess. Sometimes he'd divert Frank's attention. He'd say, 'Look over there, Frank,' and he'd knock the chess set off the table or he'd switch a piece."[16]

He wasn't above encouraging Nancy to snitch on her brothers and making a ritual out of compulsory apologies. She recalled, "He used to say, 'When I get home, you tell me what they did and I'll fix them.' So as soon as he came in the house, I'd tell him that they did something—they were bothering me or something. So he said, 'All right, boys, come here.' And he'd get a straight chair and sit in the dining room. 'All right, get down on your hands and knees. Take your sister's hand. Kiss her hand, tell her you're sorry and you'll never do it again.' Oh, boy. They hated that."[17]

They also hated the times their father would give them money for tap-dancing lessons. Instead, often as not, they'd go bowling.

But during their teen years, the Hubbard boys began increasingly to feel the brunt of their father's "absolutely maniacal temper," as Jim described it. "If he ever blew up, you couldn't say anything," he said. "His temper was monumental."[18]

Nancy, who recalled getting only a solitary spanking from her father, pointed out that "he would explode. But then he'd be over it after that and then he'd want to know what he could do for you."[19]

"Let's say he was a strong disciplinarian," said John. "He was tough. I mean tough. He used to take us all on at one time. He said, 'When you're big enough and strong enough, let me know.'"[20]

John Hubbard recalled the kind of treatment he said took him years to forgive. Once, he said, he skipped a community college class he and his father were enrolled in together. Orville caught his son in a pool hall and knocked him across one of the tables. After having been kicked out of the house twice before, John left home for good at 19, following Jim and Frank into the Marine Corps.

When Fay Hubbard accused Orville of beating her and the three oldest boys, he got her to withdraw her divorce complaints, but he also got something of a comeuppance from Jim, who, by his mid-20s, had grown to be a barrel-chested six-footer from hours of weightlifting. "I had been afraid of him physically," Jim acknowledged. "So I got a little self-confidence [to the point] where I thought he couldn't handle me anymore. One time he was after John for something, and I came down. I said, 'Why don't you leave the kid alone?' Well, we got into it. My mother screamed, 'Kill him. You've taken enough from him all your life. Let him have it.' And he went for her, and I got between them and he couldn't reach her. He said, 'Get out of my house,' and I said, 'I'll get out when I'm ready.' And I give him a shot, and boom, down he goes on the couch. Up he comes. I give him another. And he clipped me on the jaw. I didn't even feel it. He thought he still had his old shit from the Marine Corps days.

"One time we were in his office. I told him, 'I don't care what you do. If you don't like the woman, divorce her. Don't touch her anymore. Don't hit her. She's your wife, but she's my mom. You can kiss tomorrow goodbye if you're gonna continue this shit.' He said, 'You threatening the mayor?' I said, 'You can forget about being mayor. You're not gonna be around tomorrow.' He never came home again. He never touched her again, either."[21]

For several years the workaholic mayor had slept two or three nights a week in city hall, where he kept most of his suits, shirts, socks and bow ties. When he left home for good, he didn't take anything more with him.

In the years that followed, Orville Hubbard's sons reconciled with him, although it took several of them decades. John, for instance, liked to recall his father's "big, soft heart," pointing out, "He was a sucker for anybody that would come along. Easy touch, really. Hit the old man up for $20, you know. We took advantage of his good nature, and we bore the brunt of his harder side. But you asked Orville Hubbard to do something for you, he'd give you the world."[22]

Added Nancy: "My father was very generous. I don't think he expressed himself emotionally a lot. Everyone can't show their feelings, but they give you things. I always understood that."[23]

Jim noted that "he had compassion."[24]

Frank said, "He had great compassion. And he had a great sense of humor. He'd go to airports with some of his staff and hide behind the corners, and they'd say they think they lost him, and they'd run around, and he'd just sit there and laugh."[25]

"My dad was sort of a silly person," agreed Jim. "He was a jokester in a lot of ways."[26]

But Orville Hubbard's good points never quite counterbalanced his darker side, so far as Jim was concerned. "I love the old man, but I don't like him as a person. Never did. Like Mark Twain once said about somebody who was being ridden out of town on a rail and tarred and feathered, if it wasn't for the honor of the thing, he'd just as soon miss it. I can almost say the same thing about Orville Hubbard. If I'd had a choice, I wish I hadn't known him so intimately. I take that word back. I didn't know him intimately. Nobody did. He was a very, very private person. His personality is elusive. Nobody could explain Orville Hubbard. Nobody could say what he was gonna do next."[27]

John: "He was a mystery to a lot of people, even to his own family."[28]

And Frank: "He was an enigma."[29]

10

The Immature Mind

He may be found at forty, say, as a man who still gets
his own way by having tantrums; brow-beating his wife;
terrifying his children; bawling out his subordinates.
—Harry A. Overstreet, describing the pathology of
arrested development[1]

Egomaniac. Publicity hound. Bully. Clown.

Whatever tags people have tried to pin on Orville Hubbard, they always
failed somehow to explain exactly why he acted the way he did. Certainly
he had immense vanity, a driven ego. Doubtless he derived satisfaction out
of calling attention to himself and asserting his control over others. But
why? What could have spurred him to exhibit the behavior that in many
instances could be described only as pathological?

Orville Hubbard surely was among the most difficult of men to know,
and the key to his inner self can hardly be found in a word or two. Unlike
Charles Foster Kane, the William Randolph Hearst character created by
Orson Welles in *Citizen Kane*, the stroke-stricken Hubbard never uttered a
last word as he expired. There never was a "Rosebud," a favorite old sled
or other childhood fetish to crystallize his links with his early years.

And it goes almost without saying that Orvie never talked out his problems with a professional counselor. The very thought is almost laughable,
given his frequently expressed antipathy toward doctors in general. One can
only guess, therefore, about what motivated him.

He himself acknowledged a need for approval. "A compliment makes
you go, doesn't it?" he once asked me rhetorically. "I think you strive for
that." And he often talked about being brought up to have a sense of pride
and the desire to excel.

But those were only platitudes. As for what made him the kind of adult
he turned out to be, all his worst traits are readily explainable, without
getting bogged down in a morass of psychological mumbo-jumbo, by accepting

him as a child who never grew up. Several of his own children, for instance, sensed that very characteristic about him.

John Hubbard summed up his father this way in a conversation with me: "He was a grown-up kid, you know, and he never accepted things on an emotional level that an adult would do. He just liked to play, kid around a lot, so it was hard to figure out when to take him seriously and when not to take him seriously."[2]

Jim Hubbard agreed, telling me, "What made him the way he was, and as complex a person as he was, was the fact he never grew up. He was still a 15-year-old boy in a marble game who wanted all the marbles. He was a little boy at heart. I heard a radio program the other night, narrated by E. G. Marshall. He said the trouble with all great men in history from Caesar on down—Orville Hubbard jumped right into my mind—is they never grew up; they were all little boys. And little boys are more dangerous than anything there is, especially in grown bodies."[3]

In mainstream psychological jargon, this analysis holds that something in his childhood worked to make the mayor of Dearborn a case of arrested development, or fixation in Freudian terms. The concept, of course, is that Hubbard was one of those individuals whose age does not reflect their level of emotional maturity. He was an adult, and yet he was not an adult; his behavior, in fact, often was typical of a subteen.

Freud used hypnosis and a process of "talking out" to uncover in many of his patients a wide variety of unsettling childhood experiences that resulted in what he called "unresolved emotional conflicts." These conflicts typically remained buried in the subconscious as a source of feelings of incompetence or guilt.

Although some elements of Freudianism remain a source of disagreement in professional circles, the principle of arrested development is so well accepted that it appears frequently even in popular literature. As put by the eminent philosopher-educator Harry A. Overstreet in his much praised bestseller *The Mature Mind* in 1949:

> Whenever, in the formative years of life, an intense emotional conflict is left unresolved, it does not disappear but remains as a festering element that later takes the form of a severe emotional disturbance or of a pervasive uneasiness in the handling of life. . . .
>
> Instead of growing beyond such an unresolved problem—and of growing beyond its power to hurt—the individual becomes fixated at the point of development where he encountered the problem. A neurosis in adulthood is a sign that at some certain point in the formative years of life development was thus arrested. A shock experience that should properly have been assimilated and outlived was, instead, repressed into the unconscious, where it continued to operate in its infantile form. The adult, in brief, is neurotic because he is continuing to seek in infantile

ways a solution to a problem that overpowered him in infancy.[4]

There is no evidence that Overstreet, former head of the philosophy department at the City College of New York, was following the career of Orville Hubbard when he wrote his book, but no one who has known the mayor of Dearborn or read about him can fail to be struck by what Overstreet wrote. In describing a hypothetical case of arrested development, he could hardly have detailed Orvie's behavior more accurately, particularly during the 1940s and early '50s, if he had been writing a thumbnail profile of him:

> His infantile way of going at problems may well become fixed in him; and he may be thus arrested in his proper development toward mature problem-solving. Should this happen, he may be found at forty, say, as a man who still gets his own way by having tantrums; browbeating his wife; terrifying his children; bawling out his subordinates. If he happens to be in politics, instead of trying to explore political issues to their rational depths, he may simply wear down his opponents by a method equivalent to the childish method of screaming and kicking his heels.[5]

What kind of childhood experience might explain Orvie's adult behavior? As Overstreet explained it:

> A vast number of children receive their first influence from parents who are themselves emotionally and socially immature. Such parents confirm the child in his egocentricity instead of helping him to outgrow it. They may do so by making him so insecure that he is almost forced into a concentrated self-absorption; by neglecting him; teasing him; *comparing him unfavorably with other children;* quarreling over him; ridiculing him for mistakes that are, as often as not, the product of an overanxious effort to please; visiting upon him moods generated by adult worries but never so explained to him.[6]

> The boy who is forced to work his way while he should be still a secure resident of home and school easily learns to think in terms of struggle, not in terms of mutual understanding. . . . He tends to carry a once-useful belligerence into situations where it is actually a handicap. It becomes a testimony, then, not to his possession of genuine strength but, rather, to his long having had to make his weakness into premature strength, his young fear into a premature self-confidence, and his immaturity into a show of maturity. Now that he is an adult, he may have kindly impulses and the best of intentions; but instead of being the man of such tried inner confidence that he does not have to be always proving himself, he is likely to be the man of power who throws his weight around.[7]

Of course, the theory of arrested development would mean little if we knew nothing of Orvie's formative years. As it happens, however, two overriding themes in his own descriptions of his youth apply directly to Overstreet's comments. Orvie's younger brother Sylvester was his mother's apparent favorite; and Orvie worked almost frenetically at a variety of jobs throughout his childhood, eventually leaving home at the age of 16 to make it on his own after his father died.[8]

As he reflected on it, "My people were all hard workers. My brother was three years younger than I was. He was a great help to my mother. She liked him. But he didn't do the work I did."

And another time: "Recognition, I think, [is the thing] that everyone is crying for. Not everyone, but some people crave it more than others. I was not a favorite child in my family. My second brother was my mother's favorite. I don't know whether my father lived long enough to [have a favorite]."

Hubbard talked frequently enough about his childhood that a number of his top appointees and staffers shared the view that he continued to labor to win the approval of the mother who had withheld it years before. One told of the times Hubbard would visit his mother and listen to her talk about how well his younger sister treated her—and never mention the accomplishments of her famous son. Another recalled that Orvie, discussing his siblings at the time his mother died, remarked that she always liked Sylvester better. "It was a very pathetic statement," noted the observer.

Jim Hubbard postulated that his father's psychological neediness during childhood may have led him into politics. "Orville Hubbard had an overwhelming desire to be loved," he told me, "because in his youth nobody paid attention to him. His father died; his mother was too busy raising [kids]. Nobody hugged him or held him. I wonder if he just craved this adoration. He didn't have this as a child, and he got it any way he could get it. He'd make you love him. He'd beat you until you loved him. His wife and children weren't enough. He wanted everybody to look up to him."[9]

If Orville Hubbard indeed was a case of arrested development, that would explain much of his behavior to the satisfaction of a Detroit-area psychologist who maintained a years-long interest in the mayor. While cautioning me that his comments were purely speculative, he noted of Hubbard: "Arrested adolescence is common among a lot of males. He stayed an adolescent in terms of temper tantrums. Certainly an adolescent has terrific mood swings. Adolescents are awfully good at cutting down the other guy, as he was. Then there was the adolescent concern with sex. You tell five dirty jokes, now *you* tell five dirty jokes."[10] The psychologist suggested that Orvie had a number of deep-seated problems: "He was such an insecure person. Anyone lashing out as he did must have had desperate insecurities. There was no institution he approved of. He didn't like anybody—no ethnic

88

group. He certainly was a very frightened person. He always did things with groups of people. Anybody that frightened is going to take steps to try to magnify his own power, surround himself with weak people, and be in absolute control."

Why the insecurities? The psychologist said he thought parental disapproval was a likely source: "You simply cannot please that parent no matter what. They're always the holdouts—the parents—so you get everybody else to say you're the greatest."

And Hubbard's childhood pattern of work may indeed have contributed to his eccentric behavior as an adult, the psychologist acknowledged. "Is it possible he was robbed of his boyhood, had his adolescence short-circuited? It's as if he never learned to play. Did he become compulsively driven to other forms of self-indulgence the rest of his life? Look at his eating."

Hubbard's need to control others also may relate to his childhood problems, the psychologist offered. "We have a way of becoming the thing we're enraged at," he said. "He eventually took over the role of victimizer, as he had been victimized by his mother. He victimized himself—worked long hours and demanded others do the same, neglect their families, make their whole lives the city."

Some of Hubbard's activities were so highly structured as to be obsessive/compulsive: attending a travelogue series every Sunday in Detroit; rounding up a group for lunch, often at the same restaurant, nearly every day; wearing virtually identical suits every day; continuing to keep tabs on people who signed recall petitions against him. "This was driven behavior," the psychologist noted. "The thing with anybody showing a lot of pathology is the frequency and the intensity of the behavior. If you're looking for evidence of maladjustment, when behavior is that much out of the norm, it's what we use to define pathology."

If Orville Hubbard's childhood problems did cause his adjustment problems as an adult, it was also a part of his life that he continued to hold onto for as long as he could. As Maureen Keane pointed out, "Whenever he goes home for a reunion, he gets all sentimental. He gets tears in his eyes."[11]

11

Home Again

You can always tell a farmer, but you can't tell him
much.
—Orville L. Hubbard, to a Rotary Club lunch group in
Union City, Michigan[1]

Orville L. Hubbard wiped his mouth and put aside the big white napkin he
had tucked under his chin and spread across his belly like a bib. What the
hell. When you have a belly like Orville Hubbard's, it's not easy getting
anything to stay in your lap. And Hubbard had no pretensions here anyhow,
even with 70 people ready to hear him speak. He was among country
people, people like himself.

It was a bright May afternoon in 1973, and Hubbard's cinch election
to his fifteenth term was still six months ahead of him. Right now, however,
he wasn't looking ahead. Hubbard was back home where he had lived as
a boy, in the village of Union City, plunked down 115 miles due west of
Dearborn. He was here for Mayors' Exchange Day, an annual ritual in which
Michigan communities traded off their chief elected officials for a day of
ceremonial friendship. Union City's village president, Harry G. MacDonald,
meanwhile, was in Dearborn being feted by the Hubbard minions who had
stayed behind.

At 9:30 that morning, Hubbard's entourage was intercepted by Union
City Police Chief Kenneth Blue at the edge of town. A police escort led the
visitors to the home of local Michigan Week Chairman Doyle Carpenter,
where a committee of greeters handed out the obligatory carnations and
words of welcome.

Afterward, on the route to the village hall, the group passed a couple
of oak trees encircled with yellow ribbons in the saccharine manner of the
hit Tony Orlando homecoming song, "Tie a Yellow Ribbon." Farther along,
in the business section of town, was a barrage of "Welcome Mayor Hubbard"

signs in the window of nearly every store and shop.

The morning's festivities included a program by the Union City High School band, a tour of the village hall and a coffee break with a bevy of Miss Union City contestants. But the big event of the day was clearly to be Hubbard's speech at a Rotary Club luncheon in the basement of Our Lady of Fatima Catholic Church. ("Christ," a laughing Hubbard had said wonderingly a few hours before, "I didn't know they had Catholics in this part of the world. We used to shoot 'em on sight.")

Anyway, after a light turkey lunch ("no bread, no butter, no pie") at the church, Hubbard was introduced to the multitude by Rotary President Don Knief, a local insurance man who had lived in Dearborn for 22 years before moving to Union City. As the guest speaker eased his bulk up to the podium, Knief tipped a flag standard over onto him. The mayor of Dearborn remained unruffled, however, even when the adjustable podium slipped down a couple of times after he started speaking.

And the home folks, obviously delighted to have such a personage there to favor their community of 1,740 souls, grinned and nodded at virtually every word. Hubbard was in his element, and if his homey epigrams ("You can always tell a farmer, but you can't tell him much") and barnyard stories played well in Dearborn, they really went over big in Union City:

"I think the nicest thing I've seen so far is the cleanliness of your town. . . . When I was here, we had one town marshal. . . . At night he came around to make sure the merchants didn't forget to lock their doors, to see that everything was safe. During the daytime he went around with a buggy, no uniform, just an old broom, . . . just picking up horse manure on Main Street. But speaking of horse manure reminds me of another one. . . . We had a Fourth of July celebration, either that or a homecoming, where the garage is on the top of that hill. That was a livery barn. . . . Behind that barn was a big manure pile. So this fellow put on a demonstration one year, you know, to show 'em what he could do, by jumping off that barn, that livery stable, in that horse manure, with a big umbrella. Damned thing turned inside out, and he went in the manure up to his neck."[2]

The Rotarians and the rest of the audience erupted in laughter at that one, and they also obviously appreciated Hubbard's stories about the old cement factory, his old school chums and local landmarks such as "Dead Man's Hollow." Then, in an artful segue from the old to the new, he finished up with his standard Dearborn boosterism:

"If you're ever going through Dearborn, our policemen there are trained to be extremely courteous. They all have in their sweatbands in their hats four words, 'Be Nice to People.' If you get in trouble in our town—and I don't think anybody from Union City ever would—if you should get in our jail, if you can't get out, you call me up. If I can't get you out, I'll come down and sit with you."[3]

That did it. The personal touch. Even though Orville Hubbard wasn't campaigning for anything, even though, in truth, he hadn't said anything of consequence, he earned a standing ovation of the sort he wasn't accustomed to, even in Dearborn. As often as he might visit Union City (he came back nearly every year for a school reunion or a look around), he never failed to make a favorable impression.

At last, after greeting old acquaintances and acquaintances of old acquaintances, Hubbard started on a tour that would last the rest of the day. As Doyle Carpenter later put it, "We planned a tour for him, but he toured us." First was a stop at Turtle Lake, a water-filled marl pit, near where, Hubbard recalled, he once developed a bad case of poison ivy. "I was swimming in the river and had to take a crap. I took a big leaf. How the hell dumb can you be? I got it all over my back and everything." Then it was a municipal hydroelectric plant on Union Lake, where Hubbard stopped for a chat with a black man fishing from the dam. "He's from Battle Creek. Caught 15 fish, mostly bluegill. I could almost eat 'em now." Then it was a pond near the mill race of the Coldwater River, where Hubbard went into a rage over a sudden childhood memory. "A kid almost drowned me here. Son of a bitch. I'd like to get him now. Sadistic bastard. I couldn't have been over six years old. It scared hell out of me." Finally, it was the Boise-Cascade mobile home plant, built on the site of the old Peerless Portland Cement factory, where Hubbard once worked as a roustabout. "Used to be a story there were a couple of whorehouses around here, but I don't know if it was true or not."

Later on, when the "official" tour was over, Hubbard directed his party to the home of an old Boy Scout companion, Pem Little, where he turned down a facetious offer of a wheelbarrow ride. "Hell no. I'll never get out. I'm too damned fat." Soon thereafter, he vetoed a suggested stopover to visit his younger brother, Elvert. "No, hell no. You stop and you're good for all night long."

After that, there was a matter-of-fact detour to the old Riverview Cemetery, where both Hubbard's parents and his brother Sylvester were buried. It was, he said, not far from the scene of a particularly noteworthy event of his youth. "This is where I had my first piece of ass," he smilingly told the group, gesturing toward a spot that once featured a grapevine shaded by a tree near a fence. "We were both 17. She said, 'You won't like me as well after.' And I wouldn't even help her up. I didn't speak to her for several days after, and then she never did speak to me again." Then, after stopping at a four-corners with the unlikely name of Hodunk, where Hubbard had a few swallows of beer and some chips and nuts, the group started back to Dearborn.

"You fellows got a lot longer tour than you expected," Hubbard observed cheerfully from the reinforced passenger-side seat in the front of his city-owned Ford LTD. And, just like a little boy delighting in the sights, he went on, "Beautiful farmland through here, fellows. Best in the state. . . .

"Look at the cows. Did you know cows had five tits? . . . This is what you call a captive audience—nowhere to go. . . . Is this trip tiring you, Dave? You're a young man. . . . There's a boy from Africa. . . . I bet a nickel that's peppermint. . . . Look at the silos, a sign of economic distinction. . . . Look at the farmer working late, after everybody else has quit. . . .'

Everybody else, that is, except Orville Hubbard. For nearly 12 hours, it seemed, he had never stopped talking, and he wasn't showing the least sign of fatigue now. Of course, when it came to reminiscing about the country or the old days, Orville Hubbard never seemed to quit.

Baby Orville, circa 1904. (Photo courtesy of Frank Hubbard.)

Orville at 14 in his Boy Scout uniform, circa 1917. (Photo courtesy of the city of Dearborn.)

Hubbard at 20, a streamlined 159 pounds, beams with pride during his stint with the Marines in Charlotte Amalie, St. Thomas, the Virgin Islands, 1923. (Photo courtesy of the city of Dearborn.)

Hubbard at 20, in his Marine dress blues with sharp-
shooter medal, 1923. (Photo courtesy of the city of
Dearborn.)

Hubbard as a candidate for the Michigan Senate, 1932.
(Photo courtesy of the city of Dearborn.)

Hubbard as a candidate for Dearborn mayor, 1941. He
used this photo in his campaign literature as late as 1973.
(Photo courtesy of Arella Studios, Dearborn.)

Hubbard, who was founder and first commandant of the
Michigan Marine Corps League, in his gold cap and uniform, 1946. (Photo courtesy of the city of Dearborn.)

Hubbard during his fourteenth term, 1971. (Photo courtesy of the city of Dearborn.)

The entrance to the mayor's office, with its scriptural reference to Christ. (Photo courtesy of the city of Dearborn.)

Hubbard after his stroke, 1978. (Photo courtesy of the Detroit News.)

Hubbard punches in after a protest by city employees on the mandatory use of time clocks, 1944. The mayor claimed he averaged 12-hour workdays. (Courtesy of the Detroit News. *Photo by John Herrmann.)*

Hubbard greets Henry Ford I on the auto pioneer's eighty-third birthday at Ford Field, 1946. This is thought to be the only photo of the two together. At Ford's right is his granddaughter, Josephine Ford; at his left, his wife, Clara Bryant Ford. (Photo courtesy of the city of Dearborn.)

Hubbard accepts a deed to 40 acres of Ford land from Henry Ford II, 1948. The land was intended as the site for a municipal hospital, which was never built. This photo appeared in Life *in 1951. (Photo courtesy of the city of Dearborn.)*

KEEP NEGROES OUT OF DEARBORN

☒ **Vote NO on (Advisory Vote)**

(The John Hancock Rental Housing Project)

PROTECT YOUR HOME and MINE!

☒ **Vote NO on (Advisory Vote)**

(At Bottom of Column on Right Side of Voting Machine)

Blatantly racist cards like this one were distributed at Hubbard's direction by city employees to help defeat the Hancock housing referendum, 1948. (Photo courtesy of the Dearborn Historical Museum.)

Acquitted on a federal civil rights charge, Hubbard confers with Lewis McGhee, the lone black juror, 1965. (Courtesy of the Detroit News. *Photo by Carl Wienke.)*

Hubbard and DPW Director Frank B. Swapka demonstrate the city's efficient leaf collection service with a truck bearing the motto that became a code phrase for "Keep Dearborn White," circa 1950. (Photo courtesy of the city of Dearborn.)

Hubbard and son Henry meet General Douglas MacArthur
at the dedication of a war memorial at city hall, 1952.
(Photo courtesy of the city of Dearborn.)

Hubbard joins a crowd massed on Michigan Avenue to see
presidential candidate Richard Nixon's motorcade pausing
with wife, Patricia, 1960. Hubbard made Nixon an honor-
ary mayor in a brief ceremony at city hall. (Photo courtesy
of the city of Dearborn.)

Starting on his way by train to the GOP national convention in Chicago, Hubbard and two aides wear clown masks in an attempt to outwit pursuing sheriff's deputies, 1952. (Courtesy of the Detroit News. *Photo by Rolland R. Ransom.)*

Hubbard demonstrates his riding skill on a show horse at a Dearborn Junior Chamber of Commerce rodeo, 1944. This photo appeared in both Time *and* Life *in 1951. (Courtesy of the* Detroit News. *Photo by the* Detroit Times.)*

Hubbard celebrates Easter, 1953. (Photo courtesy of the Detroit News.)

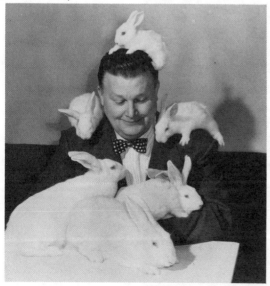

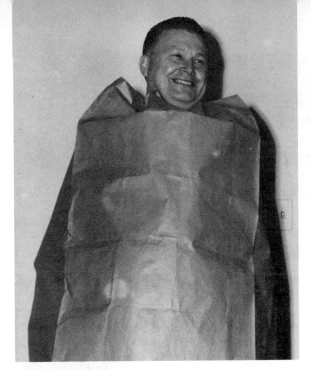

With no mayoral primary to contend with, Hubbard demonstrates that the election is "in the bag," 1953. (Courtesy of the Detroit News. Photo by the Detroit Times.)

Hubbard gleefully reprises for the cameras after being served with a subpoena during a meeting of the County Board of Supervisors, 1959. (Photo courtesy of the Detroit News.)

*Hubbard presents visiting transsexual celebrity Christine
Jorgensen with a key to the city, circa 1952. (Photo courtesy of the city of Dearborn.)*

*Hubbard welcomes former council opponent Ray Parker
"back on the team" before appointing the Fordson teacher-
coach a part-time city assessor, 1957. (Photo courtesy of the
city of Dearborn.)*

The Hubbard family, 1945: (top, from left) *Fay, Frank, Jim, Orville;* (bottom) *Nancy, Henry, John. (Photo courtesy of Arella Studios, Dearborn.)*

Sylvia Hart Hubbard, Orville's mother, circa 1970. (Photo courtesy of the city of Dearborn.)

Hubbard gets a hug from daughter Nancy, who sports a "Re-Elect Mayor Hubbard" button, 1949. (Photo courtesy of the city of Dearborn.)

Hubbard joins the festivities with Dearborn's St. Patrick's Day queen, Maureen Keane, 1959. (Photo courtesy of the city of Dearborn.)

Hubbard celebrates his sixty-third birthday in traditional city hall festivities, cutting the cake with Maureen Keane, 1966. (Photo courtesy of the city of Dearborn.)

Hubbard and his department heads swear to go on a group diet, 1974. (Photo courtesy of the Detroit News.*)*

Hubbard bolts down burgers from Art's Diner, which he had anointed as his favorite spot for them, 1969. The proprietor responded by putting "Hubbard Burgers" on the menu. (Photo courtesy of the city of Dearborn.)

Just for fun, secretary Judy Cord tries to get a tape around the mayoral chest before Hubbard's clothing sale at city hall, 1970. (Photo courtesy of the Detroit News.*)*

Less than two months after his hospital discharge following therapy for a stroke, Hubbard shares a teary-eyed greeting with Annette Ross of the Dearborn Guide *at Greenfield Village, 1975. (Photo courtesy of the city of Dearborn.)*

Dearborn's third mayor gets a bit of encouragement from his successor, John B. O'Reilly, at a Hubbard retirement testimonial at the Hyatt Regency Dearborn, 1978. (Photo courtesy of the Detroit News.*)*

This Detroit News *editorial cartoon by Draper Hill was inspired by Frank Hubbard's declaration that he was his father's choice to succeed to the mayor's post, December 15, 1976. (Photo courtesy of the* Detroit News.*)*

Sculptor Janice B. Trimpe finishes up the clay model for the Hubbard statue erected in 1989 in front of the Dearborn city hall, 1988. (Courtesy of the Detroit News. *Photo by Harold Robinson.)*

Part
II

A Chronology

12

Union City, 1903-20

The harder I work, the luckier I get.
 — A favorite Hubbard slogan

Orville Hubbard always liked to romanticize a little about being born "as near as you can get to a log cabin as anyone that lives" and being raised as "a goddamn little country kid from Mudsock." Actually, as nearly as he could tell, he was born in a small frame house on a backwoods farm in Batavia Township, just outside the tiny industrial-agricultural community of Union City in the flatlands of lower Michigan, less than 20 miles north of the Indiana boundary and about halfway between lakes Huron and Michigan. As for Mudsock, a little rural area that didn't even qualify as a four-corners, he never actually lived there, though he went to school there for a few years.

Geography aside, Hubbard had a rustic upbringing that wasn't exactly filled with pastoral charm. His father, Ralph Star Hubbard, was a sometime farmhand and full-time laborer making a dime an hour at the local cement factory. His mother, Sylvia Elizabeth Hart Hubbard, took in washing and otherwise tried to keep up with Orville and his younger siblings, two brothers and a sister.

Poverty. Christ, yeah, real poverty. No one could come from lower down the line than I come from. Nobody. I went barefoot all summer till it started snowing. Christ, I put more goddamn thistles under my feet. I didn't have electric lights in my house. The only heat was from those combination cookstoves. Didn't have water. Never had an inside toilet. Never used toilet paper. Used those smooth sheets from catalogues to wipe your ass with. I used to sit and read the Sears-Roebuck and

Montgomery Ward catalogues. I used to tell my mother all the things I was gonna buy her.

Notwithstanding his humble background, Hubbard remained intensely proud of his origins. He traced his ancestry back to a line of English colonists in the 1620s—or back to the time of the Vikings a thousand years ago, if you were willing to consider the most extreme of his meanderings about genealogy. From Massachusetts, Connecticut and then New York State, the Hubbards migrated eastward. In 1827, one Horatio Nelson Hubbard, Orville's great-grandfather, settled in lower Michigan on a farm he bought from the federal government.

I was always trying to establish that one of my ancestors was in the American Revolution, but I never could do it. I had two great-grandfathers serve in the War of 1812, Henry Dearborn's war. I paid no attention to my mother's side. Never knew if they were Scotch, English or what. My mother would say that one of our ancestors was part Indian, and I always added the comment that he caught an Indian princess that couldn't outrun him. Never knew my mother's people at first, but I met them later. They're good people, ordinary dirt farmers. But on the Hubbard side, I thought the people were a little better educated. My mother's people were inclined to be on the dumpling side. They were fat. My mother was quite a big woman at one time. My father was thin, but he was muscular. The Hubbards were all thinner. They ate like parakeets.

Hubbard's father continued the Hubbard military tradition, serving three years in the Army during the Spanish-American War, the Boxer Rebellion and a number of other expeditions and skirmishes. He was discharged as a private first class in 1901 after contracting malaria in the Philippines.

One of six children, Ralph Hubbard had been born on the old Hubbard homestead, but his mother died when he was six months old, and he was taken to live in New York with his oldest sister. After his military service, he returned to Michigan to live with his father, Sylvester E. Hubbard, and work on the family farm. There he met a young woman, Sylvia Hart, also working on the farm. They were married, and their first child, Orville Liscum Hubbard, was born April 2, 1903.

Young Orville never knew for sure, but he told people he was named after Orville Wright, even though his birth preceded the Wright brothers' first successful flight by more than eight months.[1] He was given his middle name, he was told, after Emerson Liscum, his father's regimental commander, killed in action in the Battle of Tientsin.

My father served most of his time before he got sick with malaria in Manila. He saw a lot of action under fire. He liked the Army, oh, Christ, yeah. He and my mother were married about 1901 or 1902. I hope they were married then. I was

98

born the next year. Whether my father finished high school, I don't know. My mother graduated from Union City High School, I think. But my parents didn't know anything. They just knew when it was time to eat and time to go to bed.

There wasn't much in the way of cultural enrichment in Union City anyway in the years following the turn of the century. Plunked down in the middle of some of the state's richest farmland, it was a village of 1,200 persons. The community straddled the Branch and Calhoun county line, and the St. Joseph and Coldwater rivers joined nearby. The main link to the outside was a railroad depot through which four passenger trains passed daily between Niles and Jackson. The Congregational Church boasted the largest membership in town, as well as the only gymnasium. There was one theater, the Strand, as well as a couple of hotels, a bank, a school with grades kindergarten through 12, a yeast factory and the cement factory.

Ralph Hubbard had quit his father's farm, gone to work for another farmer and finally started full-time at the cement factory. The Hubbards' next child after Orville, a son, died before he was given a name, but the others all were healthy. Another son, Sylvester, followed Orville by three years; a daughter, Omah, came two years after that; and a third son, Elvert, followed after another gap of five years. The family moved around the area as Ralph Hubbard changed jobs.

I can't say that I was unhappy. 'Course, a lot of kids did a lot of things I couldn't do. My father was strict, immaculate, spotless. He was always after me to read the papers or study something. Christ, I just hated it. I always figured my brother Sylvester was the favorite child. But I had no problems at home. We were as close as relatives could be. I would say we were close to my grandfather. My grandfather did pretty good. He had a better-than-average IQ, I'd say. And he was a very down-to-earth type of guy. But Grandfather could get along with his kids just so long. Had three sons and three daughters. He'd get mad at one and then another. He wrote more wills. They all worried about what the old man was gonna leave 'em. The Hubbard farm was in Batavia Township, and I lived there as a kid. I think it was around 275 to 300 acres. When I was about six, I went to a rural school, Hawley. A dumpy place—one room, five boys and five girls, first grade to eighth grade. I had perfect attendance, got a certificate for it. I walked two miles, carried my lunch. I can remember I had broken every glass on the telephone poles between the school and my house. Then my father left Grandfather's farm, and we moved down the street. That put me 200 feet into the other school district, in Sherwood Township, and I had to switch over to Mudsock School. One room, 38 kids. Then we moved to Madison Township, and in about fifth grade, we moved to town. I left Mudsock and went to Union City School. We lived in three different houses in Union City—I guess you'd say on the lesser side of town. I couldn't say I was a good student. But I was always a perfectionist. And I remember once in about fifth grade, the teacher said to me that I was a born leader.

99

If not an academic whiz, at least young "Hub," as he was called then, was making a mark in other ways. Though not big for his age, he was developing into a muscular, well-coordinated boy, athletic and popular, though endlessly talkative. A couple of old Union City acquaintances remembered him later.

"The whole family was mouthy," recalled Lee M. Bartlett, who continued his friendship with Hubbard after becoming a teacher in Dearborn. "He sure took after his mother. She could talk any 30 people out of their seats at once. She could talk your arm off. She was just going constantly. A huge woman. Orville's sister and later he himself were big like her. The other brothers were tall and skinny like their father. Everybody liked Hub; everybody liked him. He was a leader, even then. He was smart, a hard worker, a good athlete."[2]

Added Otto Smith, who later became a teacher in Union City and kept in touch during Hubbard's frequent visits home, "He was pretty good at breaking up fights, especially if a smaller kid was being picked on. A pretty good sergeant-at-arms. A real leader. Outspoken. He was in the darnedest scrap I ever saw in my life. He and my cousin's husband fought all afternoon."[3]

Hubbard remembers himself as a churchgoer who tried to stay out of trouble—and as a real sports buff.

As a kid, Christ, nobody went to church more than I did. I have a pin for attending without missing a day for years. Born and raised Congregationalist. I got along with everybody in school. I'd say I was a friendly, outgoing kid. I traveled basically with the kids that were not the wrecking crew. I was obstinate, always ticking somebody off, but I never got in trouble picking fights. I was always taking some guy's side that I thought got abused. I've always been a guy who's felt sorry for the underdog. I could always take care of myself. And I was a good ballplayer. I made the high school team in eighth grade. I was so small, normal baseball pants went right up over my shoulder. Paid 97 cents for a uniform from Montgomery Ward's. Originally played outfield, later shortstop and second base. The baseball coach liked me because I could hit and catch. I was a guy with big paws, never dropped the goddamned ball. Usually got on base. We had a hell of a good team, played against colleges.

Young Hubbard also pursued the usual childhood activities apart from sports. He raised pigeons, guinea pigs and rabbits. He did a little hunting and trapping. He had a mustang pony he rode bareback. He also spent five years as a Boy Scout—Troop No. 1, Black Bear Patrol—though he actually finished all the required projects before the minimum age of 12. A couple of his childhood pursuits—brief excursions into smoking and some naive sexual activity—brought him a modicum of grief.

100

Everybody chewed tobacco in those days. My father chewed Yankee Girl. He didn't smoke very much, cigars once in a while. You know how kids want to imitate the old man. I said I'd like to smoke, and he gave me a cigar. He said, "Here, take it. Puff hard and then you swallow it, see?" Oh, I got sick as a dog. For two days I couldn't eat or sleep or anything. That ended it. And then one time when I was about 12. there was this girl, and I put a straw in her pussy and blew into her. Well, she must have told her mother. Every time I'd see her mother, she'd say, "You're a bad boy." That bothered me for ages.

Life on the farm also had an influence on the adolescent Orville. It left him with a sense of raw barnyard humor that was to stay with him all his life.

Kids used to peek around under the barn to see the damn old stud horse come around. On breeding day, when the mares would be in heat, that goddamn horse, a Belgian stallion, a big son of a bitch, would come in. Had a prick on him as long as your arm and big as your wrist and a knob on the end as big as your fist. He used to shove it up these mares, pffsssht. And I remember he was a smart fucking horse. My father took him out once, got the bit in his teeth and hung onto it, and it took my old man right across the fucking barnyard, full speed. Did you ever see a rooster chase a hen across a barnyard? You hear the story about the cross-eyed rooster that was chasing two hens across the barnyard? He got tired of running, and one hen said to the other, "We'd better separate, or he'll miss both of us."

Of course, the farm wasn't all fun and games. Like most of his friends, Orville worked. But unlike most of them, he worked during every spare minute. His father saw to that.

My dad kept me busy. He had a lot of pride in everything he did. He had the reputation of having the neatest garden with the straightest rows. The rows were so straight they looked like you could shoot a bullet down the line. I had to work in the garden while the other kids played. That bothered my ass. You see, in those days life was harder. You worked from sunrise to sunset. Everybody worked, shit, yes. My people were all good, hard workers. My father was a hardworking man. My mother, though, she worked like a dog all her life. I mean a real slave. My mother would do all the fucking washing for everybody. She got 50 cents, 75 cents a bushel. That's washing and ironing. Sometimes the damn dirt from the stove would get her irons all black, and she'd have to do it all over again.

Orville worked like a dog, too. Besides working in his father's garden, he cut wood and did other chores on his grandfather's farm. He worked for other farmers, cutting thistles, weeding onion patches, harvesting hay, oats and barley, milking cows and helping drive cattle and other stock to market.

He worked as a peddler, riding his pony house to house and selling postcards and delivering *Grit* magazine, the *Detroit News* and other papers. He posted theater showbills and helped the projectionist. He worked the theater's player piano. He sorted beans. He set pins in a bowling alley. He was cleanup boy at a barber shop. He vended from his own hamburger and popcorn wagon.

But like his father and most of the other able-bodied males not farming full-time, Orville finally became a laborer part-time for Union City's major employer, Peerless Portland Cement.

I started working at the cement factory when I was 12 years old. Had a job sorting sacks. Ten cents an hour, worked 10 hours, got paid for 12. My father didn't know I had the job. He told me I could never work there. But he walked through once, and when he saw me there, he didn't object. I worked during the school year, Friday and Saturday nights when there was work available. I worked mostly in the summertime. I was on a roustabout gang. That means you do anything, anytime, wherever they want you to do it. I worked on the steamshovel that dug the clay from pits. I worked on the train that hauled the clay back from the pits. I shoveled coal from a flatcar. I pounded up bricks from the kilns with a big sledgehammer. I worked in the fuel mill. That was about the worst place of all. They'd grind the coal so it blows in like dust to keep that fire going. You're just black as a pig all the time. Oh, Jesus Christ, dust. You had it in your ears, in your eyebrows, in your throat, in your nostrils, everywhere, and all through your clothes. My father used to get cement all over his nose, inside. Later they wore this little mask, but it never was too effective. It probably contributed a little bit to my father's health problems. My old man was strong as a bull, you know. He was a scrapper. He knocked some guy through a goddamn showcase once. Oh, he worked like a dog. He used to sack cement by hand. I think the sacks weighed 96 pounds. It's enough to kill a horse, I think. He had a stroke. Didn't work for about a year. The factory gave him half pay after that. Died at the age of 43. My impression was he actually died of pneumonia. Died in the same house, same room, same bed where my grandfather had died three years before at age 86.

13

The Big City, 1920-32

I was going to be a lawyer so nobody could push me
around.
—Orville L. Hubbard, making a career decision in the
Marines

Young Orville had some tough decisions to make after his father's death in 1920. Things had been hard enough when Ralph Hubbard was working, and now there were four children, no income and no insurance. Sylvia Hubbard could continue to take in washing, but she had no real prospects beyond that.

As the oldest, Orville was two months shy of his seventeenth birthday, and he knew he didn't want to work at the cement factory the rest of his life. But he couldn't earn enough at part-time jobs even to keep himself in clothes for school, let alone help support the family. An uncle could take the youngest child, Elvert, for a few years, and perhaps Mrs. Hubbard and the other two could get by on their own for a while. That, at any rate, was Orville's thinking when he quit school in midyear and left Union City with two friends to look for work.

I always wanted to go to school, but when my father died, I didn't have any clothes, any shoes, nothing. My mother was destitute. There were too many kids around. So three of us decided to leave town. Left right after the funeral. February 4, 1920. We stayed two or three days in a Jackson flophouse. One got a job there, one went back home and I went on to Detroit.

Although he was just a country kid with a ninth-grade education, Orville was no dummy. Like most children of the era, he wore knee trousers, but he bought a pair of long pants at a pawn shop so he'd look a bit more grown-up. Then, imagining he could be a mechanic, he headed for the huge

103

Dodge Main plant in Hamtramck, a municipal enclave inside Detroit.

After standing in a couple of inches of snow with hundreds of other applicants, he got to talk to the employment manager. He showed off his Scout certificate, told the man his father had died and said he might "stay a lifetime" if he liked the work.

Orville was given a job in the Dodge service department, doing general handiwork and learning to read blueprints and micrometers and to run machines. He worked nine-hour days plus half-days on Saturday on overtime. And although he couldn't see his way clear to send money home, the paychecks were good enough to allow him to become a budding fashion plate. He bought a top-grade suit. He bought a silk shirt. He bought silk underwear, Florsheim shoes and belts with gold buckles. He bought a cameo stickpin. He even bought a watch—on credit.

After being laid off during a summer depression, he worked briefly as a stockboy, then with a road gang, carrying cement bags, mixing cement and helping lay down a roadway—by hand.

It's not likely that toting cement bags made him homesick for Union City, but at least now he had a fancy wardrobe. So, at his mother's request, he returned home in the fall, resumed school—as a freshman again—and started in again part-time at the cement factory. And maybe it was the conditioning from his dawn-to-dusk job on the road gang, but he found out something about himself: he was a football player.

I played some the year before I left, but I was really a top player the last two years of high school. Played end on offense and sometimes quarterback. Safety on defense. I was tough. Could catch the ball. Good field-goal kicker. I was a hard guy to nail down. We played freshman teams from college, junior college.

Hubbard kept few souvenirs of his athletic career, although he did have a newspaper clipping of a 61–0 rout of Homer in 1921. It reported that young Orville kicked seven field goals, caught two touchdown passes and returned punts for big yardage. He also continued to star on the baseball team and emerged as the top basketball player in town his final year. At the same time, he got some notoriety for his skill at self-defense.

I learned to be a damn good wrestler and could use my dukes, too. Guy in town used to give wrestling lessons. He was using me as the guinea pig, but I got so I could beat him. I was a strong kid, you know, had these big legs, used to squeeze him till he'd crap. Another time during a carnival, this guy offered to meet all comers on a boxing platform. He was in the Army, was a little older than I was. I challenged him, and he hit me in the nose. Jesus Christ, the blood ran all over my shirt. But then I knocked him off the goddamn platform right out into the street.

His athletic prowess helped boost Hubbard's self-esteem, and he also found it elevated him above the rank of just another poor kid in school. It made him a celebrity.

When you're the top football man, you know, Jesus Christ, you can just name your girl around a place like that. My last year in school, we had a teacher come here; she was six months older than I was. She was 18, and I started going with her. I used to think, son of a bitch, I'm gonna take her out and screw her. But I never had the nerve.

Although Orville "wasn't studiously inclined," as he later recalled, he wanted to stay in school.[1] But his mother still had no regular income, he wasn't able to help out much, and he undeniably missed some of the attractions of big-city life. None of his classmates wore clothes like the ones he'd bought in Detroit, after all.

When I'd come home, my mother couldn't believe it. I was the best-dressed guy in town. I wasn't a bad-looking kid. They used to accuse me of combing my hair on the baseball field. You got to be proud in life, what you do or who you are.

So, with mixed feelings, young Hubbard dropped out of school again. He went back to Detroit in May 1922, landing a job as a cleanup boy on an excursion boat. But collecting cuspidors and polishing brass didn't seem any more promising than working in the cement factory. The military, on the other hand, had possibilities. He'd almost enlisted in the Army at 17 to join the occupation forces in Germany, but he thought better of it and stayed home.

I used to read those ads—work for Uncle Sam and travel and make big money. I had read quite a bit about the Navy and intended to join. I was all signed up waiting for my physical, and, jeez, I saw the guys coming in and they looked like bums. So I said, "I think I'll change my mind." So then I walked down to the corner, and there was a Marine poster, like a decoy. You know, when the ducks come down, you shoot 'em. So a Marine sergeant, all dressed up like a bellhop, came up to me. Well, the first thing I know, I was sworn in to the goddamn Marine Corps. If I could change my mind the next day, I never would have gone. I thought, Well, Christ, if I don't go now, I'll be a deserter. They'll put a picture in my hometown post office. I said, "Could I go to China?" So he said, "Well, first everybody has to go through basic training at Parris Island." I thought, Christ, that'll be nice to write to my girlfriend from Parris Island, because, you know, everyone's singing, "How you gonna keep 'em down on the farm after they've seen Par-ee?"

After his June 27 enlistment, Hubbard adapted quickly to military life. At a muscular five-foot-nine, and 159 pounds, he had no problems with the physical side of basic training. And he became a real stickler for military regulations.

I was scared to death the first two or three months. But I think my basic training probably did more for me than anything else in the world. I just loved that life. Always neat and orderly. And all the stations where I transferred, I didn't have any offenses. I was very proud of that. And I was an expert rifleman. I grew up to hate Germans. I used to think, the kaiser, son of a bitch. I'd put it right between his eyes, right over the mustache.

Because of his proficiency, Hubbard drew duty as a coach on the rifle range. Then, mostly because he had brought a typewriter from home, he got transferred to clerical school at Quantico, Virginia, in September. He was a natural for clerical school, and during his six months there, he even made productive use of his weekends. He often spent Saturdays watching Congress and Sundays in the Congressional Library or the Smithsonian.

Hubbard left Quantico in March 1923 for the Caribbean. He spent 16 months in the Virgin Islands and another two in Puerto Rico as a steno aide to two colonels. During that stint, he contracted dengue fever, but he began taking correspondence courses. By the time he was finished, he had completed five.

Hubbard also had developed a sense of frugality—no more silk shirts— and he was able to send his mother $25 nearly every month from his $30 pay. He didn't date much—his finances and his studying saw to that—and he broke off with the young teacher he'd been going with back home.

In September 1924, Hubbard was transferred a final time, to the Marine barracks at the Brooklyn Navy Yard, where he drew duty as a court-martial stenographer. He also drew a promotion.

I was promoted directly to sergeant. I skipped first-class private and corporal. In those days, hell, it was almost impossible to have any rank at all, because there were so many men left over from World War I. But I had top jobs when I was in there. And I had something very strong in the back of my mind at that time—to learn my rights, so no one was gonna push me around. Courts-martial were so damn arbitrary. It didn't seem to me they got a fair deal in the service. And my feelings have always been for the underdog, so I made up my mind while I was in New York that I wanted to study law.

Seeing other Marines in trouble made an impression on Hubbard, and he continued to stay out of trouble himself, although he did beat up a barracks mate in Washington who challenged him. He also served as liaison for other Marines who wanted information about correspondence courses.

106

After all, it would have been hard to find a better salesman than Hubbard for the corps. This was a man who loved the service so much he kept all his records permanently. He even went back to visit Parris Island on the fiftieth anniversary of his discharge.

After finishing out his 36-month enlistment in 1925, Hubbard worked for a couple of months selling lots in Detroit. He went house to house but made only two sales. Then he got a typing position at the county hospital at Eloise and soon afterward a job as a steno at Ford's Highland Park plant.

But Hubbard had never forgotten about having to quit school before his junior year, and now he had his eye on law school at the University of Michigan in Ann Arbor. One catch: Latin was required for admission, and he hadn't taken any. So, on the basis of entry exams and his military background, he applied for and was admitted to Michigan State Normal College (now Eastern Michigan University) as a prelaw student in the fall of 1925.

Again, Latin was a problem, though. He was assigned to an introductory Latin class with a group of ninth-graders in Ypsilanti. At the suggestion of the principal, he transferred after several weeks to Ferris Institute at Big Rapids to study Latin and review English, algebra and the classics. He had been out of school too long to suit his new Latin teacher, but he was allowed in class over her objections. He worked hard enough to wind up with a 99 in her class.[2]

He also got back into athletics. Though he arrived at Ferris too far into the season to play football, when spring came, he made the baseball team as the starting centerfielder.

After school let out in the spring of 1926, Hubbard went back to Eloise, intending to reenroll in school in the fall. But that was before he met Fay Cameron. Her father was Dr. F. E. Cameron, the assistant medical superintendent at Eloise. Orville remembered seeing her the previous summer at the hospital and deciding she was a "pretty good-looking girl." He also recalled seeing her name in a class yearbook at Normal, though he'd never run into her at school. So when a brother of hers who knew of Hubbard's background in the Marines asked him to a picnic to meet her, Hubbard liked the idea, and they started dating.

When she took her first job teaching fifth and sixth grades at nearby South Lyon in the fall, Hubbard decided to postpone school. His decision was made a bit easier when he was promoted to assistant storekeeper at the hospital cafeteria. He also took a correspondence course in applied psychology from the Pelman Institute in New Rochelle, New York, which he later credited with helping him develop "a singleness of purpose."

Throughout the year, Hubbard continued to see Fay, though he was less than successful at winning over her mother.

I didn't know at that time that her mother was interested in breaking us up. When we were married—July 20, 1927—her mother took all of her stuff, every

*fucking thing she had, and threw it right out of the house. So that didn't make it
very nice for me to stay around Eloise.*

That September, the Hubbards returned to Detroit, where he landed a
job as a stenographer at Mathews Industries, an advertising firm. He also
took shorthand courses at night and started thinking he'd like to become
a court reporter.

Then, though he still had no high school diploma, came one of the
results of his "singleness of purpose." After arming himself with affidavits
and testimonials from people who said he would make a good lawyer, he
was accepted in January 1928 to start classes at the Detroit College of Law.
He had to borrow money from his father-in-law, and it was a grind—five
nights a week for four years—but he loved it. He got out of work at 5:00
P.M. and rushed over to class from 5:15 to 7:15. He spent lunchtime watching court sessions. But despite his tight schedule, he proved an enthusiastic,
if not brilliant, student.[3]

*My law degree—I studied like hell for it. A publishing company had a list of
500 typical bar questions. I set out to do one a day, and I did that quite conscientiously. The hardest teacher we had, constitutional law, he said I was a good
student. I got an A in his class.[4] I'd say I was probably good. I wasn't excellent.
Of course, law is an easy subject, the easiest of all I can think of. Nothing to it. It's
bullshit.*

Regardless of how Hubbard felt about the law, he ventured soon into
a closely allied pursuit: he got into politics.

*In spring 1928, that was my first taste. One of my teachers was doing some
campaigning for James Chenault. He was a Wayne County prosecutor who was
running for circuit judge. He got all the students to circulate petitions for him, and
I did it. He got elected, too. From that interest I got in it, I made application to
work as a Detroit election worker in the fall of 1928. I noticed a lot of people
running for delegate, and I wrote my name in. I got caught in the excitement of
the election. I remember I was strong for Hoover. But that election, hell, there
wasn't 10 percent of the people were Democratic. It was mostly drunks and guys
who looked like they were drunks.*

Politics was just one more outside interest to pull Hubbard away from
home, however, as far as Fay was concerned. She had enough trouble keeping his attention anyway, and they were also moving around a lot—eventually, in 1929, from Detroit into a newly built home on Hartwell in Dearborn.
Hubbard had been wanting "a better address," even though the family was
still renting, and Dearborn looked like the best bet.

I wanted Fay to get a job so I could go to school. But the last year she taught was before we were married. She never got another job. She got pregnant, and our first child was born September 24, 1928. That's Jim Hubbard. One solid year he cried. I never heard anything like it. He was a likable kid, too. Fay was always unhappy. I used to play golf with her dad once in a while. But I used to work so much, she used to say to me, "Why don't you go out like other men and play?" I worked days and was busy nights studying. Women start riding your ass. I worked Saturdays, too, five-and-a-half-day week. I used to study on the streetcar, hang on the strap. I'd get an hour of reading a day going downtown and back.

Despite his rocky home life, studies were going well. But Hubbard didn't feel he was doing well enough at Mathews, though he'd been promoted to bookkeeper and then cashier in his two years, and he'd gotten raises to $35 a week.

Then, through the same employment agency that had placed him at Mathews, Hubbard found a $50-a-week male secretary's position in spring 1929 with the Walter S. Butterfield Theatres chain. He moved on a few months later to the purchasing office at Chrysler in Highland Park at just over $60. He was there for three months, during which his most memorable task was to keep separate the checks his boss was sending to two girlfriends.

Meanwhile, Hubbard still was having problems at home. The baby was a year old. Fay was pregnant with her second child, Frank, and Mrs. Cameron still was kicking up a ruckus.

My mother-in-law said, "Why don't you leave that guy before you get some more kids?" She really raised hell. And so, Christ, my old lady—she'd get the kid and she'd run home, and I had to put all my stuff in storage when I came to Dearborn in 1929. So I moved to the YMCA for a month. I made up my mind I was going to stay in law school regardless of what happened. I told a fellow at the Y I'd been having a tough time getting back to school at night, and he said, "The Wall Street Journal wants to hire a man." I'd heard of the Ladies Home Journal; that's the only damn journal I could think of. I walked in the office, and here's the ticker going, and the guy's sitting with his hat on as if he's in a hurry to leave, and I thought, What the hell is this? Well, I said I understood they had a job for a stenographer, and he threw me a pencil. So he started reading about the market: the bear market, and I never heard of such a thing; the bull market, and I hadn't heard about the bull market, either. I didn't know what the fuck he was talking about. I typed it up. He said, "Let's see what you got." He says, "Hang your coat there," and I worked there five years. I was more a reporter than a stenographer. I did a lot of the researching. I never did get a byline. I wrote Henry Ford's obituary. Then he died so much later they forgot I even wrote it.

14

The Political Hack, 1932-39

You can't sell peanuts at the end of a parade.
—P. T. Barnum, as quoted by Orville L. Hubbard[1]

It was the middle of the Depression when Orville Hubbard graduated from the Detroit College of Law in February 1932, but you'd never have guessed it to talk to him. At 28, he was brimming with enthusiasm about his new lot in life. He was almost a lawyer, and with any luck he'd be a congressman, too.

A month after graduation, he announced his candidacy for Congress as a Republican in Michigan's new Sixteenth District. His avowed platform: a bond issue for public improvements, a soldiers' bonus, a 50-percent reduction in the federal payroll and the repeal of Prohibition.

Hubbard used to bum rides to political meetings from Otto A. Hoffman, who had gotten in the habit of driving him home after their law classes together. Throughout these contacts, Hubbard's force of personality was not lost on Hoffman. "Orville was a born mixer," Hoffman later told the *Detroit News*. "No one was too big for him to approach. He wasn't offensive about it, either."[2]

That April, in the middle of the political meetings and the congressional campaign, Hubbard came up for the bar exam.

It was a three-day examination. The last day was a half-day, and up to that time I hadn't discussed anything with anybody. A friend from Union City was taking the exam for the third time, so I asked him how he answered these mortgage questions. Jesus Christ, he convinced me I flunked it. I went home with the goddamnedest headache. But when the examinations were announced, I passed.

Hubbard was admitted to the bar, as he was able to recall four decades later, on Friday, May 13, 1932, but he continued to work at the *Wall Street Journal*. The times, he felt, were too perilous for fledgling lawyers.

I decided not to go into full-time practice right away because of the Depression. My first case was a divorce for a fellow in the office of the Journal. *He said his wife habitually used profane language and called him "vile and opprobrious names." Won the case. It was a default. His wife had run off and left him. He gave me a set of Elbert Hubbard books and a book on Napoleon. That was my retainer. No fee. He paid court costs, about three dollars. I never made any money in the law business. I'm too big-hearted a guy. I did everything free. I'd say I was a good lawyer for what I did, but I never had any real sensational case. I wouldn't represent a man if I thought he was guilty. Some people just use the law business as skinners—doctors are greater skinners—but I just couldn't do it.*

If the law game was a tough racket for Hubbard, politics wasn't proving much easier.

I took out petitions to run for Congress, and, Christ, right away I get an inquiry from Internal Revenue—how much money I make and all that stuff. I think the fellow I was running against, Frank Darin, he must have been the guy who started the inquiry. He was the whip in the legislature. They carved up his old Sixteenth District. I decided not to run for it. I withdrew and ran for state senator.

The Republicans under Hoover were still in power in the early Depression years, so it wasn't surprising that Hubbard identified himself as a Republican. But, as he later recalled, he voted for Roosevelt all four times, and the stuff he was spouting in his own campaign in 1932 didn't exactly follow the party line. He was about as much of a Republican in ideology as old-line Socialists such as Eugene V. Debs and Norman Thomas.

I ran as a Republican and started talking like a Democrat. A lot of people were out of work, and they were mad at the incumbent because he couldn't do anything for 'em. I borrowed money at 42 percent interest—that's 3 1/2 percent a month—to finance my campaign. Of course, nobody gave me a donation in those days. So I borrowed money on my furniture, and I did that every year through 1939. I ran a very strong campaign against small loan companies and this ridiculous rate of interest.

His campaign ads showed an earnest-looking, square-jawed, bespectacled young man who identified himself as an ex-service man, lawyer, farmer, reporter, stenographer and laborer. His 13-point platform was pegged to cutting government costs so that "we poor folks" could own homes. He advocated taxation relief by drastically cutting government expenses, federal control of the banking system, repeal of Prohibition, reform of election laws, reapportionment with proportional representation, old-age pension legislation, unemployment insurance, capital punishment for first-degree murder convictions, a chain-store tax, elimination of needless jobs, a ban against lobbyists in the state capital and a revision of the state tax system.

So, short on funds, out of sync with his party and almost an unknown in Dearborn political circles—he had never set foot inside city hall—Hubbard geared up for a September election against Ari H. Woodruff, incumbent Republican state senator from the Twenty-first District.

He rang doorbells, put his pictures up and even placed an extra newspaper ad he couldn't afford for an election supplement he discovered was due out the day before the vote. He had one thing going for him: his name was similar to that of a former Dearborn councilman, Edwin E. Hubbard, though they were no relation.

In retrospect, Hubbard really had no chance to win, but he did finish as runner-up to Woodruff, 12,271 to 4,811, in a field of five. And he outpolled Woodruff in Dearborn. Besides that, he did get elected to something: he became a Republican precinct delegate, and he remained one throughout the next four decades.

My campaign literature said, "Vote for the right man," and I guess they did. They voted for somebody else. There's nothing like running the first time. I was really convinced I was going to be nominated. I worked like hell in that campaign. Got a lot of baptismal experience. But, Christ, the Democratic landslide just swept Michigan behind Roosevelt. After that election, a lot of politicians switched. They all became Democrats, the whole gang of 'em. That would have been the natural time for me to have gone, but I just didn't want to be a switcher.

But the loss hardly even dented Hubbard's self-confidence. He was becoming a real political animal, and he was already an incorrigible publicity hound. Hubbard made a big impression at the time on Bill Mills, business manager of the *Dearborn Independent* and later to be Hubbard's opponent in a tough-talking 1957 mayoral election. Mills recalled the young Hubbard in an article written for that campaign:

The first time I remember seeing Orville Hubbard was a few days before Christmas in 1932. I was about to close the print shop and go home to dinner when an excited young man burst into the office. He was out of breath but happy as a lark. "I'm Orville Hubbard," he said and stuck out his hand. "I just won a new Chevvie! How about a story in the paper?" In rapid-fire fashion, the eager young man told how he spent his lunch periods staring out of his office window at a store display across the street. If he could guess the number of times the car wheel in that display turned during a three-hour period, he could win a new car. Instead of watching the wheel, Hubbard concentrated on the valve stem. With the aid of a fellow worker, he figured out the correct "guess" and won. Such cheerful stories were rare in the Depression, so Hubbard got his name in the paper.[3]

The next year, 1933, Orvie still had his job at the *Journal* and was practicing law sporadically, but despite the free car, the Hubbards were feeling the times just like everybody else.

The election was in the fall of '32, and six months later you'd think a tidal wave hit the country. Less than a year after I graduated from law school, the banks closed. That was right in the depths of the Depression, the low point, right there. Christ, the whole town was on welfare. The mayor of Detroit, Frank Murphy, was having people sell apples on the street to make a living. And, Christ, you could eat for 12 or 15 cents for eggs and bacon and tomato juice and toast and butter and jelly. I did lose a little bit in the Wayne Savings Bank. Maybe $50 or $100. The bank reopened and paid 15 cents on the dollar.

It was here that Hubbard picked up another of his rare legal cases, and this one was to make the young attorney a local hero of sorts. A man who had worked in Hubbard's campaign was charged with welfare fraud. The man, who was on the staff of the justice of the peace in neighboring Dearborn Township, had been hoarding flour he was being given weekly. Given the nature of the times, it was big news.

When I went out there, I subpoenaed everybody—the township supervisor, the guys that locked him up, everybody. It created a sensation out there because everybody was on welfare. No one had worked since 1929. They were destitute. Well, I asked for a jury trial, and I raised hell for prosecuting this poor guy on welfare. The jury went out, made an about-face and, bingo, came right back and said not guilty. And you'd have thought they were going to tear the goddamn building down. People were in the streets and all over the place. And I didn't charge this guy anything. The next day at my office at the Wall Street Journal, *about 25 of those people came down to see me. Holy Christ, was I embarrassed. Well, I became their hero out there, and the Democrats had taken over out there, mostly as a result of that case. That same gang who came out to see me were all elected. They wanted me to run. That's the time if I ever wanted to change parties, I should have done it.*

Hubbard stayed where he was—in Dearborn and with the Republicans—but he didn't need much encouragement to run again. This time, he decided to take on Clyde Ford, elected Dearborn's first mayor after the city's merger in 1929 and running now for a third term in 1933. Ford never won high marks for style—he was fat and always seemed to have soup spots on his suit or ties—but he did have a big advantage: he was a well-known Ford auto dealer and a distant cousin of Henry Ford himself.

Young Hubbard leaned even farther left than in his last election and stressed his self-made background. He described himself as "the son of a humble farmer" and as a person who had "traveled the highway of hard labor and taken the hard-knocks since the age of 16." Among reasons to vote for him, he listed: "Hubbard is a man of firm moral fiber, sterling character and rugged honesty. His word is a debt-of-honor. He has not rigged up a fancy-sounding platform to fool voters. Hubbard is not in the slightest way connected with any combination seeking to further selfish interests. He is an INDEPENDENT candidate for Mayor and comes to you with 'clean hands.'"[4]

I sure as hell was independent—I didn't get any votes at all. I was for such things as publicly owned transportation system, city-owned light plant, gas plant, electric plant—and that's just as socialistic as anything ever was. We went house to house with the damn campaign literature. I just pasted 'em up myself. I also had a slogan: "Fewer laws and more human rights." I haven't changed my tune very much.

Hubbard finished last in a field of eight with a grand total of 377 votes in the October primary, while Ford went on to win handily.

In 1934, Hubbard decided to try again for the State Senate post he had sought two years before, this time facing Darin, who had gone on to lose after nudging Hubbard out of the 1932 congressional race.

There's nothing like being young and optimistic, you know. You think every-thing's just around the corner. Darin got beat for Congress, so he decided to run for state senator again. I had the Detroit Citizens League preferred endorsement over Darin, who had served in the legislature for a long time. I thought, Jesus Christ, I'm in now, for sure. The Democrats had swept the district in '32, but a lot of people thought, well, maybe '34 it would turn back. I went through, and we covered up all Darin's signs everywhere we could. So he said, "You got my signs covered up." I says to Frank, "You covered mine up first. I'll show you." So he wanted to take me on his yacht on the Detroit River. I said, "You aren't taking me on your goddamn boat. You want to push me overboard." He says, "Let's forget the campaign." He thought he was going to win, too—thought the Republicans were going to win that year.

It turned out they were both wrong. Darin easily outdistanced Hubbard in the primary, 10,403 to 5,981, although Hubbard was the top vote-getter in Dearborn. But then Darin lost in the November election to the Democrat, Sidney Gray.

Back in the real world, away from politics, Hubbard finally decided he had had enough of the *Wall Street Journal* after five years. He quit to go into law full-time, sharing an office downtown with Raymond E. Van Syckle.

I liked it at the Journal, but my mind wasn't on that work. I didn't make very much money there anyway, about $30 a week. I could've had three, four other jobs, but I stayed put till I finished law school. I asked for a raise, and they didn't give it to me, so I went in with Van Syckle. I said I should starve my way out of it [the law]. I almost did, too.

If Orvie was vowing to starve himself out of the law business, his body wasn't going along with the program. He'd started to put on weight during his years with the *Journal*—he blamed it on a candy machine by the elevator—but he still prided himself on his robust constitution. In late 1934, he finally decided to take a part-time job as a railway clerk.

The highest-paid government job in those days was railway mail clerk, so all my life as a young man I dreamed about being one. After I passed the test, every year I got a notice to be substitute clerk at Christmastime. So I thought, well, by God, I'm gonna go down and take that job this year and see if I like it. So I go down there, and, Jesus Christ, those mail bags—are they ever big and heavy. And I started wrestling those damn bags around, and I ruptured myself. So they send me to the Marine Hospital in Grosse Pointe for an operation, and I go out there in the spring, 1935, and check in. And the fellows were coming out of the operating room, and I said, "Did it hurt?" And they said, "No, it didn't hurt. Oh, God, ohhh." So I wanted to get out. They had my clothes. I said, "Either you let me go, or I'm gonna sue every one of you."

Hubbard's double hernia was to cause him trouble the rest of his life, but it didn't dampen his enthusiasm about politics. Encouraged by his showing with Dearborn voters in his two tries at the State Senate, he decided to try his luck at a City Council seat. Fourteen candidates were nominated in the October primary, but Orvie received a shock: he finished twenty-fifth in a field of 40. The entire political situation in Dearborn was beginning to look as though it were an extension of the Ford Motor Company. Clyde Ford was still mayor, and Harry Bennett, head of the Ford security force, pretty much called the shots.

Bennett had everything. He had the whole thing tied up. This would make Hitler's own organization look like pikers, for Christ's sakes. So anyway, Clyde Ford was running for reelection. He figured the town wouldn't stick together unless a Ford was the head of the government. But Clarence Ford, nephew of the old man, was on the City Council. And he walked around here with the prestige of the name. So he was in with the city hall gang, and they decided to run him for mayor. The

115

Bennett crowd took the position that it didn't look good that these two cousins were competing for mayor. So Bennett's organization—the Knights of Dearborn, they called themselves—met poor old Clyde Ford to tell him they couldn't be with him. And Clyde decided not to run. Then a lot of his friends raised hell with him, and he finally got back in. He had a big organization. I was secretary in Clyde's campaign. They were going to make me purchasing agent. So the Bennett crowd decided to run John Carey. The story was he had a contract to sell automobile horns for Ford's. A manufacturer's agent on the side. They put the forces on the street and handed out jobs right and left. That was before the unions. You could be hired today and fired tomorrow. I heard stories that they used to put signs on workers' time cards how the hell to vote. Carey won it. He had a saying: "Carry on with Carey."

If Fay Hubbard had ever had any doubts, it was becoming pretty clear now: her husband was a politician—not a successful politician, but a politician all the same. And although she never encouraged it, at least she was getting used to it. Besides, she had enough to keep her busy. The Hubbards were a good-sized family by 1935—after Jim was born in 1928 came Frank, Nancy and John.

In those years, I don't think I ever did have what you'd call a very happy domestic life. I think things went better for us after her father died. He died suddenly at age 59 in 1934. From that time on, the old lady, her mother, didn't raise so much hell with me. I always liked him. I didn't like her.

Not only were the Hubbards comparative models of domestic tranquility, but they were homeowners, too. As renters, they had moved in 1930 from their first Dearborn address on Hartwell to Berry and later to Mead, all on the city's blue-collar east side. In December 1932, they packed again, moving a few doors down to 7055 Mead, a five-room frame house with an unfinished attic. The rent was $20 a month.

In April 1935, at an all-time low in the market, I bought that house. Had a garage, copper screen windows, awnings, carpets, everything. It was a 35-foot lot. It was built in 1928 and originally sold for $8,000. I bought it for $2,650. I couldn't believe it. I borrowed the money from an aunt.

Now a permanent Dearborn resident, Hubbard started looking again for political action outside the city. He had his eye on the 1936 congressional race, but friends decided it was time to capitalize on the popularity he had built up as a young attorney in Dearborn Township three years before. Although he himself didn't campaign, his name went on the ballot as a Democratic candidate—the only time in his life he ran as a Democrat—to oppose incumbent Justice of the Peace John Mokersky, a Republican. Hubbard sailed through the primary in March but lost the April election by a nearly two-to-one margin.

For once in his life, Orvie didn't mind losing. He really considered Mokersky more of a friend than a political rival. A few years earlier, for instance, Mokersky had done a favor for an old Union City pal of Hubbard's.

The guy's wife was pregnant, and he was looking for a piece of ass up here, so I called up Mokersky. So John said, "I'll take you out to a place." We went in there, and, and, Christ, there was a lot of babes in that joint. Some of 'em looked like old war hacks—you know, like their ass had been rode into the ground. But one gal was really good-looking. She wore a white dress and was really built. So we fixed that up for my friend. That was the only whorehouse I was ever in in my life. Christ, we were sitting there talking to another girl. She says to me, "You're next." I said, "Christ, no. I don't want to." I didn't participate, and neither did John. Later I said to my friend, "What took you so goddamn long?" He said, "I was arguing about price. She wanted five dollars." You can imagine the way times were. About three or four days later, the state police raided that goddamn place, and they took 'em all to Mokersky, and he fined 'em all.

The 1936 congressional race promised to be a bit more interesting than the Hubbard-Mokersky matchup. Nobody among the Republicans had a real chance to unseat Democrat John Lesinski, but the GOP primary would give Hubbard a chance to go up against Clyde Ford and a couple of other popular vote-getters in town. But again, it was a tough lesson for Orvie. He finished dead last among six candidates and made an almost equally dismal showing among Dearborn voters.

He did a bit better the next year in his second try for mayor. He finished far behind Carey, but he was respectably close to the other candidate, a bar owner named Michael Korte who had almost won a council seat the year before. And, as the *Dearborn Independent*'s Mills later was to write, "Hubbard didn't let defeat stop him. He went on to lose again and again. Every defeat was another lesson learned the hard way. The raw recruit became a seasoned warrior on the political battlefield."[5]

By this time, Hubbard was getting used to being thought of as a buffoonish perennial candidate. He had run and lost seven times in six years— for state senator twice, mayor twice, congressman once, councilman once and justice of the peace once.

As he was wryly to tell a *News* reporter later, "You have to campaign for something every so often and give people a chance to do something for you or they lose interest." But 1938 was the year people stopped laughing at Hubbard. He made his third try for the State Senate, and that September he became the GOP nominee, topping a field of four with 10,857 votes, nearly as many as his opponents' combined total.

That was my biggest thrill in elections to that day. It was the first time I ever got help in a campaign. Judge Ira Jayne gave me 50 bucks, a kitty of circuit judges. They thought the Republicans might win. I was going hot, 35 years of age. I used to work like a son of a bitch. I was against small loans, deficiency judgment, all those things.

Hubbard's elation was short-lived, however. In the November general election, he lost to Stanley Nowak in the Democratic rush, 47,815 to 38,378. And by the next year, 1939, Orvie at last was ready to get out of politics. He was appointed to the Michigan attorney general's office, and he was feeling good about his prospects in the law business.

I'd worked with attorney Ed Barnard on delegates, and he said, "After we win this next election"—this was 1937—"I'll put you in the attorney general's office." And he did. I was assigned mostly to the License Appeal Board, light stuff. I thought, I've run for office. I've learned what it's all about. I'll go back to the law, and that's where I'll be happier.

But a couple of friends Hubbard had made in his previous campaigns had other ideas. Frank Swapka, who had worked for Carey but befriended Hubbard in 1938, and Carl Farmer, who was chief political adviser in Bennett's crowd, decided they wanted Hubbard to take on Carey in 1939—his third run for mayor and his ninth campaign overall since 1932.

I didn't want to run at all. Oh, God, they got real mad at me. Farmer and Swapka, particularly those two guys, wanted me to run—bad. They kept coming to my house every day. They said, "This is the time to run. If you do it, we'll get you $4,000 or $5,000 for the campaign." I said, "You get me $4,000 and I'll run for president." Well, they didn't get any goddamn money. What they got, I think we had 60-some dollars. But I didn't borrow from the finance company that year. Anyway, I had old 1933 petitions, with my name in great big letters. They were the only petitions I had. I just erased 1933 and wrote 1939 on 'em. I filed the last day at the last minute. Bert Schlaff, the mayor's secretary, told me later that he objected to my petitions because of the goddamn name, it was so big on 'em. So Joe Cardinal, in the city clerk's office, said, "Let him run. He isn't going to make it anyway. What the hell difference does it make?" I met Bert coming out of the clerk's office. He said to me in a very belittling way, "Orville, I see you just couldn't stay out of a campaign, could you?" I laughed. So I went down to the Dearborn Independent, and Art Ternes, who was a coal-lumber dealer, came up to me and said, "I want to shake your hand." He was figuring on running. He was going to have all the gamblers' money and that stuff, you know, and apparently that's what our guys were telling me where I was going to get my campaign money. Ternes said, "If you win, I'm going to support you all the way, and I want you to do the same for me." I said OK.

So Hubbard and Ternes challenged Carey, with Hubbard making speeches around town and getting a good reception wherever he went. But the Ford family's choice still was Carey, and Farmer and Swapka, both Ford men, were pulled out of Hubbard's campaign and put on Carey's. Just the same, though, Hubbard managed to squeeze past Ternes for the nomination in the primary. Carey finished far ahead with 5,909 votes, although Hubbard and Ternes outpolled him with their combined totals.

The shit around town was Mrs. Ford wanted Carey. I think I may have won otherwise. See, these fellows were working for me on their own, but when Bennett gave a signal, shit, that was it. It's just like putting a red light on. Those guys all vanished. Verlin E. Doonan was Bennett's number one political man in Dearborn. He was chairman of the Dearborn Safety Commission, which ran the police and fire departments. Farmer was Doonan's number one man. The Ford crowd was spending all kinds of money. I campaigned on the theory of getting rid of Bert Schlaff. We'd never find the mayor in. The mayor was selling horns for Ford, I said. Bert Schlaff is there, and he's selling suits. I was going to clean him out of city hall. The gamblers went in and out of the police chief's office as if they were on the payroll. I remember I had a rally, and Chief of Police Brooks calls me into the back room. I had met Bennett, and Bennett says just talk to Carl. I kind of liked Brooks from meeting him. He was telling me how he'd run the soup kitchens during the Depression years. So he takes his pocketbook out and shows me a little piece of paper, and it says, "Carl, do everything you can for Hubbard. Signed, H.B." It made me feel good, but I did figure it was a phony. I looked pretty good there. I looked as though I was going to take that election. I goddamn near won it. I carried the east end of town big. I carried the south end big. But in the west end I got swamped. Carey was quite a prominent guy out there.

The final tally was Carey 9,526, Hubbard 8,609. And city hall was starting to take Orvie seriously now.

15

Beating Clarence Doyle, 1939-41

The goddamn town was the most wicked, wide-open
town in the country.
—Orville L. Hubbard, describing Dearborn before his
election

With his newfound status as something other than a political joke around
town, Orvie Hubbard figured he was now on target, for the first time in his
life, for the mayor's office. But he was still an outsider at city hall, and he
knew he might need some kind of nudge to squeeze in past the entrenched
cliqué of old-timers.

His boost—if, indeed, he needed it—came in November 1941 from a
police tabloid called *Dan Gillmor's Scoop*. With lines such as "Fear reigns in
Dearborn, and witnesses are scarce," the magazine carried a melodramatic
expose detailing, in more graphic terms than the local papers had, the "trail
of vice that coils through Dearborn from the Ford plant to the police department, and the brothels, gambling joints and hideouts of the bloody gang,
. . . the ruthless vice and gambling syndicate that has been running Dearborn for years."[1]

As described in *Scoop*, the corruption in Dearborn could be traced directly
to Ford Motor. At the top of the hierarchy, it said, was Harry Bennett, head
of Ford security and a member of the State Parole Commission. Also involved,
the magazine alleged, were Carl A. Brooks, Dearborn's police chief and a
onetime Ford investigator under Bennett; Charles W. Slamer, chief inspector
of police; and two detectives and a public safety commissioner.

Bennett already had been criticized after the Battle of the Overpass in
1937, when his service department toughs attacked union organizers while
police, under Slamer, stood by. The crooked Ford operation went this way,
according to *Scoop*: Bennett imported ex-criminals to serve as an army of
antilabor spies, and Brooks ran a job-selling operation for Ford's. Such

notorious figures as "Gentleman Johnny" Bitonti, "Black Charlie" Harrison and "George the Greek" Konstantos were said to meet regularly in the chief's office. Brooks allegedly raked in money from the gambling operation as well as from some 30 brothels under police protection around town.

The machine infiltrated the Dearborn Public Safety Commission, headed by Bennett men such as Verlin E. Doonan and Frank Schonhofen, *Scoop* charged, adding that the operation even included the judiciary. Municipal Judge Leo Schaefer, described as active in Ford's antilabor campaign, refused to prosecute presumed gang members under state law, instead assessing small fines under city ordinances, it was alleged.

Though Brooks had died of a heart attack and Slamer apparently committed suicide earlier in the year, the situation in Dearborn had been spotlighted through grand jury investigations under Wayne Circuit Judge Homer Ferguson. The grand juries already had rooted out widespread wrongdoing in Detroit and other nearby communities by the time they turned their attention to Dearborn in 1941.

The indictments, announced in May, administered "a gorgeous black eye" to "the hitherto scandal-free city," in the words of the *Dearborn Press*. Besides Brooks, the indictments covered two detectives, a former detective and nine alleged underworld figures. The charge: conspiring to protect gambling and vice. Slamer was named an unindicted coconspirator, along with Schonhofen, who served as secretary of the Public Safety Commission. Testimony before the grand jury eventually established that Brooks and the vice squad successfully protected the state's largest mutuel numbers operation, the National Daily Bankers policy house, which was operated by Bitonti and others in Dearborn's old south end. Schonhofen was named by one witness as the one who tipped off bookies and bawdy-house operators of impending raids.[2]

A few months later, the grand jury reached out to indict longtime City Councilman Ernest G. Miller in an unrelated bribe case.[3] He was accused of accepting $300 from a paving contractor for helping steer a contract award in 1936.

As described by the local papers and later by *Scoop*, the whole chain of events couldn't have happened at a better time for an aspiring young politician named Orville Hubbard.

Hubbard was running—again—for mayor, this time against Clarence Doyle, acknowledged leader of the City Council and for 17 years a prominent figure in Dearborn. Though not implicated in the grand jury investigation, Doyle at least was vulnerable as a city hall insider. That, at any rate, was the position Hubbard eventually took in exploiting the grand jury issue in the 1941 mayoral race.

The goddamn town was the most wicked, wide-open town in the country. And Bennett ran the goddamn show. Anyone that knew anything about the inner

121

*workings knew that. I really don't blame Bennett for it except in his position before
the union days of providing jobs during elections. They controlled elections through
jobs and the hope of jobs. Ford would hand out jobs by the hundreds around
election time, but then after the election you're laid off. That was a bad situation,
but it was a company-run town. To the best of my knowledge and belief, it [always]
had been a company-run town. Bennett ran the company at that time. Didn't
know him too well, but I always liked the guy. His word was good. But Bennett
in those days had unlimited power. He had a lot to say in the whole damn state
because of his influence. He called the shots all the way to Lansing, everywhere,
on all fronts. When Bennett spoke, shit, the rafters just shook; the pigeons left. The
town was running wide open. The gamblers used to sit in the chief's office. They
used the cops to take 'em over to the goddamn bank. They rode around town, wore
$150 suits when suits were $20, $25. In the meantime, the* Dearborn Indepen-
dent's *singing the praises what a clean town we've got. The vice squad—that was
the key to this town. If a patrolman saw anything going on in the street, he was
supposed to tell Brooks, then Brooks would tell the vice squad. I never heard of
anything so ridiculous. Every cop knew what was going on. And it all operated
out of the chief's office. So this guy, Johnny Bitonti—he was a real smart Dago
who came to this country at 17. He was in the numbers business. He was around
here with a big car. So they refused to stop, and, well, a couple guys in the
department, not part of the inside gang, they shot the tires off his car. That broke
it. The* Detroit Times *picked that story up and, Jesus Christ, that brought the
grand jury to Dearborn.*

Even with all the publicity surrounding the Bitonti arrest and the subsequent discovery of Slamer's body, the grand juries came up without a
single conviction in Dearborn. But that didn't matter to Orvie. The situation
automatically elevated him to the status of a valid reform candidate, even
though his opponent had an unblemished record.

Doyle had gone into the race as the odds-on favorite. He had served
six years on the City Council, six on the Wayne County Board of Supervisors
and nine on the Henry Ford Board of Education. He had won endorsements
from both the *Dearborn Press* and the *Dearborn Independent*, as well as the
UAW, AFL, CIO and several influential clubs. In addition, most of the prominent politicians in town were behind him.

The only major endorsement Doyle was missing was Ford Motor's. With
the retirement of John Carey as mayor in the aftermath of the grand jury
investigations, Ford was staying out of the 1941 election, though letting
Frank Swapka, Carl Farmer and several of its other political strategists work
for Hubbard.

Because Orvie had finished respectably close to Carey in 1939, the next
year he had stirred up some support to run as a Republican against incumbent Democrat John Lesinski for Congress. Hubbard went ahead and filed
but had thought better of it and withdrew to concentrate on local politics.

See, I'd almost clicked in '39, and then Farmer and Doonan wanted me to run for Congress real bad. I think they wanted to screw me up. The district hasn't gone Republican since it was created in 1931–32. I thought I would lose, and I could've screwed myself up for mayor. But Swapka said, "No, don't run." And I didn't. In '41, I had the sympathy of Ford's in that election. I didn't have jobs and things that they handed out in those days, but Farmer and the other fellows were active in my campaign. Local 600 [UAW] was kind of split in that election. Doyle tried to line 'em up on the other side, but they wouldn't go. They made me a life member. But Doyle was the city hall darling at that time, and my group was what you'd call a raggedy-ass army like Washington had at Valley Forge.

Going into the October primary, Doyle had contented himself with campaigning on his record and stressing the need for cheaper government without cutbacks in service. "The important thing is to continue our progress and never lose sight of the goal of making Dearborn the world's number one city," he declared at one rally, adding a pledge for "nothing but a clean campaign based in the fundamentals of true American democracy."

Hubbard waited a month and a half to declare his candidacy, finally bowing, he said, to citizens' demands for "a new and progressive leadership." He promised "not only an active and a clean campaign, but a very vigorous one as well."

The filing deadline approached, and Carey, the incumbent, ended speculation about his plans by declaring himself out of the race. The field thus was left to Doyle and Hubbard.

The campaign itself was relatively bland at first. One of Hubbard's newsletters contained photos of his family; another portrayed him unabashedly as a self-made underdog: "Oldest in a family of four children, my father (a veteran of the Spanish-American War) died when I was but 16, and ever since I have been compelled to battle my way alone in an up-hill-struggle from the farm as a laborer through a small town cement plant, the city shops and factories and the United States Marines to my present station in life."[4]

The soft-sell strategy worked. With an unusually lean turnout, Hubbard scored a surprising victory over Doyle in the primary, 5,575 to 4,705. The upstart won in 30 of 45 precincts, including Doyle's own, and declared afterward, "The people are awake. They want a change." Said Doyle, "We were overconfident."

They didn't think they were gonna lose in the primary. They didn't think I had a chance. But when I won the primary, Jesus Christ, then they pulled out all the plugs on the old lifeboat, you know. And they did get vicious as hell. You talk about a campaign. That's the most vicious campaign I ever went through. Doyle and I on the surface were good friends. He was trying to outcon me, and I was trying to outcon him. They were trying to kid me that they were gonna appoint me judge. Well, after that they acquired quite a little bit of religion in the campaign. See, Doyle was a strict Catholic, a big, loudmouth Irishman. So they started all kinds of rumors about me because I was a Protestant. Said I belonged to the Ku Klux Klan and all that shit. People who knew me knew I wasn't involved. They said I was a major general in the Black Legion; that was sort of like a Klan deal, sort of a kangaroo operation in Michigan. Lot of guys went to prison. They took a guy out and killed him because he cheated on his wife. But, hell, I was just an ordinary guy that belonged to nothing but the Boy Scouts. I never heard of the Klan till I got in the Marine Corps.

There was also some fallout from Hubbard's association with Lila Neuenfelt, a former Dearborn judge.

I was president of the Dearborn Bar Association when Lila ran for circuit judge. I worked like hell for Lila. I had $110 to my name, and I gave her a $100 donation. And she squeaked in. Then Lila worked like hell for me. She'd take me around like I was a boyfriend. They had stories that you could find me under her bed any time you wanted to look. Lila and I were real close, but I never even held her hand in my life. I treated her with more dignity than Sir Walter Raleigh treated the Virgin Queen.

Orville Hubbard hadn't lost all those elections without learning a thing or two himself, however. He countered with billboards that read, "Restore Public Confidence," and he rebutted the rumors with newsletters that warned, "Do not be misled by any false religious slander which has been brought into this campaign. I never have been against any religious group and never have belonged to nor ever will join any group that is anti-any religion. And please do not be fooled by any last minute false-and-malicious campaign propaganda or fast-and-slick campaign tricks. IT IS TIME FOR A CHANGE!"[5]

He wasn't counting on any outside help, but Hubbard got it when *Scoop* magazine went on sale. Ford, obviously embarrassed, had its people trying to keep the magazine off the newsstands, but the Hubbardites weren't about to miss a chance like that.

Christ, Bennett's gang went all over and bought those magazines up. But I had a fellow here by the name of Charlie Dapprich. Could say he was a campaign worker. He wrote to the company and bought a whole special edition. He bought about a thousand of those things, and he distributed 'em all over the whole god-damn town. Was his idea, did it with his own money.

So, with *Scoop's* serendipitous aid, Hubbard succeeded in implicating Doyle without actually accusing him of anything illegal. The strategy was simple: since Doyle was a city hall insider, he at least had to have known about the wrongdoing.

As Hubbard later was to confess to a *Detroit News* reporter, "It was lucky for me I didn't get elected in 1939, when I came so close. I'd have been blamed for everything." In one of his last newsletters before the November 4 election, Hubbard argued that Doyle did not deserve the voters' trust:

> My opponent for Mayor has been one of the senior City Hall bosses for many years. It has been said that he runs City Hall, sometimes called Treasury Island. He is in a position to know what is "going on." By sitting close to the so-called fire, as hot as the one the grand jury found flaming, my opponent should have smelt-the-smoke, and he should have known what was "going on" right-under-his-nose, but if he did not smell the smoke, and if he did not know what was "going on," then he should not be your next Mayor. And, on the other hand, if he did smell the smoke, and if he did know what was "going on" and did nothing about it, then that is all the more reason why he never should be your Mayor. You know the story.[6]

There were also Hubbard newspaper ads that raised specters of dark doings: "Now the city hall brass hats are out 'full blast' and a nonresident is in town organizing against us and another nonresident has boasted that a certain blank check has been written to finance our opposition. Your help is needed to battle this brazen political invasion of our city."[7]

Doyle's parting shot in a flyer on election day simply ran down his list of endorsements and proposed an "unbossed city" as his aim. It also referred belittlingly to his opponent as "Orv."

The turnout ran much higher than it had for the primary, and at one point Hubbard and Doyle were exactly even, with 5,353 votes apiece. But then the west end returns came in, overwhelmingly behind Orvie, giving him the lead in 27 of 45 precincts and a final margin of 9,155 to 8,129. So, after nine years of failure, Orville Hubbard finally had won an election, and by the following January, he would take office as Dearborn's third mayor.

16

Beating Jamie Johnson, 1942

We wanted a strong mayor. We got Mussolini.
—Attorney John J. Fish, assessing Dearborn's new
charter[1]

Mayor Orville L. Hubbard. The title had a nice sound to it, but Dearborn's newly elected chief executive knew he didn't have time to savor the victory he'd earned in the closing weeks of 1941. Not with the way the rest of the city's official family felt about it.

No one was happy about it. They were all mad as a son of a bitch. I didn't have a friend in city hall. It was like going into no-man's land, like a kangaroo going by and jumping into the lion's den. I really crashed the gate. Anything I did, the council was against. We were in a conciliatory mood, but they weren't. They were bitter. They were mad. They were sworn to stick together.

Hubbard worked at first to smooth things out, reaching an understanding with the vanquished Clarence Doyle after Doyle announced he had "no hard feelings whatever" after losing.

He was a likable type of guy. So I went out with him one night. He was putting on the dog: "Meet the mayor," and all this stuff. Jesus Christ, he had a roll of bills on him, $20 bills. I never saw anything like that. And he said, "I'll send over some fellows to fix up your attic." I had one of these places with an unfinished attic which has since been finished, but not with any city business or anything he had anything to do with. I wasn't as dumb as he thought I was. Said, "What you and your wife should do is go to Florida for a vacation. You've had a long campaign, you know. Just have a good time and come back." Wasn't that the goofiest thing you could ever think of?

126

One of the first problems facing the new mayor was coming to terms with his law business. He moved his downtown office immediately to Dearborn, right across Michigan Avenue from city hall. Then, he said, he thought about hooking up with a partner and trying to make some money. But that's as far as it went. He rented out the office to an old law school pal, Otto Hoffman, and although he didn't announce it formally, practically speaking, Orville Hubbard was out of the law business.

From the day I took office, I never have practiced any law, though I keep my membership active in the Bar Association, thinking that maybe someday I might. I thought, well, I'll probably be over here a couple years, maybe two terms at the most. Then I'll go back in that law office. But I worked on the theory that you can't serve two masters without cheating one. Never fed anything to the office, either. So I decided not to do any law business at all. I made up my mind that isn't the right thing to do. I'd rather go bare-ass. Prior to that I did a lot of legal work free for people. After I took office, I just didn't send 'em the bill. I had maybe $500, $600 on the books. Some paid me. Most didn't.

Not everything fell into place so easily, however. Hubbard's worst fears about his relations with city hall were realized even before he took office. One of the lingering controversies left by the Ferguson grand juries had been leadership of the police department. Hubbard had pledged before the 1941 election to promote a chief from the ranks to "conduct the department on a courteous, semimilitary basis and who will bend every effort to restore public confidence."

But John Carey, in one of his last acts as outgoing mayor, named as chief the man who had been running the department since the shakeup, Emrys Evans. Since the nation had been drawn into war by the attack on Pearl Harbor only days before, Carey decided, the city needed a permanent chief immediately.

That reasoning made little sense to the mayor-elect, however. Given the chance to comment before the council was to vote on confirming Carey's appointment of Evans, Hubbard launched into the kind of bombast that set the tone for city politics in the year to come.

"This appointment is as much a stab in the back as the Japs' attack on Hawaii," he said, neatly seizing the issue of patriotism from Carey. "If this lame-duck session of the council votes this confirmation, it is a mockery on our form of government. I don't know a thing in the world about Evans. As a matter of courtesy, however, the appointment of chief of police should be left in the hands of the new mayor. If the council wants to cram this appointment down the throats of the people, let them do it and suffer the consequences."

The council was only too happy to oblige, voting four-to-two to confirm

Evans. Doyle supported Hubbard, but only because, he said, he wanted the new mayor to appoint a chief who would be free to investigate the implications raised by Hubbard in the election about Doyle's role in the vice-gambling scandal.

Orville Hubbard took the oath of office as mayor of Dearborn as soon as he could, at 12:01 A.M. January 6, 1942. At 8:15 that evening, with baskets of flowers covering the council table and with an overflow crowd on hand, Hubbard accepted a gavel from Carey, a flag from the Marine Corps League's local detachment and a set of colors from a group of liquor license operators.

Then he invited Doyle to sit beside him at the rostrum for the business session. Doyle responded by expressing the hope that "no one will beg off or refuse to help" the man who had defeated him. The new mayor declined to make an inaugural address, stating simply that he wanted to get city affairs straightened out in view of the national emergency.

Finally, he made a modest attempt at putting the Hubbard stamp on city hall. He made a nomination to fill a vacancy on the Safety Commission, but no one supported the motion to confirm. Then he nominated a defeated council candidate, teacher Ray Parker, for the post, and the council approved the move. Finally, he offered a list of nine department head appointments for the council to consider while he was in Washington, D.C., for a conference the next week. And that was as close as the new mayor came to a honeymoon in office.

The newcomer already had challenged the council, in effect, by announcing his determination to be "mayor in fact as well as in name," a direct reference to the council's jealously guarded power of confirmation over mayoral appointments, including department heads, under the city charter. Hubbard professed to hold nothing personal against the current slate of department heads—Carey's holdovers—but insisted on the right to name his own. The council proved in the months to come that this right did not exist—and in doing so helped boost the gremlin in the mayor's office to heights even he never imagined.

Dearborn's council-mayor government dated back to the charter adopted with the vote to merge old Dearborn and Fordson in 1929. The 1941 grand jury investigations had demonstrated the difficulty of pinpointing responsibility under the charter, and that summer, attorney John Fish and the Citizens League of Dearborn announced a petition drive to place a charter proposal on the November ballot to augment the Hubbard-Doyle race.

After a number of false starts, the November election boiled down to two proposals: a yes-or-no question offered by the Fish group ("Do you favor the general revision of the existing charter?"), accompanied by a slate of 18 nominees for 9 positions on a proposed charter commission; plus a proposed amendment to the existing charter to empower the mayor to make his own appointments without council approval.

Neither Hubbard nor Doyle made an issue of the charter question, and indeed there seemed little opposition to it. The *Dearborn Press* said: "The opponents of this plan are sure to cry 'dictatorship.' This is a delusion. Dictators are not elected by a free people every two years and thereby subject to displacement such as a mayor would be."[2] And the Detroit Bureau of Governmental Research on Charter Revision predicted a new charter could give Dearborn "a model city government."

Given this climate, the charter revision question passed, 5,392 to 4,901, although the proposed amendment on mayoral appointments went down by a three-to-two margin. Fish was among the charter commissioners voted into office.

If a new charter seemed like a good idea in 1941, it started looking better and better as the feud between the new mayor and the council went on during the early months of 1942.

At the council meeting immediately after the inaugural session, the group rejected 67 Hubbard proposals for department head appointments, most of them different permutations of a dozen or so names. Even the nomination of Doyle as head of public works lost by a four-to-three vote. The only approval given was to retain the current city engineer in his post.

Council President Clyde Ford, the former mayor, seemed to reflect the general sentiment by announcing that he could support no new department heads unless the deficiencies of the old ones were demonstrated. Hubbard eventually responded by demanding that Ford remove his feet from the council table.

The pattern held for months. Hubbard would submit names of appointees, and the council would reject them. By the end of February, Hubbard had made 120 unsuccessful nominations, prompting him to resolve "to bear down and get tough."

Perhaps in spite of the threat rather than because of it, the council soon approved three appointments to the City Planning Commission, in addition to confirming Ralph B. Guy to the vacant $2,600-a-year post of secretary to all city commissions. It was the first Hubbard appointment to a paying job that the council had approved.

That was an exception, however, as was the council's confirmation of Doyle as public works head. Hubbard eventually nominated, by his count, some 450 to 500 names—all in vain.

See, they were giving me the works. They didn't confirm any job unless there was a vacancy. It was ridiculous, and we did everything we could to make it more ridiculous. It didn't matter who we put up; it would be five-to-two against it all the time. So [Anthony] Esper said to Bert [Schlaff], "Well, the mayor'll get tired of that." Bert said, "No, you know what the mayor intends to do? He intends to take the voter registration list and put every man up in town," which I did intend to do. Then I picked out these guys who were good friends of the councilmen who

129

I know were all looking for a job. Things were very lean yet. We just got in the war. And they all voted no on them. See, you have to give the council credit for this: they had a sense of decency. They'd accepted money, campaign money, from department heads. Up to that time, all you had to do to be a department head was to have four votes on the council. Many of the department heads used to go to Doyle's house. They'd go down and play poker with him and always lose to him. Then the councilmen would go on expense accounts. The department heads would take 'em to lunch. They always paid the shot. So the council just made a decision they weren't going to let any of 'em down. In the meantime, they helped wash themselves out.

Orvie soon became even more severely estranged from the council. Councilman Jamie Johnson accused Hubbard of doing the "silliest things around here I've ever seen." In April, the mayor appeared before the Charter Commission, blaming the "trouble" on a lack of a clear line of authority between the legislative and executive branches. He reiterated his complaints about the council's stubbornness. Even if he "put the Lord himself up, the council wouldn't confirm the appointment," he sniffed. If the shortcomings of the old charter ever were unclear to him before, he indicated, he now was recommending that the commission adopt a "responsible mayor form of government."

The mayor couldn't do a thing. He couldn't even turn the lights on. I never saw such a goddamn charter. Council was both legislative and administrative, which is contrary to our basic system of government. They abused the other mayor [John Carey]. He had nothing under the charter, and they gave him nothing. And they said no on everything I did.

To Hubbard's mind, even his office furnishings demonstrated his impotence. The city purchasing agent had recommended a new, $200 davenport for the mayor, and accordingly Orvie put through a requisition to the council. When Esper questioned the item, Hubbard threw a fit, tearing up the paper and berating the council. He didn't get the davenport. But he was quick to see public relations value in the situation. He began complaining, loudly and in dead earnest, that councilmen wouldn't even let him have a new wastebasket.

The charter didn't even provide that the mayor should have any quarters, so everything was subject to what the council wanted to do. All the furniture they had in the office they had gotten from Ford's before my time. I needed a new wastebasket, and the chairs had those wicker seats in 'em and they were all pushing through. So I went through the office, stuck my foot through every one of those chairs, and I just threw 'em in the corner, and when people came in, there was nowhere to sit down. I said, "Look, they won't even give you a chair to sit on."

They never gave in on it. That furniture's still around now, been reupholstered—it's up in the council chambers.

In public sessions, Hubbard and the councilmen continued to spar. At one meeting, the mayor ruled Clyde Ford out of order, then threatened to "have you taken out of here in about two minutes," finally adding he would do it himself if necessary. At the same time, the Charter Commission continued to work toward a permanent solution to the bickering.

Fish had other communities surveyed and found that the "responsible mayor" form of government did "not reveal any general abuse of the executive power." He and the other commissioners became advocates of one of the strongest mayor charters in the country.

No longer would the Dearborn mayor be simply a presiding officer at council meetings. The proposed new charter designated the executive as "responsible for the efficient administration of all departments" of the city government. He would maintain his veto power over council acts, but now he also would appoint department heads and members of boards and commissions without council confirmation, and he would remove them at his pleasure. Most departments were to be put in the hands of direct mayoral appointees, including such key jobs as corporation counsel, city controller, assessors, city engineer and the heads of public works, health and water supply. Consistent with his new responsibilities, the mayor's salary was to be raised from $4,000 to $6,500, while councilmen's pay would be reduced from $3,000 to $2,000.

Commissioners finally adopted the charter in August by a six-to-two margin, leaving it to voters in the November 3 special election. Also decided was the tricky issue of who would serve under the proposed charter. If it went down, Hubbard and the other incumbents would serve out their current two-year terms. If it passed, a new slate of officials, to be elected the same day, would begin three-year terms in January 1943.

It took only a couple of weeks for the campaigning to begin. Jamie Johnson became the first announced candidate for mayor, and he endorsed the new charter immediately. It would not promote a dictatorship, he declared, despite what its opponents might say. Joining him in the race were Clyde Ford, who had supported charter reform when he was mayor but now was opposing the new document; John F. Carey, a political unknown who was no relation to the former mayor of the same name; and Orvie.

Through early fall, the lines were drawn. Johnson was the only mayoral candidate openly supporting the new charter. All the other councilmen were denouncing it roundly. The two local papers were split, the *Press* for and the *Independent* against.

Most civic groups supported it strongly, though one, the Citizens' Committee Against the Proposed New Charter, ran newspaper ads warning of "a throne at the city hall for the kingfish" and urging voters to "join the fight against dictatorship. . . . Constant vigilance is the price of liberty."[3]

One of the strongest denunciations of the proposed charter came from James E. Greene, the corporation counsel, who said in a letter to the *Press* that the charter was "vicious and intended to accomplish a one-man government that makes him, whoever he may be, the boss instead of the people." Greene said that under the charter, the mayor "either directly or indirectly has complete control, not only of department heads, but of every city employee. . . . No matter who may be elected Mayor the party will be subject to human temptations that it is unfair to impose."[4]

Where was Hubbard? As usual, saving his best shots till the last minute. Finally, a week before the election, the man who apparently had the most to gain under the new charter came out unequivocally behind it, claiming that he had "vigorously advocated a complete revision" since 1933. This assertion failed to impress one columnist, who wrote that Orvie had "been . . . telling supporters . . . that he is for it, but leading opponents of it to believe that he isn't enthusiastic about it."[5]

I didn't get full credit for it, but without our help, without our support, it wouldn't have carried. I always did favor charter revision. When it came time for adoption, though, people were wondering whether or not I was going to go for it. Well, I couldn't have even thought of going the other way.

But there was another complication in the campaign, too, although it lay below the surface for most of the race. Ford Motor had stayed neutral in the 1941 election; Doyle was apparently too strong a personality for Bennett, and Hubbard was too much an unknown quantity. But this time around, Hubbard had taken Doyle out of the picture by appointing him DPW director.

I appointed Doyle as a matter of survival, 'cause he was thinking of running against me. And I was always sort of a peacemaker. He took it quick. That shook everybody up; they couldn't believe that one. Bennett didn't want him DPW director. They didn't like Doyle. He'd been on the Henry Ford School Board, he'd been on the council, he was wealthy, and he did a lot of things to rile their feathers. They went for Jamie Johnson. Ford came out really strong. They were really going to oppose the charter.

Hubbard worked to establish that there was a link between Ford Motor and Johnson as early as October, when he challenged the councilman's position on a Detroit Edison franchise request. "It is interesting to see how Councilman Johnson is maneuvering against this thing," Hubbard observed. "I don't know where he gets his ideas. He was sitting in [Verlin] Doonan's office yesterday. Maybe he gets them there." Johnson sprang up to insist that "my ideas are my own" and that he would sit anywhere he pleased.

Orvie insinuated throughout the last days of the campaign that Johnson was a puppet of Ford's. At a campaign rally, he passed out cards referring to "Boss" Doonan and political dictatorships, "the very sort of thing for which our men at their battle stations are now spilling their blood and dying to wipe out." Hubbard denounced the councilman at the rally and then refused to let him have the floor.

The mayor's literature continued to underscore his independent status by boasting that he was "not a stooge for anyone," and he introduced a slogan that became one of his favorites: "Reelect your unbossed mayor." He also stung both Johnson and Clyde Ford with newspaper ads that implicated them in the pre-Hubbard grand jury investigations, much as his 1941 literature had targeted Doyle: "Vote . . . to stop the return to power of the gang in authority during the period when vice, graft and corruption was in full bloom and blossomed into the blackest and biggest and rottenest police scandal that ever rocked an American city . . . remember I have kept your City clean, from vice, graft and corruption."[6]

Dearborn's unbossed mayor also took credit for a big tax cut enacted during the year, and he resurrected many of his old socialistic projects in addition to some new ones: city utility plants, city hospital, city transportation system, city airport, city railroad station, municipal parking lots and a civic community center.

And for good measure, his literature, delivered door to door, urged voters not to be "fooled by any cheap, shyster sheet put out by a screwball as a smokescreen for our odd opposition." The warnings actually stemmed not from actions by Johnson but some mudslinging by a man who wasn't even in the race: Ralph B. Guy, who had resigned as secretary of commissions after Orvie failed to back him for a vacant judge's position.

Guy was a little half-shit guy, a fair-weather guy, but he'd worked quite hard in my campaign, 1939, so I gave him the only job I had, horseshit job. But in the meantime, he was conniving. Unbeknown to me or any of our group, he was figuring on running for judge. But I had gone over to [George] Martin and [George] Belding. They had given us some money, paid for an ad or something. And that made Guy so goddamn mad he went on a real binge around town, and he said everything in the world he could say about me. Oh, Jesus Christ, he went wild. I used to have a picture in my office of Custer's last stand that was put out by Anheuser-Busch, and, shit, he said the mayor had beer pictures in his office. And on Memorial Day, I used to wear my Marine Corps uniform, being in the period when the war was going on, and Guy was talking about the mayor and his fake uniform. He was never in the Army himself; he ducked it. Good thing I wasn't as smart then as I am now. I really would have blistered his ass. Some of our fellows, they stole all of his campaign stuff. Anyway, he lost his job, and he didn't get elected judge.

With all the juicy sidelights to the election, the voting places were almost as crowded as the year before, despite the fact that this was wartime. And the results made it obvious that practically everyone blamed the council, not Hubbard, for the squabbling of the past year.

The new charter passed narrowly, 6,471 to 5,304, but Orvie swamped the field. His total was 7,061 to Johnson's 2,956, Ford's 2,212, plus 558 for the "name" candidate, Carey. The incumbent dominated the east end, carrying 37 of 45 precincts, with the other 8 going to Johnson.

This was high man take all. I think the 1942 election was the first Ford's ever took a defeat in. Up to that time, you didn't rock the boat. Even though we met head-on, we had no hostile relationship at that period. I had dinner with Bennett several times. I had lunch with 'em afterwards, and Bennett said to me— I think he was a man of his word—"Don't you appoint anyone for me. Don't you appoint anyone for anyone except for yourself. But when you appoint 'em, make damn sure they're your men." Then he said, "If you want anything from us, you call me. If we want anything from you, we'll call you." In other words, it all goes back to loyalty. That's about the best political advice you can get anywhere.

With his big margin at the polls, Hubbard could proclaim as loudly as he liked that he had a mandate. But the council, with four incumbents reelected, still wasn't buying.

At a meeting the day after the election, Hubbard presented another 10 names for council confirmation. After voting to fill a vacancy on the recreation commission with a Hubbard appointee, the council reacted with stony silence to the mayor's entreaty to help him get "started on the mechanism" of a new charter.

Things got little better in the last weeks before the charter became official in January. The council confirmed another nonpaying position, but it voted against yet another Hubbard nominee for a department head position, and the mayor accused it of "trying to sabotage and scuttle the new charter."

Every goddamn one of them except one was against the charter. They did everything possible to fuck it up. They had a big party down in the clerk's office on the last day of the year. They had a bottle of booze called Old Charter, and they all went down and took a drink to the old charter. The new one was coming in. Best damn thing that ever happened to the town.[7]

134

17

Beating James Thomson, 1943-45

> Every time Dearborn's Mayor Orville L. Hubbard writes to a citizen on official stationery or calls one on the telephone, it is strictly illegal.
> —The *Detroit News*, commenting on the city's new "gag" ordinance[1]

If there was anything Dearborn's mayor had learned in his first year in office, it was the political value of bombast. In contrast to his quickie 1942 swearing-in, this time he had an eight-page inaugural message prepared. Hubbard took his oath as the city's first mayor under the new charter at a packed council meeting on January 5, 1943.

He pinned badges on the three new councilmen—Ray Parker, Howard Ternes and Patrick Doyle—and handed over the gavel to Anthony Esper, just elevated to council president by his colleagues. Then he began his address, declaring the new charter a tribute to those who wanted "government of the people, by the people and for the people" and pledging to make Dearborn the "most efficiently governed city in the entire United States."

Next, with a hint that he intended to make full use of his new prerogatives under the charter, he singled out the Police Department as a "glaring example of wasted manpower," remediable only by "new blood and rejuvenation from top to bottom."

His declaration also signaled a climax to the yearlong fencing match with the council over department heads. Under his new power of appointment, he named Clarence Doyle to continue as DPW head, and he also named Floyd H. Smith controller; Ernest Walborn a Civil Service Commission member; Dale H. Fillmore, a great-grandnephew of former President Millard Fillmore, corporation counsel; and Otto H. Hoffman, his old law school pal, as director of public safety, with control over both the police and fire departments. This group augmented a list of six appointments Orvie had made the week before with council approval. Now the only suspense left was whether he would have Hoffman oust Emrys Evans from the police chief's job given him by outgoing Mayor John Carey a year before.

The answer came soon enough. Hoffman was sworn in on the morning of January 7, and by noon Hubbard named Erving Nielsen, an attorney who worked as a linotype operator at the *Detroit News* (and another old law school chum), to replace Evans. Responding to criticism that Nielsen lacked police experience, Hubbard observed, "He doesn't need to know how to walk a beat. His job is to direct the 150 policemen on the force."

Meanwhile, Evans had no intention of going down quietly. Instead, he complained to reporters that he had lost his job because he enforced the law. This, coupled with reports that the numbers racket was running wide open again at the Rouge plant, raised questions about the young mayor's honesty and effectiveness. The matter was settled only after Hubbard's friend, Wayne Circuit Judge Lila Neuenfelt, interceded for Evans.

Shit, he'd been part of the whole goddamn gang in with the chief over there. Everybody in town knew that the whorehouses ran and the gamblers hung around in Brooks's office. I thought it was wrong to put a fellow in charge of the Police Department who was here then. My first assignment under the new charter was to get rid of him. I was looking for him one day and couldn't find him. He was in New York. I didn't even know he'd left town. He'd just go wherever he wanted to go. That's the way they treated me around here. So he was the first guy I got rid of—within minutes. And, Jesus Christ, you'd thought the whole world came to an end. All of a sudden, Bennett's office called me, and three, four guys came over to see me. I just hid for the day. It's the first time I ever disappeared. And then your goddamn, son-of-a-bitching newspaper [the Detroit News*] writes a story that the mayor fired him because he enforced the law. Absolutely a false statement. And Judge Neuenfelt came to me for Evans. I said, "Judge, he lied like hell. All I ever asked that man to do was to enforce the law." She asked me to give him a break. I said unless he makes a complete retraction, I'd never do it.*

In January 1943, Emrys R. Evans signed the following statement for public release: "The Newspaper statements alleged to have been made by me that I was 'fired' because I enforced the laws in Dearborn never was made by me and any statement to that effect is absolutely false. The only order Mayor Orville L. Hubbard ever issued to me was to enforce the laws and I always did so without any interference from the Mayor."[2]

I wouldn't reappoint him chief. The agreement was he'd come back as an inspector to give him a chance to retire. I just did it for Lila. He retired and went to Ford's. But all that was lining things up to get rid of the new mayor. I could've gone down the chute, you know. They try to give you the works, you know, dirty son of a bitches.

With the Evans affair ended, Dearborn's new strong-mayor administration moved into more routine matters, competing for headlines with war news—scrap drives, dances for servicemen, city sons missing in action or decorated for gallantry. But it took only a few months before Hubbard had to face accusations that he was justifying the worst fears of the charter opponents of 1942: he was attempting to build up a political machine.

First there was a row in March with the Civil Service Commission. The upshot was an April election in which voters turned down a Hubbard-sponsored proposal to amend the charter by permitting him to appoint employees in Civilian Defense and in his own office without regard to Civil Service procedures.

Then there was a testy battle with the Council over the new city budget. The council figure of slightly more than $4 million brought five vetoes from the mayor, along with a tirade against several pay raises recommended by Civil Service as "the most scandalous and unconscionable skyrocketing handout" to the "favorite inner-circle city hall brass hats." Hubbard's floridly worded, three-and-a-half-page veto message prompted the council to override three of the five vetoes in its first meeting in May.

At the same time, Councilman Norman F. Edwards accused Orvie of fostering "bickering, confusion, extravagance and mismanagement never before known in Dearborn." He also asserted that the city had spent $6,500 to move the mayor's office from newly remodeled quarters on the second floor of city hall to a front wing of the first floor. Finally, he castigated Hubbard for "flighty, intemperate action" in administering the Police Department and for trying "to weaken or wreck Civil Service."

Orvie angrily interrupted Edwards's reading several times with denials, but the councilman shot back with a demand that the mayor "forget his petty, personal, political ambitions and subordinate his desire to build a Tammany machine and assume his responsibility in a dignified manner."

As an aside to the controversy, *Dearborn Press* columnist Alex Pilch agreed with Edwards that Hubbard "is guided in most issues by political considerations only. What makes this especially disappointing, yes and even revolting, is that Hubbard in talking with reporters or the public professes only noble and sublime motives."[3]

Through much of 1943, Hubbard and the council indeed did seem to subordinate their political motives to other causes, and city hall's problems were all but forgotten with such local milestones as the death of Henry Ford's son Edsel and the subsequent decision by the old tycoon—who was about to turn 80—to take over again as Ford Motor president.

But the mayor's office was shaken late in the year by accusations that further echoed the charges Evans had made and recanted. This time, Hubbard was linked with the very gambling operation he had made such an issue out of in swashbuckling his way past Clarence Doyle in the 1941 election. It began with an attempt by G. James Denny and Horace King, the two vice squad detectives suspended during the Ferguson grand jury probes, to gain reinstatement with back pay. Nielsen, however, dismissed the two in June, an action later upheld by a Civil Service ruling that the dismissal was "not for political reasons but reasons involving the good of the service." However, in mid-November, the Civil Service Board received a request for a rehearing for Denny. The petitioner was Walter S. Rae, a former assistant corporation counsel who had resigned in a huff several months earlier rather than give up spending city time on outside business. Rae's petition charged that the entire case against Denny was a conspiracy to "further the political aspirations and ambitions of Mayor Hubbard." But even beyond the supposed conspiracy, Rae went on to suggest that Orvie trafficked with such characters as Johnny Bitonti, reputed head of the Dearborn hoodlum empire of the pre-Hubbard years. Rae asserted that Bitonti and other "notorious characters" had helped in Hubbard's campaign in exchange for permission "to engage in illegal occupations" in Dearborn.

So Walter Rae wrote a petition to file against me. This is really a shakedown. [Clarence] Doyle came in for me to read it. I said, "You tell that son of a bitch to do anything he wants to with that. There isn't a goddamn word of truth in it."

Hubbard immediately responded by accusing Rae of attempted blackmail—by a threat to file false allegations against the mayor unless Denny were reinstated. The next month, Hubbard denied any conspiracy to oust Denny or any agreement to permit illegal activities in Dearborn. He declared in an affidavit: "If there is a conspiracy in connection with the Denny case, it is the rotten smear on the part of the 'behind the scenes gang' in their all-out desperate effort to return to power and to the racketeering days in Dearborn."[4]

Nielsen, the man who had dismissed Denny, also filed an affidavit supporting Orvie. Nielsen originally had charged Denny with accepting whiskey and other gifts, consorting with underworld characters, leaking information and neglecting his duty to apprehend lawbreakers. Now he accused Rae of trying to get Denny reinstated in return for withholding the spectacular allegations about the mayor. The "deal," he said, was conveyed by Clarence Doyle and turned down flatly by Hubbard. Doyle, when interviewed, denied any knowledge of it.

The next year, 1944, was ushered in by a directive from the mayor for all city employees from the mayor on down to begin punching time clocks. Early in 1943, Hubbard had created a general fuss with a demand, aimed partly at Rae, that personnel in the corporation counsel's office start punching in and out, an action that brought a tart observation from Pilch in the *Press* that the mayor himself "is hardly ever found in his office" and, when asked about it, "piously points to a sign hanging on the wall to the effect that there are no office hours for leaders." To Hubbard's protestations that he often put in long hours in the evening, Pilch wryly suggested that it wouldn't be a bad idea for him to start using a time clock.[5] Hubbard finally took him up on the proposition and applied it citywide, much to the dismay of employees' unions.

Continuing to hover in the background were speculations about whether the mayor really had any connection with the underworld. In May 1944, the council responded to a request from Hubbard, Hoffman and Nielsen to appropriate funding to help obtain evidence against numbers operators believed to be raking in $2 million a year in the Rouge plant and other industrial facilities in town. The mayor asked $15,000 in special funding but settled for a council appropriation of $1,500.

In June, Hubbard was vindicated in the Denny affair with a Wayne Circuit Court ruling that Denny had been fired properly; four months later, the Michigan Supreme Court dismissed his appeal.

The issue of Hubbard's honesty lay dormant until the next year, when it resurfaced during the 1945 election campaign. Orvie had led the mayoral field easily in the August primary, but three weeks later, who should appear in his life again but John Bitonti. This time, however, Hubbard was ready for him.

According to press reports, council opponent Norman Edwards and the editor of the *Dearborn Independent*, George St. Charles, were in Hubbard's reception room when Bitonti came in asking to see the mayor. Hubbard recognized Bitonti and then, on seeing the other two, said, "I suspect you are in on this, so you can come in, too." The gambler then accused Orvie of trying to hound him out of town. "You have police trailing me," he told Hubbard. "I'm not running any gambling places in Dearborn, so you have no right to annoy me." Then Bitonti proceeded to make other, more damaging, accusations.

> *God, this is a classic one. One day, they came to my office, St. Charles and Norm Edwards. Oh, Edwards, he was a first-class prick, the son of a bitch. Then in walked Johnny Bitonti, raising hell. He was indicted, too. He wanted me to give him a refund of the money he'd paid me. He'd say any fucking thing, how he gave the mayor money in my home, which he was never in my house in his whole fucking life. The gamblers have always claimed that they paid my campaign. They didn't. They didn't pay a goddamn penny of my campaign. And I called the chief of police over, and I said to the chief, "Lock him up." So the chief put him in the goddamn jail. First time, I think, he'd ever been in jail, because he'd had immunity from the old chief of police. Now, I don't know whether we ever swore a warrant for disturbing the peace or what it was for. Later, Bitonti came to see me. He told how he operated in this town.*

The Wayne County prosecutor's office ordered investigators to look into the situation, although officials hinted that they didn't put much credence in Bitonti's allegations. Meanwhile, Hubbard, remembering only too well that he was in the middle of a campaign, took the offensive right away by issuing a statement that reprised some of his old law-and-order themes:

> There has not been, is not and cannot be any commercial gambling, vice or racketeering so long as I am Mayor. My first and unaltered instructions to the Police Department are to vigorously enforce all laws and keep Dearborn clean from vice, graft and corruption. And I am proud to say that this has been done as every citizen, including Bitonti and his vice gang, well knows. Bitonti falsely, maliciously and slanderously said that he donated $2,200.00 to my campaign for Mayor. This is a d——— black lie. He never has at any time given me anything of any kind or description—not even a cigar. . . . Bitonti bragged that before I was Mayor, he had at Christmas time supplied a quart of whiskey for every Dearborn policeman and had given to Dearborn City officials more than $4,000 in cash for Christmas presents. And added, that he and his gang had made "lots of appointments" in the city government. He said he had not put out any Christmas presents since I was Mayor because he was not doing any business here now. . . . Bitonti has bragged around town, particularly throughout the South End, that he already has put $6,000.00 into my opponent's campaign, and that he is going to buy every vote in Dearborn to beat Hubbard.[6]

As hot as the issue was for a few days, it fizzled out soon enough when the prosecutor's office dropped the case after concluding that it was simply a political squabble. Hubbard's mayoral opponent, another old law school classmate named James Thomson, also struck out when Dearborn Judge George Martin denied a petition for a grand jury investigation of Bitonti's charges. A week later, Bitonti and a number of others pleaded guilty in Detroit Recorder's Court to charges of maintaining and operating gambling equipment in connection with the National Daily mutuel house racket investigated by the Ferguson grand juries.

And with that, by the fall of 1945, Hubbard had weathered nearly three years of accusations and sleazy innuendo, along with the predictable carping about his attempts to set up a dictatorship. Luckily for him, he discovered a few other issues to help take people's minds off the Bitonti charges as World War II wound to a close.

In October 1944, a member of the Dearborn Board of Education, Homer Beadle, appeared before the council on behalf of a homeowners' group known as the Dearborn Property Protective Association. The group was concerned about local property values, and Beadle asked the council to go on record against a federal housing project planned for Southwest Dearborn. The project was rumored to be open to Negroes.

Until then, race never had been a major issue in all-white Dearborn.

But the well-publicized race rioting in Detroit in 1943 was still fresh in the minds of many white suburbanites the next year, and Hubbard was at least as concerned as anyone else.[7] Two weeks after the request from Beadle, the mayor and four councilmen journeyed to Washington, D.C., to protest the project to the Federal Public Housing Authority (FPHA).

Dearbornites deluged city hall with calls urging officials to fight the project, and Hubbard accordingly called a special council meeting. He was only too happy to seize the publicity initiative, even though he had not been the first to bring up the subject. His message to the council declared:

> Dearborn's attitudes on racial matters are no better and no worse than
> that of any other Michigan community. It is to be expected that when
> something is forced on a community as this project apparently is to be
> forced on Dearborn by the FPHA that there shall be resistence and strong
> feeling. I don't want to see this issue forced. It isn't the first time that the
> federal housing officials have forced such a situation. They placed the
> Sojourner Truth project in a white neighborhood in Detroit only three
> years ago, despite the protests of Mayor Jeffries and the Detroit Housing
> Commission. Bad riots followed. We don't want anything like that to
> happen in Dearborn. The home owners in Dearborn face economic
> losses, and they are bitterly protesting. It is my opinion that the ordering
> of such a project would have serious repercussions in Dearborn and in
> the Ford plant where racial relations are now harmonious.[8]

A proposed resolution from the mayor for council consideration labeled the project "a direct interference with, and an invasion of the right of the City of Dearborn as a local governmental unit to determine its housing needs, and a shocking abuse of Federal power delegated in a war-time emergency. . . . We want to keep Dearborn a desirable place in which to live so that we will not break faith with Dearborn boys who have fought and died . . . in this war."[9]

The council adopted a resolution based on the Hubbard version, forwarding copies to appropriate members of Congress. Hubbard then made a second trip to Washington, this time with attorney John Fish, to continue the city's protest. Homeowners turned out by the hundreds to attend mass meetings around town and flooded their representatives' offices with complaints.

Meanwhile, the FPHA's George Schermer issued a reminder in November that the project had yet to be given final approval. However, he noted, a survey indicated that some 12,000 Negro war workers commuted daily to the Rouge and other Dearborn plants, and the war housing shortage in the area was "acute." Hubbard, who told newsmen he was devoting nearly all his time to fighting the project, said he had confirmed that only 2,000 more Negroes were working in town than before the war, so the housing problem, he argued, could hardly be urgent.

They were going to put 400 black people in an area where there were no black people at all. You can imagine the feeling in town about it. Jesus Christ, were they up in arms about it. So the mayor and council naturally took a stand against it, because they were trying to force it down our throats. One of these goddamn nigger-lover guys—I don't want to say "nigger lovers"—but one of these ultraliberal guys, Schermer—he had a warped mind—said the housing would be eliminated when the war was over. Like shit it would be. Anyone think once they got in here, they'd leave? If the war hadn't been over with, we'd have been stuck with that sure as hell.

The FPHA moved ahead in May 1945, beginning condemnation proceedings on 170 acres of Ford land just south of town. As announced, the proposal envisioned a $3.5-million package including 1,410 temporary houses with unrestricted occupancy.

The immediate response from officials in Dearborn and nearby Ecorse Township and Allen Park was to dash off more complaints to Washington about the "utter waste" involved. At the same time, Ford officials assailed the move as a "land grab," pointing out that the project was to be located between the Rouge plant, where workers were being laid off, and the Willow Run bomber plant, which was expected to close by August. Later in the month, however, a federal judge dismissed injunction proceedings brought by Ford to block the project.

Dearborn's mayor kept the controversy boiling, nonetheless, by calling for "every citizen" to protest the action. Hubbard organized a June meeting among officials from surrounding communities to show that "the people resent the high-handed, un-American, sneak actions of these self-constituted alphabetical dictators, profaning the records of our men who have died and are willing to suffer death, by justifying their actions in the name of war necessity. These ghost towns they are creating will be filled with out state citizens after the war who if hard times come will be on our hands to feed and keep."[10]

Despite the protests that followed, the FPHA began clearing the Ford land. It was not for several months that the issue was resolved, however, and then mostly because of the surrender of Japan to the Allies in mid-August. The end of hostilities meant that "war necessity" no longer could be used to justify the project, and a week later, the FPHA's local office notified Hubbard that the effort was being abandoned officially.

Whereas the end of the war with Japan preserved Dearborn's racial integrity, the end of the war with Germany already had given Hubbard a small chuckle at the expense of a group of city employees. Since 1943, a council resolution had allowed city workers to take off one day a week with pay to serve in the Coast Guard Reserve. An estimated 38 men performed maneuvers on the Detroit River, presumably patrolling for German U-boats. But with the German surrender, Hubbard wasted little time jotting off a tongue-in-cheek memo to department heads:

> Insofar as the City of Dearborn is concerned, unless good cause clearly is shown why a Bathtub Navy is necessary to the Pacific war effort, anchors shall be considered dropped, portholes opened, ships abandoned and the synthetic fleet scuttled. Then with a return of these crew members from the scuttled fleet to their full time status as city employes and liberal pensions after 20 years of abundant city hall life, will you please keep them fully occupied so that taxpayers may enjoy their undivided efforts in rendering better public service.[11]

Some five months after Hubbard scuttled the "bathtub navy," the government officially put the Dearborn Flotilla on an unassigned basis.[12] But not all the laughs in Dearborn that spring came from the mayor's ability to orchestrate events. Orvie's most serious personnel crisis of 1945, for instance, was the innocent outgrowth of his decision two years before to appoint an old boyhood acquaintance, Martin F. Buell, to succeed Dr. C. A. Christensen as city health commissioner.

Oh, Jesus Christ Almighty, that's a one-man show. Buell was always a mouthy kid, and everyone was always getting after him all his life, and I was always pulling 'em off of him. I always kind of felt sorry for him. So we had him come up here to meet the medical people in town, and they kind of took a liking to him on first sight. He acted kind of strange. Well, doctors as a whole are kind of oddballs anyway, and they recommended that we appoint him. So we did appoint Buell, and, Jesus Christ, he went on a real rampage around here. He'd come to council meetings and he'd just raise hell. He'd call 'em all kinds of names, and, jeez, the council got sort of afraid of him. He had one of these canes you could open up so you could sit on it, and he'd walk up and down behind them and swing that cane, the council ducking their heads.

Finally, in April 1945, the physician shocked those attending a council meeting by jumping to his feet during a discussion on the purchase of X-ray equipment, waving his cane in the air and yelling profanely at the councilmen to "cut out the politics." Rebuked by Council President Edwards for his language, Dr. Buell apologized but later roused councilmen's ire all over again by reading an open letter beginning, "Gentlemen, question mark, of the Council." The next week, Hubbard, obviously mortified, ordered him in writing to "immediately 'cease and desist' from your clowning and quietly settle down."

The next month, two nurses and two stenos resigned from the Health

Department, and Hubbard, complaining that Buell had disappeared with a city car earlier in the week, demanded that the doctor come in and explain things. At last, in mid-May, Buell appeared, decked out in his old Public Health Service officer's uniform, to face the mayor. When Orvie handed him an angry letter from health office employees, Buell ducked out the door with it, and then, while trying to evade a policeman dispatched to grab him, he shouted for photographers on hand to "get this one." At that, the mayor summarily fired the physician. But Buell was not finished. Abruptly, he began tootling on his ocarina, a little wind instrument he carried with him, and, after pointing out to reporters that he was "triple-tongueing it," he declared, "Wherever I am, that is where the Dearborn Public Health Service will be." A couple of weeks later, Buell was arrested on an assault charge brought by a cousin of his, and that was the last he was heard from around Dearborn city hall.

Things had quieted down by early June, and the upcoming mayoral election looked like the only remaining source of excitement. Petitions had come in from Hubbard, attorneys James Thomson and Ralph Guy and Councilmen Howard Ternes and Norman Edwards. But the city attorney's office said that only Hubbard's were accompanied by properly signed affidavits. And to complicate the matter, there were rumors that Hubbard was in line for appointment by Governor Harry Kelly to one of two new county probate judge positions, which would pay $15,000 a year compared to the mayor's niggardly $6,500.[13]

If Orvie really was serious about looking elsewhere for gainful employment, he was quickly disabused of the notion by a council challenge that did more for the young politician's popularity than anything he could have thought of himself.

Since almost his first day in office, Hubbard had tried to ingratiate himself with special-interest groups. He would routinely send out welcome letters to newcomers, write fire victims to ask about the quality of city service, hand out Gold Star pins to mothers of men killed in the service and, since the early months of the war, give pep talks to inductees as they left for active duty. By June, a jealous council had seen enough. Declaring, "We want public relations, not political relations," Edwards sponsored a measure admittedly aimed at the mayor's gimmicks. His ordinance would prohibit "all contacts by elective and appointive officers of the city with the public unless specifically authorized" by a newly established public relations bureau. But, acknowledging that 1945 was an election year, the ordinance allowed contacts "for purely political purposes of seeking election" except "under the guise of public business." In other words, almost everything that Orvie did would need approval from the new bureau, which included three councilmen, the city treasurer, clerk, mayor and senior municipal judge. Violation of the ordinance could bring a $500 fine, 90 days' imprisonment and even removal from office.

The ordinance drew instant opposition from Councilmen Ray Parker and Dr. Edward Fisher, with Parker calling it "a cheap political maneuver." But it passed by a five-to-two vote, and the outside reaction was just as negative as Parker's. Judge George Belding informed the council before the vote that he would refuse to serve on the bureau. And Orvie announced he would veto the measure as "clearly illegal," adding, "I have had to come in an hour early and work until about 10 every night to get my work done, but the people know they have a mayor who gives them service. The bureau the council would establish is simply one to do away with the mayor."

The local papers denounced the ordinance, the *Press* calling it a "Gestapo style censorship committee."[14] And the Detroit dailies ridiculed the "gag ordinance," as *News* reporter Boyd Simmons had tagged it.[15]

Hubbard vetoed the ordinance, as promised, but the council overrode him two weeks later. The councilmen, however, plainly were not anxious to force the issue. As Orvie left city hall that night with Chief Nielsen, he talked to several citizens in plain sight of the council. No one suggested that he be arrested.

A few days later, on June 27, 1945, Orville L. Hubbard delivered three-minute speeches to departing troops—at 7:25 A.M. in an American Legion hall and at 7:55 A.M. at a Knights of Columbus hall—in his official capacity as mayor without prior approval from the city's public relations bureau. Under authority of a warrant obtained by Parker in collaboration with the perpetrator himself, Orvie was arrested and then arraigned before Judge Belding. Belding released the mayor on personal bond for a July hearing.

In the weeks leading up to the trial, the mayor's arrest received almost as much publicity around the country as it did locally. Mail poured in, some of it kidding and some of it, including piles of letters from soldiers after the story was picked up by the *Stars and Stripes*, plainly indignant. Typical was a wry note from St. Louis Mayor A. P. Kaufmann labeling the gag law "a serious threat to American democracy." He observed, "From time to time it has been the happy privilege of mayors to . . . open fish fries, kiss babies, . . . and issue proclamations in observance of Be Kind to Mothers-in-Law Month, Pretzel Week or Use-Your-Own-Toothpick Day."

When the Hubbard trial began on July 12, with only a few curious citizens in attendance, it was clear that it wouldn't be much of a contest. Charles Wagner, a prominent Detroit corporation attorney who lived in Dearborn, had agreed to defend the mayor as a civic gesture. His opening address attacked the gag law as unconstitutional, as well as a violation of the city charter and Michigan law.

"I gave a talk like that once and won my case," observed Fred McCann, an assistant corporation counsel charged with the unhappy task of prose-cuting Orvie. "I'm on the wrong side here." McCann, who conceded that the council had never submitted the ordinance to his office for approval, was given a week's adjournment. But it was no secret that he and many other city officials were hoping the council would rescind the ordinance.

Sure enough, the council, recognizing the matter for the embarrassment it was, repealed the gag law unanimously on a motion from Edwards, the original sponsor. Apologizing for the notoriety it had brought on the city, Edwards blamed everything on "the mayor's everzealous desire for the limelight."

Hubbard, for his part, sat silently for once, content in the knowledge that the council wouldn't be so quick to take him on again. Two days later, Belding dismissed the complaint against the mayor, ruling the gag law unconstitutional.

I always said it was horseshit publicity. Simmons blew that thing up on a dull day, and it made the front page. He tagged it the gag ordinance, and it really went. It was just like putting a skyrocket in the air with a repeat charge on it. The justice of the peace ruled it unconstitutional. Ever hear of a thing like that? But I got a lot of mileage out of that because of pictures of being arrested and all that shit. Was one of the first times I got much national publicity.

So, with a public relations bonanza like that, Hubbard needed little else when the August 8 primary rolled around. Forgotten was Hubbard's prospective judgeship and the momentary flap about improper nominating petitions for his opponents. By this time, Ternes and Edwards had dropped out of the race anyway, leaving only Thomson and Guy to face Hubbard.

There wasn't much campaigning, and, with a rather light voter turnout, Hubbard easily led the field with 5,585 votes to 2,689 for Thomson, who thus earned a place on the final ballot, and only 1,192 for Guy. The council vote also seemed to be a show of support for Hubbard. Dr. Fisher and Ray Parker, his two backers on the gag ordinance, led the field. Then, with the housing project falling through, even the Bitonti allegations about Hubbard and the gambling apparatus couldn't hurt him much. After that, it was a bland campaign. Thomson ran thinly veiled appeals to racism in his ads ("KEEPING the City of Dearborn AS IT IS with its property restrictions strongly enforced"), and he tried to appear conciliatory with the City Council ("I will not attempt to force the Council to do my bidding by art, guile or coercion"), but he was content to let the gambling issue alone. Hubbard, apparently seeing little chance of losing, also stayed relatively quiet.

The result was Orvie's easiest victory, a margin of 13,186 to 7,180, with every precinct but one preferring the incumbent over Thomson. It was the highest vote and the biggest majority ever given a Dearborn mayoral candidate, and it was also the first time a mayoral candidate had headed the entire ballot, including candidates who ran unopposed. In addition, Hubbard supporters swept five of the seven council spots, with Dr. Fisher heading the list and Anthony Esper, Howard Ternes, Joe Ford and Ray Parker also getting in.[16] Patrick Doyle and Homer Beadle were the only outsiders to make it. Edwards, who had been ill and unable to campaign actively, finished out of the money.

The only hot ballot issue, a charter amendment providing for a city-owned hospital favored by the mayor and most council candidates, won a narrow victory as well. That vote diverted most of the attention from a $50,000 libel suit Hubbard had filed against Dr. Eugene C. Keyes, former councilman and ex-lieutenant governor of Michigan, for publishing a paper that attacked the mayor and the hospital proposition.

But with the election results of 1945 in, Orville Hubbard had passed his most critical point with voters. He had finished nearly four years in office and, manuevering all the while to keep his name constantly before the public, had begun to assert himself under the new charter.

Pleased though he may have been with the way his career was going, Orvie was not one to let things slide, however. He was reported back on the job the morning after the election, bidding goodbye at 7:00 A.M. to draftees leaving for the service.

18

Beating John Carey, 1946-47

A jerk, a liar, a flukey, a fraud and a Democrat.
—Orville L. Hubbard, during a tirade against Councilman Homer Beadle[1]

Orville Hubbard reveled in confrontation. That much was only too clear. He had already proved he had the council majority overmatched during his four contentious years as mayor. But over the next two years, Orvie was to outdo himself.

If he had tried deliberately to antagonize everybody in city government, he could hardly have done a more thorough job. By the time he had to face reelection in 1947, he had cut a swath of insults and provocations though the ranks of virtually all city employees—police, firemen and clerical workers.

His prime targets were the firemen. Soon after he took office, the mayor concluded that firemen—he never permitted them to be called fire fighters in press releases—were the most overpaid and underworked of all city employees. It was a view he never changed, once, some 25 years later, referring to them in an interview as "greedy sons of bitches."[2]

Orvie's feud with the firemen seemed in some ways almost an echo of his showdown with Police Chief Emrys Evans three years before. But this time, he had to take on the man who had organized the department and even served a term as president of the International Association of Fire Chiefs.

Roy E. Mottesheard was an officious, white-gloved disciplinarian with a penchant for encouraging firemen to enter smoldering buildings by administering a foot to their posterior regions. He had been the subject of grumbling in the ranks for some time, and a group of 78 firemen had demanded his removal three years before. Although Hubbard had protected the chief's job then, he moved at last to oust him late in1945. Public Safety Director Otto Hoffman refused to fire Mottesheard, but that didn't stop Orvic for long. In a letter dated January 2, 1946, the chief suddenly asked to be retired, effective in three months. Hubbard denied firing him, but, as the chief explained to reporters, "I was told to apply for my pension or I would be fired and lose my right to it."

The mayor had no cronies to appoint as chief, but his plans stirred things up even more than his naming of Erving Nielsen as police chief in 1943. He would replace Mottesheard with the chief's former chauffeur, a 15-year veteran named George Lewis, a low-ranking pipeman. Lewis lacked supervisory experience in the department, although he had caught Hubbard's eye in running the city's civil defense efforts during the war. A few weeks later, a committee headed by onetime Charter Commissioners Charles Wagner and John Fish trooped in to protest, and then came a resolution from a regional fire chiefs' organization decrying Mottesheard's removal as "political." Hubbard quickly backed off, agreeing to appoint a new chief based on examination scores. He held firm, however, on Mottesheard. "Now he is out and will stay out," he declared. In June, true to his word, he named Stanley Herdzik, a captain and 21-year veteran of the department, as chief.

Mottesheard was a good man. I mean, he was an efficient man. But the firemen hated him. He ran that department with an iron hand. Jeez, he kicked George Lewis right in the ass once. "Goddammit," he said, "get in there." He locked up the refrigerator so the fellows couldn't be nibbling every time they got hungry. The first year I was in office, the Fire Department all came over as a gang. They all leveled these charges against him. I said, "I'll talk to him and see if he won't quit riding the men." So then I got along all right with Mottesheard. But he drove a great big Zephyr car with a chauffeur. And I said that's bullshit. So one day, I called for the fire chief's chauffeur, and he didn't show up for about two hours. He walked in with the chief. So I said, "What in the hell are you doing here?" to the chief. "I just sent for the chauffeur." So I gave him hell. He said, "I'm going to punch you in the nose." I said, "You son of a bitch, do it. You haven't got the guts to do it." And he didn't do it. So then we fired him. Eventually he went. So I was going to appoint George Lewis chief. I took a liking to George because of his manner and his willingness and the way he worked. Jesus Christ, you'd thought the heavens were coming down. This gang came in, all these guys from the Charter Commission. They thought they made a mistake in providing the strong-mayor form of government. They wanted me to get the best man I could get, search the whole United States. That goddamn Sunday-school-teacher attitude, you know. So we agreed we'd let the Michigan Municipal League conduct examinations for all men with the grade of captain or above. They all took the test, and the low man on the test was Herdzik, and I gave the job to Herdzik, so they wouldn't just run the show.

If the firemen expected a pat on the back from the new chief, they were sadly mistaken. By January 1947, under Hubbard's direction, Herdzik began to out-Mottesheard Mottesheard. First he imposed 12-hour work shifts five days a week, abolishing the traditional around-the-clock shifts that permitted firemen to sleep and play Ping-Pong at work. When firemen blocked the move in court, Hubbard started needling them. At a fire fighters' union banquet, for instance, he took a swipe at their moonlighting activities.

"I never said that firemen are fat and lazy, as quoted in the papers," he fairly chortled. "In fact, I find that our firemen are the most ambitious of all our employees. I am amazed at the diversified interests they have." He even characterized their firehouse jobs as "sidelines" to their other pursuits.

A couple of months later, he ordered all firemen to quit their outside jobs or face suspension, as provided by department rules. And he followed up by having one longtime veteran suspended for selling real estate. The man promptly retired.

Meanwhile, Herdzik and Hubbard had been tightening up discipline. Two firemen were suspended for getting their truck stuck in a snowbank on their way to a garage fire. Another was ticketed for having two accidents on a fire call. The union president, Charles Papke, was suspended after attending a state union convention in defiance of Herdzik's orders. And through it all, the mayor never passed up a chance to make the men look bad. When a fireman suspended on a morals charge tried to deliver a summons to the mayor in an attempt to gain a court order for reinstatement, Orvie disappeared. The fireman gave up after 13 hours, and Hubbard observed later, "I'm not surprised that a fireman can't find the mayor. They can't even find a fire sometimes."

Then, in August, as Hubbard complained that "all they do is sit around and wait for their 20 years to go by so they can retire," he finally hit on an idea to "give the men something to do": they could hose down the streets at night. Elwood J. Nowka, acting chief while Herdzik was on vacation, balked at the order. But when the chief returned, sure enough, he got his hip boots and took out a contingent of men to wash down two intersections.

But the job was just beginning to wear on Herdzik. The next month, he announced he was resigning as chief and seeking reinstatement to his old rank of captain, at a sizable pay cut. Three days later the mayor talked him out of it.

Eventually, the issue of the firemen's workweek resolved itself with a compromise worked out in 1947. In the meantime, however, the mayor was not ignoring the other city employees.

Early in 1946, Hubbard had ordered police on daylight shifts assigned to one-man scout cars in an efficiency move. There was constant muttering about declining morale on the force, though most of the problems stayed out of the papers. Finally, a police lieutenant named Millard Rials filed a complaint with the city clerk alleging that Orvie had directed some officers not to write traffic tickets. Rials was suspended for circumventing department procedure, and Hubbard responded by calling the charge "just a politically inspired piece of work."

The mayor managed to alienate the rest of the city's work force through their paychecks. During 1946 budget deliberations, he vetoed a "super deluxe luxurious" pay hike of $450,000 coming on top of increases of more than 40 percent over the previous four years. Then, in August, when employees threatened to strike for a raise, he practically dared them to: "Our city employees are the best-paid people under the canopy of heaven. If they go on strike, we'll fire them all. That's anarchy. We have a waiting list of people who would appreciate a city job." The mayor won this round and pushed harder in 1947 by challenging the employee pension structure. City workers could retire at half-pay after 25 years or for reduced benefits after 20. The mayor announced that he was proposing two charter amendments to require 30 years' service, or attainment of age 60, before pension rights kicked in. Further, he vetoed another budget item, this time $300,000 as the city's contributions to the pension funds. The charter amendments, Orvie argued, would render the funds unnecessary. John Fish, representing the city unions, began court proceedings to restore the amount vetoed. The proposals went on the 1947 city ballot as scheduled, but it was not until months later that that the issue was resolved.

Overlapping with these activities, Hubbard was giving the council his customary nose-thumbing. During a flare-up in July 1946 over a Hubbard-backed proposal for a city hospital, he demanded that several councilmen resign. He even traded taunts with Homer Beadle, labeling the councilman a "faker" and earning a retort that his administration "shouldn't run a dog house." He also made a not-so-veiled threat to his old friend Howard Ternes, warning that his opposition to the hospital could cost him his post as council president.

In October came one of the low points of Hubbard's always-strained relations with the council. At a committee-of-the-whole meeting, the dapper, slightly built Ternes had challenged bidding procedures for the installation of floodlights at a city park. He was absent from the next council meeting, and Homer Beadle took it upon himself to explain why. "In my hearing," he scolded the mayor, "you told a man to beat him up." The mayor jumped to his feet and shouted, "You're a liar and a hoodlum yourself." As the two continued, the meeting was gaveled to adjournment. As reconstructed by Beadle, the story was that the mayor had ordered one of his huskiest lieutenants, purchasing agent Harold DeWyk, to thrash the 140-pound Ternes. Ternes, who had a history of heart problems, left city hall obviously shaken by the episode. Hubbard subsequently admitted only to telling DeWyk, "You ought to pull out that Hitler mustache of his." Ternes later told reporters he was resigning as council president because of the incident. "My doctor tells me I'll have to stay in bed for six months," he remarked. "I'm not resigning from the council, however, and give him [Hubbard] an opportunity to appoint another of his own crowd."

Two months later, in December 1946, Hubbard and Beadle got into it again, this time following a council meeting at which John Fish called for a grand jury to investigate Hubbard. Fish, who had increasingly become an irritant to the mayor, ticked off a list of offenses, including a catchall charge about "demoralization of city employees because of the mayor's dictatorial and arbitrary conduct." Hubbard, absent from the meeting, responded a week later by calling Fish "a lawyer and a liar" and adding, "There is not one word of truth in the whole statement." He suggested that Fish's motives were linked to his law practice; the attorney represented the Civil Service Commission, the city employees' union and individual city employees and former employees, including the suspended fireman.

Another week passed before the real confrontation came. At the next council meeting, Beadle moved a resolution on Fish's demand. But before it came to a vote, Hubbard interposed himself into the debate. His voice thick with emotion, his finger pointing in Beadle's face, his hands gesticulating wildly, Hubbard called Fish "a cockeyed liar" who "has his hands in all the politics in the city" and "should be disbarred permanently." Beadle then took the offensive, alleging that the Hubbard regime was "honeycombed with petty graft and corruption." He blistered Orvie for abusing city car privileges, junketeering and interfering with the police and fire departments, adding, "I've seen so much on the surface that the people would be surprised at the revelations a grand jury would uncover."³ Countered the mayor, "I've listened to Beadle for 13 years, and never have I met a bigger phony, never have I met a man who tells half-truths so well. All Beadle has done since he's been on this council is to heckle and snipe. If there is a shred of truth to any of these reports, I'll resign." Then, with Fish fleshing out his charges—including "threats and intimidations against citizens who dare to oppose" Orvie—the matter came to a vote: a three-three tie, with Ternes absent. At a special meeting the next week, the vote was five-to-two against the investigation, with only Beadle and Patrick Doyle supporting it. The rest, including Ternes, concluded that the evidence did not warrant formal examination.

The name-calling continued on into 1947. In May, another spat between Hubbard and Beadle elicited a *Detroit News* editorial headlined "Harsh Words, Mayor": "Out in Dearborn men in politics really speak out when they differ on public questions. For example, when Councilman Beadle questioned the propriety of Mayor Hubbard's budget procedure the mayor called the councilman 'a jerk, a liar, a flunkey [sic], a fraud and a Democrat.' Apparently anything goes in Dearborn."⁴

A couple of months after that, Beadle accused Hubbard of "alley-rat politics," and Hubbard charged Beadle with "never telling the truth." Anthony

Esper, who had succeeded Ternes as council president, had to step in and ask, "Do I need a gun up here, or what?"

The only alternative prospect for shutting up Dearborn's garrulous mayor seemed to be to defeat him at the polls. In late 1946, a committee was formed to plan ways of ousting him. Former Mayor John L. Carey was being mentioned as a possible opponent, along with retired school superintendent Harvey Lowrey and James Thomson, whom Orvie had smothered in the 1945 election.

While everyone assumed Hubbard would seek another term, he was talking about a congressional seat, and only two months before the primary, he revealed he was applying for the city manager's job in Madison, Wisconsin, at half again his salary.

With Hubbard's status uncertain, the ranks of mayoral candidates began to fill rapidly. Lowrey and Carey were the first to announce, Lowrey proposing a limit of three terms for Dearborn mayors and Carey criticizing the mayor's eccentric behavior. "There is no place for such offensive verbiage as 'liar, jerk, flukey' in the conduct of city affairs," he admonished. The other entries included two surprises: Howard Ternes, off the ailing list, and Police Chief Erving Nielsen. Also filing was Ralph Guy, back for another go-round.

Hubbard filed near the August deadline, and Ternes and Nielsen withdrew, leaving Lowrey, Carey and Guy to challenge the mayor. Nielsen released a statement praising Orvie as a "courageous leader for civic progress and a clean city," while Carey came up with an endorsement of his own—Mottesheard, who was still jabbing at Hubbard for forcing him to retire.

With the primary approaching, the three challengers came up with rather curious strategies for dumping Hubbard. Lowrey mounted an almost laughably bland campaign, citing his 25 years as superintendent, his experience on two charter commissions and his health ("enjoys playing 18 holes of golf as occasions permit; has 17 years perfect attendance in Rotary weekly meetings"). He came out in favor of such civic improvements as a servicemen's memorial and public restrooms. Guy, while expressing his disdain for Orvie's "dictation" and criticizing such spendthrift habits as out-of-town boondoggles, saved his heaviest salvos for Carey. Explaining that he had to beat Carey to face Hubbard in the general election, he joined with the mayor in attacking Carey's links to the pre-Hubbard police scandal. Carey, for his part, declined to defend his three-term administration, but he found plenty to fault in Hubbard's tenure. He pointed out that his successor had undertaken no significant public improvements during his six years in office, and he charged that city finances were "in a mess," adding that a Hubbard-engineered tax cut was based on "rigged" bookkeeping and fund transfers. Carey also vowed, "I will also get rid of the throne room in the city hall, along with its suite of air-conditioned sanctums and inner sanctums, secret dictaphones and other dime detective novel paraphernalia. . . . I will not permit the continuance of a municipal three-ringed circus for the amusement of the rest of the state and neighboring states."

Hubbard kept his campaign low-key, content to dredge up old claims about having kept Dearborn "clean" and citing his efforts at improving recreational facilities while cutting taxes.

The only new allegation popped up the day before the election—but was reported too late to have any effect on the outcome. The central figure was Howard S. Hill, husband of the mayor's old friend, Circuit Judge Lila Neuenfelt. Hubbard had appointed him assessor at the behest of the judge so that, in the mayor's words, "he would have something to do." The mayor later promoted him to head of weights and measures. But Hill abruptly resigned just before the election, angered, he said, because the mayor demanded that Hill's Civil Service staffers help address campaign literature. When Orvie coyly refused to accept his resignation because his letter came with three cents postage due, Hill blew up. "It is pretty small of him not to accept a postage-due letter," he said, "when I've had to pay 20 percent of my salary to hold my job and all the other department heads are doing it."

Mandatory kickbacks from political appointees were a time-honored practice in local government, and Hubbard, in effect, admitted the charge, explaining, "He says he paid $25 once and $50 another time. What's wrong with that? I gave him a job, and campaigns cost money. Somebody has to pay, and I don't get any money from racketeers." Other department heads interviewed by reporters denied making similar payments, however.

Kickbacks or not, Hubbard managed to cakewalk through another primary by rolling up his customary huge lead in the east end. Carey, however, actually won all but 5 of 19 precincts on the west side and finished a respectable second. The vote tally showed Hubbard with 5,763, 4,772 for Carey, 2,006 for Lowrey and 1,080 for Guy. But the mayor looked as though he were in for trouble on the City Council, as Patrick Doyle and Beadle, both Carey supporters, led the field.

Lowrey and Guy proceeded to split their allegiance between their conquerors. Lowrey said he would back Carey, while Guy announced he had settled his "trivial and insignificant" differences with Hubbard and now would "do all within my power" to prevent the return of Carey's "rotten regime."

With the primary as close-fought as it was, and with the pension proposals on the ballot sure to bring out the city employees against him, Hubbard got down to business in the weeks before the general election. His strategy of making his opponent seem responsible for the vice scandal had worked perfectly against Clarence Doyle in 1941, and he wasn't about to abandon it now.

Carey was running newspaper ads that tried to capitalize on the city's tarnished reputation under Hubbard. He said, "Dearborn's municipal circus has provided national entertainment for six years and it's time to ring down the curtain."[5] Hubbard's response was simply to resuscitate his old theme:

Wake up, Dearborn, wake up! Stop the return to power of the gang in authority when corruption was in full bloom here and blossomed into Dearborn's biggest and blackest police and vice scandal. From his ringside seat the nervous, 60-year-old former mayor who is running again saw a municipal circus, all right, yes, with an all-star cast of thugs, gangsters, racketeers, gamblers and prostitutes heading events.[6]

I remember Carey was as nervous as a whore in church. That was a real bitter campaign. A lot of hard feelings. We carried on a vigorous, hard-driving campaign to change the city pension plan. But by doing that we drove 'em all together. All the city employees and firemen and policemen united against us with their families. So they trotted out Carey to be the candidate for the city employees. See, old Carey had never been defeated at the polls. He didn't run in '42 because of the shadow hanging over him about indictments and the grand jury. Both newspapers were against us, and I lost the council. We ran five names. We made a mistake by not running seven. That was a bad campaign.

"We got licked, period." That was the way one of Carey's supporters assessed Dearborn's 1947 election. But the overall record was by no means a clear-cut victory for Hubbard. True enough, with a record turnout of more than 24,000 voters, he piled up 13,430 votes to 10,639 for Carey, becoming the city's first four-term mayor. With only the endorsement of Local 600, UAW-CIO, and with the city employees solidly against him, Hubbard duplicated his pattern from the primary. He took 30 of 33 precincts on the east side, while Carey won in 12 of 19 in the west end.

However, both of Hubbard's hotly contested pension proposals were narrow losers, and of his five backers among the council candidates, only Ray Parker, Joe Ford and Martin Griffith emerged with seats. The council majority now was against him again as he headed into his fourth term in office.

19

Beating Hancock Housing, 1948

> This issue is a volatile one and in the hands of a fanatic
> it can become dangerous to the extent of creating
> unnecessary antagonism . . . both in the white and black
> races. . . . Tolerance, we must remember, is a product of
> social evolution, not legal dictation.
> —Orville L. Hubbard, assessing a U.S. Supreme Court
> ruling on restrictive housing covenants

It was supposed to be one of the most ambitious housing projects ever built anywhere in the country. So when the John Hancock Life Insurance Co. of Chicago announced plans for a deluxe, $25-million, multiple-family development in Dearborn in September 1948, it sounded like a fine idea to most of the city's officials and most prominent businessmen. Orville Hubbard, however, seldom was influenced by what other officials thought.

The Springwells Park Development, as it was called, would house 1,200 families in 600 duplex units to be built on some 930 acres of land owned by the Ford Foundation and the Ford Motor Company. Eventually, it might accommodate 45,000 residents. Rent was to average $125 a month.

Because an interlocking directorate operated both Ford and the Hancock firm, the land changed hands without fanfare, pending rezoning action by the city fathers. Things all seemed very routine. After hearing plans for the proposed garden community, described as a model town-within-a-town, the City Planning Commission readily approved the request for a zoning change from business to residential use. Similar action was expected from the City Council.

But that was before Orvie had his say. It had been three years since the mayor had mobilized the objections of an entire consortium of communities against the Federal Housing Project Administration's proposal to provide dwelling units for Negro war workers in Dearborn or neighboring suburbs. This time, surely, there were no such objections to be made. Or were there?

The race issue, Hubbard was well aware, was on the minds of many homeowners once again. Only four months before, in May 1948, the U.S.

Supreme Court had stripped white homeowners of one of their last remnants of legal protection. The court ruled that restrictive covenants on property deeds, common in Dearborn and hundreds of other communities around the country, were not enforceable in state courts.[1]

With this as a backdrop, Ford and Hancock officials paid Hubbard a courtesy call the next afternoon, hours before a scheduled council meeting. He listened a while and then blew up. First he berated Hancock Housing Director Lucius Hill, and then he ordered a Ford real estate official out of his office. That night at the council meeting, Hubbard spewed out his protests as soon as he got the floor. "Who invited you to come here, anyway?" he barked at Hill. "You certainly got no invitation from the city government." He went on to suggest that an advisory vote on the Hancock development be put on the November ballot, and he asked, "Why allow an army of approximately 45,000 renters to march into this city, now predominantly populated by homeowners?"

Hill responded by asserting that "cities all over the country are begging us to come in" with similar developments. "We did not come here because we couldn't find any other place to spend $25 million," he said.

After the meeting, the mayor elaborated on his position: He estimated that 95 percent of Dearborn's residents were with him against the development, because, he said, the newcomers "would change the whole complexion of the population. They would change it because they would be renters, not having a real stake in the community. They would bring all kinds of people to Dearborn. Some would be the kind of people we are eager to welcome. Some would not. Anybody can afford the rentals. A single court suit would open the entire project to whoever got there first with the cash."

That seemed plain enough, but in case anybody failed to get the mayor's drift, he and his subordinates began letting it be known more explicitly around town that the Hancock project would become a "huge Negro community." The whispering campaign came out in the open at the next council meeting in October. There Hubbard recommended that the council urge Hancock "to immediately accept the invitation of our good friends and neighbors in Detroit"—where officials were on record in support of Hancock's plans—"and build just as many housing projects as Hancock finances will permit in their city."

When his recommendation was tabled, the mayor escalated the battle by reading a telegram sent to him by William R. Hood, recording secretary of UAW-CIO Local 600. Hood, himself a Negro, said of the Hancock proposal: "We are desirous of information as to whether or not these badly needed homes would give any relief to the colored population. We hope that in the preliminary discussion and in the final determination that people of all races will be taken under consideration."[2]

Hubbard postulated that such sentiments indicated a "race problem"

157

in the making, at which point several onlookers accused him of trying to stir up just such a problem. Even Ray Parker, one of Orvie's few council supporters, shouted out, "For five years I have been on the side of the mayor in the majority of cases. Now I'm ashamed that I have been with such a man." Council President Patrick Doyle finally restored order, but the council voted four-to-three against Hubbard's recommendation to put the Hancock question on the fall ballot.

However, the *Dearborn Press*, suspicious of the mayor's claim that nearly everybody in town was with him, conducted its own poll of civic leaders and others and concluded that 75 percent were actually against him and in favor of Hancock.

But Hubbard was not finished with his plan to get the issue on the ballot. He called a special council meeting the next week to consider again whether Hancock should be allowed to "invade Dearborn with a huge terrace-type rental housing project." And while he was waiting, he sent out a flyer to homes near the proposed Hancock site with photostats of a *Business Week* article describing a similar Hancock development in Brookline, Massachusetts. He also seized the opportunity to take a potshot at Henry Ford II, who had urged support of the project in several letters to Dearborn residents. "It's nice to know the young fellow is thinking of Dearborn," Hubbard chided. "It's too bad, though, he doesn't think enough of it to live here, where he makes his money, instead of on the Gold Coast in Grosse Pointe Shores."

The council meeting called by Hubbard featured a lengthy harangue in which he explained how, in cooperation with police, he discouraged Negroes from settling in Dearborn and encouraged those who had moved in to leave.[3] Homer Beadle responded by assailing Hubbard's position that the Hancock project would turn into a Negro slum as "a vicious and unwarranted assumption manufactured out of nothing." Finally, after two hours of shouting, the council adjourned to protest the mayor's tactics.

There was more of the same at an overflow meeting the following week— heckling of the council by Hubbard, boos and cheers from a divided audience of more than 600. The mayor belittled residents of the Springwells Park area adjacent to the Hancock site for caving in to Ford propaganda. "Springwells Park ought to secede from Dearborn and set up as a separate municipality," he shouted. "Then the folks down there could build multiple-type housing in their front yards, their alleys and wherever they wanted it." Then he tossed in a gratuitous slap at Ford Motor: "The Ford people want to get out of the real estate business. They'd better hurry or they'll be out of the automobile business first. If you don't believe it, try one of their new models, only take a good look first to be sure all the parts are there." He tried again to launch into one of his racial harangues, but the crowd cut him short. Then came the vote from the council: unanimous in favor of his

158

plan to put Hancock on the ballot, even though most of them already favored the project.

We got caught in this Hancock housing. I was inclined to go along with the deal, but I went to look at the Brookline housing. We took pictures of it. It was the damnedest, crummiest-looking shit you ever saw. It was just strictly row housing, just shoved together like an accordion. Meanwhile, we got this telegram from the fellow with Local 600—"How many homes are gonna be in here for Negroes?" Jesus Christ, that touched it off. So the civic associations here had a meeting, and all of them began to fall in line against this Hancock housing. I took the stand, which I've always tried to do, with the people. They were against it, and we fought it. We were stressing single-residence occupancy, not mish-mash. So we took a stand against Henry Ford. That was quite a stand to take, 'cause they just take a bulldozer and run over you. So everyone was trying to ingratiate themselves to Ford. Henry would take a crap, and they'd come like a bunch of flies. But we euchered them into putting it up to an advisory vote. Well, they started a big campaign against us, and Henry wrote either one, two or three letters, first-class mail, to every registered voter in town—many of 'em were dead—to tell 'em to vote for the project. Meantime, the News, *the* Times, *the* Free Press *were all for it; the* Dearborn Independent, Press, Guide *all for it. They had that whole steamroller against us. The Chamber of Commerce was against us, the VFW, everything was against us, everything, almost a solid front. And Henry got his ass beat. Ford got beat. They all got beat.*

In the weeks before the scheduled November 2 election, the two sides grew even farther apart than before. Hubbard charged that the project was a plot by "idle multimillionaires" to exploit the common people. He also distributed another flyer, this one characterizing the project as a "racial gamble," while every city councilman except Marguerite Johnson endorsed the development in a public statement as a way to "establish for all time an area that will act as a bulwark against any poor real estate development that might seep into Dearborn." Additionally, the project won the official endorsement of most city organizations, as well as respected voters' groups such as the Dearborn Citizens' League. The *Dearborn Press* left no doubt about how things stood. Its last preelection story, bannered under the headline "It's City vs. Mayor on Homes," proclaimed, "Dearborn . . . lined up solidly against . . . Hubbard in his one-man steamroller campaign to stop one of the Nation's biggest housing developments from coming."[4]

At last came the vote. Although it would have no legal standing, the advisory referendum was to be accepted by both sides as the final determinant. But Ford and the other proponents of the plan had not reckoned with the mayor's next move, arguably the most blatantly racist performance of his entire career and perhaps the one that best demonstrated his ability to influence events in Dearborn. Hubbard sent his top lieutenants—department heads and their aides, including some Civil Service employees—fanning out across the city's polling places with cards that said, "KEEP NEGROES OUT OF DEARBORN / Vote *NO* on (Advisory Vote) / PROTECT YOUR HOME and MINE!"[5] Other leaflets pointed out that none of the 1,500 or so Negroes working at the Rouge plant lived in Dearborn and that Hancock would be unable to keep Negroes out of the new project. "Don't be lulled into a false sense of security," they warned.

How much backing did Hubbard have from Dearborn's secret bigots? The polls left little doubt. The vote was 15,948 against the project and only 10,562 in favor. Hancock was dead in Dearborn, much to the astonishment of everyone except Hubbard.

Not that it mattered, really, but the mayor's role in the anti-Hancock campaign made him the target of continuing vilification. Beadle decried Orvie's "rottenest" tactics in making "a white project a Negro project. He lied to every civic organization in the city and every registered citizen." One of the mayor's circulars also came back at him. City Engineer DeWitt M. Coburn and his wife had been quoted in the Hubbard propaganda barrage as saying that the project would "invite all types of undesirables and floaters" and "would ruin Dearborn." Their response was to complain that Hubbard had misrepresented their feelings in what Coburn called "the dirtiest trick I ever heard of." The Coburns also filed suits totaling $20,000 against Orvie and three aides.

He sued us because we said something in the campaign he said on the housing—which he did say, too, the bastard. Well, the suit never went to trial. It just died a natural death. We put out some literature. We said it was a racial gamble. I think it had some influence, but I don't think it was the principal thing. Everyone voted for the housing except the mayor and the civic associations. And you know something? That's the best thing that ever happened to the town. Ford was so lucky they never built 'em. They'd have had a first-class slum area. Ford's admit it. They're glad they never built that shit here. A guy who'd been in their real estate division for 35 or 40 years said, "You did us the biggest favor in your life." They had the whole public relations department on that thing. We had a fellow that worked for Ford 20-some years, and they had so much conniving going on, he couldn't take that bullshit and he quit. The opposition spent, I guess, a quarter of a million dollars.

The Hancock controversy quickly extinguished itself after the election. The City Council agreed not the grant the rezoning request, and Ford announced within several weeks that the land contract with Hancock had been canceled and that the firm would not pursue its rezoning application in court.

For his part, however, Orvie continued to milk the racial issue. In addressing a group of civic association officers, he discussed the racial aspects of housing at length, pointing out that there was no legal way to discriminate but that "there were other ways" of getting the same results. He urged civic groups to organize tightly, to call for strict zoning regulations and building standards and to remain on guard against "the danger." Whether it was his goal or not, Orville Hubbard at last had preempted the race issue in Dearborn. It was all his from now on.

20

Beating Carl Matheny, 1948-49

Two down . . . one to go / Dictatorships ended / Hitler—
April 30, 1945 / Hague—May 10, 1949 / Hub—
—From a flyer for mayoral candidate Patrick J. Doyle[1]

Was Mayor Hubbard going nuts? During his first few years in office, Orvie's energy and sense of humor, along with his standing as something of an underdog, had prompted many Dearbornites to root for him. But by the beginning of 1948, in the months before the Hancock housing controversy stamped him as a spokesman for white rights, his personality took on an increasingly dark tone. He began to alienate even those who originally had taken his side. Indeed, the mayor began to look to some of his adversaries like a man who was losing control of his faculties.

Orvie had come out of the 1947 election with distinctly vindictive feelings about the vanquished. He made no secret of his delight at the defeat of Anthony Esper, a 23-year councilman and sponsor of the gag law. He also urged backers not to patronize a diner owned by one of John Carey's supporters.

A few weeks before the year's end, Police Chief Erving Nielsen and Public Safety Director Otto Hoffman deserted him. Nielsen, who already had resigned and changed his mind three times, made it final this time, citing Hubbard's insistence that he discipline two patrolmen who filed suit after they were barred from joining a police fraternal organization. Hoffman said simply that he disagreed with the mayor on several issues. Their successors, announced during the last week in 1947, were two of the also-rans from the election. The new public safety director was Howard Ternes, who had supported Hubbard often enough in the past for the two to overlook the beating threat allegedly made the year before by a Hubbard aide. And the new chief, appointed by Ternes, was Ralph Guy, who had flip-flopped

162

back over to the mayor's side after finishing last against him in the primary.

Nielsen had served on the zoning board, so I asked him one day, "Do you want to be chief of police?" Jesus Christ, he rolled back in his chair and hit the wall and said, "God, I'll have to talk to my wife." Well, that was a cue. I shouldn't have taken him, because he was weak. Hoffman resigned because he didn't like the way things went around here.

Personnel problems and defections were old stuff to Hubbard, of course. But the city was in real financial trouble now for the first time in his tenure, and much of it was directly caused by his contentious nature and his desire to make himself look good to voters.

As Carey had insisted during the last campaign, Hubbard had been on shaky ground in pushing through a tax cut of more than 60 percent. About half that resulted from transferring $800,000 from a public improvement fund to the operating fund. After attorney John Fish sued to halt the practice, a Wayne Circuit judge ruled in February 1948 that the transfers were illegal. The ruling left the city with nearly $1 million for public improvements but nothing for running the city's day-to-day operations. When a subsequent ruling prohibited the city from borrowing against tax-anticipation notes, Hubbard finally recommended pay cutbacks and unpaid leave for city workers. A month later, Fish agreed to free up the improvement funds to run the city and then restore the appropriate amount through higher taxes the next year. This helped avoid a calamity of sorts, but it was not the end of Hubbard's money woes.

There was also the matter of some $250,000 in cost-of-living raises due city employees since mid-1947 but not paid because of Orvie's obstinacy. The matter dragged on till January 1949, when the Michigan Supreme Court ruled for the employees. When it became clear that the city would have to borrow to pay up, Councilman Patrick Doyle observed, "We couldn't buy a rowboat."

Regardless of the impending monetary difficulties, the mayor and the council agreed on one thing: Dearborn needed a new program to construct public buildings. Through World War II, Hubbard had pontificated about improving city facilities, but, as his arch-foe on the council, Homer Beadle, observed, "No administration promised so much and accomplished as little."

One of Orvie's more far-fetched notions during the war years had been a vague desire to have Dearborn establish some kind of landmark recreational facility outside the city limits. Four months before he first was elected mayor in 1941, several Boy Scout leaders at a camp attended by his 12-year-old son Jim began talking up the idea. Hubbard waited to pursue the scheme until mid-1946, when, after discussing it with city recreation officials, he asked the council to set up a commission to look into purchasing land for a camp. Ideally, Hubbard said, the site would be 50 to 80 miles from town, with facilities for summer and winter sports. "It is obvious that there is a public necessity and demand for a sizeable summer vacation camp for Dearborn boys and girls," he said in a message to the council.

A month later, in August, the council turned down the request, but the next year, in June 1947, councilmen authorized a commission to study camping needs and recommend the purchase of a campsite. In October, the city's recreation commission, in concert with the 43-member ad hoc camp commission appointed by Hubbard, recommended the purchase of 240 acres in Oakland County's Milford Township, some 35 miles northwest of Dearborn. The parcel, part of the estate of one Walter T. Keller, had a woods, a stream and a 20 1/2-acre spring-fed lake—in short, all the ingredients for a rustic retreat. The cost: $40,000.

Ray Parker headed the council's procamp bloc, declaring, "This is not a potshot in the dark." But after two hours of debate, the council put the measure off to get more information. The next week, the city engineer reported that the lake was big enough for swimming, canoeing and boating, and that the cost would be only about $3,000 to cut weeds, dump sand and gravel and level out the beach. Hubbard project or not, it all sounded too good to the council to pass up. The vote was six-to-nothing to purchase the parcel and authorize a $2,500 deposit. And that was that. Now Dearborn owned the core of what was to become a recreational campsite unique in the history of American municipalities.

The next summer, on the Fourth of July weekend of 1948, Camp Dearborn opened for 7,000 residents and guests for swimming, sunbathing, fishing and camping. Augmenting the site's natural gifts were 100 picnic tables and 30 boats. Within the next few years, the city acquired enough additional land in a series of purchases and property swaps to boost the camp's total to 626 acres. And as the parcel grew, so did Hubbard's ideas of how nature should be "improved" upon. With scarcely a word of protest from any quarter, eventually he directed that five artificial lakes be dredged out, much of the woods cleared, some hills leveled, and sand and dirt trucked in. He marked out a permanent "tent village" area, campgrounds, playgrounds, picnic areas, a swimming pool/bath house, tennis courts, a concession facility and a miniature golf course.[2]

Meanwhile, Hubbard's proposal for a city-owned hospital was not faring so well, even though Ford Motor had donated a 40-acre site for the building. Plans for a privately owned rival facility had begun to roll. Although the mayor was accused of attempting to sabotage the private facility, he finally gave up on his hopes for a city-owned hospital in early 1949.[3]

Serious discussions of community development formed only an occasional diversion from the real thrust of Dearborn politics, however. The mayor's relations with the council continued to sink to the level of a grade-school playground squabble. The first council meeting of 1948 set the tone for the next two years of bickering. Patrick Doyle, named council president by his colleagues, offered his hope that "petty differences of the past be forgotten." Hubbard promised his "fullest cooperation," but he couldn't resist admonishing councilmen for being part-time legislators. "The job—and you asked for it— calls for greater responsibility than just attending the council meetings," he pointed out. So much for rapprochement. Before the meeting ended, the council had wiped out three of Hubbard's pet projects, including a new public information office, and Beadle had asked that the mayor be prohibited from participating in council debates.

In March, the mayor took what was billed as his first vacation in six years, traveling to San Diego to attend his son Frank's graduation from a Marine Corps school. While he was gone, Beadle suggested that the mayor had violated the charter by failing to notify Doyle of his absence. "Maybe we should remove him," he proposed. Doyle, poking around Orvie's office, later was accused by secretaries of rifling the mayoral desk.

Hubbard's public relations bureau, abolished by the council and then rejuvenated when the mayor vetoed the action, provided the impetus for the next round of foolishness in December. Orvie had used such curious language in his veto message—referring to Beadle's activities as "the raw and sadistic political scheming and plotting of a conniving Roamer Tweedle or his midnight shadows"—that the council clerk broke up in giggles when he tried to read it. Beadle, not at all amused, likened Hubbard's message to "the pathological ravings of Hitler," to which the mayor replied, "All I know about Hitler is what I've learned from Homer. He seems to be the expert." "And that," countered Beadle, "is why I'm able to keep my finger on all the dictatorial moves of this administration."

Things got even better at the next meeting, the last of 1948. During another harangue over vetoes, Beadle suggested that the mayor had displayed "emotional instability," and he requested that Hubbard's recent veto messages and other documents be submitted to the psychiatric division of the county medical society "for analysis and report." Without elaborating, he also attacked Hubbard for committing the ultimate heresy in Dearborn: making comments about the town's number one citizen, the recently deceased Henry Ford, "which violated every propriety of common decency exercised toward the departed." In addition, he accused Hubbard of insulting Ford's grandson, Henry II, who had taken over the firm in a showdown with Harry Bennett. He also said the mayor had rigged truck chassis bids so that the firm's competitors could underbid Ford and "tell the world that Ford products are so bad even Dearborn has stopped using them."[4]

When an angry Hubbard finally got the floor, he called Beadle's statements "the most ridiculous I have ever heard," then, laughingly referring to the councilman as "Baldy," he said, "I'm willing to go down and have my head examined if he'll go along and submit to the same examination."

The discussion degenerated even further, Hubbard referring to having seen Beadle at Camp Dearborn in bathing trunks the previous summer and thinking "it was Mahatma Gandhi," and Beadle saying he had never seen the mayor in a swimsuit, but, in an apparent reference to Hubbard's uncorrected hernias, he understood that seeing him without one "was really something." After the meeting, Beadle gave reporters a prepared statement that said, "My only feeling toward the Mayor is one of sympathy and understanding. I have personally felt for years that he is a very sick man."

But the best was yet to come. By January 1949, following the Hancock housing episode, Hubbard's support on the council had almost totally disintegrated. Only Marguerite Johnson, who recently had come over to his side, was a sure vote. So when Hubbard called a special meeting for the first week of the new year, it was no surprise that all the council members but Johnson and Doyle ignored him. What happened next was open to dispute. At Johnson's suggestion—and with the mayor's enthusiastic approval—Police Chief Ralph Guy sent officers to the homes of the five absentees. Hubbard later explained that the aim was simply to ascertain whether the councilmen planned to attend, but several complained about threats of arrest if they stayed away. Later that evening, there was a shoving match between Guy and Councilman Martin Griffith, a former Hubbard supporter.

Hubbard called another special meeting for the next week, but this time only Johnson attended, along with a swarm of reporters and photographers. However, the absent councilmen were not about to let Hubbard keep the initiative. Griffith demanded a grand jury investigation of the Guy altercation as well as Orvie's administration. "This might well uncover the use of public funds and public property for private use and would uncover some very amazing situations," he said.

A few days later, Hubbard's six intractable council opponents released an open letter to "the citizens of Dearborn":

> We will not tolerate any further unwarranted interference by the Mayor in the exercise of our duties. Neither will we permit ourselves to be bullied, coerced, framed or otherwise interfered with. . . . Any further orders by the Mayor to have the police pick us up for our refusal to attend the phony special Council meetings that he is constantly calling to stage his political carnivals, will be acted upon immediately. . . . We will not hesitate to bring charges against the Mayor for misconduct, and, if adjudged guilty by the majority of the Council, he shall be forthwith removed from office.[5]

Later that month, the council approved $1,000 for a stenographer to record the proceedings in the hope, in Beadle's words, that it would have a "sobering influence."

It was against this background that the 1949 mayoral campaign began in March, with Hubbard, Carey and several others taking out petitions.

An early indication that Orvie's popularity was being eroded came in the spring election, when voters passed four council-backed charter amendments designed to strip some measure of power from the mayor. The amendments made the corporation counsel subject to council approval, gave the council the right to appoint its own attorney for specific situations, made the council appointment to the Civil Service Board immune from mayoral veto and limited suspensions of Civil Service employees. The *Press* called it "the most significant electoral defeat suffered by [Hubbard] since he took office."[6]

The next month brought more bad news. In April 1949, Fay Hubbard filed for divorce, alleging that the mayor was "subject to violent outbursts of unrestrained rage, which as time passed became more frequent." It was an allegation that surfaced again to trouble Hubbard in the ensuing months.

A few days later, Doyle announced his candidacy with a round of carping at the mayor. A seven-year councilman who also had served three terms in the state legislature, Doyle singled out Hubbard's interference with the police and fire departments, "which have been headed by inexperienced and incompetent men who, acting on every whim and caprice of the Mayor, have completely demoralized these departments." He also invented a new category of criticism, accusing Orvie of maintaining an outmoded garbage disposal system: "I will never countenance hauling garbage 30 miles to pig farms and contribute to the trichinosis infection of citizens."

Another new entrant in the race was Arthur Wierimaa, a manufacturing plant inspector who was also the stepfather of Hubbard's secretary, Helen Bell, with whom, he said, he had "a long-standing grievance." Wierimaa declared, "Everywhere I go, people laugh when I tell them I'm from Dearborn. They've heard all about the goings-on at city hall and think the town is crazy to put up with them. I'm going to stop it if I can."

Interspersed with the campaigning, politicking continued at the council meetings. In May, Hubbard was accused of tapping city hall phones in violation of federal law, of keeping records of phone conversations for political purposes and of opening and photostatting mail addressed to councilmen at city hall. The charges originated with a disgruntled homeowner, Theodore Jamieson, spokesman for a group calling itself the Sunken Heights Suckers Club as an expression of dissatisfaction with the city's handling of complaints against a local builder. Jamieson offered no substantiation for his accusations, but Councilmen Beadle and Anthony R. Smith both said they had reason to believe that Hubbard or his staff had copied mail and made recordings of phone conversations.

A month later, in June, Hubbard took the floor to speak on a month-old strike by local bus drivers, but he couldn't resist calling attention to the fact that Beadle, who was chairing the meeting in Doyle's absence, had no necktie on. Beadle, not shy about using the gavel, ruled him out of order and called on a policeman in the chamber to "remove the mayor." When the officer stayed put, Beadle ordered Guy to "evict the mayor." When Guy refused, Beadle adjourned the meeting and walked out, along with Parker, Joe Ford, Smith and half the audience. Then, as the audience milled around, one woman called Orvie a clown, and Parker returned briefly to compare him unfavorably with Hitler and Mussolini. When Hubbard chastised the councilmen and suggested a general cleanup in the fall election, several persons in the audience suggested beginning with him.

Hubbard and the council soon had a new issue for name-calling. Two of the mayor's department heads, John Pokorney and George Brady, had campaigned openly for him and some of his slate members; they also had circulated petitions for a proposed charter amendment to prohibit office-holders from being on more than one public payroll. The proposal obviously was aimed at four of Hubbard's enemies on the council; besides Doyle's membership in the legislature, Anthony Smith and Parker were teachers, and Beadle worked for the County Register of Deeds. The council had voted to freeze Pokorney's and Brady's pay, and now Hubbard, in what Doyle characterized as a "nauseating" veto message, attacked Parker, Smith and others for making the "opening wedge of terrorism that may affect every city employee." While defending city employees' rights to participate in polit-ical action, he also accused Parker, as the instigator of the council "plot," of peddling worthless stocks to city workers. Hubbard's opponents fell a vote short of overriding his veto, but the ensuing uproar pushed the session past midnight.

Smith tagged the mayor as a "past master at the art of intimidating city employees" and labeled his department heads as "stooges who are only used as tools in the mayor's political machine." He concluded, "Our pomp-ous, bombastic egomaniac has injected homes, jobs, pensions, stocks, teach-ers, children, vacant land and the housing shortage in the veto message. . . . This type of jumbled asininity is typical of his unbalanced mind and the mayor is to be pitied more than he is to be censured."

Parker said he was not inclined to be as "cheap, mean, dirty, low, vicious, cowardly, despicable and ratty" as the mayor, but he went ahead anyway and railed on against Orvie, drawing freely from speculation about his divorce suit. Calling Hubbard a "contemptible liar" for his accusations on stock sales, Parker stated, "Perhaps, because I have never been a wife beater, I cannot follow the mad, meaningless ranting and raving in the veto message. . . . Children do not avoid me because they know I will not bend their fingers until they scream for mercy. Nor do I pull hair and twist ears until their body is wracked with pain." Parker also raised another issue—a favorite of Beadle's—that Hubbard was instrumental in maintaining a policy of making city cars available at taxpayers' expense to the "political parasites that nestle close to his throne, including his private secretary." Parker did not mention that councilmen enjoyed the same car privileges.

Clearly, the political oratory in Dearborn, such as it was, was isolating Hubbard. And mayoral candidates accordingly continued to materialize. Two more announced in August: Victor G. Rouse, who owned a home and auto supply firm, managed the Dearborn Coach Company bus line and served as a member of the city's Civil Service Commission; and attorney Carl Matheny, a past state commander of the American Legion. Rouse jumped in with a familiar-sounding denunciation of the incumbent:

> In Dearborn we have been subjected for 8 years to nationwide ridicule solely because of the present mayor's conduct of city affairs. His extravagant waste of the taxpayer's money is evident. . . . His dictatorial control of police and fire departments has impaired their efficiency. His constant evasion of the city charter by dubious means has cost the city thousands of dollars lost in lawsuits. . . . He has destroyed the confidence of every Dearborn taxpayer by his repeated attacks against private enterprise. His pleasure trips throughout the United States and Canada at the taxpayers' expense; his phony greetings bought with taxpayers' money and addressed by public employees on taxpayers' time; his distribution of thimbles to women and matches to men—all these have resulted in the mounting ridicule that has been heaped on Dearborn.[7]

With the entry of the pugnacious Rouse and the widely respected Matheny into the fray, two other candidates, Doyle and Martin Griffith, withdrew. Doyle, in fact, conceded that he had no chance against Hubbard, "who is entrenched in the city hall and who makes full use of the fiscal and material resources of the taxpayers in the prosecution of his ambitions. In addition to this, thousands of dollars are extracted from merchants." By the September 1949 filing deadline, the candidates were Hubbard, Rouse, Matheny, Wierimaa, James Thomson, salesman-bartender Harold Bartsch and George Hollman, a onetime investigator for the county prosecutor's staff who now worked as a manufacturer's agent.

In the weeks before the primary, Rouse fell in with four anti-Hubbard councilmen—Doyle, Beadle, Parker and Smith—who announced they wanted to "rid the city of a pest." Matheny, in contrast, avoided any such links. His was a quiet, sober campaign based on promises to "plan and work with the council."

Hubbard, who organized his own slate for the first time ever, teamed up with the other incumbents—Johnson, Joe Ford and Martin Griffith—along with several newcomers. Besides bad-mouthing his opponents at rallies, Orvie fell back on his time-tested themes in campaign flyers ("Forward, Dearborn! Re-Elect Your Un-Bossed Mayor"). He attacked Rouse viciously ("Rouse, who made a small fortune out of providing Dearborn with about the poorest bus transportation it ever had, is dishonestly trying to fool you about city taxes"). And he harped once more on the old vice scandal of the pre-Hubbard years, with one major change: since his opponents now did not include easy marks such as Clarence Doyle and Carey, whose careers actually reached back to the grand jury, he targeted John Fish.

Fish wasn't actually running for anything, but he was opposing Hubbard's re-election with gusto. Fish had come up with a slogan comparing Hubbard to the German Fuehrer and to Jersey City Mayor Frank Hague. The slogan, "Hitler, Hague and Hubbard," showed a tombstone indicating the imminent demise of the Hubbard regime. Fish also had begun going around to rallies, reading portions of Fay Hubbard's divorce complaint.

Hubbard's response was typically bizarre. According to a notarized statement by Fire Chief Stanley Herdzik, who had fallen out with Hubbard, the mayor gave this directive at a department head meeting: "If anybody beats up John Fish, cripples him up, does anything to get him out of my way, such a person can have any job he wants." Hubbard also circulated a flyer describing in pronouncedly antagonistic terms Fish's supposed role as a member of Dearborn's old Public Safety Commission back in the 1930s and later as an attorney filing suits against the city.

In the same flyer, Hubbard also inserted a note of praise from the vehemently antiadministration *Dearborn Press*—"He has the capacity and talents for doing a lot for Dearborn"—but, as the *Press* later pointed out, he omitted the rest of the quote: "if he only would." More representative of the *Press*'s actual sentiments was its exhortation to voters to "rid this city of the disgraceful machine that has made Dearborn the laughing stock of the country. . . . Yes, the entire country has learned of the disgrace that is ours, all based on the droolings and despicable actions of the city's mayor."[8]

Despite the rhetoric, however, there was only one issue of substance raised in the preprimary posturing, and it was instigated not by one of the so-called major candidates but by Hollman. The week before the election, Hollman charged, "Never in the history of Dearborn have the gambling and criminal elements been so free to operate as they have at the present time." Although Hubbard's supposed links to gamblers had been the subject of speculation before, Hollman's allegation, contained in a letter to the *Press*, was noteworthy simply because of the man's own background.[9] Hollman claimed he had learned while working on the prosecutor's staff in 1941, when Orvie was first elected, that the "gangster element at that time contributed $6,000 to the Hubbard campaign, and subsequent to that time they had continued to finance his campaign." He also suggested that Guy, in the prelude to the campaign, had been "forced to resign" as police chief (he had quit to run for judge) because criminals were being given police protection. Hollman's motivations may have been sincere enough, but there was ample evidence that police under Guy had been trying to stamp out gambling with some vigor. In July 1948, the newly appointed Guy had asked for a grand jury investigation of gambling at the Rouge plant.[10] He said he himself had been offered a $100 bribe the week before by a low-level union man to protect numbers operators at the plant. Although police continued to pursue the problem, most arrests were strictly small beer—pool and card games in south-end clubs, penny-ante gambling in parks, bet slips confiscated in raids.

At the time Hollman's accusations appeared in the *Press*, neither Hubbard nor Guy was quoted in rebuttal, nor was any corroborative evidence presented. Orvie promptly filed a $50,000 suit for libel against Hollman and the *Press*. H. William Klamser, coowner of the paper, responded by calling the move "just a political stunt" by Hubbard. "After all," he told reporters, "I don't know how you could possibly libel a politician anyhow."

The next day, Fish filed suit against Hubbard, demanding $100,000 for the alleged libels contained in the election circular the mayor had distributed. Perhaps Hubbard felt he had too many skirmishes brewing, and he dropped his suit.

Guy pursued the matter, however. He was denied a warrant against the *Press*, but Judge George Martin agreed to hear the charges against Hollman in Municipal Court in December. During the trial, Lieutenant Edward Mealy, head of the vice squad, testified that Guy, Hubbard and Public Safety Director Howard Ternes had ordered him to "stop all gambling in Dearborn."[11] Though Hollman never took the stand, Martin dismissed the case, saying, "There is no doubt that the statements were exaggerated, [but] they were made during a political campaign, and the public expects this sort of thing and takes it with their tongue in their cheek." A peculiar ruling—except perhaps in the context of Dearborn politics.

All the fireworks brought voters out in record numbers for the primary a week later, and the results were easy to analyze. Nobody believed Hollman or had much faith in any of the others. Far ahead was Hubbard with 12,041 votes to only 5,284 for the runner-up, Matheny. Eliminated from the final were Rouse, 3,599; Thomson, 514; Hollman, 421; Wierimaa, 205; and Bartsch, 156. In the council race, the incumbents took the top seven spots. Hubbard slaters Joe Ford and Marguerite Johnson finished first and second, with Martin Griffith fourth. In the precinct breakdown, Hubbard scored even better than usual in the east end. He took more than 80 percent of the vote in many precincts, swamping his closest rivals by such marks as 130 to 5 and 308 to 21. All told, he won 40 of 52 precincts, with the other 12, all in the west end, going to Matheny.

Hubbard called the result "just a reward for efficient public service." Matheny, content simply to have made it through the primary, said, "We have conducted a clean campaign in terms of vital issues, free from cheap bickering and name calling." Matheny also signaled that he was breaking from his policy of shunning help from organized groups. And, indeed, Doyle, Hollman and Wierimaa announced they would try to consolidate all the anti-Hubbard forces in town behind him.

Matheny spent the weeks before the November 8 election on good-government issues—chuckholes in city-owned parking lots, neglect of weeds and parkways, the possible use of city funds in surfacing a private lot. And he criticized extravagant spending, pointing out that it cost Dearborn four times as much to run the city on a per-capita basis as, for instance, it did Grand Rapids, with twice the population and half the budget.

And the rest of the opposition focused more sharply against Hubbard. Beadle spoke at a rally about the "pop-off mayor," whom the *Press* credited with having one of the most powerful political machines in the state and trying to build an organization to "make the late Huey Long look like a piker." A former councilman and police chief, Joseph Schaefer, complained that the mayor was sending out postcards erroneously suggesting that Schaefer endorsed his candidacy.

And while Matheny pledged to be "fair and impartial—playing no favorites," Orvie sent out a circular accusing the "scheming Detroit lawyer" of hiring "skidrow bums" to peddle "vicious smear sheets."

We called him "Masheeny," and, jeez, that bothered his ass, I found out later. He was a four-flushing guy. No one ever saw him. He was rolling this goddamn Masonic bullshit all over town, and the Catholics didn't like that, and he lost, the dumb bastard. He thought everyone in town was against us, I'm sure. He thought he was going to make it in '49. The first time we ran as a slate was '49, too. Up to that point, we'd print the names on our list that had my name on it and say, "This is not a slate, but these qualified candidates arranged this meeting at their joint expense so that you may hear a few campaign issues." That was so dumb. Since we've run strictly as a team, as "Elect the Hubbard Team," we've been very successful.

Successful, indeed. Although he failed to get his charter amendment on the dual public payroll through, the rest of the results were a decisive vindication of the Hubbard machine. With a record turnout of nearly two-thirds of the registered voters, Hubbard scored 16,499 votes to 12,696 for Matheny. He took 38 precincts, including the whole east end. Matheny swept 17 precincts in the west end and the upscale Ford Foundation, where he trounced Hubbard by a margin of 579 to 66.

Just as important, Hubbard carried in the three incumbent councilmen on his slate—Ford, Griffith and Johnson—with Ford and Johnson finishing first and second. Filling out the council were three Hubbard-slate newcomers—George Bondie, Lucille McCollough and Edward J. Dombrowski—plus Pat Doyle. Beadle, Parker and Smith all finished out of the running, and suddenly Orville Hubbard commanded an overwhelming six-to-one margin on the council. The only losers on the Hubbard team were James Christie Jr., a council candidate, and Ralph Guy, who was swamped in his attempt to unseat the incumbent municipal judges, George Belding and George Martin. Martin led the entire ballot with 19,361 votes.

The mayor, in a typically somber postelection statement, said, "I am very pleased at the results and deeply appreciate the continued confidence of the voters. I accept that vote as a mandate to work all the harder."

Matheny offered his congratulations to the victor but warned that the campaign to improve the efficiency of Dearborn city government was far from over.

Within three minutes after the polls closed, Ralph Guy was sworn in as police chief, barely two months after he had resigned the post to run for judge.[12]

21

The Divorce Suits, 1949, 1953

> There is something far greater and of a more lasting
> quality than mere temporary pleasures, especially those
> which are of a sensual nature, and which will lead only
> to unhappiness in the final analysis.
> —Orville L. Hubbard, from a cross bill to his wife's 1949
> divorce suit[1]

It hadn't taken Fay Hubbard very long after her marriage to discover that her new husband wasn't much of a homebody. To be sure, Orville tried to find time for her and the kids during their early years together, but law school and his increasing involvement in politics during the 1930s made it clear that his major interests lay outside the home. Then, when he finally got into city hall, he had even less time for the family.

For, say what you would about Orville Hubbard, he never shorted the city any time or energy. His days were devoted to his job—or, perhaps more accurately, to his own entrenchment—and many of his evenings were given over to meetings and classes in a variety of subjects that caught his fancy. Clearly, Fay had taken nearly all the responsibility of raising the family—subject, of course, to the same kinds of erratic tantrums her husband displayed in his public life.

By 1949, when Orville Hubbard was feeling some of the most intense criticism he had yet experienced in office, his relationship with his family was edgy, too. The two oldest boys, Jim, 20, and Frank, 19, had been only too happy to get out of the house and join the Marines, partly at the behest of their father. Still at home were the other three—Nancy Anne, 16; John, 14; and Henry, 6. But most Dearbornites didn't know much about the Hubbards' home life beyond what Orville chose to include in his periodic volleys of campaign literature.

All that changed in April 1949, when Fay Velma Cameron Hubbard filed a divorce suit in Wayne Circuit Court. The suit, seeking separate maintenance, alleged that her 240-pound husband was "subject to violent outbursts of unrestrained rage, which as time passed became more frequent," and that he beat her because he thought she was telling the neighbors about their problems.[2]

Since their marriage, Mrs. Hubbard said, she had devoted her life to raising their children—who "lived in fear of [their father's] displeasure"— and received her "only real joy" from them. The mayor's behavior caused her to "suffer severe nervous disorders and impairment of health." Things started getting worse, according to Mrs. Hubbard, when the mayor insisted on bringing home his secretary, whom she did not name but who was widely known to be Helen Bell, 25. Bell paid the Hubbards $10 a week for a room, and that, said Fay Hubbard, was the only money her husband let her handle. Beyond all that, Mrs. Hubbard alleged that Orville seldom took her out, he objected to her associating with friends and relatives, and he often beat and cursed her in front of others. Once, she charged, he beat and kicked her so badly she had to stay home for three weeks; another time, he punched her in the face, ribs, abdomen and arm. Three days after that, while Orville was away on a trip, she left. Had she stayed, she said, she was afraid he might "permanently injure and/or kill her."

At the request of her attorney, Veno E. Sacre, Judge George B. Murphy issued a restraining order to keep the mayor from moving or disposing of any property or assets. Asked for comment, Orville told reporters that "this all comes as a surprise to me" and insisted that Fay was still living at home.

Many of those who heard Fay Hubbard's sensational allegations undoubtedly believed there was something physical between the mayor and his secretary, though it later became clear that Mrs. Hubbard's bill of complaint alleged no such thing. Bell had moved from her stepfather's home soon after her mother died in 1947, and for much of the time after that she lived at the Hubbard home, sleeping in Nancy's room while Nancy moved in with her younger brothers. Mrs. Hubbard complained that Bell had been brought in "to spy on the family," not to engage in any affair with the mayor.

The next month, Hubbard filed his answer. He denied "emphatically" and "item by item" the charges that he beat his wife. He denied being subject "to violent, unrestrained rage of a progressive nature" or that he often "returned home in a belligerent mood." He suggested that it was actually his wife's idea to have Bell live in and that, far from stifling his wife's spending habits, he had "always given this Plaintiff an adequate allowance and provided her with better than the average standard of living, and her department store charge accounts alone in 1948 totaled $1,202.95." To these denials he also added an allegation of his own: that his wife's suit actually stemmed from her "interest" in a "scheming Detroit widower" for whom she had "deserted her home, her family, her children and her husband." She had told him, he said, that she wanted to marry the widower, who had "'apartment houses' and 'lots of money' and that she would not have to be 'bothered with any kids.'"[3] And despite the fact that he was "considerably

hurt when he learned within the past six months of the shameful misconduct of this Plaintiff," he asked the judge to instruct his wife that "her duty
lies at home with her family and her husband, who has always placed his
wife and family foremost and will continue to do so."

In June, Fay Hubbard replied to the cross bill. She denied living with
any widower; in fact, she was living with her mother, Mrs. George Sebert,
in Wayne. And she elaborated on Orville's physical abuse. She said he had
beaten her several times in front of the children; that he had "used his
blackjack" on everyone in the family except young Henry; and that she
feared "if given a chance he will permanently injure or kill" her.[4] At any
rate, she wished no future with Orville Hubbard "as his wife, his maid or
his punching bag."

Later in the month, Hubbard's attorney, Edward S. Piggins, requested a
change of venue. As a member of the Wayne County Board of Supervisors,
the mayor often had criticized the circuit bench and voted against salary
raises for judges, it was explained. Judge Ira W. Jayne denied the request,
saying he was "shocked" that the mayor "assumed for others that [which]
he apparently feels for himself—that a judge can't sit objectively disregarding
either sympathy or prejudice."

In the meantime, Fay Hubbard seemed content to stay away from the
house. She had filed a request for $70 to $75 a week in living expenses,
even though her husband's salary was only $125 a week. And she announced
that she would stay away unless Helen Bell left, Orville paid all household
expenses, and Orville himself either left or allowed her to bring in a woman
companion of her own choosing.

By late July, though, there seemed to be some movement. Fay, who had
taken a $20-a-week housekeeper's job and agreed to only $15 a week in
alimony, told reporters she would come home as soon as Bell left. "That is
the best place to care for the children," she said. "I am continuing to seek
my divorce. This is no reconciliation." The arrangement was fine with Orville.
"The latchstring has been out since she left," he declared. A few days later,
he was calling the papers to announce a reconciliation. It wasn't quite that
simple, however. Fay continued to stay away.

Not until May 1950 did the couple finally get together. The two met
for nearly two hours in the chambers of Judge John V. Brennan, one of the
mayor's old law school professors. Afterward, the judge mounted the bench
and announced that the suit was being dismissed on the grounds of con-
donation—Fay Hubbard had forgiven the acts she previously alleged. At
that point, an obviously dismayed Mrs. Sebert, who had always been hostile
toward her son-in-law, was overheard remarking to her daughter, "What
kind of dumbbell are you?" The two Hubbards left the downtown courtroom separately and unsmilingly. The mayor said only, "My wife and I have
decided not to make any comment whatever." The following November, the
records of the case were expunged.

176

In those times, people looked at things differently than they do now. Goddamn kids on the street hollering, "Mayor's wife sues for divorce. Extree." It bothered me. I remember the kids were all down there, and her mother said, "Well, I hope she's got enough sense to leave him." We had that constant problem. I was mad at the time, but as years go by, I didn't pay much attention to it. I went to the old lady's funeral. But these things don't add too much to domestic tranquility.

Although some of his political opponents made great sport of Orville Hubbard's marital difficulties in subsequent campaigns, his private life generally stayed out of the papers until Fay filed a second divorce suit in March 1953. At that time, a complaint filed for her by attorney Kurt J. Kremlick alleged that Orville had subjected both her and the children to mental and physical cruelty going back to his first successful election in 1941:

> [He] has assumed and practiced dictatorial control and dominion over . . . the household . . . and has been ruthless and tyrannical in his demands and orders. . . . When unable to accomplish his plans and desires politically . . . and was otherwise thwarted, . . . when home [he] would wreak his vengeance . . . by having prolonged spasms of wrath and cursing. . . . [He] has constantly verbally excoriated Plaintiff and the children [with] despicable, loathful, sinful and disgusting words. . . .[He] remains cold, cool and calculating, living in his own political world, and directing his life to the achievement of greater political power. . . .[He] has been anti-social with the family, . . . sometimes refusing to converse with anyone, but at all times domineering the home life by his autocratic methods. . . . In carrying out his bullying propensities [he] has threatened members of his family, including the Plaintiff, with physical harm and injury and other forms of retaliation and on more than one occasion has carried his threats into execution on the Plaintiff by punching her and hitting her, causing Plaintiff physical injury.[5]

In addition, Mrs. Hubbard accused her husband of breaking promises he made at the time of their earlier reconciliation, when, she said, he vowed "to mend his ways and to conduct himself as a normal person in his marriage relationship." Instead, she complained, he went back to his old ways, "but with manifested aggravated fury . . . [making] scathing rebukes . . . about her household duties, and her failure to be home at all times to suit the convenience of the Defendant." Once, she said, he broke some dishes and threatened to break other objects. His conduct made her friends afraid to visit, cutting her off from "the normal social contacts incident to living." And instead of giving her a reasonable amount of money to live on, he simply turned over an occasional $15 or $20 that he collected weekly in room and board from two of the children, even though he made her pay for her own expenses and forbade her to use his charge accounts. Lastly, she alleged, although he had demanded that she file for a Mexican divorce, he "threatened further physical violence" if she took the matter to a domestic court. Since four of the five Hubbard children were over 18, Fay was seeking custody only of the youngest, Henry, now 10.

The afternoon following the filing, Fay Hubbard told the *Detroit News*, "Either he moves out of the house or I do. I can't take any more. He is a devil to live with. All he is interested in is politics. He is a fanatic on schooling. He goes to school four nights a week studying rocks when he should be home studying family life."[6]

But that evening, something apparently happened. Suddenly, in a letter to Kremlick, she said she wanted the suit dropped and her $100 retainer returned. Kremlick, she told reporters, "wrote up the papers too fast, added a lot of lawyer talk and wrote up several untrue statements."

She come home—my daughter was there—and she said to me, "I got an injunction against you." I said, "You got a what against me? What are you gonna do with it?" And I knocked her around on her ass. That settled a couple of things, too. She didn't start any fucking more divorce [suits] against me. Shock treatment, you know. I never went through the divorce business. I never subscribed to that crap. Today it seems to be kind of a common thing for most people to do it.

22

Prelude to Recall, 1950

Chief, I want you to take a goddamn ax and . . . break
the doors down, take pictures, and raise hell there.
—Orville L. Hubbard, as quoted by Fire Chief Stanley
Herdzik[1]

Orville Hubbard had never been overly concerned about appearances. That much was clear from his ranting and endless publicity gimmicks. But by early 1950, in the middle of his marital problems and rumors that his enemies were about to launch a campaign to recall him from office, Dearborn's mayor began to exhibit behavior that qualified as bizarre even by his own lofty standards. Take, for example, his strange directive to Fire Chief Stanley Herdzik one evening in early January.

Herdzik, of course, had become used to carrying out extraordinary orders from Hubbard ever since the mayor had named him to succeed the embattled Roy Mottesheard in 1946. Having to dispatch a crew to wash down the streets in the early-morning hours had been just one incident among many. But finally, Herdzik got an order that even he was unwilling to carry out. As Herdzik explained it later, he was to go to Ford Motor headquarters and, accompanied by a city photographer, conduct a fire inspection of the premises. But he was to carry it off with a certain Hubbardian panache, by entering unannounced and chopping down the door leading to the office of Henry Ford II. According to statements later sworn to by Herdzik, Hubbard phoned the chief at home about 11:00 P.M., raving and swearing, and ordered him to embarrass Ford. "Chief," Herdzik said the mayor told him, "I want you to take a goddamn ax and go to the southwest corner of the Administration Building and break the doors down, take pictures, and raise hell there."[2]

During the next two weeks, according to Herdzik, Hubbard kept insisting he "find something wrong" at Ford's. "You are not cooperating with me," Orvie said angrily. "I want to put Ford Motor in headlines. What in the hell is the matter with you?" Herdzik continued to balk, pointing out later to reporters, "I knew the company was cooperating in every way," having spent some $100,000 on sprinklers. Why had the mayor given such an order? Herdzik didn't say, although Orvie had missed few chances to twit Ford's since the Hancock housing episode two years before, and everybody knew he was still bitter about it.

Hubbard, intolerant as ever of insubordination, relieved Herdzik of his official driver and ordered the department phone at the chief's home disconnected. Then he demanded Herdzik resign or take a demotion back to captain. Herdzik demurred, since he was 10 months shy of eligibility for his 25-year pension. A few days later, however, he submitted his written resignation and contacted the newspapers with the story.

He also tried to damage Hubbard by resurrecting old charges about kickbacks. During his tenure, he said, he and other department heads had been required to make a variety of payoffs. The first time was in January 1947, about six months after he made chief, when Hubbard summoned several of them to take care of their "share." As Herdzik described it, "I asked how much it was and was handed a letter by Hubbard which had the figure $973 typed on it. I was overwhelmed when I saw the figure and asked Hubbard if this was the regular procedure. He told me it was."[3] A couple of weeks later, he said, he was called to the mayor's office, where Helen Bell gave him the bill for $973—for thimbles and sewing kits to be distributed in Hubbard's 1947 campaign. As instructed, he banked the money and was given a cashier's check payable to a New York company.

Besides the $973, Herdzik said he also incurred a number of other financial obligations on the job. At various times, Hubbard ordered him to turn over $100 to Marguerite Johnson for her congressional campaign; $1,000 to the *Dearborn Guide*; $40 each to Councilmen Johnson, Martin Griffith and Joe Ford, on two separate occasions; $24 to some boys who had distributed political handbills; and, after drawing lots with other department heads, $10.30 to a florist. According to Herdzik, he paid all the bills except the *Guide*'s; he couldn't afford that one, he said. In addition to tattling about the payouts, the chief also told of campaigning he was required to do—circulating petitions, checking polling places and passing out literature on election day in uniform.

Hubbard was incensed at the turn of events, even though he had as much as admitted taking kickbacks from his appointees when Howard Hill made similar allegations in 1947.[4] This time, while not directly denying what Herdzik said, he declared that the chief had never contributed "a penny, dime or dollar to me in any political campaign; as to what political contributions Herdzik may have made to other people, I have no knowledge." Neither did Hubbard respond directly to the charge about trying to stir up a commotion at Ford's.[5] What he did say was that Herdzik "admitted that he never made an inspection of the fire conditions at Ford Motor in the 24 years he has been on the Fire Department." Later, he became a bit more expansive with *Press* columnist Lewis J. Betts, shouting into the phone that the allegations were a pack of lies and that Herdzik was the worst fire chief Dearborn ever had.[6] Herdzik said he had made "numerous" inspections at Ford's, and company records showed he had made 12 the previous year alone. Ford officials also said they had spent nearly $600,000 on fire prevention measures recommended by Herdzik.

Jesus Christ, he was the biggest headache we ever did have over here. That Polack asshole. All he did, he kept figuring how much his pension was going to be. He would call me every day. His wife would call me all the time. I said to him one day, "The next time your goddamn wife calls me on the P.A. on anything about you or the Fire Department, you consider the fact she makes the call your resignation, period." And I chased his ass out of the office. But break down a door at Ford's? I never said a thing like that in my life. He's full of shit right up to his asshole. He's just a goddamn liar is all.

A few weeks later, in February, Herdzik got in a few more licks. In a letter to the *Press*, he railed on about Orvie's "dirty personal treatment of me" and chided the mayor as a "dictator" of "childish mental stature." He also repeated an earlier charge that Hubbard, irked at Herdzik's plans to build a new house, "told my wife to get our things packed and take our 'brats' and get the hell out of the city." His letter said: "Self respect demanded that I leave [the Fire Department] or completely subject myself to the insatiable demands of an immature mind which seems to be filled with nothing but greed and hate. . . . No, the Mayor is not going to run my wife or me out of town. We are going to stay here and use every means and device that is ethical to expose his undemocratic and un-American Administration.[7]

Even though Herdzik was no longer with the city, however, Hubbard was not willing to let things end on that note. As a member of the city's pension board, Orvie still had an element of leverage over the 45-year-old fireman. With a hearing due on Herdzik's pension application, the mayor told reporters, "I've never yet voted for a pension for any man under 50 years old." However, after City Attorney Dale Fillmore ruled that the chief was eligible despite failing to reach 25 years' service, Hubbard was outvoted. After weeks of stalling by the controller's office, Herdzik eventually got his pension. So the Herdzik affair was over, but Orvie soon managed to disgrace himself on an entirely different issue.

Although he had finally given up his quest for a city-owned hospital the year before, he was still trying to dictate the makeup of the proposed private Oakwood Hospital. He wanted the building code amended to force the $4.5-million hospital to include an outpatient clinic. The hospital trustees were on record as opposing such a clinic, however, and there were fears that they might decide not to locate in Dearborn after all. Hubbard responded with a warning: "They better not attempt to build the hospital anywhere else, because if I am around, they will go to the jug, and it will not be a brown one, nor will it have a cork in it." A good line, perhaps, though obviously an empty threat. And it did not obscure the fact that Orvie himself was the one jeopardizing the go-ahead for Oakwood.

In early February, the Dearborn Citizens League held a "save our hospital" rally at Fordson High School, and some 800 residents turned out to protest Hubbard's interference. The meeting ended when the group's chairman, attorney John T. McWilliams, exhorted, "To arms, Dearborn. Save your hospital." That is, the meeting would have ended if Orvie had not been there with a corps of department heads and other city employees. Hubbard rose and demanded a chance to present his side. But McWilliams brushed him off, saying, "If you want to hold a meeting, go out and rent yourself a hall like I did." At this, the mayor rushed up the steps at one end of the stage, Police Chief Ralph B. Guy ascended from the other, and the two converged on McWilliams. While Hubbard argued angrily, Guy wrestled for the microphone, and McWilliams, outmatched, left the stage. Then the mayor tried to speak over a barrage of catcalls mixed with a few cheers from his entourage. Finally, he gestured toward a group of vociferous attendees at the rear and shouted, "Throw them the hell out of here." Up jumped three of Hubbard's lieutenants, one of them his son Frank, 19. But when they tried to get at one of the anti-Hubbard agitators, Police Lieutenant Edward Mealy intervened, threatening to "flatten the first man who swings." On the stage, while the mayor was ripping down several "Save Our Hospital" placards, Guy was having trouble with a 17-year-old boy. As the youth attempted to disconnect the public address system, the chief, according to one account, grabbed him, twisted his arm behind his back and told him to "get the hell out of here or I will get you good." With the electrical power thus maintained, Hubbard spoke briefly to what was left of the audience, then gave up. But, as the *Dearborn Press* observed huffily, it was "a mockery of good citizenship" that stood as "one of the most shameful exhibitions ever staged before the public by a police chief and a mayor."[8]

Ironically, the hospital controversy ended abruptly the next Tuesday, when Hubbard withdrew his objections to Oakwood before an overflow crowd of 1,500 at a council meeting. "Even the Supreme Court recognizes election trends," he conceded.

But the incident made a lasting impression. Dearbornites were starting to look at Hubbard and see a reincarnation of Hitler or Louisiana's Huey Long. One resident, Henry H. Webster, identifying himself as "an average taxpayer" in a letter to the *Press*, cited the hospital debacle and a number of edicts Orvie had attempted to impose on the city building code—no more one-story homes, no more cement block homes, no more metal awnings— and he compared them to:

Events of a few short years ago, when [a] "putsch" of a Munich beer hall was passed over lightly by a passive public. . . . It has become the ruling of a city by the personal likes and dislikes of one individual who has surrounded himself, at the taxpayers' expense, with a la Herr Himler and Goering. . . . [Not since Huey Long] has there appeared on the American scene such a threat to our fundamental principles.[9]

It wasn't long after this that Hubbard found himself beleaguered by more than just a few letters to the newspapers.

23

The Libel Trial, 1950

> He is making your otherwise splendid community the
> laughing stock of the nation with his idiotic establish-
> ment in Windsor of a "government in exile."
> —A *Detroit Free Press* commentary on Orville L. Hubbard[1]

For years, Orvie had been calling his opponents the vilest of names and
getting away with it. But in 1950, he discovered he had picked a target who
would hold him to account for his habit.

John J. Fish long had been regarded as one of the most astute and
most reputable lawyers in Dearborn. He was also a man with a keen sense
of civic duty. As a member of the city's old safety commission, Fish, a slender,
dapper-looking man with a thin mustache and an appreciation for good
cigars, had helped focus the Ferguson grand jury on Dearborn when he
and two other commissioners resigned in 1940. The next year, he led the
fight for the new strong-mayor charter to help insulate the city against
further scandal.

A casual friend of Fish's in his premayoral years, Orville Hubbard tried
unsuccessfully during his first year in office to persuade the attorney to take
the job of corporation counsel. After that, as Hubbard began to assert his
authority into more and more areas of government, the two began to drift
apart.

Fish filed some two dozen lawsuits against the city during Hubbard's
first seven years in office—suits to force the city to pay employee wage
increases over Hubbard's protests, suits to require issuance of building permits denied by Hubbard, suits to compel the city to put money into employee
pension funds that Hubbard had tried to reduce, suits to force Hubbard to
backtrack on a budget transfer meant to look like a large tax reduction.
Fish's victories over the Hubbard administration so enraged the mayor that
he began the peculiar procedure of inserting Fish's name into various veto

messages to the City Council. Most of the references, needless to say, were hardly complimentary.

In December 1948, Hubbard had attacked council foe Homer Beadle for his role in passing a Civil Service claim by two city employees represented by Fish. While concentrating on Beadle, the mayor also gratuitously appended a mention of Fish by the French version of his name, "John J. Poisson."

In September 1949, about the time Fish began circulating the "Hitler, Hague and Hubbard" slogan that had pepped up the 1949 campaign, Orvie stepped up the attack. He vetoed a council resolution engaging Fish to investigate the "Sunken Heights" housing controversy, which had stirred up resentment against the mayor and his building department. Hubbard, noting that Fish was campaign manager for Beadle and Councilman Patrick Doyle, said he was vetoing the resolution:

> 1. Because it appears more like a payoff to John J. Fish, also known as John J. Poisson . . . and, 2. Because Fish is continually trying to get money out of the taxpayers, and has sued the city about 20 times in the past few years; and, 3. Because Fish has at various stages of some cases represented adverse interests involving city litigations; and, 4. Because . . . this Council . . . certainly could select out of the more than 4,000 lawyers in this area one whose operations do not create the impression that he is of the ambulance chasing variety.[2]

Libelous? Perhaps, although Hubbard was not worried about the legal implications. His corporation counsel, Dale H. Fillmore, had told him informally that veto messages were qualifiedly privileged—immune—from libel actions.

Hubbard heard no repercussions from Fish about the veto message, so it undoubtedly seemed a small step from that to a political handbill the mayor was preparing for last-minute distribution before the September primary election.[3] The flyer looked at first like most of his others. It was filled with the old, familiar phrases: "Forward, Dearborn! For Progress and Good Public Service. Stand by the Man Who Stands by You. Re-Elect your Un-Bossed Mayor." It included the old Horatio Alger-style biography of Hubbard, tracing his rise from the farm and factory. It praised him for keeping the city "clean from vice, graft and corruption." But the other side of the handbill was something new, even for Orvie. It contained a murky, ominous-sounding chronology of alleged misdoings and schemes perpetrated by Beadle and Doyle, along with Victor Rouse, Hubbard's most vocal mayoral opponent, and two "civilians." One was Lillian Kotts, the secretary for an anti-Hubbard citizens' committee. The other was John J. Fish.

Fish was always a money guy, a sort of a semi-wheeler-dealer. At least I thought he was. John and I used to be good friends, too, for years. But he was always trying to be the hero somewhere on the other side of the fence. Fish once said he never voted for me in his life. Maybe that's true, but I supported him for justice of the peace in 1939, to show you what an ingrate he was. He was an able fellow, but he didn't like me. Back in 1949, he came out with some stickers that said, "Hitler, Hague and Hubbard." They were handing 'em out to people. Fish did that, the son of a bitch. I went to work on him. I gave it back to him—a little strong—and he got real upset about it. Fish was dishing it out. He couldn't take it, though.

The Hubbard handbill began with two passages headlined, *"LILLIAN KOTTS EXPOSED AS 'POLITICAL STOOGE' IN SMEAR PLOT FOR BEADLE-DOYLE-FISH-ROUSE!"* and *"SUNKEN HEIGHTS."* The circular vilified Kotts as part of a scheme to discredit Hubbard. It concluded, "She is just a tool and stooge for Beadle, Doyle and Rouse, who cowardly hide behind her skirts in carrying out their 'yellow' smear plot."[4]

Then, under the headline *"LAWYER JOHN FISH EXPOSED AS JOHN POISSON,"* the handbill continued:

> And just a shadow further behind her skirts is lawyer John Fish, whose real name is John Poisson. Fish fronted for the $15,000,000.00 John Hancock row-housing project last year. Fish, alias Poisson, was chairman of the old Safety Commission, which ran the police department when corruption was in full bloom here and blossomed into Dearborn's biggest and blackest police and vice scandal. Fish resigned when things got hot, and the Ferguson graft grand jury indicted the Chief of Police.

Another section, headed *"FISHY CLAIMS,"* described sketchily Fish's record of lawsuits against the city:

> Fish, alias Poisson, is continually trying to get money out of the taxpay-ers. He has sued your city about 20 times since I have been Mayor. Nearly everytime Fish files a claim against the city, Beadle and Doyle try to "out do" each other in offering him a settlement with your money, a move which too often smells like a payoff. Sometimes when the city attorney, Dale H. Fillmore, advises against and vigorously objects to such raw action, the boss of the "Big-4 Councilmen" just railroads through a settlement. Action of this nature has been so rotten that the Council even settled one case with Fish after Mr. Fillmore won it in the Circuit Court.

Continuing under the heading *"CHARITY JOHN,"* the handbill alleged, "And you can be sure that 'Charity John' got his cut. Beadle and Doyle who boss the 'Big-4 on the Council' always vote to 'cut Fish in' for a slice of the taxpayers' money." The handbill then shifted to the city's checkered school consolidation history, under the heading *"SCHOOL SHENANIGANS"*:

> The Beadle-Fish gang have been trying to capture your City Hall ever since they were caught up with on the Fordson School Board and flushed out of the school system, which they were fast turning into a political mess. For years, Beadle and Fish fought against school consolidation, and it was mostly through their high-handed shenanigans that Dearborn school children were denied equal educational facilities and opportunities.

Finally, in a grand climax headed *"POLITICAL PIRATES,"* the handbill concluded, "If this Beadle mob captures the Mayor's office, may God help Dearborn because no one else can!!"

For a man like Hubbard, as fussy and meticulous as he could be about the written word, the handbill was a real exercise in rationalization, depending heavily on implication and puns. But he believed it. He believed it all.

> *I wrote that leaflet, and to my best belief and knowledge, my honest belief in my head, we didn't say one word that wasn't true in there, though we did say it in a strong fashion, rather strong language. What we said was correct. It was positive. It was accurate. We checked everything. And we subpoenaed Fish's records. Big, strong John Fish sued the mayor. It made his business. It made him. He had no damages under it. A lot of the lawyers said to me, "Hurt me like you did Fish, will you?" Shit. The son of a bitch. He wasn't entitled to a dime.*

The handbills began appearing door to door in late September, and Fish quickly fired off the requisite demand for a retraction as a preliminary to filing a libel suit. The letter, dated and stamped as received by the mayor two days later, said, "In your desperation you have again transcended the bounds of propriety and have proven yourself ethically unfit to occupy the office of mayor or to be a member of the legal profession. . . . Do you dare meet me in fair debate, or are you the yellow, slinking coward I believe you to be?"[5]

The same day, Fish wrote the local papers, announcing that he had filed a $100,000 libel suit in Wayne Circuit Court:

> Hubbard's vicious and false attack upon me, contained in "hit and run" literature distributed under cover of darkness, is an indication of the desperate plight of this two-bit politician. . . .
>
> I challenge this un-bossed Caesar to ask the Bar Association to investigate the both of us. . . . He fears any investigation. I predict that after he leaves office in January, an investigation will reveal shocking conditions. I say to you, Orvie, as a former friend, ask the Good Lord to

straighten out your twisted moral sense and to guide your feet along the path of decency and square-dealing.[6]

Hubbard ignored Fish's correspondence, and a few weeks later, in mid-October, Fish filed a court declaration requesting a judgment of $100,000, plus costs and attorney's fees. The mayor's answer was that even though Fish had not himself been a candidate for office in the 1949 election, his antagonist's activity in politics made him a public figure. The statements in the handbill, the mayor contended, were "made under the qualified privilege of the defendant, the matter involving a public concern and interest."

Finally, on the morning of April 4, the Hubbard-Fish libel trial got under way before Circuit Judge Clyde I. Webster, hearing the case without a jury. Hubbard was first to testify, and after some fencing, Fish's attorney, Chris M. Youngjohn, began pinning the mayor down about Exhibit 1, the handbill.[7]

After Hubbard admitted composing, in a day or so, all the material in the circular, he then explained why he continued to harp on the fact that Fish's name originally was Poisson, or, as the mayor at first pronounced it, "Poison": "I did it so that it would be known that his name was originally not John Fish. . . . I think because of his activities in the campaign." Hubbard explained that he had used the "Poisson" reference in several veto messages to the council. "I never had any objections from John or anyone else about using the name before," he testified. "He never protested. As a matter of fact, it is more or less common knowledge among those who knew him intimately that his name is 'Poisson.'" Even so, the mayor added, he conscientiously endeavored to substantiate the fact before publishing the handbill. Two years before, in 1947, he had sent Dale Fillmore to Houghton, in Michigan's Upper Peninsula, where Fish's family had settled. Fillmore, he explained, returned with a birth certificate and other documents that bore out the Fish-Poisson identification.

Youngjohn next pursued the most damaging allegations in the handbill: that his client was somehow connected with the Dearborn police scandal that brought in the Ferguson grand jury.

Youngjohn: "Did you mean to imply in any way that Mr. Fish was guilty of any corruption and vice in connection with his membership on the Safety Commission?"

Hubbard: "I did not."

Youngjohn: "Have you any proof whatsoever that Mr. Fish was guilty of one wrongful act involving corruption while he was on the Safety Commission?"

Hubbard: "I have no proofs, no."

Youngjohn: "Did you investigate Mr. Fish for the purpose of trying to uncover proof of corruption?"

Hubbard: "No."

Youngjohn: "... Then why did you put these words together in this way?"

Hubbard: "Because I have always felt, and my recollection is I told John, that he lacked the courage to do the job when he had the power to do it."

Youngjohn: "Don't you know, as a matter of fact, that John Fish, from the moment he became a member of that commission, fought that police department with everything that he had?"

Hubbard: "He just fought the air."

Youngjohn: "He fought the air?"

Hubbard: "That is right—publicity."

Youngjohn: "All right. Don't you know that Mr. Fish and two others resigned from the Safety Commission after they found they couldn't do anything from the inside, and then went to the Ferguson grand jury with the evidence they had?"

Hubbard: "I thought they took a powder, because there are five members of the Safety Commission, and three constitute a majority, and the three that resigned had the power to act. Had they acted . . ."

Youngjohn (interrupting): "What did you mean by the words, 'Fish resigned when things got hot, and the Ferguson graft grand jury indicted the Chief of Police'? What did you mean by that?"

Hubbard: "What it says."

Youngjohn: "Just exactly what it says?"

Hubbard: "That is right."

Youngjohn: "Did you mean by that that things got too hot for Fish, and that he resigned to avoid indictment?"

Hubbard: "Oh, no, no, no, no! . . . I might say this if you want me to. I don't think John was a crook. I don't think he did any shady business at the time he was in the Safety Commission."

After Youngjohn noted that the grand jury investigation preceded the Hubbard administration, the attorney asked, "Let's come right down to brass tacks. You and John Fish were bitter enemies at the time you wrote this Exhibit 1, weren't you?"

Hubbard: "I have never been a bitter enemy. I am not now."

Youngjohn: "Are you friendly with him?"

Hubbard: "On my part I am. I have always been friendly to John."

Youngjohn: "You are a good friend to John Fish? . . . And you mean to tell us that you wrote this business on Exhibit 1 about a good friend of yours?"

Hubbard: "Well, he was opposing. If your friends oppose you. . . . Maybe a political enemy, but not otherwise an enemy."

Later, Hubbard conceded that he had told only his side in the circular, partly because he didn't have enough space for information that might have been favorable to Fish. "Usually during campaigns," he added, "you usually tell your side."

Proceeding to his allegations about "Fishy Claims," the mayor explained them this way: "I would say I didn't mean it was dishonest. . . . I didn't mean to convey the impression that he wasn't making an honest claim." In effect, the mayor added, it was a simple pun—claims by Fish were "Fishy Claims."

"Well," he responded to a demand for further explanation from Youngjohn, "sort of a figure of speech, at least mine in the city hall for a long time. When Fish had anything, we called them 'Fishy Claims.' . . . We felt they smelled sometimes."

In explaining what he meant by "Nearly everytime Fish files a claim against the city, Beadle and Doyle try to 'out do' each other in offering him a settlement with your money, a move which too often smells like a payoff," the mayor said, "When campaigns come along, that Fish helped out the boys financially and otherwise, and that was sort of a way of paying him back."

Hubbard enumerated some 25 cases involving Fish and the city, conceding that not all of them were begun by Fish and not all were for monetary damages. At the end of his morning testimony, he complained again about the space in his circular.

Hubbard: "I didn't have any space left. I had to cut down my message. I might be sued for $200,000 if I put everything in there that I had in mind."

Youngjohn: "I move we increase the damages to $200,000 because of the obvious malice shown here, your honor."

Judge Webster: "Motion denied. Two o'clock."

After taking the stand again, Orvie described the handbill distribution to about 18,000 homes and 4,000 apartments over a four-day period before the September city primary of 1949.

He also explained his use of the paragraph header "Charity John" by saying, "I think we intended to needle him."

Youngjohn: "With ridicule and contempt?"

Hubbard: "Well, not necessarily with contempt."

Youngjohn: "Ridicule?"

Hubbard: "A little ridicule, perhaps."

Orvie testified further about Fish's involvement in "school shenanigans." Fish had been school board attorney and opposed consolidation, he said. And, as for a reference to "political pirates," he said only that he did not mean it to be "heroic." He also defended using terms such as "gang" and "henchmen."

Following an afternoon recess, Youngjohn raised the subject of libel law in general: "Have you got the impression that just because you are mayor of Dearborn, you can say anything about anybody that you like?"

Hubbard: "After being mayor of Dearborn, you don't have any impressions about anything."

Youngjohn: ". . . Do you claim that you had a particular right to publish anything you saw fit about John Fish?"

Hubbard: ". . . We have no malice towards John. He injected himself into the campaign; and he can dish it out, but he didn't seem to be able to take it. . . . This is just mild as [compared] to what he said about us."

The next day, testimony continued, but the real news of the day was the formation of a citizens' committee to recall Hubbard from office, an event that had been rumored for months. Although there was no apparent connection between the recall and the libel suit, Hubbard's attorney, Francis K. Young, played up the angle when the trial picked up again the morning afterward. "We are here not really trying a legitimate or an honest libel and slander suit, but we are here trying a political issue in the city of Dearborn. It is quite obvious from the headlines of the two Detroit newspapers the timing of the matter perfectly to come right in the middle of the trial."

Though Fish himself might not be actively involved in the recall effort, he said, a partner of Fish's, later identified as Robert E. Wilcox, was a member of the recall corporation. Wilcox, according to later testimony, shared offices and expenses with Fish but was not a partner of his.

Judge Webster said he feared that subsequent testimony would be used in the recall fight. After a lunch recess, the trial picked up again with re-cross-examination of the mayor.

Youngjohn: "You intended to hurt Mr. Fish's feelings, didn't you?"

Hubbard: "Oh, no. This was a campaign. Mr. Fish was the leader of the opposition, and we felt the people were entitled to know of some of his activities, as much as I can relate on one side of that small sheet."

Youngjohn: "And you are not sorry now?"

Hubbard: "If I hurt his feelings, I am sorry."

Youngjohn: "Are you sorry now you published Exhibit 1?"

Hubbard: "No. It is the truth. Published the truth."

The trial eventually turned to the question of whether Orvie had had an opportunity to retract his statements in the circular, irrespective of whether he still stood on them. Young contended that Fish's demand for a retraction was sent September 24, 1949. But, he declared, the suit had already been filed and announced in the papers that day. Judge Webster agreed that Fish never really gave Hubbard a chance to consider retraction.

On the following Monday, the judge denied a motion by Young to adjourn the case "because of the current political turmoil in Dearborn." Young then introduced into evidence a number of documents, one a certified copy of Fish's birth certificate, to help establish the legitimacy of the "Poisson" references. Youngjohn called them all irrelevant. He in turn produced documents showing that Fish's father was named John D. Fish, along with diplomas, a baptismal certificate and other records to prove that the younger Fish went by the same surname.

Here Fish himself took the stand. Regarding his name, the attorney testified, "I know my father had a brother who went by the French version of the name 'Poisson,' but my father and I always have been Fish." Asked his first reaction to the handbill, Fish replied, "I was amazed and shocked. I felt sick. The charges were false, and I knew that Hubbard knew they were false." Fish also denied he had been involved in any "shady dealings," either as a school board member or as a member of the safety commission.

As testimony continued over the next few days, Hubbard showed signs of agitation. During a recess, he cursed out a *Dearborn Press* reporter-photographer, threatening to smash his camera and warning him that he'd be "taken care of" if he persisted in following the city entourage around.

Aside from the question of libel in the circular itself, Youngjohn also had to try to prove what effect it had on Fish. Was his client actually damaged, as he contended?

Three days later, Elwyn Wilcox, president of a Dearborn building firm, testified that he was given one of the pamphlets by a man who said, "Anyone with a record should get out of politics." Wilcox also said a business associate insisted that the handbill proved Fish should not be retained as the firm's attorney.

The next day, Leonora V. Baumgartner, wife of a brother-in-law of Fish's, testified that even she believed the pamphlet. "I thought Mr. Fish must be crooked or it wouldn't be printed," said Baumgartner, who did not know Fish well before the trial. "I took it for granted, he being mayor, that he would print the truth." She was especially impressed with the expression "Fishy Claims" and the reference to Fish's "alias" as "Poisson." "'Alias' sounded like gangsters," she testified.

Another witness, a process server named William F. Arnold, who called Hubbard "the hardest man I ever served with papers," testified that after trying to avoid service, the mayor disparaged Fish as "only a shyster and ambulance chaser."

When the trial picked up the following Monday, in mid-April, Fillmore was called as a witness for a second time. Before answering Youngjohn's questions, Fillmore repeatedly took time to refer to notes and to reflect on his words. The judge later criticized him for giving evasive and conflicting answers.

The subject of Fish's name came up the next Monday, when Young called City Controller James A. Hughes as his last witness. Hughes, as it turned out, had been sent to Fish's Upper Peninsula hometown of Chassell after Fillmore to dig up more evidence. Turning beet-red, he admitted he had tricked a parish priest out of a baptismal certificate by posing as "John Kelly, a very dear friend of the Fish family." After the judge called a recess, Hughes vanished, and the attorneys said he would not be recalled.

A few other odds and ends were wrapped up the next morning, and the judge announced he would render his verdict that afternoon, as if there were any doubts about his leanings. A few hours later, Hubbard, flanked by Fillmore and Ralph Guy Jr., got the bad news. As Webster read his judgment, Hubbard sat quietly and scowled darkly from time to time.

"It seems to me, after listening to all this testimony for about three weeks," Webster began, "that the plaintiff has substantiated practically every allegation . . ."

Hubbard had offered a variety of defenses—that Fish had provoked him, that everything he said was true and that, in any case, he had a "qualified privilege" to say it. Webster, however, would have none of it. The plea of provocation, he said, was not backed up by testimony. The plea of truth failed—badly, according to the judge—since the handbill contained "a few truths, some half-truths, and many untruths." And the plea of qualified privilege probably did not apply, although, he acknowledged, "there is no case quite like this where the privilege is claimed by an office-holder running for re-election, and as to one not an office-holder and not running for any election. . . ." Commented Webster:

"This is not a case of political wind, or political literature. The language used here in Exhibit 1 is full of libelous statements, statements that are libelous per se, statements that are scurrilous, insulting, damaging. . . . I believe it was thought up, designed, written and circulated by the defendant for the purpose of putting this man Fish out of business. He had annoyed him so, opposed him so many times, opposed so many of his measures, that I believe he deliberately got this exhibit up for the purpose of putting an end to Fish.

"This article is all the more libelous, all the more damaging, because it was written by a mayor who is known by everyone in the community and had reference to a prominent attorney, a man who up to that time had a fine reputation, was a good lawyer, was known as being . . . honest and truthful. . . .

"This article charges this plaintiff with being dishonest; attacks him unmercifully. I believe that this is the most vicious language of any libel case in the books in our state."

In commenting on the handbill, the judge cited the paragraph heading "Lawyer John Fish Exposed as John Poisson": "There wasn't any 'exposure'; there wasn't any occasion for using the word 'exposed.' I think that is the first cropping out of the malice." Webster also excoriated Hubbard for his continued use of the "alias" phrase. "Just like a lot of other things," he observed, "it is a slam, a slur. Sure, it does not always refer to criminals, but generally it does."

As for Fish's role on the old Safety Commission, he ruled: "There is no evidence whatever that he resigned because 'things got hot,' or because he was connected with it in any way; and the testimony shows that he was not. The testimony rather shows that he was trying just the opposite to do his best, to do something to clean up the situation there."

Webster also took exception to the mayor's reference to Fish and Beadle "trying to elect a mayor that they can control like they did the old Fordson School Board." Also unjustified, the judge said, was a reference to Beadle, Doyle, Fish and Rouse as "ganged up together . . . while the gang tries to put up a decent front." He observed, "He is practically calling these people 'gangsters.'"

Hubbard's pun about "Fishy Claims" also provoked the judge: "'Fishy Claims,' everybody knows what 'Fishy Claims' are; they are unfounded claims, unsubstantiated, no good, something wrong about them."

Webster next cited Hubbard's contention that Beadle and Doyle had often offered settlements in Fish lawsuits—"a move which too often smells like a pay-off." The judge said, "That is a direct charge that somebody got a pay-off; that Fish was involved in it. . . . That again, I say, is scurrilous, libelous per se, not founded upon any facts that justify or warrant its use."

Continuing through the handbill sentence by sentence, the judge pointed out word after word—"rotten" action, "most outrageous of the 'Fishy claims,'" a paragraph heading referring to Fish as "Charity John"—which he deemed unfair: "It, again, is insulting, it intimates an ambulance chaser, a lawyer of the cheaper kind, as known to lawyers and judges, who takes cases on claimed charity; and the language of the paragraph following, 'And you can be sure that "Charity John" got his cut.' There, again, an absolute direct charge against this plaintiff of being a crook, a shyster; no decent lawyer would get a cut."

On the balance of the questions, Webster stated: "I believe that on this record this defendant did make the statements in bad faith and with actual malice and without reasonable cause to believe them to be true. . . .

"This language, the different words that I have pointed out, are absolutely libelous per se, and not based upon any truth that would give the writer the right to write them. . . .

"This thing that is so serious to me, and this attack on Mr. Fish is so uncalled for and scurrilous, that I could fix quite a large verdict, I believe, and have it sustained by the Supreme Court. But, I have decided not to do that. . . ."

With that, Webster awarded $7,500 to Fish—$5,000 for injury to his feelings and $2,500 for damage to his business. The assessment was $1,000 more than Hubbard's annual salary. Orvie, laughing as he left court, asked, "Anybody got a dime?"[8]

If there ever was a political judgment, a horseshit decision, that was one. He should never have won that case. The judge, first, I think he got mad at me. He was an old guy. God, they get senile, the old bastards. The clerks were very influential on those old judges. Clyde Webster's clerk belonged to John Fish's church.

194

They were very close friends. The judge was a big Mason, one of those super guys, you know. There used to be two Websters on the bench. I used to say, "You mean the judge or you mean the Mason?" Arthur, the judge, and Clyde, who was a reprobate son of a bitch, the Mason. We had the Mason. I'm gonna piss on that goddamn Webster's grave. I hope I don't forget to do that before I die. Give him a good dose.

The day after the trial ended, April 26, Fillmore abruptly resigned as corporation counsel because, he said, he could "not continue to have a part in a program which injures people." Although he noted that Webster's interpretation of the facts in the Fish case "was entirely different from the view I had," the case still tainted the Hubbard administration. At Orvie's urging, however, Fillmore was back on the job two weeks later.

Meanwhile, Hubbard, who was free on $15,000 bond, announced he would appeal the verdict to the Michigan Supreme Court "and the people of Dearborn." Young, his attorney, said he hoped particularly to get Webster's finding of malice stricken, since that would prevent Hubbard from declaring bankruptcy to settle the monetary award, if it were upheld.

The next month, in May, Young asked for a new trial, contending that the verdict was "against the clear weight of the evidence" and charging 16 points of error in the trial, including a contention that the $5,000 award for injury to Fish's feelings actually "amounted to punitive damages when punitive damages had been ruled out." Several weeks later, Webster affirmed his verdict, adding that he could have assessed double the judgment he rendered, since "there was no evidence that Hubbard would have retracted his statements against Fish at any time, and he maintained that attitude to the very close of the trial."

Hubbard told reporters he was unable to pay the "punitive and excessive" judgment. In a statement filed with the court, he listed his assets at $11,125, all held jointly with his wife and encumbered by injunction pending settlement of Fay Hubbard's divorce action from the year before. Besides the family home, valued at $7,500, the mayor's assets were limited to furniture ($2,000), government bonds ($825) and a part interest in northern Michigan real estate ($800). Besides the mayor's "meager" $6,500 salary, his only other source of income was $250 a year as an ex officio member of the County Board of Supervisors. A few weeks later, in June, Hubbard said he couldn't afford attorney fees to appeal the verdict.

Fish, however, was little moved by the mayor's pleas of poverty. In July, he obtained an order empowering the sheriff to seize Hubbard's property. Fish said that if the sheriff failed to locate enough property to satisfy the judgment, he would ask for a body judgment to send Hubbard to prison as a debtor.

I had nothing. I actually intended to go into jail for nine months and take a pauper's oath and then come out with a barrel on. And I was pretty good friends with the sheriff. I figured I'd have been working the kitchen or in the office or been a trusty. But then that thing dragged on. Ever see a rabbit, ears up, and a hawk swoop down, whssht, *scoop him up? I was just like a rabbit. No one ever did catch me.*

Under the circumstances, the month of July was pleasant enough for Orville Hubbard, the rabbit. He spent most of his time at the city's Oakland County retreat, Camp Dearborn, well outside the jurisdiction of Sheriff Andrew C. Baird.

But it was his property, not himself, that the law wanted, and since Fay Hubbard had dropped her divorce action in May, the court order tying up the mayor's property was no longer in effect. A lot of good that did John Fish. A sheriff's deputy assigned to the case reported to the court that he had made nine trips to the Dearborn city hall and never once caught sight of Hubbard, much less his property. What's more, he said, a "diligent search" failed to turn up any evidence that Hubbard even had any property, no matter what the records said.

Finally, Fish, apparently suspecting that the deputy, like Baird, was a friend of Hubbard's, had seen enough. The next day, in early August, he obtained a body judgment writ that, as he had warned earlier, would consign the mayor of Dearborn to debtor's prison. He even put up $100 in advance to pay for Hubbard's upkeep in jail for four weeks.

But where was Hubbard? City hall sources reported that the mayor had left town the night before. Friends said he had boarded a plane for the East to make a personal inspection of beaches as a source for ideas to improve Camp Dearborn. By the following week, he still hadn't shown up for work, but he had been seen over the weekend at Camp Dearborn again, lunching openly with friends and department heads at a Shrine picnic. A frustrated Fish declared, "If I have to, I can get a writ in Oakland County and have him arrested at the camp."

But things were getting complicated. A couple of days later, Orvie popped up at the Blackstone Hotel in Chicago. He phoned Chicago reporters to let them know he was "that mayor they are all looking for" back in Michigan, and papers around the country ran stories about the itinerary Orville Hubbard was planning as a means of staying out of jail for the remainder of August. After Chicago, he said, he would hit the Atlantic seaboard and then Canada, adding, "I can keep ahead of the sheriff." But the mayor was covering all contingencies. Though insisting he "would not pay Fish one red cent," he conceded the possibility that he might get caught. He had already instructed Sheriff Baird to set up phones, books and a radio in a cell so that Hubbard could continue running the city. And he was planning to order stationery headed "Temporary Office, Mayor of Dearborn, Wayne County Jail, Detroit, Mich."

196

But Hubbard was still a long way from jail. The next day, insisting he was on city business ("I never take a vacation"), he lolled on the beaches along Lake Michigan and announced he would study the Chicago water-front for several days. He even saw the stage hit *Mr. Roberts.* By the end of the second week of August, Hubbard had checked out of his Chicago hotel, and DPW Director Frank Swapka, who had been accompanying him, was back in Dearborn in the mayor's city car, staying silent on his boss's where-abouts. A week later, amid conflicting reports that he had returned home or else had been touring seaside resorts out East, Hubbard checked into the Prince Edward Hotel in Windsor, Canada, just across the Detroit River from downtown Detroit. A couple of days after that, he turned up at a convention in Saskatoon, Saskatchewan. Newspapers gleefully ran wire photos of him shaving at a curbside electrical outlet designed to keep car batteries alive in the chill Saskatoon winters. "When I'm through here," Orvie obligingly informed Canadian writers, "I'm going on out to the Rockies for a little fun."

The mayor's enemies had not exactly remained oblivious to his adven-tures, what with even *Time* magazine devoting a story to "Little Orvie's" antics.[9] Back in Dearborn, Fish said he would ask for an investigation into the source of funds for Hubbard's travels. And Charles Wagner, head of the citizens' group that had been circulating petitions to recall Hubbard from office, announced that the signatures would be filed in time to put the question on the November ballot. This would give the mayor a choice of returning and facing jail or not returning and not defending himself against the recall charges.

Hubbard appeared little concerned about the home folks. Although he finally affirmed that he was paying for his trip himself, he continued his will-o'-the-wisp whistle-stopping, showing up at Toronto and Hershey, Pennsylvania, among various points on the map. Toward the end of August, he even appeared at Camp Dearborn again, just long enough to strike a tent headquarters he had set up earlier but never used. Then, after conferring with department heads, he disappeared again, turning up once at a Dear-born restaurant, where, according to one report, a sheriff's deputy just missed him. Of course, nobody believed that the sheriff's office was trying very hard. At one point, a couple of uniformed deputies were reported standing beside a plainly marked patrol car at the boundary of Wayne and Oakland counties. If anybody was going to capture the elusive Orvie, they weren't the ones.

For several weeks now, since Chicago, Hubbard had been tipping news-men that his ultimate destination was Windsor, where he would establish what he rather grandly called a "government in exile" safely across the national border and yet within cheap telephone distance of the Dearborn city hall. While many observers hooted—the *Detroit Free Press* called the plan "idiotic"—Hubbard went right ahead. After looking over the hotel earlier in the month, the mayor had begun using stationery embossed with the address and phone number of the Prince Edward, along with the identifying line "Headquarters of the Mayor of Dearborn, Mich., in Exile." But it wasn't for another week that Orvie followed through.

Accompanied by Bert Schlaff, Hughes and an entourage of other appointees, he was at first rebuffed by a desk clerk. But once Hubbard identified himself as Dearborn's traveling mayor, he got a room right away. The staff of the Prince Edward, which had been receiving calls for Hubbard all week, played right along with the game, even calling him "Your Worship," the customary Canadian term of address for mayors. Schlaff began answering calls with the salutation "Dearborn's mayor in exile," and within a couple of days, Hubbard's transplanted government seemed to be almost a functioning reality. The mayor conducted a department head meeting at the hotel and also summoned three lieutenants from the Fire Department for a ceremony promoting them to captain.

Hubbard obviously was enjoying the experience to the hilt. But he knew he couldn't stay in Canada forever. He told newsmen he'd visit Camp Dearborn again as soon as the courts closed for the Labor Day weekend and Fish no longer would be able to secure an arrest warrant good in Oakland County. Hubbard suggested that "if they really want me," Baird's deputies could probably catch him at the Ambassador Bridge or the underwater tunnel back to Detroit. "I'm telling all my men to put Baird's bumper posters on their cars," he said, adding that he'd return to city hall to "give the deputies a chance to drag me down the front steps if they want to."

There was a more serious side to Orvie's endeavors, however. For several weeks, the mayor's staffers had been negotiating with the sheriff's office to permit Hubbard to return home and fight the recall. The arrangement was to be a "jail-limits bond," which would confine the mayor within the boundaries of Wayne County, thus keeping him under the sheriff's jurisdiction without actually requiring him to stay in jail. If Hubbard were to leave the county and be caught, he would be remanded to jail, the bond would be forfeited to Fish, and the sheriff would have to seek reimbursement from Hubbard.

But until the bond actually were posted, he would make the most of the situation. During the first week in September, he sent the city clerk's office a request for an absentee ballot for the following week's election, explaining, "I expect to be absent from the city on primary election day." The letterhead was stamped, "Underground Headquarters, Mayor of Dearborn, Somewhere in Wayne County." He also sent out a tongue-in-cheek offer to reenlist with the U.S. Marines, but, at 47, he was well over the age limit and was turned down.

Hubbard's jokes didn't sit very well with his opponents, naturally. Wagner, declaring that he was ready to file recall petitions the next week, suggested that "to get out of hock, Hubbard might sell the comic strip rights of his career."

Despite the admonishment, Hubbard wasn't through sending letters. In St. Louis, en route to California, Hubbard discovered that the Michigan Judges Association was about to meet at the Dearborn Inn. Among the scheduled attendees was Clyde I. Webster. This was too good to pass up, and Hubbard accordingly dictated a letter that subsequently was hand-delivered to his libel trial antagonist at the inn. The text, in part, said, "As the Mayor of Dearborn, I want you to know that you are neither welcome nor wanted in Dearborn. Now, therefore, this is your personal invitation to 'get-out and stay-out of Dearborn.' I hope you will accept this in the same kindly spirit in which it is sent."[10]

The judge's reaction was not recorded, although it is known that a group of his colleagues on the bench discussed the possibility of having Hubbard disbarred for conduct unbecoming a lawyer. In other quarters, the Dearborn City Council considered issuing the judge an apology in the mayor's behalf, finally declining to do so and thus earning the enmity of the *Dearborn Press* for "one of the most nauseating acts of puppetry" in its tenure. However, Council President Marguerite Johnson broke with Hubbard over the issue. She suggested that he "must have intended his letter as a joke," adding that it was "in very poor taste" and "does not reflect the attitude of other officials or of the rest of the community." Joke? Taste? Orville Hubbard?

At last, on September 18, after some six weeks as a fugitive from justice, Hubbard posted $5,000 bond in return for the right to return to Wayne County and move freely within its boundaries. Surety for the bond consisted of $47,700 worth of property owned by six Dearborn residents, three of them political cronies of the mayor. The six were Ralph Guy, who had just quit as police chief to run for a vacant judgeship, $9,000; George Brady, city housing director, $6,200; M. O. Nickon, city superintendent of weights and measures, $11,500; Luigi Sesti, $10,000; Nicholas Ortopan, $10,000; and Peter Gutenberg, $1,000.

In turning over the deeds to the sheriff's legal adviser, Hubbard signed his usual inch-high signature in blue ink; he had forgotten his customary green pen in the press of business. That done, it was almost as though he had never been gone. He proceeded immediately to his first public meeting in weeks, a session of the county supervisors. That night, he attended a council committee meeting and a district GOP delegate meeting.

Straightening out his legal status wasn't the only motive for Orvie to get out of the fugitive business and back into the routine of running the city. With the recall move gathering momentum, he had plenty of reason to stay right where he was.

24

✖✦✦

Beating the Recall, 1951

> We are tired of being pushed around. More than 10,000
> citizens, in the face of threats and attacks, united in this
> committee to rid our city of this man. We have perse-
> vered without hope of any reward than to free Dear-
> born from the irresponsible hands of this petty dictator.
> —Citizens Action Committee of Dearborn, in an appeal
> to voters[1]

When *Time* magazine splashed a picture of San Francisco Mayor Roger
Dearborn Lapham across its cover in July 1946, it helped score a victory,
among other things, for good manners in politics.[2] Lapham, accused of
raising taxes and acting like a dictator, amiably agreed to sign a petition
calling for his own ouster. Then, a day after *Time*'s story on him, he won an
overwhelming vote of confidence in a recall election. The Lapham recall
may have marked a new high in deportment by a politician under fire. But
it was followed four years later in Dearborn by one that most certainly
established a new low.

Orville Hubbard did not sign his own recall petitions. Instead, he spent
nearly a year—using threats, tricks and no end of fire-and-brimstone rhetoric—trying to keep the names of other voters off.[3] It may be an exaggeration
to say that he turned his recall campaign into the most bizarre exercise in
the history of American municipal politics. But at the very least he added
a new tactical dimension to the recall procedure, which by that time had
nearly a half-century of precedent behind it.

As originally conceived around the turn of the century, the recall was
to be a lever against the corrupt, machine-backed hacks running many city
halls and state capitols. If an official betrayed his trust, reasoned the reform-
ers, why wait until the next election? Circulate petitions, call a special election and vote the rascal out ahead of time. Although it was used for a couple
of decades in the Progressive Movement's battles against bad government,
by the time the recall concept was resurrected against Lapham and Hubbard,
it was something of a political relic. But what else was left? Orvie obviously

still commanded enough support to beat anybody who might challenge him head-to-head. If he had no one to attack, however—if he were forced instead to defend his own record—he might be vulnerable. And even if he couldn't be dumped, at least he could be embarrassed.

People started talking openly about recalling Hubbard in early 1950, after he and Ralph Guy had tried to take over the "Save Our Hospital" meeting. About a month later, in March, a group of 80 housewives and church clubbers announced a drive to remove the mayor. The group's leader was Rona Scott, wife of a city DPW worker and herself a onetime Hubbard supporter. Scott, who indicated that the Hubbard camp had been threatening her and spying on her for her efforts, followed up her original announcement by marching some 20 of her cohorts to a council meeting to accuse the mayor of various charter violations and conduct unbecoming a city officer. They demanded that the mayor resign within six days. If he refused, they said, they would ask the council to impeach him. If the council refused, they would ask Governor G. Mennen Williams to remove them all from office. What they would do if the governor refused to act was left to the imagination. The council filed a copy of the demands, and Orvie, rather uncharacteristically, smiled and declined comment.

At the next council meeting, a letter was received from a former Republican congressional candidate named Fred Rush. The letter, charging Hubbard with "corruption" and with being a "fake champion of the ordinary citizen," demanded that both the mayor and Council President Marguerite Johnson resign. Johnson brushed Rush off, saying, "I do not feel that this council is a sounding board for any crackpot idea you might have." Rush's sentiments, however, were not so easy to dismiss.

By law, no movement to recall an elected official could begin until at least 90 days after his term of office began. Hubbard's 90 days were up April 1, and, sure enough, within a week a nonprofit corporation filed to remove him. But this was no political disappointee, no clique of busybody do-gooders. Calling itself the Citizens Action Committee (CAC) of Dearborn, it boasted the names of 30 civic leaders as directors.

I came out of court one day, and a big headline in the Detroit News, *that son-of-a-bitching paper, faces me in the goddamned eyes: "Corporation formed to recall Hubbard." I can see it today. So they started a recall against us, and I had every fucking thing in town against me—the* News, *the* Free Press, *the veterans associations, Ford Motor Company. Everything in the world was against us except the Lord, I guess.*

The president of the group was Charles A. Wagner, a corporation lawyer with a long background in civic affairs. He was the man who 10 years before had served as chairman of the commission that spawned the strong-mayor charter responsible for entrenching Hubbard in office. He was also the onetime Hubbard supporter who fought the gag ordinance case of 1945.

Wagner and the other recall leaders immediately attempted to shroud the recall movement with almost the aura of a holy crusade. "One-man government must be ended," Wagner solemnly announced. "There is no room for a dictator in this city." The recall petitions accused Hubbard of:[4] joining with Guy to take over the hospital meeting in February and nearly causing a riot; seeking to prevent an independent audit of the city's books by the Dearborn Chamber of Commerce;[5] attempting to deny a pension to Stanley Herdzik, who had quit as fire chief several months before; appointing unqualified department heads and requiring that they "act in accordance with his personal edict"; and using police to tack up signs boosting Guy as municipal judge during the previous primary campaign.

Hubbard brusquely denied the charges, although it was not until the next month that he finally got around to making a point-by-point rebuttal. Among his comments: he had attended the hospital meeting simply "as a citizen and voter"; the books needed no audit, since "there wasn't even a penny out of sight"; Herdzik didn't deserve a pension, since he should not be "all worn out at 45, while I am 47"; loyalty among appointees is a more important trait than training; and the police simply were following orders to put up Guy posters they already had torn down illegally, as "anyone who knows Dearborn knows the policemen aren't for Hubbard."

Orvie also made a shrill promise: "I knew this was coming. Let them go to it. We'll give them a real licking this time, one they'll never forget." He brushed off his opponents as "stuffed shirts," labeling Wagner as "the stuffiest of the bunch."

The Wagners had built a lot of stuff around town. There was even a Wagner hotel. It was an old family here. Well, up to that time Charlie Wagner had been friendly to me. But Charlie was always the uppity guy in the community. He was one of these guys like the Archbishop of Canterbury. Everybody kind of tiptoed around, and it was like they were saying: "Be careful. The monsignor just walked in." Charlie was always the kind of a guy that if you don't play ball the way he wants to play it, why, he'd just take his bat and ball and go in the house. He was basically a mean son of a bitch.

According to Wagner, the recall machinery already was well oiled by the time it was made public. The CAC had been meeting secretly for two months and was ready to start circulating petitions. But Hubbard had done a bit of homework himself. When he said he knew the recall was coming, he was not speaking idly. Hours after Wagner received his petitions from the printer—the night before 300 circulators were to blanket the city—strange reports began filtering into recall headquarters. Somebody had jumped the gun. Circulators already were out covering the city's finest residential areas, where opposition to the mayor traditionally had been strongest. Two recall officers said they saw a woman circulating petitions in the Ford Foundation, the most vehemently anti-Hubbard area in town. She was being followed in a car by Guy and a plainclothes policeman. Other stories came in. Policemen's families were circulating petitions. The Levagood Park area and other high-income neighborhoods on the west side were being covered. Eleven high school girls got 300 names in two hours. Yet none of these circulators had been sent out by recall headquarters. A dismayed Wagner guessed the worst: the mayor somehow had procured copies of the petitions and begun circulating them through his own people.

We actually circulated their own petitions before they did. We had a good espionage system going. One of their men got 'em for us, double-crossed them. The law says you can only sign one petition, so our theory was, if they'd sign our petition. they couldn't sign a real one or they'd be in trouble with the law. We thought the place to circulate those petitions was where the vote was heaviest against us, so we went over to the Foundation, and, Christ, those people grabbed those damned petitions just like a rock bass that hadn't had a worm all summer. We did all kinds of shit. We muddied up the water and did everything we could do. You see, they changed their whole tactics when they went with the petitions in the street. They'd say to the Italian people and Polish people that were my friends, they'd say, "This is for the mayor, to give you a chance to vote for or against the mayor." They used that divorce shit, too, house to house, all over town. Piece of recall literature said the mayor has a broken heart. They said if you couldn't manage your own home, how are you gonna manage the city? This fucking game they talk about Nixon and Watergate—that's just a Sunday school picnic.

The mayor announced that all the signatures he had were from genuine petitions given him by "disgusted" recall workers. But the real strategy was apparent to the CAC. Wagner countered by announcing he would sign every recall sheet, adding that "anyone forging my name on false petitions will be liable to arrest." This thwarted the mayor, but only momentarily.

The day the real petitions went into circulation, Hubbard filed $25,000 libel suits against seven persons who had signed the bogus petitions circulated in the Foundation. He proclaimed he would retaliate with similar suits against all signers, though he soon amended this to include "just those able to pay." The recallers cited the ploy as an example of Orvie's "tyranny," and Wagner promised to defend anyone thus persecuted by the mayor. "The idea of suing for libel for signing a recall petition is ridiculous," he declared, "at least in America." The homeowners threatened by Hubbard announced they had joined the CAC and signed legitimate petitions. In a press release invoking a host of democratic clichés and labeling Hubbard "an enemy of liberty," they vowed, "We will not abandon our heritage of freedom." The CAC then circulated pamphlets placing Hubbard in the company of Hitler, Stalin, Mussolini, George III and Huey Long: "He made the same mistake they all made. He thought we wouldn't fight but we are going to stand up for our rights. His threat to sue . . . is an open and obvious attempt to intimidate the entire community."[6]

Hubbard's response was another threat to sue, this time the recall leaders. Before the month was out, however, the mayor dropped this line of attack. His backers threatened to press trespassing charges against petition circulators approaching their homes, but Hubbard failed even to follow up his libel action, and Wagner had the matter dismissed in court.

Throughout the rest of April, Hubbard was kept continually off-balance fending off accusations. In the ensuing months, the charges and countercharges were hard to keep straight. First the recallers charged that several petition circulators had been threatened by Hubbard men. Next they accused the son of one of the mayor's department heads of snatching a petition from a circulator who had called at his home; the CAC would sue for the return of the paper, they said. The next charge involved Stanley Herdzik, who had begun working in the recall after his split with Orvie. Just after he and his wife had turned in petitions, Mrs. Herdzik claimed, a phone caller had threatened her life. Then, she said, a "not-very-intelligent-looking" man in a dark topcoat confronted her. "We want you and your husband out of Michigan within 48 hours," she quoted him. "If you value your life, beat it." Next another recaller, real estate dealer Harry E. Smiley, reported a phone threat to "shoot his stupid head off." Wagner also reported some threats, once from a caller who told his wife she had "better get your husband out of this or something may happen to your children." Wagner declared that his group would "hold Orville Hubbard personally responsible for any violence should something happen to any recall worker." He also said he would ask State Police protection for workers. And, he warned, he would ask Governor G. Mennen Williams to step in "if there is any further intimidation of our people."

Hubbard, naturally, denied knowledge of any of the acts alleged by the recallers. But he added, a bit ominously, "We are at our best in a situation like this. We have our own men on their committee, even on their board of directors. We are going to run Wagner out of town. He'll have to win this or move on."[7]

How the recall was going was anybody's guess. Despite the mayor's prediction that "they're about to give up," the CAC was claiming success even in Hubbard strongholds. In a few weeks, Wagner said, the group had collected two-thirds of the 7,000-odd signatures needed to put the recall on the ballot.

The recallers claimed the next publicity coup when they got the signature of Otto Hoffman, the mayor's onetime public safety director. The two had been law school classmates and had set up law practice together near city hall. When Hubbard was elected, Hoffman stayed on as a renter, though

Hubbard's name still was on the door and the telephone remained listed under his name.

They wanted to make it look real bad. One of the headlines said, "Hubbard's law partner signs recall petition." He never was a partner of mine. He was a tenant of mine.

A more serious setback came the next week, when it became apparent to Hubbard that the Fords had joined the opposition.

Never a favorite of old Henry Ford, Hubbard was resented more and more by the late automotive pioneer's grandson, Henry Ford II, now the company president. After enduring Orvie's continual attacks on the family and the firm, Ford at last saw a chance to get rid of the gadfly mayor. The matter came to a head in a letter to Ford, whom Hubbard accused of allowing recall petitions to be circulated in the Ford administration building, less than two miles from city hall. Hubbard wrote: "Reports tell us that petitions are shoved under the noses of employees while at work. . . . As your friend, may I suggest that you familiarize yourself with the Michigan election laws relating to the corporation or its agents coercing, threatening or intimidating its employees."[8] Several days later, Ford spokesmen acknowledged that some petitions had been circulated, nearly all during lunch periods and after hours. Within two weeks, young Henry wrote back to Hubbard, confirming that the company had supplied the recallers with a list of employees living in Dearborn. "As you know—or should know—the Michigan election law has no application to this matter," he wrote.[9]

Later, Hubbard publicly accused Ford's of financing and planning the recall attempt. Why? Partly, he said, because the firm wanted to convert large tracts of vacant land in the city into housing for "cheap labor," including Negroes. Perhaps Hubbard realized that he was overplaying his hand, because he stopped short of making race a major issue in the recall. However, he also accused Ford officials of refusing to cooperate with attempts to stop gambling at the Rouge plant. At one point, Ralph Guy said Dearborn was "probably the cleanest industrial city in the United States," even though police were arresting "about two gamblers a week at the Rouge plant."

We never carried an ax for Ford. We had no feud with them. But everybody who wanted to ingratiate themselves with Ford ran over at that time. There was more intrigue going on in that campaign. You know what Ford's did, the bastards? They used all their goddamned corporate billboards—"Had enough? Vote Yes." We couldn't even buy any billboards. They were all gone. But we had a Mercury dealer in town. He did have me on his billboard. We had "Unfair recall. Vote No." One guy who quit after 24 years at Ford's brought all the negatives and plates of the stuff they'd put out. He figured it out, that Ford's had spent more than $100,000 on that recall.[10] Ford. He was a fucking faker. That's real money going after you.

They were paying people four and five dollars to sign the recall petitions. They did have all kinds of guys working against us. There was John Bugas, an FBI guy they brought in behind the scenes. Then they brought this big fat guy, Tom Reid. He was supposed to liquidate me. How the hell he was going to do it when the FBI wasn't smart enough to do it. And Ford used to have a goddamned half-ass public relations man. He was a no-good son of a bitch. He set an hour aside daily— he actually shut the blinds, took the phones off and sat an hour—to hate Hubbard. That was what he said: to hate Hubbard. He was a real prick. We had a rally, and I said, "I know they've got court stenographers here. I used to work as a stenographer myself, so I'll take it slow enough so they can get it down. That [public relations man] is a queer in the crudest meaning of the term. Go back and tell him I said that." He didn't dare make one fucking thing out of it.

In the early weeks of the recall effort, there was almost no dialogue between Hubbard and CAC officials. The first such opportunity, a meeting scheduled at Fordson High School, got a big buildup when John McWilliams, president of the sponsoring Dearborn Citizens League, requested State Police surveillance, ostensibly because of Orvie's conduct at the February hospital meeting. Governor Williams denied the request, suggesting that Dearborn police would be more appropriate to the occasion. Hubbard confirmed that police under "high-line officers" would attend, then announced that he would boycott the meeting. He sent his son Frank to take notes of the proceedings, but there was little to report. The 700 who attended simply heard further denunciations of the absent mayor. "Unfortunately, we have a man who uses his power as if he were king," Wagner said. "This is a kind of tyranny we fought against in the war."

The recall campaign ground down in mid-May, when Wagner announced he had well over the number of signatures needed to force a vote. To avoid a summer election that probably would be poorly attended, however, he said he would postpone filing the signatures a few months. He said the extra time also would give the CAC a chance to collect another 2,000 or so names.

If Hubbard was worried, he still was not letting it show, but he let it be known that he was keeping his options open. He said he had 16,000 names on petitions asking him to run for Congress. The offers, he said, "have been coming in like rain." He stopped talking about it as the recall progressed, however.

Over the summer, Orvie continued to make news even though the recall was stalled out. In May, his wife, Fay, dropped her divorce suit, and then he embarked on his low-comedy hide-and-seek game with lawmen after the Fish libel trial.

The recall was back in the forefront in September, when more of the mayor's support had eroded. The house organ of Ford Local 600, a steady Hubbard booster over the years, this time editorialized for his recall. The

206

publication criticized his opposition to employee pension rights and his penchant for appointing "former goons of Harry Bennett" as staff members. A week later, Local 600 President Carl Stellato tried to patch things up, announcing that the union was officially taking a hands-off policy on the recall.

The moment the recallers had all been waiting for finally came in December, and Wagner wasn't about to let it slip past without a touch of showmanship to rival Hubbard's. On the morning of December 5, an armored truck pulled up to city hall, double-parking on Michigan Avenue. Revolvers drawn, two Brinks guards emerged, carrying bags stuffed with petitions bearing the names of 8,720 Dearborn voters. Orvie himself held the doors open, and when Wagner walked in with the guards, the mayor barked, "There goes the number one rat." He also apportioned out insults to John Fish and other recall officers accompanying Wagner. As the guards proceeded to the city clerk's office with the petitions, Hubbard moved quickly to a phone. His orders: he wanted a scout car at city hall instantly to ticket an illegally parked armored truck. But by the time officers arrived, the truck was nowhere to be seen.

Hubbard appeared unfazed when he talked to reporters later. "They haven't got a Chinaman's chance," he said. Wagner, calling Hubbard a "carpetbagger," was equally confident. The signatures, he said, represented a "comfortable margin" over the required number of 7,755, one-fourth the total that voted for governor in the previous election. "I don't think there is any question but that we will defeat Hubbard," Wagner said. "By intimidating citizens, Hubbard angered them into signing. Also, the mayor's actions of the past few months have antagonized even his very close supporters."

The mayor tried stalling. Guy attempted, unsuccessfully, to obtain perjury warrants against two petition signers who admitted they had added the names of their spouses. A couple of weeks later, Hubbard filed suit to block certification of the petitions, alleging a long list of irregularities. A circuit judge denied Hubbard's request for an injunction, and the Michigan Supreme Court denied his appeal without explanation at the end of the next month. In the interim, the campaign got bogged down in the same pattern of baiting and diversionary tactics that had marked the previous months.

Hubbard actually seized on the Korean emergency to try to make his fight against the recallers an issue of national welfare. Conjecturing that his ouster "might give aid and comfort to the Kremlin," he sent Wagner a letter appealing "to you and your political disappointees to withdraw your phony recall movement at once." He also urged Wagner to volunteer for Civil Defense "so you can do something useful" in light of the fact that "your personal vendetta masquerading as a recall is doomed to failure anyhow."

In a less patriotic vein, Wagner accused Hubbard and City Controller James Hughes of making threatening phone calls to petition signers, adding,

"I don't know how many persons they have called that are afraid to tell anyone about it." Hubbard scoffed at the charges. "The only person I know who has been intimidated," he replied, "is an elderly woman whom Wagner frightened into signing the recall petition." Soon afterward, he warned city employees not to circulate petitions or take part in the movement, however. At the same time, the recallers accused him of ordering city employees to "persuade" petition signers to withdraw their names. The charge came from an insider, Clyde Hale, Hubbard's housing director of two months. Hale resigned his job, saying he found it "impossible to go along with Hubbard's policies." Hubbard replaced Hale with William Hyde, a former Ford printer and the man who had supplied the incriminating documents about the auto firm's involvement with the recall. As events developed, the defection of Hale, who took a job with Ford, was just one in a series of setbacks for the mayor.

First there was another incident involving Herdzik. According to the former fire chief, he had been in the city clerk's office perusing petitions on a Saturday, when Hubbard "came in and began to storm and curse at me. He ordered me out." When he refused to move, he said, Hughes "jumped" him from behind. Herdzik, sporting a black eye and cut cheek, pressed charges, and Hughes was arrested and released on bond. Hubbard's version to reporters was that Hughes was "just standing there innocently" when Herdzik, swearing, shaking his fist and "jumping up and down like a chimpanzee," swung on Hughes. Hughes, calling Herdzik a "case for a lunatic asylum," confirmed that the former chief had attacked him. But at the trial the next week—despite testimony from Orvie's men that Hughes was defending himself, raising his hand as Herdzik lowered his face into it—Hughes was convicted and fined $50 by Judge George Martin. The pivotal testimony came from Deputy City Clerk Joe Cardinal, who said he saw Hughes deliver "a beautiful punch to Herdzik's face." "This case," Martin said, "shows many features of a totalitarian government, when Mayor Hubbard's officials have reached the stage where they slug people in city offices." Hughes's conviction subsequently was overturned on appeal by a circuit court jury in 1951, but the damage to Hubbard was done.

It was horseshit. He never should have been found guilty. Martin was a black-hearted son of a bitch.

The next incident involved Frank B. Swapka, the city's public works director and Hubbard's closest confidant since he helped persuade him not to drop out of politics a dozen years before. In mid-December, Hubbard announced that one of his department heads had been "playing around with the recall bunch," that the mayor had cut off his pay and that the man had resigned as a result of their differences. The man was Swapka.

*I would consider the guy here who was my best friend was Frank B. Swapka.
He was a goddamned Polack who was playing a double game with this whole
goddamn recall. What Swapka did, the cocksucker—he's lucky to be alive—I gave
those petitions we'd collected to Swapka for safekeeping, and the son of a bitch
double-crossed us and turned them all back to them, and they filed them against
us. Hitler took his best friend out behind a fucking building in Berlin and shot
the cocksucker for double-crossing him. If we had been in South America, where I
could've got ahold of him, I would've shot Swapka. Frank was a worker, though;
I'd have to say this for him. In my heart, I don't have any bitterness, but, you
know, those little things erode you. He's been friendly with me since.*

For his part, Swapka expressed shock at being "fired in a cheap, low-
down way—without notice." And, he added, "Hubbard is completely nuts.
He has a psychotic way of doing things. He is just simply gone crazy. No
wonder his old friends are leaving him. I wish I could understand what has
happened to him." Hubbard's rejoinder: not only was Swapka fraternizing
with the enemy, but he was guilty of a conflict of interest. The DPW chief,
Orvie alleged, owned a plumbing and heating firm that did business with
the city. He had known of Swapka's involvement for months, he said, although
he had waited to take action. Swapka confirmed that he "was in sympathy"
with the recallers, but he denied having joined the movement, as he denied
being involved with any heating firm. He also went on to detail the mayor's
behavior in private situations. Orvie was an eccentric, he said, often keeping
department heads at meetings for hours while reading from books such as
Grimm's Fairy Tales and *The Boyhood of Robert E. Lee.* He was paranoid, using
police at city hall switchboards to monitor calls to department heads. And
he was a tyrant, habitually carrying a gun, often going into such rages that
city officials "fear for their lives." The mayor denied carrying a pistol, then
declared, "I have more on him than he has on me."
    Almost lost in the controversy was the fact that City Assessor J. Joseph
Schaefer became the third department head to desert Hubbard. The mayor
announced Schaefer's resignation at the same time as Swapka's, and for
similar reasons. There were also reports that others besides those two and
Hale were planning to leave, and the mayor accused the recallers of trying
to engineer a defection a week "to make it look worse."

*Swapka and Maggie Johnson were screwing around. See, they really had a
conspiracy. Each department head would quit, one a week, and that way give you
bad publicity. And I called [City Assessor Carl] Farmer, and Farmer says, "Mayor,
I have to tell you the truth: you're absolutely, 100-percent right. I don't know how
you figured that out."*

The only comment from Wagner and Johnson was praise for Swapka
as one of Hubbard's few competent appointees. As it happened, a fourth

Hubbard man, Don F. Martin, director of veterans' affairs, also resigned in December.

To offset these desertions, the mayor could claim only one recruit. Joining him as Schaefer's replacement, the mayor announced, was George A. Martin. Martin—no relation to the judge—was presented as a "disillusioned" recall member whose support Wagner had tried to "buy."[11] The council reacted to Martin's appointment by firing him under a never-invoked provision of the charter. Hubbard outflanked his foes by appointing Martin a veterans' counselor a few days later.

As January and the new year came, the council continued to put pressure on Hubbard. During the first meeting of 1951, the council voted to hire an attorney to investigate charges that Hubbard was using city labor and equipment to fight the recall. Originally surfacing with Charles Wagner and Clyde Hale, the accusations had escalated in December when two recallers secured an injunction to prohibit the practice. Their complaint was supported by Hale's statement that Hubbard's clerks had typed names from petitions onto filing cards; the mayor then handed out the cards to department heads and told them to get the signers to withdraw their names.

Finally came the ultimate break between the council and the mayor. The council, at least its new anti-Hubbard bloc, was joining the recall. In an open letter in January, five of the seven councilmen declared themselves solidly against "this miniature Mussolini" in city hall. "We have now reached the solemn conviction that the city is in danger," they wrote. Urging petition signers not to be scared off by Hubbard or his "goon squads," they promised, "We will protect you to the fullest extent of our powers."

The letter was signed by Hubbard's longtime nemesis, Patrick J. Doyle, along with four members of the mayor's victorious 1949 slate: Marguerite Johnson, Martin Griffith, George Bondie and Joe Ford. Only Edward Dombrowski and Lucille McCollough stood with Hubbard now. The mayor's sneering response to the five signers: "They have written their own political obituaries."

While the political byplay was going on, the recallers were making sure they had enough signatures. Wagner appeared at city hall in mid-January to file another 1,900-odd names. Hubbard met him at the door and demanded an accounting of the money spent by the CAC. Wagner brushed by, declaring his refusal "to talk to that man about anything." Within a week, City Clerk Myron Stevens announced that "considerably more" valid signatures had been filed than were required. The final tally was 9,215 verified names, or nearly 90 percent of the total turned in. And since a county primary already was scheduled for February 19, Stevens said, that would also be the date for Orville Hubbard's recall.

In the weeks before the election, Hubbard adopted a favorite campaign technique of his, launching a series of neighborhood civic rallies at city schools. They featured door prizes, acrobats and "starlets from stage, radio and television," who generally ended up being students from local dancing schools. Just the same, the crowds were heavy, often turnaway, and enthusiastic. Dombrowski and McCollough made speeches for the mayor, and he seemed confident.

But Hubbard's opponents on the council weren't through with him yet. They would begin an immediate investigation of "every department and officer" of city government, they declared, and they would do it before the recall. "We will begin as soon as possible and stay in session every day if necessary," said Johnson.[12] Hubbard countered with an accusation that the council had a "pricetag attached" to its motives, and he threatened to petition for a grand jury to investigate the council itself.

A few days later, the council followed up by resurrecting the long-discredited allegations that gamblers and racketeers were flourishing under the Hubbard regime and may even have contributed to his campaigns. Also passed was a vote to ask Estes Kefauver's Senate crime investigating committee to look into "any connection between politics and crime in Dearborn."

The move drew a hair-trigger response from Hubbard during a belligerent session of name-calling. Jumping to his feet, red-faced with anger, the mayor shouted at his council antagonists, "You had better include the Ford Motor Company in that request." Then he added, "I'll give anyone a hundred-dollar bill if they can prove the existence of rackets or gambling in Dearborn," and, swinging around to point at Ralph Guy, he promised, "And if it is proved, I'll fire Guy and the whole vice squad." Johnson retorted dryly, "If the Rouge plant is in Dearborn, you have just admitted what we originally charged."[13]

Two weeks later, in early February, the mayor turned another council meeting into a pie-throwing contest by submitting vetoes of both the council investigation and the request for the Kefauver investigation. However, after a testy discussion interrupted by off-color heckling from female Hubbard supporters in the audience, the council voted five-to-two to override both vetoes. The council would press on.

After one postponement, the investigation finally got under way just 10 days before the recall. A parade of witnesses—Clyde Hale, George A. Martin, Frank Swapka, Carl Farmer—answered questions from special counsel Walter M. Nelson. The testimony corroborated Hale's charges that Orvie was using city equipment and personnel to fight the recall. Swapka provided another inside look at the mayor as a man who spent department head meetings criticizing individuals and making fun of ethnic groups. Hubbard mocked the Poles; Hubbard ordered appointees to give councilmen the "fisheye treatment"; Hubbard decreed that garbage should not be picked up in some areas. But out of all of it—some two weeks' worth of testimony—there was only one serious accusation: that Orvie had ordered reductions in property tax assessments to two businesses, a small one of $3,500 to the U.S. Printing Co. and a large one of $221,850 to a clothing firm, People's

Outfitting Co. Hale, Farmer and former assessor J. Joseph Schaefer confirmed the story, and Hubbard probably would have to justify it someday.

Now was not the time, however. Hubbard kept silent, content to let the
council play out its drama till the end. That came two days before the
election with one more attempt, by Councilman Doyle, to link the mayor's
name with gamblers. Doyle said a number of retired policemen had told
him that gamblers were contributing money to Hubbard's campaigns. But
when he had Lieutenant Edward Mealy of the vice squad take the stand
and asked him if he recalled telling Doyle in 1949 that a certain gambler
was "getting tired of supporting Hubbard," Mealy squelched that line of
questioning altogether. "No," Mealy replied. "I said I had rumors that gambling money was available to back you if you wanted to take it." Mealy
acknowledged that Doyle had refused the money, some $5,000 to $10,000,
and withdrawn from the race, but the session was a victory—and an unso-
licited one—for Orvie.

The recallers also struck out with the Kefauver committee. Ralph Guy
testified in Detroit about an attempt to bribe him in 1948, but he received
nothing but compliments from the investigators for his attempts to clean
up the Rouge plant.

Just the same, the recallers were predicting success. Some of them already
had Orvie's successor picked out, in fact. They would hold a straw vote to
decide whom to back in the scheduled April 2 city primary. Judge Martin,
for one, said he could be drafted, and Wagner predicted the judge would
be an easy winner.

The CAC deluged Dearborn with literature in the two weeks before the
recall. In a letter addressed to "Fellow Enemies," coyly picking up on Orvie's
label for petition signers, the recallers warned that Hubbard could "be expected
to do anything—and we mean anything!—between now and the election."
The CAC declared that it would take "many thousands of words even to
summarize Mayor Hubbard's dictatorial actions. It is a shameful record of
quarrels, fights, insults, libels, plots, threats and irresponsible antics." Besides
Hubbard's wide-ranging indiscretions, the CAC said, he had "persisted in
misleading the people to believe that he is responsible for Dearborn's low
taxes," while in fact he had "mismanaged the finances of Michigan's richest
city until Dearborn is almost broke." Beyond everything else, the recallers
concluded, "we cannot trust this man with his city departments staffed with
stooges and spies."

The committee's 200-word message for the February 19 ballot was a
bland recounting of grievances already listed against him, everything from
taking over the hospital meeting to using police in Ralph Guy's campaign
for judge in 1949.

However, the newspapers printed a much longer indictment of Hubbard
the week before the recall under the signature of CAC member Edward N.
Long. Besides rehashing familiar criticisms of the mayor and accusing him

of raising "phony issues," it also attempted to turn the topic of race back on him:

> If Negroes ever move to Dearborn in large numbers, Hubbard will be to blame, because his constant use of the race issue as a phony political dagger is causing responsible Negro leaders and organizations to consider Dearborn as a number one target for infiltration as a matter of principle. Unless we get rid of Hubbard and his political use of the race issue, we may really have trouble.[14]

Hubbard's final public statement, issued the weekend before the election, avoided answering any specific charges. Instead, and typically of Hubbard, it went on the offensive. The recall was a plot based on "the possible gold mine in rackets and real estate" to be reaped by his successor. The plotters, including Ford officials, wanted a mayor "they can own and boss. The mayor's office under Orville L. Hubbard is not for sale at any price." His opponents were stooping to "every foul trick, frame-up and smear. The big money involved in the recall has attracted every type of political termite, parasite and barnacle." Voters, he said, "will be awake and alert and realize they must turn out at the polls and whip the black conspiracy to capture city hall."[15]

The 200-word text Orvie prepared for the ballot was even more farfetched, but much more effective than the recallers' version. Voters going to the polls on February 19 were confronted by this miniature masterpiece of political flimflam:

> The recall is unfair. Cooked up by a gang of political disappointees, scheming lawyers and real estate sharks, their reasons for it are a pack of lies! Why are they plotting to capture your City Hall? Who is putting up all the money? Why the phony newspaper talk to fool citizens? What do they hope to gain?
>
> Is John Hancock back with his Boston bankroll hiding behind Ford ghosts ready to "haunt" Dearborn with another housing project? Hubbard won't sell out Dearborn. He is against undesirable housing!
>
> Within 7-months you vote again for Mayor. Why keep Dearborn in a political turmoil? Hubbard provides good public service. He keeps Dearborn Clean, your books clean and your taxes low.
>
> Camp Dearborn was his dream. He fought hard to help provide it for you. Always on the job, never too busy to see anyone, Hubbard is for the people and devotes his full time to community problems.
>
> The unfair recall—not a word of truth in their reasons for it—is a plot by the same sneaky gang, beaten election after election, who hope to sneak one over in zero weather. They are poor losers and need a good lesson in American sportsmanship.[16]

Political analysts in Dearborn were predicting a close vote. If enough of the 50,000-plus registered voters turned out, they said, Hubbard probably would be retained. If not, his dictatorship would be over.

On election night, when it became apparent that the turnout was a record of nearly 30,000, campaign workers and supporters filled Orvie's offices and overflowed into the outer corridor to follow the ballot count and cheer him on.

February 19, 1951: I remember that date like when Columbus discovered America. We won that son of a bitch. They timed it so it would be in zero weather, and nobody would come out except those that might be mad as hell. Jesus Christ, that west side was murder. The Ford Foundation, all the stuffed shirts over there, they really came out against us. But I just knew in my bones that I would win that son-of-a-bitching election. I never doubted for one moment I was gonna win. And election day I was positive I was. The sun was out, the day was good, and people just streamed in here to say, "I voted for you," and they had.

Sweeping 14 of 17 precincts in the south end and 14 of 25 in the northeast sector, both heavily blue-collar, Hubbard totaled 16,872 votes to 12,732 for ouster. Only in the white-collar areas in the northwest and southwest did he suffer reversals. But even a 629-to-77 swamping in the Ford Foundation wasn't nearly enough to stop him.

After spending an hour shaking hands, an ebullient Hubbard offered a few postelection platitudes, even calling himself "just a farm boy trying to get along in the city." He described his reaction to the vote as "deeply humble and greatly appreciative." The election, he said, served as a "civic hypodermic," and the "phony" recall "has already boomeranged" against the "gang of political schemers whose chief aim is to exploit the city and line their own pockets." Then, even more pointedly, he suggested that if anyone were "tired of living under our clean, safe, sane and excellent administration," he could move out of town. As a case in point, regarding his enemies in the Ford Foundation, he said, "I think I'll call a special advisory vote to be put on the April 2 ballot and get rid of 'Snob Hill.'"[17]

The recallers appeared far from resigned to accepting defeat, however. "We are resolved to carry on," Wagner said. "The people offered their efforts unselfishly in the fight. They would feel let down if we stepped aside just because we lost."

Marguerite Johnson noted that the council still was loaded five-to-two against Orvie—"and it will stay that way." But would it? At the council meeting the night after the election, a packed audience of Hubbard supporters booed the bloc of antis and cheered as Dombrowski and McCollough handed the clerk a request that their opponents resign forthwith. Johnson's response was a venomous "I've never seen such conceit," and she promised to continue the fight. But after the meeting, Orvie gave a pep talk to those who stayed behind. He urged his backers to bring in petitions "so we can begin to get them out of office. Let's begin with Johnson." He also asked the audience to "bring your friends and neighbors. It's better than a movie and a lot cheaper."

The same could have been said of his entire tenure in office, of course. But there was no underestimating the importance of Hubbard's victory. As one analyst put it, "He knew he was king of Michigan's wealthiest city, knew his reign was now threatened only by a mumbling in the corridors."[18]

25

Beating Carl Matheny, 1950-51

Be Nice to People.
                    —Orville L. Hubbard's new slogan

With the recall safely behind him, Orvie permitted himself the luxury of a
few quiet months in 1951. True, he did throw one of his famous tantrums
when *Time* magazine came out with an unflattering two-page spread on
him in March; he made a major production out of hopping up and down
on the story for the edification of department heads and newsmen.[1] Then
there was the time in May when he lost his temper after Ford's balked at
giving the city 40 acres for a park. The firm had agreed to donate the land
after Hubbard and the council threatened to condemn it, but then the council received a letter from Ford Vice-President Ernest R. Breech, scolding the
city for failing to submit project plans for approval. "Now I've heard everything," Hubbard shouted hoarsely at a council meeting. "Why don't they
just give us that little piece of stinking land? If they really had a heart, they
would develop the land themselves. Ford has never done anything for this
town—absolutely nothing. They're just too cheap, that's what." Then Hubbard pounded the table and yelled, "Why, if I see that guy Breech, I'll punch
him right in the nose." And he instructed the council clerk to say so in a
note to the company.

Beyond that, the mayor fell into the regular routine of the job. He
continued his feud with police, criticizing them as "discourteous" and "gruff,"
complaining that they "herd people around like a worker herding elephants
with a bull hook" and threatening to set up a "courtesy school" for the
department. He plugged energetically for one of his pet projects, a youth
center he envisioned on a 200-acre parcel he wanted Ford to donate. He
tried unsuccessfully to get voters to approve an April charter amendment

setting up a city-owned transit system. And he pushed through the newly obeisant council a list of proposed amendments for the November ballot, including measures giving regular cost-of-living raises to elected officials—including himself, of course—and to boost terms of office from two years to four.

In truth, Hubbard had been gearing up for the fall election since filing his petitions in January. He even put out a snappy little press release then, saying, "Orville L. Hubbard, Dearborn's politically fast-stepping mayor, today showed fine scorn for his current recall annoyance by tossing his natty hat into the suburb's mayoralty race—eight months away." As the election drew closer, he created a momentary diversion by feigning interest in a judgeship made available by the resignation of George Belding. The council actually voted four-to-three to give him the job, and Hubbard told reporters he was "seriously considering" the offer. His serious consideration lasted three weeks, at which point he backed off, saying he "just wouldn't have the heart to put people in jail." The council filled the position by appointing Guy, who had hinted he would rather be a judge than a police chief.

Meanwhile, the list of sacrificial victims for the September mayoralty primary began to grow. Erving Nielsen, the old Hubbard police chief, took out petitions in May, announcing he wanted a "full-scale investigation of the Hubbard administration." The next to announce was one Matthew O. Cassini, a policeman turned chinchilla rancher. A month after that, it was John T. McWilliams, the attorney who ran the "Save Our Hospital" rally Orvie had crashed the year before. In August came the real opposition. The primly respectable Carl Matheny, convinced he had not given Hubbard his best shot in 1949, took out petitions and promised a campaign that would be "far from quiet."

McWilliams opened up by criticizing traffic enforcement, only to draw a tasteless rejoinder from Orvie about "running over his own daughter five years ago." McWilliams explained that an accident in which he struck his daughter Ruthanne in the driveway at his home "got me interested in safety." McWilliams later distributed a leaflet so brazenly self-congratulatory that even Hubbard called it undignified. "At last, here is the colorful, courageous leader Dearborn has been waiting for," the leaflet trumpeted.

Also declaring themselves in were Patrick Doyle, perhaps Orvie's most formidable challenger, and a housewife, Velma Pamment, who instantly stamped herself as the least dignified. Promising to conduct "a louder and cornier campaign than Hubbard," Pamment announced her candidacy at an August meeting by holding up a gold-tinted toilet seat and promising, "If the public wants the kind of government they now have, they can elect me and be sure that I will follow the stupidity and extravagance of the present administration. I will see that we have gold toilet seats throughout Camp Dearborn, a stop sign on every corner and messenger uniforms for all department heads." A week later, she became the first woman mayoral candidate in Dearborn history by filing her petitions for mayor wearing overalls, a checkered shirt and straw hat and carrying a sign mimicking the mayor's frequent references to his rural background. It said, "I'm just a farm girl myself." After that, she continued to wear cowboy cap pistols at her side because, she insisted, Hubbard normally carried a gun. A week after that, she withdrew to concentrate on running for a council seat.

Doyle also removed himself from the list of eligibles by agreeing to run for council on Matheny's slate, along with such disillusioned Hubbard boosters as Martin Griffith and Ray Parker. City Clerk Myron Stevens and Treasurer William F. Kaiser also aligned themselves with Matheny.

The final field thus consisted of Matheny, McWilliams, Nielsen, Cassini—and Hubbard, whose petitions included 100 signatures from the "Gold Coast snobs," as he liked to call them, from the Ford Foundation area.

Two weeks before the primary, Matheny began his sniping. For the first time since 1935, he said, challengers would be used at the polls to help "in preserving the purity of elections and in guarding against the abuse of the elective franchise." Did that mean Hubbard was guilty of somehow finagling illegal votes? Matheny didn't say, and he soon had to abandon his poll challenger plan because his staff failed to meet state procedural requirements.

Hubbard, by contrast, tried to keep things quiet. His campaign slogan was "Be Nice to People." His billboards peppered the town with the reminder that he "kept Dearborn clean." His workers distributed hundreds of gold-colored petitions proclaiming, "You deserve re-election, Mayor Hubbard."

The calm was interrupted when, barely a week before the election, Matheny complained that someone had thrown a brick through a window at his headquarters. It happened, he said, shortly after his leaflet distributors accused Hubbard of threatening them. Matheny, stopping just short of charging the mayor with the deed, said, "Vandalism is part of the whole picture of Hubbard's vicious campaign." Hubbard, with a countercharge that his own leaflets were being stolen from porches by Matheny people, denied any responsibility for the brick incident. "None of our people would do a thing like that," he said. "They [Matheny's backers] probably did it for a publicity stunt."

That squabble almost obscured a tidbit of insider's gossip that Matheny had included in his campaign literature. Ford Motor, he said, was planning a "decentralization" of the Rouge plant, and its effect on the city might be devastating. Hubbard, however, was quick to answer, calling the story "vicious campaign bunk to make it look like Ford is pulling out of town." Given the antagonism between Orvie and Ford's, it might almost have been worth the auto maker's while to back up Matheny's claims. But, as it happened, the firm announced a few days later that it would spend "millions of dollars for expansion of the Rouge plant." Orville Hubbard, miraculously, had been vindicated by the Ford Motor Company.

That was a mean election. Matheny ran with the goddamnedest line of bullshit
I ever heard of—Ford was moving out of Dearborn, and the town was gonna be
a ghost town because of Hubbard. But that was Carl Matheny.

For all Matheny's newfound aggressiveness, the September primary
looked almost like 1949 all over again. With about half the registered voters
turning out, Hubbard rolled up his biggest primary vote ever, with 13,841
votes to 8,378 for Matheny, 1,369 for McWilliams, 416 for Nielsen and 240
for Cassini. Matheny, who had to be content with drawing 3,000-odd votes
more than any primary opponent of Hubbard's ever had, asked the other
losers to "join with me for final victory."

The mayor called the vote "another civic hypodermic," reprising his
comment from the recall election and cooing, "We shall continue being nice
to people and try to win more friends to support our program."

Doyle led the council field, setting up a confrontation between Hubbard
slaters led by Lucille McCollough and Matheny slaters led by Martin Griffith. Far back with the also-rans were Stanley Herdzik, the onetime fire
chief; Velma Pamment, who found that clowning alone was no guarantee
of election, not even in Dearborn; and George Hollman, who two years
before had accused Hubbard of being in cahoots with the gambling fraternity.

Despite his unpromising showing, Matheny continued to attack Hubbard in October. First he ridiculed Hubbard's youth center proposal as the
latest in a series of vote-getting deceptions. The mayor, he said, had "come
up with a cheap political 'gimmick' every two years—just before election
time—trying to cover up his repeated failures to deliver."[2]

A few days later, he followed up on his earlier hints that something
was wrong at the polls. This time, he demanded that a grand jury investigate
"startling and shameful" evidence of voting fraud as well as indications that
the city was spending "hundreds of thousands of dollars" illegally every
year.

The next week, he went on television accusing the Hubbard administration of taking kickbacks in return for permitting vice, gambling and other
illegal enterprises. The city, he charged, was "ruled by terror and corruption,"
and Hubbard was guilty of "forcing businessmen to pay 'tribute' under
threat of tax increases." Matheny also repeated his charges of election fraud,
contending that "hundreds of voters in the recall election were not citizens
of Dearborn." He concluded by asking the state attorney general's office to
investigate.

Hubbard, predictably, responded in kind, declaring, "Any attorney who
makes outright, malicious, dishonest statements should be disbarred."

The candidates met at the Dearborn Kiwanis Club the week before the
election. There Matheny accused Hubbard of improperly assigning 31 new
city autos, including one for his secretary, Helen Bell. Orvie demanded that
Matheny recant—"or I'll punch you in the nose." But no retraction was

forthcoming, and the mayor declined Matheny's request for a second debate.

Shortly afterward, Hubbard received an exoneration of sorts from Attorney General Frank Millard. An investigation into the voter fraud charges, he said, turned up evidence of "some irregularities" but "not wholesale or methodical." Only 16 of 121 names submitted by Matheny seemed "questionable," he said; on balance, the voting was "without evidence of fraud." The news seemed to interest Orvie only minimally, however. "Running the voting is a function of the city clerk, not the mayor," he noted, "and while I believe the voting to be honest, the city clerk is on Matheny's election slate, not mine." It was true. Although the incongruity apparently had eluded both Matheny and City Clerk Stevens, the charges of election fraud were deflected right back at them.

Things got a bit hotter. A few days before the election, Matheny filed a $100,000 slander suit against Orvie for saying the attorney should be disbarred. "This is not connected with my campaign for mayor," Matheny said somewhat disingenuously.

Hubbard had his own threats, however, revealing he had ordered three separate suits prepared against Matheny. "We've been taking notes at every one of his campaign meetings," he said, "and our only problem is to decide which one to sue for. I'll enjoy winning a suit for a change."

Hubbard literature that went out the weekend before the election contained the same kind of paranoid warnings as many of his previous ones. A handbill announcing a school rally said, "Meet, see, hear your un-bossed mayor at his fighting best . . . rip, strip and expose the scheming, double-talking Detroit lawyer, and the behind the scenes gang with a bag of money who are smearing Dearborn with a pack of lies and again trying to capture your city hall."[3]

Another one raised the old specter of crime, contending "no vice, graft or corruption is tolerated under Hubbard."

November 6 was ushered in by a heavy blizzard lasting through the afternoon and evening, and Matheny's chances seemed to improve with every minute the snow swirled. The anti-Hubbard faction would show up no matter what, but would the mayor's precinct workers be able to get enough of his supporters out? Ringing doorbells and pushing stalled cars, the Hubbard forces helped turn out nearly 60 percent of the registered voters and give the mayor his sixth term rather handily, 16,050 to 11,101. It was a bit better than he had done against Matheny in 1949, and he even managed to collect 96 votes (to Matheny's 411) in the Ford Foundation.

Tempering the victory was a decisive defeat for several Hubbard-sponsored charter amendments, including the cost-of-living allowance and four-year terms for the mayor and other elected officials. Also going down were his proposal for a youth center and the establishment of new recreation and sanitation departments. The lone proposal to pass was one Hubbard had opposed, a plan of Judge George Martin's to cut back to one full-time municipal judge, thus reducing Ralph Guy to part-time status as a $1,000-a-year associate judge.

The council race was a mixed bag. Doyle again led the field, bringing with him two Matheny slaters, ex-Hubbardites Parker and Griffith. Hubbard managed to slip in four of his slate members, although he considered only two of them, McCollough and Edward J. Dombrowski, reliable. The others, Joe Ford and George Bondie, had opposed him during the recall. The major shock was the showing of incumbent Council President Marguerite Johnson, who finished only twelfth. Amid speculation that Hubbard had offered to make her police chief if she quit the council, she had withdrawn from the race "in the interests of teamwork and good government." But the mayor "drafted" her right back onto his slate, saying she had supported him "better than any other councilman," aside from the small matter of working against him in the recall. Even Orvie's gracious endorsement couldn't get her elected again, however.

Marguerite was a switcher. She was a switcher and a bitcher. I called her a witch, a political witch. She was gonna sue me for that. She was the ringleader when the sons of bitches double-crossed us that year on the recall. So she wanted to make peace, which we were willing to do. So the fall election came, and people wouldn't vote for Maggie.

Hubbard's victory statement was a rehash of previous efforts. "I have never felt so humble, proud and grateful," he said. Added Matheny, restating the obvious, "We were unable to convince the voters of the real jeopardy our community is in."

He also was unable to convince the new owners of the *Dearborn Press*, who had adopted a policy of "constructive neutrality" credited by the Hubbard camp with helping in the victory. Whereas the Klamser-run paper for several years had ridiculed, attacked or ignored "the chubby mayor," as it often called him, the publication now treated him fairly, if not fawningly. In December, the *Press* named Orvie one of its citizens of the year for his "two sensational triumphs at the polls."[4]

26

The Clown Mask Caper, 1952

One of the things I'll do in Chicago is to punch Carl
Matheny in the nose.
—Orville L. Hubbard, describing his agenda at the
Republican National Convention[1]

The early-morning train from Detroit to Chicago had come and gone, and
Orville Hubbard wasn't on it. He had promised reporters he would attend
the 1952 Republican National Convention to vote as a delegate for Robert
Taft. He was going, he said, even if he had to disguise himself to evade arrest
under terms of his bond in the Fish case—an arrangement that technically
made him a prisoner within the boundaries of Wayne County. But there
was no mistaking a man of Hubbard's girth, and when newsmen gathered
in downtown Detroit to watch for him to board the 7:13 A.M. New York
Central *Wolverine*, as promised, he was nowhere in sight. Was this another
case where Orvie had made a wild promise and then failed to follow through?

Some reporters thought so, but those who stayed around were rewarded
for their time. A few hours later, as passengers prepared to board the noon
train to Chicago, down the Michigan Central Depot platform bounded a set
of big-bellied triplets. All were carrying tan leather suitcases, wearing green
shirts and hiding their faces behind identical clown masks with idiotic grins
frozen on them. The mayor of Dearborn was going to the GOP convention
disguised as a clown.

Finally, not three years after he had been found guilty of libeling John
Fish, it had come to this. Hubbard obviously was prepared to do anything
to get out of paying off the $7,500 he still owed Fish from 1950. Not that
he hadn't tried to figure out other ways to circumvent his obligation. By
July 1951, with the recall well behind him and his next dismantling of Carl
Matheny's candidacy still ahead of him, the mayor thought he had hit on
a way to pay off Fish without really having to pay him off. At a special

council meeting, with Patrick Doyle and Martin Griffith absent and unable to challenge him, Hubbard railroaded through a package of proposed charter amendments for the September ballot. One of them asked, "Are you in favor of making Lawyer Fish help pay his own $7,500 libel judgment against Mayor Orville L. Hubbard by amending the Charter to provide special compensation therefore?" The council was actually going to ask the voters to pay off Hubbard's bill, along with $450 interest, about $60 in court costs and any tax liability resulting from the ballot proposal.

As Fish was to comment later, "It's the same old story. The deadbeat wants the people to pay his bills."

Hubbard didn't have quite such an easy time with the state of Michigan as he had with the council, however. The attorney general's office ruled the proposition illegal as a private use of public funds. Under state law, the council now had to approve the measure by a two-thirds majority to overcome the objection. But this time, with Doyle and Griffith present and with Hubbard loyalists Lucille McCollough and Edward Dombrowski voting no, it went down. It lost again several weeks later, even after Orvie had it reworded to satisfy the state's "phony" objections.

Hubbard wasn't the only one who owed Fish money, however. The attorney was having difficulty getting his due from the city, too, thanks partly to two mayoral vetoes of council resolutions to pay Fish for representing the Civil Service and retirement boards in court.

The mayor obviously was feeling less than contrite about the Fish libel trial. He continued to write veto messages the way a schoolkid would use a squirtgun, one of them calling his antagonist a "schemer and political disappointee operating behind the shady scene of last year's recall to smear his clean city in conniving and plotting that black, rotten deal."

Fish threatened to sue again for libel and for his still-unpaid fee, "although," he conceded, "I suppose that would be pointless." He eventually collected $4,000 in fees, although he had to sue the city again when the mayor vetoed another $2,500 due for representing Marguerite Johnson after the council cut her salary as public safety director in 1953.

Despite the name-calling in public, Hubbard had been wheedling Fish in private for months to get him to wink at proposals for the mayoral itinerary. From October 1950 to December 1953, Orvie wrote Fish 30 requests for permission to leave the county without forfeiting his jail-limits bond.[2] In October 1950, he asked to attend a U.S. Conference of Mayors meeting in Washington, D.C., on civilian defense, noting, "One of the principal dangers facing all American Cities, and especially Dearborn, is that of an atomic attack." Fish refused, but that didn't stop the mayor from asking the next week for permission to go to New York for a public works congress and the Army-Michigan football game. To sweeten the offer, he offered a $10,000 airline insurance policy to enable Fish to "'get yours first' and please turn the balance over to my wife and five children." He signed himself, "Your

223

Un-Bossed Mayor." Fish ignored the letter. Two weeks later, the attorney got a council request to let the mayor attend a sewage disposal conference in Oakland County. Fish sent back a letter of refusal, along with a recommendation that Orvie be removed from office.

After a few more unsuccessful tries, Hubbard eased off on his routine for a while, then started again with requests for trips that included appearances at the wedding of son Jim in Big Rapids and at the Mudsock School reunion back home. To many of these requests, Hubbard appended a folksy little reply that Fish could sign and adopt as his own. A request to visit his mother in November 1951 was accompanied by this sample note of consent: "Go on down to Sturgis for Thanksgiving with your mother. It is OK with me, but drive safely and don't eat too much." And a request to undergo a physical examination at the Mayo Brothers Clinic in Rochester, Minnesota, in February 1952, "because of being somewhat under the weather," contained this: "After all, I have an interest in your good health. . . . Good luck to you and stop in to see me when you return." Fish, not noticeably impressed at Hubbard's sense of humor, continued to ignore the requests.

Permission or no permission, however, Orvie had his own way of dealing with things. And in June, he came up with a new way of tormenting his judgment creditor. As one of 46 Michigan delegates elected to the GOP convention the next month, Hubbard was determined to make an appearance. "When I get ready to go to Chicago," he told newsmen, "I'll pick up my bag and go. Chicago is a big place, and Fish can come down and look for me." Fish returned Orvie's taunts in kind, urging the mayor to be sure to see the GOP favorite, Dwight Eisenhower, on his scheduled visit to Detroit the following weekend. "This will be his last chance to see the general," Fish quipped. "The minute the mayor starts for Chicago, I start for circuit court."

A few weeks later, Hubbard told newsmen he had spent the Fourth of July weekend in Chicago and would return for the roll call of delegates. As for Fish: "He's got to catch me first." His plan was this: he would leave early July 9 on the NYC *Wolverine* and be in Chicago to cast his ballot that night. Oh, and one other thing, he told newsmen: so that Fish couldn't identify him in court from photos or TV footage, he might wear a mask.

The night before the convention, the mayor's number three son, John, showed up at the Michigan delegation headquarters at the Congress Hotel, asking for his father's credentials. Delegation Chairman Arthur S. Summerfield refused to turn them over, phoning the mayor to say that the national chairman, Guy G. Gabrielson, had ruled they would have to be claimed in person. With that, Hubbard's tickets, papers and delegate badge were locked up in the hotel safe. That was the doing of the custodian in charge of credentials, one Carl Matheny.

Back in Detroit, with newsmen milling around the train station on convention morning, the *Wolverine* pulled in—and then pulled out again without Hubbard. Later, however, when the three "clowns" showed up, they were surrounded by reporters, photographers, a newsreel cameraman and various curiosity-seekers. One of the clowns identified himself as Orville Hubbard, but he refused to name the others, since "they might be used as witnesses to prove I left the county." Even with all the hoopla, the clown conceded his plans were beginning to unravel. He acknowledged he probably wouldn't be allowed to vote without signing for his credentials. "That will prove to Fish I was in Chicago," he said. "Orville Hubbard isn't such a sucker as that." Just the same, the clowns would make their presence felt at the convention. "All three of us will wear our masks and we'll raise cain," he said, promising that "one of the things I'll do in Chicago is to punch Carl Matheny in the nose." After boarding the train, the clowns posed obligingly for photos. All the papers ran pictures, bestowing on Hubbard the title of "most clownish mayor in the United States."

In Chicago that night, the whereabouts of the three clowns was a bit of a mystery. One of them had his picture taken at the Congress, although nobody knew for sure whether it was Orvie. The convention itself went on with its decorum intact. The mayor of Dearborn was reported seated with the Puerto Rican delegation at one point, but he never picked up his credentials, never made it to his seat to vote, and, in truth, never was identified positively on the convention floor or anywhere near it.

The next night, he was back in Detroit with two roly-poly men in clown masks to meet with reporters in an NYC train shed, where crew members of the *Twilight Limited* said they believed the three passengers had been on the train all the way from Chicago. Hubbard's story seemed to have some holes in it, however. He said, in effect, that convention officials "stole" his credentials by giving them to an alternate delegate. "They even sold the guest tickets which were legally mine," he said. "The purpose in not giving me my credentials was to keep me from voting. They are all Ike men and I was for Taft." Despite the obstacles, he said, he had stayed at the Congress and, wearing buttons for both Taft and Eisenhower, sat in the convention gallery for two and a half hours during the voting. Not everyone was convinced of his veracity, however, even though several papers had reported him present in Chicago.

Fish, for example, wrote a quite different version in a letter to a fellow attorney the following week. "Actually," Fish said, "Mr. Hubbard did not leave Wayne County and did not go to the Chicago convention. As a matter of fact, last Friday he came to my office asking for forgiveness."

What really happened did not become apparent until months later, and then through no doing of the mayor's. It was during a grand jury probe of the Hubbard administration in early 1954 that his administrative assistant, Norbert C. Schlaff, testified that his boss didn't go to Chicago after all. Instead, Schlaff said, Orvie gave reporters the slip and got off the train in Jackson, about 50 miles west of the county line. As had been arranged, Schlaff picked him up and drove him back to Dearborn.

I wanted to go to the convention. Ed Brand—he was a reporter for the Detroit Times—*he called my hand on it. I was just bullshitting around a little bit, telling Ed we'll have the other guys go along, and if they should pick up the wrong guy, we'll sue them for false arrest or some goddamn crap like that. So Ed put me on the spot on it. He went downtown and bought three masks, brought them out here to us. Well, Christ, I couldn't very well renege after all the copy I'd had on the thing. So I went down, got on the train. The* Times *had two guys were supposed to stay with me all the way. So I had gone to the washroom or something and I got off the damn train in Jackson. Ed was right with me in the car, but he never dreamed I was going to get off. The other two guys were [Harold] DeWyk and [Jimmy] Dick, all about the same size at that time. They had to wear those goddamn masks all the way to Chicago. DeWyk had a belt that had H on it for Harold. They thought it was Hubbard for sure. They never would give 'em my credentials.*[3]

The summer of 1952 wasn't all clowning around for Hubbard, however. He was still trying to get the taxpayers to help him settle his libel judgment. He turned in petitions calling for another ballot proposal, this one for the upcoming November election. Although the petitions didn't specify any connection with the Fish verdict, it was hardly a secret: the proposal would give the mayor an expense allowance of $7,500. The way Hubbard figured it, the average taxpayer would be out about a nickel, and Ford Motor would have to pay $4,500. "I have had numerous individuals and special groups offer to pay off the judgment for me," Hubbard said in explaining the scheme. "I have refused because I did not wish to be under obligations for that sum." He obviously felt more comfortable being under obligation to the voters. The attorney general disapproved this proposal, too, however, thus raising the likelihood of a court challenge if voters passed it. Dearborn went for the Eisenhower-Nixon ticket in the November election—the first time since 1928 that the city had voted for a Republican president—but there was no need for any legal complication on the mayor's expense account. Voters turned it down, 25,601 to 9,790.

It was more than a year later before Hubbard was forced to think again about having to pay off Fish. In January 1954, his wanderings turned up in court during ouster proceedings against him. Testifying before Circuit Judge Wallace W. Waalkes of Grand Rapids, Schlaff admitted that his boss had been out of the county with him on city business at least four times since the jail-limits bond took effect in 1950. There was a trip to Washington, D.C., in June 1952, two to Long Island in July 1952 and July 1953 and one to Toledo, Ohio, in October 1953. Was this at last the proof Fish needed to revoke the mayor's bond and have him jailed? He demanded that Wayne County Sheriff Andrew C. Baird arrest Orvie, but the sheriff refused, insisting that Fish was required to bring suit while his debtor was physically outside the county, not after the fact. Schlaff further corroborated the mayor's meanderings several weeks later during a second appearance before Waalkes. Hubbard, he said, had "outsmarted" Fish by leaving the county more than 200 times. One of the trips was the clown mask episode, he said, but most were predawn jaunts to Camp Dearborn.

If Orvie was worried by the revelations, he wasn't letting on. A few months later, in May, he asked Fish for permission to go to tiny Chesaning, 30 miles west of Saginaw, for Mayors' Exchange Day. Fish told him, "Orville, I am going to slip it to you if I can," and that was all the prodding Hubbard needed. He showed up in Chesaning the evening before the official festivities and proceeded to address city fathers on such topics as street cleaning and keeping dogs out of gardens. He also toured a dairy, a slaughterhouse, a coop elevator and the town swimming pool. Then, at a minute after midnight, with Mayors' Exchange Day officially arrived, he had his picture taken next to the village limits sign, waving his hat. Fish, who had heard about Hubbard's ploy, phoned the village attorney, John Quinn, asking him "to slap papers" on Hubbard. Quinn refused.

Later in the month, the mayor invented a new way to violate his bond: 2,000 feet in the air and 120 miles an hour. When a brewery made a DC-3 available to city officials, Hubbard came up with a laundry list of ideas for an aerial tour, including a chance to size up the effectiveness of a police helicopter to help with traffic jams and stop low-flying planes. Orvie himself demurred as he helped see off a load of councilmen, department heads and newsmen for an hourlong flight. "Not me," he said. "I can't leave the county." When the flight returned, he ushered a second group aboard, and, with the photographers all heading back for their cars, he scrambled on and slammed the door shut as the plane taxied off.

A year later, in May 1955, Hubbard was promising another Mayors' Exchange Day appearance, this time in Hastings, southwest of Lansing, and Fish was threatening to be there, too. But the day came and went, with Fish's operatives keeping tabs on Hubbard in Wayne County while a three-car entourage of other Dearborn officials did the honors in Hastings. The ceremonies had ended, but at 1:00 the next morning, another group of Dearborn officials showed up in Hastings with a photographer—and Orville L. Hubbard. And there, rousted out of bed to greet them, were three aldermen and a local chamber of commerce official, still in their pajamas. After 10 minutes of handshakes and small talk, Hubbard was whisked away again. "It was him, all right," said the chamber's Phil Schumbert. "He never stopped talking, and when he told those men with him to move, they jumped." Said a chagrined Fish the next day, "One of these days, I'm going to catch him."

It took another year, but at last Fish thought he had what he needed. In early July 1955, he filed suit to collect $10,000 from Sheriff Baird for permitting Hubbard to violate his bond. This time, thanks in part to sur-

227

veillance by men with two-way radios, there was proof that the mayor had been at Camp Dearborn on July 6–7, according to Fish's attorney, Chris M. Youngjohn.

With this, Hubbard became downright reckless. In late July, the local papers ran a photo of him at Camp Dearborn astride a pedal boat and wearing a loud Hawaiian shirt. A couple of weeks later, he sent a *Dearborn Press* editor a postcard from California. In late August, he was reported in Fort Knox at the invitation of the U.S. Army. In late November, he was reported in Miami for a meeting of the American Municipal Association. "He probably thinks he has nothing to lose," Fish conjectured. "He's wrong, and I'm going to show him so."

Wrong or not, Hubbard kept right on traveling. In May 1956, unable to resist the lure of another Mayors' Exchange Day, he put in a daylight appearance at the Upper Peninsula town of Escanaba. "Under the old Northwest Territory ordinances, Escanaba is right in Wayne County," he explained enigmatically.

By August, Fish announced he had the goods on Hubbard. His proof did not center on the Camp Dearborn trip he originally had cited, however. This time, he had documentation that Orvie was at Miami's Biscayne Terrace Hotel, room 907, the previous November 27–30 with the city's motor transport head, R. William Hill. He also had testimony from Detroit Mayor Albert E. Cobo and other airline passengers who said they saw Hubbard on the trip. A September hearing was scheduled in Wayne Circuit Court. But first they had to find Hill and Hubbard. Hill turned up only after a bench warrant was issued for his arrest. Orvie, meanwhile, was his old elusive self.

It wasn't easy for Fish to find someone to serve the mayor a subpoena. Nobody from the city or the municipal court would do it. Finally, an old Hubbard adversary, Godfrey Glomb, volunteered. But after Glomb tried the mayor's home at 2:00 one morning, getting no answer and driving off, he suddenly found himself in trouble. A few miles away, he was stopped by a Dearborn policeman and arrested for disturbing the peace. Later, it was discovered that the arresting officer was Patrolman Jim Hubbard, and Fish, tired of "fooling around with Hubbard and his stooges," said he might sue for false arrest. Later that month, Associate Municipal Judge John T. McWilliams found Glomb not guilty, and he scolded Jim Hubbard for arresting the process server without a warrant and for failing to give his correct name when asked for identification.

A few days afterward, Glomb and another man, Nick J. Tremba, "eased up on Hubbard in the shadows as he stood at a soft drink stand" at Camp Dearborn—and successfully served him. The two did "a lot of unnecessary work," the mayor said. "All they had to do was call me on the telephone and I would have accepted the paper." Hubbard appeared promptly for the hearing, but threatened to go back to Miami when he found his case was being shifted to a different judge.

228

Under threat of arrest, he returned that afternoon before the new judge, Miles N. Culehan, and confirmed what William Hill already had sworn to that morning: he had indeed gone to Miami the previous November on city business. However, he added, Fish had given him verbal permission more than a year earlier to go "anywhere on official city business."

Fish denied this, and Circuit Judge Thomas J. Murphy, who eventually took over the case, couldn't believe it either. Ruling for Fish the following year, in January 1957, Murphy said, "By a preponderance of evidence I find that Fish never gave Hubbard consent—either oral or written—to leave the county. The mayor may have drawn the conclusion that Fish gave oral permission, but I am afraid the wish was the father of the thought." Hubbard, apparently reconciled to the judgment, congratulated Murphy on "the fine manner in which you try lawsuits" and complimented him on his "beautiful courtroom."

Fish, asked by Murphy why he never had tried to garnishee the mayor's salary, replied, "I wouldn't do that because he is making only $6,500 a year, and I didn't want to make a martyr of him." The way Orvie and his friends orchestrated things, however, that was the effect anyway.

The court said Baird would have to pay Fish the $5,000 posted by Hubbard's original cosigners on the bond, but Fish would have to look elsewhere for another $5,101 in interest and expenses he claimed. A few weeks later, Baird sued Orvie for the amount for which the sheriff was not liable.

The next week, the *Press* ran a front-page story carrying a suggestion from an anonymous letter writer that Dearbornites voluntarily pay off the libel judgment. By March, a fund drive was officially under way and had a chairman, Vic Rouse, Hubbard's most vitriolic opponent in the 1949 campaign. "This is a drive for the little fellow," Rouse said in announcing establishment of the Freedom Fund for Mayor Orville L. Hubbard. "Donations will let Mayor Hubbard know that the people of Dearborn appreciate all he has done for them."[4]

Vic Rouse—he was against me in the goddamn recall. Politics makes strange bedfellows. People made donations to it all over. I had nothing to do with it at all.

The *Press* continued to shill for the fund, and at last Rouse announced a presentation ceremony at city hall for mid-June. Before a small gathering made up mostly of city employees, Rouse turned over a $5,000 check to Sheriff Baird in compensation for the forfeited bond and another check for $3,549.25 to Fish's attorney, Youngjohn. An additional $750 came in by late July, and Rouse said he knew the mayor "will be very happy to make up the difference" between the amount collected and the $10,000 plus Fish figured he had coming. Fish said he'd get the rest, even if he had to go ahead and attach the mayor's salary.[5]

For his part, Hubbard was very happy to turn the whole thing into one more excuse to needle Fish. "I've always paid my own way," he said. "I have never been primarily interested in money. My job is more fun than making money. I hope if Fish and his family use it to make their proposed trip to Europe, they have a pleasant vacation."

27

The Grand Jury, 1953

It is a bitter pill to swallow, realizing that two men and
their click [*sic*], . . . after twelve years of trying to strike
and inflict their venom on the people of Dearborn, are
finally successful in seeking outside help to try and
blacken the name of the greatest mayor in the United
States.
—Dearborn resident Earl E. Orr, commenting on accusations brought against Orville L. Hubbard[1]

It seemed an innocent enough encounter when, one winter day early in
1950, Dearborn's three tax assessors got together to discuss the property
assessment of a budget-priced furniture store known as People's Outfitting
Company. The way one of them, bespectacled, white-haired Clyde Hale, was
to tell it later, sometime after he quit his job over a disagreement with
Hubbard, he and fellow assessors Carl Farmer and J. Joseph Schaefer met
with a tax expert from People's who "approved of the valuation and commended us for a 'fair job.'"[2]

Hubbard, who was planning his strategy for his much-rumored recall
and his libel trial, couldn't have cared less about the People's meeting. But
the events that followed it proved to be a greater threat to him than either
of his other concerns.

A week or so later, according to Hale, Farmer was saying that City
Planner Joseph Goldfarb had told an official at People's he could "get the
taxes lowered if he knew the right people." In Dearborn, the "right people"
clearly included Hubbard, and a few weeks after that, the mayor was meeting at a Detroit restaurant with Farmer, Goldfarb and People's officials.

Soon afterward, Hale continued, Farmer came up with a directive: "We'll
just have to cut People's taxes." When Hale and Schaefer objected, Farmer left
for a while, then came back and repeated the order. "We said again that we
disapproved," Hale said, "and Farmer told us that we'd have to cut the tax or
be out of a job. He said he would go up and see Hubbard about it. When he
returned, he said, 'Well, I'm going to cut the taxes on People's whether you
want to or not.' Schaefer and I were still against it. He said, 'Well, it's cut anyway.'"

Seven or eight months later, Farmer himself apparently began to feel regrets, Hale indicated. He said Farmer and Public Works Director Frank Swapka picked him up and took him to Detroit's Book Cadillac Hotel, where they met Councilmen George Bondie, Joe Ford, Martin Griffith and Marguerite Johnson. "Farmer asked the councilmen if they would remove Hubbard from office if he provided the sworn affidavits concerning the tax reduction at People's," Hale said. "He was insistent on Hubbard's removal and said that this instance was only one of the times Hubbard had had tax assessments cut. . . . Farmer said, 'It will be easier to get Hubbard out this way than to recall him.'" But the councilmen "refused to accept the idea," Hale continued. "Their view was that it seemed to be more democratic to let the people remove him from office. I agreed with them."

Hale's recounting of the People's affair didn't get much of a rise from Dearborn voters, even though it received considerable press coverage as part of the council's flimsy attempt to discredit Orvie just before the recall election.

Though little else was said about the tax reduction for another year and a half, the mayor's enemies had not given up. In September 1952, the People's case resurfaced in a petition demanding a grand jury investigation of various "irregularities" in the Hubbard administration. The petition did not accuse Hubbard or anyone else by name, and the "criminal violations" were no more specific than those cited the year before by Carl Matheny. This time there were vague allusions to officials pocketing public money, mishandling funds, rigging contract specifications to favor certain bidders, and conspiring to reduce assessments illegally.

It sounded like a rehash of earlier accusations. But Charles A. Wagner, the recall leader who was also the moving force behind the new petition, noted that six months of legwork went into this effort, and there was a good reason not to list specific charges: witnesses might be tampered with. "We have something this time," he assured reporters, "and we will tell it to the jury."

Hubbard said the charges were too vague to comment on, though he said Wagner was "peeved recently" because the city was putting up an archery range and a parking lot near his house. "I suggested that Charlie never enter his backyard without an apple on his head," Hubbard quipped. "Must have irked him."

It didn't take long for Orvie's lightheartedness to become heavy-handed, however. He ridiculed the petitioners as the "same old gang" of spiteful outsiders that "lost its case before the grandest of grand juries, the people, at every election." In truth, the petitioners were all signers in the recall effort. Besides Wagner, there were Earl Hole, George H. Kessell, Harold Cordell, Joseph G. Nemethy and Loran G. Stoops. Hole had been head of the Dearborn Historical Commission at a time when Orvie had derided it as the "Dearborn Hysterical Commission."

Hubbard went for the big headline, offering $100 "to anyone who can show me any vice or gambling in this town. It is clean. It is known to be clean. That's the way I stay in office." He also stepped up his counterattack, filing his own petitions denying Wagner's "wild and general" charges and demanding that any grand jury find out where his election opponents got their funding. Of particular interest, he indicated, was Wagner's backing by "gambling and other predatory interests." He charged that a "big" gambler had been offering $1,000 bets six weeks before that a grand jury petition would be filed against the mayor. Wagner promised to study the statement for libel action.

A few days later, Wagner had another of Hubbard's familiar red herrings to deal with. In an affidavit filed with Circuit Judge Miles Culehan, appointed to confer with Wagner's group about the charges, Orvie accused the Panhandle Eastern Pipe Line Company of being the secret force behind the grand jury request. There was a certain circumstantial logic to the claim. The mayor had thwarted the gas company the previous March, vetoing a council resolution authorizing it to pipe surplus natural gas directly to Ford Motor and other local industrial firms. Hubbard had accused Panhandle of being "hog hungry for more profits." When Wagner casually mentioned that the Hubbard investigation also had begun six months earlier, that obviously had set the mayor to looking at his calendar. And when Wagner revealed that one of his investigators had been Gordon Gillis, a former assistant prosecutor and a member of the old Ferguson grand jury investigating team, that clinched it for Hubbard. Gillis, as it happened, also had been working for Panhandle for five years and, according to Hubbard, had "virtually camped on the doorsteps of various councilmen in a desperate effort to have the council favor Panhandle." Orvie called Gillis a "busy bee" in "a long campaign of harassment of me 'because Hubbard won't let anyone make a fast buck in Dearborn.' That applies equally to a petty, chiseling numbers runner or to a multimillion-dollar utilities gang." Wagner observed that Hubbard's attempt to link the grand jury request with the Panhandle campaign was "ridiculous."

There was a big struggle going on then, particularly—Jesus Christ, I'm getting so fucking mad about this I'm liable to say something I shouldn't—the struggle for gas. Panhandle wanted to come in and take off the commercial market. They were working with Ford's. You know, they [Ford's] didn't give a goddamn about anything. They had the money, put a streamroller over you and forget you. They needed four votes on the City Council. So Ford's were putting the pressure on everybody around here for them to grant the Pipe Line people permission to sell direct to Ford's. So we said the hell with 'em. We cast our lot with Michigan Consolidated Gas Company, because they claimed that if Ford and other industrial users were able to take off the cream of the business for industrial use, they'd lose that business and that would necessitate increasing rates to homeowners.

A few weeks later, in October, the circuit bench authorized Prosecutor Gerald O'Brien to look into the charges of wrongdoing in Dearborn and decide whether a grand jury were warranted. Hubbard's response was instantaneous. He filed three affidavits with the court, asking to appear for a grilling. "You are urged to fire questions at me about the 'wild and weird' Wagner-Panhandle charges," he said, "and, on my honor as an officer of your court, I will tell you the truth quick and fast, and produce for you within minutes any city record."

As events progressed, Orvie cooled a bit on the notion of making court appearances. But before he needed to do so, he took a tack that might let him make any probe of his administration seem politically inspired. In mid-December, he announced he was a judicial candidate, sending out Christmas cards and enclosing petitions to be circulated on his behalf for a circuit court race the next April. Not long afterward, in January 1953, the circuit bench voted unanimously to conduct a one-man grand jury probe into Dearborn as "necessary in the interest of public justice." O'Brien and Michigan Attorney General Frank Millard said there was reasonable cause to believe the Wagner petition. Hundreds of witnesses had been questioned, they said, and many others refused to appear unless compelled to by a grand jury. The grand juror was to be Miles Culehan, who said he would begin as soon as possible. Hubbard, predictably, accused the judges of using the event to hamper his run for a court seat.

A couple of months later, there were increasing signs of animosity between Hubbard and Culehan, who was running for reelection to the bench. Hubbard had told reporters that, if elected, he would "put the rest of the ciruit judges to shame by opening court at 8 A.M.," and Culehan had responded that "the hours kept by Wayne Circuit judges are set by law, but Hubbard, never having practiced law, would not know this."

The mayor showed up to ask Culehan about the quote—and about a comment that the judge might look into a gun permit issued to Hubbard. Instead of meeting with him, Culehan called court into session, giving Orvie a chance to say that he had no current gun permit and that he had practiced law for nine years, even though he was unaware of the law setting court hours. And, added Hubbard, "I still don't think it's fair for the grand jury to make cracks about me in the papers." Conceded Culehan, "You're right, Mr. Hubbard." After the mayor left, Culehan told reporters, "This is not a Hubbard grand jury, as the mayor thinks it is. I'm not going to fight with him."

As the grand jury got under way in late January, with the judge calling Wagner as the first witness, Hubbard was active himself. He began checking out the finances of the inquiry and complained that regular court funds were being "misappropriated" to fund it. And he demanded that O'Brien issue a criminal warrant against Panhandle's Gillis for acting as a private detective without a state license or proper bonding. The mayor also asked Joseph A. Moynihan, presiding circuit judge, to name an "impartial outstate judge" to run the grand jury. Culehan's appointment, Hubbard said, had been "scandalous and improper because he and I are running for the same office."

The whining from the mayor had no effect except to prompt the State Bar of Michigan to say it was observing Hubbard's conduct "with a great deal of interest."

Since the grand jury's proceedings were kept secret by law, Hubbard had no legal way of knowing what was going on. But in early February, he came up with a scheme. He showed up as attorney for City Controller George Brady and Deputy City Treasurer Peter Kruthers. Culehan, after determining that Orvie was a paid-up member of the bar, barred him from court anyway.

It was not until April that the mayor had a chance to appear as a witness. When a State Police detective tried to subpoena him at the County Building downtown, Hubbard managed to pirouette away as the paper floated to the floor. "You don't have to subpoena me," the mayor said. "I'll appear any time."

He did show up to testify, but he was still looking for ways to stymie the inquiry. As an ex officio member of the county's Board of Supervisors, Hubbard had been trying to block a Culehan request for $10,000 to pay steno expenses. In April, he asked his colleagues to table the measure "as a courtesy to a fellow member." With his hands upraised, he declared, "The future will show that you'll never have to feel that you served with a crook on this board." The supervisors voted to give Culehan his money, but since the yes votes fell four short of a majority of the full board, the resolution was defeated. The inquiry proceeded with expenses being paid out of regular jury and witness fees.

A parade of witnesses appeared before the grand jury, including Farmer, Goldfarb, Swapka, City Attorney Dale Fillmore, all seven councilmen and newly named Public Safety Director Marguerite Johnson.

Farmer, with an inkling of what was coming, released a Hubbard-style statement criticizing the "false and malicious gossip" about the People's assessment cut "cooked up in the clouded and revengeful mind of a double-talking disgruntled former associate," an obvious reference to Clyde Hale. Farmer's side of the case was straightforward: People's assessment in 1950 had indeed been cut $221,850 from the previous year, including $132,600 for real estate and another $89,250 for personal property. But what had not been pointed out before, he said, was that the adjustment corrected an unwarranted increase for the company between 1948 and 1949. The assessment for People's land and buildings more than doubled—from $370,000 to $884,140—from 1948 to 1949 before the assessors cut it back to $751,540 in 1950, he said. Nonetheless, Farmer was indicted in April for perjuring himself during his appearance before Culehan. "There's no doubt about it," Farmer told reporters. "We raised the taxes and we reduced the taxes. We've never denied that." Culehan's warrant quoted Farmer as saying, "I did tell Schaefer that the mayor told me to go over the thing and see if there was anything wrong." The warrant also said Farmer lied when he denied to the grand jury that he had told several persons he had enough on Hubbard to oust him from office.

In May, the grand jury accused Goldfarb, the city planner, with misfeasance and malfeasance, including his refusal to pay a bill of $656.02 to People's after the tax cut. The next month, Goldfarb resigned "to practice architecture and planning." The charges against him were "absurd," he said, but his $6,500 salary "does not make up for all the abuse I have to take."

But at least Goldfarb did not have to answer to criminal charges. Pretrial examination for the unlucky Farmer began in late May before Detroit Recorder's Judge George Murphy. The first witness was Hale, who stood by the story he had told the City Council in 1951, saying he and Schaefer signed the tax rolls despite misgivings. Under questioning from Farmer's attorney, Edward N. Barnard, however, Hale admitted he didn't know the People's assessment had been hiked more than $500,000 in 1949. He said he simply objected to the 1950 reduction because the People's tax expert said the old figure was fair. Barnard attacked Hale as an "incompetent" who "couldn't assess a baby buggy" and didn't know an assessment "from a hole in the ground."

A few days later, in early June, the Farmer exam escalated into the kind of grilling that Hubbard, months earlier, had claimed he welcomed. Sitting as an observer at Farmer's defense table, an astonished Hubbard was called to the stand. Barnard objected, but Judge Murphy overruled him. "You have nothing to hide," Irving Beattie, assistant attorney general, said to the mayor. Barnard snapped back, "You should hide your face. You did this for a little publicity."

When the mayor took the stand, Beattie asked pointedly, "Did you ever receive any gift or gratuity from the People's Outfitting Company?" "I did," Hubbard replied. But a moment later, he added, "I think the gift was from one of the officers, and not from the company. As a matter of fact, I don't know what it was, whether it was from an officer or the company." He said he received the gift "some time after" the tax cut.

Beattie also read into the record Orvie's refusal during the grand jury to answer questions about gifts from People's. Barnard objected to further questions, all but blowing up: "They apparently didn't get anything at the grand jury. Now they are trying to get it here. They have run out of their case against Carl Farmer, and they are trying to use you, Your Honor." Murphy upheld the objection but permitted Hubbard to testify about his 1950 lunch with Goldfarb, Farmer and Henry and James Wineman of People's. He could not recall discussing taxes, he said, but he added that the Winemans paid for the lunch.

Afterward, when reporters asked Hubbard about the gift, he refused to answer, even under Barnard's prodding: "Oh, go on and tell them. I understand you got a television set."[3] Hubbard later collected himself and gave the press his rationale: "This looks bad in the papers, but I did absolutely nothing for People's other than give the same courtesy I extend to a dozen firms or citizens every year who come in protesting assessment increases." He said that after the Winemans protested the new figure, he called Farmer in "and asked him to reexamine the situation. Eventually Farmer was able to give some relief. Since then People's has made three requests for assessment cuts, which have been refused."

Hubbard, who later described the TV as a large black-and-white RCA console, acknowledged that he frequently received small gifts from acquaintances. "I've even received bushel baskets of tomatoes from friends," he said, "and as long as I am not under obligation, I see no reason for not accepting them. Sometimes it would be embarrassing to turn down such homey gifts from honest, well-meaning citizens. Maybe I should have passed People's gift on to some institution—I even thought of it at the time—but I didn't, and it's too late now."

They complained about their assessment being so high. It did look funny, you know, when your assessment's suddenly doubled. And I had Farmer come up to explain what had happened. I asked for nothing. They offered nothing. Then Jimmy [Wineman] called me up after. He said, "We're gonna send you over a TV." I said, "For what?" He said, "Just because you treated us so decent when we were in your office." I just treated them the same as I would any other citizen. They did send the TV. And even now I don't see anything wrong with accepting it. Except maybe today I wouldn't have done it. Maybe better judgment would have been not to accept it. I don't know. Truman, Eisenhower accepted things. It was a complete surprise to me. It had no connection as far as influencing me was concerned. So what happened then, the grand jury, he asked me a question, if I'd received any gifts, any gratuities, and at that point I declined to answer on the grounds that it might tend to incriminate me. Christ, he really thought he hit a hot spot. So anyway, he adjourned the whole grand jury quick. In the meantime, they indicted Farmer. I think what he said, he had enough on Hubbard to hang him. And I think that television set was what he was talking about. Farmer was quoted as having said this at a party. And before the grand jury, Farmer denied he ever said it. That's what he was cited for perjury on before the grand jury. They were pretty thin on it.

Two weeks later, Judge Murphy ruled Farmer would have to stand trial on the perjury charges. It was not until December 1954 that the indictment was quashed, when Recorder's Judge Joseph A. Gillis ruled that Farmer's testimony was not material to the inquiry into the Hubbard administration.

In the meantime, the Culehan grand jury had turned its attention away from Hubbard to look into unrelated charges of labor racketeering in the area. But if Orvie thought the grand juror had forgotten about him, he stood corrected in October 1953, when a couple of State Police detectives showed up at his office with subpoenas for Helen Bell and Bert Schlaff. The mayor barged in on the scene, shouting, "Get out of here. You lazy cops, you should all be shot." When Detective Fred Chrispell shot back, "I've got one for you, too," Hubbard ran out, but Chrispell cornered him in an outer office and served him. At that point, the mayor called police to help with the intruders. Six officers responded, but they refused to follow an order from Hubbard to eject the two. Finally, the detectives left, promising to return the next week, with Hubbard shouting after them, "You look like pigs."

A few days later, clearly bent on one-upping Culehan, Orvie petitioned the court, demanding Culehan be replaced as grand juror and accusing him of "prejudice" and "harassment, disrupting the affairs of the city of Dearborn and preventing city employees from doing their work." Additionally, he gave 21 reasons why the grand jury should be dissolved, claiming it had been active only when he was running for office.

Although he hadn't had much time to worry about it, Hubbard did have another mayoral election coming up November 3. Since he had only one opponent, a car salesman and onetime athlete named James Christie, he had no primary to enter. In the weeks before the election, joshing with reporters after finishing a session with Culehan, he predicted he would be indicted by the grand jury just before November 3. "Of course," he grinned, "you can see how worried I am."

28

Beating Jim Christie, 1952-53

Of two-faced double-crossers, we've_had our fill; Council fakers don't fill the bill. So vote for 7 from these 18
to help Hubbard Keep Dearborn Clean.
                              —From a Hubbard political flyer[1]

Orville Hubbard and George Martin had hated each other for years. There
was something about the judge that rubbed Orvie the wrong way. It was
more than seeing him as a rival for the adulation of Dearborn voters. The
mayor just plain detested him. Martin, the son of Irish immigrants, was an
erudite man whose looks and speech reminded some people of Adlai Stevenson. He had been valedictorian of Fordson High's first graduating class
in 1925 and, as he liked to tell the story, dug ditches to support his widowed
mother while he studied law at the University of Michigan. He practiced
law, beginning in 1931, served on the Dearborn Board of Education from
1933 to 1941 and then became a justice of the peace in 1942, the year
Hubbard took office. Since then, the two had battled so incessantly that
Martin eventually began calling his court "the last true bastion of democracy and justice in Dearborn." "Hubbard has control of everything else," he
once told the *Detroit News*, "and it would be a dreadful state of affairs if he
captured the court, too. But he knows he can't while I'm here. In fact he
becomes livid when I tell him I could beat him for mayor any time I want
to try."[2]

Their already antagonistic relationship soured even further in 1951
when Martin got voters to cut back the city's other full-time municipal
judge, Hubbard lieutenant Ralph Guy, to a $1,000-a-year part-time post.
Guy was continuing to work full-time, pending a Michigan Supreme Court
ruling that eventually upheld the charter amendment pushed by Martin.[3]

Over the next year, Orvie was facing enormous, albeit self-imposed,
pressures from the grand jury, the unpaid Fish libel verdict and the usual

name-calling bouts with councilmen. But in 1952, the Hubbard-Martin wars escalated beyond all bounds of political convention. In August, the judge attacked Hubbard and Guy for a "scandalous, horrible record" of traffic court policies that had produced the nation's worst traffic enforcement statistics, according to the National Safety Council. Blaming his adversaries for a three-year backlog of unserved warrants, Martin excoriated Guy as the "mayor's stooge judge who fixes traffic tickets right and left." Before that, he asserted, the police under Guy had "developed a pernicious habit of losing tickets before reporting them to court." Guy called the charges "a pack of lies," adding, "I don't know anything about fixing tickets, but if I have suspended fines, it was for a good reason."

Orvie's response was to demand that Martin resign unless he could produce evidence of his charges. He also called the judge "a glorified justice of the peace who has quietly done a deluxe ticket-fixing job and now tries to credit his associate for his own scandalous and shocking shenanigans." Hubbard said Martin had "fixed 471 of 508 parking meter tickets he has handled the past year." He also said the judge should pay for them himself. Martin's explanation was that he had asked police months before to cancel some 15,000 tickets written on "defective" parking meters. Calling the mayor "a great ticket fixer himself," Martin recalled: "The last time I saw Hubbard was when he spent two and a half hours in my office in February trying unsuccessfully to get a pal's ticket fixed. We have a no-fix ordinance, and he has been trying to get it repealed."

The best was yet to come. Hubbard phoned Martin, and the judge hung up on him. Miffed over such a blatant breach of etiquette, the mayor had Martin's interoffice phone service cut off. The brouhaha moved to the council the next week, when the judge charged that the phones "were removed because I wouldn't stand for the mayor's filthy abuse." At this, Orvie jumped up and shouted, "You accused me of fixing tickets. You can't show me one bit of evidence. You are a stinking liar." By this time, the two were nose to nose, separated only by a waist-high railing in front of the council table. "You are intellectually dishonest," Martin barked. "I can show you where you and Guy fixed 865 tickets. You are a filthy liar. You are the worst mayor this town ever had." Shot back Hubbard, "You have been getting away with a lot in this town, but now I'm going to put the finger on you. You shake down every merchant you fix a ticket for. You're the biggest chiseler to hit this town."

As Dearborn's mayor and senior judge thus faced off, the crowd of some 150 was on its feet booing the performance. "Throw Hubbard out," someone shouted. "Throw the dictator out. This is America, not Russia." When a photographer's flashbulb startled the two combatants, Council President Patrick J. Doyle restored order. "I want to apologize to you citizens of Dearborn and to the press," he intoned, "for the behavior of the man who is supposed to represent Dearborn as its mayor. I could have him thrown out, but that would only put the policeman on duty on the spot."

The council pursued the matter in proper parliamentary procedure. First, in accordance with a resolution by Councilman Ray Parker, the mayor agreed to restore Martin's phone service. Then Parker read a letter from Martin that appended evidence of his original charges against Guy. "Never before in the history of the Dearborn courts has one judge [Guy] suspended sentence on so many traffic tickets in so short a time," Martin's letter said. Attached was a record of 500 tickets purportedly fixed by Guy; a list of the remaining 365 was to follow.

Then Hubbard and Martin resumed their conversation. "If you took a lie detector test, you would break the machine," Hubbard shouted. "If you don't watch out, I'll throw you in jail." Martin countered, "I can take care of you any day of the week."

The issue simmered for the next year until, in November 1953, Hubbard proposed a schedule of hefty discounts for prompt payment of parking tickets and minor traffic tickets, with no court appearance required. Martin called the idea outrageous, dangerous and probably illegal, quipping, "It would be a pity if Hubbard got killed in an accident at 25 cents a crack."

A week later, the two reached a truce of sorts, announcing a new program that would require violators to take care of unpaid tickets before renewing their driver's licenses. And to clear up a backlog of some 15,000 unpaid tickets, police officials began signing complaints so warrants could be issued.

In the meantime, Orvie had been demonstrating judicial yearnings of his own, for the first time since he had gotten walloped running for justice of the peace in Dearborn Township in 1936. Perhaps it was just another attempt to show up Martin, but after announcing his candidacy for the April 1953 circuit court race, he promoted it to his enemies as a "good way to get rid of me" as mayor. He also pointed out that incumbent Guy A. Miller of Dearborn was retiring, and voters thus could replace one Dearbornite with another.

But the Hubbard bandwagon would have to get started without Miller, who, asked for reaction, protested that Orvie had "absolutely no qualifications to be a judge." Although he himself was leaving public life at age 76, he said, if he "thought Hubbard had a chance to win, I'd run against him."

Undaunted, Orvie collected his nominating petitions and, in an extraordinary display of political trust, turned them over to Doyle, of all people. The councilman, who was also a state representative, was going to be in the capital anyway, Hubbard reasoned, so why not have him file the petitions? Doyle went along with the game, and, amid reports that Hubbard supporter Edward J. Dombrowski was to succeed him as council president, he suddenly was reelected seven-to-nothing.

What was going on here? A simple deal, according to political observers. Hubbard wanted a shot at the judgeship, with a salary of $21,000, and

Doyle liked the idea of moving up to Hubbard's old job. "I might not be able to beat Hubbard for mayor," Doyle explained. "I can beat any of the other candidates, and I want to get rid of him. We've had Hubbard around Dearborn too long, and I'll be happy to give him to the county." A half-serious attempt to speed up the anticipated succession fizzled when Hubbard vetoed a council resolution making Doyle mayor because of Hubbard's announced candidacy.

In March 1953, a few weeks before the judicial election, Fay Hubbard filed for divorce again, for the second time in four years, and then withdrew her petition almost immediately. Orvie explained his latest embarrassment by saying his wife had been tricked in an attempt to sabotage his candidacy.

He didn't make much of a race of it in any case. In his first defeat since becoming mayor, Hubbard finished only twenty-first in a field of 29, with the top 18 earning seats. It was small consolation that he led the Dearborn balloting, outpolling even his old friend, incumbent Lila Neuenfelt, who finished first overall.

With that diversion out of the way, Hubbard could get back to doing what he did best: arguing with the City Council. But not everyone enjoyed the show. As the *Dearborn Press* observed, "Why the Mayor lets himself get trapped into inane outbursts of anger and poor judgment is a moot question. . . . Don't blame all the Mayor's outbreaks on his unusual temperament. There's childishness on both sides."[4]

The latest round of bon mots had begun in April 1952, when Doyle, Parker and Martin Griffith had walked out of a budget session to protest Hubbard's "interference" and "the hopelessness of fighting a ruthless political machine." In May, Parker accused the mayor of spending "the taxpayers' money like a sailor on a spree."

In September, Orvie called Doyle a "black liar" and a "goddamn liar" in a quarrel over the mayor's failure to deposit a check from a sign company. Doyle threatened to fight "if you ever dare call me that on the street." Later, in a speech at a church, Hubbard called Doyle a liar again and offered to punch him in the nose. In one of the pettiest squabbles of all, the council in November condemned Hubbard for pressuring city employees to make United Foundation contributions. The mayor vetoed the resolution and fingered Parker as "the only councilman who failed and refused to give anything to the City of Dearborn's quota" for the charity. Parker said he gave as much as the mayor did.

Through much of 1953, Hubbard was occupied with the Culehan grand jury.[5] It was not until August that he and Doyle had another set-to. The councilman accused the mayor of meeting with Johnny Bitonti, the gangster Hubbard had clashed with before, and promising to "give" Bitonti the numbers concession in town in return for a campaign contribution of $4,000. He said Orvie then reneged on the deal and refused to refund the money. And he said he could prove it. Hubbard and his accuser then erupted in an all-too-familiar-sounding exchange before the council.

"Pat, you are a liar, a black liar and a yellow liar," Hubbard yelled. "Bitonti never was in my office. He or no other racketeer has ever operated in Dearborn during my administration. But I'll tell you this—he did have concessions and operated openly in the four years prior to my administration when you were one of the big four."[6] The ruddy-faced Doyle responded, "Oh, he was in your office, all right. You're the one who's lying."

A week later, the two clashed during a discussion on whether taverns were selling whiskey in Dearborn on Sunday. "Ask Doyle," Hubbard suggested to an interrogator. "He knows more about drinking than I do. I never use the stuff." "You're a liar, mayor," said Doyle. "Just the other day you took me out and bought me two grasshoppers." What that settled was problematical.

By late August, however, it was clear that the mayor's precarious four-to-three majority on the council was in real jeopardy. His only sure votes were Dombrowski and George Bondie. Slate members Lucille McCollough and Joe Ford occasionally sided with Doyle, Parker and Griffith to produce the votes necessary to override a veto. They had done so the previous spring when the council had made 161 changes in the mayor's budget and then overrode 12 of 13 line items vetoed by him. "We clipped your wings, brother, for the first time in 10 years," a jubilant Parker shouted at the time.

And now in August, McCollough, who had stuck with Orvie through the recall, had given him an ultimatum: "a week's time to brace up, get on the ball and serve the people, or I'll have to part ways with you." In trying to blame Hubbard for a recent property tax increase, McCollough sponsored a resolution criticizing "the Mayor's efforts to conceal and hide his expensive, inefficient handling of city government and . . . the Mayor should be severely censured for conspiring to fool the people, hide the truth and defraud the taxpayer."

Hubbard bounced right back with a veto message attacking his opponents as "the worst council Dearborn ever had." He pelted them with such extravagant terms as "polluted" and "politically warped," but he saved his best shots for McCollough, who, he noted, had made her mark in the budget debate by supporting chimes and goldfish ponds at fire stations. He complained that it was unfair of the "frustrated council financial amateurs" to try to extricate themselves from the budget hassle by saddling "their sad and pitiful mistakes upon an efficient, hard working and honest administration." And he derided McCollough as "an out-of-tune nagger"—an insult that moved her, white-faced and shaking with anger, to threaten to run against him. The mayor sat smiling in silence as the council, with two members absent, failed to muster enough votes to make even the symbolic gesture of overriding his veto of her resolution.

Finally, Parker, a high school civics teacher and onetime Hubbard slater, launched into perhaps the most bizarre performance—and the only pantomime—on record at a Dearborn council meeting. First he dropped to his knees and waved his arms in mock supplication, depicting the way he himself once had obeyed the mayor's every command. Next he did one of the best Orville Hubbard impressions ever seen in public, puffing himself up and striking a series of campaign poses. Lastly, in execrably bad taste, he plopped down in Councilman Joe Ford's vacant chair and mimed knock-kneed terror. Ford, who had stayed on Hubbard's side, was home recuperating from a heart attack suffered when he was summoned to testify before the Culehan grand jury. For once in his life, Orvie could sit back and enjoy the show. Neither McCollough nor Parker got a rise out of him.

A few weeks later, in mid-September, Hubbard again chided McCollough and declared that the "small big-four councilmen," as he had taken to calling them, were writing their own "political obituary" by advocating a police union.

By now it was the eve of Dearborn's 1953 city election, and Hubbard clearly was gambling on his ability to reclaim a council majority. Strangely, though, there had been only a modest buildup for the election. There was some speculation in June that Hubbard might face yet another challenge from Carl Matheny. Other possibilities were Doyle and the city's new associate judge, John T. McWilliams. Hubbard had said he would rather run against Doyle than Matheny. As it turned out, he did neither.

Matheny had filed petitions, as had Doyle, Griffith, Hubbard staffer George A. Martin and political unknowns Anthony Perna and William Cooper.[7] But just before the deadline, Matheny also filed for James Christie, a local Ford sales manager. Then Matheny, Doyle and Griffith withdrew from the race. Perna and Martin withdrew. That left only Christie and Cooper to face Hubbard, and the next week Cooper was disqualified for failing to meet a charter requirement that a candidate own property in Dearborn. Suddenly, Christie was anointed as the people's choice. Matheny still was backing him, and now Doyle, Griffith, Parker and McCollough were throwing their support to him.

Christie was undeniably a striking-looking candidate. At 32, he was a husky six-footer with wavy hair, blue eyes and a square jaw. Born in Scotland, he had been an all-state basketball player at Dearborn High in 1938, had graduated from Albion College as a physical education major and had spent six years as an outfielder with the Philadelphia Phillies farm system. He even had some political experience, having run for council as a Hubbard slater in 1949 and an independent in 1951. Christie announced that he was in the race to debunk the "calculated myth of low taxes and efficient government which has lulled Dearborn into complacent acceptance of the most expensive and inefficient administration in the history of the city." He attacked Hubbard's "gang of political hirelings," pronounced the administration guilty of "vulgarities" and vowed that his own team would be "public servants instead of tricking and cynical masters."

Hubbard was little impressed. "Matheny is evidently afraid to run himself," he sniffed. "I'm surprised Matheny is tying his kite to a sinking ship."

Since Christie and Hubbard were the only candidates for mayor, both were spared the superfluity of a primary election. Instead, they focused on September's council race. Hubbard fielded a slate of 18, headed by Dombrowski, Bondie and Guy. Christie put together a slate of 7 that looked like the strongest coalition ever to challenge the mayor. Aligned together against Orvie's team were Matheny, Doyle, Parker, Griffith and McCollough. The two sides fought to a draw in the primary, each getting 7 of the 14 nominations. Dombrowski and Bondie led the field, followed by Doyle, McCollough, Guy, Parker and Matheny.

Hubbard and Christie both professed to be pleased. "When Pat Doyle slips to third place, that is an indication of what's ahead for him," Hubbard said. "We'll elect five men sure." Christie called the outcome "a tremendous success for the good government forces of Dearborn."

He also challenged the mayor to a debate. And, he added, he would "not tolerate any of the physical threats thrown at other candidates in past elections. Any threats will have to be carried out on the spot." There were no threats—and no debate, for that matter—but the candidates went at each other with a degree of political gamesmanship that was impressive even by Dearborn standards.

Christie's newspaper ads urged voters to "end machine control of our City; end waste and incompetence in the administration of our City Government; remove political hacks from responsible jobs as department heads; bring decency and honesty to our City Hall."

Hubbard filled his ads with his traditional doggerel: "Stand by the man who stands by you; clean out the Council wrecking crew. Tuesday, November 3rd, is the date. Vote the Hubbard slate—vote it straight." In other ads, the mayor attacked "double-crossers" and "fakers" on the council, while tossing in a slap at Christie's manhood: "'Scheming back-room bosses' want to make a stooge Mayor out of a used-car salesman, who brags about being a great athlete, and even though 21 when Pearl Harbor was bombed, he failed to serve his Country in World War II."[8]

The two camps also campaigned aggressively by billboard, although Hubbard had a stranglehold on the choicest locations. Christie accused the mayor of having a deal with the dominant billboard company, Walker & Company: the firm could maintain permanent signs on city property without charge, in return for the obvious favor at election time.

One Christie sign, displayed at several locations not controlled by Walker, said, "Christie or clown? To mayor your town. It's up to you." It carried a caricature of Orvie in his clown mask disguise from the GOP convention trip. But Walker refused to post the sign because, as company President D. D. Blessed explained it, "Our company is only trying to keep political advertising on a high level." Christie, dubbing his sign "the picture they wouldn't let you see," sued the firm for $25,000 for breach of contract. He eventually accepted the firm's offer of free signs and a cash settlement.

The candidates also ran afoul of each other in a more traditional billboard controversy. Three men were charged with vandalizing one of the mayor's signs early one morning. The three turned out to be figures active in the 1951 Hubbard recall.[9] Christie never was tied in with the episode.

But the highlight of the campaign was a pamphlet entitled "Dearborn Facts," published by the Citizens for Christie for Mayor Committee.[10] The pamphlet, which all but accused Hubbard of being a crook, carried the transcript of the recorder's court examination of Carl E. Farmer, thus graphically rehashing the issue of the TV set Hubbard received from People's Outfitting. It also had cartoons. One showed a diabolical-looking "Little Orvie" putting money from People's into his pocket. Another depicted him with his hand out, with the caption, "This shouldn't be necessary to do business in Dearborn." Other features in the flyer included an article alleging that the "present administration is ridden with admitted grafters." It named former City Plan Director Joseph Goldfarb, who had resigned under pressure. And there was an article that, using the best Red-baiting techniques of Wisconsin Senator Joseph McCarthy, linked Hubbard with three minor political figures whom "the sworn testimony made before the House Committee on Un-American Activities names as responsible Communist Party Functionaries." Four days before the election, Christie's committee sent 60 men out to distribute the pamphlet. A few hours later, about half of them had been rounded up by police. Of those, three were charged with violating a 1947 city ordinance making it illegal to print or distribute literature that "tends to expose any individual or any racial or religious group to hatred, contempt or obloquy" unless the name and address of the person or group publishing the material were included. Orvie labeled the flyer "the most libelous and scurrilous piece of literature I have ever seen put out on the streets." Christie, who paraded for hours in front of the police station and city hall, responded, "I bought those papers with the last bit of money I had. They went to two sets of lawyers before they were published. Everything in them is true. They point up the corruption, dictatorship and acts to suppress opposition in every manner and means possible in Dearborn." The three pamphleteers were released after their lawyer, Michael Berry, himself a Hubbard recall officer, observed, "It is very strange that Hubbard, who has made a career of the character assassination of others, is so exercised at the exposure of his own nefarious activities." A day later, he got a court order allowing the distribution of Christie's literature.

In the meantime, Hubbard was missing few chances to take pot shots at his council opponents. In fact, McCollough already had filed suit against him for slander after he accused her of keeping her mother-in-law under treatment at city expense in Wayne County General Hospital.[11]

Beyond that, Orvie was continuing to campaign vigorously, making appearances at schools and halls and staging his now-familiar election eve rally at Fordson High, featuring "starlets of stage and screen," plus organ music and door prizes.

Hubbard expected that he would handle Christie easily enough at the polls, but even he couldn't have foreseen the extent of his victory. Thanks to a record turnout, he pulled some 9,000 votes more than ever before, collecting 71 percent of the vote and rolling up a margin of 25,572 to 10,322. He swept all precincts except the Ford Foundation, and even there he was beaten only 342–270. "I suppose we'll have to consider them citizens again," he conceded wryly.

And his campaign slogan against the city's "worst council" produced the most stunning sweep in the history of Dearborn politics. Doyle was out. Parker was out. McCollough was out. Griffith was out. Orvie had pulled in his entire slate and suddenly enjoyed a seven-to-nothing council margin, even better than the six-to-one majority he boasted for a while in 1949. Dombrowski led the field, followed by Bondie, Guy and four rank underdogs: former Councilman Anthony Smith, Robert Vezzosi, William Broomhall and Charles Gilbert. Trailing were Doyle, Parker, Griffith, McCollough and, in twelfth place, Matheny.

"I still can't believe it," Orvie said. "This is the most gratifying thing that has ever happened in my political life." Christie confessed, "I am equally amazed. The result of the vote shows the power of his political machine."

Hell, we really ran a hard campaign that year. And, by God, we caught Doyle, who seemed to be invincible, and McCollough at the same time. We cleaned the whole goddamn gang up. They all went down the chute.

Almost lost in the excitement was the approval of two charter amendments that Hubbard was backing to use as leverage against Doyle and Parker, and perhaps Judge Martin someday. One barred elected officials from being on more than one public payroll, and the other prohibited officeholders from running for another office without first resigning the current one.

Of course, Hubbard never figured that both Doyle and Parker would lose, or that the charter propositions would backfire on one of his own slate members, Smith. Smith, like Parker a schoolteacher, filed suit to make the council certify his election victory, then voluntarily gave up his right to his seat.[12]

But that was only a minor annoyance for Orvie. After all, he now had a mandate from the voters—and an entire City Council to back him up.

29

The Removal Hearings, 1954

> They may send me to jail someday for contempt, but
> they'll never send me for being a crook.
> —Orville L. Hubbard, answering grand jury charges
> against him

Hubbard didn't have much time to savor his trouncing of James Christie in the 1953 election. Two days later, on November 5, Miles N. Culehan, the Wayne Circuit Court's one-man grand juror, demanded Orvie's removal in a petition to Governor G. Mennen "Soapy" Williams. The 35-page petition contained 20 specific charges emanating from the yearlong probe of the Hubbard administration. Hubbard, served a copy when he appeared under subpoena in court that morning, later groused to reporters, "This whole thing is ridiculous and pathetic." The petition charged the mayor with malfeasance, misfeasance and willful neglect of duty. Under the law, the governor could hear the charges himself or designate a probate judge to review them.

Hubbard said he would open the books of the city to the press and answer all charges. Typically, he also accused Culehan of being "biased and prejudiced and using high-handed, Gestapo tactics." He said he himself would petition the governor for Culehan's removal, saying the judge had "consistently failed to comply" with a law requiring semiannual reports on cases heard. But then the mayor pinpointed the most significant element in Culehan's findings: that the judge had *not* leveled criminal charges against him. "This petition is a confession by Culehan that he has not been able to find cause for indictment," Hubbard announced.

The charges were essentially a warmed-over version of earlier allegations dating back to the recall.[1] They stated:

(1) When questioned before the grand jury regarding the reduction of

1950 tax assessments of People's Outfitting Co., Hubbard refused to answer questions relative to his receiving a gift from an official of the company on the ground that his answer might tend to incriminate him.

(2) . . . Hubbard gave directions to assessor Carl E. Farmer, and Farmer reduced the tax by more than $120,000. Shortly after, Hubbard told an official of the store he wanted a certain make and type of television set, and he accepted such set as a gift.

(3) Hubbard obtained pay raises for Farmer before the three-year term of office held by Farmer had expired, . . . contrary to a charter provision. . . .

(4) Hubbard appointed George E. Brady controller in charge of city finances of approximately $10 million a year, knowing Brady was not a qualified, experienced and competent bookkeeper and accountant, as required by the Dearborn charter.

(5) Hubbard entirely deleted from the 1952–53 budget any sum for an audit, although the charter requires an audit to be made each year.

(6) Hubbard, contrary to state law and the charter, has willfully directed and permitted overspending of budget appropriations.

(7) In violation of state law and Dearborn charter, Hubbard has ordered, directed and permitted the purchasing agent, Harold DeWyk, the controller, Brady, and other department heads to illegally contract, purchase and pay for property and services.

(8) Hubbard has and does now order, direct and permit a system of warrants and verification open to fraud in that the controller relies solely on a vendor's affidavit and the signature of a city department head, though certified public accountants and others have repeatedly recommended a system requiring the vendor to furnish an invoice. . . .

(9) Hubbard . . . ordered and permitted use of Dearborn public money, material, machinery, equipment and labor to pave or surface parking lots for bars, businesses and churches.

(10) Hubbard ordered, directed and permitted unnecessary trips by city officials and employees to distant points in the United States and Canada at public expense, and did not require any accounting or receipts for transportation, lodging, meals and other expenses.

(11) Hubbard failed and refused to follow recommendations made by certified public accountants year after year, regarding systems of accounts. . . .

(12) Hubbard ordered enforcement officers and others to refuse and neglect to sign complaints necessary for issuance of warrants by the Dearborn Municipal Court, and there are 12,423 cases pending where the Municipal Court is unable to enforce . . . laws . . . for the years 1951, 1952 and 1953 as a result of such policy.

(13) Hubbard failed to keep council fully advised as to financial condition and needs of the city, . . . vetoing a request of the council for a report of total amounts paid each month to city employees.

(14) Though city council overrode his veto, Hubbard has neglected

and refused to furnish this to the council and has . . . required all [payroll statistics] to be turned into his office and is holding them there.

(15) . . . Hubbard advised Dearborn officials and employees against appearing before a preliminary investigation into the merits of the citizens' petition for a grand jury. . . .

(16) Oct.12, 1953, Hubbard told Sgt. Chrispell of the Michigan State Police that Helen Bell, his private secretary, and Norbert Schlaff, his executive secretary, were not in, knowing that the officer had subpoenas to require their attendance before the grand jury, when in fact Hubbard knew that Bell and Schlaff were in Hubbard's office at that very time.

(17) The evening of Oct.12, 1953, Hubbard instructed employees in the mayor's office that if police officers returned with subpoenas for Bell and Schlaff to tell the officers they were not in.

(18) On Oct.14,1953, . . . Hubbard tried to evade service by running away, and when served in spite of such efforts, he used profanity toward the officers in the presence of women in his office.

(19) On Oct. 12, 1953, Hubbard willfully ordered and agreed to permit Helen Bell to absent herself from the state of Michigan, knowing a subpoena had been issued. Hubbard agreed and permitted her to obtain an advance on her salary, . . . and he permitted her to obtain a check for $379 for travel expenses. . . .

(20) On Oct. 12, 1953, Hubbard ordered and agreed to permit Norbert Schlaff to leave the state of Michigan . . . and permitted Schlaff to draw advance pay. . . .

Shaking with anger, the mayor responded to the grand jury charges two days later. He denied most of the allegations altogether, accusing Culehan of deliberately falsifying some. Other charges, he said with some justification, were "trifling." As for the most serious charge, the People's Outfitting assessment cut and the TV set, Hubbard already had explained himself publicly, and he was incensed that Culehan had accused him of asking for the gift. "The gift was made but was never solicited," he said. "If it had been solicited, it would be a criminal action, an indictable offense. The judge knows it is a lie or he would have indicted me."

The mayor was almost as angry about the judge's allegations about paving private parking lots. Of 19 addresses listed by Culehan, according to Hubbard, 14 were churches. "I've always done that, and I'll continue to do it as long as I'm in office," he declared. "What's more, I'll continue to get the snow off the lots, too, every Sunday, and I'll use city equipment." Of the other five parking lots, identified as being owned by a nightclub, a fraternal club, a restaurant, a drycleaner and a supermarket, Hubbard categorically denied any illegal deals.

Responding to the charge of circumventing competitive bids for purchases, the mayor conceded that the city sometimes rushed things through or broke down large billings into smaller ones. Usually these involved Camp

Dearborn, he said. "It is a bad practice, and I don't approve of it," he said, "but it certainly contains no fraud. What happens is that we need something fast or we need a particular type of equipment, and so it has been bought this way."

On the lesser charges, Hubbard said that Farmer's pay raises, like those given other department heads, were debated openly before the City Council; he affirmed Brady's competence; he denied blocking the city audit or illegally transferring money for employee overtime; he acknowledged approving advance vacation pay for Bell and Schlaff, though he denied it was to hamper Culehan's investigation; and he conceded that some employees could be padding their expense accounts.

If the governor held hearings on Culehan's petition, he said, he would subpoena the grand juror himself as a witness. "I want to testify with a lie detector strapped on my arm," he said, "and I will invite other witnesses, including the judge, to do the same. They may send me to jail someday for contempt, but they'll never send me for being a crook."

That goddamn snakeskinner. That son of a bitch. He was one of the biggest pricks that ever lived. He really was. If you gave Culehan everything, he really was. Forget my case. He was a faker of the first order, a faker of the first order, a faker of the first order. He thought he could be another Homer Ferguson, you know. Culehan came in with an ax to grind. He subpoenaed everything around here. The State Police were looking for me to subpoena. I had one big guy used to come to my house. He'd run, get in the car. State Police would chase him all over. Then I'd come out, get in the car and go the other way. Keystone Kops. Finally, he had me down there, and I said, "Culehan, you're just wasting your time here. You may find that we've stretched the law a little bit here and there, but you won't find that we're involved in any dishonest or crooked deals. You just look to your goddamn heart's content." Then he was asking me where I had money hid in Canada, how much I had in outstate banks and stuff like that. "I have nothing," I said. But that didn't satisfy him. That rotten son of a bitch. I'll piss on his grave twice. He died of cancer of the throat, and he deserved to die, too. Just 'cause you put a black robe around a lawyer doesn't make the son of a bitch a saint. Lawyers do that, then they call a judge a grand juror. Christ, you'd think he's a goddamn angel or something. Well, anyway, he winds up with all of this horseshit stuff. He didn't have one place to hang his hat.

In mid-November, Hubbard filed a $250,000 libel suit against Culehan in circuit court, contending that the claim about soliciting the TV set was not protected by judicial immunity. In early December, Hubbard amended his libel action to maintain that all grand jury activity since July 23, 1953, had been "illegal, unauthorized and void," because the probe had not been extended under a state law setting a time limit of six months for such an inquiry. Presiding Circuit Judge Ira W. Jayne ruled that the extension had been ordered in June, although the action had not been entered into the court record. Hubbard tried again, arguing that the judges had extended the grand jury illegally during a "secret" meeting at the posh Detroit Athletic Club. The next month, the suit was dismissed by Judge Charles O. Arch of Hillsdale, visiting in Wayne Circuit Court. Arch said that the meeting at the athletic club might have been open to criticism but was not illegal. He also said that the principle of judicial immunity from civil liability was "indispensable to the maintenance of the judicial system."

In the meantime, Governor Williams had announced a hearing officer for the Hubbard removal charges: Wallace Waalkes Jr., a freshman probate judge from Grand Rapids who had been a law school classmate of the governor's at the University of Michigan. Waalkes, who said he didn't "know Hubbard from Adam," was to make no decisions but simply conduct the hearing on the charges and certify a record of the proceedings to Williams.

The Waalkes hearings started out badly even before they began. The assistant attorney general in charge of the proceedings, Irving Beattie, met with the judge in Grand Rapids, and Culehan went along. Hubbard soon heard of the "secret trip" and demanded that the governor replace Waalkes, since he could no longer "obtain a fair and impartial hearing" from him. Hubbard also demanded Culehan resign as a judge because of the "scandalous and unscrupulous" meeting with Waalkes. The mayor scored Culehan's "inquisitorial enthusiasm," adding, "Anyone who may be threatened and abused in Judge Culehan's Gestapo mental torture chamber will know that he is about as impartial as a bloodthirsty saber-tooth tiger." The governor permitted Culehan and Waalkes to stay on, of course, praising the Grand Rapids juror's "impartiality" while criticizing Culehan directly. "The meeting between Beattie and Judge Waalkes was perfectly proper and necessary," the governor said, "but the fact that Judge Culehan came along was certainly unnecessary and improper, and it is regrettable that such a circumstance should have occurred to give rise to this question."

Orvie was finding other avenues to harass Culehan as well. In November, the mayor's "inquisitor" had 18-year-old John Hubbard subpoenaed, and the next month, after Culehan had the mayor's son in for questioning a second time, the grand juror himself became the target. As Culehan emerged from his office, John Hubbard served him with a summons connected with the mayor's libel suit. The judge tried to grab the film of a photographer who was on hand and, obviously irked, then lectured several reporters and cameramen about the importance of keeping grand jury activities secret. Twitting the judge for lacking a sense of humor, a *Free Press* editorial later concluded, "All we can make of it is that dealing with Orvie is very wearing on the judicial temperament."

The Waalkes hearings began in Detroit January 4, 1954. The judge said he would permit an informal atmosphere with "great leeway" for both sides in questioning witnesses. The first witness was the secretary of People's

Outfitting, James Wineman, who backed up Hubbard's story right down the line. Wineman, son of the company's president, Henry Wineman, said that he and his father were "shocked" over the assessment increase in 1949 and decided to contact Hubbard.[2] "The mayor listened but made no promises to us," he explained. As for the TV set, which People's bought wholesale for $287 and gave Hubbard in the spring of 1950, Wineman said, "At no time did Hubbard ask for a gift, nor did he infer or imply that he wanted one. I insisted he was going to get one, and we'd like to make it a TV set. I suggested the best on the market then, and he said OK." The next day, Wineman testified that Hubbard had been spooked by the grand jury, that the mayor telephoned without identifying himself, complaining that the grand juror was "trying to crucify me." He suggested meeting "to get our stories together," Wineman said. Wineman said he refused, reminding Hubbard he was under oath not to discuss the matter.

A few days later, former assessor Clyde Hale took Waalkes through his version, repeating that he and Joseph Schaefer had objected to the tax cut, although they signed the rolls anyway. By this time, nearly two weeks had passed, and Waalkes was threatening to run the hearings 10 hours a day. "There is no reason for this to go on for months," he observed.

Things picked up following testimony from City Controller George Brady. "Do you consider yourself competent to audit the books of a peanut stand?" Beattie asked him. "I can audit a hardware store," Brady shot back, noting that he had taken college extension courses in bookkeeping and accounting and had learned a lot on the job. "We have never ended a fiscal year in the red in Dearborn," he said, "and no audit by a private firm has ever shown so much as a penny shortage of Dearborn funds."

The next week, Waalkes considered the charges of the suspicious expense accounts. Hubbard's attorneys, Frank N. MacLean and Lawrence Burns, saved the judge a week or two by conceding that the mayor had authorized funds for trips without requiring itemized accountings. But they said they could justify the city formula of rail fare plus $20 a day expenses.

Bert Schlaff damaged Orvie's cause a bit when he answered Beattie's questions about being sent out of town by the mayor to avoid questioning by Culehan. Schlaff testified he had left for Virginia the previous October, stopping in Toledo, Ohio, to meet with Hubbard and others. He said he returned when the mayor told him Culehan had ordered him back.

The subject of parking lot paving came up several times over the ensuing weeks. DPW Director Harry A. Hoxie acknowledged that the city had expended a total work value of some $9,800 in constructing or repairing lots adjacent to 13 churches. His administrative assistant, John L. Kadela, observed that the policy had been a campaign issue in two regular elections and the recall. "It was no secret we were working on these parking lots," he said. "We didn't try to conceal it at all." Frank Swapka, fired as DPW director during the recall, testified that the mayor had ordered him to pave lots for Shore's Cafe and the Club Gay Haven, two of the private businesses named by Culehan, along with a supermarket, a fraternal club and a dry-cleaner. A current councilman, Robert Vezzosi, testified he had made a deal with Swapka to have to club's parking lot surfaced and graded in exchange for a load of topsoil. Hubbard was not consulted beforehand, he said. Later, the supermarket owner explained that the city had smoothed and oiled his unpaved lot as a convenience for area residents who parked there.

The charge of circumventing the charter on bidding out items over $500 was explained by Deputy City Controller William B. Godette as simply a convenience. "We have honest people out in Dearborn," he declared.

An unfriendly witness, Municipal Judge George T. Martin, told Waalkes about his problems with traffic ticket enforcement as a result of Hubbard's policies. He also said he once paid a speeder's fine after the mayor insisted it be fixed.

Hubbard, meantime, was staying away from the hearing amid reports that State Police were unable to find him. Fearful that process servers might come disguised as postmen or newspaperboys, the mayor was said to be refusing to accept mail or papers. And his subordinates were insulating him from potential service at city hall. At one point, the opposing attorneys sparred over the issue after Beattie called State Police Detective Pat Detzler to the stand. When Beattie asked about Detzler's failure to serve Hubbard successfully, MacLean interrupted, asking, "Are you trying to show how inefficient these officers are?" "No," Beattie replied. "I am trying to show how elusive your client is." "He is not hiding," MacLean objected. "Everybody else seems to be able to find him. Photographers were taking pictures of him all over the Dearborn city hall yesterday, and yet you say you can't find him." Detzler's companion officer, Fred Chrispell, explained, "He has too many people on the lookout. He has more lieutenants out in front of him than they have guards at Jackson Prison."

In the seventh week of the hearings, when it became apparent that Orvie would not appear, Beattie asked to use answers given to the Culehan grand jury. Waalkes refused.

Finally, on February 24, 1954, the Waalkes hearings concluded after 17 sessions, 43 witnesses and some 800,000 words of testimony—none of them from Hubbard.

The next day, the Redford State Police Post in Detroit got a corpulent visitor asking if there were a subpoena for him. Told he was no longer being sought, Orvie sighed, "It's too bad I never received official notice of the hearing."

He also marked the occasion by telling the press he might challenge for the attorney general's job held by Frank G. Millard, who, he said, "has been sticking his nose into one of the very cleanest cities in the United States."

Almost unnoticed during the Waalkes hearing was the fact that at midnight on January 22, 1954, exactly a year after it began, the Culehan grand jury quietly expired, as provided by state law. Its legacy included no indictments but simply a pending perjury charge against Carl Farmer, the forced resignation of Joseph Goldfarb and the conclusion of the removal hearings against Orville Hubbard.

In late March, Waalkes turned over the hearing transcript to the attorney general's office. In early August, Millard gave the governor Beattie's 270-page summary, as well as the complete 1,770-page transcript and the accompanying 86 exhibits. Millard made no recommendation on a course of action. What would Williams do? According to speculation, the governor had been skeptical about the charges. Indeed, he and Orvie were well acquainted, and he had favored the city of Dearborn for the last six years by appearing in its Memorial Day parade, although this year he had arranged to walk some distance behind the mayor and had avoided being photographed with him.

At last, in September, Williams announced his decision: Hubbard would stay on as mayor of Dearborn. Although Orvie had shown "bad judgment" in some matters, he said, Culehan's charges remained unproven and "do not justify" removal. He said, "No corruption and no venality on the part of Orville Hubbard was shown by the evidence. Careful examination of the evidence fails to reveal a case of malfeasance, misfeasance, willful neglect of duty or willful misconduct . . . which would justify the use of the governor's extraordinary power of removal."[3]

Of Culehan's 20 specific charges, only three were worth commenting on, Williams indicated. On the gift of the TV set from People's Outfitting: "There is affirmative evidence that Hubbard made no commitments to the taxpayer. There is no direct evidence in the record that the mayor ordered any change in the assessment. The evidence in the record is that he did not solicit the gift. There is no question but that this incident involved bad judgment and poor policy, but it is not sufficient grounds for ouster."[4] On the paving of the parking lots: Hubbard was "not solely responsible" for the practice, established before he took office, and he "derived no personal gain from its continuation," although the practice should be investigated by the City Council. On obstructing Culehan's investigation: "The grand juror has available to him the traditional powers of punishment lodged in the judiciary. If he found it inappropriate to use them, it would be presumptuous of me to invade his province."[5]

Culehan, questioned while attending a judicial meeting, had no comment for reporters, but Hubbard was ebullient. Complimenting Williams for his "fairness and impartial conduct," the mayor issued a statement lambasting the "greedy, grabbing gang" that instigated the grand jury. The statement, naturally, also contained Hubbard's familiar litany of self-adulation: "I am deeply grateful to Governor Williams for his action in refusing to be a party to about the blackest and rottenest scheme ever concocted and plotted against an able, honest and courageous public official by a gang of political disappointees. He is one of the best governors Michigan ever had, and I hope that my friends everywhere are equally as grateful as I am."[6]

I always liked Williams. We'd worked like hell for Williams in the early days. I voted for him all the time. Not intimate with him, but closer than the average politician. I didn't say one word to him about it [the removal hearing].

With the grand jury and the removal hearing behind him, the City Council and the recall threat taken care of, Hubbard was running out of challenges.

30

Beating Ray Parker, 1954-55

I'm so used to winning, it's a little difficult to think up
some victory comment that sounds different.
—Orville L. Hubbard, after winning his eighth term

Orville Hubbard was getting bored. His $6,500-a-year salary had looked all right 12 years before, but now he was no longer a young attorney desperate for a toehold in public office. He was 50 and ready for something more important.

After all, with the governor's removal hearings behind him and no dissenting voices left on the council, politics in Dearborn wasn't even fun anymore. Hubbard failed to attend the opening council session in January 1954 ("Why should I steal the show?"), and he didn't show up at any meetings until late May.

In the interim, Hubbard was left to such mundane chores as a photo opportunity with a Brownie troop to mark a scouting anniversary. His most newsworthy announcement in months was a gimmick requiring department heads to begin each day with a half-hour at their desks to wait for a burst of inspiration. "They are to shut themselves in their offices, take no phone calls and see no one," the mayor explained. "They are supposed to sit and think. If they think enough, they may have ideas. That is the way Newton discovered the law of gravity." Actually, the plan wasn't as screwy as it sounded. The annals of Dearborn record no scientific breakthroughs as a result of Hubbard's "think sessions," but, what was more important to him anyway, he got a two-page photo spread in a February issue of *Life* magazine.[1]

Despite Hubbard's low salary, these were boom times in Dearborn. Ford Motor reported record profits and turned over its biggest tax payment ever to the city treasurer. The disparity was not lost on Hubbard.

257

In July, he heard about a job opening that appealed to him. He showed up at a Detroit City Council meeting to apply for the $18,000-a-year post of auditor general. He was careful to say that he always regarded Detroit as Dearborn's big brother, and he made sure the council got some leftover campaign literature listing his accomplishments and personal history. His performance failed to win the job, however, and when the group adjourned without settling on a candidate, Councilwoman Mary Beck commented dryly, "This fiasco has had everything. All we need now are the trained dogs and the acrobats."

In November, voters turned down cost-of-living raises for the mayor and other Dearborn officials, sending Hubbard off to circulate petitions for a second try at a circuit judgeship. Though people didn't take him entirely seriously when he first ran in 1953, he sounded much more determined now. "I like my present job," he said in announcing his candidacy, "but I've always looked on it as merely a detour in my ambitions as a lawyer and a judge. I don't know what I would do with the $24,500 salary a circuit judge receives, but I might like one of those trips to Europe or South America."

Running again was something of a calculated risk. This time, he would have to deal with the charter amendment he had railroaded through in 1953 to get rid of Councilmen Ray Parker and Pat Doyle and to discourage Judge George Martin from running for mayor. The amendment barred anyone from running for office if he already held one public job, and now Hubbard fit the bill. As the filing deadline neared, the mayor promised to resign and even went so far as to recommend Dombrowski and Councilman Robert Vezzosi as his successor. But before he actually made the break, he asked City Attorney Dale Fillmore for an opinion on the charter provision, and Fillmore advised him to stay in office. Hubbard stayed in office.

In mid-January 1955, Hubbard turned in twice as many signatures as he needed to file. And later that month, he went to work to try to gain an "equal advantage" in his designation on the judicial ballot. Since the two incumbents, Wade McCree and Theodore Bohn, both were listed as "circuit judge," Hubbard thought he should be identified as "mayor of Dearborn." But the county elections board turned down his request, and so did the federal district court.

In the February primary, Hubbard led the field of eight in Dearborn and did well enough in several western suburbs to make it as one of four nominees for the two positions. Though well behind the front-runner, McCree, he finished third overall, giving him a real chance in the April election. At least he thought so. "Believe me, I was surprised," he told reporters. "I did no campaigning, actually spent no more than the postage necessary to mail out petitions necessary for filing. I didn't even make a campaign speech."

Surprised or not, Hubbard already had decided what kind of judge he would be. He would carry his lunch, he said, and ask lawyers appearing before him to do the same. He would set up a night court and ask the other judges to clear their dockets any way they could. He would do his best to discourage golf outings, quasi-official meetings at private clubs and long vacations.

For all his good intentions, Hubbard was going to need lots of help to get elected. He got a little when Circuit Judge Arthur Webster ruled in March that the mayor could run in spite of the city charter stipulation. That thwarted the efforts of his longtime opponent, attorney James Thomson, who had sued to make him resign before running.

A few days before the election, Hubbard told reporters he was "tired of kicking around" as mayor of Dearborn and was ready to be a judge. But just in case, he also would be a candidate for a vacant $17,500-a-year job as city manager in Grand Rapids.

In the meantime, Hubbard also was trying to cover his bets back in Dearborn, attempting to push through charter amendments to extend his term from two to six years and to hike his pay from $6,500 to $24,500. Although Thomson failed to keep the mayor's name off the ballot, he sued to block the amendments. And when Judge Webster got a look at the wording, he quickly sided with Thomson. The amendments asked, "Are you in favor of paying the mayor the same rate paid each Wayne County circuit judge?" And "Are you in favor of the mayor's term of office being the same as a circuit court judge?" In granting Thomson an injunction, Webster said, "This attempt to tie the mayor's office in some way to the judicial office . . . raises at once a suspicion of some political motive behind the peculiar wording." Thomson had more than a suspicion. He then got another circuit judge, George B. Murphy, to block a different proposal, this one recommended by the Dearborn Bar Association and setting the mayor's salary at $16,500. Still Hubbard was not finished. He asked Fillmore and his staff to recast the stalled amendments as advisory propositions, which would not carry the force of law but would indicate community sentiment. Fillmore balked. The mayor, incensed, fired Fillmore and his five assistants, although he soon hired them all back. Fillmore stayed away several weeks before returning, while his chief assistant, B. Ward Smith, was back in 24 hours. Four junior attorneys never left, saying Hubbard couldn't fire them in the first place.[2]

The judicial election itself was almost an anticlimax. Hubbard outpolled his three opponents in Dearborn two-to-one, but overall he trailed well back in last place as McCree and Bohn easily retained their seats. With the judicial race out of the way, at last it was time for a taste of politics as usual in Dearborn.

In August, a squabble with the CIO local representing most city employees caused a minor rift with the City Council—the first since the new slate came in the year before—but it also gave Hubbard a new forum to elicit sympathy about his job. At the mayor's behest, the council had stripped the union of its exclusive bargaining rights and a dues-checkoff system for city workers. Now the union members were picketing city hall, and two councilmen, Dombrowski and John Baja, marched with them. While the council reacted skittishly to the union demands—at first giving in, then pulling back and finally granting the concessions once again—Hubbard just kidded. "I picketed with them myself a week ago," he joshed. "I had a sign that said, 'No pay raises since 1942. I demand more pay, less work, shorter hours, rest periods, security on earth and in heaven.' They've got it made. They got my job beat all to hell."

If that was really the way he felt about his job, he still liked it well enough for another crack at the polls. The rest of 1955 was a prelude to another mayoral campaign. But the only controversy that came up involved one of his own staff, a former grocer named M. O. Nickon, whom the mayor had hired as superintendent of weights and measures and who later put up his home and cottage for the Fish jail-limits bond. Nickon showed up late with nominating petitions for the September filing deadline, and when Hubbard upbraided him as "the lousiest, most undependable man" in city hall, Nickon got mad. He quit, pulled out of the Fish bond, threatened to join the opposition and filed a $100,000 suit against the city for injuries suffered by his wife, Pauline, in an auto accident the previous spring involving another Hubbard appointee.[3]

This fellow, Nickon, was running around like a nut. I should have been fired for ever giving him a job in the first place. I chewed his ass out, and he said, "I quit, I quit." He jumped up and down, pounded the goddamn table. I had a couple of the boys talk to him, but he didn't cool down. He finally wound up going house to house against us in that election. On election day he put a sign up, a great, big sign: "Hitler, Hague and Hubbard." Had it out at Henry Ford School, and he stood out there all day at that voting booth fighting me, and I got the biggest vote in my life in that precinct. I wish I had two more guys like that around town. I still run heavy over there.

As for the opposition on the ballot, there was Ray Parker, the Fordson High social studies teacher who had served nine years on the council when the Hubbard slate swept him out in 1953; two real estate salesmen, Charles J. Nemeth and Leo A. McCarthy; and a Notre Dame law student, Edward J. Robinson Jr.

Only Parker was a known quantity, and how could he beat Hubbard if he couldn't even get himself elected to the council his last time out? Based on his record as a pop-off antagonist of the mayor's after jumping the Hubbard team in 1949, however, maybe he could embarrass Hubbard. The low point in their relations came in 1951, when he gave Hubbard a little of the mayor's own style of bullying. As a councilman-elect who had been out of government for two years, Parker had begun to speak from the audience during a council meeting, only to find himself drawing Hubbard's fire.

The mayor called him a liar and added, "You aren't even a man." That was too much for Parker, a strapping, lantern-jawed former University of Michigan wrestling star. He took off his coat and responded, "Come outside and I'll show you whether I'm a man or not." Hubbard hesitated a moment and backed down. "No," he said, "I won't go outside with you. What would that settle? You're a bull. You look like one and you think like one." Parker finally sat down, as one exasperated observer piped up, "They talk like a couple of old women arguing over the back fence."

But the 1955 election failed to live up to even that level of interest. Hubbard promised not to take it easy on his opponents, protesting, "Strange things happen in politics, and I don't want to get caught flat-footed." In fact, however, he all but ignored them throughout the campaign.

Actually, he had been busy patching up old animosities, inviting ex-Councilman Pat Doyle and former Fire Chief Stanley Herdzik onto his council slate. Doyle, the state rep ousted in the purge of 1953 after 11 years on the council, joined the fold with a slap at "people who talk about the mayor's faults but leave the fighting to a few of us." Also on the Hubbard slate were incumbents George Bondie, William Broomhall, Charles Gilbert, Ralph Guy and Dombrowski. Off were John Baja, who was trying to make headway by labeling himself an independent, and Robert Vezzosi, who was under indictment in a credit union scam.[4]

Parker, who was running a strangely bland campaign himself, emphasized his concern about efficiency in government and promised to "work harder than any Mayor you have ever had." Elsewhere, Nemeth, who had been a director in the old Hubbard recall campaign, issued a statement saying Orvie ruled by "fear." And James Thomson, capitalizing on his anti-city hall lawsuits, organized a council slate with himself at its head.

Hubbard's by-now-familiar newspaper ads emphasized teamwork and "the Hubbard way" and cautioned, "Wise home owners vote the Hubbard slate."

He really didn't need to do more. With less than 30 percent of the registered voters turning out, he swept every precinct in the primary, totaling 11,075 votes to 4,368 for Parker, 651 for Robinson, 580 for Nemeth and 346 for McCarthy. His five incumbents were nominated, along with Doyle and slater Natale Micale. Also nominated was Thomson, who again blocked a package of amendments by pointing out that the charter barred them from a primary ballot. One amendment would have set a minimum salary of $12,000 for Hubbard, and another would have lengthened elective terms to four years.

Without a real challenge from Parker, Hubbard spent the weeks before the November election focusing on his old nemesis, George Martin, who was running for his third six-year term as municipal judge. The mayor was supporting former city controller Duane Dunick against Martin; he also favored B. Ward Smith against Associate Judge John McWilliams.

The two judges had solidified their reputation for independence the year before. In July 1954, when the Hubbard council repealed Martin's "no-fix" traffic ticket ordinance, the judge asked the council to put it on the ballot. The ordinance, which made it illegal to cancel or solicit the disposition of a ticket, needed no such help, however. The council voted it back into effect at its next meeting, because, as Baja explained it, "people already were plaguing us to take care of their tickets."

McWilliams had his own cause célèbre. Council President Guy, who earlier had lost the associate judgeship to McWilliams, helped engineer a move to turn over the judge's courtroom to a city department and let McWilliams use the council chambers as needed. When McWilliams found his bench and other fixtures piled outside the court building as he returned from lunch one day in February 1954, he turned the situation into a public relations coup. With reporters and photographers looking on, he mounted the bench and declared court in session on the spot.

That fall, the Martin-McWilliams court was named the country's best by the National Safety Council. Perhaps most irritating to Hubbard, however, a ballot proposal to raise Martin's pay from $6,500 to $15,000 was having no difficulties similar to the Hubbard-sponsored measures being stymied by Thomson. So Hubbard's newspaper ads ignored Parker, who was claiming he could save the city $1 million a year without cutting services, and instead singled out Martin. Railing against "production line justice," the ads urged voters to attend "another sensational 'show of shows'" sponsored by Hubbard and hear "the shocking facts about the foxy Judge—how he fooled and deceived you with a tricky charter amendment." The ads also warned against housing project proposals by which "Dearborn could be ruined." And they resurrected Orvie's perennial warning against shadowy outside forces: "Hear how scheming rascals would like to fleece Dearborn and why home owners should be sure to vote in this quiet election. . . . Hear Hubbard Hammer Hell out of the plotting political pirates who have tried every trick in the bag to grab and control your City Hall."[5]

The outcome was never in doubt. Some 53 percent of the voters turned out November 8 to help bury Parker, 21,063 to 8,961. The council race also went strongly for Hubbard, with Doyle leading with 17,532 votes. He was followed by Orvie's five incumbents—Dombrowski, Bondie, Guy, Broomhall and Gilbert. Baja, running on his own, edged Thomson for the last seat.

Martin's popularity continued to frustrate the mayor, though. He beat Dunick almost three-to-one, while McWilliams disposed of Smith by a comfortable margin. And Martin's pay raise proposal passed narrowly, while Thomson again blocked Hubbard amendments for salary increases and four-year terms.[6]

But if Hubbard couldn't get rid of Martin, at least there were no other obstacles in his way. As the once-hostile *Press* oozed after the election, "Mayor Hubbard is paid homage because Dearborn people regard him as a fine administrator and know him to be strictly honest in his handling of city affairs."[7]

31

The Interview, 1956

> I am for complete segregation, one million per cent on all levels.
> —Orville L. Hubbard, explaining how Dearborn deals with the race issue[1]

When a stubborn black seamstress named Rosa Parks refused to give up her seat on a bus to a white man in Montgomery, Alabama, in December 1955, she had no idea that she was ushering in the modern civil rights era. And when Orville Hubbard agreed to speak his mind on segregation three months later to a Montgomery newspaperman, the mayor didn't realize he was making his own special contribution to the movement by demonstrating that racism was not confined to the South.

Hubbard got involved when the *Montgomery Advertiser* responded to the Parks incident by publishing a series of articles on Jim Crowism in the North. One staffer, William T. Johnson, wanted to interview Hubbard. But the mayor, despite his reputation as an unabashed segregationist, hadn't said much for public consumption recently. Would he talk now?

Johnson phoned Hubbard, and when he started asking questions, he found he could hardly get the mayor to shut up. Johnson taped more than enough for an article, published March 26, that was designed to validate the paper's "sorrowful" contention: "That wherever in America the Negro migrates in significant numbers, he encounters rejection, candidly in the South, pharisaically in the North."

Johnson found Hubbard "a friendly firecracker with a ready wit, a sense of humor and a robust willingness to talk." Hubbard, for his part, undoubtedly intended the exercise as a primer for southern readers on how to control the racial situation. Perhaps he didn't realize—though he should have—that it might eventually have wider readership in his own locale than it did down South.

It was only a matter of days before the *Michigan Chronicle*, a black-oriented weekly published in Detroit, reprinted the entire interview.[2] The article, headlined "Why No Negroes Live in Dearborn," was the definitive statement on Hubbard's racial position. It read in part:

"I am for complete segregation, one million per cent on all levels. I believe in economic equality [for Negroes] but social equality is a horse of a different color.

"If a man works, I don't care what color he is—he ought to be paid. But I'm against any of this social dream stuff.

". . . They can't get in here," says Hubbard. "We watch it. Every time we hear of a Negro moving in—for instance, we had one last year—we respond quicker than you do to a fire. That's generally known. It's known among our own people and it's known among the Negroes here." . . .

Q. Has the NAACP ever called on you?

A. "No, we'd chase 'em to h———l out of town."

Q. When is the last time any Negroes called on you?

A. "I think when I was running for circuit judge. A colored fellow brought me a petition. I gave him a can of beer and two bucks or something. He's from Detroit. He wanted to see me. He said he'd heard I had horns. . . .

"We're for complete segregation, no ifs, ands, or buts about it. That is my position and I tell the Negroes the same thing. I say, 'We don't have equality among the whites and you don't have equality among the Negroes. Why stir up something when you're getting along all right?' . . ."

Q. But how are the Negroes kept out of Dearborn?

A. "We say it's against the law to live here," says Hubbard. "They say, 'You know what the Supreme Court says.' I tell them we're talking about the law of custom, the law of habit. . . ."

Q. In other words, all the property owners would have to be in agreement with you.

A. "Well, that's why I'm still mayor, 15 years."

Q. They just won't sell to Negroes?

A. "That's the way you do it."

Hubbard, proceeding with my higher education in Northern race strife, said the population of Dearborn has been doubled since 1950 by a large influx of Poles and Italians who were "crowded out of Detroit by the colored people coming in."

Those people, he said, "are so anti-colored—much more so than you in Alabama, if you took a vote on it.

". . . Now don't misunderstand me: I'm not against a man necessarily because of his color, but I feel bitter about this aggression in trying to force them upon each other. I think it's morally wrong to force one race upon the other.

"... Like the colored fellow said to me. He said, 'You think the Negro's all right in his place.' I said, 'You're right. I have nothing against the Negro, but don't push us around. Quit pushing the whites around. We've been pretty good to you. We've nursed you along, we've kept you here since the Civil War, put shoes on your feet. Don't push us around.'"

I didn't have the slightest idea he was taping it. But I don't deny it. I just told the truth about it, but people, it didn't sound good to 'em, that's all. What's wrong with it? I just told 'em the truth. Why should I be sorry about it?[3]

It may have been Hubbard's truth, but it wasn't everybody's. And it wasn't long before he was bombarded with criticism, this time not coming from other politicians.[4] His main antagonist this time was the Right Reverend Richard S. Emrich, bishop of the Episcopal Diocese of Michigan. In a statement cleared with church attorneys, Bishop Emrich declared that Hubbard's position violated fundamental teachings of Christianity, adding:

It is the duty of every pastor and Christian to oppose him. Mayor Hubbard espouses views which are opposed directly to the Constitution of the United States and to the beloved tradition which brought so many freedom-loving people to America. He not only has a disregard for American law but also for larger American interests. Mayor Hubbard's views, picked up by the press and spread to Africa, Southeast Asia and Japan, are worth many Russian divisions.[5]

I took on that goddamn phony. The NAACP gave him some award for attacking me. Christ, he gave me the royal treatment. But I went out and got a picture of his goddamn house out there in Palmer Woods. I really checked him out. He didn't practice what he preached. Palmer Woods. How many niggers do you think live around there? Bullshitting people about God. He isn't a bad guy, despite what I said about him. Since then he's invited me to his church.

Hubbard further defended his stand in the press: "Dearborn has been a segregated white community since 1790, and if there are any unhappy souls living here, they won't have to travel far to live in another neighborhood. . . . Dearborn is the cleanest town in the world, physically and morally."[6]

Though Hubbard at first threatened to sue the bishop for his comments, he let it slide. In the meantime, a number of church groups in Dearborn and around the state voiced support for the clergyman's stand.[7] But Hubbard, who kept insisting that his views represented those of his constituents, suggested that there seemed to be "a strong segregationist movement in Michigan." Segregationist councils from Alabama had been attempting to organize chapters in the area, he revealed.

That was the end of it, as far as Hubbard was concerned. The episode had solidified his reputation as a racist, and he certainly had done nothing to soften its effect afterward.

32

Beating William L. Mills, 1956-57

People all over town say, "Well, Hubbard picks up my
rubbish and he keeps the colored people out." But he
doesn't do either one—you do.
—Mayoral candidate William L. Mills, in a campaign
speech to voters

Keeping Dearborn white was only one of Orville Hubbard's preoccupations
in the mid-1950s. Now, in 1956, Hubbard had the big picture all planned
out. He would, in making his third attempt at the office, find himself elevated
to the circuit bench. Failing that, he would so encumber Municipal Judge
George Martin that the "glorified justice of the peace" would be totally
impotent as a rival. Next he would merge the police and fire departments
as a grand model of law enforcement for the rest of the country. Not content
with that, he would merge his city with 15 neighboring townships and
make Dearborn the second-largest community in the nation, a ravenous
monster covering 400 square miles, with himself at the head, of course. And
perhaps most grandiose of all, he would expand Dearborn's influence all
the way to Florida, gobbling up 1,000 acres of free land for a seniors' retirement haven, even if the Michigan attorney general said he couldn't do it.
At least this was the dream Orvie had for himself and his city while others
railed on about his racial pronouncements.

First things first. He had tested his judicial appeal twice before, in 1953
and 1955, but those failures hadn't convinced him he had no future on the
bench. In June 1956, voters gave Hubbard his first raise since he took the
mayor's job in 1942, boosting him from $6,500 to a much more respectable
$17,500, effective in 1958. But if he could snare a court vacancy, he would
jump all the way to $24,500. The mayor's first move that month was to try
to dispose of an old rival, Frank Darin, but the Michigan Supreme Court
rejected Orvie's claim that some of Darin's signatures were invalid. Hubbard
wound up a lame third in the August primary, behind Darin and the even-

266

tual winner, incumbent Victor Targonski. Orvie alibied that he "didn't even spend a nickel for a cigar" and was encouraged enough by his performance to want to try again.

"I've loved my job, but I'm an old man of 53," he told reporters. "Being mayor of Dearborn is hard on me." Indeed, it was as hard as he made it. He continued his never-ending quest to make Judge Martin's life miserable, and this time he brought most of the rest of Dearborn's elected government into the fray. In June, Hubbard got the council to eliminate the court's probation officer from the budget, even while he was proclaiming that the court needed a second full-time judge. "If Hubbard really wants to help my court, he can give me a probation officer and stop padding my budget with things I don't need," Martin said.[1] Martin also complained that the city jail was grossly inadequate, and to prove it, he began sentencing misdemeanants to terms there instead of in the county lockup. That sent Public Safety Director Marguerite Johnson into a snit. She described Martin's tactic as "a spoiled-brat temper tantrum." In September, Martin renewed his complaints about traffic enforcement, blaming the council for repealing—for the second time—his "no-fix" ticket ordinance of 1954. Then the tiff spilled over into the council, when John Baja blamed Johnson for the problem, and she demanded he quit the council and devote his energies to a tavern he owned instead of harboring ambitions to become "Dearborn's first bartending mayor." Despite the sideshow, Martin kept on complaining, right through the next year, when the National Safety Council again rated Dearborn's traffic enforcement as the worst in its population class. Martin derided Hubbard as "notorious for doing his utmost to discourage proper traffic law enforcement." For his part, Martin was named Michigan's best judge in 1957 during an April conference of the Michigan Municipal Judges Association, of which he was president. Hubbard could do nothing to tarnish that distinction, although he did get in a few more digs. In July, Martin grumbled that the mayor was delaying the installation of a window air conditioner in his court office, and in September, he complained that Orvie was trying to eliminate him from the governmental mainstream by transferring the court from the police building to a house near the office of gadfly attorney James Thomson. "As long as Thomson and Martin spend so much time together anyway," the mayor said, "it will be more convenient for them to have their offices close by. They can sneak back and forth across the street to plot against me to their hearts' content."

The mayor eventually discarded his notion of giving Martin the bum's rush from the police building. But in a separate maneuver involving the police, he began a partial merger of the police and fire departments. He had announced plans in January 1957 to train police to fight fires, and two months later he said he hoped to abolish the Fire Department. Hubbard said the plan would take several years to implement but ultimately would "revolutionize the whole concept of police and fire operations in the United

States." In October, the city sent out a fleet of station wagons manned by police trained to fight fires. The wagons—flame red and white and emblazoned with the old Hubbard slogan, "Be Nice to People"—were equipped with fire extinguishers, flares, hydrant wrenches and other fire-fighting paraphernalia.[2]

The police-fire merger wasn't the only consolidation Orvie had in mind. He was thinking grand thoughts on several fronts. In February 1957, a month after announcing his police-fire plan, he urged 15 area township boards to consider merging with Dearborn to realize "obvious advantages" of scale. The resulting city, he pointed out, would boast a population of 500,000, about quadruple that of Dearborn.[3] Not only that, but the new city would expand Dearborn's 24.5 square miles to 400—bigger than New York, almost twice as big as Chicago and three times bigger than Detroit. Only Los Angeles, with 451 square miles, would rank ahead of Dearborn. Orvie said in a "Dear Friends" letter to the townships:

> There are now 44 different, independent local governments in Wayne County, and townships are continuously being sliced up to make even more costly and unnecessary communities. . . .
> Meanwhile, the "courting of Dearborn" by some of our neighbors points up the advantages to them of joining Michigan's fourth largest city rather than trying to form a new consolidated community of their own. . . .
> They see in annexation to Dearborn, their becoming part of a community acclaimed far and wide, as well as by its own residents, for its good public service, cleanliness, fine recreation and low taxes.[4]

Reaction was mixed. One official, Dearborn Township Supervisor Lyle E. Miller, conceded, "We've been clamoring to get into Dearborn for years," but, he noted, Dearbornites would "be screaming if Hubbard tries to annex all those townships." In Dearborn, the response was less than enthusiastic. Baja suggested that the mayor's "insincere daydream" would cause "more headaches and a higher tax dollar just so we can say that we're the second-largest city in the United States." Dearborn Township leaders scrambled to start a petition drive to take advantage of the scheme.[5] Orvie, meanwhile, continued to tout the idea in speeches.

But turning Dearborn into some mutant creation of suburban sprawl was not his most extravagant plot during 1956.[6] Even before the township merger plan, Hubbard had become smitten with the notion of a Dearborn stronghold in the South. The idea came to him after visiting Florida in 1950 and 1951, when he decided it would make an ideal retirement home. As he later explained it, "I thought, 'All this property available and people up North freezing to death.'" Now, in a torrent of news releases in early 1956, Hubbard found himself plugging "a paradise in the sunny Southland" or, as he took to calling it, his "dream of sunbeams." What he wanted to do, he said, was to get federal aid for a kind of Florida version of Camp Dearborn, a low-cost, high-grade development of small rental cottages for Dearbornites with limited retirement incomes. The louder Hubbard trumpeted the idea, the better it sounded, at least in the local weeklies. A week later, in March, he declared the response "fantastic." The Dearborn Board of Realtors endorsed the idea, a development company tried pitching Arizona instead of Florida as a site, and even U.S. Senator Hubert H. Humphrey, who knew Hubbard from conventions during Humphrey's days as mayor of Minneapolis, declared that the plan had merit. "It is a most imaginative and stimulating proposal," Humphrey wrote Orvie. "It is so provocative that I intend to bring it to the attention of my fellow senators."

Hubbard's plans bogged down in January 1957, when his old nemesis, James Thomson, secured a court injunction against spending tax money or using city workers to promote the project. The mayor responded by getting the council to put a Florida proposal on the upcoming April ballot as a charter amendment. Thomson had blocked an attempt to get an advisory referendum on the February ballot, contending that the project was a "scheme to unload thousands of acres of bog-land, swampland, sand dunes and undesirable property upon the taxpayers of Dearborn." Orvie called Thomson "one of the little hurdles civilization must get over from time to time."

In February, Circuit Judge Horace Gilmore approved an advisory question for the April ballot asking whether the mayor should appoint a committee to recommend a development site. He also gave the city the go-ahead on a charter amendment that would allow the city to acquire and develop grounds, construct buildings and conduct a recreation project in Florida. The only hitch was that the state attorney general's office ruled the scheme unconstitutional, in the absence of any explicit authorization for a city to acquire land in another state. That meant the proposal could stay on the ballot, but, if approved, it likely would be challenged in court.

A week before the April election, a Florida developer offered the city 1,000 acres north of Lake Okeechobee, 30 miles from the Atlantic coast. The land, which he said was worth $2 million, could accommodate 3,000 homesites, and, because a development would enhance the value of another parcel he owned nearby, he would give the 1,000 acres to the city for free. You could almost feel Hubbard salivating: free land in Florida. But voters failed to echo the mayor's enthusiasm. By a ratio of more than three to two, they turned down both the charter amendment and the advisory referendum. Hubbard couldn't believe it. He engineered another advisory vote in June, and this time the measure went down almost four to one. A gleeful Thomson dubbed the aborted project "Swamp Dearborn." The Scotch-born attorney, who had filed more than two dozen suits against the city over the years, thus got the results he wanted without having to go to court one more time.[7]

The next year, in January 1957, Thomson took on Hubbard again, this time alleging that "privileges and immunities are sold and purchased in Dearborn city government." Most serious of Thomson's accusations, all of them denied by the mayor, was a charge that unnamed city employees accepted payoffs for building permits, certificates of occupancy and permission to violate zoning ordinances. Thomson made the allegations in a request to extend an ongoing grand jury investigation into Dearborn.

Thomson never was able to provide enough specifics to interest the grand jury in Dearborn, but Hubbard faced a detailed layering of accusations of a different sort later that year. The source was the *Dearborn Independent*, and the venue was the best-conceived, most vigorously contested mayoral campaign Hubbard would ever face. William L. Mills was a stubby, bald, ruddy-faced man who had worked for 32 years as copublisher and business manager of the *Independent*. Although he and the paper had backed Hubbard enthusiastically at first, their relationship soured in the late 1940s. Now, as a candidate, Mills had a ready-made outlet for his anti-Hubbard platform, and he wasn't averse to using it.

The first challengers to take out petitions surfaced in March. By the filing deadline, the list numbered eight. Besides Mills, they were Samuel J. McSpadden, a pizza cook; Timothy M. Mulroy, an advertising agent; John Kadela, former Dearborn city controller; Edward Robinson, who had joined the U.S. Marines after working a few months as Hubbard's administrative assistant; Charles J. Nemeth, a motel night clerk and sometime real estate salesman who helped run the 1951 recall; Ray Parker, a teacher and former councilman; and Eugene C. Keyes, an attorney-dentist-physician and former councilman. Parker, Robinson and Nemeth all had been obliterated by Hubbard in the 1955 race. The mayor took out his petitions in late August.

McSpadden dictated the early course of the campaign. A bow-tie-wearing cigar smoker, he crusaded against parking meters and asked voters, "Why Keep a Bad 'un? Win with McSpadden." Recognizing that Orvie's big advantage was his sense of publicity, McSpadden unveiled a daring plan to outdo the master. In an apparent attempt to make it known that he was being persecuted by Hubbard, McSpadden spent a week in jail on a reckless driving charge after refusing to post bond. His tactics also included racking up a series of 15 traffic tickets in a week and agitating a woman who complained he had been sleeping in a car in front of her house.

Among the most vigorous of the remaining challengers was the 57-year-old Keyes (rhymes with "Eyes"), who had gained a wide enough following that he was elected Michigan's lieutenant governor as a Republican for two terms in the 1940s. Getting elected to state office was a far easier matter than unseating Orville Hubbard, of course, but Keyes persisted valiantly, telling reporters, "I can find a better candidate than Hubbard by looking into my own mirror," and running newspaper ads that pleaded, "Help Dr. Keyes Defeat the Boss." Keyes also distributed flyers calling Hubbard's the "most extravagant" city administration in the country. The allegation, similar to ones raised by Orvie's opponents in the 1940s, noted that Detroit, with its population of 2 million, budgeted less than $74,000 for its mayor; the total for little Dearborn was almost $76,000, not including car expenses. The first volume of Keyes's *Dearborn Citizen*, distributed in August, sniffed, "The stunts and buffoonery of our mayor have shocked not only the citizens of Michigan but almost all of the United States, so much so that visiting anywhere in the country, when it is learned that you are from Dearborn, the stock comment is, 'Oh, that's where you have that "nut" for a mayor.'"[8]

Mills stamped himself as a serious challenger in September with a half-page- plus newspaper ad that urged voters to "end the dictatorship." He proposed limiting the mayor to three consecutive terms, keeping the police and fire departments separate, cutting back city jobs, abandoning any annexation plans, halting interference with the court, and building fire stations. In addition, Mills urged:

Eliminate persecution and fear of reprisal by a too powerful political machine. Stop wasting public funds for publicity stunts. Stop juggling tax rates to fool the voters and get phony tax cuts during election years. Restore the good name of Dearborn and make it a city which decent citizens can be proud to live [in]. . . . Stop raising controversial issues which rouse the base instincts of fear, greed and prejudice to bait the voters.[9]

That ranked as one of the first references to Hubbard's racist tactics by any mayoral opponent in 16 years.

Dearborn's voters seemed little impressed by the rhetoric, however. Hubbard was in bed with the flu for 10 days before the primary, and the rallies put on by the other candidates were largely ignored. A Monday night rally at Lowrey School featured 17 candidates and attracted an audience of 18. But Orvie was back in fighting trim at his traditional Fordson rally the Sunday before the primary, and more than 1,000 came to hear him take on the 56-year-old Mills.

Mills ran a big front-page editorial, and it challenged the mayor to debate any time, any place, and he'd pick up the tab. I was down with something, but I read that, and it made me so goddamn mad I got out of my goddamn bed. I wrote him a goddamn letter and told him to be there and have the money. The place was jammed to the roof. And he came down front to debate. He wrote a check. I said, "No, we want cash on the barrelhead. No goddamn checks." So he gets up on the platform, and this is my meeting, and he says I'm a Hitler and a dictator. And I says, "Well, take a look at Mills. Take a look at me. Who looks more like Mussolini? Who looks like the dictator?" He really looked like one. Jesus Christ, they went wild over it. They almost hauled him out of the schoolhouse.

271

Mills tried hard to climb out of the hole the mayor's quips had put him in. When he was forced to ask the audience if anyone would cash his $99 check for the auditorium rental, he accepted a $100 bill from a relative of his wife's and made sure he demanded a dollar change from the Hubbard camp.

He hammered at the mayor's record, calling him a "dictator who runs the city to suit his own whims with no regard for anyone" and pointing out, "His stooges are paid $188,000 of your taxes every year to keep the machine in office." He promised to "eliminate government by trickery, defeat the rascals on the push-button Council" and throw out Johnson as safety director. Then he touched on the subject that had become all but taboo for anyone but Hubbard to mention: the Negroes. Mills was smart enough to know he wasn't going to beat Hubbard by becoming the city's integration champion. So he couched his criticism of the mayor's racist posture in terms the voters might accept—that they, not Hubbard, deserved the "credit" for keeping Dearborn clean. Said Mills, "People all over town say, 'Well, Hubbard picks up my rubbish and he keeps the colored people out.' But he doesn't do either one—you do. The rubbish collections are paid for with your taxes and were done better by four administrations before Hubbard's. And twenty-three of the thirty-one large communities in the Detroit area have no Negro populations. The only way this is going to change is when individual residents begin to sell their homes to the people you have been keeping out."[10]

Orvie was not through with his theatrics. He shouted at his challenger, "Why don't you ever tell the truth? You never stand for anything. You have opposed everything I have tried to do." He gave a serious answer to Mills's charge of machine politics: "We operate strictly according to the city charter, and Dearborn has one of the best ever written." He then wound up the half-hour debate by ripping up a copy of the *Independent* and throwing the scraps on the floor. Mills, he said, used "the Hitler technique of repeating the 'big lie' in his rag."[11]

The September 23 primary went pretty much according to form. Nobody really thought Mills was telling the "big lie," but neither was he telling Dearbornites what they wanted to hear. With 42 percent of the registered voters turning out, Hubbard piled up nearly a two-to-one margin over Mills, with 14,174 votes to 7,216. The also-rans were led by Parker with 1,859, then Keyes with 1,442, followed by Kadela, 615; Mulroy, 298; Nemeth, 203; Robinson, 98; and McSpadden, 70. All seven Hubbard slaters in the council race won nomination, including incumbents Edward Dombrowski, George Bondie, Ralph Guy, William Broomhall and Charles Gilbert, plus Robert Johnson and Nick Mondella. John Baja led the field.

Hubbard, irked at not doing even better in the primary, said he would try to counteract Mills's appeal with "more of our famous public service charm in the areas where we weren't as strong as we believed." Mills simply

272

promised to get the "vote out in November and we will beat him."

Both sides lined up their support. Mills attracted a council slate that included Baja, James Thomson and former Hubbard Police Chief Lawrence Schaefer. In addition, Martin also was apparently backing Mills, having appeared at rallies with him and been photographed with him. At Hubbard's request, the council asked the city attorney to investigate whether the judge had violated the Michigan Bar Association's code of ethics.

The mayor, meanwhile, received the endorsement of Parker, who wore a football helmet and jersey in a publicity photo intended to illustrate that Orvie's "old quarterback" on the council was "back on the team" after years of opposition. The reunion spurred rumors that Parker was about to get a city job.

Hubbard's newspaper ads strung together many of his favorite slogans: "Stand by the man who stands by you. Support Mayor Hubbard with a council team that will keep Dearborn clean. If you like things done the Hubbard way, vote the Hubbard slate on election day. Wise home owners vote the Hubbard slate. You expect more from Hubbard and you get it. It takes teamwork to get things done."[12]

Mills continued to campaign against the "lack of integrity in the city government now dominated by one man whose chief interest is perpetuating himself in office and not facing the real problems of the city." The challenger also made extensive—and arguably unfair—use of his newspaper to lampoon and critique Hubbard. One issue of a preelection *Independent* featured an all-but-blank front page marked with a "censured" (*sic*) stamp from "The Dictator," obviously intended to satirize the mayor's control of the local press. The only story on the page was a mock testimonial that said, "Orvie Liscomb [*sic*] Hubbard is the most wonderfulest mayor that has ever been elected to public office in any city, any place in the whole world."[13]

More telling was a series of stories written by Mills and printed earlier in the year by the *Independent*. The series, called "How Dearborn Got a Dictator Mayor," was condensed and reprinted in the *Detroit News*. Hubbard called it a "vicious, bitter and distorted attack," but many observers found it generally accurate. One reporter, James Sullivan of the *Free Press*, called it "a fairly objective, dispassionate review."[14] The series, which began with Mills's version of how he first took a liking to Hubbard as a political novice in the 1930s and eventually helped convince him to file his petitions for mayor in 1941, brought an immediate denial from Orvie. "The first time I ever knew Mills had been a supporter of mine was when I read it in that smear sheet," he told reporters. Mills explained his position this way: "Orville Hubbard proved a good mayor for his first six years in office. But with each succeeding victory he became more greedy for power. He could not stand any opposition. One by one, he began to purge each department in the city government, replacing department heads who refused to bend to his will with hand-picked puppets." Retorted Hubbard: "I have known Bill Mills for over 20 years, and he is a pathological liar."

The Independent *at that time wanted to take over city hall. Bill decided to run for mayor, so the* Independent *threw everything it had into it. The* Independent *just published all the shit that people just knew wasn't true. And they made it so bad that they lost subscriptions. I don't think I've changed one bit. I'm still a farm guy I ever was. I've got some recent letters from Charlie Wagner before he died telling me what a good job I've done. He said how right I'd been all along.*

The two warriors set up one last clash the night before the election, with Hubbard vowing in a flyer to "hammer Hell out of the gang who operate behind the scenes and use every trick in the bag to grab control of your City Hall" by running a "cocky stooge for Mayor, who acts and looks like a dictator." The only catch was that Hubbard failed to appear after a crew from a local radio station showed up. The station went ahead and broadcast a 15-minute speech in which Mills threatened to "nail Hubbard's hide to the wall if he ever showed up." The pro-Mills crowd heckled the Hubbard-slate council candidates who appeared—particularly Guy, who cracked, "So many people are laughing at me, I ought to go to Hollywood and get a job." Mills's coup de grace against the absent mayor was to display a large caricature showing Orvie with fangs and horns with the slogan, "Big Brother is watching you."

Dearborn voters obviously loved Big Brother, however. A record turnout in the November election gave another Hubbard foe a walloping, this time by a vote of 25,169 to 14,721. Mills won only 13 of 107 precincts, mostly in West Dearborn's upper-income precincts. Hubbard, as usual, dominated in East Dearborn, where the *Independent*'s circulation was concentrated, even winning Mills's home district, 231–161. Mills blamed his defeat on Hubbard's "machine of tax-paid department heads. I thought we would do better, but neither I nor my paper will stop fighting the dictator." Baja led the council field, but four Hubbard slaters gave the mayor another majority— Dombrowski, Guy, Bondie and Broomhall. Voters defeated Hubbard-backed proposals for six-year terms for elected officials, pay boosts for councilmen and reestablishment of a second full-time judge.

Hubbard told well-wishers at city hall afterward that he intended to "reward" Golfview Estates voters for going heavily for Mills by extending a road through the subdivision, a suggestion that had been bitterly opposed by residents. The council turned down the proposal a few days later.

But the power in Dearborn still lay with Hubbard, in case there were any doubters. The next month, when Bondie tried to delay pay raises for department heads, Orvie shouted, "Either you pass these pay raises tonight, or you can walk out of here backwards and never come back." The raises were approved.

As for Mills, he became sole owner of the *Independent*, then sold out to the rival *Dearborn Guide* in 1959 and moved to San Francisco to sell real estate. A few years later, he sent Hubbard a postcard of Alcatraz prison. It said, "I wish you were here."

33

Beating Roger Craig, 1958-59

> I just squawk.
> —Sign on the cage of a live duck at a Hubbard campaign rally at Fordson High School

With an impish grin spread across his face, the rotund figure gathered himself in midair, knees bent and fists clenched, as he prepared to land, with all the force of his 300-plus pounds, on a sheet of paper that looked more than a little the worse for wear after being kicked, stomped and sworn at. The paper was a subpoena demanding appearance before the State Labor Mediation Board, and the character taking such delight in abusing it so, of course, was Orville L. Hubbard.

Hubbard had been served in March 1959, during a meeting of the County Board of Supervisors, on which he held a seat by virtue of his position as Dearborn mayor. The controversy that elicited such an effort from him was whether his city would be forced to recognize Jimmy Hoffa's local of the Teamsters Union as bargaining agent for some 325 rubbish collectors. It was the union's first attempt to organize public employees in the area.

The epic battle between subpoena and servee was captured on film by enterprising newspaper photographers who had arrived an hour late for the performance but were treated to an encore after pleading, "Do it again, Orvie!" The photo that resulted from the obligingly energetic Hubbard epitomized the labor problems that beset him in 1959. It also resurfaced later as he campaigned for his tenth term in office against the new hope of Dearborn's liberals, Roger Craig.

Craig, a 25-year-old attorney and onetime athlete, the year before had become the youngest person ever elected to the Dearborn Board of Education. He was also, as it developed, much too young to present a serious challenge to Hubbard. Any kind of challenge would do, however, even if it was only another chance for the mayor to elude a subpoena.

The Teamsters were claiming they had the backing of well over the 50 percent of the city's DPW workers required for a union to be certified. But Hubbard, concerned about racketeering charges that had followed the union even after Hoffa had replaced the ousted Dave Beck as president, wasn't cooperating. In order to certify Local 299, the Labor Mediation Board needed city records showing employees' names and signatures. The city had not produced the records, and Hubbard had refused to meet with the board to discuss the matter. Telegrams from the board to the mayor were returned unopened—five times.

While Teamster pickets marched in front of city hall, two State Police detectives tried in vain to serve Hubbard and DPW Director James Dick. The pair gave up after a two-hour wait. The next day, one of the detectives, Jack Wooley, confronted Hubbard after roll call at the supervisors' meeting downtown. Wooley tried to stick his subpoena in the mayor's suit pocket, but Orvie let the document flutter to the floor. "I wish I was on the state legislature," the mayor snapped. "I would cut your budget." After the officer left, Hubbard kicked the subpoena away. But when the photographers showed up, he sprang back into action, stomping it, then jumping on it. Many of his fellow supervisors roared with amusement, but two, both union officials, called for his censure. Another said the State Police should be censured "for invading a legislative body in session." Hubbard spat on the subpoena, still lying on the carpet, as he left, but Councilman Ralph Guy put it in his pocket.

Although the mayor later claimed immunity from summons during a legislative session, officials said the privilege applied only to the state legislature. The issue evaporated when Dearborn Personnel Director Dudley Sherman produced the city records in question, but the acrimony persisted. "Never, never as long as I'm mayor will we recognize these gangsters, bogeymen, hoodlums in our clean city," Hubbard vowed. Responded Teamsters Business Agent Charles O'Brien, "We'll march 'round Dearborn until he comes to his senses."

What the mayor had in mind was more like a feast for the senses. As the union began picketing city hall, Orvie set up loudspeakers to broadcast his inspirational declamations and such tunes as "Jailhouse Rock." That continued for a week or so, until attorney James Thomson secured an injunction on behalf of former Councilman Eugene Keyes, who operated a nearby hospital and complained the racket was bothering his patients. The city threatened court action of its own against the union. And Orvie announced he would seek bids from private firms to pick up rubbish so "we won't have to shell out all sorts of fringe benefits to a bunch of loafers."

The Teamsters weren't about to give up, however. From New York, Hoffa dispatched an assistant, Larry Steinberg, who told cheering DPW workers that the union "will spare no funds" in the battle. "In the meantime," he said, "go home and tell your friends, your community and the whole world that you are being mistreated by a nincompoop." Steinberg also lectured the workers about the importance of following supervisors' instructions. "You may even be branded racketeers from a corrupt union," he said, "but behave. The resistance you are facing in Dearborn is happening all over the country wherever the Teamsters are trying to organize."

A few weeks later, in April, the dispute had simmered down, and Orvie was targeting a pay raise proposal that police and firemen had managed to get on the spring ballot.[1] Police and firemen estimated the request would average $340 a man. But to Hubbard, the request was "one of the biggest raids ever perpetrated on the citizens of Dearborn" and would total up to $1,608 a man, including fringe benefits. "Schemers and cheaters, that's what they are," he stormed. He tried the same kind of intimidation as he had with the Teamsters. The city was studying a proposal to farm out police work to private agencies, he said, and fire protection duties could be turned over to Detroit. And, he warned, there would be no pay raises at all, not even the modest ones he was willing to give voluntarily, if the ballot proposal failed.

In the last days before the vote, firemen complained that local businessmen were being "intimidated and harassed" if they dared display posters backing the pay raise. Thomson got a court order prohibiting the city from interfering with the campaign, and, when the city was accused a few days later of ripping down posters, Thomson tried to have Public Safety Director Robert Keith Archer found in contempt. Orvie also flooded the city with literature decrying the "tax grab," but when police and firemen began handing out their handbills, he ordered them arrested. The leaflets, he said, were illegal because they lacked the signatures, names and addresses of distributors. Several of the men gave themselves up, but the mayor declined to sign a complaint against them.

Despite his differences with city employees, Orvie wanted it known he was still one of the guys. So a few days before the election, he dropped in at the West Dearborn fire hall so the men could help celebrate his fifty-sixth birthday. He had been invited by fireman Daniel Zahari, who was not a member of the union. And in case not all the men were pleased about the little party, Chief George Lewis ordered them all to the dining hall. The mayor, accompanied by a city photographer, had coffee and cake with the firemen and then asked them all to chip in to pay for the refreshments. No, he wasn't kidding, and no, the firemen weren't paying. Zahari finally picked up the tab.

As for the election itself, Dearborn voters never had been known to give money away voluntarily, particularly after years of being pampered by Hubbard's long-standing policy of keeping the tax burden off homeowners. The vote was reasonably close, but the pay raise went down, 18,831 to

13,704. Deriding "the gang which connived, lied and conspired to jam down the throats of Dearborn taxpayers an outrageous $500,000 pay raid," Hubbard accused police and firemen of seeking help from 200 nonresidents who "invaded Dearborn on election day to help their greedy kind." Other villains aiding the cause, he said, were "Jimmy Hoffa's bogeymen in dark glasses and black Cadillacs," as well as Judge Martin and the Democrats. And now that the returns were in, Orvie warned, police and firemen would have to buckle down. He asked citizens to report "any cops loafing on the job" and any firemen "who may be robbing others of work by holding two jobs." Those who didn't like it, he said, could submit their "immediate resignations."[2] The following week, at the mayor's recommendation, the council voted minimum pay raises of $250 a year for firemen and $300 for police. It was less than the employees were asking but still more than Hubbard originally had proposed.

The mayor's efforts to hold down personnel costs could hardly have been lost on voters in 1959. But while he was busy boosting himself as a champion of low costs, and thus low taxes, the man who would challenge him at the polls was establishing himself as a proponent of increased residential property assessments, and thus high taxes. And, though no one would admit it, Roger Craig all but took himself out of serious contention as a candidate even before the campaign began.

Craig's decision to run climaxed nearly two years of uncharacteristically strained relations between city and school officials. In years past, a few school people had gotten into politics: teachers Ray Parker and Anthony Smith and former school trustee Homer Beadle all were long-term councilmen. The mayor himself had stayed largely out of school affairs, however.

His record of self-restraint disintegrated in 1957, when the school board proposed building a new high school. Over the previous two decades, Dearborn had established a greenbelt known as Crowley Park as a buffer with the blue-collar, largely Negro community of Inkster.[3] But the park was precisely the spot the school board had chosen for a new school for southwestern Dearborn's growing teenage population. In January 1958, the council voted, over Orvie's objections, to sell 55 acres of the park to the school board for $500,000. After ridiculing school officials as "a bunch of do-gooders" who had "gone screwy," Hubbard the next month vetoed the sale, saying it would "be the open gateway for the invasion into Dearborn of certain people, the kind of which thousands of local residents have moved to Dearborn to escape as neighbors." If that weren't clear enough, he also warned that the legislature might make Dearborn take pupils from Inkster and eventually consolidate all the school districts in the county in order to meet financial pressures. Then, he declared, "Dearborn schools will have to accommodate all of its barefoot neighbors." School spokesmen disputed his claims as "utterly fallacious" and began condemnation proceedings to force the sale. But in the meantime, Hubbard had maneuvered the council into putting the issue up for an advisory vote on the November ballot. With the Chamber of Commerce urging a no vote, and with Hubbard distributing a door-to-door broadside, voters streamed to the polls to voice their disapproval by a three-to-one ratio.

Faced with a rebuff like that, the school board announced in January 1959 that it was reluctantly abandoning its plans. That didn't stop Hubbard from squaring off with school officials over several other construction projects in 1958, however. At one point, when board members were discussing ways to improve cooperation with the mayor, Trustee Ralph Bell observed dryly, "That's like trying to get along with Russia."

Relations were helped little when Robert Keith Archer, Hubbard's resident expert on school affairs, ran for a seat on the board in June 1958. Even with Orvie's backing, however, Archer finished last in a field of five. The winner was Craig, who had run dismally in the 1957 council primary but suddenly stamped himself as a rising political star. A year later, Craig announced he would try his luck against Orvie. "There has been a good deal of pressure on me to run," he said. "Someone has to give Hubbard a fight."

Perhaps the Craig camp thought voters had forgotten, but the young school trustee had committed a political gaffe a few months before by proposing an end to property tax breaks for homeowners. In April, he had demanded the city assess homes at 100 percent of true cash value, as provided by the state constitution. The prevailing level of assessment, Craig pointed out, was less than 33 percent, while businessmen were forced to make up the difference with assessments of over 80 percent. Craig's plan was quietly dropped two weeks later, but the damage was done. Even the Chamber of Commerce, whose members presumably would profit the most from the proposal, conceded it "would have shocking results for the taxpayers in this city."

The rest of Hubbard's challengers were hardly more credible. They were Leo A. McCarthy, a real estate and insurance salesman who had brought up the rear in the 1955 race; Charles Nemeth, a real estate salesman and hotel clerk who had run far back in both 1955 and 1957; and Donald A. Calkins, an attorney and civics teacher making his first run for office. Calkins was the best known of those. He had accused Hubbard two years earlier of going into a profane pique and breaking a tape recorder during an interview with Calkins's students. He also had been working toward the same kind of property reassessment as Craig had. In fact, he had filed suit in August to make the city return property tax money collected because homes were being underassessed. He had made three previous legal attempts since 1956 to get assessment procedures changed.[4]

The primary campaign offered little to scare Hubbard. Calkins's newspaper ads promised a "complete eradication of racial rabble rousing by the Mayor's office" and urged voters not to "confuse clean streets with clean government—you are entitled to both." Craig and the rest were scarcely heard from. The mayor's billboards boosted a slate of four council incumbents: William Broomhall, Ralph Guy, Edward Dombrowski and George Bondie. The opposition was less than well coordinated, with some candidates complaining that they were shorted billboard space because Craig and several others were calling the shots. The only flare-up before the primary came when the mayor took off against Councilman John Baja, calling him a "two-faced double-crosser" who "was born that way and will die that way." Baja had earned the fusillade by charging that Hubbard was ignoring the needs of east enders by pushing a plan to build up the area near the Rouge plant into a solid industrial zone. The two simmered down only after Guy threatened to have police toss Baja out of the council meeting disrupted by the tiff.

At his traditional preelection rally at Fordson High, Hubbard emphasized the importance of teamwork. "If you feel the opposition councilmen should be elected," he said, "don't vote for me." He also displayed a live duck with a sign, rife with symbolism, that said, "I just squawk," and he entertained the audience with duck calls throughout the evening. At the close, he invited the 1,300 attendees for a free malted at a nearby drive-in, where city police, under orders not to give parking tickets, directed the swarm of traffic.

It probably wasn't the malted that did it, but Hubbard carried every precinct in racking up 12,004 primary votes to 3,466 for Craig, 1,369 for Calkins, 773 for McCarthy and 720 for Nemeth. He got his four incumbents, plus three other slate members, nominated for council, but his three opponents—Baja, Vincent Fordell and George Hart—led the balloting.

The mayor refused to view the council results as a setback. He was, he said, "deeply grateful for this amazing citywide vote of confidence." Then he added, "It takes a heap of teamwork to get things done, and the job is hard enough without a bunch of jerks on the City Council sniping, bucking and opposing every move when they should be working shoulder-to-shoulder with each other and the mayor." He wasted no time picking on Craig, who, he said, "should resign from the board so someone who is genuinely interested in school matters can take over the job he doesn't want."

Craig fired back in kind. "Why didn't Hubbard resign when he ran for circuit court?" he asked. "In every campaign Hubbard has dragged in personalities. He gets his bloodhounds out looking for personal information to use against his opponents. He tried it with me and he didn't get very far. If he wants to carry on that kind of campaign, he should remember he lives in a glass house." As for his chances, he said, "I know I look like a sacrificial lamb to some people, but I'll put up a darned good fight and blow the whistle as loud as I can on the machine that has run our city too long."

Hubbard's control over the council continued to be the only issue in the election. The independents ran a newspaper ad attacking Hubbard's incumbents as "Charley McCarthys" and "abject stooges of the administration" who were "only interested in being a part of the city hall political machine." Baja and Hart called for outside studies on "extravagance and inefficiency" in the Hubbard administration. The proposal, which was simply tabled for study, was labeled by Hubbard as "political crap" inspired by Judge Martin. Craig put out literature accusing Hubbard of hiding behind the Fifth Amendment and hiring political hacks, including a convicted felon.[5] The brochures, picturing Craig in a swimsuit and the mayor jumping on the subpoena served during the county supervisors meeting in March, obviously were intended to depict Craig as a vigorous challenger taking on an incumbent who held his office up to ridicule.

It is likely that some were simply reminded, however, that an untested youngster was trying to take on a cagey veteran who was, moreover, a genuine original. Orville Hubbard stuck by his formula, reprising his old slogans on teamwork and loyalty. The *Dearborn Press* endorsed the mayor, noting that Craig had decided "not to wage an all-out fight" and concluding that his campaign was "little more than token."

There wasn't much suspense on election day, in truth, and the returns soon showed that the exact status quo would hold. Hubbard trounced Craig by a vote of 22,730 to 9,782, and all the council incumbents kept their seats, with Baja, Fordell and Hart leading the way ahead of mayor's four-man team. The ticket leader, Baja, said he was "delighted" with his showing in spite of "the mayor's smear campaign."

Hubbard called the result a "wonderful vote of confidence" following "one of Dearborn's strangest and quietest elections." He said, "We accept the protest vote as a challenge to do better, and we wish the opposition to know that we are not angry with anyone about anything."

But, after all, why should Orville Hubbard be angry about anything? He was ready to move into the 1960s with the absolute certainty that he never again would meet with significant opposition. With the young darling of the school board crowd dispatched, there was simply no one left to challenge him.

34

Beating Gene Wagner, 1960-61

Take a look at Martin's eyes and his face. You'll never
see anything so phony.
—Orville L. Hubbard, describing his relationship with
George Martin[1]

For a fiery young liberal with good political connections, Roger Craig had
turned out to be a disappointingly easy mark for Orville Hubbard. But just
when city hall was ready to write him off, Craig injected himself with so
much vigor into Hubbard's ongoing feud with George Martin that he restored
single-handedly the quaintly combative nature of old-style Dearborn politics. The only problem was that he landed in jail on assault charges in the
process.

After shellacking Craig in 1959, Orvie had missed few chances over the
next two years to aggravate Martin. But the judge, who three times had
earned the American Bar Association award for having the nation's best
court, was able to keep his equilibrium over the mayor's provocations. Craig
was not. Though not one of Hubbard's intended targets, Craig found himself
drawn into a simmering dispute over new court facilities that opened in
early 1961 over Martin's protests.

In May 1959, the judge had ridiculed Hubbard's plans to tack a courthouse onto the rear of a proposed new police headquarters in the civic
center. Orvie at first wanted to build a fire station there, but after the foundation was laid, he ordered up architectural plans for a court-police building. When Associate Judge John McWilliams said he liked the change, going
so far as to provide some design ideas, the City Council approved plans and
cost estimates. But Martin turned up his nose, calling the facility a "glorified,
glass-enclosed chicken coop, a disgrace, a costly mistake and a bargain basement dime store." The Dearborn Bar Association agreed, more or less, calling
it "inadequate, undignified, disrespectful and shortsighted." Martin even tried
to block the project in court but soon gave up.

A few months later, Hubbard tried to open a new wound, demanding that somebody investigate Martin's supposed favoritism in court. Since the mayor already had arranged to have a monthly audit and get daily records of how Martin disposed of his cases, the judge scoffed at the new demands. "The mayor had daily proof that I allow no favoritism in the Dearborn courts," he said. "The mayor's big grievance is that my policy of no favoritism includes the mayor." There matters lay for two years until the court finally opened. Martin, needless to say, was as unhappy as ever. A drive-in window proposed by McWilliams was too high for motorists to reach, doorknobs kept falling off, and Martin was little appeased by the fact that a closed-circuit TV and most of McWilliams's other innovations had not materialized.

We asked Martin to develop a plan for the court, and he outright refused. So we asked McWilliams. Martin hated that court. He didn't like it because it was built in the back of the building, and he wanted everything green. So we made his toilet paper green, so he could wipe his fucking ass on it. I think we put green fixtures in his toilet. He was so goddamn Irish.

Beyond that, Hubbard was bucking for a ballot proposal to dilute Martin's influence by promoting his associate judge into a full-timer, as the job had been before 1951. He also rebuffed Martin's attempt to get a proposal on the ballot for a police youth bureau, calling it "Martin's baby—let him rock it."

Things came to a head in late April, when Orvie ordered Martin's parking spot in the municipal garage spruced up a bit. The Irishman's space was painted green and roped off on three sides; and, dangling from the ceiling, just at windshield height, was the pièce de resistance—four green styrofoam balls, intended either as parking guides, if you believed city hall, or as the mayor's "latest needle," if you believed Martin. In any case, the balls disappeared, and Hubbard's public safety director, Robert Keith Archer, ordered a stakeout of the garage in case the thief struck again. The trap worked to perfection: the culprit turned out to be Martin's secretary, Irma Clark, who was duly apprehended and then hired Craig to get her out of the mess.

Craig, now 28, was a onetime Fordson High football player and swimmer who had been a Little All-American halfback at Wayne State University. He responded in a way that Clark did not anticipate. As Craig later explained it, "When you see someone goose-stepping in public, you either join him or sock him in the eye. I walked into Archer's office thinking, 'How can people use the law for something like this?' And I became infuriated, jumped over the desk and hit him." That pretty much coincided with his antagonist's version. Archer, 30, who had succeeded to the safety director's job when Marguerite Johnson died in 1958, said, "I made no attempt to fight back. He was in a towering rage and said he was going to throw me out the window. My glasses were broken, and I had blood in my eye so I couldn't see to defend myself. I was almost paralyzed by shock." Archer got six stitches, and Craig got a court date in May—before Judge Martin.

A few days later, Craig dashed off a letter to Orvie about Archer's "vicious misuse of power." Hubbard subsequently read the letter to the council, taking the opportunity to point out three misspelled words and adding, "This doesn't speak too well for a school board trustee with two college degrees."

Martin sent the mayor his own letter, criticizing police involvement in the Craig-Clark incident. "Let me suggest that you find cheaper ways to harass the court in the future," he said. "From past experience, I'm sure you can do it." Hubbard responded that the judge was "cracked."

As for Craig's trial, Martin postponed it until June, when, before a visiting judge, a jury deliberated one and a half hours before acquitting the defendant. Craig, decrying Archer's "Hitlerite" tactics, hailed the verdict as a "lesson to the boys at city hall." Archer had no comment.

Actually, Hubbard had maintained—for him—a rather low profile in 1960–61. There was a peripheral confrontation with civil rights activists, but he made only an occasional splash with his projects and schemes, most recycled from years past. He opened a city youth center in early 1960 as the first building on a parcel donated by Ford for a civic center, and the new police-court facility followed a year later. But he was stymied trying to pry land away from Ford for a municipal golf course, and his plans for a sports arena fizzled in May 1961, along with a proposal to attract a pro bowling team. A proposed helicopter taxi service never got off the ground, and another advisory vote on Orvie's "dream of sunbeams," the apartment project in Florida, went down by more than three-to-one. Even one of his best publicity coups seemed like an accident: getting photographed with Richard Nixon as the presidential candidate's motorcade passed city hall.[2]

He was more in command of the situation when it came to dealing with the integrationists. The possibility of a racial confrontation was raised in March 1960, when a TV interviewer asked Hubbard whether Dearborn could be compared to Little Rock, Arkansas, where President Eisenhower had sent in federal troops to oversee the integration of Central High School in 1957. "Yes," the mayor answered unflinchingly. "General [Douglas] MacArthur was born in Little Rock and once visited Dearborn." Asked if anyone, even Negroes, could live in Dearborn, Hubbard retorted, "There are no restrictions. Negroes could live here. The property's a little high, though."

Reporters questioned Dearborn's housing practices again a couple of months later, when Grosse Pointe, an old-money suburb just east of Detroit, was revealed to be using a "point system" to keep out Jews, Negroes and other "undesirables." Noting that Michigan Attorney General Paul Adams was examining the Grosse Pointe situation, H. Gordon Wood, a lawyer for property owners there, remarked, "If Adams wants publicity, he sure could get some if he spent some time in Dearborn." That brought a raft of denials from Realtors and civic association members about discrimination in Dearborn.[3]

It was not until July 1961 that Dearborn's racial attitudes actually were challenged. The Congress of Racial Equality (CORE) announced it would send freedom riders in to test public facilities there, and Hubbard was quick to respond. He called the integrationists "misguided troublemakers" who would encounter no segregated public facilities except for toilets, some for boys and others for girls. And he pointed out that thousands of Negroes worked in Dearborn, even though only about 100 lived there, almost all of them domestics. ("Most Negroes prefer to live in Detroit.") He also promised that the freedom riders would have no problems in Dearborn as long as they "obey the traffic laws and don't throw garbage on the streets." In fact, he said, "I'll greet them on the steps in front of the city hall if they come." No such greeting was forthcoming, but neither was there any trouble when a racially mixed group of nearly 50 CORE members and Michigan Young Democrats, most of them from Ann Arbor and Detroit, ventured into Dearborn. "It is well known all over the country that Dearborn is a Jim Crow town," reported Anna Holden, chairman of the Ann Arbor CORE chapter. "But we found that public facilities in Dearborn are much more open than we had expected. We are pleased." She said that managers or other employees were "hostile, nervous or insulting" in perhaps a third of the 23 restaurants or bowling alleys visited, but "in many cases, Negroes were treated as any other customer." In only two restaurants, she added, were Negroes denied service, told at one place that they needed reservations and that the other was about to close. And that was the opening salvo, such as it was, for integration in Dearborn.

Hubbard's next challenge was to find somebody to run against him in the 1961 election. Craig, who was named school board president by his fellow trustees a month after the Archer trial, was no longer a viable candidate. But who else was there? Of the four candidates who filed for the September primary, none rated so much as a backward glance from Orvie. There was Charles Nemeth, who had run far back in the last three primaries; Eugene R. Wagner, a teacher-coach in the western Wayne County suburb of Wayne and nephew of old Charles Wagner, leader of the recall; Thomas J. Bruce, a Ford employment interviewer; and Daniel Zahari, a city fireman.[4] Wagner and Bruce had run twenty-fourth and dead last, respectively, in a field of 39 in the 1959 council primary. Zahari had never run for office before. Of a handful of other possibilities, none materialized. Friends took out petitions for Orvie's oldest son, Jim, a Dearborn policeman, but he never filed them. And John Baja, who looked increasingly like the only remotely anti-Hubbard councilman in town, said he would wait another two years to run. Overall, according to Harry Arnott of the *Dearborn Press*, the opposition was "badly shaken by quarrels and defections." Councilman George

Hart had come over to the Hubbard team, and Vincent Fordell no longer was closely aligned with Baja.

Zahari opened his campaign on a conciliatory note, saying he would fire Archer but "keep Hubbard's talents in some capacity, such as director of his long-proposed retirement village in Florida." The city fathers were not so charitable with Zahari, however. As soon as he filed his petitions, he ran afoul of the old charter amendment engineered by Hubbard to keep officials off two public payrolls at the same time. The Civil Service Commission denied his request for a leave of absence, and he was removed from the city payroll. As for the rest of the opposition, it was all but invisible. Nemeth announced a platform pegged to increased care for the aged. The campaigns of Wagner and Bruce were so low-profile they seldom made the local papers.

Hubbard hammered away at the theme of teamwork in government. His only real concern, after all, was that he might lose one of his council backers. "If you like things done the Hubbard way," urged his singsong ads, "vote the Hubbard slate on election day." His slate this time included five incumbents: the recently enlightened Hart; Irving ImOberstag, a businessman who had been named to replace William Broomhall, now a department head; Ralph Guy, who had continued on as council president for the last two years; George Bondie; and Edward Dombrowski. Rounding out the Hubbard slate were Thomas Dolan, Larry Williams, Walter Blankertz and Joseph Martin.

One disillusioned council candidate not aligned with Hubbard was Lillian Dale, who told reporters the mayor quoted her a cost of $1,200 to get on the slate, including expenses for billboard space. In fact, she said, it would have cost her $150 just to have her name included in house-to-house literature and to get a chance to speak for six minutes at the mayor's Fordson High rally the night before the primary. The rally lacked its usual pizzazz, though. Hubbard tried to make it interesting by taking some shots at Baja, but most of the combatants devoted their energy to making it clear they really weren't against Orvie at all.

The vote in the September primary went pretty much according to form, although Wagner and not Nemeth finished second to qualify as Hubbard's opponent in the November runoff. The vote was 18,611 for Hubbard to 2,925 for Wagner, 1,341 for Nemeth, 1,032 for Zahari and 805 for Bruce. All the mayor's council slaters were nominated but Blankertz and Martin.

The six-foot-four Wagner, 28, was a graduate of Dearborn Sacred Heart High and a former member of the old Vagabond Kings pro basketball team. He realized he had no chance of making things close, and he cemented his position by refusing to campaign aggressively. He even showed up sporting a Hubbard lapel pin at a restaurant opening.[5]

On election day, it was Baja, not Wagner, who provided most of the action. He plastered car windshields with cartoons of puppet councilmen dancing as Hubbard pulled the strings, but as fast as he passed them out, the mayor's crew removed them.

To no one's surprise, Hubbard scored his biggest win ever, earning 77 percent of the votes, for a gap of 26,583 to 7,957 over Wagner. With Hart leading the council race, all seven incumbents retained their seats, leaving only Baja and Fordell to battle the mayor. George Martin earned an easy victory over Hubbard slater William Hennes for municipal judge.

The election also gave Hubbard a chance for one last Punch-and-Judy swat at Martin before the year's end. Voters in recent years had been turning down ballot proposals engineered by the mayor, including two earlier in the year that would have extended terms of office from two years to four and raised council pay from $2,000 to $4,500. So it was with little optimism that Hubbard maneuvered four propositions onto the November ballot. A civic auditorium proposal lost, but the others all passed. One extended terms of office to three years, one expressed voter sentiment for selling the city hall complex and building a new one at the civic center, and, much to Hubbard's glee, the third required the court to be open 33 1/2 hours a week, including three nights.[6] This was not aimed at Martin, Orvie had protested in urging passage, but "judges have been known to cork off," and court hours "ought to be set for convenience of the public." After the returns were in, the mayor called Martin a phony and accused him of "feeding candidates money on the side." Martin in turn said Hubbard "wore a false face upon occasion." But name-calling aside, what more could Hubbard wish for? He had a big win and an extra year tacked onto his new term—and George Martin had to work nights.

35

Beating Charles Nemeth, 1962-64

We are beginning a campaign that will not end until
Dearborn is desegregated. We are not afraid.
—Detroit NAACP Executive Director Arthur L. Johnson
addressing demonstrators at Dearborn city hall

In any other community, it might have been called a period of unrivaled
hostility. In Dearborn, however, it was simply business as usual for Orville
Hubbard during his first three-year term. In fact, the way events struck Bill
Ross, editor of the *Dearborn Guide*, the early months of 1962 were the quietest in the two decades since Hubbard first took office. And at the end of
the year, Ross observed that the mayor seemed more kindly disposed toward
his enemies, friendlier and mellower. It was, Ross noted, truly an "era of
good will."[1] Perhaps it really was so. Ross was not the only observer impressed
by Orvie's statesmanlike conduct; the Dearborn Chamber of Commerce
named him its distinguished citizen for "aggressive community leadership
and outstanding service to the people."

Notwithstanding all the plaudits, there were some elements of Dearborn's political life that had a decidedly familiar texture to them. Six months
after the opening of the new court facility, George Martin was still unhappy
about it. To anyone who would listen, the judge complained that the roof
leaked, the drive-in window let cold air in, and phone wires were strewn
around. Hubbard's response was a note to Martin demanding he "quit complaining about imaginary faults in your beautiful new courtroom." Orvie
was not above making changes, however. Four months later, in June, he
ordered 12 lights turned off to save on electricity. The judge subsequently
announced that several people attending night court sessions had walked
into plate glass doors and "narrowly missed" walls. To avert a similar fate
himself, he had begun carrying a lantern. A few months after that, Hubbard
was nagged further about the court, this time by a woman who complained

at a council meeting about loose phone wires stretching across the carpet in Martin's chambers. When she persisted, Hubbard told her to "get lost," adding, "I agree that Judge Martin needs wiring. Why don't you and the judge get wired together?"

Eventually, the wiring and the rest of the problems were fixed up to Martin's satisfaction.[2] The judge also was able to resolve his unhappiness over the new court schedule imposed on him by the charter amendment the mayor had pushed through. He circulated petitions for another charter amendment, this one expanding the schedule from 33 1/2 to 42 1/2 hours a week and including evenings and Saturday mornings only "as necessary." The proposal carried easily in November, and Martin was back on days and presumably would have no further use for his lantern.[3]

Hubbard made one more sally against Martin, trying to have him removed from the Election Commission on the pretext that he was overworked. But the council balked, with Vincent Fordell calling the proposal "a practical joke through the ballot."

John Baja and Fordell both got involved in further imbroglios with Hubbard. After Baja badgered Orvie about street lighting, he and the mayor turned a June council session into a kindergarten spat, trading names such as "pig" and "rat." The tiff between Fordell and Hubbard was sparked by a spectacular fire that destroyed Ford's world-famous exhibition facility, the $15-million Ford Rotunda, in November. It was the costliest fire in the nation in 1962. Fordell, picking up on a theme raised by Detroit fire officials, requested an inquiry into the department's staffing and equipment. Hubbard responded angrily by calling Fordell "the worst councilman in the 21 years I have been mayor." Fordell answered back, "Khrushchev could take lessons from you." The mayor later vetoed the investigation, contending the building was "doomed" when its plastic roof collapsed despite the efforts of 83 firemen. He also cited a letter from Henry Ford II praising the department's efforts.

As close a rein as Hubbard always had tried to keep on the council, he generally had picked his spots more carefully before entering into public debate with the school board. Now, however, he began to speak out more frequently on school affairs. In early 1962, he attacked the board when it voted to sell a vacant school to a Catholic seminary instead of turning over the land for a new housing development.[4] Later that year, he threatened to begin recall proceedings if the board carried through with plans to merge with the tiny Fairlane District of neighboring Dearborn Township. The board ultimately headed off the showdown by rebuffing the proposal.[5]

Hubbard could point to a number of civic accomplishments during his 1962–64 term. In mid-1963, the city opened Townsend Towers, the first of a projected series of senior citizens' apartments. In early 1964, the city bought another 40 acres to tack onto Camp Dearborn, bringing the total up to 626 acres. And a few months later, the city began its first urban renewal project by starting to buy up homes near the Ford Rouge plant.

There were also a few pet projects that the mayor continued to nurse along. After Detroit passed a city income tax in 1962, he recommended the Dearborn City Council follow suit, just as he had proposed in 1946. He backed off again, however, after voters expressed their distaste in an advisory referendum in November. He also maneuvered an advisory proposal on his Florida retirement project onto the April 1963 ballot, but it was defeated decisively by voters for the fourth time. And, though he hadn't finalized his long-planned police-fire merger, he continued to train police in fire fighting. Finally, lest anyone think he had completely lost his touch in thinking up city services with public relations potential, he set up a free babysitting service in mid-1964 to stimulate local business. The service was available to mothers who made a purchase of a dollar or more at any local store.[6]

Orvie was somewhat less successful in manufacturing public relations coups out of the racial confrontations that were thrust on him as the city increasingly became a focus of the civil rights movement. If nothing else, however, Dearborn's most famous racist found a larger forum than ever for his rhetoric. The issue of integration had not been raised in Dearborn since the CORE freedom riders' foray in 1961. But in June 1963, the Detroit chapter of the NAACP announced it would stage the city's first racial demonstration. The goal, according to spokesman Abraham Ulmer, was to have "colored people living in Dearborn by the end of the summer." "Dearborn has become the Birmingham of the North," Ulmer said. The NAACP couldn't secure a parade permit, so organizers were expecting a confrontation with police, perhaps even a police blockade. Dearborn, meanwhile, was gearing up for any eventuality. Police leave days were canceled, and all available officers were given assignments, many of them in plainclothes, on the day of the scheduled rally, June 22, a Saturday. Orvie had been invited to speak, but unfortunately he would be out of town inspecting garbage disposal equipment, according to Alex Pilch, his information director.

Saturday came, and a group of about 220 Negroes and 80 whites met on Michigan Avenue, a few blocks east of city hall. With police barricading the streets to traffic, the protesters walked along the sidewalk. Their signs said, "10,000 Negroes Work Here; Not One Lives Here," "Dearborn Can Be Clean—And Integrated," and "Wallace and Hubbard, Two of a Kind." As the marchers gathered on the steps of city hall, some of them were pelted with peanuts from the crowd, estimated at several thousand, that massed on the lawn and spilled over into Michigan Avenue. Joined by more than a dozen Dearborn ministers, the demonstrators began a program of prayers and speeches over the jeers of the crowd. Hecklers tossed eggs and firecrackers, though no one was hit. One demonstrator had his sign taken from him. But the program proceeded without a major confrontation.

"This is the real beginning of the desegregation of Dearborn," remarked Arthur L. Johnson, executive director of the Detroit NAACP chapter. "We are beginning a campaign that will not end until Dearborn is desegregated. We are not afraid." Other speakers supported his sentiments. Edward M. Turner, president of the Detroit NAACP branch, declared, "If necessary, we're going to call on the federal government to come into Dearborn, just as it has in Alabama and Mississippi." And Ed Robinson, onetime Hubbard assistant and the Dearborn Young Democrats secretary, added, "Integration is coming to my hometown. Let's do this peacefully, as brothers in Christ."

After an hour of this, the marchers returned without incident to their cars. A total of six troublemakers had been removed from the crowd by police. One of those, a Dearborn man, was held briefly after a toy pistol was found on him. Given the concerns on both sides before the demonstration, the event had to be considered a success by any yardstick. As the *Guide* said in an editorial, "All in all, Dearborn did not react in the same light as Birmingham, Alabama, or Jackson, Mississippi, . . . which makes one wonder whether the Negro community in the metropolitan Detroit area had it all wrong about Dearborn, in the first place."[7]

Scarcely two months later, there was another episode with racial overtones in Dearborn, but this time it did not resolve itself quietly. In what came to be known as the Kendal Street incident, a crowd gathered in an east-side neighborhood on Labor Day 1963, and, as police looked on, vandals damaged the home and car of one Giuseppe Stanzione. The reason: neighbors thought, mistakenly, that Stanzione had sold his home to Negroes.[8] The event immediately raised concerns throughout the city. Several weeks later, a crowd of more than 300 jammed a council meeting to hear the issue discussed. "We can't kick it under the rug anymore," attorney Thomas Brennan told the council. "It is inevitable that our Negro brothers will eventually move into Dearborn."

Hubbard, meanwhile, had defended his police in the press, saying there was no need for any action. "The Negro," he said, "is not abused in our community, either in employment or in restaurants. And one Negro told us once that our policemen are the most courteous he had ever met. We don't invite or encourage them to move in, but we can't keep them out." He said the Kendal Street stories were "played all out of proportion" in the papers and should go "in the back pages where they belong." The media were unwilling to cooperate, however. Even *Newsweek* and *Time* carried stories.

The whole racial issue was kept alive when the newly formed Dearborn Community Council asked Hubbard in March 1964 to remove "inflammatory" clippings from city hall bulletin boards.[9]

With all the attention being given to race, it was a wonder that anybody had time for another political campaign, much less one that was relatively free of racial overtones. But Hubbard's term was coming to a close in 1964, and once again it was time for mayoral candidates to come forth to be slaughtered while trying to slay Dearborn's unslayable dragon.

If the prospects of finding a St. George—or even a reasonably presentable sacrificial virgin—were slim in 1961, they were all but nonexistent in 1964. Early that year, Hubbard began soliciting suggestions from citizens on how to run the city. He reported later that he actually got a few good ideas, but the process underscored his utter dominance over the city. "We have a Mayor with a solution who is looking for problems," observed Bill Ross. ". . . The opposition seems to have melted away."[10]

Charles J. Nemeth, selling real estate in addition to holding down a hotel job, took out petitions for his fifth run against Hubbard. Also in were William B. Cooper, a salesman who had run in the last council race, and Daniel Zahari, the outspoken ex-fireman. Zahari, now working as an accountant, had lost a $1-million suit against the city in federal court in 1963, arguing that he had been fired for political reasons when he ran for mayor in 1961. The court upheld the charter provision barring persons from holding two public jobs at the same time.[11]

The campaign, such as it was, began rolling in August, when the council okayed the posting of campaign signs on small, city-owned lots. Councilman John Baja protested that Orvie would "gobble up" all the spots, while the Hubbard team suggested that the additional locations actually should help the opposition. "The administration has no trouble getting any signs," said City Attorney Ralph Guy Jr. "It's a long-established custom." Guy Jr., a baby-faced 28, had been promoted to the job in 1958 upon Dale Fillmore's death. He had a passing familiarity with long-established Dearborn customs, having grown up observing his father's career and practicing law for a year with him before joining the city's legal staff. As for the signs, Hubbard got most of the best spots, and Zahari, for one, later griped he was having trouble getting any.

The mayor focused his attention on plugging for his council slate. He had five incumbents—Ralph Guy Sr., George Bondie, Edward Dombrowski, George Hart and Irving ImOberstag—along with five others. Against this lineup was matched an "independent" council slate announced by Fordell and including Baja and a dentist, Ronald J. Banish. "One-man rule is not good," Fordell said. "Mayor Hubbard is only human, and he can be quite vindictive." Banish added ominously that Hubbard had "the strongest political machine in the history of municipal government in the U.S."

As for the mayoral candidates, Zahari complained about Hubbard's mistreatment of local businessmen and urged a complete reorganization of city government. He also accused one of his opponents, Cooper, of being Hubbard's "boy," put on the ballot to divert votes from Zahari in southeastern Dearborn. Other than that, however, the mayor's opposition was silent.

On September 26, in what city officials said was the first Saturday municipal election in U.S. history, Dearborn voters turned out in record numbers to nominate Hubbard by the laughable margin of 21,691 votes to 2,472 for Nemeth, 1,329 for Cooper and 644 for Zahari. With his five incumbents leading the council ticket, followed by Fordell and Baja, Hubbard pulled 8 of his 10 slate members into the November election. Orvie rehashed his old victory statements, declaiming, "We are humbly appreciative of the wonderful vote of confidence given this administration."

Despite Hubbard's obvious advantage, the gray-haired Nemeth predicted he himself would win in November by 2,200 votes. Computer projections, he said, gave Hubbard 10 percent more votes than in the primary and Nemeth everything else. "Let us watch the rich Hubbard machine squirm and tremble," he said. "The boot is now on the other foot after 21 years."

The effect of the racial issue on the vote was uncertain. Although a national Lou Harris poll indicated there was general anxiety over the civil rights movement, there had been no overt racial references in the Dearborn primary. The *Guide*, however, acknowledged the likely impact of Hubbard's well-known position:

> The Mayor, of course, attributes his growing popularity to good public service and a satisfied electorate. However, . . . much of the pro-Hubbard vote in Saturday's primary can be attributed to the so-called [white] backlash vote which some say does not exist in Dearborn. It most certainly does. The Mayor lately has been able to sway votes in neighborhoods that were strongly aligned against him years ago.[12]

In the weeks before the November election, the issue cropped up occasionally. Nemeth took pains to point out at one juncture that Orvie was not responsible for keeping Negroes out of Dearborn. The challenger, sounding as though he wanted some "credit" himself because of his real estate job, said, "Mayor Hubbard has very little to do with it. It's the citizens and the real estate salesmen. But Hubbard gets the votes of the people."

Nemeth, while predicting that "the end is near" for the mayor, somehow managed to make Orvie sound like a sort of Robin Hood by saying he "takes the money from the rich—they are few—and gets the votes from the poor—they are many." Nemeth also purported to find a Hubbard pattern of vetoing "every major park improvement in the city." In addition, he said, Orvie jumped on the Camp Dearborn bandwagon only after the city's Recreation Commission had boosted it for a year. "Today people move into Dearborn, see all the parks, and give Mayor Hubbard the credit," said Nemeth.[13] His own platform, Nemeth declared, included such ideas as limiting the mayor to three terms, auditing certain city funds, constructing a "fitting" war memorial, building public restrooms near city hall, painting city cars with a logo to cut down on personal use, and having an elected Camp Dearborn commissioner.

Hubbard kept his public statements to a minimum, but he really didn't have to say a word. Despite his so-called computer projections, Nemeth had to rank as a bigger underdog than Republican Barry Goldwater, who was trying to wrest the presidency from Lyndon Johnson. And on November 3, with the Dearborn municipal election coinciding for the first time in history with a national election, Johnson rolled up a record margin, and Hubbard did even better. Orvie swept all precincts to run up a personal high, with 40,269 votes to 7,849 for the challenger. His percentage of the vote was 83.4 (compared to Johnson's 61.3), topping his previous record of 77 percent against Gene Wagner. The mayor also carried his five incumbent slate members, with Guy leading the balloting and Fordell and Baja filling out the rest of the victorious holdovers.[14] Hubbard's only setbacks were the usual attempts at pay raises and a longer term in office. In September, a proposal to allow the council to set the pay of elected officials went down. This time, a measure to raise the mayor's pay from $17,500 to $24,500 lost by more than two to one, and similar raises for other elected officials fared worse still. Voters also defeated a proposal to extend the term of elected officials from three years to four.

Hubbard's recycled victory statement said that winning "makes us as proud today as we were in 1941 when first elected. With a good council working shoulder-to-shoulder with your mayor, we will be able to accomplish more with less fussing and feuding and to proceed full speed ahead with the many projects now in progress."

Seven weeks later, in December, another Hubbard project in progress proceeded full speed ahead, but this one was not at the mayor's instigation. Dearborn Police Chief Garrison Clayton and Public Safety Director George Lewis were indicted by a federal grand jury and arraigned under a civil rights law with roots dating back to 1870.[15] They were accused of violating the civil rights of Giuseppe Stanzione in the 1963 Kendal Street incident.

As for now, Hubbard himself was not involved in the proceedings. All that would change soon enough, however.

36

The Kendal Street Incident, 1963-66

This was a time for honesty, not race. Just honesty.
—Negro juror Lewis McGhee, explaining his vote in
the civil rights trial of Orville L. Hubbard

At first, there was no obvious reason why Giuseppe Stanzione shouldn't have been able to get along with his neighbors on Kendal Street. Like a lot of other East Dearborn residents, he came from an East European background. Born in Sicily to an American mother, he had claimed his U.S. citizenship when he immigrated in 1958. He started out as a construction laborer, then went into business for himself as a cement contractor. By 1963, he owned a car, a dump truck, a cement mixer truck and a pickup truck. But he had a habit of parking some of the trucks in a vacant lot next to his home, and a number of neighbors had called police at times to complain about it. Stanzione, 27, also had a few other habits that failed to endear him to the neighbors. As they told it, he had been living for two years with a woman he wasn't married to, he hosted loud drinking parties and poker games on weekends and, whenever he lost his considerable temper in arguments on the block, he would threaten to sell the house "to niggers" and move to California. So it was with special interest that the neighbors observed two men and a pregnant woman begin moving furniture and miscellaneous furnishings into Stanzione's old two-story house at 7427 Kendal on the afternoon of September 2, 1963, Labor Day. As it happened, all three were Negroes.

A while later, Stanzione parked his 1961 Cadillac convertible in the driveway and went into the house. During the next 29 hours, according to Stanzione, a crowd of up to 400 gathered and pelted the house with rocks, bottles, eggs and vegetables; they broke seven windows in the house; they scratched and dented the car. Stanzione, according to his later words, also

296

was assaulted with a bed rail and "vilified and threatened by the crowd." Where were the police while all this was going on? Oh, they were there, all right, but, according to Stanzione, they just stood around, without making a single arrest, ordering the crowd to disperse or taking any action to protect his property. All this, he said, was done under direct orders from Orville Hubbard to make an example of what happens to a white person who tries to sell a home in Dearborn to Negroes.[1]

Of course, it really didn't matter that Stanzione wasn't selling his home at all—and certainly not to Negroes. The week before, he had agreed to rent out his upper flat to a white man whose parents lived nearby. The man lived with his Japanese wife and their five-year-old daughter.[2] The three Negroes? They were movers. But apparently nobody in the crowd knew it.

Hubbard tried to play down the incident, but he didn't get much cooperation. Three local clergymen who had been on the scene turned up at a City Council meeting to complain about the lack of police action. The mayor responded with praise for the police, calling the city "one of the safest and cleanest places in the world to live." Of the clergymen, Hubbard said they should stick to preaching "instead of trying to revolutionize our community." The mayor said he first learned of the incident after the fact "and didn't think there was much to it." But the next Thursday, the *Dearborn Guide* came out with a "sensationalized" story, and the Detroit papers picked it up the next week.

Then there was the little matter of the *Time* reporter who was given the bum's rush out of city hall when he tried to follow up the Labor Day incident for his magazine. The reporter, Ben Cate, said he would press charges against the men involved. Hubbard, predictably, was unimpressed by Cate's plight. "If *Time* magazine wants any facts, let it subscribe to the local paper," he said, adding he was still "sore" over *Time* articles in 1950 and 1951 that he felt pictured him as immoral.[3] Hubbard also said the media had exploited the race issue, adding that "it would be no problem at all" if the papers "would play those stories back in the classified section where they belong." But Stanzione wasn't about to let that happen.

In March 1964, attorney Ellsworth K. Hanlon filed a complaint in Federal District Court, charging that Stanzione had been denied the privileges and immunities of a citizen and denied equal protection and due process of law under the Fourteenth Amendment. After the Labor Day mob scene, known locally as the Kendal Street incident, police had failed repeatedly to respond to his calls for protection. He had been forced to leave his house after a fire of unexplained origin did $5,000 damage in January, he said; in addition, people had thrown stones, rattled windows and doors at all hours and left hate literature on his porch. He wanted a permanent injunction restraining city officials from failing to protect him and his property. And he also wanted something else: a judgment of $250,000, plus additional relief, against Hubbard and his top two law-enforcement officers,

Public Safety Director George Lewis and Police Chief Garrison Clayton, as well as 13 other policemen.[4] The monetary figure was quite a step up from the amount Stanzione's previous attorney, G. Daniel Ferrera, had offered to settle for out of court—$260, including $200 in attorney's fees—but Stanzione had fired Ferrera when he found out about that offer from a reporter.

Stanzione's complaint, as later amended, alleged that Hubbard had violated a city charter provision making him responsible to see that all laws and ordinances were enforced;[5] all the defendants had violated the Michigan Riot Act, requiring them to disperse any crowd of 12 or more armed persons or 30 or more unarmed persons who were unlawfully or riotously assembled, with penalty of six months in jail and a $250 fine;[6] and Hubbard, Clayton and Lewis, "motivated solely by racial prejudice," had violated federal laws on deprivation of rights and conspiracy.[7] The defendants, Stanzione alleged, withheld police protection "to demonstrate to those who might otherwise rent or sell real estate . . . to Negroes that the police . . . could not be relied upon to protect from violence the property or persons . . . involved." Their objective, Stanzione charged, "emanated from and was generated by [Hubbard], who, to perpetuate himself [as mayor], has deliberately used that office to encourage feelings of contempt and hostility for Negroes and to exclude them from residence or participation in the affairs of the city of Dearborn." The charges had the same ring as statements Stanzione had made a week after the incident. "We pay taxes for nothing in Dearborn," he had said. "I called the Dearborn police at least 20 times Monday night, but all they did was cruise around the block, never interfering while the mob wrecked my car, threw bottles and rocks at my windows and yelled insults at me."

Newsweek had picked up part of the statement, a fact that was not lost on city officials when they made their answer in court in May, June and July: a countersuit asking $20,000 for each defendant, including $10,000 in exemplary damages, for the "libelous, slanderous and defamatory" statements.

The defendants' version of the crowd scene on Kendal Street differed substantially from Stanzione's. Police arrived at the house at 6:30 P.M. Labor Day, the city's statement said, when the crowd dispersed at the request of police. However, another crowd assembled about 8:30 P.M.; police returned and succeeded in getting some to leave, but others kept coming. Objects were thrown at the house, causing minimal damage, from 10:00 P.M. till about midnight, when the crowd went home. A small crowd assembled again at 5:30 the next afternoon, though it dispersed when police arrived again; no damage was done that day. Police, the statement concluded, had no knowledge of damage to Stanzione's car. Beyond that, Stanzione had suffered no physical harm at all, and police had used their best efforts to disperse the crowd throughout the episode.

What was Orvie's part in all this? Contesting Stanzione's allegation that he had been giving police orders on strategy, Hubbard submitted an affidavit asserting his complete innocence. He had been at Camp Dearborn on Labor Day, he said, and didn't find out anything about the incident until he got home at 11:00 that night. He received a police report the next morning and was told the situation had been handled with no personal injuries and a minimum of property damage. He went to Kendal Street at 10:30 P.M. following a council meeting the day after Labor Day and was told by an officer that everything was calm. That was his only appearance at the house, he said. Hubbard stated he "never issued an order, directly or indirectly, formally or informally, or by implication, to treat any person or class of persons differently by reason of their race, color, creed or national origin, nor has such order ever been conveyed by innuendo or otherwise." Neither, he said, had he conspired or discussed with anyone "as to the treatment and protection to be afforded members of minority groups or persons dealing with minority groups." He also affirmed that he had "never conspired, discussed or otherwise communicated with any person . . . as to techniques, schemes or plans to prevent or discourage sales, leases or rentals of Dearborn property to members of minority groups" and "has always insisted that such laws be enforced without regard to race, creed, color or national origin." Further, he said, he "did not conspire, discuss or communicate with any persons . . . for the purpose of withholding police protection or allowing damage to persons or property by individual or group action as to this plaintiff or any other individual or group."

Clayton, Lewis and the other defendants likewise denied issuing or receiving any order to discriminate against anyone. They also denied discussing the matter with the mayor.

Also included in the city's motion was an explanation for the mysterious fire that Stanzione had cited as an example of the lack of police protection. The city submitted an affidavit from a special agent for the National Board of Fire Underwriters who said that shortly before the fire, Stanzione had increased his fire coverage from $12,000 to $16,000. Stanzione also had been behind in his mortgage payments, but the agent said a polygraph test had cleared the homeowner of setting the fire himself. Did someone else set the fire? The agent said Stanzione implicated an ex-convict who had been renting the house and who apparently got mad when Stanzione went to California with relatives but refused to take him. The city's part in the fire? The agent said the house could have been leveled except for the police and fire departments.

City Attorney Ralph Guy Jr.'s motion also asserted that no federally protected right was infringed upon, that police actions were "discretionary" and that in any case the mayor was immune from suits arising from the performance of his duties in office. Guy asked that the case be dismissed.

Hearing the motion was Judge Theodore Levin. He denied Guy's request, holding that Hubbard had no immunity. As for the contention that police action was "discretionary," he retorted angrily, "Have you ever heard of police standing by while houses are destroyed? I never heard of people being denied police protection for 29 hours regardless of the reason."

It was to be more than two years before Stanzione's civil suit was cleared up. But in the meantime, Hubbard, Clayton and Lewis got bad news on another front. In December, a federal grand jury indicted the mayor's two subordinates for failing to perform their duty on Kendal Street under the Michigan Riot Act. A citizens' organization, the Dearborn Community Council, asked the mayor to suspend Lewis and Clayton, pointing out that the city often had taken such action in previous cases, "even for something as little as smoking in a squad car." Hubbard disdainfully told reporters he would not honor the request. "If they aren't happy," he said, "they ought to be able to find a place where they will be happy."

Then, in February 1965, the grand jury added Hubbard to the indictment and brought another charge against Clayton and Lewis: conspiring with the mayor to deprive Stanzione of his rights. The conspiracy charge carried a five-year jail term and a $10,000 fine, the substantive charge a one-year prison sentence and $1,000 fine. The substantive charge against the three was filed under a civil rights statute with antecedents in a Reconstruction law passed in 1870.[8]

The indictment alleged that the defendants "did willingly and knowingly combine . . . to commit an offense against the United States, that is to willfully fail and refuse to use their authority to prevent violations of the criminal laws of the state of Michigan and to thereby deny to Giuseppe Stanzione equal protection of the laws of the state of Michigan"—and, being aware that a crowd was gathering at Stanzione's house, committing vandalism and assault, they "did willfully fail and refuse to use their authority to prevent . . . violations and apprehend . . . those persons responsible."[9]

Lewis and Clayton were arraigned before Federal Judge Fred W. Kaess and, after already having stood mute on the substantive charge and then pleading not guilty on the conspiracy charge, were released on $1,000 bond. But Hubbard failed to appear for arraignment, and U.S. Attorney Lawrence Gubow declared, "It has now reached the stage where Orville Hubbard, the citizen, or Orville Hubbard, the mayor, or Orville Hubbard, in any capacity, thinks himself bigger than the federal government." A warrant was issued for his arrest, but U.S. marshals searched in vain at city hall, Camp Dearborn and elsewhere. They expended 170 man-hours in the exercise, according to testimony.

If the government didn't approve of the way things were going, others were having a good time with it. A Dearborn motel posted a message on its marquee: "Is Orville here?" Somebody pasted a huge valentine on a Hubbard election billboard, saying, "We still love you, wherever you are." And a Ford welder from nearby River Rouge collected $140 from "15 little people" as a defense fund "because we believe the federal government is supporting radicalism and that Mayor Hubbard is fighting it."

On the fifth day of the manhunt, William H. Merrill, Gubow's chief assistant, asked the FBI for help, though he agreed to hold off after Guy Jr. called in to say the mayor would appear for arraignment that afternoon. When he finally showed up, Hubbard was in a good mood, accompanied by aides who handed out a two-page press release calling the charges against him "a rotten abuse of the mighty power of the federal government." It also said:

> The accusations, based on one-sided distortions, are tragic examples of personal persecution for political purposes by the federal lawyer in charge. I was not present at the Kendal Street incident, and the federal lawyers know it. . . . I could not possibly have conspired with police officials, and the federal lawyers know it. . . . We're reliably informed that the FBI made two investigations of this incident and found no cause for action, and the federal lawyers know that, too.[10]

He went on to tell newsmen, "I think the federal government bribed witnesses to get them to change their testimony before the grand jury. I may get a warrant charging bribery." Then, under arrest at last, he sniffed before entering court, "You'd think the federal government would have something else to do."

Hubbard was a bit less sure of himself inside the courtroom, stammering several times as he pleaded not guilty and acted as his own attorney during arraignment before Federal Judge Thaddeus M. Machrowicz. Given several minutes by Machrowicz to read a copy of the indictment against him, Hubbard said, "This whole thing is ridiculous," but the judge cut him off. "The only reason you are here is to set bond," Machrowicz snapped. "I want to hear no speeches and no talks."

The mayor then asked to be released on his own recognizance. But Merrill, acting for the government, objected, citing Orvie's failure to appear for arraignment the week before, as well as similar failures going back to his "government in exile" in Windsor 15 years before. All things considered, he said, Hubbard was a bad risk: "These facts seem to indicate an attitude, more a feeling being above or beyond the law." Merrill also was obviously unimpressed by the mayor's press release, which, he said, went into "considerable detail" on the case, "which is a clear violation of the canons of ethics, which I think he must be aware of as an attorney."

Hubbard responded to Machrowicz, "There are a lot of shenanigans going on with this whole grand jury that if the court knew about it, the court might feel differently about it. I have been 24 years in public office, and my word is my bond, and I am requesting a personal bond. If I am supposed to be here, I will be here. I came in voluntarily today." He told the judge he had missed the scheduled arraignment the week before because he had left Friday for New England to inspect theaters designed by a consultant being considered for work in Dearborn. When he returned Sunday, he said, he wasn't "feeling too good. I am 61 years of age and carry an awful lot of weight, and I was resting yesterday." Machrowicz, unimpressed, refused to concede that a three-day trip could explain a week's delay in appearing. Hubbard responded, "After all, it didn't seem to me this case was that important. This case is a year and a half old."

"It is not for you to say when you will be in court," the judge replied. "When warrants are issued out of a court, as an attorney, you know it is you duty to appear in court, and no man, whether he is a mayor, a judge, a governor or a president, has a right to disregard that."

Hubbard, explaining why he hadn't tried to contact Merrill or return his phone calls, said he had not received notice of the arrest warrant "other than the newspapers and radio." To that, Machrowicz declared sternly, "I am sure that when you went to law school, if you paid attention, you heard that this is a nation governed by laws and not men, and no man can set himself above the law, no matter how great he is or how great he thinks he is. We are now being troubled throughout this country because of the lunatic fringe, because of the radical right and the radical left, who are taking the law in their own hands, and when a public official like you lends them aid and assistance by acting as you did this last week, it is a very bad day for this nation." With that, he set bond at $5,000, which Hubbard posted.

It was almost four months before the trial began, with Lewis and Clayton losing a motion before Federal Judge Wade H. McCree to delay the scheduled June 2 opening because a recent *Free Press* series had been "prejudicial" against them. McCree, later to become U.S. solicitor general, had been picked by lot for the trial, and he was a noteworthy choice: he was a Negro. "I'm glad I'll be tried before McCree instead of that jerk from Hamtramck," Orvie said in an obvious dig at Machrowicz. "I know McCree and I respect him. He will give me a fair shake."

The jury, picked June 3, consisted of five men and seven women. One of them, Lewis McGhee, a Detroiter who worked on a Chrysler assembly line, was a Negro. That there was a jury at all was no doing of the defendants'. Their attorney, George E. Woods, a former assistant U.S. attorney, had waived their right to a jury trial, but Merrill, handling the case for the government, insisted on one. Woods, who had taken over the case from the Dearborn city attorney's office, also was unsuccessful in an attempt to mold the jury. He objected in vain to Merrill's questioning of prospective jurors on possible racial prejudice and the likelihood they would give special weight to the testimony of public officials. In addition, he lost a request for 10 peremptory challenges, though he wound up using only one of the three allowed him—to dismiss a Negro woman.

The trial itself began June 8 in a jammed courtroom. In his opening statement to the jury, Merrill described the failure of Dearborn police to disperse the crowd at Stanzione's house. He asserted that "the motive in this incident was to keep Negroes from moving in—an attempt to show whites what would happen if they sold their homes to Negroes and what would happen to Negroes if they tried to move into Dearborn. We will prove this was a willful denial of the protection of law, and a conspiracy. We will prove that Mayor Hubbard knew what was going on and did nothing to halt it."

The first two witnesses were Clifford E. Korsedal, a reporter for the *Dearborn Guide* at the time of the incident, and the Reverend Richard W. Morey, then minister of Dearborn's Cherry Hill United Presbyterian Church. Korsedal arrived on Kendal Street about 8:30 on the first evening, he testified, and asked Clayton what was going on. Clayton, he said, responded, "Nothing," and added, "I have the situation in hand." Korsedal said he later asked Clayton—who, along with Lewis, was among only a few policemen he observed at the house—why he had not "at least chased the crowd away." Clayton's reply: "I have a family to feed, too, you know." Stanzione had come out of the house several times, Korsedal recalled, to shout at the crowd in English and Italian. He yelled that he had a bayonet inside "and would take them on one at a time," Korsedal said. The crowd in turn was screaming anti-Italian and anti-Negro epithets, also challenging Stanzione to "come on out and fight" and shouting, "Why are you hiding?" Korsedal and Morey finally entered the house together. "I saw a distraught man, weeping, sitting in the living room," Morey said. It was Stanzione, surrounded by stones and broken glass and within reach of an unsheathed bayonet. A few minutes later, Morey said, Ferrera appeared with the deed and abstract for the house, waved the papers from the porch and shouted, "Here is the title. It has not been sold." This seemed to mollify some people in the crowd.

Another witness, Dearborn Patrolman Nils Strang, testified that he was sent away by Inspector Karl Parchert, then returned an hour later and was told by Clayton to "circulate around" and "prevent any damage to the house." Strang, who said he stayed on duty till 6:30 the next morning, then provided what was to be the most specific testimony linking the mayor to the incident. "Mr. Lewis said to me that he had to check with the mayor at Camp Dearborn and let him know exactly what the situation was," Strang said. "He said he had to check with the mayor every 45 minutes or hour to let him know what was going on. He said he had talked with him and would have to check again shortly."

Hubbard disputed Strang's testimony in a later interview. "How can that cop say that?" he asked. "I wasn't being called up during the incident."

I knew nothing about that till the following morning. Lewis called me [to report] there had been a riot the night before. Dirty son of a bitch, you talk about what they do to people. Merrill came out to see Lewis on the q.t. He'd have done anything to get Lewis to say that the mayor said not to enforce the law. I never said anything to anybody about it.[11]

On June 9, the second day of the trial, Stanzione took the stand. Speaking in broken English in a low voice, Stanzione gave his version: arriving home at 5:30 P.M. to find a crowd gathered, calling police a half-hour later, with two officers responding, and making another 14 or so calls for help. "People came to me and started calling me names," he said. "They didn't believe me. They wanted to know what the colored pregnant lady was doing there. I didn't know. There was no way to explain. They started screaming and calling me liar, traitor, other things. They accused me of selling to colored people. They said they moved to Dearborn because property values were ruined in Detroit, and now they were going to have to move all over again. Some wanted to fight." When he tried later to explain things to Clayton, the chief had him address the crowd from the porch. People continued to shout at him, he said, and when he turned his back, he heard something hit behind him. It was a bed rail. The movers were cowering nearby and finally ran away, he said. Police eventually removed their truck, with some of the furniture still in it. Despite being urged by police to stay inside, Stanzione conceded he came out five or six times to look for help and talk to the crowd. "I told them to go home," he said. "I told the women to go clean their houses."

"That's all you said, the way you said it?" Woods asked.

"Well, maybe I was mad and probably swore," Stanzione replied. He said one neighbor said he wished a policeman standing nearby "would give him his gun so he could shoot me. I told him I didn't know why he would want to shoot me. I told him to go home." Another man, he said, carried a rope and yelled, "See that tree? We're going to hang you."

"Were you frightened?" Woods asked.

"Yes, I was, I'm sorry to say," Stanzione conceded.

For much of the evening, he said, he sat in a corner of his living room to avoid being hit by stones and bottles thrown through the windows. Occasionally, he saw a police car drive by, and sometimes an officer would stop for a few minutes. His own car, still parked in his driveway, was badly damaged, he said—the convertible top burned, the body dented and scratched, a tire slashed, sugar put in the gas tank and salt in the crankcase, and the dashboard stained with eggs and vegetables.

Woods pressed him about his continuing interaction with the crowd: "Isn't it true that you told the neighbors that you had killed American soldiers during the war and you wondered how you had missed more?"

"No, I did not say that," Stanzione responded emphatically. "I'll tell you what I did say. Someone in the crowd called me a traitor. And I said, 'What do you think I did—kill American soldiers? I was only six or seven when the war was over.'"

Stanzione said he left the house at 12:45 A.M. that night and came back at 10:30 in the morning. The crowd, he said, stayed till about 9:30 the second evening.

His first contact with the mayor came September 9, a week after the incident, he said. He was sitting in Ferrera's office near the phone when Hubbard called, and Ferrera let him listen. "The mayor said he did not like the publicity he was getting," Stanzione said. "He doesn't like what's happening, and if I don't stop it, he would have me deported to my country."

At that point, Hubbard said to his lawyers, within earshot of reporters, "He's a damn liar."

Stanzione said he met with the mayor when Hubbard phoned to make a peace overture three weeks before the trial: "He said he'd like to meet me. I said, 'All right, you can meet me. I don't see anything wrong with that.' He asked me to come to his office. I said I wouldn't do that. I'd meet him anyplace else. I had no auto. I was staying with my aunt. He'd have to come and get me." Less than an hour later, he said, Hubbard was at his door.

In the car, the mayor asked, "You're not scared, are you?"

"No," Stanzione said he replied, "I'm not scared."

The mayor apologized about the incident, Stanzione said, adding, "He told me he didn't have anything to do with it. He was out of town. He wished he could have done more. I told him somebody goofed; they should have informed you." He said Orvie wound up buying him four drinks and dinner.

After Stanzione was finished, Merrill announced that his last—and, as it developed, most important—witness would be someone who wasn't even in Michigan during the incident: William T. Johnson Jr., the Alabama reporter who conducted the controversial interview on Hubbard's racial attitudes in 1956. Woods objected heatedly and had McCree excuse the jury before he and Merrill debated the relevance of hearing Johnson. Woods contended the interview no longer could be expected to reflect the mayor's attitudes on race. In addition, he said, the case was based on the alleged violation of Stanzione's rights and was not an indictment of Negroes' treatment in Dearborn. Merrill responded that Johnson's testimony could establish "proof of motive and intent" by Hubbard and could describe the mayor's official policy in 22 years in office.

"If this goes in, the case is over," Woods protested.

Although he later was criticized in the Negro community for sending the jury off to deliberate with instructions favorable to the defense, McCree ruled Johnson could testify. Johnson, brought in under subpoena, was permitted to read the account of his taped interview with Hubbard.

I said read the whole thing. Put it all in there. Don't just object to this or that. Let the judge hear it, too. Might do him good. I've never said anything about race that I don't say today. I think it's basically wrong for any group of people to

305

try and force themselves upon another group of people. That's what they tried to prove a conspiracy about: I conspired because of my attitude.

As had been well publicized nine years before, the article quoted Hubbard as saying, "I am for complete segregation, one million per cent on all levels." And more significantly, in McCree's mind at least, Hubbard explained the "unwritten law" that supported this policy: "They can't get in here. We watch it. Every time we hear of a Negro moving in—for instance, we had one last year—we respond quicker than you do to a fire." After Johnson's reading of the article, Merrill closed the government's case with a summary of how Michigan law and the city charter were violated during the Kendal Street incident.

The next day, Woods called for a directed verdict of acquittal on both charges for all three defendants. He argued the government had failed to show that Stanzione had been deprived of equal protection under the law, though, he conceded, the protection offered may have been inadequate. Also, he said, Hubbard still had not been shown to be directly involved.

McCree refused to dismiss the charges, holding there was enough evidence to be considered by the jury. "I think that if he hadn't given this interview, I would have granted your motion," McCree told Woods. The judge did order one of the two charges—the substantive charge of violating Stanzione's civil rights—dropped against Lewis, since he was an administrator and not a police officer under the city charter.

Woods then made his opening statement. He said he would show that much of what happened was a matter of Clayton's judgment and would explain why that judgment was made. He promised to show some "falsehood" in the prosecution testimony. And he said he would prove the mayor did not know what was going on at the scene and "these defendants could not have a willful intent or evil mood or evil purpose in exercising their judgment." He conceded there "probably had been a violation of the Michigan Riot Act," adding, apparently as an afterthought, "There's no question about it." But, he said, there was no intent "to deny Giuseppe Stanzione equal protection of the law." Woods also argued that there really was not enough evidence to show that Hubbard had any connection with the incident, though, as Merrill rebutted, there were "bits of evidence" that made it "circumstantial logic that he couldn't help knowing about it," if only because of his all-powerful position in the city.

Woods began his case for the defense with testimony from Patrolmen Bernard R. Dunlap and Stephen E. Crowell. Dunlap, who had just bought a house on Kendal across from Stanzione's, said he helped monitor the crowd from about 6:00 to 8:00 P.M. Just before dark, he said, he went back to his new house and watched for an hour or so before returning to his old house. "When I left, I thought everything was all over," he said.

Crowell testified he ordered Stanzione back inside his house twice because of angry words with his next-door neighbor. He contradicted Stanzione's earlier testimony, quoting him as saying, "During World War II I killed American soldiers."

"That was his parting shot," Crowell said. "That's why I ordered him back in the house."

A few days later, the trial explored Stanzione's deteriorating relations with his neighbors before the incident. Crowell said several residents complained Stanzione had threatened often to sell, "I quote, 'to niggers,'" and move to California. "This had been going on for six to eight months," Crowell said. "Every time Mr. Stanzione got in an argument, he would say he was going to do this."

Asked by Merrill about ordering Stanzione back inside, Crowell conceded he had not done the same to the neighbors. And, asked if Clayton or Lewis had ordered anyone off the sidewalks or threatened to arrest anyone, Crowell replied, "No, sir."

After several other officers testified about Stanzione's exchanged insults with the crowd, Parchert, one of those named in Stanzione's civil suit, defended police tactics. Bystanders were "in no mood to be moved without violence," he said; the department decided against "direct action" in trying to move them. Asked by Woods whether things should have been handled differently in hindsight, Parchert responded, "No, sir. The proof of the pudding is in the eating." Asked to explain, he added, "Based on my experience, someone might have been injured; based on the results, no one was injured."

Testimony on June 17 from a pair of young men who lived in the neighborhood cast real doubts on Stanzione's claims about vandalism. Andrew Bercheny and Walter J. Piotrowski Jr., both 18, said Stanzione had asked them to "ruin" his car. Also as a result of his urgings, they said, they had driven up and down Kendal, shouting, "Kill him, kill him," and another young man had thrown an empty pop bottle at the house. Bercheny, who said he had known Stanzione more than five years, drove him to a store to buy a shotgun and ammunition, and then he and Piotrowski went into Stanzione's house with him. "Why don't you ruin my car?" he said Stanzione asked him, adding, "He wanted us to put gravel in the crankcase. We didn't want to do it, so we opened the hood and took the oil cap off, but we didn't put anything in." In describing the scene outside the house, Bercheny said, "There were a lot of old people around—old ladies and old men, you know. I thought it was a ball." He said Stanzione invited them and several others to a party at his house on the second day of the incident, adding, "Joe [Stanzione] was angry and bitter toward the crowd and said to me, 'If anybody starts making any trouble, I'm going to blow their brains out.'"

Ferrera next contradicted some of his former client's allegations. Ferrera, a former Dearborn assistant city attorney who said he provided considerable legal aid to Italian and Polish residents of East Dearborn, said

Stanzione's reputation for telling the truth was "not very good." And, he added, there was no truth to Stanzione's claim that the mayor had threatened to have him deported. "I'm an immigrant myself, and if the mayor had said anything like that, I would have called the newspapers right off the bat," he said. Ferrera also testified that Stanzione had been receiving funds from the American Civil Liberties Union, the *Michigan Chronicle* and attorneys representing him in his $250,000 civil suit.

Under cross-examination, Merrill tried to show a close link between Ferrera and the defendants. Ferrera, who had worked in Guy Jr.'s office in 1956, said, "Oh, yes, we're good friends. I know them all." But he denied this influenced his testimony. Asked why he quit his city job, Ferrera said, "The mayor's just like a general I had in the Army, and I didn't want to be in the Army anymore." Ferrera said he had talked to Hubbard about Stanzione's complaints of continued harassment after the incident, and the mayor had offered to send two plainclothes officers to sleep in Stanzione's house. "But Stanzione turned it down," he said, "saying he would have his cousins stay with him."

Finally, it was time for the defendants themselves to take the stand. Clayton, 46, insisted that the decision not to use force was his, not Lewis's and certainly not Hubbard's. He said he told his officers "we were going to disperse the crowd by talking to them," and Lewis "had no police experience to speak of," even though he was the administrative superior present. He also said neither he nor Lewis, so far as he knew, had talked directly or indirectly to Hubbard, though Lewis had tried to call the mayor twice that evening from the police station. Under questioning by Woods, Clayton explained at length why he had not taken more decisive action against the crowd, which he said included many women. "It would have been a sadistic move if I had taken any stronger action against these people," he said, adding that he had ordered additional officers to the scene when people started throwing things at the house. This, he said, ended the throwing.

"Did you have an evil motive or bad purpose in mind?" Woods asked him.

"No, sir," Clayton said.

"What was your purpose?"

"I had in my mind to keep someone from getting hurt that night."

"Did you intend to deprive Mr. Stanzione of his equal rights?"

"No, sir."

Clayton also complained about Stanzione's "loud, vociferous and vulgar" arguments with the crowd. "I told him several times to stay in the house, that he was merely aggravating the group," Clayton said. "When he was in the house, some of the crowd would leave and the noise would drop off. When he reappeared, the crowd would start up again—him yelling at the crowd and them yelling back at him."

The next day, it was Lewis's turn. At 57, with three years' service as public safety director, Lewis had charge of the fire, police and signal departments. He had stepped down as fire chief after 33 years in that department. Lewis swore he never issued any orders to anyone at the scene, noting Clayton had full control. And he denied he had told Nils Strang that he, Lewis, had to report regularly to Hubbard. Lewis said he got no answer when he tried to phone the mayor that night, once at his home and once at city hall. He said he knew of no one talking to the mayor that night.

Woods rested the case for the defense that day with the testimony from Clayton and Lewis. What about Hubbard? Since he never had been linked directly with the incident, Woods never put him on the stand.

Merrill called several rebuttal witnesses: Stanzione, who denied getting aid from the ACLU or asking the teenagers to damage his car or commit other unlawful acts; and James T. McShane, chief U.S. marshal in charge of government troops at various mob scenes. McShane testified that he would have used techniques different from those Clayton used, though Woods got him to agree that the ideal situation was one in which the "least amount of force possible could be used."

McCree told the jury of four men and eight women (one of the men had been replaced with a female alternate after talking about the case outside of court) that the case would be given to them the following week. He later denied another defense motion to dismiss the charges, and Merrill ended the government's case with two futile efforts to introduce as evidence a piece of race-oriented propaganda from the mayor's 1961 reelection campaign. The literature referred to "persons and problems who would lower property values" being kept out of Dearborn. It also pumped the merits of Camp Dearborn: "37 hours to Africa, 37 minutes to Belle Isle, but who wants to go to either place?" McCree turned down Merrill's request because, he said, the authorship of the literature had not been established.

We have never used a nigger campaign strictly as a campaign. We've said in our campaigns it's so many hours to Africa and less than an hour to Belle Isle, but who wants to go to either place? You can put any interpretation you want on it. I have never done anything to encourage black people being here, and I don't know if I've ever done anything to discourage them from coming here. But they come; they get the same treatment here as any other citizen. And I think the evidence shows that.

On the trial's final day, June 23, Woods and Merrill summarized their cases. The government's real purpose, Woods suggested, was to put Hubbard on trial because of his racial attitude. "If you are going to put politicians in jail on the basis of attitude, you're going to have to make the jails a lot bigger," he said. He described the Kendal Street incident as basically a problem between a neighborhood pest—Stanzione—and his neighbors—"old ladies, kids and probably, wouldn't you imagine, a few rubbernecks and curiosity-seekers as well as a few loudmouths and a few racists." What occurred, he said, was a "mutual fanning of their prejudices, of their likes and of their dislikes," much of it Stanzione's fault. "Some of these neighbors had a reason, other than because they thought he had sold to Negroes, to hate his insides," Woods said. "Stanzione was not about to win any popularity contests on Kendal Street before Labor Day, 1963." As for Clayton's strategy, he managed to avoid a "king-sized pack of trouble that would have lasted for days and days, weeks and weeks," by moving quietly among the crowd and trying to disperse it without a show of force, Woods said. Woods pointed out that despite the racists and stone throwers in the crowd, Clayton handled things "without anybody getting so much as a hangnail out of it."

In the prosecution's summation, Merrill countered that the government had no intention of criticizing Hubbard's attitudes, but it was assuredly interested in preventing a denial of Stanzione's rights as a means of implementing those views. And he asked the jurors to put themselves in Stanzione's place, asking, "Is this the kind of protection an American citizen should receive? Is this the kind you would want to receive?" After all, he added, "How long would such a mob be allowed to stand in front of the home of Mayor Hubbard?"

McCree's charge to the jury took one and a half hours. Hubbard later characterized the instructions as "very scholarly and brilliantly done." Said the judge, "No one is on trial here for his attitudes about race, whatever they may be." He emphasized that the only issue was whether one man's civil rights had been violated.

Thus instructed, the jury began deliberations at 11:17 A.M. on June 23. Hubbard, asked by reporters for a prediction, said, "I'm not much of a prophet." With time off for lunch, the jurors deliberated until 4:30 P.M. They resumed at 9:30 the next morning. About noon, the jury foreman sent the judge a note saying, "It appears that we are unable to unanimously agree on a verdict on either charge." At that point, it was later revealed, the vote was 10 to 2 for acquittal on the conspiracy charge and 11 to 1 for acquittal on the substantive charge for Orvie and Clayton. There had been considerable movement from their first vote, tied 6 to 6 on the conspiracy and leaning 9 to 3 for acquittal on the substantive count, but the jury needed additional instructions from McCree. After lunch, he instructed them again and sent them back. After having told them the day before that they should disregard racial matters in seeking the verdict, he reminded them now that "we are not trying attitudes or philosophies but an assertion that certain acts or omissions occurred on that date." He also answered the request for new instructions on the racial question. He said jurors could consider racial evidence only as it pertained to the defendants' motives. He stressed that if jurors had a reasonable doubt, they should resolve it in favor of the defense. Merrill was to indicate later that he thought the judge's remarks had damaged the government's case. As juror Helen Hallar, a librarian, explained later, "When the judge instructed us to disregard the racial issue, everything seemed to fall in line." Other jurors agreed, saying the only remaining question was whether the police acted with evil intent.

When the jurors filed into the box at 4:15 P.M., many of them showing signs of strain, Woods expected the worst. Many courtroom observers had expected a hung jury. But the foreman had a verdict to announce: all defendants innocent on all counts. Merrill had McCree poll the jury to confirm it.

As the jury emerged from the courtroom, Hubbard strode into the corridor and threw his arm around McGhee, the Negro juror. "It must have been hard for you," Hubbard said. "The pressure, I mean."

"This was a time for honesty," McGhee said. "Not race. Just honesty." Asked whether he had ever had any trouble in Dearborn, McGhee said, "I always go through without stopping."

Talking to reporters, Orvie said he never expected to be found guilty, adding, "Each day was the same as any other for me. That's the way it is when you don't have a guilt complex. You thank God for democracy."

Passersby paused to ask about the verdict. A Negro man grumbled, "What's this, Montgomery?" A white man said, "They didn't have a thing on him." A third man, also white, observed, "Engaging scoundrel, isn't he?" And a little boy—Negro—sneaked into one of the wire service photos, holding up two fingers in an ironic victory sign.

Several of the jurors had invited Orvie out for a drink afterward, but instead he started lining up city cars and herding the jury inside. The mayor was actually taking the jurors, as many of them as he could find, out to dinner. Seven of the jurors went along, together with the three defendants, several other city officials and Hubbard's son John. They wound up for two hours in a private dining room at the Continental Congress Inn in Dearborn. Several jurors were concerned about propriety, but the mayor allayed their fears by pointing out that he couldn't be tried again on the same charges, "even if I said I was guilty." Everybody laughed. At one point, Orvie presented the women jurors with plastic thimbles bearing his name and the date he took office—the same thimbles he often gave away at city hall and usually carried in his pockets. And for the lone Dearborn juror, Phyllis M. Brooks, a psychiatrist's secretary, Hubbard noted she had had her fiftieth birthday the day before, so he autographed a menu for her and passed it around for the others to sign. Three city officials led a chorus of "For He's a Jolly Good Fellow," and the jurors joined in.

The mayor told reporters at the dinner, "I didn't lose a minute's sleep over this damn case, not a wink. All the government had was a lot of fiction and no facts." He was a bit surprised, however, at the blanket acquittal, he admitted; he had expected that the jury might find Clayton guilty.

Hubbard proceeded to astonish the jurors at the table by producing a "box score" on their conduct during the 11-day trial, noting whether they paid attention, favored either side, smiled, looked at the defendants or flirted with Merrill. "I picked eight of them as being on our side," he explained, also conceding he had misjudged McGhee. "I never thought he would vote for us. I give him credit for his honesty. I invited him to come to the dinner, but he just disappeared. I told him back at the Federal Building that if he had any trouble in Detroit, we might move him to Dearborn and get him a job."

McGhee and one other jury member held out for conviction on the conspiracy charge until the last of the nine or so ballots, according to other jurors.

And so the dinner ended cordially, with Hubbard seeing each juror to the door after signing checks for $226.70 and $34.20, telling reporters, "And I'm paying for this, not the city."

It was just a spur-of-the-moment thing. Never gave any thought about it at all, wasn't planned. I probably wouldn't do it again. It looks as though I was trying to reward the jury, but it was done innocently and thoughtlessly. An expression of appreciation. But it had the appearance of wrongdoing.

Not surprisingly, a number of local judges thought so, too. Among their comments: "Very improper." "Rather in poor judgment." "Certainly offends decency." Despite all the huffing and puffing—a few judges even talked about having the state Bar Association look into the situation—nothing happened. After all, who else but Hubbard would ever do it again?

It was to be another year before the Kendal Street incident was closed officially, with Judge Theodore Levin scheduled to sit in on Stanzione's civil suit. Because Levin had been one of the judges who scolded the mayor about the dinner, Orvie said he thought the judge should disqualify himself from the case, but Levin pooh-poohed the idea. "I wasn't criticizing anything except a violation of a general principle," he said.

In the aftermath of the incident, Stanzione had moved to another home near his old neighborhood. But he also had been hospitalized for two months with tuberculosis. He claimed he had not worked and had no money for further litigation.

Hubbard offered to settle out of court for $4,500, and on July 13, 1966, Stanzione accepted, and Levin dismissed the case. Guy Jr. noted that the settlement was not an admission of liability, adding, "It is still our position that Dearborn officials acted properly at all times." The mayor was unavailable for comment.

We shouldn't have paid 'em a dime. We went along with the lawyer's recommendation—we got enough money in donations from the defense fund, might as well pay him from it. How the hell could we be responsible for what the neighbors did to his goddamn car? I guess because we didn't protect him. I think he did it

312

to his own goddamn car is what I believe. I don't believe those neighbors did anything to his car or his property. Every neighbor around there hated him. He disappeared, you know. I'm glad they didn't charge me with his disappearance.[12]

Stanzione may have disappeared, but the Kendal Street incident had not. Even if there was no conspiracy, there might as well have been one. Negroes had been put on further notice that they weren't welcome in Dearborn. And Hubbard's reputation as a racist had been even more firmly established. After all, his comments were now a mater of record in federal court.

37

The Bulletin Boards, 1964-69

> There's freedom of speech and freedom of the press.
> Isn't there freedom to clip?
> —Orville L. Hubbard, reacting to a state Civil Rights
> Commission order

Even apart from the trial, Kendal Street wasn't the end of Orville Hubbard's problems with the race issue. Not everyone in town was willing to let things simmer down of their own accord. Members of Dearborn's branch of the American Association of University Women wrote the *Free Press* to affirm that the city "is NOT composed of a group of rock-throwing bigots. The overwhelming majority of its citizens are law-abiding and hard-working." And barely a month after the Labor Day incident, about 300 citizens formed a nonprofit organization known as the Dearborn Community Council. Its avowed purpose: "To work toward a community in which there is a harmonious relationship among people of all backgrounds and races." Orville Hubbard obviously was the prime threat to such harmony.

In March 1964, the Community Council wrote asking the mayor to remove "racially inflammatory" materials from bulletin boards at city hall and several other city buildings. Signed by the group's president, Fabian V. Stempien, the letter said the materials, mostly clippings from newspapers and magazines, "tend to inflame racial hatred, downgrade the Negro race, and impress those who see it that there is strong opposition to community integration of the Negro and white races."

Receiving no reply from Hubbard, the Community Council next asked the brand-new state Civil Rights Commission to investigate whether Dearborn had a "public policy" of racial discrimination. Stempien told the commission that the bulletin boards were "symbols of the generally accepted theory that the official attitude of the city of Dearborn is one of racial bigotry. The problem is that we allege that this is the official policy. The mayor won't say anything. It's like struggling in the dark. You know it's there, but there is nothing to grab hold of."

Following a suggestion from Stempien that a public hearing might "clear the air," officials from the NAACP, the Detroit Urban League and a number of area church groups met in May to discuss Dearborn. Also present were representatives of the Civil Rights Commission, empowered by the state's 1963 constitution to deal with rights violations over a broad spectrum. Burton I. Gordin, executive director of the commission, told those present that if Dearborn's racist policies were to be exposed, evidence of actual discrimination would be needed. One person suggested having Negroes sit in a Dearborn park to see whether anyone asked them to move.

The next month, Gordin received a staff memo based on interviews with a dozen or so attorneys, newspapermen and civic leaders. Although each felt that Hubbard's official position was "antipathetical toward the Negro as a race," none of them could come up with any documentation that the city discriminated. The memo advised that additional interviews probably would fail to produce anything more concrete.[1] But there might be another way to pressure Hubbard into embracing a policy of equal opportunity. The commission, it was suggested, should focus on the narrower issue raised previously by the Community Council. And thus was born the great Dearborn bulletin board case.

Always an avid reader and follower of current events, Hubbard also was an incorrigible saver of items of interest. He started cutting out clippings in kindergarten and had been doing it ever since. "I'm the neatest clipper of newspaper clippings I ever saw in the world," he once told me. Almost from the day he first took office, he had posted news items on city bulletin boards, depending on "how busy I am and what captures my attention from time to time. The stuff is up there if I want it up there." Some entries he underlined in red, and others he embellished with comments. As later summarized during a rights commission hearing, the items he was sharing— some of them three years old— included the following, posted at city hall, the Youth Center or the drivers' license bureau at the police station: six letters to newspapers opposed to integration; two carbons on demonstrations, riots and violence by Negroes and civil rights activists; an article on a Negro demonstration and resulting violence; an article on the social ostracism of a Negro family moving into a white area; three articles on violent assault by Negroes and the subsequent formation of citizen patrols; five photos and articles on riots in Harlem; one article and photo on a Negro convicted of murder; one article and photo on a Negro convicted in a numbers swindle; one photo of a Negro lying in front of a bulldozer; two articles on Congressman Adam Clayton Powell's notion to boycott Santa Claus; and two letters to Hubbard opposing forced integration.

According to Stempien, many residents were offended by the material. As a father of nine, he said he didn't think "my children or any children of the city of Dearborn should be exposed to this kind of thing." Further rebuffed by the mayor, Stempien's group filed a formal complaint in October with the rights commission. Two days later, the commission sent a team to city hall to take photos.

"Hubbard came waddling into the hall outside his office at the first flashbulb," a commission staff memo reported.[2] "He appeared more resigned than angry, talked about past years, made no attempt to hinder us and motioned a detective away who had trailed him. . . . He kept insisting that the board display was an old one 'from the public press' and that he had as much right to display it as publishers had to print the original material."

On January 4, 1965, at the precise time that the federal grand jury was preparing its indictment against Hubbard in the Stanzione case, the rights commission held a public hearing on the first case to come before it. Its target: Orville Hubbard and the Dearborn bulletin boards. Meeting on the University of Michigan–Dearborn campus before a crowd of about 200, the commission's three-member hearing panel listened to 10 witnesses and inspected photos of the boards. Neither the mayor nor the other official named in the complaint, DPW Director James Dick, was present. Nor was anyone from the city attorney's office. In fact, Ralph Guy Jr. already had advised the commission that the city disputed its jurisdiction and that in any case the offending clippings already had been removed. A commission staffer verified this, except for the Santa boycott clippings. But the panelists, chaired by former Federal Judge and state Republican Party Chairman John Feikens, were unimpressed. They ruled that the clippings were "degrading and derogatory" toward Negroes, and they announced they would recommend that the full commission order the city to stop posting such materials.

On January 26, the commission upheld the panel's recommendation by issuing its first cease-and-desist order. Blasting Orvie as a "foe of integrated housing," the commission forbade the city to post materials in public buildings that "taken as a whole or separately tend to degrade, humiliate, defame or hold up to public ridicule and contempt the Negro race." Such materials, the commission ruled, violated U.S. and Michigan constitutional guarantees of equal protection.

But if Hubbard had not exactly been cowed by the federal government's attempt to convict him, it wasn't likely that a state commission would hold many terrors for him. The Dearborn Community Council, which had started all the trouble, was "a collection of oddballs, if there ever was one," he said. "They were just do-gooders trying to tell us, 'Do as we say, not as we do.'" As for the commission hearing, he said, "I wasn't about to dignify such a trite kangaroo court with our presence." He observed that the city had "no race problems." Beyond that, he declared, "There's freedom of speech and freedom of the press. Isn't there freedom to clip?" Hubbard also told reporters the rights commission "should go to the newspapers where these clippings are written and presented. We don't write it. We don't circulate it. We don't print it. All we do is put some of it on our boards, and how many people ever look at our boards?" The mayor said that "we talk frankly" about race, although, he added, "There are a few misguided whites in town who talk differently than what they do. I liked the clipping about this white pastor who married a colored girl. He's not hypocritical. He's living up to what he believes. I like anyone who lives up to what he believes." As for city policy, he said, "We treat everyone here equally. We're not anti-Negro. We're not anti-anyone."

A few days later, in an interview on WJR radio, Orvie downplayed the thought of a court showdown, saying, "All they want is publicity anyway." He dismissed Feikens as "a loud and mealy-mouthed type of a guy," "nasty," "mean" and a "sort of a shriveled-up thing anyway." He also offered up Dearborn as a pillar of the principle of justice for all: "We have never, in the years I've been in this town . . . had a complaint from one colored person—when I say colored, I mean Negro person—about the treatment, being abused, being refused any accommodations or anything in our community. Matter of fact just yesterday they were telling me that one fellow that the State Police had picked up, he said, well, he wished it had been the Dearborn police 'cause they had treated him decently."

Not all observers were convinced, however. Bishop Emrich, the Episcopal churchman who had taken on Hubbard nine years before for his comments on segregation, addressed Dearborn in his regular column in the *News*: "Mayor Hubbard's present discomfiture is a logical development of his unjust and immoral policy . . . ," he wrote. "One can predict that his career in Dearborn will be coming to an end."[3] Several Negro legislators in the state at that time were working toward that very goal. Two of them, Senators Basil Brown and Coleman Young, both Detroit Democrats, sent the mayor a copy of a bill they were sponsoring. It proposed that any person convicted of civil rights violations be disqualified from holding office in Michigan for 10 years. With the bill, they sent a note to Hubbard, who then was being sought by federal agents in the Stanzione case. It said, "Dear Mr. Mayor: Wherever you are, try sticking this on your bulletin board."

Meanwhile, the commission had been keeping tabs on the situation in Dearborn for weeks. A staffer noted in mid-February that the city hall board contained "almost all new material, and displayed both stories for and against Negroes. . . . Compared to the material which was presented at the Janary 4 hearing, this material appears to me to be innocuous if stupid."[4] The commission announced just the same that it would seek to have its order affirmed in court the next month. It was an unwieldy procedure but the best the commission could do, since the constitution had invested it with no enforcement powers.

Wayne Circuit Judge Edward S. Piggins set a hearing date for April. As a former law school classmate and later divorce attorney for Hubbard, the judge offered to step aside if either side wanted him to. But neither did, and

Piggins stayed on. At the next hearing, held in July, Guy Jr. moved for dismissal. "Whenever the name Hubbard appears, there is a tendency to try the myth, not the man," he said. "This is nothing but another effort to make Dearborn officials the whipping boys for the commission and to showcase their activities. . . . We are not violating the order now, nor do we intend to in the future." Assistant Attorney General Carl Levin, noting that the city had refused to "conciliate or discuss" the issue, answered that compliance was no defense, that Dearborn contended all along it had the right to post clippings under provisions of free speech and in any case the commission had no jurisdiction over a municipality. Piggins promised a decision by August.

With the Stanzione trial now safely behind him, Hubbard appeared ready for a collision with the commission, when, at the end of July, Guy Jr. made a surprise move. He signed an agreement that Dearborn would abide by the commission's order. Although the maneuver was not an admission that "defamatory" material had appeared on the boards in the past, the city agreed not to post other such material. Hubbard was prepared to let the matter stand, although, needless to say, he was far from reconciled philosophically.

The Civil Rights Commission had nothing to do. I put those clippings up, things Negroes were doing. I said, "Well, Christ, I didn't write it." They said, "You underlined it." "Well," I said, "isn't that too bad? People should know what's going on in the world, shouldn't they?" That's [George] Romney's legacy he left [as a major influence in writing a new state constitution, which established the commission]. He's the biggest asshole that ever came in this business, and I voted for him twice.

It was more than three years before the issue of the bulletin boards came up again. In 1969, Dearbornites began noticing that material of a racial nature was going up again at city buildings. The worst example, according to observers, was a scurrilous article from a southern paper alleging that the Reverend Ralph Abernathy had been caught in bed with a 15-year-old girl and then chased by her husband, meat cleaver in hand. In July, a complaint was filed with the commission by residents representing the Dearborn Inter-Faith Action Council, a human relations group. The council proceeded to rip down several of the clippings, including the one on Abernathy. Guy Jr. informed the commission that the Abernathy article had been removed and that no discriminatory material remained up. But the commission went ahead and filed a petition in court to have its 1965 order enforced.

Hubbard remained disdainful of the commission's work, despite the evidence against the city. "I don't know anything about any racist clippings," he told reporters. "It's a pathetic situation when you have an agitating committee of busybodies with a solution looking for a problem." Arguing that the clippings merely reflected a broad spectrum of current events, he said he "wouldn't object" if the commission itself posted material.

As late as October 1969, commission attorney William F. Bledsoe was threatening to get a court order against Dearborn. Hubbard kept on posting clippings, but no more complaints surfaced, and the commission moved on to more pressing matters. From a legal standpoint, the mayor had earned no better than a standoff, but, as usual, he seemed to have gotten in the last word—if not by outmaneuvering his antagonists, at least by outtalking and outlasting them.

38

Beating Charles Nemeth, 1965-67

Learn to shoot and shoot to be a dead shot.
—Orville L. Hubbard, on coping with the aftermath of
the Detroit riots

Orville Hubbard was, he admitted, "really scared" for the first time in his life. At first, he had dismissed the Detroit riots of 1967 with a quip. "Instant urban renewal," he called the burning, looting and rioting that left at least 40 dead and 2,000 injured after police arrested several Negroes at an after-hours bar, or "blind pig," on Detroit's near west side.

But on July 24, a day after the mayhem began, Hubbard embarked on a tour of the riot area, accompanied by two department heads and a reporter. At the wheel of an unmarked city car, without police protection, the 300-plus-pound mayor spent three hours maneuvering around barricades, fire-fighting equipment and crowds of milling Negroes. At one point, on Twelfth Street near Clairmount, where the violence had broken out, he was having difficulty changing lanes to get around rubble from a burned-out building. "Let's get the hell out of here," he barked, cutting into traffic amid hostile glances from Negro motorists. At that, he made a quick left turn out of the area.

Hubbard's reaction as a close observer was surprisingly sympathetic. Shaking his head as looters defied police and guardsmen, he observed, "What if they shot one of these kids? That would only make everything worse. I feel sorry for the honest Negro citizens who are obviously being hurt more by this situation than anyone else."

Several days later, his view of the situation hardened. He announced that he had set up a task force of Dearborn police to defend the city's borders around the clock, with orders to shoot looters and arsonists on sight. He also set a curfew. Hubbard then made a second tour of the riot area, this time with two police armed with a carbine and a submachine gun. The mayor, disguised in a straw hat and necktie, directed the group toward sniper fire at one juncture. Later, he stopped to pose for a photo with several Detroit Edison workers, one of them Negro.

A week after the rioting began, order was restored to Detroit when 4,700 federal paratroopers and 8,000 national guardsmen were called out. Dearborn was spared any real spillover from the riot. A hardware store near Dearborn's northeast border with Detroit was looted by a group of Negroes who witnesses said smashed two windows. There was a scuffle involving Negro youths and local whites in southwestern Dearborn's Crowley Park. Three local youths were arrested for firing weapons at police; also arrested were nine local men for carrying loaded weapons in their cars.[1] The only Negroes arrested in Dearborn were three men and a woman who were riding around with liquor and a sawed-off shotgun.

At the following week's council meeting, Hubbard showed up to assess the riot situation. "Such things wouldn't have happened here," he said. "I would put a curfew into immediate effect and shoot any looters or troublemakers on sight. This is war. When you have mad dogs running around, brute force is needed." The mayor was quick to blame civil rights activists. "Rabble-rousers such as Dr. King and Stokeley Carmichael have been firing them up," he said. "H. Rap Brown says, 'If America doesn't come around, we'll burn it down.' It's amazing what a few people can do." He also said the current wave of rioting was "just the first bite of it. It's a very dangerous situation. Be prepared for it. Learn to shoot and be a dead shot." The mayor moderated his remarks by pointing out that not all Negroes were involved. "Some were looting," he said, "but you don't indict a whole people for it." Just the same, the entire episode served only to solidify his racist reputation, coming as it did after his civil rights trial and the ongoing controversy over the city bulletin boards.

But race relations encroached only slightly into Orvie's agenda in the three years after he swamped Charles Nemeth in the 1964 election. During his twelfth term in office, while passing the age at which most men retire, Orville Hubbard continued to keep his name in the news.

A few days after his acquittal in federal court in June 1965, Hubbard said he probably would run again for circuit judge, obviously undismayed by his three losses in the 1950s. A week later, George Martin said he would run, too, setting up a head-to-head race with Hubbard for the first time in their careers. Martin, in his twenty-third year as a municipal judge, inundated the area with billboards, posters and speeches.

Hubbard, meanwhile, was doing almost no campaigning. But that was not to say he hadn't been busy. Dearborn voters had turned down a proposal the previous April to raise the mayor's pay from $17,500 to $21,500. And by the end of the summer, the council had voted onto the ballot two more referendums, one to hike the salary to $23,500 and another to raise it to

$25,000. Was his campaign for judge a plot to make it somehow easier for voters to give him another pay raise? Hubbard wasn't saying. He did explain at one candidates' forum why he wanted the job. "Mayors get spit on," he said. "I thought if I got me a judgeship, they'd stop spitting on me."

But he was giving mixed signals about his intentions. At one point, he warned that at age 62, "this will be the last time I'll be running for anything." Another time, he noted archly that he planned to stay on as mayor but was giving his enemies a chance to get rid of him by making him a judge. But who would vote for Orville Hubbard for judge? Certainly not Detroit's burgeoning Negro voters. And perhaps not even his local supporters, who would want to keep him on as mayor. Hubbard did well enough in the outcounty suburbs to earn a spot on the November ballot, finishing sixth in the September primary, with eight nominated. However, his showdown with Martin produced mixed results. While Martin finished only tenth, trailing Hubbard in total votes, 48,300 to 29,689, he outpolled the mayor in Dearborn, 8,346 to 3,808. Hubbard blamed his "poor showing" on a "hard-core anti-Hubbard vote in Dearborn." However, he said he felt "highly flattered" by the fact that his pay raise proposal came within 500 votes of passing.

Hubbard was flattered beyond all reason in the November election. He got his pay raise to $25,000, a positively lofty figure compared to the $6,500 he was making as recently as 1958, when voters had upped it to $17,500. The judicial race? He didn't come close to winning one of the four open spots, finishing seventh in a field of eight. He admitted he was disappointed, of course, though "except for a few appearances in Detroit, we did not campaign at all."

A year later, in November 1966, Martin improved enough to earn a circuit seat, finishing third in a field of six. The next month, the council named its president, Ralph Guy Sr., to succeed Martin as municipal judge. And that effectively ended Martin's feud with Hubbard, who no longer could call his rival a "glorified justice of the peace."

At the time of Martin's election, however, Hubbard had moved so aggressively into a national policy debate that he hardly took notice of Martin's departure. Orville Hubbard—ex-Marine, law-and-order patriot and nationally known racist—was crusading for the United States to pull out of the Vietnam War. To those struck by a need for ideological consistency, it may have seemed like another publicity stunt. But those close to Hubbard were convinced that, for once, he was espousing a cause on its own merits. He first started talking about Vietnam during his federal trial, suggesting that the war was being pushed by lawmakers whose own safety was not at risk. "In the old days, kings used to lead their troops into battle themselves," he observed. In 1966, Hubbard, who had declared that if he were of draft age, he would go to jail rather than follow orders to fight in Vietnam, called a "town hall" meeting for October to discuss the subject. The result was a unanimous vote in favor of putting an advisory referendum on the November ballot. When the council took up the issue the next night, Vincent Fordell and John Baja opposed it. "It can hold us up to ridicule," Fordell protested. "We're doing nothing but performing a publicity stunt." The rest all sided with Orvie, however, voting to hold what apparently would be the nation's first local test on the war.

The proposal, as adopted, read, "Are you in favor of an immediate cease fire and withdrawal of United States troops from Vietnam so Vietnamese people can settle their own differences?" The wording was loaded so as to elicit a yes vote, of course, by implying outside intervention into an internal problem. But that was just the way the mayor wanted it. The skewed phrasing became an issue a few days later between Hubbard and a congressional "hawk," Democrat John Dingell, whose district included Dearborn. Before an audience of 250, the pair turned a breakfast forum into a shouting match. Dingell complained that the wording was "really just a choice between a fight to the death or abject withdrawal." Hubbard, rising in rebuttal, declared the administration was drafting youths "to kill barefoot boys who haven't done anything to the United States. If our country were attacked, it would be a different story, and if this were a volunteer army, it'd be different." Then he said Congress didn't have the courage to declare war officially—"and neither does Dingell."

The next week, Hubbard resumed the weekly coffee-and-doughnut sendoffs he had started for inductees in World War II. Meanwhile, the issue was attracting considerable national attention. Hubbard appeared on national TV, and the story popped up in papers all over the country.

Two weeks before the election, Harold M. Ryan, a former GOP congressman from the suburb of Grosse Pointe, sued in federal court to keep the question off the ballot. Ryan said the proposal "harms and endangers the national security of the United States," and he accused Hubbard and his council of acting as if the city were "larger than the United States itself." Ryan argued during the subsequent hearing that the referendum violated his civil rights, including his right to be "immune from being covered with propaganda." Federal District Judge Fred Kaess scoffed: "What are you going to do, enjoin the newspapers, television? We're all talking about Vietnam." He tossed out the suit, accepting the city's argument that his court had no jurisdiction.

But the referendum did not go Hubbard's way in November. With Republicans George Romney and Robert Griffin winning election as Michigan governor and U.S. senator, respectively, the hawks beat the doves on the Dearborn Vietnam question, 20,628 to 14,134. Nearly 10,000 voters declined to express an opinion on the question.[2]

Hubbard went on national TV to grump, "All those 20,000 people who voted for this war should go over to the recruiting office and join up and put their bodies where their votes are." The mayor also blamed the white-collar districts in West Dearborn, where he himself traditionally had been weakest, for the no vote. "Where the cars are the shiniest and the homes the nicest and the children the fewest, it gets the most no votes," he said.

Hubbard stayed involved in the issue even after the vote. Early in 1967, he posted a Vietnam billboard outside his office, showing lists of war casualties and aircraft lost, as well as a color photo of injured and burned Vietnamese children. A few months later, he appeared in an antiwar protest at Detroit's Wayne State University. He was jeered by liberals on the race issue, and he also was picketed by a right-wing campus group called Counterthrust. The mayor drew a laugh and an ovation, however, when he responded, "All these young men who are hot for this war, your recruiting offices are open." Later in the year, Hubbard joined a list of sponsors of a newspaper ad urging President Johnson to end the war. Among the signers was the Reverend Martin Luther King Jr. As far as anyone could tell, it was the first time Orville Hubbard and Dr. King ever had lined up together on the same side of an issue.

With the Hubbard conspiracy trial over, Dearborn seemed ready to pass out of its crisis stage in race relations. That view was confirmed in July 1965, about the time the city was feuding with the Civil Rights Commission over bulletin boards. Two Dearborn college students, Pat Quinlan and James Wadsworth, arranged a test of city policies on integration at Camp Dearborn. The two got a mixed group admitted to the camp for lunch and a day of softball. They elicited a few catcalls from campers, but there were no incidents. Several days later, however, troublemakers set an eight-foot-tall cross afire in the neighborhood of Wadsworth's parents.[3] Police said the Wadsworth home was the apparent target. No arrests were made.

It was not until two years later that the city got its biggest racial scare—and then only because of its proximity to the Detroit riots. After his declaration about who was to blame for that particular catastrophe, Hubbard further interjected himself into the civil rights arena by recommending a so-called stop-and-frisk ordinance to give police extended search powers. Similar laws were facing court challenges in other states. Hubbard said he couldn't understand why innocent people would object, although one robbery suspect, a Negro, had filed a complaint against Dearborn with the Civil Rights Commission recently after he had been searched by police. The council voted in mid-August to put an advisory referendum on stop-and-frisk on the September ballot. Voters approved it by a margin of better than five to one, and the council then voted to support legislation at the state level.

Dearborn was not in much of a mood for another mayoral fight. Hubbard had taken 83 percent of the vote against Nemeth the last time around. How much of a surprise could there be now? Nonetheless, Nemeth took out petitions in May to try for his sixth time since 1955 to unseat Hubbard. Only two other opponents emerged. They were yet another of the Wagner clan, Anthony H. Wagner, who managed the family's stores, apartments, hotel and other properties; and Jerry D. Hurley, a former constable and now general foreman at General Motors.

Hubbard took out his petitions four days before the August deadline and filed them the same day. Hundreds of Hubbard billboards popped up in the last week of August, featuring the mayor and his five council incumbents—George Bondie; George Hart; Edward Dombrowski; Thomas D. Dolan, an insurance salesman appointed to fill Guy Sr.'s seat; and Van D. Mericas, a chiropractor appointed to succeed Irving ImOberstag, who had committed suicide in May. By the week before the September primary, the mayor's slate had ballooned to include 14 of the 30 council candidates. One of them was his son John, 32, a trucking firm dispatcher making his first try in politics. "I won't be a rubber-stamp councilman," announced John Hubbard. "Mayor Hubbard has had the say in everything. Maybe a member of the family will have something different to say." John Hubbard's nomination provided the surprise of the primary. Billing himself as an independent even while appearing in his father's newspaper ads and election eve rally, he finished seventh behind six incumbents but ahead of Mericas.

Orville Hubbard? His 16,347 votes gave him 85.6 percent of the returns, another personal best. Nemeth scraped together 1,057 to earn the dubious honor of opposing Hubbard in November, while Wagner got 1,034 votes and Hurley 653.

Nemeth, a "night person" who sold real estate and worked as a hotel-club clerk in the evening, was keeping such a low profile that one reporter referred to him as the "ghost" of Dearborn politics. He hardly said a word at a Hubbard candidates' breakfast and left before he could shake hands with anyone or have his picture taken with Hizzoner. A week before the election, he announced his strategy—he would not campaign. "I want to see how an election will go that is very, very quiet without any hysteria," he explained, pointing out that Hubbard thrived on hysteria. "He'll still win the election. There's no question about that, but he'll get 8,000 votes less."

Nemeth's prediction proved conservative. Hubbard fell off fully 14,000 votes from his peak in the 1964 presidential election. As a result, he scored only 26,448 votes to his opponent's 3,940—87 percent, another personal record. John Hubbard jumped up to third place in the council balloting, behind Hart and Bondie and ahead of Dombrowski, Dolan, Fordell and Baja. Guy Sr. won Martin's old judicial seat. However, voters again turned down a package of pay proposals, including one to up the mayor's salary from $25,000 to $27,500 and one to add a fourth year to elective terms of office.

Nemeth complained that the Hubbard machine had sent out so many campaign workers that "the voters could hardly get through to the polls." He also saw a sign of things to come. "The old man's getting tired, and maybe they're grooming the son for his job," he said. "We'll have Hubbards around for a long time."

Orvie, little moved by his own showing or his son's, simply dredged out an old victory statement, pledging "to continue to plow deep while others sleep and to work harder than ever."

But after a mandate like that, Hubbard could be pardoned for feeling he could do anything he wanted. Accordingly, the following Sunday, he called a special council meeting to approve a bid to buy an apartment building in Clearwater, Florida. Voters had turned down similar proposals four times before, but Hubbard couldn't resist the chance to snap up a bargain and convince the townsfolk afterward that they'd like it, too.

Actually, the mayor was lagging behind on civic projects. Throughout 1965, he hyped a site near Ford and Greenfield roads, near Henry Ford I's old farm home, for a giant sports stadium. He all but shelved the project the next year, though, when William Clay Ford, owner of the Detroit Lions football team and brother of Henry Ford II, indicated he was not interested.[4] Next came a scheme in 1965 to buy the Ambassador Bridge and perhaps the Detroit-Windsor Tunnel, the area's major auto routes to Canada. A New York investment counselor, Robert M. Sherritt, proposed that the city sponsor a nonprofit corporation to own and manage what he described as "the last two such facilities in the United States that are privately owned." According to Sherritt, the corporation would float $22 million in tax-exempt revenue bonds to buy out the bridge's stockholders and then try the same with the tunnel. Any profits would go to the city; any losses would be borne solely by the bondholders, since the city would not be required to pledge its full faith and credit to the project. Hubbard loved the idea. "It sounds too good to be true," he told the council at a January meeting. "But we could do it if everything went through. We could earn money and we'd have no risk." If it was such a good idea, why hadn't somebody done it already? Well, said Sherritt, both the state and the city of Detroit had turned down the proposal because of politics. No such problems in Dearborn. Hubbard backed the plan. The council went along. And then everything fizzled. For once in his life, Hubbard chickened out—and later regretted it for years. Another Hubbard project that fell through was a municipal golf course. In 1967, he went so far as to threaten to condemn a parcel of Ford land for a course, but he never followed through.

There were a few civic projects that came off. Ground was broken in 1966 for the city's second senior citizens building and for the Henry Ford Centennial Library, to be built on a 15-acre parcel donated by Ford Motor near the civic center.

And then there was Dearborn, Florida. The mayor had proposed in 1956 that the city purchase land for a community of rental units for Dearborn retirees. But attorney James Thomson blocked the project in court. Then, when Hubbard got a proposal on the ballot in 1957 to implement the project, voters turned it down overwhelmingly. They snubbed it again in advisory votes in 1957, 1961 and 1963, but Orvie continued the hype.

He even put up a sign at Camp Dearborn that said, "Drive Safely. Live to Enjoy Dearborn, Florida."

And at last the mayor got his chance. In 1967, he spotted a brochure from the Federal Housing Administration (FHA) describing an eight-story, 88-unit apartment building on a 1.8-acre plot in Clearwater on Florida's Gulf side. The structure had been built in 1960 for $2 million but went into default and was acquired by the FHA in 1963. Now it was for sale. Hubbard liked the looks of the building, which he said reminded him of the city's two local senior citizens' buildings, and he went with an entourage to inspect it in late October.

Then, at the first council session in memory ever called for a Sunday, with most city department heads and two reporters in attendance but without a single citizen, the council voted seven-to-nothing to bid on the property. City Attorney Ralph Guy Jr. and City Controller Daniel S. McCormick flew to Washington, D.C., the next day to deliver the city's top bid of $1.5 million. The day after that, less than 48 hours after the special council meeting, the FHA announced that the high bid—the last one opened—had come from the city of Dearborn. The purchase price, $1,076,111, was nearly $500,000 under the city's top, but it was also $20,000 higher than the next bid. All 27 other bidders were private firms.

A week later, the council renamed the building Dearborn Towers, and the city announced that more than 150 residents had applied for apartments there. The city's purchase was reported around the country, and phone calls, letters and telegrams poured in, most of them expressing strong interest and support, officials said. "This is like Columbus landing," Hubbard was quoted by *Newsweek*. "It's never happened before."[5]

But no one had reckoned with James Thomson. In a reprise of his 1956 suit, the attorney obtained a temporary restraining order in circuit court, with a hearing to be held at the end of November. Thomson's brief called the purchase "a plan to provide a happy land for a chosen few with a minimum of benefits at great expense and liability to the taxpayers of Dearborn." He also objected to the Sunday council meeting as a charter violation with "overtones of secrecy which is repugnant to the American concepts of democracy." Finally, he said, the purchase violated a state law governing municipal acquisitions. Guy Jr., speaking for the city, responded that state law permitted a city to own property outside its corporate limits. "We know of no restrictions against us doing this," he said. In late November, Circuit Judge James N. Canham agreed, rejecting Thomson's arguments and giving the city the go-ahead.[6]

In December, the city leased the first two units to Dearborn residents. By the end of the year, Hubbard was grandly predicting a second Florida building.[7] "The Hubbard administration definitely is not going to rest on its laurels," he said.

39

Beating Doug Thomas, 1968-70

Support Your Local Dictator.
—Legend written on a portrait of Orville L. Hubbard
hanging in the office of Teamsters Local 214 President
Joe C. Valenti

One could only imagine what Orville Hubbard was thinking in March 1969, when he arrived for a civic function at the picturesque old Dearborn Inn. He was about to have lunch with a black—and a black, moreover, who was active in the increasingly contentious arena of civil rights. Scheduled to address the Dearborn Rotary Club was Atlanta minister Ralph D. Abernathy, who had taken over as head of the activist Southern Christian Leadership Conference after Dr. Martin Luther King Jr. was shot dead in Memphis the year before by James Earl Ray. Hubbard was known to have regarded King as a "son of a bitch" who had stirred up trouble wherever he went. Would he say so today and dare Abernathy to contradict him? Would he say the same of Abernathy? Would he invite Abernathy to leave town, as he once had demanded of a Detroit judge who had offended him? No matter what happened, the meeting promised to be an event.

When Orvie spotted Abernathy, he made a beeline for him. "Welcome to Dearborn," he said with a broad grin, reaching out to shake hands. "We'd like to have you living here."

"Thank you," responded Abernathy, appearing somewhat nonplussed. "It may be when I finish solving the problems of hunger and inequality, I may retire here in Dearborn."

"You're doing a good job," Hubbard added as the two went off to lunch together.

The conversation had to rank among the unlikeliest exchanges in the history of Dearborn social amenities. Perhaps Hubbard believed that his cordiality would diffuse the impact of Abernathy's remarks. If so, the hope was short-lived. The minister went on to admonish the Rotarians, "Regardless of how safe and secure you may feel in Dearborn, you never will be free until your black brothers and sisters are free." The scolding elicited several standing ovations from the group, but later Orvie reflected, "There are still a lot of questions I would like to ask him: What's the remedy? Where else has the black man done as well as he has here? Who got the black man out of the jungle in the first place?"

Orville Hubbard's feeling on the race issue hadn't really changed any over the years, but the mayor had turned 65 as the decade of the 1960s neared an end, and it was apparent that he was less strident on the subject than he once was. In fact, a civil rights group, the Dearborn Inter-Faith Action Council (DIFAC), went so far as to request a meeting to discuss integrating the city. The mayor did not respond.

Hubbard had begun his thirteenth term in January 1968 by pushing Michigan's first local stop-and-frisk ordinance through the council. The ordinance, which permitted police to search "suspicious" persons, was sponsored by the city's newest councilman, John Jay Hubbard, the mayor's number three son.[1] There was no mention of race, though that was clearly on the mayor's mind when he proposed the measure in the aftermath of the Detroit riots. Detroit followed with its own version.

In June 1968, Michigan Governor George Romney signed a new open-housing law. To the surprise of many, however, Dearborn was already integrated—or had been until just a week before Romney signed the measure. At that time, a family described as the city's only black residents announced they were moving out because they were "never made to feel welcome" there after two and a half years of renting from a black landlord. The Reverend Arthur Knight told newsmen that he, his wife Dorothy and four children were moving back to Detroit, where he was pastor at a Baptist church. They did so that fall, but Dearborn had not heard the last of the Knights. A few months later, in January 1969, Hubbard became an overnight target of Roy Wilkins of the NAACP. Labeling the mayor the nation's "meanest man in race relations," Wilkins called him "a more dedicated segregationist (if that be possible) than Strom Thurmond, James Eastland or George Wallace."

What prompted the elevation of a small-town northern mayor into a ranking with a trio of redneck southern politicos? The Knights, it turned out, had accused Hubbard of refusing to add the name of their son, MacArthur Knight, 20, a Vietnam War victim, to a war memorial in front of the Dearborn city hall. The reason, the Knights charged, was strictly racial. Declaring that Orvie had "descended to the lowest level" in his "incredible refusal" to post the name of the Knights' son, Wilkins said, "The segregationists ought to get rid of him in sheer self-preservation."

When told of Wilkins's comments, Hubbard's press aide, Doyne Jackson, chuckled, "Who's Roy Wilkins?" But on a more serious note, he also had what sounded like a plausible explanation: "The reason the soldier's name isn't on the memorial is simply because he never lived in Dearborn. To our knowledge he never set foot in the state of Michigan, let alone Dearborn." The mayor, Jackson said, would have no comment. But a local veterans' group corroborated Jackson's contention that the memorial was only for residents and local school attendees.

Hubbard later gave his opponents a number of more legitimate opportunities to accuse him of racism. At a council meeting in January 1969, he had invoked the specter of a black "invasion" of Dearborn's east end to justify selling a small park for residential development instead of improving it for recreational purposes. The latter, he said, "would be an open invitation for nonresidents to invade our city. We'd have a worse mess than we ever had on Kendal Street."

But Orvie scored points with the local liberals a few months later with his genteel treatment of Abernathy, and he surprised almost everyone in September when he endorsed a black, Richard Austin, for Detroit mayor.[2]

But if he was trying to repair his image, he certainly wasn't working at it full-time. In May 1969, he snubbed largely black Inkster during the annual Mayors' Exchange Day program matching Michigan cities. He dispatched Councilman George Bondie to substitute for him without explanation.[3] And during the summer and fall of 1969, the old bulletin board controversy flared up again, dying a natural death after a circuit judge dismissed the case in October.

Orvie further enhanced his standing among whites' righters when the United Klans of America met in Dearborn in 1970. Hubbard already had laid some groundwork during the 1968 presidential campaign by appearing at a rally in Dearborn on behalf of former Alabama Governor George Wallace. Wallace, an American Independent Party candidate with impeccable credentials among the segregationist bloc, was Hubbard's choice, even though the mayor went around town wearing a button for Democrat Eugene McCarthy, whose opposition to the Vietnam War he echoed. Wallace didn't show up for the Dearborn rally, held in October at the Youth Center, but Lester Maddox did. The Georgia governor, who once had used an ax handle to discourage blacks from patronizing a restaurant he owned, addressed an audience of 700, including a large contingent sitting in silent protest. Hubbard welcomed Maddox with the declaration, "This is Wallace country," following with an elaborate introduction that reached back to DeSoto's landing in Georgia in 1540. Hubbard expected Wallace to do well in the November election. But even with the mayor stumping for him, Wallace trailed far behind Hubert Humphrey and Richard Nixon among Dearborn's voters. In a local note of interest, however, Dearbornites confirmed Hubbard's belief that sentiment was growing for a U.S. pullout from Vietnam. An advisory referendum almost identical to the one that appeared on the Dearborn ballot in 1966 resulted this time in a clear mandate for a cease-fire. The mayor did not make a personal appearance at the Klan rally, held before 400 sympathizers at the Youth Center in February 1970. However, State Senator Roger Craig, Hubbard's mayoral opponent in 1959, said to some 700 protesters outside, "We are probably no better or no worse than any of the other all-white suburbs in the Detroit area, and yet we allow ourselves to become a symbol of race hatred like this. I think it is offensive and a source of embarrassment to most Dearborn residents that we are singled out for these meetings."[4] Hubbard tried to distance himself from the controversy, but when local attorney George Lewis assailed him at the next council meeting as a "bigot who is too gutless to admit it," the mayor responded angrily with a threat to "roll one off your goddamn nose." That ended that.

The mayor was only slightly less combative when it came to employee relations. His stubbornness was largely responsible for setting off the city's first-ever labor strike. The city had been on uneasy terms with the Teamsters Union since 1967, when the union's Local 214 was certified as bargaining agent for some 450 blue-collar municipal employees. When the union threatened a walkout in the fall of 1968, the mayor responded crisply: "If they want to walk out, they had better keep walking, because they won't have a job here." Finally, in February 1969, about 325 workers walked off the job in a wildcat strike. What set them off was a statement from DPW head James Dick that they should "eat around their sandwich bags" instead of taking extra wash-up time for lunch. True to Hubbard's threat, the city fired the strikers and then refused to take them back after their grievances were upheld in circuit court. For 23 days, the strike continued, marred by fighting and vandalism. Several stewards were suspended after the dispute was settled, and several union members were prosecuted on criminal charges. Even though the mayor had not taken an obvious role in negotiations, the Teamsters understood who was making the decisions. Pickets hanged him in effigy during the strike.

A year later, with the union still mired in contract squabbles, the president of Local 214 lit a cigar and gestured at a smiling portrait of Orville Hubbard on his office wall. Under it was the legend, "Support Your Local Dictator." "There's no doubt in my mind that Dearborn is the most strongly anti-union public employer in the state," said Joe C. Valenti, who had taken to calling the mayor "superboss." "And that's the man who's responsible. As long as Hubbard is mayor, he will have unilateral control over the city."

The Teamsters were not the only union challenged by Hubbard, however. A few weeks before the Teamster strike, he had castigated police, firemen and other employees for demanding "irresponsible and unreasonable" 15-percent wage hikes. "It's been honey and cream for the employees and nuts to the taxpayers for too long," Hubbard said in a press release. "We're going to try to reverse that diet." His best line he saved for the firemen: "Through their lobbying in Lansing, they are in the fire hall so little, it's a miracle they can find it." Later, in August 1969, the mayor ordered the Civil Service Commission to begin accepting applications for volunteer firemen as a prelude to cutting back department strength by one-third. Employees finally settled for raises under 10 percent.

But the mayor reprised the same themes in February 1970, when employees demanded raises of 15 to 18 percent. He even released a time study showing firemen spent only 1.3 percent of their work time putting out fires, compared to 55.4 percent eating, on coffee breaks and in leisure activities. "It appears," he said wryly, "that some of our residents are moonlighting as firemen." City workers got 8-percent raises that year, though firemen later received 14.8 percent through binding arbitration, a figure Orvie disparaged as "ridiculous and outrageous," even as he threatened to challenge the legality of the procedure.

No one doubted Orvie was just trying to solidify his reputation for keeping taxes low. After all, he would be up for election again later in 1970. But he was still such a sure bet that people were starting to pay more attention to how his son, freshman Councilman John Jay Hubbard, was faring. Young Hubbard, a crewcut blond with the physique of a small refrigerator, took on the air of an independent almost from the start. Although he used Jackson's press release on the stop-and-frisk ordinance he sponsored, he challenged his father on a spate of proposals during early 1968. Among them was a $55,000 appropriation for Camp Dearborn supplies. John Hubbard was in the minority on that one, prompting his father to observe, "Everyone who's ever opposed Camp Dearborn is no longer around here. That goes 20 years back."

But by the fall of 1968, John Hubbard had taken to admonishing his father in public. At one council meeting, he began a gently sarcastic monologue this way: "We are dignified by the presence of the mayor tonight for the third time since January. Although you are twice my age—and perhaps twice my weight—Your Honor might be surprised to know . . ." The following year, he questioned whether his father was keeping an honest tab on the time clock he had been punching in since the early 1940s. "I know that you punch a time clock," he said, "but when I stop by to see you, I don't find you in. May be that somebody is punching you in." The mayor absorbed it all in silence, telling reporters at one point, "If he sits down for a couple of years with his ears open and his mouth shut, he'll learn something."

Although not everyone bought the image of an independent-thinking Hubbard son on council—17-year council veteran John Baja, for instance, snorted, "Hubbard would love to see his son as mayor"[5]—John Hubbard said, "There's one thing in this town that Hubbard dreads, and that's me on the council. He has some of these guys in his hip pocket, but he knows he can't control me. He never could." While denying he had mayoral ambitions, he acknowledged he had been working on his image, "so I could be considered as an individual" instead of an Orville Hubbard clone. "When your name is Hubbard," he said, "you're automatically branded a racist and a hate-monger. I'm not an extremist either way on the race issue, and I want to be known for my own ideas."

By March 1970, however, John Hubbard was no longer a councilman. When City Clerk R. William Hill died, the council appointed the younger Hubbard to fill the vacancy. The job paid only $9,800, compared to the $13,000 he was making as a dispatcher for a local trucking firm, and he also had to give up his $2,000 as a councilman. But now he had a full-time job in politics, and his father was rid of a gadfly on the council. The maneuvering led to speculation about the prospects of a Hubbard dynasty in city hall. Despite John Hubbard's protests, many saw the clerk's job as a logical stepping stone to the mayor's job. And Orvie's two older sons, Jim and Frank, had expressed interest in politics as well. Jim, a Dearborn policeman, announced his possible candidacy for mayor after his father retired. Frank, a county Road Commission employee, had taken out petitions for council in 1964, though he did not file. The talk of a dynasty was premature as long as Orville Hubbard was alive and running, however. And despite his status as a senior citizen, he had announced in January 1970 that he would run again for mayor. Would anyone run against him?

In late May, a burly blond named John Jay Hubbard became one of the first to take out petitions for mayor. Telling reporters he would "make a hell of a good candidate," he declared, "Maybe we need some new blood in the office. I think Orville Hubbard is the greatest thing ever to come along in the history of U.S. politics. I'm convinced that no one in the country could beat him for mayor. But if you push a good man too long and too far, he gets to the point where he needs a rest." The mayor said simply, "It's a free country."

By the June filing deadline, three candidates were in the race. They were Jerry D. Hurley, a former city constable; Beverly A. Bazzy, a Dearborn Schools bookkeeper and wife of a Teamster; and Douglas B. Thomas, an insurance agent.[6]

John Hubbard? He had filed for clerk. "It would have ended up in a disaster," explained the younger Hubbard after withdrawing from the mayor's race. "I didn't have any more chance against the Hubbard machine and the mayor's cronies than anybody else would have. What happened was that I had a couple of Manhattans, called up one of the local newspaper editors and told him I wanted to run. The mayor had said I'd be 'all washed up' in this town if I ran against him, and I decided he was right. I'm the first to admit that I couldn't be in politics today if it weren't for my name."

With or without John Hubbard in the race, it was apparent the mayor was not overly concerned about his opposition. A week after the filing deadline, he announced another of his famous municipal innovations. This time, he would personally conduct a rummage sale of old clothes that no longer fit him. He opened up his office the following Monday with about 160 items, including 28 suits priced from $5 to $25; three topcoats at $20 each; plus assorted hats, bow ties, Masonic fezzes, belts, shirts, shoes, slippers and a pair of silk pajamas. In his shirtsleeves to mingle with the crowd ("You've got to do something about that waistline," he advised one buyer), Hubbard moved $702.60 worth of merchandise in three hours. Curiosity-seekers who wandered in later pushed the take to more than $800. Orvie said he would use the proceeds for his campaign. "Do you think this is what people mean when they say it's time to clean out city hall?" he chuckled later.

Meanwhile, Thomas quickly emerged as a serious candidate with a barrage of press releases prepared with the help of a Detroit ad agency. The son of William Thomas, an old Hubbard backer who had served for years on the City Plan Commission, the 37-year-old Thomas opened up with the most obvious issue he had: the mayor's age. Current problems, he said, could not be solved "with the ideas and tactics that were used in the 1950s." Over the next few weeks, Thomas blamed Hubbard for such diverse matters as city employee problems and a decline in the city's population from 112,007 to 103,870 since 1960. And while he was at it, Thomas also railed against Orvie for closing parks, proposing to spend $4 million for five ice arenas, purchasing the Florida building "against citizens' wishes" and failing to stem the deterioration of retail areas.

Of the other two challengers, Hurley stayed pretty well out of sight, and Bazzy spent much of her time explaining her status as the first woman to run for mayor in Dearborn.[7] "Hubbard has been mayor here so long, people think it's his city," she said. "But it's not. It belongs to everybody here."

Hubbard, meanwhile, was hardly even campaigning, though he had taken in nearly two-thirds of all council candidates—16 of 25—onto his slate. The only notable omission from the 1970 Hubbard team was Baja, who had flopped over onto the mayor's side with enough fervor that Hubbard had engineered his designation as council president. However, Baja had become a political liability, partly because of a business reversal that had landed him in court on a bankruptcy petition.

The mayor's only disappointment in the August primary was that he failed to beat his record of 87 percent of the vote. This time, he collected "only" 77 percent, with 17,615 votes to 3,051 for Thomas, who thus made the November runoff. Farther behind were Bazzy with 1,261 and Hurley with 891. Eleven of the mayor's 16 council slaters won nomination, led by incumbents George Bondie, Edward Dombrowski, Thomas Dolan and Van D. Mericas, who had been named to fill young Hubbard's seat. Baja was fifth, followed by Hubbard backer John Grecu and independent Ken Budny. Longtime Hubbard foe Vincent Fordell was retiring from the council, running instead for one of the city's new district judgeships—with the mayor's backing. And Hubbard slater George Hart, the remaining council incumbent, had opted to try for a State Senate seat.[8]

John Hubbard trounced the other candidates for clerk.

However, four charter amendment proposals lost, even with the mayor's backing: a "fair cost-of-living" pay hike formula for elected officials, plus raises for the council, clerk and treasurer. It was the second defeat that year for a council pay raise and the nineteenth since the 1942 charter took effect.

Thomas lost no time resuming the offensive, at least as much of an offensive as one could mount against an institution. "I think Hubbard can be beaten," he said. "There is a base of 10,000 to 11,000 anti-Hubbard votes still here, I think." Thomas, whose only previous attempt for office was a failed campaign for State Senate as a Republican in 1964, acknowledged that he faced a "recognition" problem, that perhaps only one voter in five even knew who he was, compared to "at least 99.9 percent" for the mayor. "I can't imagine anybody not knowing the name of Orville Hubbard, but I suppose there might be somebody," he said.

Thomas wound up spending much of the next three months releasing a carefully orchestrated sequence of press statements. He attacked Hubbard with the observation, "All the tax money that Ford pays tends to cover up the spending problem. Most people probably are thinking they've got an efficient government when actually it has been a very costly one." He criticized Hubbard for allowing East Dearborn's business district to deteriorate, while holding on to "a dilapidated city hall" that took up "the most desirable corner in the city." Thomas said he would like to sell the site to a developer and turn East Dearborn into "a little Georgetown." Later, he proposed amending the charter to limit mayoral terms, declaring, "After eight years, it becomes a question of empire-building." Finally, in a maneuver that Hubbard himself would have been proud of in his most combative years, Thomas began letting it be known in early October that the mayor's health was failing. Thomas told a police group that Hubbard had suffered four "attacks" of an unspecified nature, adding that the mayor planned to resign after the election and then "turn over the keys to city hall" to John Hubbard through council appointment. He contended that the mayor had been "strangely absent" from numerous public functions during the last year because of the "attacks," the last two of which he said occurred in Denver during July and in Dearborn in September.[9]

Where was Hubbard during all this? The mayor, who had started to put up his billboards only a week or so before, had decided early on not to make any comment about his opponent. But this was too much. "I don't have any health problems," he snorted. "Hell, the Hubbards live forever. All my people have lived into their 80s." The mayor pointed out that his mother had died a few years before at age 89, but he neglected to mention that his father had died at 43, even though that was part of his official biography.

Thomas stuck with his story and continued to widen his attack. In mid-

October, he accused Hubbard of "doing the city damage" with his racist stance. "Dearborn is no different than the suburbs around any big city," he said, adding that integration probably would come within three years, no matter who was elected. "Dearborn is what the people are, not what Mayor Hubbard is." In the last weeks before the election, the challenger ran ads in the local papers attacking a Hubbard proposal for a 1-percent city income tax that had been voted down in an advisory referendum the summer before. Another ad grumped, "Dearborn's City Government is in a rut. It's out of date. It's tired."

Toward the end of October, the incumbent and the upstart challenger took turns calling each other names. The mayor denounced Thomas as a "cunning opportunist" who was trying to deceive voters in much the same fashion as most of the other opponents he had faced and defeated since 1941. "And he's going to take the same route as all the others," he predicted. "I've been smeared so often it's unbelievable. Hardly any of these guys who ran against me ever told the truth, and you can't believe what these damned newspapers say, either." When told that Thomas had characterized him as "one of the dirtiest campaigners around," the mayor exploded. "That son of a bitch," he yelped, pounding his desk. "I'm the cleanest campaigner I ever heard of—although I've used what you might call rabbit punches in some campaigns. I've never looked for a fight, but I've never run away from one, either."

A week later, the mayor at last resorted to one of his "rabbit punches": he challenged Thomas to prove he had a legitimate line of work. "Anybody who doesn't list an occupation in the directory or phone number in the phone book appears as though he's trying to hide something," he said. Thomas answered by identifying himself to reporters as an independent insurance contractor since 1966, adding, "I ran this campaign because I felt I could afford to run. The issues are not my employment. I've got a wife, two children, a home and a car to pay for, so I just think those charges are asinine."

All things considered, it was the toughest, most aggressive challenge to Hubbard since he ran against Bill Mills in 1957. The result, however, was much the same as in the primary. Hubbard swept to his fourteenth term with 74 percent of the vote, taking 31,110 votes to 10,939 for Thomas. He won all precincts, including Thomas's, 229 to 143. He also got five of the seven council seats, with Bondie leading the field, followed by the newcomer, Budny, then Dombrowski, Dolan, Baja, Mericas and Grecu. Baja, who had tried and failed to interest the nonaligned candidates in forming a slate to oppose the mayor, reportedly got under-the-table support from Hubbard and his aides at the last minute.[10] Young Hubbard was an easy winner in the clerk's race, as was Fordell in the judicial race. A Hubbard-backed list of 10 charter amendments lost, however, including one to increase the mayor's pay to "as much as the superintendent of schools" made. Other proposals would have lengthened officials' terms to four years, given the mayor the authority to appoint the city clerk and treasurer and raised councilmen's pay to "one-third as much as the city dogcatcher" made.[11]

Orvie said he interpreted the vote as a mandate to continue to "do things the Hubbard way." He also called Thomas a liar: "If my opponent had stuck to the facts and offered the people a positive community improvement program instead of falsely spreading the untrue and malicious story about my having two heart attacks and trying to convey the impression that I might be dead before the election, he might have impressed people as being a more fair-minded and desirable candidate. The only 'attacks' I have suffered over the years have been from phony, creepy opponents." He also repeated one of his time-honored challenges: "We would like to invite and encourage all unhappy people who continuously oppose the Hubbard administration to move to a place where they would be more contented. In line with our reputation for courteous, efficient service, we will be happy to provide them with police escorts to the city limits."

Thomas offered no apologies for the stories about the mayor's health. He also chided Hubbard on his victory statement. "I'm certainly not getting out of town," he said, adding that it sounded "like Hitler or one of the leaders behind the Iron Curtain who would like to get 100 percent of the vote all the time." And, he said, he was planning to run again in 1973 as "the loyal opposition for Orville Hubbard." To that end, he noted, he was printing up bumper stickers that said, "Bye, bye, Orvie."

40

Beating John Pazzanese, 1971-73

I do the best I know how, the very best I can, and I
mean to keep on doing this down to the very end.
—Abraham Lincoln, as quoted by Orville L. Hubbard
in a newspaper ad for his mayoral campaign

Dearborn was "Wallace Country." Orville Hubbard already had proclaimed as much in 1968 during former Alabama Governor George Wallace's unsuccessful campaign for president. So what could have been more natural three years later than for the mayor to show up to welcome Lester Maddox to the Dearborn Youth Center for another rally for Wallace's American Independent Party?

In October 1971, as Orvie pulled up to the building in his chauffeur-driven city car, he found a two-pronged demonstration in progress. A number of young people were picketing and chanting, in the manner of the antiwar protesters, "Hey, hey, ho, ho. Orville Hubbard's got to go." But they were being drowned out by a larger group yelling back, "Ho, ho, hey, hey. Orville Hubbard's got to stay." Flattered by at least part of the welcome, Hubbard walked past the pickets and saw to it that the counterdemonstrators got in without paying the three-dollar ticket fee to hear Maddox speak.

The mayor, there to introduce the Georgia lieutenant governor to the crowd of some 400, quickly turned the rally into a mass denunciation of cross-district school busing. Picking up on rumors that Dearborn pupils were to be bused to the inner city, Orvie urged residents to fight a Detroit busing plan under advisement by Federal District Judge Stephen Roth. Busing, the mayor declared, "is against all moral principles. How can one judge shove this down millions of people's throats and tell them what to do?" Maddox echoed the theme by stepping up and decrying forced busing as "communistic" and symbolic of "tryanny in government." Two days later, Roth directed the Michigan Board of Education to prepare a package of

338

school integration proposals, including one for busing pupils to and from suburban districts.

Hubbard, it turned out, had touched on an issue more incendiary than any since the start of the Vietnam War. Other local officials followed suit, but it was Orvie who soon became a symbol of antibusing sentiment in Michigan. Although he turned down most of the invitations he got to antibusing meetings, Hubbard did announce he was sponsoring a Dearborn rally in response to hundreds of requests. One such request came from a woman, not a Dearborn resident, who suggested the option of assassinating Judge Roth.

Hubbard's rally, billed as the largest political gathering ever in Dearborn, drew some 1,600 people and featured a slew of politicians anxious to express their dismay over forced busing. The mayor chided the U.S. Supreme Court, saying he doubted people would "let those old judges who are practically senile tell us what to do." He called for a "revolution" and, injecting his standard segregation rationale, added that "people have to be accepted" and he himself wasn't welcome in the posh Dearborn Hills subdivision "unless I spray myself with Chanel No. 5." Other speakers were equally forceful. Irene McCabe, a housewife who had founded an antibusing organization called the National Action Group (NAG), was undaunted when Hubbard mixed her up with another speaker and finally introduced her as "Mrs. McCab." "I will go to jail," she told the crowd, "but I will not give up my freedom of association to any tyrannical district judge." She drew standing ovations before and after her talk. One official was all but booed off the rostrum. Thomas J. Brennan, a Dearborn resident and member of the State Board of Education, hardly got a chance to speak his piece against forced busing after he dared to say he favored racial integration.

By early 1972, the city's antibusing fervor had coalesced even further. The school board voted in January to join other suburban districts in challenging Roth's busing plan. And the City Council moved in March to put three advisory propositions on the May presidential primary ballot. One, recommended by Hubbard, asked, "Are you in favor of amending the United States Constitution to prohibit forced busing and guarantee the right of each student to attend his neighborhood school?"

Meanwhile, McCabe had embarked on a 44-day, 600-mile walk from her home in Pontiac, north of Detroit, to Washington, D.C., to protest busing. Orvie joined her five times in her first week, giving her a cash donation at each stop as she smooched him on the cheek. Later on during her trek, Dearborn department heads working as "volunteers" helped her with a sound truck and did some advance publicity for her.

A local delegate to the Wallace party's national committee had said several months before that she would ask Hubbard to run for the U.S. Senate the following year, "because he'd be one of the few people we could support." A Hubbard spokesman brushed aside that idea, but by April, Orvie was threatening to run for Congress as a protest candidate on the busing issue. Eventually, the mayor thought better of his threat, just as he had in 1966 when he talked about taking on longtime incumbent Democrat John Dingell on the Vietnam issue.

The antibusing forces got a boost that month when Wallace himself, now campaigning for the Democratic nomination, brought his presidential bandwagon to the Dearborn Youth Center. Hubbard said he couldn't attend but sent Police Chief John B. O'Reilly to introduce the governor. Before a crowd of 3,000 inside the building and another 3,000 outside, Wallace lambasted busing, big government, liberals and his other favorite targets. Several dozen pickets walked outside.

Among those who arrived too late to get a seat in the Youth Center was a onetime Milwaukee busboy and janitor named Arthur Bremer. Bremer had taken a car ferry across Lake Michigan from Wisconsin. Then, hoping to reach Dearborn before Wallace did, he got lost and had to settle for a spot outside a ground-level window near the stage. The glass was reinforced with wire mesh, but Wallace came within 15 feet once before his speech. According to a diary made public later, Bremer wrote, "Two 15-year-old girls got in front of me. Their faces were two inches from the glass. They were sure to be blinded and disfigured. I let Wallace go just to spare those stupid, innocent, delighted kids."[1] No such impediments stood in Bremer's way six days later in Laurel, Maryland, when he shot Wallace in the back as the candidate shook hands in a shopping-center parking lot. The next day, Wallace, whose injury would render him a paraplegic, swept every precinct in Dearborn's Democratic primary, with 61 percent of the vote against 23 for the national nominee, South Dakota Senator George S. McGovern. Dearborn also approved Hubbard's antibusing question, 29,037 to 5,409.

In June, Judge Roth finally issued his busing ruling, setting up a panel to draft an integration plan that named Dearborn one of 52 suburban districts to be paired with Detroit in 1973. The next week, Hubbard predicted "massive resistance." He also jibed at Roth as an immigrant who "should be crated up and shipped back" to his native Hungary. As implementation of the Roth decision dragged out, it became clear that the worst fears of the suburban busing foes would not be realized. In July 1974, Roth died. Two weeks later, the U.S. Supreme Court killed his busing plan in a five-to-four decision supporting the concept of local autonomy. Detroit thus was left on its own to solve its school segregation quandary.

While the busing controversy was simply the latest manifestation of a racial dilemma that affected most of white suburbia, Dearborn had its own special ethnic problem that was tied to increasing industrial activity in its southeastern section. Long a Hubbard stronghold, the south end traditionally was home to East European emigrants drawn by Orvie's blue-collar appeal. However, after decades of steady immigration from the Middle East, the area by 1970 was said to be the largest and longest-established Arab enclave in North America. About half the south end's 5,500 residents were Arab Moslems. Anchored by Ford's Rouge complex, the area had always had to cope with heavy pollution from automaking, as well as from slag and cement companies, trucking firms and brickyards. Perhaps it was coincidental, but as the south end became increasingly Arabic, some felt the area seemed to become more and more a stepchild in the eyes of city hall. Under terms of a 1961 master plan, the city had launched a "community development" program in 1964. The idea was simple: the city would move in more industry and move out most of the homes. By 1970, however, residents were beginning to grouse about the burgeoning urban renewal program. In June 1971, faced with increasing pressure from city hall to sell their homes, residents voted to sue to halt the program. In the words of community spokesman Alan Amen, the city wanted to "change the character of the south end."

Don't think that city hall went down there and tried to start this urban renewal. We were only doing what they asked us to do. If they want to sell, it's their business. If they don't want to sell, it's their business. What the hell do I get out of going to the south end and bothering them? We have never chased a man out of his home in this town. People in the south end know that when they deal with the city hall—those who just aren't trying to steal the show—that we deal honestly, fairly and squarely with them.

Hubbard was involved directly in September when about 100 south enders went to a council meeting to complain. Yawning through a two-hour debate, Hubbard listened as one resident after another attacked the renewal plan. One, an attorney named George Lewis, called him a "racist pig" and snapped, "You and your silent, cowardly henchmen on the council are enemies of the working people." Amen added, "We will not stop until we defeat or change this city government." The mayor's retort was that most critics were misinformed about the city's plans. "I guess I'm just an SOB," he said, "but I can tell you there isn't a section of town we have greater sympathy for." He promised home repair permits to anyone having problems with city hall's building department.

In the eyes of city officials, difficulties had been minimal. Records showed that of 174 homes razed since the program started, 30 were owned by absentee landlords and 9 were vacant. Of the rest, 87 owners moved elsewhere in the city, and 48 moved out of the city. Unimpressed with such statistics, residents filed suit against the city in federal court in October 1971 to stop all urban renewal in the south end and the nearby Eugene-Porath neighborhood.[2]

At a press conference announcing the suit, Detroit attorney Abdeen Jabara castigated the city's urban renewal program as "a form of cultural genocide." Jabara, a Lebanese emigrant who had helped defend Sirhan Sirhan on appeal of his conviction for assassinating Robert F. Kennedy in 1968, declared, "The administration of Dearborn is seeking to destroy this community. I've never seen such a display of utter contempt for the people."

In March 1972, Federal Judge Ralph M. Freeman issued an order restraining the city from acquiring further property in the two urban renewal areas. That did little to close the rift between the residents and city hall. At a council meeting a week later, the mayor all but kissed off Freeman's ruling, saying, "We're ready to buy any property that residents want to sell, and we're going to continue to do it." As a parting shot, he told Amen's "crew of malcontents" that their lawsuit "should be thrown out like a bomb and you along with it." At that, Amen and some 60 supporters walked out, and Orvie told the stragglers, "This is what I'd call their last hurrah." It was hardly that. In February 1973, after nearly a year and a half of delays, the Dearborn urban renewal trial began in federal court in Detroit.

Jabara's team called 46 witnesses over the first five weeks of the trial. Not surprisingly, Hubbard, who somehow was never around when subpoena servers went looking for him, was not among those who testified. In rebuttal, the city called 21 witnesses over two more weeks to testify, among other things, that the south end got better city services than the rest of the city.

In August, Freeman issued a preliminary ruling that city officials "have taken the plaintiffs' property without due process of law" and "have destroyed the private market" in the two areas. He did not, however, find the city guilty of violating the provision of equal protection of the law, indicating that he did not think the city was acting because of the ethnic or economic makeup of the south end. The judge awarded no monetary damages but said that those who had sold their homes to the city could file for damages on a case-by-case basis if they were unsatisfied. Four months later, in December, Freeman confirmed his preliminary ruling, prohibiting the city from acquiring further property except by condemnation. That effectively ended the city's urban renewal efforts in the south end. But even though Freeman's ruling technically absolved Orvie of accusations of anti-Arab sentiments, the entire case nonetheless affirmed his reputation as a racist.[3]

Much more damaging to Hubbard was another set of land transactions that came to light in April 1972, a few weeks after Judge Freeman first issued his restraining order. At that time, the *Detroit News* disclosed that the mayor's 29-year-old son Henry, the city's superintendent of motor transport, had made money on property he sold to the city. The *News* also reported that Maureen Keane, 32, director of the city's complaint department, had profited on a similar sale. According to the *News* story, young Hubbard had bought a home in 1968 for $16,000 and sold it to the city less than three years later for $24,950; Keane had bought a home in 1969 for $6,000 and sold it for $8,950, also in less than three years. Both buildings were demolished by the city, Hubbard's for a park and Keane's for an urban renewal project. The Michigan attorney general's office said the sales apparently violated the state's 1968 conflict-of-interest law.

Keane defended her deal, saying, "All of my land transactions have been on the record. There has been nothing underhanded." The mayor said he had no comment, telling the *News*, "I don't care what you print as long as it is accurate." But later, in a taped interview with Joyce Hagelthorn, editor of the *Dearborn Press*, Hubbard sounded just short of apoplectic.[4]

In the interview, portions of which were deleted in the *Press*'s version, Hubbard raged over the apparent leak in city hall responsible for tipping the *News* about the land deals: "I'd like to get the son of a bitch who instigated the goddamn story, . . . and I'd put it [a gun] right between his eyes and I'd pull the trigger, right through his goddamn brain, blow it right out of his head, whoever he is. . . .

"It never was his [Henry Hubbard's] idea. It was mine. He never did want to sell. He doesn't know anything about real estate. He sold his house for less than anybody else. . . . Miss Keane . . . bought the same as anyone else can buy property. . . .

"The whole inference is that someone stole something or did something illegal or something wrong, and there was nothing wrong in the world about it. . . .

"I've been in this town since 1929. I have one piece of property, the only piece I ever bought. If I'd been interested in making money in this town, . . . I could've gotten rich, the way property is moving up."

Within a week of the disclosure, State Senator Jack Faxon, a Detroit Democrat and coauthor of the conflict-of-interest law, asked the attorney general to issue an opinion on the land deals. And two Dearborn homeowners' groups, one of them headed by the mayor's old antagonist Doug Thomas, requested an investigation by the county prosecutor or perhaps a grand jury.

Eight months later, in December, the prosecutor's office announced it would not pursue either the Keane or the Henry Hubbard case, even though they might involve misdemeanors. "While there apparently is a conflict of interest in each of these cases," Assistant Prosecutor Leo Cahalan told reporters, "our investigation revealed no fraud or collusion." A report by the prosecutor's staff noted that both deals were handled in routine transactions with the city and that real estate experts concluded that the prices were reasonable. The report advised the city to follow condemnation proceedings in future land dealings with city employees.

It may have appeared to many to be a curious approach to law enforcement, in effect absolving public officials of wrongdoing because neither they nor their public employer recognized a conflict of interest when it occurred. However, a few months later, when the next city election campaign was under way, the Dearborn land deals never even became an issue.

By 1973, Orville Hubbard was in his thirty-second year as mayor, and his most formidable obstacles were well behind him. Now, as he approached his fifteenth term in office, he launched a campaign that was one of the city's most historically significant—and also surely one of its least suspenseful.

In March, the mayor's first challenger for the August primary made himself known. He was Walter A. Roman, an unemployed marketing analyst whose primary qualification was that he had run thirteenth in the 1970 council race as a Hubbard slater who tried to establish his identity by urging voters to "keep Dearborn clean with Roman cleanser."

Two more candidates announced by June: Irene M. Strong, a housewife, and John A. Pazzanese, a government teacher at Detroit's Austin Prep School. Strong said she would base her campaign on the "need for telling the truth," adding, "Politics is a dirty word, and I won't have any part of it." Pazzanese, an old friend of Henry Hubbard's, had run dead last in a 14-person field as a Hubbard slater in the 1970 council race. Now he said he wouldn't attack Orvie and, if elected, would ask him to stay on as an adviser. "I want him as our elder statesman," he said. "He should be out on the 'Johnny Carson Show' and out at conferences telling people about Dearborn." Pazzanese also pledged to work for a public transit system with modest fares, a daycare program for the children of working mothers and a 5-percent cut in property taxes.

Hubbard, issuing a campaign statement noting, "There's no substitute for experience," filed his petitions in June—as usual, just before the deadline.

One noteworthy absentee among the candidates was Doug Thomas, who had taken out petitions in June but then decided against another run at Orvie.

Strong began her campaign by improving on an old Hubbard tactic and using her high school graduation picture in her literature. She announced a platform that included requiring a five-dollar "license" of patrons at go-go joints and restoring the onions in the hamburgers at Camp Dearborn.[5] Pazzanese, in a move hardly calculated to boost his prospects, revealed that his students had conducted a poll in July showing that 82 percent of the sample preferred Hubbard and only 7 percent himself.

With hardly a sidelong glance at his challengers, Hubbard barreled through the primary with an 84-percent majority, totaling 12,664 votes to 1,321 for Pazzanese, 539 for Roman and 473 for Strong. Fewer than 25 percent of the registered voters bothered to go to the polls, and the mayor didn't even call out his traditional "pony express" service to bring in tabulations. He carried every precinct, with a low mark of 59 percent in the south end and 76 percent in Eugene-Porath. He even beat Pazzanese 116 to 28 in the challenger's home precinct. Council incumbents swept the top seven spots. Of the 24 candidates, 14 had managed to find a spot on the Hubbard slate, including all the incumbents except independent Ken Budny. Two weeks after the primary, the council put a proposal on the November ballot to raise the mayor's pay from $25,000 to $32,000, later amending the figure to $35,000.

The closest Hubbard and Pazzanese came to a confrontation was at a neighborhood association meeting two weeks before the general election. Pazzanese politely criticized the mayor's volunteer fireman program and a few other aspects of his administration, then said, "I admire the mayor. There's plenty Orville Hubbard can contribute, but he should do it as our elder statesman." Hubbard snapped back at the volunteer fireman statement. "This young man doesn't know what he's talking about," he said, but concluded by urging him, "Don't give up. If you hang on, someday you might make it."

But someday was not this year. With less than 48 percent of the voters turning out, the lowest percentage for a general election in Dearborn history, Hubbard collected more than 82 percent of the vote, 24,952 to 5,301. Again, he swept every precinct, including a vote of 209 to 63 in the challenger's home precinct. Even the pay raise proposition almost passed, losing out only 14,179 to 14,092. Only Budny broke up the Hubbard stranglehold on the council race by finishing fifth. The other Hubbard incumbents—Ed Dombrowski, Thomas Dolan, John Grecu, Van Mericas, John Baja and William Reeves—all won reelection. The mayor's remaining slate member, Henry Doman, finished eighth. And John Jay Hubbard easily won reelection as city clerk.

Hubbard's only postelection promise was to watch his health by losing another 75 pounds during his new term. "As long as the people desire my services and as long as I feel physically and mentally able to serve," he said, "I will serve until my last breath."

41

The Stroke, 1974

I'm all shot. I'm all shot.
—Orville L. Hubbard to Maureen Keane[1]

Almost everything seemed to be going Orville Hubbard's way as he settled into his fifteenth term as Dearborn's mayor. Even though voters had turned down a $10,000 pay raise proposal in the last election, Hubbard became eligible for a raise of $11,000, boosting his salary to $36,000, effective in 1974. The windfall was authorized a few weeks after the election by a compensation commission appointed by the mayor and confirmed by the council under a 1972 state law. The commission also voted raises for the clerk, treasurer and council. By this time, the mayor also could sit back as construction began on an $18-million luxury hotel, the centerpiece of Ford's massive, central-city Fairlane development project and part of the biggest building boom in Dearborn's history. In addition, he unveiled the latest version of his annual community improvement program, a $50-million package that included a new auditorium, a golf course outside the city, an outdoor tennis complex, an outdoor pool and three more apartments for seniors.

And he appeared healthier than he had in years. Although he often cheated on his rice diet, he claimed his weight was down to 249, the lightest he had been in perhaps 20 years. His diet kick even turned out to be a publicity bonanza for him when he ordered 18 department heads to lose weight or lose their jobs. A weigh-in for his slimmed-down appointees a few weeks later netted the mayor live interviews on network TV and radio, as well as front-page stories in newspapers in Los Angeles ("Dearborn mayor orders an end to waist in government"), Miami and other cities around the world.

Hubbard appeared to be enjoying himself thoroughly, devoting less energy to the daily routine of city hall and, under a 1972 state law, beginning to perform marriages in a big way, often as many as 20 or 30 a week.

In August, he smoothed over a flare-up with son John, who had threatened for the second time to resign as city clerk. This time, John had tried to fire a female staff worker, only to have his father transfer her to the mayor's office. "I found out he has the real power around here," groused young Hubbard as he stalked off the job. But a week later, returning after a long talk with his father, he announced contritely, "I guess I bit off my nose to spite my face."

The only political activity around town in 1974 was a scheduled election to replace the retiring Ralph Guy Sr. as district judge. The contenders were the city attorney, Joseph J. Burtell, and a local lawyer, Royal Targan. Burtell, who had resigned his city post to run, had collected endorsements from several councilmen, although Orvie himself was staying neutral. He was staying neutral, that is, until Targan made him so mad he decided to go all out for Burtell. Since Burtell was using photos of himself and the mayor together, Targan got Orvie to pose with him, too. But the attorney's flyer, distributed door to door the Friday before the November 5 election, went a step farther. Accompanying a photo of Targan and the mayor was a statement, juxtaposed with Hubbard's flamboyant signature, calling Targan the only qualified candidate. As reported by the *Dearborn Press & Guide* later, the implication that the mayor was supporting Targan sent him into a fury that lasted the whole week. "I've worked for the mayor a long time," Doyne Jackson told the paper. "I have seen him mad, and I have seen him cuss. But I never saw Orville Hubbard as mad as he was over that political pamphlet. He got to talking so fast and furious that his words were sticking together."[2]

The next day, Saturday, Hubbard performed 10 weddings he had scheduled, but after each ceremony, he was back on the phone to Jackson with new orders for getting even with Targan. Jackson prepared a press release describing the mayor as "damn mad" and accusing Targan's camp of forging his signature. "Never have I witnessed such a foxy, unethical, malicious, immoral and dirty campaign scheme," the release quoted Hubbard. The mayor also left it to Jackson to work out details of a flyer zinging Targan and to arrange a Sunday morning meeting with Burtell and his campaign manager, Fred Hoffman, managing editor of the *Press & Guide*. Then Hubbard went out for dinner with son John, Maureen Keane and longtime friend Floyd Haight, a retired teacher and member of the City Historical Commission.

"The mayor had been complaining of a headache all day," Keane later was quoted. "He was really grouchy over this political campaign incident. He was acting pretty mean." The group ate at Detroit's Roma Cafe after leaving the mayor's favorite restaurant, Joe Muer's, where, Keane said, he "blew up and began yelling at the head waiter."

After stopping at Haight's home after dinner to look at old photos, Hubbard nodded off, and Haight remarked that he looked ill. Then the mayor and Keane left for her apartment on Dearborn's northeast boundary with Detroit. Still out of sorts over the election and still bothered by his headache, Hubbard ate half a chicken and nearly a pound of grapes before going to bed. The next morning, he felt worse, and Keane called Jackson to cancel the meeting with Burtell.

While Keane was on the phone with her father, Hubbard got up to open a window. Moments later, he staggered back and fell, and Keane rushed over. She later described the scene to the *Press & Guide*.[3]

"I'm all shot," Orvie sobbed. "My teeth are no good. Now my hand is gone. My feet are gone. I'm all shot. I'm all shot."

She helped him up from where he was kneeling and guided him to the kitchen table. She poured him a glass of orange juice, but he dropped it. He wanted to lie down. As she got him to the bed, his right hand fell over his face. "Get your hand off my face," he yelled.

"That is not my hand," she answered. "It's yours."

Keane then got on the phone, summoning the mayor's youngest son, Henry Ford Hubbard, and Dearborn Fire Chief Gino Polidori. About two and a half hours after the attack, Polidori called for an ambulance. Two minutes later, fire fighters Jerome Vigilante and Jerry McLean arrived, strapped the mayor onto a stretcher and took off for Detroit's Henry Ford Hospital.

An arteriogram indicated a clot in a major artery on the left side of the brain. Early Monday morning, attendants wheeled Hubbard into surgery, and a half-hour later a team of neurosurgeons went to work. The clot they removed after two and a half hours was as big as a tennis ball. Later, as he lay in critical condition, doctors said that Orville Hubbard was paralyzed on his right side and had suffered some speech impairment. The stroke would have killed 75 percent of its victims, and the surgery would have claimed another 5 to 10 percent, they said.[4]

"He's doing as well as can be expected for a man who has been through what he has in the past 24 hours," said Dr. H. Speed Rogers, one of the surgeons.

42

Life with Keane, 1966-74

What was he doing in Miss Keane's apartment that
Sunday?
> —Pete Waldmeir in the *Detroit News*[1]

The first thing men noticed about Maureen Keane—nobody ever called her
by her given name of Mary Josephine—was her hair. Strawberry blond,
combed back from her forehead, cascading down to her shoulders. She was
short, only five-foot-two, but a looker. Full-breasted, blue eyes, good teeth,
high cheekbones. She had a sort of hard, streetwise air about her, but maybe
that was just the natural result of growing up in a family with four brothers
and a father who was known around town as a hard drinker. "I'm not as
brassy as some people think," she once had protested.

Not everyone at city hall appreciated her self-assured, take-charge style—
or the inside track she obviously had with Orville Hubbard. When the
mayor went out with a group for lunch, Maureen was usually along, and
he seemed to have more time for phone calls from her than from his other
department heads.

Once, during one of our talks in his office, he displayed an easy familiarity on the phone with her that didn't exactly bespeak a standard employer-
employee relationship. "She's telling me that she loves me," he said in a
whispered aside. Then, bantering with her: "I'm not telling Dave about your
love, no. Oh, no, no. You tell Dave. You're in better position than I am. You
know what the next word is goes with 'love'? . . . 'Loyalty.' You remember
a queen getting her neck cut off for being disloyal?"

Most of the time, however, Hubbard was much more guarded. Maureen
Keane was the one subject he wouldn't talk about. Toward the end of our
interviews, when asked what he wanted me to write about their relationship, he replied, "If you're smart, you won't do anything with it. Nothing.
She's a friend of mine." End of discussion.

But in the weeks that followed Hubbard's stroke in November 1974, Maureen Keane wasn't so easy to dismiss.

The day after the stroke, the *Detroit News* reported that the mayor was stricken while working at city hall; the paper attributed the information to his son John. The next day, the *Free Press* said, without attribution, that he had suffered the stroke at home. Two days after that, the *Dearborn Guide*, also without attribution, said the attack came in the mayor's East Dearborn home on Mead; the account said family members had been with him and had called the Fire Department.

It was not until several weeks later that gadfly *News* columnist Pete Waldmeir disclosed that Fire Department records placed the episode in Keane's East Dearborn apartment, on Tireman near Hubbell. "What," Waldmeir wanted to know, "was he doing in Miss Keane's apartment that Sunday? There may be a perfectly logical and plausible answer to that one. But if so, why the smokescreen?"[2] According to Waldmeir, the official report of the run to the apartment was removed from Fire Department records after Fire Chief Gino Polidori "coached" the ambulance attendants to doctor the document. When Waldmeir sought clarification from city spokesman Doyne Jackson, Jackson wouldn't give him any. "He had it at home, Pete," Jackson said. "I've gone through this with a lot of people. That's all I'm going to say."

The unspoken questions, of course, were more delicate. Did the mayor of Dearborn, all 300-odd pounds and 71 years of him, really have something going with a 34-year-old blonde? How could he? And where was his wife through all this?

As the Detroit papers began to raise questions, Orvie and Maureen fast became a favorite topic of gossip around town.

Finally, even *Guide* Publisher Bill Ross, long a social friend of the mayor's, had to acknowledge that something was up. In trying to shield Maureen from the rumor-mongering, Ross tried to explain in a column six weeks after the stroke that she was a "gal Friday" to Hubbard.[3] "Maureen, as most folks around town have long known, has been Mayor Hubbard's constant companion for years," he wrote. "Among other things, she has been his personal chauffeur and unofficial confidante."

In fact, their relationship was more serious and more stable than most of their acquaintances knew.

As she later described things to reporters, the two had been living and traveling together for more than eight years, since sometime after the mayor had left Fay Hubbard and moved his clothes and other personal effects to his suite at city hall. In leaving his home on Mead, he also left Fay in the middle of remodeling the downstairs, with the walls stripped down to the studs.

John Hubbard insisted several years later that he had had no inkling that his father actually was living with Keane. And Jackson said he had found out only after Maureen gave him her phone number when he needed to reach the mayor on business.

Orvie had taken some pains to keep things quiet. He had a standing rule for the city photographer. In group shots that included both Maureen and him, she was to be at one end or the other so the two of them would not appear to be together and so she could even be cropped out if need be before the photo went to the newspapers. And when they were out together, Orvie tried to disguise the fact by dragging along some friends or coworkers. Often, the two would drive to events separately, or at least try to make separate entrances, and they tried to avoid sitting together at public functions. If they left in a group with others, Hubbard was careful to see that he got dropped off at city hall first, and then he would meet Maureen at their apartment.

As secretive as Orvie had tried to be, Maureen occasionally was more open. Once, a few years before, she had leaked a story to the *Free Press* that the two of them were going to marry and that a glitzy, three-carat diamond she was flashing was an engagement stone from the mayor. Hubbard was quick to deny the story, but Keane raised the topic from time to time, particularly after Hubbard began performing marriages in his office.

One such occasion was a September morning in 1972, when it was raining too hard for the mayor to take one of the half-hour walks he had begun under a regimen prescribed at Duke University's weight reduction clinic. Hubbard repaired to the Dearborn Inn to eat a breakfast of six prunes and coffee with Keane, another city official and me.[4] Regaling the group with a story about a "big, fat guy" and a "little, tiny girl" whose wedding he had officiated at recently, he mused, "You wonder who would ever want her and who would ever want him. But they wanted each other."

"Look at you and I, Orville," Maureen put in.

Then, wondering aloud why January and June are such popular months for weddings, he asked, "If you're gonna get married, why the hell don't you get married, instead of waiting . . ."

"Yeah, why the hell don't we?" she interjected. "Ha, ha."

". . . For seven months?" he asked, finishing his own question.

"Or 13 years?" she shot back.

The next morning, back at the inn after his morning walk, the pair continued their teasing. The mayor, noting that he had 20-20 distance vision even though he wore glasses for reading, noticed that a nearby waitress had brown eyes.

Keane: "You just keep looking straight ahead, Orville. Someday I'll find somebody that wants to support me."

Hubbard: "Is that what you're looking for?"

Keane: "No. I just want you. I want to stay around and make your life miserable. Ha, ha."

Hubbard: "You're doing a good job of it. . . . You're doing all right.

Sort of a charmer.... I've been nice to you since you were a little girl."

Keane: "Yeah, little girl. I've been captured, like they go out in the jungle and capture the baby cubs."

Actually, the simile wasn't all that far-fetched. When she was six, as she recalled it, she had wandered into city hall, a half-block from her parents' East Dearborn home, on her way to school. One of the mayor's secretaries, thinking her lost, took her in to see him, and Maureen explained, in a precocious bit of smart-assery, that she wasn't lost but that her brothers were. "He sat me on his lap and told his secretary he was available any time I came in," she told me.[5] The little girl came back the next day, and the visits got to be something of a habit. "My parents didn't believe me at first when I said I knew the mayor, but we really got to be friends," she continued. "He'd give me good advice, too. Sometimes he'd give me a nickel and he'd tell me to go brush my teeth. He even taught me how to type when I was about nine."

In July 1957, when she was 17, Maureen Keane took a job in the mayor's office as a part-time receptionist and recording secretary. After graduating from Fordson High School the next year, she took the job full-time. She attended business and psychology classes at Henry Ford Community College over the next two years while working at city hall, but she left in February 1960 to take a job as a United Air Lines stewardess. Hubbard helped her get the job.

The mayor had been taking a personal hand in promoting her interests before that, however. In 1959, when Municipal Judge George Martin was organizing a St. Patrick's Day program, Hubbard assigned Maureen and Veteran's Bureau Director John O'Reilly to help out. When it came to selecting a parade queen, it happened that Hubbard knew of a Dearborn girl whose parents had come over from Ireland and moved practically next-door to city hall. She was five-foot-two, 107 pounds, a blue-eyed blonde who was a freshman at the community college. Best of all, her birthday was on St. Patrick's Day; she would turn 19 on the day of the parade. What else could he do? The mayor picked Maureen Keane as the city's St. Patrick's Day queen. "March 17, 1959," Hubbard later recalled. "Jesus Christ, was that a cold day.... I remember she had nothing to wear. Christ, she looked like a lobster that had just been boiled, she was so red."

While working at city hall, Maureen was dating a young man who worked as a city hall publicist, and, she recalled in a later interview published by the *News*, Hubbard "made it possible for me to be where my young man would be most of the time. The mayor really tried to help me hook him, short of ordering him to marry me, of course." But, she added, after three years of dating, the young man began going with an airline stewardess, and she took the job with United. A few years later, the young man proposed to Maureen, and she turned him down.

When she left for stewardess training, Hubbard gave her a small photo of himself with this message typed on the back: "To Maureen: One of the nicest and sharpest secretaries we ever had. I have admired you since you were a little girl. You have grown up so fast and left us, and we miss you and your smiling blue eyes. We need you and hope you will return soon. With love and my very best of good wishes to you, and I hope you'll always be cheerful and happy and that your pretty blue eyes will always sparkle. Pops."[6]

At first, she told interviewers later, her "love for him was that of a daughter for a father," and she "became one of his children." But when he flew to Denver to pin her United graduation wings on her, she realized there was more to it than that, she said. "It was a strange feeling, but I knew that more than anything in the world I wanted to be with the mayor, and I found he wanted to be with me as much," she told the *News*.[7] She said he phoned her and wrote letters every day, and, as she later explained it to *Monthly Detroit* magazine, "There was never anything romantic between us until I went away. It was the first time I had ever been away from home and I was naturally scared. His phone calls and letters kept me going. He was my advisor and protector."[8]

When the airline transferred her back to Detroit in 1966, Maureen began working part-time in the city's Service Department, although she continued officially with United until July 1967. In August, Hubbard hired her to head the department full-time at $14,000 a year. "When I came back to town and he asked me to run the citizen complaint bureau, that's when I fell in love with him," she told *Monthly Detroit*. "He had been separated from his wife for years."[9] She told the *News*, "I knew I had to be near him. I probably could have married a millionaire or two while I was flying, but as I look back, I know there really has never been anyone else for me but the mayor."[10]

Judy Cord, a good friend of Maureen's since grade school, had come to work for the mayor at Maureen's encouragement in 1959. As she recollected, Maureen had a burgeoning friendship with Hubbard for several years before that. "I always remember her talking about knowing him as kids," she said, "and on her sixteenth birthday she asked if I wouldn't go with her to 'Cinerama,' that he would take us. He took us down to 'Cinerama' and then to dinner at the Dearborn Inn. I think that was probably the first time I had seen them together. She said to me one time, 'He can do anything, and I mean anything. If you want anything, he can do it.' . . . She really felt that he was all-knowing and all-powerful."[11]

Not surprisingly, Hubbard's obvious affection for his young protégée produced its share of tension in the office, especially when Fay Hubbard came around. Cord recalled, "He got very angry at me one time over the fact that he took Mrs. Hubbard to get glasses or something, and Maureen was looking for him. And he told me, 'Don't tell anyone where I'm going.' And she said, 'Oh, please tell me,' and I told her, and, oh, he had a fit. Did he holler and scream. 'And I'm gonna fire your ass out of here'—that's what he told me. He put his finger up to my nose. 'I'm gonna tell you something right now. I am never gonna marry that girl, no matter what she tells you. If you wanna work for me, you don't tell her anything.'"12

Hubbard moved into Keane's two-bedroom walkup apartment after she returned to Dearborn in 1966, although she continued to tell reporters she lived with her parents.

The mayor himself became increasingly protective about his relationship with her. No longer so altruistic about her other beaus as he had been when she was a teenager, Hubbard went to great lengths to solidify his position. "Whenever she had a boyfriend, Orville would destroy it," Judy Cord recounted. "He would somehow miraculously get the fellow's name and address, and he'd write him a letter and sign her father's name, or call him, tell him it was her father and that would be the end of them. But she never knew how he got it. There was a dignitary that came from Washington for Memorial Day stuff. He was a lieutenant colonel or something, and evidently was smitten with her at the time he was here and went back to Washington and wrote her a love letter, was gonna divorce his wife. And then somehow Orville got a hold of it and mailed it to his wife."13

The Hubbard-Keane pairing—almost inevitably, it seemed—was a combative one. Friends and observers often remarked that the two always seemed to be fighting but that both seemed to enjoy the tension and that their affection for each other did not suffer because of it. A few months before their father's death, the mayor's two oldest sons, Jim and Frank, compared notes about the battles.

"I was in a car with her one time driving," Jim recalled, "and Keane reached across the backseat and whacked him right in the face. Man, I'd never seen my old man struck in the face before. He'd turn around in the car and he'd be whacking her out in the backseat. One time, he was chasing her around the filing cabinets, and O'Reilly just happened to walk in, and she'd say, 'Chief, save me.' And the old man said, 'Get out,' and O'Reilly ran out, jumped in his car and went to a bar somewhere."14

Put in Frank: "They had an argument in a restaurant one time. She stuck a fork in him. I guess he knocked her off the stool or something."15

Jim Helmrich, who accompanied his wife, Mary, on frequent out-of-town trips with Maureen and the mayor, added, "She could give him hell and talk up to him. You couldn't drive with them for an hour without them fighting about something. But they'd forget about it. I honestly do believe that they both thrived on this."16

Through all the fighting, the machinations and the petty jealousies, and despite the hazards of public disclosure, Maureen Keane and Orville Hubbard endured as a couple. Hubbard's dynamic personality continued to fascinate the younger woman, though some of those who knew them figured it was just a matter of time before she extracted what she wanted from the relationship and then moved on to something else.

When the stroke cut him down in 1974, they were sure of it—at first. As she herself had acknowledged, most people thought of her then as "the mayor's hussy" or "the harlot."[17]

But some observers were more sympathetic, even those who were not aligned with her at city hall. Observed Doyne Jackson, "She paid a price. She was branded to the whole world as just a glorified whore—high-paying job because she slept with him. But I've got no doubt at all they loved each other."[18]

Helmrich said he and his wife had a more charitable view than most of the mayor's more casual acquaintances. "We saw a side of Maureen that was one of a very caring, loyal person," he told me. "It was an unusual relationship, but it was one that he just reveled in, you might say, because of the brightness she brought into his life. Maureen dearly loved that man, but I think as a father more than anything else."[19]

Shortly after the stroke, Maureen Keane and her brother Noel, a Dearborn attorney whom Hubbard several years earlier had encouraged to enter law school while working as a police clerk, began soliciting $1,000 donations from city department heads and others to buy the mayor a $34,000 condominium to live in after his release from the hospital.[20] But they failed to collect enough to complete the plan after John Hubbard told reporters, "The Hubbard family does not endorse begging. There is adequate space in his children's homes or in his own home when he's released from the hospital."

Meanwhile, Maureen had been taking charge of things at the hospital, spending uncounted hours at Hubbard's bedside and constantly shooing others out of his room. She served as his personal nurse around the clock, except for appearances she put in at city hall to see how her department was doing. The *Guide*'s Fred Hoffman later credited her "constant care and concern" with saving the mayor's life during his recovery.[21] As Jackson later put it, "She slept down there in his room. Your wife would hire a nurse to do things for you that Maureen did for that man. Yeah, she was paid all the time she was doing that, but there were no other department heads that were working their 40 hours a week to enhance his life. She was."[22]

However, her devotion to Orville Hubbard seemed only to antagonize the mayor's family members, most of whom looked in on the patriarch only infrequently. City hall insiders told of drawn-out arguments between Maureen and Fay Hubbard in the hospital hallway. Then there was the time when Fay and her daughter, Nancy Dmytro, reportedly squared off with Maureen over the mayor's release from the hospital. "They were arguing— Fay and Nancy with Maureen and the mayor," recounted Annette Ross, whose husband, Bill, lay dying in the hospital room next to Hubbard's. "And the mayor was saying, 'No, no, no, no.' They [the family] were all set to take him from there. Maureen was set to take him back to her apartment. Fay and Nancy were really fighting to take him, and he would not go with them. They left, and he was crying. He went with Maureen. I was right there."[23]

But if Maureen Keane had put herself in the position of having to battle with her old friend's family over his care, it was not a decision she had made lightly. Annette Ross, who, with her husband, often went out with the mayor and his younger companion, told of a heart-to-heart talk she had with Maureen in the mid-1960s:[24] "She was 25 at the time. I said, 'You're a beautiful girl. You know he's never gonna divorce Fay. He's never gonna marry you. You have a right to a family and children. You know what's gonna happen: 10 or 15 years down the road, he's gonna be an old man and you're gonna be in the prime of your life. He's gonna have a stroke or a heart attack, and you're gonna end up being a nursemaid.' And she says, 'Annette, I love him enough that if that's the way it's gonna be, I'll take it as it comes.'" Some nine years later, as Annette Ross was visiting her husband at Ford Hospital, she recalled, "Maureen and I went out and we were eating, and she looked at me and said, 'I remember what you told me when I was 25 years old, and my answer today would be the same as it was then.'" And the two women went back to tend to their men. Orville Hubbard was permitted to leave the hospital with Maureen Keane, and Bill Ross died the next day.

43

The Last Hurrah, 1974-77

You know, when Orville is not the mayor anymore, we
will lose the most colorful and glamorous politician
that has ever lived.
—Frank Hubbard, announcing that his father would
not run again

At last, Orville Hubbard had suffered the ultimate irony. The acknowledged
master of political bombast, the man who had choked off one opponent
after another with a torrent of press releases and nonstop vituperation, had
been silenced. He could not read or write, and when he tried to speak in
sentences of more than one or two words, his brain twisted everything up
into an incoherent babble. In medical terms, he was a victim of aphasia, an
impairment in language powers. Even in the most fortunate cases, doctors
knew, the condition cleared up only after years of speech therapy.

In addition to his speech problems, Hubbard was paralyzed on one side.
He could sit up in a wheelchair, but he couldn't use his right arm or leg.
One good sign, however, was that Ford Hospital visitors and medical staffers
alike remarked right from the start at how alert the patient was and how
well he seemed to understand what was said to him. The month after the
stroke, Doyne Jackson told reporters, "He's got total awareness, but he's not
up to coming back and making decisions yet."

But at least there seemed to be some hope that Hubbard might make
it back to city hall. Dr. Boy Frame, an internist who was his attending
physician at the hospital, released a statement that noted he had "shown
significant improvement, particularly in the area of speech therapy."

In the meantime, the city was running on the equivalent of automatic
pilot. As provided by the charter, Council President Edward Dombrowski,
58, assumed some of Hubbard's duties, although as acting mayor he had
no veto power over the council and no removal power over department
heads. Dombrowski, whose nearly 25 years made him the city's longest-

tenured councilman ever, was regarded as Orvie's most dependable supporter. But he was a tight-to-the-vest politician who could be counted on not to rush major decisions. His colleagues were sure enough of his lack of ambition that they reelected him council president unanimously the next month, in January 1975, so that he could continue as acting mayor and leave everybody else at an equal disadvantage when it came time to name a permanent successor to Hubbard. A few weeks later, Dombrowski caused a bit of a stir when he announced he would ask Hubbard to recommend him for the job "if the mayor feels he should retire," but, getting no immediate encouragement, he decided not to work full-time at being mayor. Instead, he told reporters, he would keep his job as a project engineer at a broach and machine company and work evenings and weekends at city hall. To coordinate the daily routine, he named one of the brightest but most abrasive personalities on the Hubbard team as chief administrator: Recreation Director Robert Keith Archer, who held a master's degree in public administration.

By late January, Hubbard's reported weight was 245, his lowest since the 1950s, and he was reported continuing to do well with speech therapy. In addition, his daily sessions with a physical therapist had gotten him to the point where he could walk a few steps. His doctors let him make a brief visit to his office one Sunday afternoon and also gave the go-ahead for weekend trips to Camp Dearborn and elsewhere.

The mayor's itinerary failed to quiet rumblings about his inability to perform in office, however. Among the most impatient was Doug Thomas, who appeared at the first council meeting in February to demand that officials "clear the air" by getting a definitive statement on Orvie's condition. A month later, Thomas presented the city clerk with a petition demanding an ouster hearing for Hubbard under charter provisions mandating the mayor's removal if he were absent from his duties for 60 days.

Hubbard, who had passed the 60-day mark in early January, was recuperating from his first major setback since his original stroke. Although newspapers reported that he had suffered a small second stroke in February, doctors concluded that his problem was a urinary tract infection. The medical staff had to catheterize Hubbard at that point, and the mayor became such an uncooperative patient that Keane terminated his inpatient rehabilitation programs. "I sat there one afternoon," Jackson said in an interview, "and they worked with him over an hour on the word 'water.' He'd throw things at the therapist—books, flower vases—he'd get so frustrated. She cut that off. There's no reason that you can't continue to take walking [rehabilitation] from a catheter, but Maureen determined that that upset her Orville. Once they stopped the oral rehab and the physical rehab, he seemed to degenerate down to just an existence."[1] Dr. Frame issued a statement noting deterioration in Hubbard's mobility, as well as further impairment in speech and writing: "There is evidence that he still comprehends what is being said to him. His minimal ability to communicate makes this difficult to thoroughly assess."[2]

As if to refute Dr. Frame, Maureen Keane took her charge out for three rides the next week, one of them delivering him to city hall minutes after Thomas's petitions were filed. The mayor's response on being told about his old antagonist's maneuver was simply to shrug.

The mayor had his believers, though. A laid-off janitor collected more than 1,000 signatures on pro-Hubbard petitions in three days, and several councilmen indicated they were prepared to let the mayor stay on indefinitely. "There's just no way that we're going to kick him out of office," remarked Councilman Van Mericas. "No way."

Hubbard was discharged from the hospital in mid-March, 19 weeks after his admittance. Keane took him back to her apartment, arranging for him to undergo speech and physical therapy on an outpatient basis at Ford Hospital. In one of his first public appearances, he rode in Detroit's annual St. Patrick's Day parade.

Petition circulators filed more than 4,000 signatures supporting Hubbard in March. And on his birthday, the first week of April, he received several hundred greetings.

Meanwhile, Thomas was having trouble with his petitions. City Attorney William Hultgren invalidated most of Thomas's signatures—for technical reasons, he said. Thomas said he would file more petitions and accused the city of delaying. Thomas made good his threat, but not before he was upstaged by Councilman John Baja, who signed papers calling for a council hearing on the mayor's competence, thus eliminating the need for the petition procedure. "I'm not here to knock the mayor down," Baja declared at a May council meeting. "I think this town needs a mayor immediately, and I want to have a hearing to take the pressure off the council." Baja, a sometime Hubbard opponent who had run on the mayor's slate in 1973, stood firm when John and Frank Hubbard accused him of trying to further his own mayoral ambitions by participating in the "opportunistic onslaught."

Nearly in tears, John Hubbard asked Baja, "as a fellow public official," to withdraw his request. "When a man is down, give him a chance to get back up," he said. A few minutes later, his brother, now serving on the City Plan Commission, added, "When Mayor Hubbard operates at 100 percent, there is nobody who can match his energy. At 75 percent he still has more faculty than Councilman Baja or Mr. Thomas put together at 100 percent."

The council, however, accepted both the Baja request for a removal hearing and a new petition from Thomas. The hearing was to be held within 30 days after the mayor was served with the paperwork. Dombrowski adjourned the meeting just as Thomas left his seat to speak.

At the next council meeting in May, Baja, who was on record saying that the council would keep Orvie in office, nonetheless moved to grant him a pension of $36,000, equal to his salary, if he decided to retire. No one seconded the motion.

While the machinery for his removal had thus been started, Hubbard apparently was perking up. He had begun taking drives again and watching school parades connected to the city's annual cleanup campaign. Residents would applaud the familiar figure in the dark blue Ford, and children would gather to shake hands or take his picture.

In June, as he was being wheeled into the Youth Center for a dinner honoring 25-year city employees, he was intercepted by a young woman who asked, "Are you Mayor Hubbard?" When he said yes, she dropped a piece of paper into his lap and ran off. Hubbard hardly seemed to notice it, but Maureen Keane grabbed it and threw it to the floor. The young woman was Thomas's daughter Debbie, 19, and the paper was a copy of the removal petition. Hubbard had been served.

Councilmen scheduled the competency hearing for their next regular meeting, June 17. They would receive medical testimony and then would vote on removing the mayor as incompetent to discharge his duties under the charter. Hubbard himself would not testify and would not even be required to attend. The meeting was to begin at 8:00 P.M. By 6:30, all 200-odd seats in the council chamber were taken, and during the next hour and a half, another 600 pilgrims ventured out into the muggy evening air to see firsthand whether their mayor would be stripped of his duties. They stood against the walls of the council chamber, spilling out into the hallway, down the circular staircase, through the first-floor corridor and out into the parking lot behind city hall. City officials, who already had set up loudspeakers through the building and parking lot, said it was the largest crowd ever to attend a Dearborn council session. Many of the attendees, caught up in the spirit of the moment, spent four dollars each on green-and-white "I Support Orville L. Hubbard" T-shirts being hawked by Keane's brother Jerry, a printer, who said proceeds would go to the mayor's legal fund or favorite charity. Doug Thomas arrived with his attorney a few minutes before 8:00 to a round of hissing from a cross-section of the audience.

As the first order of business, Deputy City Clerk William Karr began reading the charges of "physical and/or mental incompetency" against the mayor. He was interrupted when the crowd outside the chamber let out a roar. Orville Hubbard, smiling and waving from his wheelchair, was being borne up the circular staircase like an imperial potentate by four burly attendants, one of them his policeman son Jim. As he was rolled in to take his usual spot beside the council table, the crowd jumped up and cheered. For six minutes they cheered. News photographers and TV cameramen rushed over as the mayor of Dearborn waved to his subjects with his good left hand and exchanged a teary-eyed greeting with Fay Hubbard, there with other family members in the fourth row.

Then Karr, returning to the matter at hand, finished the charges and

360

started reading affidavits on Hubbard's condition. Ford Hospital's Dr. Frame, on the basis of a recent examination, wrote that the mayor's "modest recovery" after his stroke "has now plateaued and I would not expect him to exhibit any additional significant improvement in the future with regards to his paralysis or ability to speak."[3] A more optimistic assessment came from Dr. M. Meyer Pensler, a Dearborn Medical Center surgeon who said he examined Hubbard several times in the hospital and after his release.[4] "There has been good progress," he wrote. ". . . He is mentally alert, clear, and understands anything that is told to him." Noting that the mayor could speak many short words clearly, was learning to write his name left-handed and could walk with a leg brace and cane, the physician said he felt that with more therapy, "the outlook for more improvement is good." Two other affidavits—from physical therapist Harish Bisht and speech therapist Mitzi Weitzman—also remarked on the progress Hubbard had made since they began working with him in April. Weitzman, noting the mayor's strong motivation to regain his language skills, said, "Further recovery can surely be expected."[5]

According to Jackson, Dr. Frame's assessment came as a surprise to city officials, and Dr. Pensler's opinion was solicited by Keane. Dr. Frame, Jackson said in a subsequent interview, "is the guy that kept telling us, 'There's always a chance,' but when he put it on paper, he said he [Hubbard] was done.'" As for Dr. Pensler, Jackson said, "That was Maureen's doing. She's a good friend of the Penslers."[6]

Speaking for Thomas and the removal petition signers, attorney Dwight Vincent did his best to act as though the outcome of the hearing were still in doubt, arguing that the mayor should resign if he could not assure the council that he would return to work shortly. Vincent was booed roundly.

Hubbard's attorney, B. Ward Smith, delivered a rebuttal, arguing that the medical affidavits tended to support Hubbard's staying on the job. Smith pointed out that there was no evidence the mayor was failing to perform his duties. Indeed, he said, his client had been attending ceremonial events in recent weeks and had attended that night's hearing when he didn't have to. Smith also observed that Hubbard didn't have to recover all his abilities in order to return to work. He quipped, "It's not the duty of the mayor to sign his name with his right hand."

Actually, as Smith saw things, there was no legal reason for the council even to bother hearing witnesses. He had told councilmen before the meeting, "What you have on your hands is a political decision. You don't have to justify it. Council does not need a reason not to remove Hubbard under the charter." That meant that the whole proceeding, in effect, was just show-biz. After several councilmen made brief statements of support for the mayor, John Grecu cut the hourlong hearing off with a motion to retain Hubbard in office for the duration of his term. To no one's surprise, it carried seven to nothing.

Bedlam. The crowd cheered madly. Men rushed up to shake the mayor's hand. Women rushed up to kiss him, including one in dark glasses and a brown wig who still was unmistakable as Maureen Keane. Thomas stalked out.

"This is Russia," grumbled Thomas, already upset because his father had died of a stoke earlier in the day. "We didn't get the facts tonight, and there aren't too many people—even Hubbard supporters—who do not think this was a whitewash. The mayor didn't prove he was competent. All he proved is that he's got seven of his boys up there on the council."

As for Hubbard, who stayed on as the council took up its slate of routine business after the hearing, the perfunctory vote must have seemed no less a victory than his 1941 upset of John Carey or his 1951 crushing of the recall forces. It meant that the Hubbard regime was securely in place for another two and a half years, until 1978. Toward the end of the meeting, Councilman William Reeves provided just the right touch of cornball obeisance, telling Orvie, "You've shown again tonight you're the king of mayors." Hubbard waved and nodded.

Though he was under no direct pressure to do so now, the mayor started back to work the next week, attending his first department head meeting in more than seven months.

According to a local newspaper column written later by Archer, Dombrowski's choice to supervise the city's daily administration, the mayor had lost little of his sense of command. Archer walked in two minutes late for Hubbard's second department head meeting, he wrote, and the mayor, sitting at the head of the table again, "looked at me, frowned, slapped the table decisively with his left hand and pointed at the clock. With a lump in my throat, I took my seat and thought, 'Mayor Hubbard, it's good to have you back.'"

But for all the appearances, it was problematical how much influence Hubbard really could have running city hall. When asked later about the extent of the mayor's input, Jackson replied, "Zero. I think in the very early stages he could comprehend, but no one will ever know if he was comprehending like an 8-year-old or a 68-year-old. If we could've gotten an authoritative statement from the Henry Ford medical crew very early in the game that this man would never be able to function again, the thing to have done would've been to purge him out of office gracefully and politely. If I knew what I know now, and I could turn the clock back, I think I'd have told the newspapers, 'This man will never be able to rule again,' and give them the parts of Frame's quotes that fit the situation. That is hindsight, and you rule out emotion and everything else."[7]

Hubbard continued to attend the department head meetings almost daily, although his speech limitations kept him from presiding. He also attempted to reintroduce other elements of his old routine, even if some of them seemed to border on self-parody. In August, he married his first couple since his stroke, raising his left hand as Keane recited the words and later scrawling his name left-handed on the marriage certificate. In November, he was readmitted to Ford Hospital with another urinary infection, spending several days in intensive care.

If Doug Thomas was frustrated at the outcome of the competency hearing, he was able to extract a measure of revenge by the end of 1975. In December, the state treasurer's office, acting on a previous complaint by Thomas, released a 38-page report detailing a five-and-a-half-month investigation into alleged irregularities by the Hubbard administration. At about the same time as the Hubbard ouster hearing in June, Thomas had asked the state to monitor the city's practice of providing cars to officials and to review the financial implications of Hubbard's wedding ceremonies. As the state began its review, city cars were turned in by three members of the Hubbard family: Fay, Jim and a granddaughter, Nancy Dmytro, who worked in the mayor's office. In July, Thomas turned over another complaint to treasury auditors. He accused department heads of paying off pro-Hubbard councilmen with cash gifts at Christmas in return for loyalty to the administration. It was a rehash of charges made several times against Hubbard, going back to the 1940s.

One former department head chose to respond publicly to the accusation. Ralph Guy Jr., former city attorney who now was federal district attorney in Detroit, acknowledged that he gave Christmas gifts to councilmen as a matter of goodwill, and he said he assumed that other Hubbard appointees did the same. He said that when he first was appointed, most department heads gave whiskey, but he gave flowers and later cash. "The concept of giving somebody $25 as a bribe is ludicrous," he said. "And because no specific vote was involved, in no way could this even remotely be considered as bribery."

If anyone else had major concerns, they were not apparent to federal officials. Guy was nominated for a federal judgeship only days after the state audit report was made public.[8] The audit report suggested no criminal activity by city officials, but it did cite a number of areas of concern. Besides confirming the conflict-of-interest findings made by the county prosecutor's office in a 1972 probe of the city's land deals with Maureen Keane and Henry Ford Hubbard, the audit found that the city's fleet of 113 cars was to be used strictly for official business, but no records were kept to indicate whether any also were used on personal business. New cars were provided to councilmen every six months under a Hubbard policy dating to the mid-1950s, apparently in violation of charter restrictions against extra remuneration and use of city property. Cars also were provided to other elected officials, department heads and other employees, including five assigned to the mayor's office. Other findings: Councilmen received nearly $10,000 in retirement and insurance benefits, another apparent charter violation. Nine units at the city's Florida apartment building were leased in conflict with announced policy that senior citizens were to have preference; Councilman Baja held one of the leases. The city had failed to collect off-street parking assessments of nearly $367,000 due from 54 business firms in lieu of paved parking facilities under a 1964 arrangement. The mayor had performed 1,745 weddings between July 1972 and November 1974, collecting $35,638 and turning back only $3,490 to the city under an ordinance requiring that a two-dollar fee be charged for each ceremony.

Although the auditors said no such thing, Thomas declared that the report proved the Hubbard administration was "corrupt." "The mayor should resign," he said. "He has been discredited and his aides have been discredited. He has violated the charter right down the line, and he owes Dearborn over $30,000 that he has pocketed from city hall weddings." He also said Keane, Henry Hubbard and several other city officials should resign with the mayor.

Predictably, most city officials pooh-poohed the report. Ken Budny, the only councilman not on the Hubbard team, called the investigation "a fishing expedition." City Attorney Hultgren reported that Orvie "did not appear overly concerned" about it.

Most damaging to Hubbard on a personal basis was the clear implication that his kitschy persona as purveyor of quickie weddings was nothing but a coverup for siphoning off money that belonged to the city. The records showed that he made $3,274 from 155 weddings in 1972, $15,967 from 905 in 1973 and $16,397 from 685 in 1974. He ranged from a low of 10 in August 1972 to a high of 98 in October 1974, the month before his stroke. Hultgren said the fees paid beyond the official two-dollar requirement were not public moneys but personal contributions, which, in any case, the mayor reported on his income tax returns. He said 54 of the weddings were free, though the mayor still sent two dollars to the city for each. As for costs incurred by the city, six photos were provided free to each couple. "He just loved doing it," Jackson later said of Hubbard's marrying bent. "He was a showman. He loved being center stage on that stuff. I think [the notion of making] the money came after the enthusiasm. I don't say it was totally unimportant, but I don't think it was the prime motivation. It was an ego thing. You know, these people really fawn over you after you marry them. He would buy 'em gifts and all that other stuff. At one point, he was giving away flowers to the brides. He bought the white runner for his office. He bought some music. I think he'd probably given away $6,000 or $8,000 [worth] of stuff. I don't think Hubbard ever dreamed that the wedding funds would be a controversy of any sort anywhere down the line. He was from the school, if you got married by the local J.P. or the mayor, you gave 'em 10 bucks. It's done all over the country."[9]

After the report was released, Thomas called for a citizens' grand jury and an investigation by Michigan Attorney General Frank Kelley. Thomas said Kelley rather than Wayne County Prosecutor William L. Cahalan should handle the probe because of a possible conflict of interest. "It's fairly common knowledge," Thomas said, "that Cahalan has been dating Maureen Keane. I don't know if there is a conspiracy between them to cover anything up, but Cahalan should disqualify himself from any investigation."

Cahalan, a widower, acknowledged Keane to be a "very dear friend of mine," but, he added, "we won't allow personal considerations to affect our operations." In any case, he said, Kelley should handle the probe because of county budget cuts.

While Kelley's office was reviewing the treasury audit, Thomas kept sniping away at Hubbard. In February 1976, he accused the mayor of an unethical deal involving the estate of a Dearborn man. He said the man, Pasko Purdoff, was moved into a senior citizens' apartment even though his assets and income were too high to qualify. The quid pro quo, according to Thomas, was that Purdoff had willed his estate to Hubbard before dying in 1973 at the age of 68. The estate was $22,290 after expenses, although sources said Hubbard later split the money with two of Purdoff's nephews who had complained about being left out. Keane, who was familiar with the case, told reporters of Purdoff, "He came into the mayor's office, and the mayor always took care of things for him. He thought he was being cheated and was deserted by his family, and he told the mayor that he was the only one who was helping him. I was there when Mr. Purdoff told the mayor about the will, and I remember the mayor protesting. I also remember Mr. Purdoff saying, 'I can give what I've got to whoever I want.'"

In March, also at the behest of Thomas, the federal Department of Housing and Urban Development (HUD) began an inquiry into Dearborn's housing commission policies of tenant selection in senior citizens' apartments. Federal funds had been used for the city's first three senior citizens' buildings. A HUD audit report in August called for administrative changes in city procedures, including improvements in file keeping.

It was not until January 1977 that the attorney general at last reported on what had become a yearlong investigation of the treasury audit. Kelley said he would prosecute no cases himself but would turn over to Cahalan the possible misdemeanor prosecution of officials who made personal use of city cars. The report noted that Baja, Dolan and Councilman George Bondie admitted such use. But, Kelley noted, while the charter seemed to prohibit personal use of cars, it set no penalties.[10]

As for the Keane and Henry Hubbard land deals, Kelley said prosecution was not warranted because the two apparently were unaware that they were violating the law. In addition, he said, they made "no attempt to hide either transaction," received only an inflation-level profit and apparently had no inside information that the city would buy the properties from them.

The report said there was nothing illegal about the fringe benefits for councilmen, the failure to collect off-street parking fees from businessmen or the leasing of apartments in Florida to tenants who were not senior citizens. The report also said the law was not violated in the Christmas gift controversy because there was no evidence that councilmen solicited the gifts. Although some told investigators that Hubbard ordered department heads to give compliant councilmen cash gifts of up to $200, others said he did not have such influence.

On the most serious charge raised by Thomas, the report said that Hubbard apparently violated the law by pocketing the extra marriage fees. Under normal circumstances, such a misdemeanor conviction could bring a 90-day jail term and $100 fine. However, according to Kelley, this case could not be prosecuted, either. The reason: the one-year statute of limitations in the case expired in November 1975, a month before the treasury audit was turned over to his office. "Every mayor in the state of Michigan was starting to marry and collect at the time," Jackson recalled. "Hubbard used to get letters from other mayors saying, 'Could you send me a copy of your wedding ceremony? How much do you charge?'"

Thomas, predictably, was incensed at the report. "It proves," he sniffed, "that it is who you know and who you can't get to as criteria for staying in office, and the action which would be criminally prosecuted for the average man is not an offense to an elected official."

Jackson, speaking for the city, said the investigation confirmed the honesty of the Hubbard administration. "Kelley isn't indicting anybody," he said. "In the wide range of things, most of these issues were aired in public view by the mayor himself during his political campaigns. All this stuff was washed before the public, and still they elected him. You can talk about criminal violations, but what Kelley is really questioning is administrative policy. If, after 35 years in office, if this is all they can rake up on Mayor Hubbard, then by political standards the man is a saint."

Thanks to the investigations and audits dating back nearly two years, Hubbard's past was undergoing much more intensive scrutiny than his present. Since his 1975 competency hearing, the mayor had continued to attend department head meetings and take his auto tours of the city. But his speech capabilities, as predicted by Dr. Frame, had indeed plateaued, and he continued to be plagued with urinary tract infections; he was hospitalized for a week in early 1976. The result was that he found himself relegated increasingly to the role of a figurehead.

In February 1976, he posed for photos with President Gerald Ford and Vice-President Nelson Rockefeller, in Detroit for a campaign. And on a note of lame-duck tokenism, in May, he was elected a GOP precinct delegate for the twelfth time since 1932.

And in between the ceremonial tasks, the mayor of Dearborn apparently was doing a lot of thinking about the old days. One day late that year, he had his driver take him to the East Dearborn home of Iva Fish, widow of his old antagonist in the 1950 libel suit. Mrs. Fish went out to the car to chat a few minutes and thank him for stopping by, and that, she thought, was that. But when the mayor repeated the visit the next day—and a few days after that—she finally asked him, "Mayor, does your conscience bother you for what you did to Jack Fish?"

"And he nodded his head," Mrs. Fish recounted. "And I said, 'You did a terrible thing to an honest man. Shall I tell you something? He forgave you a long time ago. I've forgiven you, too, so let's forget about it. And thank you for coming.' And he just kind of smiled and he left. I think he had a conscience."[11]

While Orvie was tending to personal affairs as best he could, most of the Hubbard team's decisions in 1976 were made by his cadre of department heads under the direction of Thomas Dolan, who was elected by the council that January to replace Dombrowski as acting mayor and council president. A longtime insurance agent and a councilman since 1967, Dolan took over the mayor's job full-time, asking for a salary of $20,000 but settling for $10,500, a raise of $5,000 over the existing standard. He also decreed that Archer no longer would function as chief administrator and that the council would make decisions committee-fashion. In reality, Archer, Jackson and Hultgren ran the day-to-day governmental operations.

"Decisions were made by the acting mayors," Jackson recalled later, "with a lot of help from the department heads. When Dombrowski was acting mayor, Archer had the most influence. When Dolan was acting mayor, I had the most influence. When [Van] Mericas was acting mayor, [Fred] Hoffman [who had quit his newspaper job to become director of the city beautiful department] was the guy doing all the orchestrating. Hubbard just became the ceremonial mayor in the true sense of the word."

Soon after his colleagues chose him, Dolan became an increasingly visible presence at city hall. He issued new guidelines for the use of city cars, ordered the closing of loopholes in Florida apartment rental, reinstated an assistant city attorney fired by Hultgren for insubordination, confronted John Hubbard after the council cut off funds for several of the clerk's pet projects, merged several departments and reduced the size of the mayoral staff, explaining diplomatically, "Let's face it. The staff in the mayor's office was built and expanded to suit the mayor's mode of operation. He was a pretty dynamic guy and had to have sufficient personnel to carry out his many projects." He also became an effective city spokesman when Doug Thomas began demanding that a long list of department heads be fired. "In answer to you, Mr. Thomas," Dolan quipped at one council session, "look in the mirror and you'll see a horse going north." Another time, he snapped, "If I were as unhappy as you, I'd leave Dearborn. I don't like you and have no use for you. You don't know what you're talking about."

Despite—or perhaps because of—his performance, Dolan fell victim to a palace revolt in January 1977. His council colleagues, convinced of his mayoral ambitions and unwilling to grant him an even bigger head start, refused to reelect him council president and acting mayor. Instead, they crowned Mericas, a chiropractor who had been on the council four terms. Mericas, professing to have no interest in succeeding Hubbard, promised to "keep the Hubbard team intact," run an "open administration" and rely on the mayor for "whatever assistance his health will permit him to give."

That assistance wasn't much. Hubbard continued to play a minimal role as the months ran down on his last term. But even if he served no function as an administrator, he still had value as a symbol. It was, after all, an election year, and Orville Hubbard might have some thoughts about passing on the baton.

If Mericas didn't see himself as a candidate, there was no shortage of other prospects. In February, John B. O'Reilly, the police chief, became the first to announce. In the process, he stirred up his potential opposition when he acknowledged that he hadn't informed Hubbard of his intentions. "I have not talked to Mayor Hubbard," he was quoted. "He does not communicate. Anyone who says he does is a liar." Later, O'Reilly apologized, explaining he meant simply to convey the notion that Hubbard was unable to carry on a conversation. Just the same, O'Reilly's early announcement— while he still held a highly visible city job—immediately brought calls from Baja and Thomas to resign. John Hubbard distributed a press release attacking the chief as an opportunist.

Later that month, Frank Hubbard made it clear that he was in the running, too. Frank, now 47, had worked 19 years with the Wayne County Road Commission and spent 3 years as a member of the City Plan Commission. Although John Hubbard once looked like the heir apparent, the family now had settled on his older brother. Frank already had declared that his father was backing him as his successor, and now, at a $10-a-head fund raiser, Frank told 400 supporters at the Al Matta Club that, if elected, he would make the old man "lifetime mayor emeritus of Dearborn" and use him as an unpaid consultant. "We could set up an office for him in city hall," Frank Hubbard said, "and he could travel with us on all official ceremonies. If I am elected, Dearborn will have two mayors." That sounded like a pretty good idea to the crowd. The 400 jumped to their feet cheering when the mayor was wheeled onto the stage, as a band played a medley that included the inevitable "For He's a Jolly Good Fellow." He waved, nodding and smiling, as his fans crowded in, hugging him and telling him how good he looked. His eyes teared when his son introduced him as "the best public servant the state of Michigan ever had." The next Thursday, Orville showed up at a department head meeting with a campaign button that said, "Win with Hubbard."

The mayor still had more than nine months before he had to give up his job officially, but in March he unofficially lost his office. A moving van hired by his family drove off with his files, furniture and memorabilia.[12] Later that month, as part of a departmental realignment, Mericas aborted a four-year-old Hubbard experiment by eliminating the volunteer fire brigade.

In late March, Frank Hubbard unwittingly greased the skids under his father's wheelchair even further. Irked that Mericas had decided to let O'Reilly wait till the end of May before retiring from the police force, Frank and three of his father's appointees met with Orville to demand that he fire the chief. The mayor would have none of it, but things didn't end there. Mericas, who had been vacationing in Greece, was properly furious when he heard about the incident upon his return in early April. He slapped a two-week suspension on Frank's coconspirators—Phil Ciccarelli, a onetime Teamsters Union steward whom the elder Hubbard had appointed sanitation director; Eugene Forbes, the former city attorney who now was working as Hultgren's deputy; and James Hughes, the old-line Hubbard weights-and-measures director. "These three men were guilty of insubordination," Mericas explained at a press conference, "and had I not acted, I would have become impotent as an administrator."

Forty-five minutes after making the announcement, Mericas found himself enmeshed in a charter crisis. Ciccarelli was dropping off copies of a letter from Orville Hubbard at city hall. It notified Mericas that he—Hubbard—was rescinding the suspension. "The city charter says that the mayor pro tem can only act in the absence or disability of the mayor," Ciccarelli told reporters. "Mayor Hubbard is neither absent or disabled. He knows what's going on. I'm going back to work. As long as Mayor Hubbard is here, he is still my boss."

Five minutes after the letter arrived, Mericas and the department heads sequestered themselves. Then, after the regular afternoon department head meeting, Mericas sat down again with Hubbard, his son Henry, Hultgren, Jackson and Maureen Keane. Within the hour, after shouts of "No, no, no" from the old man, Mericas called a press conference. "In order to uphold a unified organization," he explained, "the ruling will stand. I have to call the shots. There has to be some sort of corporate head here in Dearborn."

Asked if he agreed, Orvie answered grimly, "Yeah." But when asked how he felt about the turn of events, he just shrugged.

The crisis of authority was thus averted, but it was a painful accommodation for Hubbard. He had kept his job, but he had lost everything that went with it. He had acknowledged something he never even thought about before in 35 years as mayor: somebody else was boss in Dearborn.

"We explained to the mayor there had to be a line of command," Mericas said in describing the new "compromise." "I told the mayor that either I should run the city or I can go home. The power has to be here."

As for what had set off Hubbard during the meeting, those present said it was a warning that a further confrontation with Mericas would hurt him and embarrass Frank's campaign for mayor. He agreed to back down, accounts said, when Mericas assured him there would be no further sanctions against the three mutineers.

As Jackson explained it later, "Mericas had the leverage, and Hubbard

369

didn't realize it at this point. I had to tell him that he couldn't do anything anymore, that he was at the mercy of Mericas, that he could be removed from the office. I played heavy that day. Didn't want to do it. All Hubbard had was what little pride was left in year three of the stroke. He was yelling, 'No, no, no,' that Mericas couldn't run the city. He was yelling to me. Whatever relationship I had with Hubbard ended that day.'"[13]

Ironically, Mericas lifted the suspensions soon afterward when it looked as though the council might overturn his disciplinary measure.

With Hubbard thus emasculated and the acting mayor forced to keep looking over his shoulder at the council, the race began in earnest to determine a successor to a city legend.

Frank Hubbard's campaign signs began appearing in shop windows—signs that substituted the son's photo for the father's and recycled an old Hubbard slogan that said, "Good Service—Clean City / Hubbard / Elect the Hubbard team." As yet, there was no Hubbard team, but presumably that would come.

Another entrant, declaring, "I'm in the race to win," was the 1976 council president and acting mayor, Dolan. "I am the only candidate to date to have the actual experience of being mayor," he said, "and I will stand on my record."

Also announcing were a trio of throw-in candidates—Arthur Dombeck, Henry Miga and Irene Strong—and Doug Thomas, who took on as his campaign manager Orville Hubbard's former executive secretary, Herb Amthor. Thomas, continuing to cast himself as a leader of the disloyal opposition, said, "This town needs a choice. Dearborn won't have a choice from among the gang of candidates presently running for mayor."

In June, Frank Hubbard blanketed Dearborn homes with circulars announcing Orville Hubbard's endorsement of him for mayor. Bearing a facsimile of Orville's famous inch-high green signature, the circular sounded almost word-for-word like one of his old campaign broadsides from the 1940s and '50s: "Beware of slickers, double talkers and fence straddlers, who try to out-fox you with weasel words. . . . [Frank Hubbard] is for the people all the way, and 'he'll fight like a tiger' to expose any sharks, schemers or shysters who might attempt to skin Dearborn citizens or homeowners."[14] The circular kicked up a cloud of protests. It seemed to be printed on city stationery and distributed illegally in mail boxes, and how could a victim of aphasia compose and sign it? Frank Hubbard denied that it was printed on city stationery or at city expense. He also said his father signed the original with his left hand after having it all read to him. "He went over it in very fine detail and approved every word of it," he said. "That's the way he's always expressed himself."

Poor Orville Hubbard. First stripped of his authority and now reduced to having his signature stamped under a ghost-written endorsement on mock city stationery. Perhaps it got to be too much for him, knowing that it would soon be over—the media attention, the adulation of the little old ladies and the kids, the kowtowing of department heads. Or perhaps it was the more mundane realization that he soon would be reduced to living on a small city pension and would lose his police chauffeurs. At any rate, a month later, a familiar burly figure was wheeled into the city clerk's office on a Friday afternoon. He apparently had come for something but left after Maureen Keane arrived to argue him out of it. But the next Monday, escorted by his two full-time police guards, he returned. This time, he spoke out clearly enough that there was no doubt about his intent: "I want petitions."

Deputy Clerk William Karr described what happened then: "I asked the mayor if he was sure he wanted to do this, and he told me yes. He seemed to be intent."

Intent or not, Frank Hubbard said he was sure this was just another prank by his father, irrepressible even in his debility. "Orville Hubbard," he told reporters that night, "is the world's greatest clown. He just wanted to show everyone that he is still the mayor of Dearborn. When I found out what my father did, I asked him if he was serious about running for mayor. My father laughed and said, 'Hell, no.' Then I asked him who he was going to vote for and he said, 'Frank Hubbard.' You know, when Orville is not the mayor anymore, we will lose the most colorful and glamorous politician that has ever lived."

Six days later, the most colorful and glamorous politician that has ever lived dumbfounded his friends and family by filing petitions containing the requisite 100 signatures with his son John in the clerk's office. Both Mericas and Keane tried to talk him out of it, but Orville Hubbard was having too good a time to quit now. "The mayor was clearly serious about filing his petitions," Jackson observed. "He indicated he wanted a city photographer to record the event."

In interviews with the reporters who suddenly wanted to talk to him again, Hubbard answered questions in monosyllables. "No," he didn't intend to retire. "Yes," there would be changes in the way acting mayors were appointed and given power if he were elected.

Maureen Keane was plainly distressed, though she said she would support his candidacy. "I didn't want to see him run again, but what can I do? He is afraid that there will be nothing for him if he retires."

Fay Hubbard, the long-suffering, long-separated wife, had an explanation only a mother's son could love: "Orville pulled this stunt to get publicity for Frank."

Even Frank wasn't buying that, though. He filed petitions for himself for both mayor and council, telling the press, "We will not oppose Mayor Hubbard in any way. If he is serious, I will place my entire campaign staff at his disposal."

The other candidates were unswayed by Hubbard's maneuver. "I believe that Mayor Hubbard is not able to take over the job of running the city," O'Reilly said. "We are running a campaign against the administration, and it doesn't matter if Frank or Orville Hubbard is setting up the fence," offered Thomas.

Perhaps Orville could continue to run Dearborn in the same muted style forced on him since his stroke. Regardless of his handicaps, perhaps he could be elected once again by voters unwilling to break the city's link with the past. The *Press & Guide*, however, focused on the problem that would pose for the city:

> The void of dynamic leadership left behind when Mayor Hubbard suffered his stroke was never completely filled. What the city has seen over these past three years is a series of stop gap measures. . . .
>
> Throughout his political career, Orville Hubbard has staked his claim to fame on the grand gesture. He should perform one last grand gesture by passing the torch on to a new era in Dearborn politics.[15]

Passing on the torch. Maybe that's what it was. In any case, during the last week of July, a day before the deadline for doing so, Orville Hubbard withdrew his petitions and officially dropped out of the 1977 mayor's "race." With tears in his eyes, flanked by John and Frank Hubbard, he sat at his conference table as newsmen gathered around. "I've just talked with the mayor," John Hubbard told the attendees. "He handed me this letter. The subject of it is his notice of withdrawal."

The letter, endorsing Frank once again, explained his decision as "better for the city and better for me personally." Frank described it as one of several letters submitted for his father's approval after he indicated he wanted to withdraw. "The mayor selected the one he wanted to sign," Frank said.

Asked if he had been pressured, the mayor replied, "No." Asked if he had been serious about running, he nodded yes. Asked if Frank's campaign influenced him, he nodded again.

"I think he'd be running today if he could do the job that's required of the mayor," John Hubbard said. "He's a hell of a swell guy and he's been a great mayor. He cares."

On that note, as good a political epitaph as any, Orville Hubbard became a former candidate—after nearly 45 years of running, losing, finally winning, then never giving up ground.

In the five months that remained in his fifteenth term, he would sit back and watch his heirs battle his old machine. He would try to help out Frank, even going so far as to try to get his department heads to sign a loyalty oath that might be interpreted as a pledge to support his son. But mostly, he would just go through the motions, attending department head meetings, taking drives around town, collecting his paycheck.

And at the end of 1977, Orville Hubbard would leave city hall and try to get through what remaining time he had left with the young blonde woman who had become his most loyal protégée.

44

The Probate Fight, 1977-81

> I'm going to be with Orville till the day he dies. None
> of them are.
> —Maureen Keane, responding to a suit by the Hubbard
> family

The changing of the guard in Dearborn, the city's first since 1942, came on a wet, snowy New Year's Day in 1978 with 1,500 citizens jammed into the Dome Room of the Youth Center. As two bands played the National Anthem, a three-man Army honor guard escorted the city's new mayor to the bunting-bedecked center stage. Then came the living icon, the head of government for three generations of Dearbornites.

Orville Hubbard, grinning, waving, tears in his eyes, was wheeled up to the front of the auditorium, and the citizens rose to acknowledge him with several minutes of cheers and applause.

The brief swearing-in ceremony for the Hubbard successor was conducted by Federal District Judge Ralph B. Guy Jr., the former Dearborn city attorney who now had found himself on a fast track in the U.S. judiciary. Guy, performing the requisite obeisance to his onetime mentor, told the audience it was "a tribute to the community" that so many had turned out "to acknowledge this great mayor. . . . There will never be another mayor of such distinguished duration as Mayor Hubbard."

Then, following more cheers and applause, former Dearborn Police Chief John B. O'Reilly, now the fourth mayor in the 49-year history of the community, pledged "an open city government with enlightened leadership."

The adulation bestowed on Orville Hubbard that day, the first day in 36 years he had not been mayor, was fine as far as it went. But it was becoming apparent that the good citizens of Dearborn were unwilling to demonstrate their appreciation for their longtime leader in more tangible ways. During the previous September's primary, as voters were selecting

O'Reilly and Frank Hubbard to face off in the general election, they also declined to approve continued police protection or improved pension benefits for the mayor. They voted 19,792 to 10,448 against allocating a payout of some $37,000 for two police officers and transportation expenses. They voted 18,228 to 11,750 not to grant a pension of two-thirds of Orvie's top salary of $40,000. That left Orville Hubbard with a pension calculated at $4,128.24 a year, in addition to a life insurance policy of $1,000, for which he was paying an annual premium of $20. The maximum pension figure, $6,000 terminating with the pensioner's death, had been rejected by the mayor in favor of the lower figure, which would be paid to his wife if he died first. The only concession from the city: he could purchase his old 1970 Ford LTD for $600.

To compensate for what the voters had refused to give, Hubbard supporters scheduled a retirement testimonial, but by the week before the February 5 affair, only 300 of the $10 tickets had been sold, including exactly 38 to the folks at city hall. Groused Doyne Jackson, "It seems as though people have forgotten all about Orville Hubbard." Last-minute appeals improved attendance to 1,126. The final take, boosted by some donations of up to $200, was more than $16,000 to go toward the mayor's expenses. Among those who took notice was the partially paralyzed George Wallace, who sent along a letter of congratulations.

Later, the City Council favored the former mayor with a resolution proclaiming April "Thank You Mayor Hubbard Month."

Hubbard had deleted department head meetings from his daily routine after O'Reilly's swearing-in, but Maureen Keane was doing her best to preserve most of his life-style, such as it was, now that he was divorced from city hall.

She herself was in the same situation. Her $27,000 job as head of the Service Bureau had been eliminated by O'Reilly in a wave of cost-cutting. Hubbard cried for two days when she told him about it, she said. But she became an upscale entrepreneur the next month, opening a chocolate shop in Detroit's new Renaissance Center riverfront development.

Her charge's life remained busy despite her new responsibilities and the loss of his old contacts. As she explained to reporters, "He still talks to some people at city hall. But most of his department heads were never comfortable with Orville in a social setting. He was a tough boss."

His new routine depended on a crew of part-time attendants, most of them college students working for four dollars an hour, to help dress, wash, carry and drive him. He typically awoke at 8:00 A.M., watched TV in bed for an hour, had breakfast in bed, listened to someone read him the newspapers, then watched more TV—"Donahue" was among his favorites. He took a nap from 11:30 to 1:30, then went for lunch and a chauffeured drive around town. Among his stops were parks, senior citizens' apartments, the public works yard, and the homes of friends, family members and acquaintances from his hospital stays. He was normally back home by 5:30 for another nap, would get up for dinner with Maureen at 7:30 and retire for the night after she read to him in bed and watched the local news at 11:00 with him.

Not surprisingly, the routine was a considerable drain on Hubbard's finances. Maureen was sharing rent, utilities and food expenses equally, but the mayor's attendants were costing more than $1,000 a month, and his family was concerned.

Fay Hubbard had died in March 1979, and by the next September, John Hubbard filed a petition in Wayne Probate Court seeking guardianship and estate rights on behalf of the ex-mayor's children. Orville Hubbard, the petition said, was mentally incapable of handling his own affairs. "All of us are concerned for our father's happiness and physical well-being," said John Hubbard, "but at the rate his expenses are allocated, he will be a pauper in less than three years." Not counting life insurance and other indeterminate assets, the family was estimating the estate at $130,000. It included a bank account of $22,000 and valued the family home at up to $50,000. It was not a large amount, but it was all there was.[1] John Hubbard attempted to make it clear that preserving his father's funds, not changing his life-style, was the family's goal: "Dad can live anywhere he chooses, but a conservatorship must exist to ensure that he won't end up a pauper."

Maureen Keane's response was predictably bitter: she would fight. "I'm not trying to become his guardian because I don't choose to go to court and say he's incompetent," said Keane, who already had power of attorney. "I'll go and fight his right for his competency. They'd put him in a home because none of them want to take care of him. They've all said it. I'm going to be with Orville till the day he dies. None of them are."

She had been dating a prominent Dearborn businessman for some time, she said, but that did not affect her devotion to Orville Hubbard. Their romantic relationship had changed over the years to a deep friendship, she explained. "I love another man very much," she told the press, "but I would never let the mayor down. I'm his best friend and I love him. He took care of me when I was a child. I'm going to fight. I may lose. But if I lose, the mayor's really the loser."

The probate hearing was scheduled for mid-October, but 10 days before, Hubbard was admitted to Ford Hospital with his fourth urinary tract infection since November 1975. Early the next morning, he went into convulsions and lapsed into a coma. "He is not responding to treatment," said Dr. Boy Frame. "He has severe metabolic problems. A man his age and in his condition, I would say he has less than a 20-percent chance."

The next morning, after he had been administered the last rites of the Roman Catholic church, Maureen Keane read him the newspaper headlines about his condition. As she later recounted it, she said, "Orville, they're counting you dead. C'mon, show these guys." A half-hour later, she said, he opened his eyes.

Less than two weeks later, Hubbard had been released from the hospital, and the probate hearing was moved back to November. In the meantime, Keane and the Hubbard children continued to reproach each other in the local press. "I'm not taking shots at her or anything, but she's not medically trained to handle the problem," said John Hubbard.

Keane responded, "He is not going to a convalescent home. He would die in a convalescent home. He may live to see John in a convalescent home."

John Hubbard soon yielded a bit. He said he would be willing to hire a nurse for his father at the family home, where John and his brother Jim were staying with John's daughter and paying Orville rent. "As far as we're concerned," John said, "the home on Mead Street is his. The place is paid for and remodeled. Why doesn't he want to come home? Maybe he's being held captive there."

By the time the family appeared in probate court with Keane, John Hubbard had answered his own question, noting, "Orville Hubbard has in fact forsaken his children and chosen to live with this 39-year-old, good-looking woman."

That morning, Orville Hubbard smiled for reporters and nodded his approval at the way things were going. Later, an ecstatic Keane declared, "We won. It's an election day, don't you know. We're all going to be fine. We're all for him. Things will be the same."

Probate Judge Willis Ward had approved an agreement reached the night before by attorneys for both sides. It granted Keane conservatorship over Hubbard's estate without going into the question of his competency. Under the arrangement, the aides could stay on, but she was to limit spending to $80 a day, and she was to post bond to cover any excesses.

John Hubbard and Keane hugged each other for the cameras, and he conceded, "Our father has a right to live wherever he chooses and to spend the money that is his." But, he added, "I haven't changed my mind about my father going broke. He's still going to go broke. If this is my father's wishes, let him do as he will." Even at that, though, he conceded that life with Keane should help his father stay well. "It's a complex and private thing," he said.

45

Keane for Mayor, 1981

This town always used to look like a shiny new penny.
Now parts of it look like a shantytown.
  —Maureen Keane, running for mayor of Dearborn[1]

If this was Orville Hubbard's apartment, it wasn't immediately evident. Where were all the photos of Hubbard with Henry Ford I and II, Hubbard with President Nixon, Hubbard with sex-change celebrity Christine Jorgensen, Hubbard with a boa constrictor encircling his arm?

In this apartment, a decorator's touch was apparent everywhere. Scattered around the living room were displays of crystal glassware and stemmed bowls, modern paintings, statuary and houseplants. Suspended over the table in the dining el was a gaudy crystal chandelier. Multihued Persian-style rugs set off the yellow walls and matching carpet.

But there, sitting on the mantel over the fireplace, a few feet from a stuffed monkey, was a more personal touch, a photo of a self-assured-looking man in his 50s beside a younger blonde woman in a T-shirt that proclaimed, "Maureen Keane for Mayor."

The blonde was Maureen Keane, all right, but the man was not nearly ponderous enough to be taken for Hubbard. He was Wayne Doran, chairman of the Ford Motor Land Development Corporation and Keane's intended. And the T-shirt was no joke. On this night, September 15, 1981, Maureen Keane was running for mayor of Dearborn.

Tonight, she would sit in her luxury Fairlane East townhouse, the one she still shared with Orville Hubbard after six years, engagement or no engagement, and she would await primary election returns. The results would tell her whether she would face the incumbent, John B. O'Reilly, the old Hubbard chief of police, in the November general election. Should that happen, the election would prolong for four more years the unofficial trappings of the Hubbard era in Dearborn.

The preceding months had been more than a little reminiscent of Hubbard's heyday in the 1950s. O'Reilly was running on a platform of increased efficiency and good intentions. Keane, whose previous administrative experience consisted of 10 years as head of the city's Service Bureau, had swashbuckled her way into the race by carping about the town's deterioration since the Hubbard years. "This town always used to look like a shiny new penny," she told a magazine free-lancer. "Now parts of it look like a shantytown. I tell you, it's criminal."[2]

Maureen Keane's entry into the race had scared out most of the major anti-city hall personalities in town, and she adopted a strategy that made it clear that she intended to try to throw a bit of a scare into O'Reilly, too. She attacked O'Reilly's spending record and his failure to head off a state-mandated property assessment increase. She faulted him for supporting a city income tax proposal that voters already had turned down. She mounted a door-to-door campaign to capitalize on her feisty personality. She walked up to strangers and told them her analyst wanted her to run to help resolve some inner conflicts.

More daringly yet, she began talking openly with reporters about her past liaison with Orvie. Instead of the town's worst-kept secret, it became, remarkably, her major qualification for office, a sign of loyalty, a familiarity with the Hubbard ways. "I will take care of him until his last breath," she told the press. "He will not die without dignity in his own town."

But if her devotion to Hubbard had invested her with the ambition to be mayor herself, this was still emphatically her election, not his. She had planned a postelection party at an American Legion post not far from the town hall, but she already had brushed aside an inquiry about whether Hubbard would make an appearance there. "I wouldn't do that to him," she said curtly. "That's going to be a zoo over there."

At the Keane-Hubbard townhouse on the city's east side, a handful of campaign workers and supporters was awaiting developments. It was 8:00 P.M., the polls had just closed and neither the former mayor nor the candidate was in evidence. Keane was due back from dinner any minute, and Hubbard, it was said, was napping in the second bedroom.

He had been taken out earlier for his daily 3:00 P.M. meal at nearby Bill Knapp's restaurant—always bean soup, a hamburger and ice cream—and then for his usual stops to see his grandchildren and his former secretary, Helen Bell. He did not mark the day with a trip to the polls, however. Wheelchair-bound as he still was, he had done his voting already, with Keane's help, by absentee ballot.

The candidate arrived presently, looking properly executive yet glamorous in a black suit and heels and lavender blouse tied with a bow. After excusing herself briefly to pin up her hair, she tended to the next order of business: rousing Hubbard. Stealing back to his bedroom with her nephew Chris and several friends, she found him lying on his right side, his still-hefty figure in purple print pajamas. His hair was steely gray now that it was no longer being tinted. And the right side of his mouth and face drooped noticeably. And yet, when Keane slipped onto the bed beside him, the old man perked up.

"Wake up, Mayor," she said brightly. "Say hi to Chris and his friend Mark. And you remember Dave Good? He's writing a book about you." Hubbard extended his left hand smilingly to his visitors as Keane stroked his shoulder and reminded him about the big event of the day. His grip was still firm. "Are we going to win?" she asked him. "No," came the response. She asked the same question, her arms around his shoulders, and this time the answer sounded like "Yeah."

That plateau reached, she continued to coax. "Show Dave what you can say. He can say, 'Keane,'" and her charge repeated, "Keane," crisply and with obvious pride. "He can say, 'Ice cream,'" and he did. "He can sing," she continued, but the mayor lay there silently. "He's going to get up later," she explained, ushering out the visitors.

Later, Keane's campaign manager, a Lansing political strategist named Jerry Roe, poked his head into the living room to update a handful of people drinking white wine and piecing off a tray of canapes: after the absentee ballots, it was Keane 1,535 and O'Reilly 2,109, with the others well back.

Keane, now minus her shoes and jacket, said to no one in particular, "Pull up a seat and have a breakdown with me."

But Roe, whose early-year poll had shown O'Reilly trouncing Keane 80 percent to 20, was elated. If the votes for the also-rans were pooled with hers, he noted, she'd be ahead.

Keane, appropriately bolstered, said, "And you guys thought I couldn't do it. This is the man I hired to tell me I couldn't win. I'm so excited."

By now a *Detroit News* photographer had shown up. After talking her out of putting her jacket back on, he shot Maureen hugging her sister-in-law, Kathy Keane. Somebody suggested she pose with the mayor, but she nixed that. "I don't want to have a picture with him," she said. "We've already done that to death."

A little after 9:30, Hubbard finally was up, sitting in the wheelchair beside his bed, his pajama top still on, a white towel spread across his lap. His hair had been combed for him, and now that he was in direct light, it was plain that his right eye was partially closed and the droop was more pronounced than it appeared before. Most disconcertingly, his feet were purplish from an apparent circulatory problem. However, he looked pleased at the attention as a small line of greeters formed in his bedroom, which, it was now also plain, was filled with plaques, service awards, photos and other memorabilia. He extended his good left hand to each visitor.

Keane allowed that the election was having its effect on the old man, even though he wasn't in it. "He's so proud," she said. "Aren't you proud, Mayor? He's so proud." Hubbard, remaining silent, went teary-eyed.

Soon after 10:00 P.M., the last of the vote totals came in. "We're right on target," Roe declared. "We're 40.9 percent, 10,431. O'Reilly 11,330 for 45.7 percent. You know now you can win this election."

A few minutes later, a call came in from WWJ radio, and Keane, sitting not far from a tinted photo of a young Orville Hubbard, gushed, "I'm ecstatic, yes. I'm really overwhelmed. We thought we'd do well, but I'm really encouraged by the support we received. Now we're really going to roll up our sleeves."

After hanging up, she went back into Hubbard's bedroom for the last time. "Mayor, we did it. By God, we're in. We did it." Outside the bedroom, Keane had bid the old man good night and was ready to leave for her campaign party.

"Let's go get 'em," she said to herself as much as to anyone else. "Don't make me cry, you guys."

Maureen Keane had wiped away some tears, and now she was doing her best to keep from sounding disappointed. Six weeks had passed. It was about 10:30 P.M. on November 3, 1981, in the Hubbard Ballroom of Dearborn's Hyatt Regency Hotel, and she was consoling a throng of supporters after her runoff with O'Reilly. Despite the close primary, the incumbent's margin this time was 23,634 to 15,067, almost 60 percent to 40.

"I love my town, and I have made so many new and great friends, and I'm sure all of you have, too," Keane was saying. "We really didn't lose tonight. The town has been woken up, and I'm sure the mayor'll do a good job." Later, she conceded to reporters, "I just feel very hurt."

For his part, Roe explained that Hubbard was not exploited more because "we wanted this to be a Maureen Keane race, not an Orville Hubbard race." He added, "We couldn't knock O'Reilly, except to say that he's bland, colorless and unimaginative."

Colorless or not, O'Reilly had rolled up an even bigger margin than he had in disposing of Frank Hubbard four years before. Orville Hubbard's coattails, it turned out, were not long enough to reach from a wheelchair. And with Maureen Keane's defeat, the Ghost of Dearborn Past, as one wag had named him, was exorcised from the town hall.[3]

46

The Funeral, 1982

It looks like we are losing our friend.
—Maureen Keane, assessing the decline in Orville
Hubbard's health

The gossip columnists had been predicting it for months. And at last, in a wedding that one weekly newspaper described as a twentieth-century fairy tale come true, it happened. The time: 7:00 P.M., February 5, 1982. The place: San Francisco's Hyatt on Union Square. The participants: Maureen Keane, unsuccessful Dearborn mayoral candidate, slimmed down and glamorous, her strawberry-blonde hair falling to her shoulders, her gown a white satin original by Yves Saint Laurent. And Wayne Doran, the man responsible for developing downtown Detroit's monstrous RenCen, pudgy, moon-faced but still somehow a man who looked to be in charge of things.

The couple had met nine years before, when Doran, formerly vice-president of the Del E. Webb Corporation, a Phoenix-based construction and development firm, was in Dearborn during the planning stages of the Fairlane Town Center. They had been dating for three years as the health of Keane's live-in companion continued to deteriorate. She had sold her two RenCen stores, Maureen's and Godiva's Chocolatier, as a preliminary to her marriage. And as for her run at Jack O'Reilly the year before, she told an interviewer, "Probably the luckiest thing that ever happened to me was losing that race. I would be in my office now trying to straighten out the financial messes in this city. Instead, I'm nervous." She said she hadn't decided whether to work or be a stay-at-home wife, though she'd "be cutting down my life-style somewhat."

Then came the wedding, a black-tie affair attended by nearly 75 friends and family members. The happy couple glowed for photographers and announced they would postpone the honeymoon until May, then take a two-week trip to Austria.

Two weeks after the ceremony, Maureen Keane-Doran abandoned the condo she had shared with Orville Hubbard since 1975. She said, as she loaded her car with belongings destined for Doran's Farmington Hills home, that the mayor would soon move to a house she hoped to turn into a sort of museum of Hubbard memorabilia. He was to continue to have around-the-clock care. She told the local press that the separation was hard on her. "I didn't think it would ever be this difficult," she said. "He's really happy for me. He's laughing, and I'm crying. He's being very supportive. He's my dear, dear friend."

In early March, Orville Hubbard, looking as dignified as possible for an old man who could do little more than grunt, grin and cry, was wheeled up a ramp to the front porch of an old brick house on Wellesley near city hall. The house had been Keane-Doran's campaign headquarters in 1981 and was only four doors down from the house where she had grown up. Asked by Wayne Doran's wife whether he liked his new home, the mayor nodded assent. But he was moist-eyed just the same.

"This is the closest he's been to city hall since his stroke," Keane-Doran said. He's really back home here. I think he's excited."

Hubbard was to occupy a first-floor bedroom. A bodyguard and a companion-aide would take two other bedrooms. The living and dining rooms already displayed photos of the mayor. Some knickknacks—rubber stamps, signs and other political odds and ends—had been disposed of earlier by Keane-Doran in a Dearborn resale shop. Most went fast.

Eight months had passed since the day Hubbard had moved into the house on Wellesley. Maureen Keane-Doran's name appeared more and more frequently in society columns. But though she still managed to find time for her old friend, his condition clearly was getting worse. On November 18, he started suffering fainting spells, and three days later, when attendants were unable to rouse him, she had him dispatched by ambulance to Ford Hospital.

There, a comatose Hubbard, suffering from what doctors described variously as convulsions, spells of unconsciousness and a type of seizure, underwent a series of tests. The medical team said he apparently had not suffered a major new stroke and predicted he would be able to return home later in the week.

Frank Hubbard, designated spokesman for the family, told reporters, "At this point, there's nothing to be alarmed about," but Keane-Doran confessed, "I don't think he is going to come back this time, and I've never given up hope before."

The patient was being fed through a tube to his small intestine, while a crew of eight, including Maureen, massaged his body and bathed him in cold water to stimulate his circulation. His condition was amended from "stable" to "guarded" to "serious," and tests confirmed another stroke, this one on the right side of the brain; his 1974 stroke had been on the left. Except for one precipitous drop in his blood pressure, his vital signs remained strong, but the death watch had begun.

"It looks like we are losing our friend," Maureen said.

Finally, at 1:00 A.M., December 16, 1982, some three and a half weeks after entering the hospital, the ex-mayor of Dearborn died of heart failure. He was 79. At his bedside were his daughter, Nancy, and Frank's wife, Dorothy.

The flag at the Dearborn city hall flew at half-staff that day and for a month thereafter, and a moment of silence was observed in the city's schools. The body, laid out the next day in a closed casket at Howe Peterson Funeral Home on Michigan Avenue, was visited by an estimated 3,000 persons during an 11-hour period. The flag-draped casket was flanked by members of a Dearborn police honor guard. Behind it hung a painting by local artist Joseph Maniscalco, portraying a firm-jawed Orville Hubbard, in command, standing at his conference table beside his favorite picture of Washington on horseback.

Maureen, holding up well even though obviously tired, greeted most of the sympathizers, sharing the scene—uncharacteristically—with little apparent rancor toward the Hubbard family. "I'm so proud to have been able to share his life," she told more than one visitor.

Lest the event pass without incident, however, one wizened-looking woman demanded, as she paid her respects, "Why is the casket closed?" Keane-Doran gestured over to Nancy Hubbard Dmytro, standing nearby. "I don't know," she said. "Ask her. I thought he looked pretty good." The crone promptly accosted the mayor's daughter. "Why is the casket closed?" she asked again. "I'd have loved to see him. He couldn't have looked that bad." Dmytro, with a gallant effort at suppressing her exasperation, replied, "That was our decision. He didn't like people staring at him. That was the way he was."

The way he was—in all its nuances—also was the subject of considerable attention in the media that day. The wires portrayed Hubbard as a racist and the nation's "most clownish mayor." The *New York Times* ran a 10-inch obituary plus a photo.[1]

Locally, the *News* and *Free Press* ran front-page features, followed the next day by back-page photo spreads. Both obits were sprinkled with references to Hubbard's racist reputation, and a *News* editorial disparaged him as "a racist and a bully who enjoyed acting the buffoon."[2] The two Dearborn weeklies marked the occasion with laudatory specials on him the next week.

Among the public officials who sent condolences to the Hubbard family were President Reagan, who noted that the mayor's tenure "was marked by distinction and integrity," and Michigan Supreme Court Justice and former Governor G. Mennen Williams, who remarked on his "good relationship" with the mayor "despite the fact that some of the things he stood for I absolutely abhorred and probably he was opposed to many of the things I stood for."[3]

On the day after visitation, a chilly, overcast Saturday, an estimated 800 mourners filled Dearborn's Sacred Heart Catholic Church nearly to capacity for a 10:00 A.M. mass. Occupying the first several rows were the families of four Hubbard children—Nancy, Frank, John and Jim—although Jim himself stayed at the rear of the church. Henry, the youngest, had moved out of state and did not attend. The Dorans sat behind the family. Also attending were a number of local officials, including Mayor O'Reilly, Wayne County Prosecutor William Cahalan and a prominent black, William Lucas, Wayne County sheriff and newly elected county executive. Notably absent were Detroit city officials and representatives of the legal community.

Then, with a TV camera whirring in the background, the coffin was carried in under the high, vaulting arches of the sanctuary, where the half-timbered-and-plaster walls were adorned with Christmas wreaths. A contingent of U.S. Marines trailed the coffin, and a police honor guard stood at attention in the vestibule. The program featured a soprano and a baritone, along with a violinist, a flutist and an organist.

The idea of such a ceremony would have brought a chuckle from the Orville Hubbard who once cracked jokes about people "shooting Catholics on sight" in his hometown. However, according to a memorial program, Hubbard had converted to Catholicism in February 1975, three months after his first stroke. Maureen Keane had had the last laugh about that. But at least this ceremony had the right mix of decorum and showbiz, what with the Marines, the police, the musicians and the TV crew.

In his homily, the Reverend John Child, pastor of Sacred Heart, suggested that many aspects of Hubbard's life had been obscured by the race issue and the headline-seeking. "He was called an accomplished politician, charismatic, colorful," pointed out Father Child. "He was referred to as a segregationist, as an opportunist. . . . However, I didn't see much reference to the quiet phone calls that he made to his citizens over the years, the patience with which he listened to the problems and complaints of the citizens of this community as they sought help and support from him—and in most instances received it."

After a communion offering, Federal Judge Ralph B. Guy Jr., too, found a way of assaying Hubbard's good side in the best tradition of sugar-coated eulogies. It marked one of the few times anyone outside the family had referred to the mayor as just plain "Orville" in years. Guy described Hubbard as a man of integrity, courage, loyalty, perseverance, forgiveness, humility and pride. And, in an extravagant ending that would have made even Hubbard flinch, he concluded, "Well, Orville, your service is at an end, and you can enjoy a much-deserved rest. . . . I do have a few thoughts to share with the management. . . . Meaning no disrespect, I hope all those harps are shined and all those angel wings are on straight. And there better not be a piece

384

of litter anywere around. And maybe, maybe just for one day, you could change the name on those big gates to read, 'Citizens' Country Club.' Orville would like that. You're getting one very tough—and very good—man."

Then the Marine pallbearers carried the casket past the saluting honor guard into a hearse for the ride to Union City's Riverview Cemetery. He always had wanted that. Not to be buried in his adopted city of Dearborn or with his wife, Fay, in Flat Rock, but with his parents, back home in farm country.

Epilogue:

✲

The Politics of Confrontation and Theater

What a man does for himself dies with him—what he
does for his community lives forever.
—Slogan embossed on official City of Dearborn
stationery

He said he never wanted anything to be named after him. It's a quirk that
seems strangely out of character in an elected official who labored as hard
on his own behalf as Orville Hubbard did for nearly four decades. Perhaps
it was false modesty. Perhaps it was just good politics. But "Orville L. Hubbard, L.L.B., mayor of Dearborn since Jan. 6, 1942," as he dubbed himself
on city envelopes and letterheads, insisted repeatedly that he did not want
any memorials to himself.

"Basically I'm not interested in landmarks," he once said. "You saw
what happened to all of the monuments to Stalin in Russia and Batista in
Cuba."

True enough, he did allow an existing road in town to be renamed
Hubbard Drive during his next-to-last term in office, and he lived to see
two city-built senior citizens' apartment buildings christened Hubbard Manor
East and West, as well as a room at the Hyatt Regency Dearborn named the
Hubbard Ballroom. And in 1988, six years after his death, a tavern near city
hall was named Orville's Food & Spirits after him. Finally, despite his cau-
tionary statement about the destruction of the Stalin and Batista monuments, there was a statue—a bronze, life-sized likeness of a middle-aged
Hubbard, waving and striding as if in a parade. The work of local sculptor
Janice B. Trimpe, the statue was unveiled in front of city hall in April 1989,
on what would have been the subject's eighty-sixth birthday. It had been
commissioned with a $60,000 drive engineered by Noel Keane and funded
primarily by small contributions from friends and admirers. Predictably, it
brought a round of criticism about Hubbard's racial stand even before it

was installed. The NAACP's Arthur Johnson told the *Detroit News* in late 1988 that the statue's proponents "are obviously saying they think it doesn't matter that he was a racist."

If Orvie himself was lukewarm about landmarks, he was much more enthusiastic about the municipal innovations he championed—Camp Dearborn, his "citizens' country club" in the next county; or Dearborn Towers, his Florida apartment building for local retirees, for instance. Or the sense of pride that he helped engender among residents of his town as a result of its superb services and fine recreation facilities. Or perhaps the look of the town—the elimination of substandard buildings, the closing of alleys, the proliferation of neat-as-a-pin neighborhoods consisting of well-built, albeit largely undistinctive, homes.

But Hubbard's most enduring legacy, as illustrated by the controversy over his statue, may well turn out to bear no relationship to his innovative ideas or even to the brick and mortar he left behind. Instead, it may be the lingering tendency, nearly a generation after his last public pronouncement, for outsiders to brand his city a haven for bigotry. In a sense, it's almost as if Dearborn has been unable to exorcise Orville Hubbard's ghost.

In one notable sighting, the specter materialized in December 1985, when a coalition of church and labor leaders challenged an ordinance passed by Dearborn voters the month before to make most city parks off-limits to nonresidents. NAACP and American Civil Liberties Union (ACLU) officials, among others, criticized the ordinance as a transparent means of keeping blacks out of Dearborn's parks, and the coalition retaliated by calling a black boycott of the Fairlane shopping center and other Dearborn businesses. City officials had been about to sign an agreement to postpone enforcement of the ordinance until a court test. What held things up, according to city hall spokesman Doyne Jackson, was that the coalition's written complaint proved its leaders wanted "the city of Dearborn, the people of Dearborn and the ghost of Orville Hubbard on trial." A few months after that, in fact, Detroit ACLU Director Howard Simon allowed that maybe the mayor's spirit *did* need to be exorcised from Dearborn, that even though the rotund, motor-mouthed Hubbard was gone, his city continued to practice his peculiar, nose-thumbing brand of bigotry. Although the ordinance was never enforced, it was invalidated in September 1986 in Wayne Circuit Court and subsequently became bogged down in appeals.

It was, in a twisted kind of way, a tribute to the flamboyant style and public relations genius of Orville Hubbard that his community, from World War II through Korea and Vietnam, spanning the modern civil rights era, remained so thoroughly identified with one aspect of a complicated and colorful personality. For, although the Hubbard years were peppered with a long series of racist pronouncements from the mayor's office, there was little in the public record to back up the contention in the boycotters' complaint, for example, that "Throughout the years, public officials of the city of Dearborn have publicly stated that blacks were not welcome to reside in Dearborn, and at various times acts of violence were committed against black persons attempting to reside in the city of Dearborn."[1] In fact, the "public officials," in nearly every case, were Hubbard and Hubbard alone, and the "acts of violence" consisted of one angry scene in 1963, when a white Dearborn man had his home besieged by neighbors who thought he had sold to blacks.

An observer is tempted to conclude that Dearborn-bashing continued to be a popular pastime not primarily because of what actually happened in the city over the years, but because of what one man said over the years. And even the simple exercise of dismissing Hubbard himself as a racist is to miss some important nuances about him.

Orvie was not a white supremacist in the traditional sense of the term—he did not believe that blacks are genetically inferior to whites, for example—but he was, as he himself often acknowledged, a segregationist who fought for the "right" of whites to keep apart from blacks. Orville Hubbard's stance was the racism of a politician with a streak of shameless opportunism, who, despite obvious gifts as a leader, an innovator and a promoter, was willing to pander to the fears of a homogeneous white community. Instead of trying to ease racial tensions, instead of being a molder of opinion, as he was on most other issues, he settled for reflecting and, indeed, agitating community prejudices.

Orville Hubbard spouted his own suburban-oriented brand of white-rights rhetoric whenever it suited him, not so much because he was a race hater but sometimes just because he thought a well-timed red herring would help him at the polls. And not so much because Dearborn was a particularly bigoted community but because racism, on a more subtle level than preached by Hubbard, was at the very core of suburban development in general. It could be argued, after all, that racism was a major reason for the existence of many of the nation's suburbs, or at least for most of their growth. In fact, despite the public statements of its headline-grabbing mayor, Dearborn's stand on race was essentially the same as that of any other white northern suburb. Its attitudes were similar, even if its reputation had been exaggerated.

Even as it applied to Hubbard himself, the race issue was overemphasized. And despite what, if anything, posterity may remember about him, his tenure was more remarkable for his one-man dictatorship than for his racial attitudes.

If Orville Hubbard was not a machine politician in the standard definition of political scientists, he still qualified as a boss by almost any available gauge of his influence over the daily fabric of life in his community. He broke from the machine stereotype chiefly in that he had no patronage appointments other than his department heads and that his administration was relatively free of corruption.

Of all the bosses he was compared with, Hubbard was most like a northern version of Huey Long. Like the onetime Louisiana governor and U.S. senator, Hubbard was an unschooled but whip-smart country boy who made himself a lawyer, earned a reputation as a populist, assumed an almost socialist political philosophy and fancied himself a champion of the downtrodden, even while openly scorning authority figures and many of the institutions of a democratic society. Also like Long, Hubbard was a dynamic personality and persuasive orator with a bizarre sense of the comedic, a perverse gift for invective and a pathological need for power. Outside of Long, Hubbard's personality and his administrative style made him perhaps the most arrestingly original elected official of twentieth-century America.

With his subordinates and his family, he often was a sadistic tyrant; with his political opponents, he was a formidable strategist who, if he couldn't outmaneuver them, would simply resort to outshouting them or concocting some gimmick to distract them from the issue at hand.

He seized political control of a company town historically dominated by a generous, community-spirited auto manufacturer that had become consumed with trying to squash a fledgling labor movement, and he had replaced one set of abuses with another. He moved, as he often said, to "keep Dearborn clean of vice, graft and corruption," but, despite his background as an attorney, he lowered the overall level of political dialogue in the city, instigating a long list of threats and slanders against opponents, an ongoing state of warfare with city employees, and endless bouts of litigation based on whim.

Part of the formula that made Orvie what he was in Dearborn was a set of essentially unreplicatable circumstances. He was welcomed in as a reform candidate in a corruption-ridden town. He became the beneficiary of a new charter that positioned him to become one of the strongest mayors in the nation. And perhaps most importantly, he was the inheritor of the huge Ford Motor Company tax base, which made Dearborn one of the richest communities in the nation, enabling him to entrench himself in office by keeping homeowners' taxes low and the level of services and quality of public facilities high. It was Ford tax money, of course, that permitted him the luxury of running an administration that frittered away funds on extravagances and became bogged down in meaningless details, even as he built a reputation as a master of efficiency and budgetary penury.

For all its individuality, Orville Hubbard's Dearborn was close to qualifying as a microcosm of America, a place named for a Revolutionary War hero, a place where, in an almost storybook example of the wonders of capitalism, a local industry wound up changing the way Americans traveled and lived. Yet, despite its newfound status, it remained a small town in personality as well as in size. If Henry Ford was Dearborn's biggest fish, then Orville Hubbard was a great white shark, an alien, predatory species that, thrashing around and darting hungrily this way and that, devoured all its political competition and overwhelmed its little pond of a city.

The Hubbard style was essentially a blend of politics as theater and the politics of confrontation, and it was this, almost as much as his racist image or his personalized delivery of Dearborn's much-touted municipal services, that made him an invincible presence at the polls for 36 years. If nothing else, Orville Hubbard's politics of confrontation proved that bombast and belligerence can be an effective strategy—at least on a small, municipal scale. And his sense of politics as theater showed that sometimes a good laugh is all that's needed to interest people in government. For, say what you will about him, Orvie never bored anybody.

Curiously, Hubbard's personal problems and certain aspects of his political success both stemmed from the same source: a maladjusted personality rooted in childhood difficulties that seemed to qualify him as almost a textbook case of arrested development, or fixation, in Freudian terms. This condition, somewhat reminiscent of that afflicting the potty-mouthed Mozart crafted by playwright Peter Shaffer in *Amadeus*, often rendered Hubbard incapable of dealing with situations as a mature adult—witness his childish tantrums, name-calling bouts and hide-and-seek sessions with process servers. The visionary who builds a "citizens' country club" and buys a Florida retirement complex also harasses a municipal judge with such distractions as having the courthouse phones cut off. The patriot and ex-Marine who opposes the Vietnam War on principle also stoops to libeling a political antagonist in a sleazy pamphlet. The civic servant who boasts of providing the "world's best public service" also is accused of withholding trash pickup from selected neighborhoods. The self-described friend of the underdog, a man who makes his reputation doing extraordinary favors for ordinary citizens, keeps tabs for more than two decades on signers of recall petitions against him. And yet, no less than his undeniable successes, his dare-anything behavior, erratic as it often was, undoubtedly endeared him to at least a portion of his constituency.

Having Orville Hubbard for your mayor was a lot like having the Mt. St. Helens or Kilauea volcano plopped down in the middle of your town. You might worry about the damage from those pesky eruptions, but at the same time you had to admire the power and the majesty of such a terrible force of nature, and you surely had to enjoy the notoriety it brought to the place.

So pervasive was the Hubbard mystique that many voters assumed he retained control at city hall after the debilitating stroke he suffered in the apartment he shared with the young blonde woman he had appointed a city department head several years before. Actually, in a scene somewhat reminiscent of the poststroke months of Woodrow Wilson's administration, Orvie's last three years passed with a team of his lieutenants at the helm, while the wheelchair-bound mayor was shuttled around to maintain the fiction that he still was making decisions.

When his police chief, longtime loyalist John B. O'Reilly, emerged from the pack of city hall insiders to become his two-term successor, it was a different Dearborn that he became heir to. As Hubbard often remarked, "I pity the poor son of a bitch who follows me." Chief among the problems faced by the new mayor was a citywide property reassessment mandated by the state to correct the decades-long favoritism shown to Dearborn homeowners at the expense of Ford and other industrial firms. Orvie's answer had been to forestall such problems. But his successor had to take action, by downsizing city government and approving what in Dearborn passed for austerity budgets.

As for Orville Hubbard's successes, some of his associates felt he was simply the right man in the right place at the right time, that he stumbled into a situation made to order for him and that he seized on every circumstance to enhance his power base and become simply through happenstance a municipal figure unique in U.S. history.

But in a sense, Hubbard was born too late. He would have been better suited to the life of a soldier-king heading some medieval city-state—fearless, decisive, able to inspire others to follow, ruthless when not given absolute obeisance. But his time was twentieth-century America, and he and his self-styled "Hubbard team" had to be content with making politics the same kind of macho display as, say, a football game.

However, because of the idiosyncrasies of his personality and his style, there remains a lingering doubt about how he might have fared in a larger political arena, even granting the stipulation that he might have been electable on a state or national level. As his notoriety grew, neither Democrats nor Republicans wanted him as a candidate for anything. Orville Hubbard wanted to be a judge, though he hardly had what could be described as a judicial temperament. At various times, he wanted to be a state legislator or a congressman. Perhaps, though he never said so publicly, he wanted to be governor. As he once remarked to me in a nostalgic comparison with a former governor, "I once counted for more in the Michigan Republican Party than Harry Kelly."

A more impartial observer who was convinced that Orvie had the right stuff for a bigger job was respected *Detroit News* political columnist Will Muller. Never exactly an unabashed fan, Muller noted that Hubbard had left behind "a long history of gasconade and frog-pond putsches. He has concerned himself always with little things, petty personal triumphs and publicity with a purple tinge. Even his victories are without meaning."

And yet Muller nonetheless tabbed him as "a politician who could have done lasting things. Under the drive of Hubbard's imagination, industry and ingenuity, Dearborn could have blossomed into a model city." He wrote:

Hubbard is articulate and dynamic. He is fearless. Not a little of his
charm derives from his audacity. He has devoted his life to political survival and has asked no other things from life. Such industry and dedica-

tion properly oriented could have lifted him far above his municipal playground. With the right motivation, a background of community accomplishment which could have been his, it would have been possible for Orville Hubbard to have sat in the executive office in Lansing. . . . With . . . his own persuasiveness and extraordinary talents, Hubbard could have become a community builder of national stature. . . . Yet . . . Hubbard's chief wrong to his community . . . lies in the deliberate wastage of precious talent for small ends. . . . His crime—and crime it is—is in not becoming the public figure he might have been. The country was ready for a man like that.[2]

It hardly seems like an unreasonable stretch to see Orville Hubbard's life as something of a Greek tragedy. It's the classic American success story: small-town boy with humble agrarian roots grows up as self-made success, lionized by small children and little old ladies. A fundamentally decent man, honest, hardworking, talented, creative. Except that somewhere along the way, he goes wrong. His behavior begins to be dominated by a personality quirk stemming from his immaturity. His fatal flaw—his meanness, his pettiness, his smallness, as remarked on by a newspaper columnist and countless mayoral critics—severely diminishes this otherwise heroic figure.

Still, as often criticized as he was, the man who took over the hometown of Henry Ford undeniably did his share of good over the years. It is remarkable that Hubbard escaped the ultimate cliché about power. He came about as close to absolute power as is possible in a modern democracy, and yet he was not so much corrupted by it as he was seduced and made complacent by it.

Hubbard ranks near the top of the rolls for political longevity in American history, but his Victoria-like hold on the mayoralty of a suburb of 100,000 was as much an evidence of his ultimate failure as it was a testament to his political acumen.

The tragedy of Orville Hubbard was not that he turned out to be a racist or a dictator or a petty, self-aggrandizing egotist. It was that these traits condemned him to 36 years in Dearborn's city hall instead of permitting him to move on to higher office. In a very real sense, Orvie's long mayoral tenure was not his glory but his badge of mediocrity.

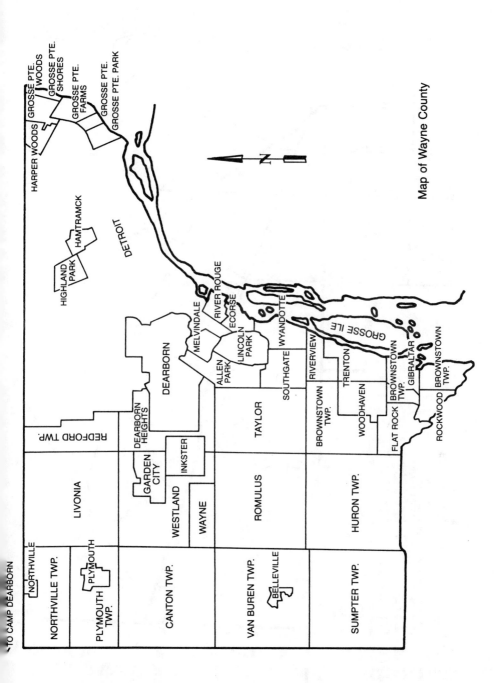

Map of Wayne County

393

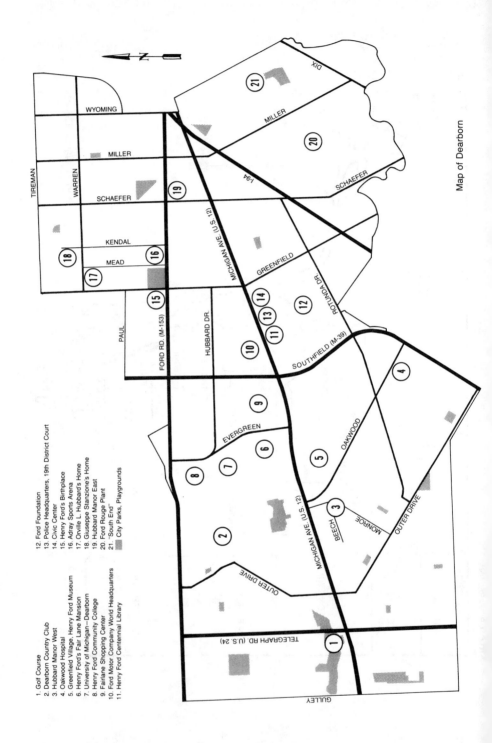

Map of Dearborn

1. Golf Course
2. Dearborn Country Club
3. Hubbard Manor West
4. Oakwood Hospital
5. Greenfield Village, Henry Ford Museum
6. Henry Ford's Fair Lane Mansion
7. University of Michigan—Dearborn
8. Henry Ford Community College
9. Fairlane Shopping Center
10. Ford Motor Company World Headquarters
11. Henry Ford Centennial Library

12. Ford Foundation
13. Police Headquarters, 19th District Court
14. Civic Center
15. Henry Ford's Birthplace
16. Adray Sports Arena
17. Orville L. Hubbard's Home
18. Giuseppe Stanzione's Home
19. Hubbard Manor East
20. Ford Rouge Plant
21. "South End"
      City Parks, Playgrounds

394

Appendix

Table 1. Hubbard in Dearborn Mayoral Elections:
Voting Returns

YEAR		DATE	CANDIDATES	VOTES	PERCENTAGE
1933	P	Oct. 9	Ford, Clyde M. *	5,357	47.7
			Jones, David L.	1,402	12.5
			Bovill, Reginald V.	1,256	11.2
			Beadle, Homer C.	1,139	10.1
			Thomson, James	748	6.7
			Hovey, Oscar C.	507	4.5
			Rich, Peter	437	3.9
			HUBBARD, ORVILLE L.	377	3.4
1937	P	Oct. 11	Carey, John L. *	6,196	66.6
			Korte, Michael	1,738	18.7
			HUBBARD, ORVILLE L.	1,376	14.8
1939	P	Oct. 9	Carey, John L. *	5,909	45.2
			HUBBARD, ORVILLE L.	3,799	29.1
			Ternes, Arthur A.	3,357	25.7
1939	G	Nov. 7	Carey, John L. *	9,526	52.5
			HUBBARD, ORVILLE L.	8,609	47.5
1941	P	Oct. 13	HUBBARD, ORVILLE L.	5,575	54.2
			Doyle, Clarence A.	4,705	45.8

YEAR		DATE	CANDIDATES	VOTES	PERCENTAGE
1941	G	Nov. 4	HUBBARD, ORVILLE L.	9,155	53.0
			Doyle, Clarence A.	8,129	47.0
1942	S	Nov. 3	HUBBARD, ORVILLE L. *	7,061	55.2
			Johnson, Jamie L.	2,956	23.1
			Ford, Clyde M.	2,212	17.3
			Carey, John F.	558	4.4
1945	P	Aug. 7	HUBBARD, ORVILLE L. *	5,585	59.0
			Thomson, James	2,689	28.4
			Guy, Ralph B. (Sr.)	1,192	12.6
1945	G	Nov. 6	HUBBARD, ORVILLE L. *	13,186	64.7
			Thomson, James	7,180	35.3
1947	P	Sept. 22	HUBBARD, ORVILLE L. *	5,763	42.3
			Carey, John L.	4,772	35.0
			Lowrey, Harvey H.	2,006	14.7
			Guy, Ralph B. (Sr.)	1,080	7.9
1947	G	Nov. 4	HUBBARD, ORVILLE L. *	13,430	55.8
			Carey, John L.	10,639	44.2
1949	P	Sept. 26	HUBBARD, ORVILLE L. *	12,041	54.2
			Matheny, Carl C.	5,284	23.8
			Rouse, Victor G.	3,599	16.2
			Thomson, James	514	2.3
			Hollman, George A.	421	1.9
			Wierimaa, Arthur	205	0.9
			Bartsch, Harold	156	0.7
1949	G	Nov. 8	HUBBARD, ORVILLE L. *	16,499	56.5
			Matheny, Carl C.	12,696	43.5
1951	R	Feb. 19	HUBBARD, ORVILLE L. * (NO)	16,872	57.0
			(YES)	12,732	43.0
1951	P	Sept. 24	HUBBARD, ORVILLE L. *	13,841	57.1
			Matheny, Carl C.	8,378	34.6
			McWilliams, John T.	1,369	5.6
			Nielsen, Erving	416	1.7
			Cassini, Matthew Orpeth	240	1.0
1951	G	Nov. 6	HUBBARD, ORVILLE L. *	16,050	59.1
			Matheny, Carl C.	11,101	40.9

Appendix

YEAR		DATE	CANDIDATES	VOTES	PERCENTAGE
1953	P	Sept. 28	(No mayoral primary)		
1953	G	Nov. 3	HUBBARD, ORVILLE L. *	25,572	71.2
			Christie, James (Jr.)	10,322	28.8
1955	P	Sept. 26	HUBBARD, ORVILLE L. *	11,075	65.1
			Parker, Ray F.	4,368	25.7
			Robinson, Edward J. (Jr.)	651	3.8
			Nemeth, Charles J.	580	3.4
			McCarthy, Leo A.	346	2.0
1955	G	Nov. 8	HUBBARD, ORVILLE L. *	21,063	70.2
			Parker, Ray F.	8,961	29.8
1957	P	Sept. 23	HUBBARD, ORVILLE L. *	14,174	54.6
			Mills, William L.	7,216	27.8
			Parker, Ray F.	1,859	7.2
			Keyes, Eugene C.	1,442	5.6
			Kadela, John L.	615	2.4
			Mulroy, Timothy M.	298	1.1
			Nemeth, Charles J.	203	0.8
			Robinson, Edward J. (Jr.)	98	0.4
			McSpadden, Samuel M. (Jr.)	70	0.3
1957	G	Nov. 5	HUBBARD, ORVILLE L. *	25,169	63.1
			Mills, William L.	14,721	36.9
1959	P	Sept. 28	HUBBARD, ORVILLE L. *	12,004	65.5
			Craig, Roger E.	3,466	18.9
			Calkins, Donald A.	1,369	7.5
			McCarthy, Leo A.	773	4.2
			Nemeth, Charles J.	720	3.9
1959	G	Nov. 3	HUBBARD, ORVILLE L. *	22,730	69.9
			Craig, Roger E.	9,782	30.1
1961	P	Sept. 12	HUBBARD, ORVILLE L. *	18,611	75.3
			Wagner, Eugene R.	2,925	11.8
			Nemeth, Charles J.	1,341	5.4
			Zahari, Daniel	1,032	4.2
			Bruce, Tommy	805	3.3
1961	G	Nov. 7	HUBBARD, ORVILLE L. *	26,583	77.0
			Wagner, Eugene R.	7,957	23.0
1964	P	Sept. 26	HUBBARD, ORVILLE L. *	21,691	83.0

YEAR		DATE	CANDIDATES	VOTES	PERCENTAGE
			Nemeth, Charles J.	2,472	9.5
			Cooper, William	1,329	5.1
			Zahari, Daniel	644	2.5
1964	G	Nov. 3	HUBBARD, ORVILLE L. *	40,269	83.4
			Nemeth, Charles J.	7,849	16.6
1967	P	Sept. 12	HUBBARD, ORVILLE L. *	16,347	85.6
			Nemeth, Charles J.	1,057	5.5
			Wagner, Anthony H.	1,034	5.4
			Hurley, Jerry D.	653	3.4
1967	G	Nov. 7	HUBBARD, ORVILLE L. *	26,448	87.0
			Nemeth, Charles J.	3,940	13.0
1970	P	Aug. 4	HUBBARD, ORVILLE L. *	17,615	77.2
			Thomas, Douglas R.	3,051	13.4
			Bazzy, Beverly A.	1,261	5.5
			Hurley, Jerry D.	891	4.0
1970	G	Nov. 3	HUBBARD, ORVILLE L. *	31,110	74.0
			Thomas, Douglas R.	10,939	26.0
1973	P	Aug. 7	HUBBARD, ORVILLE L. *	12,664	84.4
			Pazzanese, John A.	1,321	8.8
			Roman, Walter A.	539	3.6
			Strong, Irene M.	473	3.2
1973	G	Nov. 6	HUBBARD, ORVILLE L. *	24,952	82.5
			Pazzanese, John A.	5,301	17.5

Key: P Primary election (2 nominated)
      G General election
      S Special election
      R Recall (NO, against recall; YES, for recall)
      * Incumbent

Table 2. Hubbard vs. Mayoral Opponents: Voting Percentages

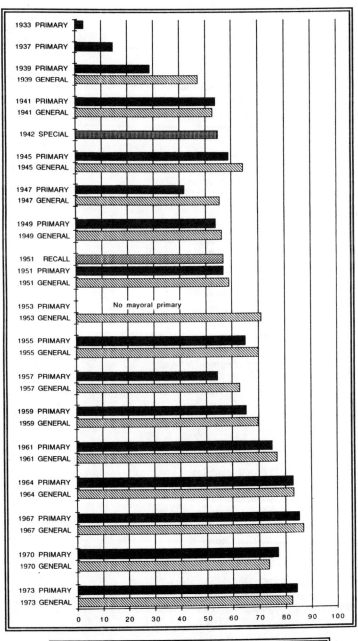

Table 3. Hubbard in Nonmayoral Elections:
Voting Returns

YEAR		DATE	CANDIDATES	VOTES	
				DEARBORN	TOTAL
1932	P	Sept. 13	State Senate, 21st District, Republican		
			Woodruff, Ari H.	1,519	12,271
			HUBBARD, ORVILLE L.	1,856	4,811
			Dwyer, Edward H.	2,253	4,389
			Welday, Donald F.	311	2,157
			Kurtz, Arthur J.	306	1,960
1934	P	Sept. 11	State Senate, 21st District, Republican		
			Darin, Frank P.	1,361	10,403
			HUBBARD, ORVILLE L.	1,719	5,981
			Turecki, Paul	189	936
1935	P	Oct. 14	Dearborn City Council (14 nominated)		
			Esper, Anthony M.		4,467
			Miller, Ernest G.		4,372
			Oglesbee, Carl C.		3,877
			Schaefer, Joseph W.		3,589
			Doyle, Clarence		3,371
			Henson, William		3,072
			Beadle, Homer C.		2,815
			Fisher, Edward F.		2,733
			Korte, Michael		2,604
			Bovill, Reginald V.		2,592
			Johnson, Jamie L.		2,560
			Johnson, Marguerite C.		2,543
			Keyes, Eugene C.		2,489
			Hughes, Caspar B.		2,388
			Doyle, Patrick J.		2,067
			Behrendt, Gustav C.		2,009
			Justice, Clarence S.		1,917
			Fordell, Joseph F.		1,683
			Fukalek, Frank		1,559
			Klein, Albert A.		1,518
			Moore, William		1,444
			Rachow, Warren J.		1,424
			Neisler, George H.		1,388
			Guinan, James		1,224
			HUBBARD, ORVILLE L.		1,076
			MacDonald, Roderick F.		1,035
			Oehmke, Fred C.		836
			Jones, David L.		695
			Vyant, Adrian J.		656
			Catana, Nicolai H.		633

Appendix

YEAR	DATE	CANDIDATES	VOTES DEARBORN	TOTAL
		Snyder, Lucille		577
		Briggs, Clifford		554
		Miller, George H.		537
		Moore, Clyde		511
		Decker, Clayton A.		325
		Grace, George		279
		Lavine, George		272
		Weishuhn, Floyd		232
		Pellow, Frank		193
		Provost, Jose D.		190
1936 G	Apr. 6	Justice of the Peace, Dearborn Township *		
		Mokersky, John (R)		734
		HUBBARD, ORVILLE L. (D)		390
1936 P	Sept. 15	Congress, 16th District, Republican		
		Ford, Clyde M.	1,421	6,660
		Fisher, Edward F.	977	5,057
		Miller, Ernest G.	1,378	3,039
		Kreger, Ira J.	56	2,517
		Mayrand, James S.	180	2,300
		HUBBARD, ORVILLE L.	382	1,482
1938 P	Sept. 13	State Senate, 21st District, Republican		
		HUBBARD, ORVILLE L.	2,678	10,857
		Harvey, J. Mark	1,334	5,538
		Kurtz, Arthur J.	297	3,831
		Tingle, Walter	228	2,023
1938 G	Nov. 8	State Senate, 21st District		
		Nowak, Stanley (D)	8,141	47,815
		HUBBARD, ORVILLE L. (R)	7,946	38,378
		Nauta, Mint (Socialist)	33	148
		Welch, John (Const. Dem.)	17	140
		Sekulich, John (Soc. Labor)	9	60
1953 G	Apr. 6	Circuit Court, Wayne County (18 elected)		
		Neuenfelt, Lila M.	6,729	172,515
		Maher, Thomas F.	4,069	172,143
		Jayne, Ira W.	3,811	166,303
		O'Hara, Chester P.	3,896	165,256
		Fitzgerald, Frank	3,426	152,474

YEAR	DATE	CANDIDATES	VOTES	
			DEARBORN	TOTAL
		Brennan, John V.	3,365	149,848
		Murphy, Thomas J.	3,381	147,481
		Moynihan, Joseph A.	3,794	146,230
		Weideman, Carl M.	3,433	145,635
		Toms, Robert M.	3,428	142,307
		Webster, Clyde I.	3,528	139,531
		Murphy, George B.	3,204	139,020
		Webster, Arthur	3,174	136,680
		Fitzgerald, Neal	2,919	134,699
		Marschner, Adolph F.	3,119	130,839
		Ferguson, Frank B.	3,018	122,831
		Culehan, Miles N.	3,353	121,968
		Brennan, Vincent M.	2,328	103,509
		McNally, James N.	2,668	101,342
		Sempliner, Arthur W.	1,803	76,225
		HUBBARD, ORVILLE L.	7,006	76,063
		Bashara, George	1,539	68,458
		Griffiths, Hicks G.	1,904	68,019
		Lutomski, Anthony L.	1,626	61,349
		Montante, James	1,474	57,179
		Salowich, Nicholas	1,758	52,318
		Leib, Samuel W.	831	49,378
		Kane, John F.	1,181	44,844
		Bartholomew, Frederick D.	1,175	39,091
1955 P	Feb. 21	Circuit Court, Wayne County (4 nominated)		
		McCree, Wade H.	951	76,372
		Bohn, Theodore R.	1,274	57,782
		HUBBARD, ORVILLE L.	3,851	40,007
		Branigan, Edgar M.	1,120	39,631
		O'Brien, George D.	874	35,298
		Dingeman, Harry J. (Jr.)	828	34,131
		McNally, James N.	957	32,430
		Bartholomew, Frederick D.	235	8,488
1955 G	Apr. 4	Circuit Court, Wayne County (2 elected)		
		McCree, Wade H.	4,481	179,689
		Bohn, Theodore R.	5,316	157,426
		Branigin, Edgar M.	5,827	134,035
		HUBBARD, ORVILLE L.	11,561	110,801
1956 P	Aug. 7	Circuit Court, Wayne County (2 nominated)		

YEAR	DATE	CANDIDATES	VOTES DEARBORN	TOTAL
		Targonski, Victor	3,030	127,044
		Darin, Frank P.	2,039	80,824
		HUBBARD, ORVILLE L.	4,909	68,812
1965 P	Sept. 14	Circuit Court, Wayne County (8 nominated)		
		Moody, Blair (Jr.)	2,929	81,080
		Farmer, Charles S.	985	78,859
		Foley, Thomas J.	1,605	69,987
		Dingeman, Harry J. (Jr.)	1,823	64,236
		Sullivan, Joe B.	1,181	56,434
		HUBBARD, ORVILLE L.	3,808	48,300
		Szymanski, Anthony	1,523	41,993
		DeMascio, Robert C.	502	41,719
		Kennedy, Cornelia G.	1,262	41,660
		Martin, George T.	8,346	29,689
		Targonski, Victor	1,302	27,624
		Stempien, Ronald R.	1,255	26,597
		Ryan, Harold M.	367	26,008
		Murphy, Robert D.	650	22,142
		Evans, Robert Lee	94	21,601
		Watts, Lucile	557	21,522
		Bradley, Michael W.	322	18,130
		McDonald, Charles W.	551	17,426
		Cyrowski, Arthur J.	440	16,055
		O'Connell, James D.	242	14,336
		Hathaway, James A.	233	13,691
		Krueger, William	613	12,662
		Markowitz, Seymour	270	12,587
		McManus, Lee C.	166	11,907
		Dunn, Richard D.	600	11,146
		Schmier, Abe A.	121	9,969
		Edwards, Dee	220	9,481
		Moore, Warfield (Jr.)	124	9,415
		Brashear, Lonnie H.	162	9,009
		Allen, Julius E.	165	8,892
		Liddy, Mary Jane	215	8,582
		MacDonald, John E.	237	8,470
		Keating, Patrick J.	220	8,392
		Tobias, George W.	165	7,553
		Williams, Ben L.	234	7,410
		Breen, John E.	124	6,557
		Callanan, Evan H.	228	6,344
		Austin, J. Connor	89	6,283
		Bonfiglio, Antonio	807	5,728

YEAR	DATE	CANDIDATES	VOTES DEARBORN	TOTAL
		Koch, Paul M.	129	5,555
		Harty, Paul	114	5,334
		VanWiemeersch, Robert P.	99	5,170
		Targan, Royal G.	1,954	4,752
		Ponder, William N.	79	4,121
		Safran, John	135	4,040
		Howard, Austin A.	105	3,681
1965 S	Nov. 2	Circuit Court, Wayne County (4 elected)		
		Moody, Blair (Jr.)	11,415	313,825
		Foley, Thomas J.	9,383	251,111
		Farmer, Charles S.	5,410	219,351
		Dingeman, Harry J. (Jr.)	9,846	212,527
		Sullivan, Joe B.	6,487	196,295
		Szymanski, Anthony	6,932	149,757
		HUBBARD, ORVILLE L.	9,204	139,106
		DeMascio, Robert C.	3,546	124,393

Key: P Primary election (1 nominated unless otherwise noted)
     G General election (1 elected unless otherwise noted)
     S Special election
     * From the *Dearborn Independent*, April 10, 1936. Dearborn Heights (formerly Dearborn Township) City Clerk retained no records for general election or for March 2, 1936, primary election.
SOURCES: Dearborn City Clerk, Wayne County Election Commission.

Notes

Prologue

1. Dan Gillmor's Scoop 2, no. 27 (November 1941).

2. Michael Sayers, "Vice Gangs Rule America's Defense Arsenal," *Dan Gillmor's Scoop* 2, no. 27 (November 1941): 7-11.

3. Dearborn and Fordson effected only the second successful city merger in Michigan history, according to the state Boundary Commission; the first paired Saginaw and East Saginaw into the new city of Saginaw in 1889.

4. Sayers, "Vice Gangs Rule," 9.

5. For details on the Slamer affair, see the *Dearborn Press* (July 31–August 7, 1941) and the *Detroit News* (May 23–August 14, 1941).

6. For a fuller description of the grand jury, see the *Detroit News* (May 23, 1941–May 24, 1942).

Chapter 1

1. William Serrin, "Mayor Hubbard Gives Dearborn What It Wants—and Then Some," *New York Times Magazine*, January 12, 1969, 92.

2. Hubbard still had a feeling that Ford was on a roll. He won eight dollars in a pool with his appointees when Ford became Nixon's choice to succeed Spiro Agnew as vice-president on October 12, 1973.

3. Although Dearborn city officials continued as late as 1988 to credit Hubbard with being the all-time record holder among full-time mayors, that distinction is more aptly claimed by Erastus Corning II, Democratic machine mayor of Albany, N. Y. Corning served 41 years, taking office five days before Hubbard, on January 1, 1942. He was into

his eleventh four-year term when he died at age 73 on May 28, 1983. Hubbard's fifteenth and last term expired January 1, 1978. For a fuller description of Corning's administration, see William Kennedy, *O Albany! An Urban Tapestry* (New York: Viking, 1983).

4. William T. Noble, "Dearborn's Great White Father: 26 Years of Pride and Prejudice," *Detroit News Sunday Magazine*, June 25, 1967, 12.

5. Michigan election laws permit absentee ballots to be issued on election day only on an emergency basis, at the discretion of the city clerk's staff.

6. See official vote totals for 1973 in Appendix.

7. Hubbard declined a request to meet with Young before the Detroit election, according to a September 27, 1973, column by Fred Hoffman in the *Dearborn Guide*. Hoffman said a former associate called to make the request, telling him Young believed "there are only two effective mayors in the country today, Orville Hubbard and Richard Daley." Hubbard reportedly replied that he was flattered, but pointed out that when he endorsed another black, Richard Austin, for Detroit mayor four years before, Detroiters wrote letters telling him to mind his own business. Hubbard told Hoffman, "I'll be happy to meet with whichever one of them wins after the election and tell them exactly how we do things in Dearborn, but I believe in first things first, and I certainly don't want to get involved in that race." Young was quoted in the *Detroit Free Press* on October 3, 1973, that "besides obvious philosophical differences" that Young had with Hubbard and Daley, "they are representative of mayors who get things done." A spokesman said Young considered the two "typical models" for efficiency in keeping cities safe, clean and livable.

Chapter 2

1. John C. Dancy, *Sands Against the Wind: The Memoirs of John C. Dancy* (Detroit: Wayne State University Press, 1966), 18.

2. U.S. Marines occupied Haiti from 1915 to 1934 based on claims that such action was justified by the Monroe Doctrine and the principle of humanitarian intervention.

3. Noble, "Dearborn's Great White Father," 28. Hubbard denied the allegation.

4. Hubbard discussed race with a class of seventh graders in March 1965, after his federal indictment. Asked what he would do if a Negro moved next door to him, he hesitated, then said, "I'd move." Asked why, he replied, "For personal reasons." Asked about voter registration problems in Selma, Ala., he said, "If I were in Alabama, I'd register these people to vote and I'd let them pray." Asked what if the situation were in Dearborn, he said, "Same thing. I'd let them go, as long as they don't tear things down."

5. Besides retaining the words *Negro* and *Negroes* wherever originally used in quoted statements, I have used those words where appropriate in narrative parts of the text covering the period up to the late 1960s, when *black* and *blacks* became the preferred usage.

6. Hubbard was not alone among Dearborn politicians whose actions were influenced by race. The civil rights record of another Dearbornite, Congressman John Lesinski, was considered instrumental in his 1964 Democratric primary defeat by Congressman John T. Dingell when their districts were merged. Lesinski was the only Democrat from a northern industrial state to vote against the original version of the 1963–64 Civil Rights Bill. He subsequently was censured by the state and district Democratic committees.

7. A *Dearborn Guide* editorial said July 1, 1965: "In all the years that Hubbard has been mayor of Dearborn, there haven't been any instances of Negro mistreatment. As a matter of fact, Negroes have been accorded full respect in the community in recent years."

One instance of a formal complaint against the city was registered in August 1965 by a Detroit black, Charles Spencer, 40, who told the Michigan Civil Rights Commission he had been arrested without cause by Dearborn police, then beaten and starved for a week while being held incommunicado. In October, he admitted in Detroit Recorder's Court that he had made up the story to avoid being fired from his job in a bakery after missing a week of work. Found guilty of making a false report of a crime, he was sentenced to 30 days in jail and two years' probation. For a condensed discussion of Dearborn's racial history under Hubbard, see David L. Good, "The Ghost of Orville Hubbard," *Michigan: The Magazine of the Detroit News*, April 20, 1986, 8–25. See also Epilogue, herein, note 3.

8. Serrin, "Mayor Hubbard Gives Dearborn," 26.

9. A *New York Times* version of the quote in 1968 was more blunt: "If you have integration, first you have kids going to school together, then next thing you know, they're grab-assing around, then they're getting married and having half-breed kids. Then you wind up with a mongrel race. And from what I know of history, that's the end of civilization."

10. Noble, "Dearborn's Great White Father," 28.

11. Judy Cord, tape-recorded interview, Dearborn, Mich., November 18, 1981.

Chapter 3

1. John Bartlett, *Familiar Quotations*, centennial ed. (Boston: Little, Brown, 1955), 622. The statement, attributed to Ford in 1919, sometimes is rendered, "History is more or less bunk."

2. Ford ended free Rouge plant tours on June 27, 1980, citing a desire to save $1.5 million in costs in the face of a weak economy and uneven production schedule. Nearly 8 million people had toured the plant since 1928.

3. One observer, Mark H. Forsthoefel, concluded that Hubbard's pugnacity was a strategy to attract Ford workers' support and did in fact gain him more votes than it lost.". . . Since over 20,000 Ford employees lived in Dearborn, many would recall the harsh treatment that they had received in the thirties at the hands of a company that was then fighting attempts at unionization," Forsthoefel wrote in "Some Phases of the Hubbard Administration in Dearborn, Michigan, from 1942 to 1951," master's thesis, University of Toledo, 1955, 170.

4. John J. Fish, tape-recorded interview, Dearborn, Mich., undated, 1972.

5. Ronald R. Stockton and Frank Whelon Wayman, *A Time of Turmoil: Values and Voting in the 1970's* (East Lansing: Michigan State University Press, 1983), 27.

6. Ibid., 12-13.

7. Ibid., 40.

Chapter 4

1. Orville L. Hubbard, conversation with associates during auto trip from Dearborn to Union City, Mich., May 21, 1973; normally he downplayed talk of such ambitions.

2. Hubbard was a longtime admirer of Elbert Hubbard, but he said he was never able to find evidence that they were related. As for the slogan, a city hall spokesman said in 1988 that its origin was uncertain, although the mayor had it reprinted on the cover of Elbert Hubbard, *A Message to Garcia*, Special Printing for the City of Dearborn, Mich. (East Aurora, N. Y.: House of Hubbard, Memorial Edition, 1967).

3. William L. Mills, "How Dearborn Got a Dictator Mayor," *Dearborn Independent* political supplement, September 1957.

4. A major victory for Hubbard came when the City Council voted 4–3 to pass his proposal requiring conformity in type of construction in neighborhoods, as reported in the *Dearborn Press* on April 20, 1950. Two months earlier, a group of builders had accused him of trying to "subvert the city to his will."

5. Frank Hubbard, tape-recorded interview, Dearborn, Mich., July 10, 1982.

6. Doyne Jackson, tape-recorded interview, Dearborn, Mich., April 19, 1986.

7. William V. Shannon, "The Political Machine I: Rise and Fall/The Age of the Bosses," *American Heritage* 20, no. 4 (1969): 29.

8. Booton Herndon, *Ford: An Unconventional Biography of the Men and Their Times* (New York: Weybright and Talley, 1969), 342.

9. Conventional political science wisdom holds that Hubbard does not qualify as a machine boss. Charles R. Adrian and Charles Press, *Governing Urban America* (New York: McGraw-Hill, 1977), 48: "Hubbard does not have a machine in the traditional sense. He has almost no patronage appointments. There are no ward or precinct organizations." Political scientist Austin Ranney, following a talk at Henry Ford Community College, Dearborn, on November 21, 1980, agreed that Dearborn's low patronage level disqualified Hubbard as a boss.

10. Jackson interview, April 19, 1986.

11. Ibid.

12. Ibid.

13. From a 1953 Hubbard campaign flyer. Hubbard credited an aide, George Martin, with composing the jingle.

14. Jackson interview, April 19, 1986.

15. Ibid.

16. Ford challenged Dearborn's 1981–82 assessments on part of the Rouge complex, and the firm in 1984 won favorable rulings from an administrative law judge for the Michigan Tax Tribunal, later appealed by the city. The case was before the Michigan Court of Appeals in March 1985 when Ford and the city settled the dispute. The agreement gave Ford tax refunds totaling $32.5 million (including $10.1 million from the city, the rest from the Dearborn schools and from Wayne County) for the years 1981 to 1984. Cash value of Ford property in the city was established at $575 million for those years, a reduction of $300 million for each year. Ford agreed to accept a lower interest rate on the refunds than awarded by the tribunal.

17. Jackson interview, April 19, 1986.

18. Joseph J. Burtell, tape-recorded interview, Dearborn, Mich., December 7, 1981.

19. Doug Thomas, tape-recorded interview, Dearborn, Mich., November 8, 1987.

20. Jim Hubbard, tape-recorded interview, Dearborn, Mich., July 10, 1982.

21. Mel Ravitz, interview, Detroit, Mich., June 19, 1972.

Chapter 5

1. *Dearborn Citizen* 1, no. 1 (August 5, 1957).

2. Ronald R. Stockton and Frank Whelon Wayman, "New Suburban Populism: Changing Values and Politics in a Northern Community," an unpublished portion of *A Time of Turmoil*, 1.30.

3. Cord interview, November 18, 1981.

4. "The Political Observer" column, *Dearborn Independent*, July 22, 1949.

5. Cord interview, November 18, 1981.

6. Ibid.

7. See Chapter 43 for details about a state audit report on the Hubbard wedding ceremonies.

8. *Annual Statement of the Financial Condition of the City of Dearborn, Wayne County, Michigan*, fiscal period ending June 30, 1975, compiled by Office of the City Controller.

9. Jackson interview, April 19, 1986.

10. Stockton and Wayman, "New Suburban Populism," 1.29–30.

11. Ibid., 1.31–32.

12. Ibid., 2.23.

13. Adrian and Press, *Governing Urban America*, 49.

14. Serrin also errs in "crediting" Hubbard with creating Dearborn's bathtub navy. For a fuller discussion, see the *Dearborn Press*, June 7, 1945. See Chapter 17 (notes 11, 12), herein.

Chapter 6

1. *Dearborn Press*, January 6, 1977.

2. Orville L. Hubbard, tape-recorded interview by Joyce Hagelthorn, editor of the *Dearborn Press*, Dearborn, Mich., April 5, 1972.

3. Fish interview, 1972.

4. William L. Mills, tape-recorded interview, Dearborn, Mich., June 29, 1982.

5. Fay Hubbard spelled her first name "Faye" in her early years on such legal documents as her divorce complaints and her children's birth certificates, and newspapers in the 1940s and '50s used that form. Frank Hubbard said she dropped the *e* later, and her name appears as "Fay" in her obituary notices.

Chapter 7

1. Hubbard, Hagelthorn interview, April 5, 1972.

2. "Up Rose Little Orvie Then," *Time*, March 5, 1951, 23-24. See Chapter 24 (note 17) and Chapter 25 (note 1), herein. See also "The Ordeals of Orville," *Time*, August 21, 1950, 13. See Chapter 23 (note 9), herein.

3. Edward E. Malkin, "Dearborn's Madcap Mayor," *Coronet*, September 1958, 66–70.

4. Adrian and Press, *Governing Urban America*, 48.

5. The *Independent* was not connected with Henry Ford's periodical of the same name, which had been labeled anti-Semitic by critics and was withdrawn from publication. Ford granted the publishers of the weekly *Independent* permission to use the name.

6. Under new ownership, the *Press* adopted a policy of "constructive neutrality" after the recall of 1951.

7. Despite some razzing, Hubbard used a 1941 photo of himself on his campaign literature through the 1960s. "Well, they haven't ever changed the picture of Washington on the dollar bill," he told me. "If it isn't Hubbard, who is it?" As he recalled it, he had 25 photos taken by Arella Studios of Dearborn—"and didn't like any of 'em. I changed my shirt, changed my necktie, went back, took about 10 more. Used to put 'em up at the

fireplace in my house. People come over, I'd say, 'Out of all those pictures, which one do you like best?' And nearly everybody picked that one picture out. And that's the one I used. It isn't just because the picture is when I was younger. It costs about $500, $600, $700 just to change the negatives on the literature." The photo, like its successor, was somewhat ubiquitous, also showing up in such places as the Dearborn driver's license bureau, where applicants were directed to look at it while being photographed.

8. Jackson interview, April 19, 1986.

9. Thomas Jefferson, in a letter to John Norvell of Danville, Va., June 11, 1807, *The Life and Selected Writings of Thomas Jefferson,* ed. by Adrienne Koch and William Peden (New York: Modern Library, 1944), 581–82.

10. Serrin, "Mayor Hubbard Gives Dearborn." According to Doyne Jackson, the action was timed to divert attention from Roy Wilkins's criticism of Hubbard as the nation's "meanest man in race relations."

11. "'History Is Bunk'—Mayor Seeks Facts," City of Dearborn Research and Information Department, handout issued for release January 15, 1969.

12. Robert Ankeny, *Detroit News*, April 5, 1972.

13. Hubbard, Hagelthorn interview, April 5, 1972.

Chapter 8

1. James Helmrich, tape-recorded interview, Flint and Pontiac, Mich., December 14, 1987.

2. Fish interview, 1972.

3. Cord interview, November 18, 1981.

4. Jim Hubbard interviews, August 1 and 22, 1982.

5. Jim Hubbard interview, August 22, 1982.

6. Maureen Keane, tape-recorded conversation, Dearborn, Mich., September 14, 1972.

7. Raised Congregationalist, Hubbard established a pattern of attending many churches in the city during his early terms in office as a tactic to make members of each congregation think he was a member. When I asked him how religious he was, he replied, "Oh, Christ, I don't know. I'm not a disbeliever. I just think, you're dead, you're dead; that's all. Some people believe [in an afterlife]. I don't know."

8. Helmrich interview, December 14, 1987.

9. Fred Hoffman, tape-recorded interview, Dearborn, Mich., December 1, 1987.

10. Annette Ross, tape-recorded interview, Dearborn, Mich., November 30, 1987.

11. Helmrich interview, December 14, 1987.

Chapter 9

1. Jim Hubbard interview, August 1, 1982.

2. Gary Farrugia, *Dearborn Times-Herald*, September 4, 1975.

3. John Hubbard, tape-recorded interview, Dearborn, Mich., October 19, 1981.

4. Frank Hubbard interview, July 10, 1982.

5. Jim Hubbard interview, July 10, 1982.

6. Nancy Hubbard Dmytro, tape-recorded interview, Dearborn, Mich., January 21, 1989.

7. Jim Hubbard interview, July 10, 1982.

8. Frank Hubbard interview, July 10, 1982.

9. Jim Hubbard interview, July 10, 1982.

10. Jim Hubbard interview, August 1, 1982.

11. Nancy Hubbard Dmytro interview, January 21, 1989.

12. Jim Hubbard interview, July 10, 1982.

13. Frank Hubbard interview, August 1, 1982.

14. Jim Hubbard interview, July 10, 1982.

15. Frank Hubbard interview, August 1, 1982.

16. Jim Hubbard interview, July 10, 1982.

17. Nancy Hubbard Dmytro interview, January 21, 1989.

18. Jim Hubbard interview, August 1, 1982.

19. Nancy Hubbard Dmytro interview, January 21, 1989.

20. John Hubbard interview, October 19, 1981.

21. Jim Hubbard interview, August 1, 1982.

22. John Hubbard interview, October 19, 1981.

23. Nancy Hubbard Dmytro interview, January 21, 1989.

24. Jim Hubbard interview, August 1, 1982.

25. Frank Hubbard interviews, July 10 and August 1, 1982.

26. Jim Hubbard interview, August 1, 1982.

27. Jim Hubbard interviews, July 10 and August 1, 1982.

28. John Hubbard interview, October 19, 1981.

29. Frank Hubbard interview, July 10, 1982.

Chapter 10

1. Harry A. Overstreet, *The Mature Mind* (New York: W. W. Norton, 1949), 25. The book was quoted by former Dearborn Councilman Anthony Smith in a letter about Orville L. Hubbard to the *Dearborn Press*, March 30, 1950.

2. John Hubbard interview, October 19, 1981.

3. Jim Hubbard interview, August 1, 1982.

4. Overstreet, *The Mature Mind*, 23.

5. Ibid., 25.

6. Ibid., 66; italics added.

7. Ibid., 162–63.

8. Hubbard's younger brother Elvert was quoted in the *Detroit News* on April 17–18, 1950, as saying he remembered little about Orville's childhood, though he remembered being impressed seeing him play football once. As an adult, he said, "I don't see him too much. Lived with him for awhile when he was just starting to run for things, but I had enough of that. . . . I helped Orville tack up the posters over other fellows' posters and tear down the other fellows' when they tacked theirs up over ours. Nuts. I wouldn't be in his shoes for a million dollars. All he has is uproar."

9. Jim Hubbard interviews, August 1 and 22, 1982.

10. Interview with clinical psychologist who asked that his name not be used, Dearborn, Mich., August 31, 1987.

11. Keane conversation, September 13, 1972.

Chapter 11

1. Orville L. Hubbard, tape-recorded luncheon speech, Union City Rotary Club, Our Lady of Fatima Catholic Church, Union City, Mich., May 21, 1973.
2. Ibid.
3. Ibid.

Chapter 12

1. Even Hubbard's official biographical press handout, released and updated annually by the City of Dearborn, pointed out that Wright's flight at Kittyhawk, N. C., took place December 17, 1903.
2. Lee M. Bartlett, interview, Dearborn Heights, Mich., May 23, 1972.
3. Otto Smith, conversation, Union City, Mich., May 21, 1973.

Chapter 13

1. Hubbard scored 61 in elementary algebra, 90 in general science and 76 in English for the first semester, followed by 92 in general science and 84 in English for the second semester, as recorded in January and June 1922, respectively, in the *Union City High School Register*, 310. In applying for admission to the Detroit College of Law on January 26, 1928, he claimed high school credits of one unit each in algebra, general science, English, ancient history, bookkeeping, typewriting and shorthand, plus one-half credit for arithmetic.
2. Hubbard's Detroit College of Law application claimed high school credits of one unit each in Latin and business English, plus one-half credit in public speaking, from Ferris Institute. It also noted that he studied but did not finish classes in European history, mathematics and English.
3. Along with Hubbard's application, approved a day after its submission, he turned in a seven-page, single-spaced, typewritten paper entitled, "A Synopsis of the Experience of Orville L. Hubbard after Being Graduated from the Eighth Grade of the Union City Public Schools, Union City, Michigan/June 20, 1920 to January 26, 1928." Hubbard's grades in four years of law school: 3 A's, 5 B+'s, 25 B's, 1 B-, 2 C+'s, 15 C's, 1 D+, 18 D's and 3 "passed" notations.
4. Hubbard actually pulled three B's and a "passed" in his four semesters of constitutional law. His only A's came in first-year criminal law, first-year (summer class) bailments and fourth-year suretyship.

Chapter 14

1. Hubbard sometimes attributed the quote to himself and sometimes to Barnum in literature he handed out at city hall.
2. *Detroit News*, April 18, 1950.
3. Mills, "How Dearborn Got a Dictator Mayor."
4. Orville L. Hubbard, "To the Independent Thinking People of Dearborn," undated

political flyer, September/October (?) 1933. Copied from the files of Orville L. Hubbard.

5. Mills, "How Dearborn Got a Dictator Mayor."

Chapter 15

1. Sayers, "Vice Gangs Rule," 7 and front cover.

2. Schonhofen and nine others eventually brought to trial in the Dearborn vice-graft conspiracy case were acquitted in March 1943 after a trial of nearly a month. Wayne Circuit Judge DeWitt M. Merriam said, "I am convinced that there was considerable crime and vice in the city of Dearborn and that some of the defendants here were involved. However, I am not satisfied that there was a conspiracy under the laws of Michigan." Two police detectives, James Denny and Horace King, were among those acquitted. Six of the defendants—including John Bitonti, reputed leader of the Dearborn underworld, and Charles Muradian, his top aide—admitted participating in gambling activities. Bitonti testified that he, Muradian and two others each put up $1,000 to set up the National Daily policy racket in 1938. He said that only about 10 percent of its business was in Dearborn and that the best days brought in $1,200. Bitonti denied making payoffs to police, and the judge ruled that testimony failed to show conclusively that there was collusion between police and racketeers, even though the transcript of Inspector Charles W. Slamer during a preliminary examination in July 1941 indicated otherwise. Schonhofen, Denny and King took jobs with the Ford Motor plant protection force after their indictments.

3. Miller was indicted and bound over for trial in Wayne Circuit Court in September 1941, after witnesses before the Ferguson grand jury testified that he had accepted $300 for exerting his influence in the awarding of a $57,000 contract for sidewalks in 1936. Miller, protesting his innocence and claiming that he was at a hunting lodge in the Alpena, Mich., area at the time of the alleged bribe, lost a reelection attempt in November 1941, finishing twelfth in a field of 14 nominees. Governor Murray D. Van Wagoner denied a petition to oust Miller from office, however, and Miller finished his term through December 1941. In January 1943, Miller was acquitted of the bribery charge by Wayne Circuit Judge DeWitt M. Merriam when the prosecution conceded it was unable to break his alibi, despite incriminating testimony from a contractor and two employees. Miller took a job with Ford Motor Company after his indictment.

4. Orville L. Hubbard, political flyer announcing September 21 rally at Knights of Columbus Hall, Dearborn, September 17, 1941. Copied from the files of Orville L. Hubbard.

5. Orville L. Hubbard, political flyer announcing November 2 radio broadcast on WXYZ, undated, October 1941. Copied from the files of Orville L. Hubbard.

6. Ibid.

7. *Dearborn Press*, October 23, 1941.

Chapter 16

1. Susan Morse, *Detroit Free Press*, December 17, 1982.

2. *Dearborn Press*, October 2, 1941.

3. Ibid., October 22, 1942.

4. Ibid., October 29, 1942.

5. Ibid. Hubbard named the author, Alex Pilch, city director of public relations in June 1948.

6. Ibid.

7. The charter lasted until July 1, 1980. A new charter was approved by a vote of 3,052 to 2,623, with less than 10 percent of registered voters turning out, in November 1979. Under a 1977 mandate from voters, the new charter retained the strong-mayor form of government. The changes made were regarded as predominantly technical. A first proposed revision that would have restricted mayoral powers severely was turned down overwhelmingly in June 1979.

Chapter 17

1. *Detroit News*, June 20, 1945.

2. Emrys R. Evans, open letter to Orville L. Hubbard, January 9, 1943. Copied from the files of Orville L. Hubbard.

3. Alex Pilch, *Dearborn Press*, May 13, 1943.

4. *Dearborn Press*, December 30, 1943.

5. Ibid., February 25, 1943. Hubbard eventually made public relations fodder out of punching in early and punching out late.

6. Ibid., August 30, 1945.

7. Stirred by unfounded rumors that whites had thrown a Negro woman and her baby off the Belle Isle Bridge, groups began battling each other on June 21, 1943, in three days of racially tinged disturbances that left 35 dead and 530 injured. Some 4,000 federal troops joined state troops under a state of emergency declared by Michigan Governor Harry Kelly. A total of 1,188 persons were prosecuted on felony charges.

8. *Dearborn Press*, November 16, 1944.

9. Ibid.

10. Ibid., May 31, 1945.

11. Ibid., June 7, 1945.

12. Ibid., November 1, 1945. The enlistment plan was credited to the commandant of the Coast Guard, Vice-Admiral Russell R. Waesche. The Dearborn Flotilla numbered Judge George Martin and other Hubbard foes among its members.

13. Hubbard's official city biographical press handouts said, "Mayor Hubbard remained loyal in May 1945 to those who had supported him in earlier elections by declining an appointment by then Governor Harry F. Kelly to one of two new Wayne County Probate Judgeships created by the Legislature."

14. *Dearborn Press*, June 7, 1945.

15. *Detroit News*, June 6, 1945.

16. Ford ran newspaper ads on August 2, 1945, referring to the proposed federal housing project and declaring, "We shall fight to keep Negro housing out of Dearborn."

Chapter 18

1. *Detroit News*, May 22, 1947.

2. *Detroit Free Press*, April 22, 1971. "The needy are going to starve while these greedy sons-of-bitches get fat," he said after the Michigan Supreme Court ordered pay

raises and retroactive pay for firemen. Soon thereafter, the firemen's mothers complained about the "profane and unseemly statements."

3. Abuse of city cars was a favorite topic of Beadle's. The councilman charged repeatedly that Hubbard's appointees and relatives were given free use of city cars, and he suggested several times that the cars be marked plainly as city cars to discourage abuses. It was not until 1950, after Beadle was voted off the council, however, that his hope was realized. In December 1950, during the Hubbard recall campaign, the council decided to require that some city cars, not including their own, be marked. Following a closed meeting between Hubbard and the council, during which the mayor apparently coerced them to include their own cars, councilmen voted to have all city cars except certain police vehicles marked. See Chapter 43 (note 10), herein.

4. *Detroit News*, May 23, 1947. "Flunkey" is a misquote.

5. *Dearborn Press*, October 30, 1947.

6. Orville L. Hubbard, political flyer, undated, November 1947. Copied from the files of Orville L. Hubbard.

Chapter 19

1. In a St. Louis case, *Shelley v. Kraemer*, 334 U.S. 1 (1948), the court ruled in a unanimous five-man decision that judicial enforcement of restrictive covenants constituted state action in violation of the Fourteenth Amendment. A companion case in Detroit, *Sipes v. McGhee*, brought the ruling even closer to home for Hubbard and his constituents. In that case, the court's ruling overturned a 1947 Michigan Supreme Court decision that would have denied Orsel and Minnie Sims McGhee the right to occupy a home they purchased in 1944 in an all-white neighborhood on Detroit's near west side. The spread of restrictive covenants had been one result of a controversial Detroit court case in the 1920s. In June 1925, a Negro physician, Dr. Ossian Sweet, and his wife purchased a home in an all-white neighborhood. When a rock-throwing mob formed after the Sweets moved in, an exchange of shots killed a neighbor, Leon Breiner. Dr. Sweet and other family members were arrested and charged with murder, and the NAACP brought Clarence Darrow in to defend them. The case resulted in a hung jury.

2. William R. Hood, Western Union telegram to Orville L. Hubbard, September 29, 1948. Copied from the files of Orville L. Hubbard.

3. Never elaborated on in the *Dearborn Press*. It may be an urban legend, but some Dearbornites tell anecdotes about city harassment of Negro families who occasionally moved into town in the 1950s. In one case, police and firemen made hourly calls throughout the night in response to supposed requests for aid. The family is said to have moved out shortly afterward. There is no record in the press of any such happenings.

4. *Dearborn Press*, October 28, 1948.

5. *Dearborn Independent*, November 4, 1948. Examples of the cards were retained in Hubbard's files and in the Dearborn Historical Museum.

Chapter 20

1. Patrick J. Doyle, campaign flyer, undated, September 1949. Copied from the files of Orville L. Hubbard.

2. The layout of the camp and its tent village reminded some observers of Marine

camps such as Camp LeJeune, N. C., with olive-green tents laid in row after row.

3. Hubbard held on to the deed awhile. In March 1950, the council resolved that the deed should be returned. In December, the council gave the mayor 15 days to return it or be ousted from office. He turned it over to the city clerk's office for forwarding within the time limit.

4. *Dearborn Press*, December 23, 1948.

5. Ibid., January 13, 1949.

6. Ibid., April 7, 1949.

7. Ibid., August 18, 1949. The statement apparently was written for Rouse. In a tape-recorded interview, Dearborn, Mich., May 5, 1985, Rouse said he remembered nothing about it.

8. *Dearborn Press*, September 22, 1949.

9. Hollman himself had several run-ins with the law the next year. In April 1950, a municipal court jury found him guilty of possessing horse-betting slips. Judge George Martin fined him $100. Several months before that, he was involved in an accidental shooting, after which police confiscated a revolver belonging to him.

10. In February 1951, Guy, resplendent in his gold-star-studded uniform, testified before the Detroit staff of the Kefauver Senate Crime Committee about gambling in Dearborn. He reiterated the story of his bribe offer, saying that a Ford union committeeman named Edward Hester had offered him $5,000 a month for the gambling concession at the Rouge plant. When Hester, thinking that the chief was cooperating, turned over a list of seven pickup men to be protected, Guy had them arrested the next day. As Guy told it, a month later, with detectives hidden in his office, he received a $100 payment from Hester, then had the union man arrested on the spot. Declared a member of the committee, "You acted very effectively and are to be commended."

11. The subject of gambling in Dearborn came up again during a City Council investigation of the Hubbard administration in 1951. See Chapter 24, herein.

12. *Dearborn Press* City Editor Lewis J. Betts wrote in a column on January 19, 1950, that Hubbard had ordered Guy to run so that the incumbent judges would have to campaign themselves instead of having time to snipe at the mayor.

Chapter 21

1. *Dearborn Press*, May 19, 1949.

2. *Detroit News*, April 13, 1949. Details that follow are from *Detroit News*, April 13-August 4, 1950; *Dearborn Press*, May 19–June 23, 1950; and court records copied for the files of John J. Fish before they were expunged from the record. The cases were filed as *Hubbard v. Hubbard* in Wayne Circuit Court, no. 445–891 (1949) and no. 501–571 (1953).

3. Although the widower in question never was identified publicly, a Detroit building contractor named Joseph W. Good (no relation to the author) was described by the *Dearborn Press* on March 2, 1950, as a "friend" of Fay Hubbard's. Good, who previously had helped build a home in Wayne for Fay Hubbard's mother, filed a complaint with Detroit police in March 1950, alleging that Jim and Frank Hubbard had thrown a beer bottle through the front window of his home. The investigation was dropped for lack of evidence. The *Press* said on November 9, 1950, that after Orville Hubbard had reconciled with his wife, Good again filed a complaint with police, this time against the mayor. Good told investigating officers he had picked Fay up near her home on a Saturday night and driven off, when he was shot at from a following car. Good said he let Fay out and retraced

his route on foot to look for witnesses. Suddenly, he said, Mayor Hubbard and another person appeared and began beating him with blackjacks. He dropped his car keys in the scuffle and ran off, he said. Orville Hubbard laughed off the charges, telling reporters, "I was an expert rifle shot in the Marines and I wouldn't have missed." Fay Hubbard failed to confirm Good's story, saying she was out of town at the time. Good, unable to produce evidence beyond a .38 bullet hole in his car, withdrew his complaint.

4. *Dearborn Press*, May 19, 1949.

5. Copied from the files of John J. Fish. The *Detroit News* ran a shorter version on March 18, 1953.

6. *Detroit News*, March 18, 1953.

Chapter 22

1. Stanley Herdzik, notarized statements, January 12 and 20, 1950. Copied from the files of John J. Fish.

2. Ibid.

3. *Dearborn Press*, January 26, 1950.

4. In a front-page "Points of View" column on January 26, 1950, the *Dearborn Press* commented that the charges were "serious and involved," but added, "They tell a story that is neither new nor unusual. It's the story of politics and political machination of almost any era. . . . The so-called 'kick-back' or monetary support that appointees make to hold a job, certainly brands the entire system as cheap and not conducive to efficiency. The system has been known to exist not only in Dearborn but in many cities throughout the nation—it has almost become an accepted practice—yet it cannot be justified." In April 1950, Hubbard threatened to sue Herdzik for libel if he failed to retract his allegations about the kickbacks within three weeks. The mayor took no action, however.

5. Hubbard kept his sense of humor about how silly the order was. A few weeks later, he held a closed meeting with union officials on the issue of the new hospital. Councilman Patrick Doyle, barred from the meeting along with several other mayoral opponents on the council, phoned Frank Gilligan, Herdzik's successor as fire chief, and asked him to come to the mayor's office. "I want you to chop down the door to the mayor's office," Doyle chortled. Gilligan declined, of course. Later, asked why Doyle and the others weren't admitted, Hubbard said, "They were never invited. The last time Doyle was here, he stole some tickets out of this office." And when told of Doyle's request of Gilligan, he observed wryly, "Maybe he's responsible for all these reports going around about chopping the doors down at Henry Ford II's office." He then ordered his administrative assistant, Bert Schlaff, to have the chief of detectives investigate the connection.

6. Betts concluded in the *Dearborn Press* on January 26, 1950, that Hubbard was "the most convincing prevaricator, or does the most convincing job of stretching the truth, of any politico the writer has encountered."

7. *Dearborn Press*, February 9, 1950.

8. Ibid.

9. Ibid., February 16, 1950.

Chapter 23

1. *Detroit Free Press*, August 22, 1950, editorial page.

2. Orville L. Hubbard, veto of council resolution 9–1653–49, September 6, 1949. Copied from the files of John J. Fish.

3. Orville L. Hubbard, election flyer, undated, September 1949. Copied from the files of Orville L. Hubbard.

4. Rouse later chaired a drive to pay off Hubbard's libel judgment. See Chapter 26 (note 4), herein.

5. John J. Fish, letter to Orville L. Hubbard, September 24, 1949. Copied from the files of John J. Fish.

6. *Dearborn Press*, September 29, 1949.

7. This and subsequent testimony copied from transcripts in the files of John J. Fish. Judge Webster's comments are from *Fish v. Hubbard*, Wayne Circuit Court, no. 258-129 (1950).

8. Hubbard was not quick to change his ways after the court judgment against him. The following year, the mayor continued to issue veto messages containing derogatory references to Fish. In one, issued in January 1951, he referred to "John J. Fish, formerly known as Joseph John Poisson and also formerly known as John D. Poisson."

9. "The Ordeals of Orville," *Time*, August 21, 1950, 13. The article twitted the "loud-mouthed, 225-lb. 'Little Orvie'" for his "lightheaded antics and heavy-handed rule," for stocking his office "like a gift shop with articles to pass out to voters," for his divorce troubles and, finally, for plans for a government in exile.

10. Orville L. Hubbard, letter to Clyde I. Webster, September 7, 1950. Copied from the files of Orville L. Hubbard.

Chapter 24

1. *Detroit News*, February 18, 1951.

2. "City I Love," *Time*, July 15, 1946, 23–25.

3. For years after beating the recall, Hubbard remained obsessed with converting signers of the recall petitions over to his side. As late as 1973, the city hall publicity department still was issuing press releases about residents requesting that their names be removed. According to the releases, more than 500 such requests had been made, all of them completely spontaneous. A typical statement from a petition signer: "Signing the petitions seemed the popular thing to do and I've regretted it ever since. I've been thinking about removing my name since I signed that stupid thing."

4. *Detroit News*, April 6, 1950.

5. The firm of Sovell, Wellington and Company, hired belatedly to conduct the city's annual audit, reported a number of irregularities and made several recommendations for improved accounting methods. Among the practices criticized was the assignment of personnel to Camp Dearborn while continuing to assign costs to the departments to which they were officially attached instead of to a camp fund. A second audit, performed by the firm of Ernst and Ernst at the behest of the Chamber of Commerce, alleged a number of charter violations, including the failure to bid out some items costing more than $500.

6. *Detroit News*, April 11, 1950.

7. Hubbard never quite forgave Wagner. The mayor forced him to appeal all the way to the Michigan Supreme Court to get building permits to build on his property at Morley Court near Ford Field in 1957. He took his court order to get the permits in April 1957. Hubbard also tried in late November 1957 to widen Wagner Court from 22 feet to 50 feet, but the Hubbard-dominated council refused, calling the move vindictive. Wagner's land would have been condemned for the widening.

8. Orville L. Hubbard, letter to Henry Ford II, May 6, 1950. Copied from the files of Orville L. Hubbard.

9. Henry Ford II, letter to Orville L. Hubbard, May 10, 1950. Copied from the files of Orville L. Hubbard.

10. Two years after the recall, Hubbard's allegations were repeated by Marguerite Johnson, who was appointed by him as public safety director after a reconciliation following the recall. In testimony on an unrelated matter in Detroit Recorder's Court, she said that several top Ford officials had helped plan the recall. Ford Vice-President John Bugas was in charge of getting jobs for Hubbard department heads and other supporters who would agree to desert the mayor "on a timetable," she said. Thomas R. Reid was imported by Ford "expressly to get rid of Hubbard," she added. Ford public relations officials later said in interviews with the author that they could neither confirm nor deny the firm's involvement in the recall, and they indicated that Ford Board Chairman Henry Ford II would have no comment. Reid, executive director of civic and governmental affairs, denied any personal involvement in the movement and characterized the other allegations as "the wildest of conjectures." Bugas had no comment. Two former CAC officials, Robert Wilcox and Michael J. Berry, said in interviews with the author that they had no knowledge of Ford funds having been used in the recall.

11. Fire Chief Frank Gilligan announced that he was postponing his retirement because "it would surely be used in the recall propaganda." The Pension Board ruled he could be reappointed.

12. Johnson admitted in testimony in Detroit Recorder's Court two years after the recall that the council inquiry was "just a publicity stunt."

13. Later, Ford announced it "has taken and is continuing vigorous and effective measures to stop gambling in the plant." The announcement cited records of employee discipline for gambling but conceded that the firm was hindered by a union contract provision that fired employees could be reinstated by appealing to an umpire.

14. *Dearborn Press*, February 8, 1951.

15. Perhaps intended as a pun with racial connotations, although he occasionally used "black" simply to mean "wicked."

16. *Dearborn Press*, February 1, 1951.

17. The mayor was quoted in "Up Rose Little Orvie Then," *Time*, March 5, 1951, 24, as saying: "I am writing the mayors of Lincoln Park, Inkster and Melvindale suggesting that they annex it. If they want it, they can have it. [Meanwhile] it's going to be tough to get snow-removal trucks in there between now and spring."

18. Russell Harris, *Detroit News*, February 20, 1951.

Chapter 25

1. The article that provoked Hubbard was "Up Rose Little Orvie Then," *Time*, March 5, 1951, 23-24. The article capsulized the "irrepressible" mayor's troubles with his wife and his libel judgment, in addition to the recall campaign against him. It accused him of "jealously" blocking Ford from donating Oakwood Hospital to the city, "presumably because Ford had insisted on making its gift through the Great Detroit Hospital Fund." It related his view of the late Henry Ford's importation of Negroes to the North: "'The good grandfather went down south in 1917 and brought 'em up by the trainload,' he bawled. 'They wooed, and they cooed, and they multiplied.'"

2. A bit of an exaggeration. See Chapter 5 (note 13), herein.

3. Orville L. Hubbard, handbill for rally at McDonald School, November 2, 1951. Copied from the files of John J. Fish.

4. *Dearborn Press*, December 27, 1951.

Chapter 26

1. *Dearborn Press*, July 10, 1952.

2. The following material was copied from the files of John J. Fish, including Orville L. Hubbard, letters to John J. Fish, October 2, 1950; October 12, 1950; November 21, 1951; and February 27, 1952.

3. A third clown was on the train to take Hubbard's place after the mayor got off, according to William "Don" McGrew, in a tape-recorded interview, December 3, 1987, Dearborn, Mich. McGrew identified him as Al Novack, a New York Central Railroad policeman.

4. Rouse ran a vitriolic mayoral campaign against Hubbard in 1949. See Chapter 20, herein.

5. In March 1958, Fish wrote Youngjohn that he still was considering garnishment on the balance of more than $900 due from Hubbard. He never followed through, however, and years later, in a 1972 interview, he said the mayor never had paid the final several hundred dollars in the matter.

Chapter 27

1. Earl Orr, letter to Wayne Circuit Judge Miles N. Culehan, published in the *Dearborn Press*, January 29, 1953.

2. Transcript of City Council hearings on alleged corruption in the Hubbard administration, published in the *Dearborn Press*, February 15, 1951.

3. *Detroit News*, June 2, 1953.

Chapter 28

1. *Dearborn Press*, September 24, 1953. See Chapter 4 (note 13), herein.

2. *Detroit News*, March 7, 1959.

3. The court ruled against Guy in October 1952, and Guy resumed his law practice to supplement his judicial income. He expanded his practice further in April 1953, when he lost the associate judge's seat to John T. McWilliams, but he was elected to the City Council in November 1953 as a Hubbard team member.

4. *Dearborn Press*, February 14, 1952.

5. In June 1953, Parker said he had information he would use against Hubbard in the city election. Hubbard asked at a council meeting, "If it's so good, why didn't you give that to Judge Culehan, too?" Parker replied with a laugh, "It's too juicy to give to Judge Culehan."

6. The mayor was mistaken, apparently confusing Doyle for the moment with Clarence Doyle, former councilman who lost the 1941 mayoral election to Hubbard.

7. Martin filed petitions from time to time, often when Hubbard expected Judge

George T. Martin to run. Judge Martin told reporters earlier in the year that he had assured Hubbard he wouldn't run "as it stands now—but if I ran I would beat you." Never one to shrink from gamesmanship, the mayor obviously figured that a "name" candidate might muddy the water if the judge decided to run.

8. Hubbard's ads omitted the information that his opponent tried to enlist in the Marines in 1941 and later in the Army but was turned down each time for medical reasons—a vision defect and a heart murmur, respectively, according to Christie.

9. Charles J. Nemeth and Godfrey A. Glomb of the Dearborn Independent Voters League and George Hart, process server for Judge Martin. Glomb had been an unsuccessful council candidate in 1951; Nemeth went on to run against Hubbard in 1955, 1957, 1959, 1961, 1964 and 1967; and Hart became a longtime councilman and state senator. The charges against them were dropped.

10. "Dearborn Facts," September 1953. Copied from the files of John J. Fish.

11. McCollough hired attorney Michael J. Berry but dropped the slander action before it went to trial.

12. His vacant seat was filled in January 1954, when the council named John Baja Jr., Hubbard's city housing director, to replace him. Baja, at 27, became the city's youngest councilman ever.

Chapter 29

1. *Detroit News*, November 5, 1953.

2. The primary source for information on the hearings were issues of the *Detroit News*, January 5–March 22, 1954.

3. *Detroit News*, September 3, 1954.

4. Ibid.

5. Ibid.

6. Williams later gave this version of the removal hearing episode, his first encounter with Orvie: "I gave careful study to the report that there was nothing actionable in the whole record. . . . At the next election Orville Hubbard called me several times during the election evening and recounted my victories in all or almost all the precincts in Dearborn, I am sure more because of his personal campaign (on my behalf) than mine. I had already told Orville that I would have thrown the book at him if the cards had come out that way and that he owed me nothing. But as this story makes apparent the man's gratitude was great and he responded in a very warm and human fashion which I appreciated." G. Mennen Williams, Lansing, Mich., letter to the family of Orville Hubbard, Dearborn, Mich., December 18, 1982. From the files of Frank Hubbard.

Chapter 30

1. "Speaking of Pictures . . . ," *Life*, February 22, 1954, 14–15.

2. Fillmore at first said he wouldn't come back unless Hubbard made the first overture, adding, "I never asked for the job in the first place, and I'll be damned if I'll ask for it now." Several weeks later, the mayor, deciding that Fillmore's absence would be regarded as vacation time, capitulated, wiring him a request to report back for work. "We have missed you around city hall," he wrote. "Your books need dusting and your chair needs warming, but no one is indispensable." Fillmore came back.

3. Nickon and his wife were awarded $15,000 in November 1956 for his wife's injuries in the accident with longtime Hubbard appointee C. King Boring.

4. Vezzosi, former treasurer of the Ford Rouge Employees Federal Credit Union, was indicted in July 1955 by the federal government for conspiracy to defraud the credit union. He did not run in 1955 for his city council seat, but Hubbard appointed him housing director in December 1955. He was given two years probation in March 1956, after pleading guilty to a charge of filing a false financial statement. The conspiracy charges were dismissed in January 1957. See Chapter 33 (note 5), herein.

5. *Dearborn Press*, November 3, 1955.

6. In March 1956, Wayne Circuit Judge George Edwards upheld the constitutionality of Dearborn's municipal court after city attorneys had tried to block Martin's raise by having the court declared unconstitutional. The pay raise stood up.

7. *Dearborn Press*, November 10, 1955, editorial.

Chapter 31

1. William T. Johnson, "Publish It Not in the Streets of Askelon . . .," the *Montgomery* [Alabama] *Advertiser*, March 26, 1956. Exhibit in the 1965 civil rights trial of Orville L. Hubbard.

2. Ibid.

3. The *Dearborn Guide* dismissed Hubbard's comments as "dramatizing." In an editorial on July 1, 1965, the paper said Hubbard "was not really sincere when he made all those irresponsible statements."

4. The politicos did not ignore Hubbard totally, however. State Representative Charles M. Diggs, a Detroit Democrat, said on the House floor, "This man Hubbard ought to be examined by psychiatrists and put away for the safety of the state." (Diggs, a Negro, was not related to Charles C. Diggs Jr., Michigan's first Negro congressman.)

5. *Detroit News*, April 19, 1956.

6. Hubbard bought a full-page ad in the Dearborn weeklies in April 1956 to reprint a *U.S. News & World Report* article from April 13 on Negro migrants moving from the South to Chicago and increasing welfare rolls, problems with health, housing, jobs and schools. Hubbard appended an introduction saying, "When Negroes move north, many problems of the South—and others, too—come with them." He did the same thing in July 1957, this time with a report from the magazine on civil rights and racial problems in the South. The magazine protested the unauthorized use of the reprint both times but said Hubbard failed to respond.

7. The Dearborn Council of United Church Women issued a resolution noting that they "deplore the attitude" of Hubbard. He replied, "If they want to practice what they preach, they should move two miles to the west [to the integrated village of Inkster]." The Dearborn Pastors' Union resolved to endorse the churchwomen's statement.

Chapter 32

1. Dearborn voters restored Martin's probation officer in November 1957, after the judge got an initiative proposal on the ballot.

2. Hubbard continued through the 1960s to encourage joint training for police and firemen, but a series of unfavorable rulings on grievances brought under binding arbitra-

tion with the police and fire unions under Michigan Act 312 eventually discouraged the mayor from trying to merge the departments.

3. Dearborn's peak estimated population actually was 112,000, rather lower than Hubbard's estimate at that time.

4. *Dearborn Press*, February 21, 1957.

5. In April 1958, Dearborn voters overwhelmingly turned down a proposal to annex a three-and-a-half-square-mile area of southern Dearborn Township. Hubbard, who backed the annexation, at one point castigated school board members and others as "the same old gang of political disappointees for their unfair attempts" to mislead voters in opposing the annexation. In April 1959, voters easily defeated another proposal to annex a five-square-mile section of northern Dearborn Heights. Hubbard stayed out of that election. The topic of merger kept cropping up through the mid-1960s, but nothing ever came of it. In October 1965, Hubbard and Dearborn Heights Mayor John L. Canfield announced they would meet with the mayors of neighboring Allen Park and Melvindale to discuss recurring suggestions of merger. Hubbard said, "Many residents of Allen Park, Dearborn Heights and Melvindale are former Dearborn residents. Many are sons and daughters of longtime residents, and the feeling persists that they'd like to have their cities become a part of Dearborn so they could share in and enjoy its prestige and high standards." In December 1966, Hubbard urged Dearborn Realtors to take the lead in encouraging merger with Dearborn Heights. Eventually, Hubbard gave up.

6. When Hubbard testified before the Michigan Constitutional Convention in December 1961 in favor of the principle of annexing small townships, convention delegate Clarence Bell of St. Ignace commented, "As far as I can figure it, Hubbard is in favor of a strong type of government as long as he can be the head of it."

7. Thomson had less success in a court showdown 12 years later. See Chapter 38 (note 6), herein.

8. *Dearborn Citizen* 1, no. 1 (August 5, 1957).

9. *Dearborn Press*, September 12, 1957.

10. *Detroit News*, September 23, 1957. The *Dearborn Press*, which on October 3, 1957, endorsed Hubbard and assessed Mills as a candidate who "plainly lacks glamour," editorialized on October 31, 1957, that the paper's publishing rival "screamed all over town that it is . . . not Hubbard that keeps Dearborn 'white.' The scheme backfired. All it accomplished was to antagonize people who feel that because Dearborn is white is no reason to blab to everyone about it."

11. The previous January, Hubbard tore up a copy of the *Dearborn Independent* during a ceremony marking a Ford Motor Company gift of 50 acres to the city for a civic center site. He called the paper's contents "bold-faced lies."

12. *Dearborn Press*, October 31, 1957.

13. *Dearborn Independent*, October 18, 1957.

14. James Sullivan, *Detroit Free Press*, October 27, 1957.

Chapter 33

1. Teamsters Local 299 never was certified as the DPW workers' bargaining agent. It was not until 1968 that another Teamsters unit, Local 214, finally negotiated the first contract with the city on behalf of some 400 DPW employees. In February 1969, the union staged a 23-day walkout over working conditions, the first strike in the city's history.

2. The comment drew a critical editorial the next week from Ford Local 600 Pres-

ident Carl Stellato. In an editorial in the union publication, he called it "reminiscent of the preunion days at Ford's" and asked if the mayor were "trying to deprive the city employees of joining the union of their choice."

3. The population of the tiny village swelled in the 1920s, when Negro auto workers, many of them migrants from the South, built small homes south of Michigan Avenue, the unofficial demarcation line between Negro and white neighborhoods. Henry Ford bailed out residents during the Depression by building an IOU food commissary and a school.

4. In July 1956, Calkins told the Michigan Tax Commission that the city had a double standard for residential assessment, 32 percent for homes built after 1946 and 12 to 18 percent for homes built before then. The city acknowledged two assessment standards, current cash value for homes built after 1946 and the 1941 cash value plus 10 percent for homes built before then. See Chapter 4 (note 16), herein.

5. Hubbard-slate Councilman Robert Vezzosi was indicted in July 1955 on federal charges of conspiracy to defraud the Ford Rouge Employees Credit Union, of which he had been treasurer. He declined to run for reelection in 1955 but was appointed city housing director by Hubbard in December 1955 and then made city sanitation director in December 1956. He subsequently pleaded guilty. See Chapter 30 (note 4), herein.

Chapter 34

1. *Dearborn Press*, November 11, 1961.

2. The *Dearborn Guide* ran the photo on page 1 on January 16, 1969, before Nixon's scheduled inauguration as president. The photo was something of a public relations masterstroke, helping dilute the impact of two negative stories, one on Roy Wilkins of the NAACP calling Hubbard the nation's "meanest man in race relations" and one on the mayor imposing a form of censorship on press interviews following Serrin's unfriendly story in the *New York Times Magazine*.

3. George Morrison, president of the Dearborn Federation of Civic Associations, said that screening prospective buyers by race was "not practiced outright" in Dearborn. "I know of no organized screening system practiced by Realtors, the city administration or the civic associations," he said.

4. Three years later, before the city's 1964 primary, Zahari claimed that Wagner had been "planted" in the race by Hubbard to discourage other candidates. Wagner said in a brief interview on November 27, 1988, that the charge was "absolutely false" but acknowledged that his father, Anthony H. Wagner, entered the 1967 mayoral race with Hubbard's encouragement, finishing third in the primary.

5. *Dearborn Press*, October 26, 1961, and November 2, 1961. Wagner said his only chance would have been, say, if Hubbard had suffered a sudden heart attack. He said he had a $30 budget, most of it spent on campaign literature. He also said he wore the Hubbard lapel pin "kiddingly."

6. The city hall had been for sale for several years before that, with no takers. Hubbard continued without success to sell the property, going so far as to display a lawn full of "for sale" signs from local Realtors on the property in November 1962.

Notes

Chapter 35

1. William L. Ross, *Dearborn Guide*, April 26, 1962.
2. In March 1963, workers took care of the loose wires in Martin's office. Later, Hubbard approved a request from Martin to finish off the building's second courtroom, which had been used as a storeroom for the city clerk. "We want to make the judge happy, contented and satisfied," Hubbard said.
3. The original schedule of hours—before the Hubbard-engineered change—appeared not to impede the court's dispensation of justice. In August 1962, Martin's court was named by the American Bar Association as the nation's best in cities over 100,000 population. Martin's court had been similarly honored several times in previous years in a category for cities in the 50,000–100,000 range. U.S. Supreme Court Justice Tom Clark was on hand in Dearborn to present the award to Martin in October, but Hubbard and most of the rest of his city hall crew boycotted the event.
4. The city held up building and occupancy permits for the buyer, the Pious Society of St. Paul, until ordered to grant them in Wayne Circuit Court in July 1962.
5. Dearborn annexed Fairlane in 1972, after voters in the Dearborn Heights district sanctioned a March ballot proposal. Dearborn already had approved the annexation on a December 1971 vote of the Board of Education; no ballot proposal was required.
6. To help publicize the service, Hubbard showed up on the first day, calling himself "Mother Hubbard" and reading the story of "Bouncing Bear" to kids. He even tried bottle-feeding one infant, finally admitting he was "out of practice" after trying several armholds on the child.
7. *Dearborn Guide*, June 27, 1963.
8. See Chapter 36, herein.
9. See Chapter 37, herein.
10. William L. Ross, *Dearborn Guide*, January 2, 1964.
11. His suit was treated the same as one filed by former Councilman Patrick J. Doyle, who had served without pay after his dual election to council and the State Senate. His suit for back pay of $3,375.48, including interest, from January 3, 1956, to August 10, 1957, was dismissed in Wayne Circuit Court in 1962 and the Michigan Supreme Court in 1963.
12. *Dearborn Guide*, October 1, 1964. This argument, of course, ignores the point that Hubbard ran out of credible opponents following the 1951 recall attempt. A 1964 survey of residents in the twelfth State Senate district, covering West Dearborn, Dearborn Heights and Redford Township, indicated that opinions about civil rights there were similar to those in other northern U.S. suburbs. Conducted by the staff of Edward Robinson during his successful 1964 campaign, the survey indicated that 45 percent felt that integration was being pushed too fast, while 9 percent thought it wasn't fast enough and 32 percent thought it was about right. A similar question in a George Gallup poll among northern whites produced figures of 45, 12 and 31 percent, respectively, in the same categories.
13. See Chapter 20 on Camp Dearborn, herein.
14. Hubbard slater George Hart, who appeared to win reelection by finishing seventh in the council race, was disqualified in December in Wayne Circuit Court because he had also run for, and won nomination for, a State Senate seat. This violated the Dearborn charter amendment that also had tripped up Zahari. Roger Craig, runner-up to Hart in the Democratic primary, eventually won the Senate seat after Hart was disqualified from that race as well. The controversy was resolved when the Dearborn City Council named Hart in January 1965 to fill the vacancy created by his own disqualification.

15. The same law was utilized to prosecute 20 men in the 1964 murder of civil rights workers James Chaney, Andrew Goodman and Michael Schwerner in Philadelphia, Miss. When state authorities failed to charge the men, federal officials brought them to trial for conspiracy to violate the civil rights of the three victims. Seven men, including a sheriff's deputy and the imperial wizard of the Ku Klux Klan, were convicted by an all-white jury and sentenced to federal terms in 1967.

Chapter 36

1. A precursor to this incident occurred on July 22, 1950, according to the *Dearborn Guide*. Police were called to settle a disturbance at 6456 Steadman on Dearborn's east side. The owner, a widow named Alma E. Boyd, reported that loiterers threatened a Negro couple responding to an ad she placed in Detroit papers. Noting that neighbors had accused her of seeking Negro tenants, she explained, "I did no such thing. I only advertised for colored help. I offered to provide living quarters to a colored couple in exchange for domestic services." She told police that neighbors had beaten her dog and insulted her family.

2. The couple, Jerry and Michiko Kilgore, separated before actually occupying the house. Mrs. Kilgore and her daughter moved in without incident.

3. See Chapter 7 (note 2), herein.

4. The case was *Stanzione v. Hubbard et al.*, Civil Action no. 25099 (E. Dist. Mich., S. Div., 1966). Also named besides Hubbard were George Lewis, Garrison Clayton, Thomas Shaughnessy, Blaine Dannenberg, Clifford Gowing, Karl G. Parchert, Frank J. Scanlon, Lawrence J. Cameron, John T. Connolly, Albert D. Farrell, Louis Hinkel, John M. Lindsey, Dennis O'Brien, Richard O'Brien and William Roberts. Stanzione's suit subsequently added a request that $50,000 in exemplary damages be assessed as well.

5. Section 8.3 of the Dearborn City Charter makes the mayor "a conservator of the peace and [he] may exercise, within the city, the powers conferred upon sheriff's [*sic*] to suppress disorder." Dearborn is a home rule city under Act 279, Michigan Public Acts of 1909.

6. Michigan Statutes Annotated 28.789-96.

7. Title 42, U.S. Code Service, Section 1983 provides that "every person who, under color of any statute, ordinance, regulation, custom or usage, of any state or territory, subjects or causes to be subjected, any citizen of the United States or other person within the jurisdiction thereof to the deprivation of any rights, privileges, or immunities secured by the Constitution and laws, shall be liable to the party injured in any action at law, suit in equity, or other proper proceedings for redress." Section 1985 holds that if two or more persons conspire to prevent officers from doing their duty under law or conspire to deprive persons of equal protection, they are liable for recovery of damages.

8. *U.S. v. Hubbard et al.*, Criminal Action no. 41367 (E. Dist. Mich., S. Div., 1965). The law was Title 18, U.S. Code Service, Section 242, passed June 25, 1948, based on the act of March 4, 1909, and ultimately derived from the so-called Enforcement Act of May 31, 1870. The Enforcement Act was part of a package of civil rights acts designed to ensure Negroes the full protection of the Thirteenth, Fourteenth and Fifteenth amendments. For a fuller discussion, see Alfred H. Kelly and Winfred A. Harbison, *The American Constitution: Its Origins and Development* (New York: W. W. Norton, 1963). See also *Dearborn Guide*, February 18, 1965. Section 242 states, "Deprivation of rights under color of law: Whoever, under color of any law, statute, ordinance, regulation, or custom, willfully subjects any

inhabitant of any State, Territory, or District to the deprivation of any rights, privileges, or immunities secured or protected by the Constitution or laws of the United States, or to different punishments, pains, or penalties, on account of such inhabitant being an alien, or by reason of his color, or race, than are prescribed for the punishment of citizens, shall be fined not more than $1,000 or imprisoned not more than one year, or both; and if death results shall be subject to imprisonment for any term of years or for life." The defendants also were charged under Section 371 of Title 18, "Conspiracy to commit offense or to defraud United States."

9. Ibid., *U.S. v. Hubbard.*

10. *Dearborn Guide*, February 18, 1965.

11. Hubbard contradicts his earlier affidavit, in which he said he first heard of the incident at 11:00 the first night.

12. Spokesmen for the FBI and the Dearborn police said in 1988 that they had no information on Stanzione's whereabouts following a report in May 1969 that the FBI was looking into the possibility that he was a victim of gangland violence in Chicago or Detroit. Two months before that, he had been indicted by a federal grand jury in a plan to smuggle aliens across the Detroit River from Canada; he later was reported free on bond in the case. In January 1969, he had been evicted from an East Dearborn house he had moved to after the Kendal Street incident. See Chapter 38 (note 1), herein.

Chapter 37

1. Mitchell Tendler, memorandum to Burton I. Gordin, June 9, 1964. From the files of the Michigan Civil Rights Commission.

2. Russell Harris, memorandum to Mitchell Tendler, October 23, 1964. From the files of the Michigan Civil Rights Commission.

3. *Detroit News*, February 21, 1965.

4. Russell Harris, memorandum to Carl Levin, February 18, 1965. From the files of the Michigan Civil Rights Commission.

Chapter 38

1. Among those arrested was Giuseppe Stanzione, the victim of the 1963 Kendal Street incident. Stanzione, who had moved to Detroit, was arrested while driving through a store parking lot after hours. He was ticketed for excessive noise and charged with weapons violations after being found with a shotgun, an automatic rifle and other firearms. See Chapter 36 (note 12), herein.

2. Two years later, in November 1968, a referendum worded virtually identically went the other way, by a vote of 20,936 to 15,674. Hubbard, curious whether public sentiment had swung away from involvement in Vietnam, did not orchestrate a prolonged public discussion this time. The vote, however, received national media attention amid coverage of Richard Nixon's victory over Hubert Humphrey and George Wallace in the presidential election. See Chapter 39, herein.

3. The home, on Mead in East Dearborn, was within two blocks of Hubbard's home.

4. The scheme died in July 1968, when Ford Motor told the city neither of the company-owned sites proposed for the stadium was available. The other was by Rotunda and I-94.

5. "Hubbard's Hotel," *Newsweek*, December 4, 1967, 80A.

6. In February 1969, the State Appeals Court upheld the city's purchase of the building on a unanimous decision of a three-judge panel. Hubbard called the decision "a tremendous social victory." The Michigan Supreme Court upheld the city on a four-to-three vote in April 1971. The case was *Sabaugh v. City of Dearborn*, 384 Mich. 510, 16 Mich. App. 182 (1969).

7. There was no second building. In May 1968, the Michigan Civil Rights Commission urged the FHA "not to be a partner in future property transactions which will result in reinforcing and extending segregated housing patterns" and to take "specific steps" to avoid federal assistance to Dearborn Towers. The subsequent controversy over rental of units lasted several years. A city report showed the building earned slightly more than $50,000 in net operating income in its first year and was 100 percent occupied; only 13 of 88 units were rented by Dearborn residents, however. The rate of return on investment was 4.7 percent.

Chapter 39

1. Young Hubbard's father-in-law, John D. Denison Jr., wrote a letter to the *Dearborn Guide*, published January 11, 1968, complaining that the stop-and-frisk legislation would help Mayor Hubbard "make a Gestapo of the Dearborn Police Department." The mayor, he said, had a "Hitlerian attitude," and the ordinance was "hate" legislation. He said he had campaigned for his son-in-law because he said he opposed the measure, but now, he added, "it would appear that [the mayor's] Councilman-son will rapidly become the court jester."

2. Wayne County Sheriff Roman Gribbs defeated Austin in the November election.

3. Hubbard also snubbed the western Wayne County community of Livonia, which was all-white, in April 1970, because, he said, he had sent out letters on behalf of the unsuccessful candidate for mayor there earlier in the month. He worked out a Mayors' Exchange Day switch with the outstate Michigan community of Belding.

4. The city sent a bill for $14.46 for alleged property damage to the sponsor of the demonstration, the Interfaith Center for Racial Justice. The center paid only after city officials pressed the issue.

5. John Hubbard had predicted in late September that Baja would lose his council seat, prompting the obviously irked Baja to retort, "He hasn't the ability or knowledge to predict anything. The only thing John Jay has on his side is his name. His two years on the council only showed the public that he is incapable of ever becoming mayor."

6. Missing from the list of candidates was Charles Nemeth, who had vowed in 1967 to keep running as long as Hubbard did. Nemeth ran instead for state representative in August 1970, losing to the incumbent, Lucille McCollough, in the Democratic primary by a seven-to-one margin.

7. Dearborn housewife Velma Pamment had filed petitions to run for mayor against Hubbard in 1951 but withdrew a week later to run for City Council. See Chapter 25, herein. Bazzy thus was the first woman to make the mayoral ballot in Dearborn.

8. Hart ran a weak third in the Democratic primary that August, behind Lucille McCollough's son Patrick, the eventual winner, and Roger Craig.

9. Thomas said the strokes occurred during 1970 trips to Denver, Seattle, San Francisco and one other city. He said his source was a Dearborn councilman (Thomas interview, November 8, 1987). James Helmrich said he noticed that Hubbard suffered from

the effects of altitude during a trip they went on in June 1970, adding, "He did remark about having difficulty breathing and not sleeping well. It wasn't an attack. He did not curtail any of his activities. I remember going for a swim in the hotel pool. I was having a hell of a time breathing" (Helmrich interview, December 14, 1987).

10. See Chapter 4, herein.

11. After 19 unsuccessful attempts at getting a raise, perhaps the council could be excused for trying to muddy the issue. As passed in August, the wording originally asked for "as much as councilmen received in 1942," or $3,000.

Chapter 40

1. *Detroit News*, August 4, 1972. The diary was read during Bremer's trial in Maryland's Prince Georges County Court. Bremer was convicted and sentenced to 63 years in prison.

2. *Amen v. City of Dearborn*, 363 F. Supp. 1267 (E. Dist. Mich., S. Div., 1973); 718 F. 789 reversed, 532 F. 2nd (6th Cir. Appeals, 1983); cert. denied 104 S.C. 1596 (Sup. Ct., 1984). The case was filed on behalf of Amen's mother, Katherine Amen. Alan Amen was elected in 1987 to the Dearborn Board of Education, the first Arab-American in the city elected to public office.

3. Appeals to higher courts dragged out for more than a decade. The suit was filed in U.S. District Court on October 14, 1971; the city was enjoined from acquiring property in the area on March 22, 1972. Freeman issued his opinion on August 14, 1973. The case was appealed to the U.S. Court of Appeals, Sixth Circuit, and remanded back on March 25, 1976, when the court ruled that Freeman's court lacked jurisdiction because plaintiffs failed to show damages of more than $10,000. That requirement was negated by a 1978 U.S. Supreme Court ruling that federal courts have jurisdiction over all cases involving constitutional rights regardless of the amount of damages. The appeals court issued its opinion on October 6, 1983, permitting damage claims filed by 180 homeowners to be considered individually. In 1984, the U.S. Supreme Court refused to hear the city's final appeal. The city declined to pursue urban renewal plans in the two areas, and both were rezoned residential under city master plan amendments.

4. Hubbard, Hagelthorn interview, April 5, 1972.

5. Hubbard restored the onions himself before the primary, effectively removing one campaign issue from the opposition.

Chapter 41

1. Gary Farrugia, *Dearborn Press & Guide*, November 3, 1977.

2. Ibid.

3. Ibid.

4. Unknown to Hubbard and his physicians, the mayor may have suffered a series of small strokes before being stricken in November. Nearly a full year before Hubbard's stroke, the author played one of the mayor's interview tapes to a speech pathologist, Robert Schad of Saskatoon, Saskatchewan, who noted that several of Hubbard's speech mannerisms were consistent with those of stroke victims.

Chapter 42

1. Pete Waldmeir, *Detroit News*, December 9, 1974.
2. Ibid.
3. Bill Ross, *Dearborn Press & Guide*, Dec. 12, 1974.
4. Hubbard and Keane, tape-recorded conversation, Dearborn, Mich., September 13-14, 1972.
5. Keane, interview with the author, *Detroit News*, August 15, 1968.
6. John Miller, "Mayor Hubbard's Girl Friend Talks about Their Life Together," *Detroit News Sunday Magazine*, September 28, 1975, 15.
7. Ibid., 18.
8. Don Kubit, "Living with the Ghost of Dearborn Past," *Monthly Detroit*, September 1981, 65.
9. Ibid.
10. Miller, "Mayor Hubbard's Girl Friend," 18.
11. Cord interview, 18 November 1981.
12. Ibid.
13. Ibid.
14. Jim Hubbard interview, August 1, 1982.
15. Frank Hubbard interview, August 1, 1982.
16. Helmrich interview, December 14, 1987.
17. *Detroit News*, October 11, 1979, and September 6, 1981.
18. Jackson interview, April 19, 1986.
19. Helmrich interview, December 14, 1987.
20. In 1976, Noel Keane pioneered the concept of brokering surrogate motherhood contracts after a Dearborn couple asked him to help find a surrogate to bear a child for them. He placed ads in college papers announcing, "Infertile couple wants test tube baby." Over the next 12 years, he arranged more than 150 surrogacies, leading eventually to the controversial "Baby M" case. As executive director of the Infertility Center of New York, he arranged for Mary Beth Whitehead to be artificially inseminated by William Stern under a $10,000 surrogacy contract. Whitehead decided she wanted to keep the child she bore, but in a first-of-its-kind case, a New Jersey judge awarded custody in 1987 to Stern and his wife, Elizabeth.
21. Fred Hoffman, *Dearborn Guide*, August 7, 1975.
22. Jackson interview, April 19, 1986.
23. Ross interview, November 30, 1987.
24. Ibid.

Chapter 43

1. Jackson interview, April 19, 1986.
2. Dr. Boy Frame, medical statement released by Doyne E. Jackson, *Dearborn Press & Guide*, February 27, 1975.
3. Dr. Boy Frame, notarized letter to the Dearborn City Clerk, June 16, 1975.
4. Dr. M. Meyer Pensler, notarized letter to the Dearborn City Council, June 16, 1975.
5. Mitzi Weitzman, notarized copy of affidavit sworn June 17, 1975.
6. Jackson interview, April 19, 1986.

7. Ibid.

8. After his appointment by President Ford to the U.S. District Court bench in Detroit in 1976, Guy was named to the U.S. Sixth Circuit Court of Appeals in 1985 by President Reagan.

9. Jackson interview, April 19, 1986.

10. See Chapter 18 (note 3), herein.

11. Iva Fish, tape-recorded interview, Dearborn, Mich., December 12, 1988.

12. Hubbard's voluminous personal files at city hall were removed by the family during his poststroke recuperation. Many were disposed of, some were turned over to persons cited in the material and 45 archival boxes worth of paper items and other memorabilia were turned over to the Dearborn Historical Museum in January 1977 under a 25-year seal. The seal was lifted and the records made public by Maureen Keane in January 1983, the month after Hubbard's death, under her power of attorney. The material was still being catalogued in early 1989.

13. Jackson interview, April 19, 1986.

14. *Dearborn Press & Guide*, June 23, 1977.

15. Ibid., July 28, 1977, "Our Points of View" editorial.

Chapter 44

1. The family later determined that the mayor had accumulated an additional $98,500 in custodial accounts for many of his grandchildren, in addition to a $5,000 account for Fay.

Chapter 45

1. Kubit, "Living with the Ghost of Dearborn Past," 63.

2. Ibid.

3. Ibid.

Chapter 46

1. *New York Times*, December 17, 1982. The error-strewn obituary mistakenly cited Hubbard's age as 80.

2. *Detroit Free Press*, December 16, 1982; *Detroit News*, December 17, 1982, editorial page.

3. Ronald Reagan, Washington, D.C., letter to Frank Hubbard, Dearborn, Mich., January 4, 1983. From the files of Frank Hubbard. G. Mennen Williams, Lansing, Mich., letter to the family of Orville Hubbard, Dearborn, Mich., December 18, 1982. From the files of Frank Hubbard.

Epilogue

1. *Detroit Branch, National Association for the Advancement of Colored People v. City of Dearborn*, Case no. 85-531629 CZ, Wayne County Circuit Court (1985). See Good, "The Ghost of Orville Hubbard."

2. Will Muller, *Detroit News*, February 24, 1965.

Bibliography

Books

Adrian, Charles R., and Charles Press. *Governing Urban America*. New York: McGraw-Hill, 1977, 48-53.

Overstreet, Harry A. *The Mature Mind*. New York: W. W. Norton, 1949.

Stockton, Ronald R., and Frank Whelon Wayman. *A Time of Turmoil: Values and Voting in the 1970's*. East Lansing, Mich.: Michigan State University Press, 1983.

Pamphlets and Handbooks

Hubbard, Elbert. *A Message to Garcia*. East Aurora, N. Y.: House of Hubbard, Memorial Edition, 1967.

Larson, Robert Henry. *The Dearborn Story*. Dearborn, Mich.: Dearborn Historical Museum, undated.

League of Women Voters Dearborn–Dearborn Heights. *Dearborn*. Livonia, Mich.: Robins Printing Company, 1976.

Manuscripts

Forsthoefel, Mark H. "Some Phases of the Hubbard Administration in Dearborn, Michigan, from 1942 to 1951." Master's thesis, University of Toledo, 1955, 180 pp.

Hubbard, Orville L. "A Synopsis of the Experience of Orville L. Hubbard after Being Graduated from the Eighth Grade of the Union City Public Schools, Union City, Michigan/June 20, 1920 to January 26, 1928," 1928, 7 pp.

Jackson, Doyne E. "Mayor Orville L. Hubbard of Dearborn, Michigan," City of Dearborn press release (Hubbard biography), April 1970, 5 pp.

Mohamed, Marietta. "An Analysis of Katherine Amen, et al., Plaintiffs, v. City of Dearborn, a Municipal Corporation, et al., Defendants." Bachelor's degree thesis, University of Michigan–Dearborn, 1987, 25 pp.

Pilch, Alex. "Hot Ideas on a Cold Day," City of Dearborn press release (Hubbard biography), undated (1960?), 20 pp.

Stockton, Ronald R., and Frank Whelon Wayman. "New Suburban Populism: Changing Values and Politics in a Northern Community," unpublished portion of *A Time of Turmoil*, 450 pp.

Magazine Articles

American City. "Baby-sitting for Shoppers." December 1964, 117–18.
———. "Complaints and Service Calls Handled Quickly by Complaint Department." February 1953, 111.
———. "Dearborn Builds Water Wonderland." November 1954, 80.
———. "Dearborn Buys Florida Retirement Home." February 1968, 75.
———. "Dearborn Establishes City Beautiful Commission." March 1952, 7.
———. "Dearborn's Research and Information Department Proves Worth to Civic Groups, Media, Industry." May 1958, 188–89.
———. "Mayor Plans a Sunny Southland Paradise for Retired Dearborn Families." April 1956, 173.
———. "Operation Eyesore Stops Urban Decay." May 1963, 165–66.
Business Week. "Dearborn Voters Say No to Buying Florida Haven for Their Oldsters." April 6, 1957, 54.
———. "A Ford Collides with Dearborn's Mayor; How Mayor Hubbard Mothers Dearborn." January 10, 1970, 66–68.
Christian Century. "Churchwomen and Bishop Rap Dearborn Mayor." May 2, 1956, 540.
DeMott, John S., reported by William J. Mitchell. "Shop Here, but Don't Stop Here." *Time,* March 10, 1986, 46.
The Economist. "Keep Off the Grass." June 21, 1986, 33–34.
Good, David L. "The Ghost of Orville Hubbard." *Michigan: The Magazine of the Detroit News,* April 20, 1986, 8.
Holland, B. "Camping for the Community: Camp Dearborn." *Recreation,* May 1950, 68–69.
Hoxie, H. A. "Kitchen Garbage Grinders Mean a Cleaner City." *American City,* May 1954, 150–51.
Hubbard, Orville L. "Corporals for Dearborn, Mich., Police." *American City,* September 1955, 7.
———. "How We Care for Our Trees." *American City,* August 1957, 112–13.
———. "New Lights Increase Police Efficiency." *American City,* August 1969, 34.
———. "'Operation Eyesore' Stops Urban Decay." *American City,* May 1963, 165–66.
———, and R. K. Archer. "Ice Skaters Enjoy 'Heat Breaks.'" *American City,* December 1963, 86–87.
Jones, Wade. "Dearborn's Uninhibited Mayor." *Pageant,* September 1955, 90–95.
Kubit, Don. "Living with the Ghost of Dearborn Past." *Monthly Detroit,* September 1981, 62–67.
Kursh, H. "Has Your Town a Gripe Center?" *American Mercury,* September 1956, 26–28.
Life. "Little Orvie Rides Again." March 5, 1951, 34–35.
———. "Speaking of Pictures . . . These Show Attitudes of City Officials during the Mayor's THINKing Hour." February 22, 1954, 14–15.
McCann, Hugh. "Mayor Hubbard and Dearborn: The Story of a Curious Love Affair." *Detroit/The Detroit Free Press,* November 29, 1970, 32–42.
Malkin, Edward E. "Dearborn's Madcap Mayor." *Coronet,* September 1958, 66–70.
Miller, John. "Mayor Hubbard's Girl Friend Talks about Their Life Together." *Detroit News Sunday Magazine,* September 28, 1975, 14–24.
New Republic. "Think." March 1, 1954, 4.
Newsweek. "Hubbard's Hotel." December 4, 1967, 80A–B.
———. "One-Man Gang." November 16, 1953, 30.

433

———. "One Million Per Cent." July 5, 1965, 27–28.

Noble, William T. "Dearborn's Great White Father: 26 Years of Pride and Prejudice." *Detroit News Sunday Magazine*, June 25, 1967, 10–30.

Pilch, A. "Dearborn Provides a Country Club for All Residents." *American City*, July 1953, 96–97.

Rich, Marney. "What Hath Orville Hubbard Wrought?" *Monthly Detroit*, November, 1984, 10–11.

Sayers, Michael. "Vice Gangs Rule America's Defense Arsenal." *Dan Gillmor's Scoop* 2, no. 27 (November 1941): 7–11.

Serrin, William. "Mayor Hubbard Gives Dearborn What It Wants—And Then Some." *New York Times Magazine*, January 12, 1969, 26.

Shannon, William V. "The Political Machine I: Rise and Fall/The Age of the Bosses." *American Heritage* 20, no. 4 (1969): 27–31.

Swapka, F. B. "Dearborn Requires Grinders in Commercial Establishments." *American City*, August 1950, 13.

Time. "The Ordeals of Orville." August 21, 1950, 13.

———. "Tell It Not in Gath." April 23, 1956, 62.

———. "Up Rose Little Orvie Then." March 5, 1951, 23–24.

Vernier, Evelyn G. "Mayor Hubbard's Marriage Bureau." *Woman's Life*, Fall 1955, 13–16.

Newspapers

Dearborn Guide. January 4, 1962–December 30, 1976. Including Hubbard tribute supplement, May 6, 1967; Dearborn vacation supplement, summer 1973.

Dearborn Independent. January 8, 1948–December 29, 1949; January 3–December 24, 1957.

Dearborn Press. January 30, 1941–December 28, 1961; January 6, 1972–December 30, 1976. Including Hubbard tribute supplement, March 6, 1975.

Dearborn Press & Guide. January 6, 1977–December 29, 1988. Including Dearborn progress supplement, January 25, 1979; memorial supplement, December 23, 1982.

Dearborn Times-Herald. Selected issues, 1967–88. Including Hubbard tribute supplement, August 27, 1975; Dearborn salute supplement, August 9, 1979; Hubbard memorial supplement, December 23, 1982.

Detroit News. May 6, 1941–December 31, 1988.

Barron, James. "Parks New Racial Issue in Dearborn." *New York Times*, January 19, 1986.

Bussey, John. "Stores in Dearborn See Profits Decline Because of Boycott." *Wall Street Journal*, December 31, 1985.

Grangenois Gates, Mireille. "They're Upset with Outsiders in Dearborn, Mich." *USA TODAY*, June 16, 1986.

Johnson, William T. "Publish It Not in the Streets of Askelon . . ." *Montgomery* [Alabama] *Advertiser*, March 26, 1956.

Joseph, Frank S. "Mercurial Mayor of Dearborn: One-Man Show in a Tidy Paradise." *Washington Post*, August 17, 1975.

Mills, William L. "How Dearborn Got a Dictator Mayor." *Dearborn Independent* political supplement, September 1957.

Risen, James. "Town Finds It Hard to Shed Racist Image." *Los Angeles Times*, January 6, 1986.

Putnam, Stan. "Dearborn's Mayor—Orville Hubbub," and subsequent parts of five-part series. *Detroit Free Press*, May 12–16, 1965.

Simmons, Boyd. "Enemies Vanquished, Hubbard Now Battles His Erstwhile Pals," and subsequent parts of three-part series. *Detroit News*, April 17–19, 1950.

Interviews

Bartlett, Lee M. Interview by author, May 23, 1972, Dearborn Heights, Mich.
Berry, Michael J. Interview by author, November 21, 1973, Detroit, Mich.
Boring, C. King. Tape-recorded interview by author, December 1, 1987, Dearborn, Mich.
Burtell, Joseph J. Tape-recorded interview by author, December 7, 1981, Dearborn, Mich.
Cord, Judy. Tape-recorded interview by author, November 18, 1981, Dearborn, Mich.
Dmytro, Nancy Hubbard. Tape-recorded interview by author, January 21, 1989, Dearborn, Mich.
Eberhard, David. Interview by author, undated, March 1973, Detroit, Mich.
Fish, Iva. Tape-recorded interview by author, December 12, 1988, Dearborn, Mich.
Fish, John J. Tape-recorded interview by author, undated, 1972, Dearborn, Mich.
Greene, Walter R. Interview by author, undated, March 1973, Detroit, Mich.
Helmrich, James. Tape-recorded interview by author, December 14, 1987, Flint and Pontiac, Mich.
Hoffman, Fred. Tape-recorded interview by author, December 1, 1987, Dearborn, Mich.
Hood, Nicholas. Interview by author, undated, March 1973, Detroit, Mich.
Hubbard, Frank. Tape-recorded interviews by author, July 10, August 1 and 22, 1982, Dearborn, Mich.
Hubbard, Jim. Tape-recorded interviews by author, July 10, August 1 and 22, 1982, Dearborn, Mich.
Hubbard, John. Tape-recorded interview by author, October 19, 1981, Dearborn, Mich.
Hubbard, Orville L. Tape-recorded interviews by author, September 12–15, 1972; November 13–17, 1972; December 11–14, 1972; November 6, 1973; March 4–8, 1974; August 26, 1974, Dearborn, Mich; May 21, 1973, Union City, Mich.
———. Tape-recorded interview by Joyce Hagelthorn, April 5, 1982, Dearborn, Mich.
Jackson, Doyne E. Tape-recorded interview by author, April 19, 1986, Dearborn, Mich.
Keane, Maureen. Tape-recorded conversations with author, September 13–14, 1972; September 15, 1981, Dearborn, Mich.
Lancaster, Roy. Tape-recorded interviews by author, March 30, April 26, 1985, Dearborn, Mich.
McGrew, William "Don." Tape-recorded interview by author, December 3, 1987, Dearborn, Mich.
Mills, William L. Tape-recorded interview by author, June 29, 1982, Dearborn, Mich.
Ranney, Austin. Interview by author following lecture, November 21, 1980, Dearborn, Mich.
Ravitz, Mel. Interview by author, June 19, 1972, Detroit, Mich.
Reid, Thomas R. Interview by author, undated, 1973, Dearborn, Mich.
Rogell, Billy. Interview by author, undated, March 1973, Detroit, Mich.
Ross, Annette. Tape-recorded interview by author, November 30, 1987, Dearborn, Mich.
Rouse, Victor G. Tape-recorded interview by author, May 5, 1985, Dearborn, Mich.
Smith, Otto. Conversation with author, May 21, 1973, Union City, Mich.
Thomas, Douglas R. Tape-recorded interview by author, November 8, 1987, Dearborn, Mich.
Van Antwerp, Philip J. Interview by author, undated, 1972, Detroit, Mich.

Wagner, Eugene R. Conversation with author, November 27, 1988, Dearborn, Mich.
Wierzbicki, Anthony J. Interview by author, undated, 1972, Detroit, Mich.
Wilcox, Robert. Interview by author, undated, 1973, Detroit, Mich.

The author expects to donate to the Dearborn Historical Museum the Orville L. Hubbard interview tapes cited herein. The other tapes will not be made public during the interview subjects' lifetime except in cases where written authority is granted.

Primary Documents

Files of Orville L. Hubbard, Dearborn, Mich.
Orville L. Hubbard archival files, Dearborn Historical Museum, Dearborn, Mich.
Files of John J. Fish, Dearborn, Mich.

Index

437

David L. Good has worked at the *Detroit News* for 23 years and is currently an assistant feature editor with the newspaper. He holds the M.A. degree from the University of Michigan.

The manuscript was edited by Wendy Warren Keebler. The book was designed by Joanne E. Kinney. The typefaces for the text and display are Linotype's Meridien and Meridien Medium. The book is printed on 50-lb. White Champion and is bound in Holliston Mills' Roxite over 88 pt. binders' boards.

Manufactured in the United States of America.